S0-BRJ-082

Managing the small business

# Managing the small business

DONALD P. STEGALL, D.B.A.
University of Colorado

LAWRENCE L. STEINMETZ, Ph.D.
President
High Yield Management, Inc.

JOHN B. KLINE, J.D.
University of Colorado

 1976   Revised Edition

RICHARD D. IRWIN, INC.   Homewood, Illinois   60430
Irwin-Dorsey International   Arundel, Sussex   BN18 9AB
Irwin-Dorsey Limited   Georgetown, Ontario   L7G 4B3

Revised Edition

*First Printing, April 1976*

ISBN 0-256-01784-0
Library of Congress Catalog Card No. 75–35091
*Printed in the United States of America*

# Preface

The authors of this revised edition of *Managing the Small Business* consider it a substantial improvement over the first edition. In addition to updating the text material to reflect all the latest developments in small business management since 1968, several sections were completely rewritten, some new sections and numerous new charts and other graphic materials were added, and the entire manuscript was carefully edited to make it both more concise and more readable. The result is a comprehensive treatise on the subject that is shorter in length (by some 200 pages) and easier to understand, with a fresh, new approach in many areas.

Despite these changes, our purpose in this revised edition has remained unchanged; that is, to offer a practical approach to the grassroot, real-world problems the small business manager faces in the complex, dynamic, risk-ridden economy of today. The intent in this hard-nosed, down-to-earth treatment was to design a text that would prove both pedagogically rewarding to the student and economically rewarding to the entrepreneur.

In more specific terms, the following features are representative of the many elements that make this revised edition unique:

1. Chapter 3 presents a complete and expanded treatment of the several sources of aid available to the entrepreneur—from the franchisor to the Small Business Administration.
2. Chapter 6 provides a new approach to the subject of buying and selling a small business that is unique to this text.
3. Chapters 8, 9, and 10 have been extensively rewritten to provide an improved, hard-hitting treatment of the management function.
4. A completely new Chapter 19 dealing with insurance and risk management in the small business provides a better, more practical treatment of the subject than do most other small business texts available.
5. Chapter 26 includes an expanded and completely updated bibliography of reference materials and management aids that is unique to this book.

v

6. Finally, *Managing the Small Business* has not presented the subject material in a retailing and accounting format, as is typical of most small business texts. As a result, the authors have avoided the tendency to write a book that appears to be a junior version of an accounting or marketing text.

Consistent with our desire to present the best treatment of small business management possible, any and all comments, criticisms, suggestions, and reactions of those who study and use this revised edition are solicited and will be sincerely appreciated. As is customary, the authors assume full responsibility for any errors that may have eluded us.

*March 1976*                                      DONALD P. STEGALL
                                                 LAWRENCE L. STEINMETZ
                                                 JOHN B. KLINE

# Contents

planning. Establishing plans of operation: *The time to dream and the time to be conservative and realistic. Strategies and tactics of master planning. Benefits and advantages to long-run and master planning. Formalizing the plan.* Other planning methods: *Short-run planning. Planning for special events. Crisis planning.* Manpower planning—an example of the problems encountered in planning for the daily operations of the small business: *Indivisibility of employees. Lack of facilities for developing managers. Lack of economies of scale. Personality complications. The chore of planning.* Plans that fail.

keeping function: *Use of the computer in small business record-keeping.*
Concluding remarks. Appendix.

*Considerations about the media.* Assessing your advertising efforts. Developing a good advertisement: *How to write advertising copy. Principles of effective advertising copy.* Using an advertising agency: *Role of the advertising agency. Selection of the advertising agency. Compensating the advertising agency. Doing it yourself.* Selling and sales promotion.

# 1

# Introduction to small business management

The small business has played a significant role in American economic history since the beginning; and there is little evidence to indicate this will not continue to be true in the future. The spirit of entrepreneurship is widespread. Americans by the millions, at some time in their lives, have aspired to own and operate their own businesses. Entrepreneurship has always represented an American's right to make it from "rags to riches." In light of this phenomenon, this book is dedicated to those, both present and future, who seek to realize the "great American dream."

The purpose of this introductory chapter is to consider two basic questions designed to put the "dream" in its proper "realistic" perspective. First, why should a person start a business? And second, what are the most common stumbling blocks to success in small business?

## The why?[1]

Fortunately for those who try to "make it on their own," the larger segment of the population has an aversion to risk. They prefer the security and comfort of working for someone else. The regular pay checks, paid vacations, seniority and job security, and a good program of fringe benefits are too inviting.

But every so often an individual comes along who turns a deaf ear to "security." What are the reasons for doing so? Are some reasons better than others? Instead of asking why start a small business, might it be more appropriate to ask, Why not?

It appears the most successful small businesses are started by those who simply are unhappy with their present standard of living, and desire to make more money. The dollar is a powerful stimulus to those bent on the

---

[1] Some of the ideas expressed in this section were based on comments made by Gordon B. Baty in his book entitled *Entrepreneurship, Playing to Win* (Reston, Va.: Reston Publishing Co., 1974), chap. 1.

"better things in life." So it seems that those who want to make money "try harder."

The second best chance for success appears to rest with those who desire to directly reap the benefits of their professional competency instead of selling it to an employer. They realize the value of their ideas and wish to gain professional recognition by accepting full responsibility for its development.

Beyond the desire to make money, or exploit one's professional competency, other reasons for going into business are far less likely to generate success. They include the following:

1. The desire to be one's own boss; to work when one wants to work; to look up to nobody.
2. The self-made objective that it is necessary to succeed in entrepreneurship to "prove" one's abilities.
3. A social consciousness that compels one to "do something" for science, or technology, or society, or whatever the cause.
4. An involvement because of real or imagined talents outside one's present job or profession.
5. A vindictive attitude, expressed in the desire to "give it to the competition."

Of course, in reality, human motives are mixed. In any particular case, the reason for selecting entrepreneurship as a "way of life" will be some combination of justifications—any of those cited above and any based on the individual's unique background, training, or experience. But in the final analysis the question is whether the reason or reasons justify the costs, sacrifices, and risks of "being on your own."

The premise of this book is that the central objective of the small business venture is to make money for the owner-manager-entrepeneur. All else should be secondary, regardless of the motive. To the extent the owner-manager seeks to accomplish a variety of objectives, energies are diluted. If the firm does not survive, there are no objectives. Thus, all efforts should be directed to keeping the firm alive, and that means making money.

This is not to say there is something inconsistent with proving one's abilities and making money; or doing something for society and making money; or creating competition and making money. It is simply a matter of recognizing that only those ventures that profit will make any lasting contributions to society, technology, or the competitive system.

### The why not?

For those with the talent and ambition to become successful entrepreneurs, the "why?" should be complemented with "why not?"; i.e., why not start a small business? From this point of view, the reasons reflect the advantages of entrepreneurship.

1. At no time and in no place has the climate for new small business been so good. Venture capital is more plentiful today than at any time in the past, and things keep getting better. Commercial banks, investment bankers, commercial finance companies, and others have become increasingly aware of the essence of capitalism reflected in entrepreneurship.

2. People tend to overestimate the difficulties and problems in starting a new business. Given some minimum level of talent, initiative and drive are the more important ingredients, particularly in view of the professional services available at reasonable cost, on either a part-time or full-time basis. Inventors, consultants, lawyers, and vendors are ready and waiting to help design, manufacture, and package a product to the entrepreneur's specifications.

3. The American economy, like no other, provides variety of distribution channels to accommodate virtually any type of product. Commission representatives, distributors, wholesalers, and jobbers of every description stand ready to service the entrepreneur in almost any conceivable distribution effort.

4. There are vast numbers of skilled, competent individuals in the economy's labor force waiting for "the right move." To the extent the entrepreneur needs help, it can be bought. In today's world it is not unethical to even buy the competition's talent. No stigma is attached to changing jobs. That segment of the labor force with talent and expertise is more mobile than ever. Additionally, it is not uncommon for professionals to join the effort for part ownership instead of cash, which can be to the advantage of both parties.

5. Government is becoming increasingly helpful to small business. The Small Business Administration at the federal level not only represents a potential source of funds, but also provides a wealth of information and assistance in its regional offices across the nation. At the regional and local levels, various development authorities and Small Business Investment Corporations offer assistance. The tax structures are also designed to provide incentives to the small business.

6. Finally, the personal and professional risks of entrepreneurship are usually overestimated. Leaving the "security" of being an employee and investing some amount of capital in a small business is not an irreversible position. In a complete failure, the entrepreneur loses his/her savings and has to find another job. But the experience has undoubtedly been of great personal and professional value. This is not to say that risk-taking does not involve a cost. But most things worth doing at all involve risk.

In summation, it seems many people with ability fail to take that first step into entrepreneurship because they have overestimated the hazards and underestimated the potential advantages. Furthermore, small business failures can be traced to a number of basic causes that can be avoided with a little foresight.

## SMALL BUSINESS FAILURES

In 1972 Dun & Bradstreet reported 9,566 business failures with unpaid liabilities in excess of $2 billion. And in nearly 56 percent of the cases the bankrupt concerns failed within the first five years of operation.

Year after year the record on business failures shows that in nine out of ten cases, the cause of failure is managerial inexperience or ineptitude. Among the major problems that plagued the bankrupt firms, insufficient sales generally headed the list, followed by "competitive weakness," and problems with receivables, or poor credit management.

Unfortunately, the general attitude of many entrepreneurs is that extra cash is the answer to most every problem. The evidence shows, however, that if a company has everything but good management, it may prosper for a while, but eventually it is doomed. On the other hand, if the firm's strongest asset is management it will succeed one way or another.

Businesses that fail, both large and small, seem to repeatedly make the same management errors. Thus, one of the best ways for the entrepreneur to learn management skills is by studying the mistakes of others. Bank of America's *Small Business Reporter* publication entitled "Avoiding Management Pitfalls" cites eight areas of management incompetency that generally lead to small business failure.

### Downgrading the need for experience

Most small businesses are founded on one person's abilities; the owner-manager. If this individual lacks the necessary skills and versatility to either perform or supervise the tasks of finance, accounting, marketing, production, personnel work and other aspects of management, the venture is destined for failure.

In the new firm, the best solution for lack of experience is adequate training prior to entrepreneurship; and the acquisition of people that add the necessary elements to the abilities of the management team. In the going concern the owner-manager must detect the missing parts of his/her experience and close those gaps with knowledgeable employees, partners, business consultants or counselors; and possibly an emergency self-development program.

### Poor record-keeping

Poor financial records create problems in ever facet of the small business; yet the need for a good accounting system is frequently overlooked.

A study of ten unsuccessful small businesses showed all had accounting systems so imprecise that the state of the business remained unknown even to the owners. In contrast, a similar study of ten successful ventures revealed complete accounting systems, and well-informed managers who knew how to use the financial data in running the company.

Although a knowledgeable accountant can set up an effective system and keep it going; the entrepreneur must understand the financial information derived from the system and be able to use it in decision-making.

## Poor cash management

The failure to maintain a stable and adequate financial position is a serious management error. A "cash poor" firm has little or no bargaining position, and must waste a good deal of time struggling to appease creditors.

The nearsighted entrepreneur often allows capital to reach dangerously low levels. Bills cannot be paid with machines, or inventory, or accounts receivable; nor can these assets provide funds in an emergency.

In the new firm the problem is one of undercapitalization—simply not putting enough capital into the venture to really get started. In the going concern, on the other hand, too much capital can get tied up in fixed assets, slow-paying receivables, or obsolete inventory, if growth is not properly controlled.

In dealing with the cash flow problem the entrepreneur should consult with the accountant as well as with the banker. After studying the firm's records and financial statements these advisers can suggest ways to control costs and conserve cash. Furthermore, the manager should ask the accountant for instructions in proper budgeting and money management techniques to accomplish cost and cash control.

## Failure to plan

Professional business consultants generally agree that one of the most frequent causes of small business failure they observe is the lack of planning. The rapidly changing marketplace of today demands forward-looking strategies. Well-formulated plans permit the entrepreneur to take better advantage of opportunities as they arise and head off management difficulties before they become too serious.

Planning is not simply "thinking ahead." It involves the establishment of objectives and determination of methods for reaching the objectives. Without these elements the entrepreneur is merely indulging in wishful thinking, not planning.

## Misuse of time

The typical entrepreneur has too much to do in too little time. A normal work week may average 50 to 60 hours. Experience shows that in many cases owner-managers spend as much as half their time on trivial matters, and leave vital jobs undone.

Good time management is learning to control the job rather than letting the job control the person. The objective is to work "smarter," not harder. Proper management of time is a matter of self-discipline. Effective managers put "first things first"; they rank duties according to importance.

A critical aspect of time management involves delegating appropriate jobs to subordinates, to free the entrepreneur from the routine, operational duties. A manager who fails to properly delegate can become so involved with everyday activities that important jobs, like planning, are often rushed. A further problem is the perfectionist, who rationalizes his/her reluctance to delegate by claiming the employees are incompetent. Such persons are afflicted with the "I can do it better and faster myself" malady.

## Inattention to marketing

Sales is the secret to success in any business venture. The best of products, personnel, and physical plant is of little use without customers. Unfortunately, some entrepreneurs have the false impression that their products or services will sell themselves. They dislike the thought that the product or service must be "marketed."

The truth is, few things sell themselves. An organized and vigorous marketing program is essential to build customer awareness. Some view poor sales as an isolated problem rather than as a symptom of an inadequate marketing effort. In such cases, the entrepreneur attempts to stimulate sales through price cutting, aggressive sales tactics, or advertising gimmicks. But these short-run measures will not work unless the solution fits the specific marketing problem. Reduced prices are not a substitute for a poor location, and advertising will not sell an obsolete product.

An objective analysis of the firm's products or services, its present marketing effort, the competitive situation, and the genuine needs of customers will show the ways to solve sales problems.

## Ignoring the human factor

Many entrepreneurs encounter serious personnel problems. They complain about poor workmanship, absenteeism, long coffee breaks, and the failure of employees to follow directions. Experience shows that malcontent workers not only waste time and materials but also tend to drive away customers. Some 70 percent of all customer losses can be attributed to poor service and employee indifference.

Most employee difficulties result from poor personnel administration. Too many entrepreneurs spend all their time worrying about production, sales, and finance, and solve personnel problems on a "crisis" basis. A loyal and efficient work force can be built only if adequate attention is given to the hiring, training, and managing of employees.

## Failure to assume the proper role

The success or failure of any business venture depends on the quality of management. The same capital, materials, and machinery that produce profits for one may generate losses for another.

The skills and talents required to be a good manager change as the company changes. The managerial know-how necessary to run a one-man operation in the early years is much different from the needs of a growing firm five or ten years down the line.

As the firm grows to new stages of development the entrepreneur must adopt his/her role. The transition from operator, to manager, to executive must be smooth. If the entrepreneur sticks with the comfortable, familiar jobs, organizational growth and personal growth are both slowed.

## Concluding remarks

The eight pitfalls described are by no means a complete list, but alone or in combination, they emerge as the most significant factors accounting for small business failures. However, regardless of the specifics of the situation, one generalization is valid: the success or failure of any venture depends basically on one person, the entrepreneur.

Those who are destined to fail ignore the standards of good business practice and operate on the basis of trial and error. They go from crisis to crisis, always struggling with the same basic problems.

Those who succeed are able to admit their shortcomings and learn from their errors. They face problems head-on by improving their managerial skills. When necessary, they hire experience and expertise for assistance. The strong entrepreneur produces the strong organization.

## QUESTIONS

1. Which of the "motives" for becoming an entrepreneur seems to produce the most success? What is the second most successful "motive"?
2. What are the distinct advantages of entrepreneurship as you see them?
3. Year after year, what is the most common reason for small business failure?

4. Would you agree with the statement that if the entrepreneur can make it through the first five years, his/her chances for success improve?

5. Although many entrepreneurs have the general attitude that extra cash will cure all ills, what is the "real" key to success in small business?

6. Discuss briefly each of the eight most common "pitfalls" to success in small business.

## PROBLEMS

1. Examine, by interview if possible, three or four very successful small businesses in your community. Identify the factors in each case that appear to contribute to the firm's success.

2. Try to get some idea of the small business failure problem in your community. Attempt to examine some recent failures and identify the underlying causes as you see them.

3. Go to the nearest library that represents a government documents depository and survey the materials published by the Small Business Administration on small business failures; and factors contributing to success in small business.

4. Visit the nearest regional office of the Small Business Administration and discuss small business failures with an appropriate SBA official.

## BIBLIOGRAPHY

Baty, Gordon B. *Entrepreneurship: Playing to Win.* Reston, Va.: Reston Publishing Co., 1974. This book is an excellent treatise on entrepreneurship. It is required reading for anyone who aspires to operate his own business venture.

Klatt, Lawrence A. *Managing the Dynamic Small Business Firm: Readings.* Belmont, Calif.: Wadsworth Publishing Co., 1971. Another winner. This book is a collection of recently published articles that provide good sound advice to the entrepreneur. It is highly recommended.

# 2

# Why operate
# a small business?

There are many reasons why men and women want to start their own business. If the typical small business owner were asked why he or she elected a small business as a source of livelihood, probably the typical answer given would be "to be independent" or "to make money." However, these answers are often superficial. Much like the mountain climber who says he climbs mountains "because they are there," the small business owner may be inclined to give the answer he or she feels the interviewer is seeking rather than the true answer which lies deep within the man's or woman's mind and psychological structure.

Whether or not the typical small businessperson has any true insight into his or her basic motivations, it is true that usually small business is elected as a way of life on the strength of certain appealing advantages. These advantages are usually listed as: (1) being your own boss, (2) doing something you like, (3) job security, (4) community development, and (5) the all-important element of personal status. These factors therefore merit individual consideration.

## Being your own boss

The independence of being your own boss is a frequently sought goal. Obviously the freedom and independence of action which goes along with business ownership appeals to many individuals. Being your own boss, of course, has a variety of meanings for those who are seeking self-direction. To one person it may mean being able to close up shop and go fishing, to another it may be the freedom to do the work in the sequence he or she elects, or not having to kowtow to the whims of another person, or simply the privilege of making decisions in all matters pertaining to oneself. There is little question that the desire to be your own boss is a strong and obtainable factor in electing small business as a career.

9

## Doing something you like

Owning a small business entitles the individual to engage in a line of work which is enjoyable. Such freedom is closely linked to the independence gained from being your own boss. However, the freedom to do something you like goes further than merely being able to determine when you want to do something; it also includes the freedom to elect not to do something and to tell others what to do. It should therefore be recognized that the freedom of doing something which one likes is an advantage to small business ownership in and of itself.

## Job security

A surprisingly large number of small businesses are owned and operated by men or women who are seeking security or lack of dependency upon an employer. For example, one study found that about 25 percent of small businesses are started because of a need for providing the small businessperson with a job or some source of income. There is, obviously, a great advantage in being the owner of a small business from the standpoint of job security: few people have been known to fire themselves.

Whether or not many people start their own small businesses because of the anticipated or real loss of a job may be a debatable point. However, a large percentage of the population does tend to find themselves in jobs for which they are not particularly suited, which do not particularly appeal to them, and which they take no pride in doing. When this happens, they often are motivated to start their own business.

## Community development

Another area of major advantage to operating a small business lies in public service. Many people who own and operate their own small business have initiated these enterprises because they feel a responsibility to the community and need to shape and develop it. This feeling of responsibility toward the community is not a common feeling among all entrepreneurs, but those individuals that do feel that they have an obligation toward their community, state, and nation often find an opportunity for serving their communities via small business management.

## Personal status

There is one final advantage which many people seek by means of owning their own small business. That advantage is the personal status and recognition which they feel will be theirs as an entrepreneur. The general feeling in respect to the personal status which an individual attains as a small business manager is that he will be recognized as an independent businessperson. However, while the fact is that many people do feel they obtain status, recognition, or prestige by being successful small business managers, it is questionable whether small business management really is a source of such status and recognition. For example, some authorities feel that the image of the entrepreneur as the great inventor, promoter, or daring risk-taker simply does not square with the facts.

Although operating a small business may not bring with it the personal status and recognition sought, many people elect small business management in hopes of attaining such status and recognition.

## SHORTCOMINGS OF OPERATING A SMALL BUSINESS

Choosing the field of small business certainly has its merits. However, before jumping in head first, the disadvantages should also be considered. These disadvantages can be serious.

### Having to serve undesirable customers

One of the major disadvantages of operating a small business lies in the area of freedom the small business manager has. Although it may be true that an individual operating his or her own business is not dependent upon an employer's dictating how, when, and where to do a job, he or she is really *everyone's* subordinate. The cliche "the customer may not be always right, but is always the customer," certainly contains more truth than fiction. Furthermore, the customer is only one of the groups that is always right so far as the small businessperson is concerned. For example, a small business manager in trying to renew a short-term loan to carry him or her over to a period of low sales might discover that bankers are right—or at least like to be treated as if they are right. By the same token, distributors who are extending credit like to feel that they are right or— if they are wrong—that they have the privilege of delivering at their convenience rather than at the "right" merchant's convenience. And similarly, the landlord, the plumber, the newspaper editor, and the city councilman may or may not be right, but at least they are easier to get along with if they are treated as if they are right.

### Paper work and other chores

Another problem in operating a small business is the paper work and other chores involved. Most persons who enter small business management recognize that there will be paper work. However, many do not recognize the amount involved, particularly if their business happens to be a booming success. Oftentimes they do not realize that in addition to ordering new stock, they must also keep records of inventory, billing, payroll, collections, insurance, income tax, employee withholdings, employee insurance, etc. This paper work is not insurmountable; nor do all people detest such work. However, some individuals who (for example) like to work in electronics may not care about "pushing paper." By the same token, other people are of such a bent that they gladly—perhaps even gleefully—attend to the minutest of detail in paper work, only to neglect the real purpose of their business.

## Possible low income

Another real problem with operating a small business is the potentially low income. While everyone thinks they will "hit it big," the odds are that they will fail, losing their assets in the process. One authoritative source found that the typical small business will only provide a minimal income and practically no return on investment to the person(s) operating that business. A prominent national speaker on the subject of small business management even advises his clientele not to start a small business (even after they already have!).

## Long hours and demanding work conditions

Yet another disadvantage to operating a small business is that of long hours and hard work. Few people who successfuly run small businesses do so with short hours. Even fewer have plush work conditions. The overhead and other expenses in a small business certainly do not lend themselves well to ostentatious living. But those who are dedicated to the small business nevertheless will find the challenge worth the inconveniences.

## CONSTRAINTS ON OPERATING A SMALL BUSINESS

The preceding portion of this chapter has been designed to point out some of the advantages and disadvantages of electing small business as a way of life. However, two points should be made clear before proceeding further: First, an individual who chooses the life of a small business manager must recognize that his or her decision does not guarantee that he will be successful. Second, although the individual who elects small business can control his or her environment to a very large degree, how this is done can make life either a dream or a nightmare. The following discussion points out some of the additional factors which the small businessperson must cope with if he or she is to be successful.

## The market for the small business product or service

To a great degree most of the above advantages are inherent in small business management. However, there are some factors impinging upon the small business manager which may serve to his or her advantage or disadvantage, depending on managerial ability. One of the first of these is the working of the market itself. True, the small business manager may be totally victimized by a change in the market for the product or service. But by the same token, there may be an opportunity to capitalize on a market change. This does not apply to those instances when the market tends to "fall in one's lap" or is stolen by a competitor. Such caprice of the market often is uncontrollable. Rather, what is meant here are the times that the small business manager works the market to his or her advantage (or disadvantage) by taking some kind of action to gain control or influence over opportunities or changes in the market. This point can be made more appropriately by the following case.

Bob Smith, a carpenter, lived with his wife and two children at a trailer park. One of his routine chores on Saturday was to replace his bottled gas containers as needed since such service was not available in his trailer park. Bob was a young, friendly individual, and his neighbors felt no compunction at asking him to pick up their bottled gas in his truck.

Obviously, here was a need for a bottled gas distributing service. Bob saw this need and quite profitably met it by (1) getting a franchise arrangement with the bottled gas distributor in his area, and (2) informing his neighbors (many of whom were friendly only on Saturday mornings) that he was starting a business and would be charging for his services.

The moral of the above case is that Bob recognized a market and captured it. It must be recognized, of course, that the very advantage which created the need for, and profitability of, Bob's services could be lost just as capriciously. For example, it might be that a natural gas pipeline would be installed in his area. The true small business manager having entrepreneurial qualities, however, would be prepared for such an encroachment and would have an alternative enterprise when the need arose.

## City codes and city councils

The activities and events of the city council (or other govermental agencies) can go a long way toward determining whether a small business will be a boom or bust. Again, using Bob as an example, what would happen (as actually did occur) if the city council suddenly gave rights to a Public Utility to install natural gas lines in Bob's sales area?

Because of his awareness of the needs and activities of others, Bob had been looking around for other business activity. Seeing that no amount of lobbying on his part would prevent the activity of the council, Bob attempted to broaden his market area to more isolated areas. This he did, and he continued to maintain a reasonable profit, although not as great as before.

## Other business problems

Continuing with our story of Bob, subsequently he ran into another business adversity. A customer with a sizable bill was unable to pay what he owed. The customer was a stonemason and was nothing more than a financial liability to Bob until he hit on the idea of giving the man the opportunity to work off the debt. Bob was a good carpenter and he determined that the stonemason was a good bricklayer. It seemed clear that all Bob needed to start his own house construction crew was to hire plumbers and electricians and people from a few other trades. Bob soon found himself in the business of speculative home building. He made a tidy sum not only recovering the bricklayer's arrearages but earning a markup on the man's work. This soon became a successful home construction business.

While the above may sound like luck to some, Bob's success was a combination of drive, energy, determination, and the myriad of other entrepreneurial characteristics which create success in small business management. He had the ability to perceive the market needs, to keep current on what was happening by way of legislation which would affect his business, and to keep up with what his competitors and customers were doing. Had Bob not possessed such ability, he might have wound up working for the stonemason upon whom he capitalized.

## DETERMINING IF YOU ARE READY TO START A BUSINESS

By now the reader should be fairly conversant with the role of small business in the American economy and the role of the individual in operating a small business. However, this knowledge is not sufficient for the individual to actually select himself or herself as a manager of a small business. Entirely too many people enter their own business without knowing whether or not they are qualified to manage it. The usual train of thought which lures a person into this trap is as follows: (1) I know what it takes to be a small business manager, (2) I will look out for my own best interests, and (3) I therefore have sufficient managerial knowledge and drive to make myself a successful business manager.

Such logic is not altogether true. The problem is that the potential small business manager is often guilty of not being able to see the forest for the trees. In short, although all systems may appear to be "go" from the standpoint of the person considering whether or not to start a small business, one problem still exists—the selection of the manager. Almost inevitably the person selected to manage the small business is the entrepreneur himself or herself. This does not mean that the person will be a successful manager. In fact, one might be better off not going into business if one must select oneself as his or her own manager. The following topics, therefore, are designed to probe the ins and outs and whys and wherefores of selecting oneself as a small business manager. It is hoped that the discussions will either discourage or encourage the reader to select himself or herself as his or her own company president.

## An entrepreneurial person—who is he or she?

Economic studies of all types have been conducted to evaluate the feasibility of new business formation. Large corporations continuously engage in such activity, investigating the opportunity, resources, and support elements needed in stimulating the development of new business opportunity. However, such studies are really only feasibility studies, for the final recommendations are directly related to the existence of individuals who are capable of perceiving, interpreting, and acting upon such opportunities. The final determination for starting a new business venture depends upon the availability of managerial talent. The existence of capable individuals is taken for granted by large corporations—they develop the managers they need. However, such an assumption is not always correct for the person wanting to start his or her own small business. Whereas big business recognizes the value of trained managers and will not expand operations without qualified individuals to take over the management, people starting small businesses often fail to recognize the requirement for managerial talent.

The reason that the need for managerial talent is not recognized lies in the fact that small business does not expand in proportionally smaller increments, like large corporations do. Rather, small business is either (1) initiated from scratch, or (2) expanded into an area which will perhaps double its operations. Therefore, it can reasonably be said that small businesses need good, well-developed managerial talent the minute they open their doors, whereas large corporations can grow and develop them as needed. In substance the problem is that too often the presumption is made that the person who wants to start his or her own small business is capable of leaping right in and becoming a *complete* manager of a total enterprise with little or no prior training as a general manager.

Because this fallacious assumption is often made by the potential small business manager, many investigations have been undertaken concerning the characteristics of the kind of person who becomes an enterprising individual. The findings are particularly relevant to any persons interested in managing their own business because they shed light on the types of individuals who have been *successful* as small business managers.

There are significant differences between the typical small business-person and the typical large business manager in the United States. The typical small businessperson grows up in a family of working class origins, with better than half of them having fathers whose principal occupation was either farming, clerking, selling, or unskilled, semiskilled, or skilled labor. Further, it has been found that nearly two thirds of the people who become successful entrepreneurs have had a poor, and oftentimes under-privileged, early family life. Although this is not always true, it is argued that one of the reasons that blacks and other minority groups form an increasing percentage of successful small businesspersons is because of their backgrounds and the extraordinary achievement drives they have developed as a result of these backgrounds.

## Education levels of enterprising people

It is frequently argued that education is the key to success, and that to be successful in managing a business, one must have high levels of educa-tion. However, many studies find that the educational levels of small business entrepreneurs is quite diverse, being almost equally distributed between those with no high school education, those with some high school education, high school graduates, those with some college education, and college graduates.

Thus, it could be argued that higher education offers little advantage to the small business manager. But, there may be some question as to the causal relationship between success as an entrepreneur and the possession of a high school or college diploma. The argument might be made that a man is successful as an entrepreneur *despite* his high school or college diploma rather than because of it, but the argument could also be made that some small businesspeople succeed because they do possess high school or college diplomas.

## Age and sex

Age is one factor which is always considered important by people in evaluating someone's worth. The young think the old are just taking ad-vantage of having been born earlier, while the old feel the young have no seasoning, no experience to rely on when things get rough. Actually, both points of view possess elements of truth, but various studies have shown that for the small business manager, age is *not* a relevant or differentiating criterion for success. Although small business owners tend to be older, with a median age of 40 years, this is primarily a result of need rather than ability, drive, or desire. For example, when faced with unemployment, younger people are more apt to continue their schooling; but for those who have reached middle age, starting their own business is often the only alternative. Furthermore, starting a business usually requires capital—something youth does not always have and is often placed at a handicap in acquiring.

Another factor, once considered in the same category as age, is that of sex. This factor is complicated by the fact that in recent years women have become an increasing percentage of the work force. The fact may be that women sometimes can stay in business because they are not breadwinners. On the other hand, it may be just as true that women are often discriminated against as managers. No valid conclusions can be drawn in respect to sex as a criterion for success as a small business manager, but it is true that an increasingly large percentage of today's entrepreneurs are women or come from minority groups.

## Sociopsychological attitudes of the entrepreneur

While the foregoing would tend to indicate that neither the background, educational level, age, or sex is significant to the success or failure of the typical entrepreneur, there is an element which does appear to be indicative of the possible success or failure for the small businessperson in general. This element is his sociopsychological attitude toward life.

For example, it has been indicated that the most significant difference between entrepreneurs and executives in established organizations is their attitude toward authority figures and interpersonal relations. The successful business executive usually has a positive attitude toward authority, whereas successful entrepreneurs are often people who have little regard for authority figures and have failed in their attempts to achieve traditional and highly structured goals and objectives available to them in society. They seem to have found outlets for their creativity, drive, and energy by creating their own businesses. One psychologist using a Thematic Apperception Test found that, in fact, there were dominant themes or traits which run through the "typical" entrepreneur's personality. These themes include the following: (1) social value systems steeped in middle-class mores; (2) lack of social mobility drives—i.e., no desire to climb up the social ladder; and (3) unremitting pursuit of tasks.

In summary, the successful small business manager who set about formulating and managing his or her own business will often be a derivative of a lower income family, who may or may not be well educated, but who is striving, unrelenting, unyielding in terms of pursuit of his goals and objectives, yet a person who might even be contemptuous toward authority figures. The successful manager of a small business also strongly believes in the worth and need for his or her product or service, and is willing to risk all in pursuing his or her objective of independence from others.

## Comparing yourself to the models of success

Awareness of the above factors should go a long way toward helping a person determine whether he or she is capable of managing a small business. The unfortunate part of the above analysis is the fact that, like many things, when one wants to compare onself to the standard and even tries to be wholly objective in that comparison, the standard is still loose enough that one can generally say that he or she personally "fits the pattern." It is too easy for persons to rationalize that, because they came from a wage-earning family, they are "an exception," or they are hard-hitting, driving, enthusiastic, and not awed by authority figures, and thus can become successful managers of small enterprises. Therefore, simply tracing the characteristics of the successful small business manager may contribute little or no insight into one's potential selection of oneself as an entrepreneur. What is needed is more insight into the specific characteristics of successful small business managers. Since certain personality traits seem to distinguish the successful small business manager from those who fail to succeed, these will be examined in greater detail.

## The success model—a personality profile

One study, directly concerned with the personality characteristics of successful small business management, identifies five factors which can be considered relevant to success as a small businessperson. These include the personality characteristics of drive, thinking ability, human relations ability, communications ability, and technical knowledge. What is meant by these five factors, how they contribute to one's success, and how they can be identified will now be considered:

*1. Drive.* The element of drive includes one's willingness to accept responsibility, one's vigor, initiative, persistence, and health. While the study indicates that successful small business managers possess a great amount of all these factors, various elements of this trait should not be subjected to self-evaluation. Rather, they should be evaluated by customers and suppliers or by means of psychological tests. This, then, implies that a potentially successful small businessperson will possess a great deal of drive as measured by objective observers but not necessarily as measured by himself or herself.

*2. Thinking ability.* Thinking ability is defined as the ability for original thinking, creative thinking, critical thinking, and analytical thinking. Again there appears to be a correlation between one's ability to think creatively, originally, critically, and analytically and the success of the small business manager. However, the important *measurement* of a person's thinking ability is a function of other people's evaluation—not in how individuals perceive themselves. Thus, while thinking ability can be proven as a requisite for success of small business managers, they themselves may not be capable of evaluating their own ability to think. Perhaps more important than whether or not persons can evaluate their own thinking ability, however, is the fact that one's thinking abilities can be developed, if need be. That is, the enhancement of one's thinking ability —the ability to solve problems, make effective decisions, evaluate alternatives, discern between hazy alternatives, etc.—is the gist of all our educational programs and is the one long-lasting asset which can be gained by attending college, night school, etc. Furthermore, by their grading standards, such educational institutions tend to provide a very accurate feedback and evaluation service to individuals wanting to evaluate themselves on their thinking ability.

3. *Human relations ability.* The characteristic of human relations ability is composed of the elements of ascendancy, emotional stability, sociability, cautiousness, personal relations, consideration, cheerfulness, cooperation, and tactfulness. As in the case of drive and thinking ability, there is a significant correlation between success of the small business manager, and how he or she is rated by customers on human relations ability, and other related factors. However, it is the ratings given the small businessperson by *others* which is considered related to success, not self-evaluation—or the evaluation made by family or friends.

4. *Communications ability.* Communications ability includes verbal comprehension, verbal communications, and written communications. There seems to be a definite relationship between communications ability and the success of a small business manager. Again, this relationship was established on the basis of verbal comprehension tests and on customer and supplier questionnaires on the subject of the small business manager, and not on the basis of small business managers' self-evaluations. Thus, although everyone feels they communicate effectively, the ability to communicate is more effectively measured by people who must associate with the communicators rather than by the communicators themselves.

5. *Technical knowledge.* The technical knowledge element, as treated here, is all-encompassing. Possession of technical knowledge relating to the business appears to be a correlate of success as a small business manager. However, as with the other factors mentioned, technical knowledge can best be measured by the judgment ratings of customers and suppliers. Those who must deal with a person are in the best position to evaluate whether the person is knowledgeable on a given subject. Use of the technical knowledge criterion is, therefore, a very tenuous self-selection criterion, for few people are willing to admit that they don't know all there is to know about their jobs. Yet lack of job knowledge accounts for a great deal of small business failure.

In summary, research shows that drive, thinking ability, communications ability, human relations ability, and technical knowledge are all correlates of success of a small business manager, but the existence of these traits usually are discerned accurately only by outsiders and not by small business managers themselves. Further, it should be recognized that an ample possession of one quality will not necessarily serve to offset a shortage of another quality. That is, there appears to be a requirement for the small businessperson to be rated high on all factors—drive, thinking ability, communications ability, human relations ability, and technical knowledge—if he or she is to be a success.

Thus, the requirement for success for the small business manager presents itself as almost entirely a function of the small business manager's psychological makeup and personality profile. The successful small business manager is a person who has rebelled against authority, possesses drive, creative thinking ability, human relations savvy, communications ability, and has thorough technical knowledge. In contrast, the person who is doomed to failure is awed by authority, possesses little drive and initiative, is not a creative thinker, is not gregarious by nature, is not particularly adept at communicating, and is not very knowledgeable in his or her job.

## SUMMARY

This chapter has discussed some of the pitfalls, problems, and promises involved in operating a small business. It was determined that successful small business managers come from poorer, laboring class families and that there may be little correlation between their success and their educational attainments, age, or sex. On the other hand, their sociopsychological attitude or personality is critical to their prospective success.

The difficulty in a person evaluating himself or herself as a prospective small business manager is that it is hard to be wholly objective about oneself. This lack of objectivity is complicated by shortcomings inherent in the various self-selection guidelines commonly used in determining whether or not an individual should go into small business management. Therefore, it is of extreme importance that reliable, objective opinions be obtained concerning the individual's qualifications before he or she starts a small business. Unfortunately, since the final decision with respect to going into small business management resides with the individual, in all likelihood the self-styled entrepreneur will make his or her decision on the basis of their own desires and not as a result of cold, critical evaluation. Once the decision is made, it can only succeed if individuals commit themselves unequivocally. Without such commitment, failure is virtually assured. With such commitment, a bad situation may be saved and a good situation may triumph.

## QUESTIONS

1. Describe the risks inherent in a person selecting himself or herself as the manager of his or her own business. Why is subjective bias not the only problem inherent in such self-selection?

2. How important is education to the probability of a person's success as a small business manager? Are any particular kinds of educational background more likely to predict the success of someone as a small business-person?

3. Is there any pattern or stereotype which one might present as a "typical" personality of today's small businessperson? Explain your answer.

4. Is "thinking ability" relevant to an individual's probable success as a small businessperson? How can persons (a) evaluate their thinking ability and (b) improve their thinking ability?

5. What kind of program would you use to evaluate yourself if you were thinking of starting your own small business? Develop such a plan in detail.

6. What are the probabilities of financial loss if one does go into business for oneself? What are the probabilities of gain? Explain fully how you believe these probabilities are evaluated by prospective small businesspeople.

7. The desire to be independent or to make more money is often listed as a reason many persons want to manage their own small business. Are these valid reasons? Why or why not?

8. Is it true that the small business manager can always do those things that he likes and avoid doing those things which he dislikes doing? Why or why not? Qualify your answer if you stated: "It depends."

9. What would be your reply to a person's statement that there is a major advantage to owning and operating one's own small business because of the feeling of public service which one receives from such activity?

10. What would be your comment to a person who states that "the entrepreneur is a great inventor, promoter, or great and daring risk-taker?" Present both your reply to this question and what you would anticipate someone's rebuttal to your reply would be.

## PROBLEMS

1. Georgia Burkes is a sometime beautician who has decided to open her own fashion boutique. Her friends tell her she will fail, and the bank absolutely refused to advance her any money. She has asked you to back her.

    What would you look for, what information would you expect, and on what basis would you (a) back her financially, (b) assess her probability of success, and (c) decide on her ultimate credentials as a small business-person?

2. John Towne and his wife Maria were both college graduates. John had his bachelor's degree in business and his wife had hers in art. Both of them were ambitious and had worked their independent ways up the corporate

ladder in the companies where each had gone to work subsequent to their graduation from a small state college. John was now Head Bookkeeper in the company he worked for and Maria had been promoted to Senior Buyer in the large department store for which she worked.

Both John and Maria have wanted to go into business for themselves for a long time. Both their families' backgrounds are entrepreneurial and John's sister has been a successful local distributor for a large cosmetics firm that sells door-to-door. Both John and Maria feel that they have what it will take for success if they open a fabric and upholstery shop. Maria knows buying and materials and John can certainly handle the bookkeeping.

- a. Do you think John and Maria will be successful? Why or why not?
- b. What would you, as their friend, advise them to consider before starting their own business?
- c. Develop a list of five items that you feel are critical indicators for success to John and Maria's endeavor, assuming they pursue it.

## BIBLIOGRAPHY

Allen, Louis L. *Starting and Succeeding in Your Own Small Business.* New York: Grosset & Dunlap, 1968, 156 pp. A good, basic book for anyone interested in starting a small business.

Baumback, Clifford; Kelly, Pearce; and Lawyer, Kenneth. *How to Organize and Operate a Small Business.* 5th ed. Englewood Cliffs, N.J.: Prentice-Hall, 1973, 672 pp. A foundation book for anyone wanting to become an entrepreneur.

Dible, Donald M. *Up Your Own Organization.* Santa Clara, Calif.: Entrepreneur Press, 1971. An excellent book on the financial aspects of starting and managing a new business. Contains a very good bibliography.

Steffire, Volnew. *The Small New Business.* Springfield, Va.: Clearinghouse for Federal Scientific and Technical Information, 1969. This text deals directly with the problems of getting a new business going. Contains much financial matter.

# 3

# Sponsors of
# small business

The world of small business operation and management can often be a very lonely existence. Many of the operators of the smaller business are very small. There may be as many as 10.5 million small businesses, based on the figures compiled by the National Small Business Association,[1] and of this total perhaps one third will never develop sales of over $20,000 per year. When you are small and in a remote community somewhere, you may have the company of others like yourself, but not much of anyone to help you.

Fortunately for the small business entrepreneurs and managers there are agencies, companies, financiers, and advisers who do make it their business to help small business operators. Many supporters expect adequate return for their efforts, but expect that the small business will be equally benefited in the process. Others help because small business is a part of the economic system and deserves its share of the available expertise. Others are benevolent in their efforts and derive personal satisfaction in helping others to succeed.

Support tends to develop from the following kinds of sources:

1. U.S. Small Business Administration
2. Minority enterprise agencies and associations
3. Small business investment companies
4. Venture capital firms
5. Franchisors
6. Trade associations
7. Bureaus of business research (state universities)
8. Economic development associations
9. Commercial banks
10. A variety of federal, state, and local governmental agencies

[1] *The Case For Small Business* (Rocky Mountain Industries, January 1975), pp, 22–24. Comments by John E. Lewis, Executive Vice President of National Small Business Association.

## SMALL BUSINESS ADMINISTRATION

The Small Business Administration (SBA), which is now a permanent agency of the U.S. Government, has been in existence since 1953. During this period of over 20 years, the SBA has engaged in a wide range of activities. Because the SBA is an important factor in small business activity, the more important agency activities are summarized under a number of categories following this introduction.

For the purpose of making loans the SBA specifies business size which must in general meet the following criteria:

1. Wholesale—Annual receipts from $1 million to $5 million, depending on the industry.
2. Retail or Service—Annual receipts from $1 million to $5 million, depending on the industry.
3. Construction—Annual receipts of not more than $5 million, averaged over a three-year period.
4. Manufacturing—from 250 to 1500 employees, depending on the industry.

The prospective entrepreneur or owner must realize that the above listings are a means of establishing operating and maximum sizes for types of direct loans and *do not* limit assistance through other methods such as participation loans or guaranteed loans through banks or other agencies.

### Financial assistance

Businesses needing financial assistance can contact an SBA office for advice. The agency may help in providing information to enable the individual or group to secure a conventional loan. If this seems unlikely, SBA may consider a participation loan with a bank or guaranteeing a bank loan up to 90 percent. A direct loan might be made if funds are available, but most SBA loans are made in cooperation with banks. The funds obtained can be used for construction, expansion of the business, acquiring machinery, equipment, supplies and materials, and for use as working capital.

Under the loan guarantee plan, the SBA can guarantee up to 90 percent of the bank loan or $350,000 (whichever is less) with an interest rate set by the bank, within limits set by the SBA. These limits vary from time to time.

### Economic opportunity loans

These loans are made to disadvantaged businessmen or women to enable them to own their own businesses. These loans are based on the inability of a family unit to generate basic family income needs or conventional financing not being available because of social or economic disadvantages. Each applicant must prove some ability and is expected to have some money or other available assets.

## State and local SBA development companies

The state development companies are formed to promote business within a state. Where small businesses are involved loans are available up to the amounts generated from other sources.

The local development company loans are community-oriented and depend on a number of people who put up local money to finance development. Such loans are often in participation with other organizations which are concerned with the local community development and betterment.

## Disaster loans

The disaster loans are based on such circumstances as storms, floods, and earthquakes and also on other circumstances such as displacement due to urban renewal and hardships brought on by compliance with new legislation.

Because these loans are so variable, no details are given here. The actual loan may be handled by the SBA but dependent on action by some other federal agency. A presidential proclamation or action by a presidential cabinet secretary may generate loans to meet the various needs of businesses that have suffered a qualifying disaster.

## Lease guarantee program

Under this program the SBA will guarantee through an insurance policy the lease of a businessman or woman who is lacking in the credit rating necessary to secure a good lease location. Special conditions are involved in this program, but the SBA is favorable to the program and it should be investigated by the business operator who needs a good or improved location.

## Procurement assistance

The SBA is charged with the responsibility of making sure that small businesses participate in certain federal government contracts. Often the contract is written with a specific "set-aside" which must be filled by some small business. Often these will be subcontracts which are let out by the prime contractor to the smaller business. There are a number of activities associated with the procurement assistance program which help the smaller business. Meetings and seminars are held to inform firms how to bid. Efforts are also made to inform firms of pending contracts and to sell surplus property to small business.

## Management assistance

A number of different programs have been devised by the SBA to provide direct management assistance to small businesses.

In the training programs SBA conducts courses, conferences, problem clinics, and workshops. The courses are set up to help in the setting of policies, implementing objectives, and other functional activity which is deemed useful in any particular business.

Conferences deal with particular and specific topics, whereas clinics are concerned with various types of problem-solving. Workshops also concentrate on the area of problems and problem-solving.

## SCORE

The word SCORE is formed by the initials for Service Corps Of Retired Executives. These persons are ex-business executives who offer their services to help small business operators. Generally an initial visit is made, some time is spent with the businessperson, and some suggestions are made which are based on the executive's background of experience and knowledge.

The SCORE group are not paid consultants, nor do they recommend any specific firms to implement their suggestions. They may, however, suggest that certain help be obtained, which may include the services of a professional consultant such as a CPA.

## MINORITY BUSINESS ENTERPRISE

The increased emphasis on minority business enterprise is primarily based on efforts of the federal government. Growing dedication to helping minority groups is a part of the total effort to improve the economic position of all minorities, and in particular to do so by enabling them to assume an expanded position in the areas of business activity.

Positive results to the mid-1970s are still very limited, but some progress is being made. A number of different aid programs have been initiated and some direct funding of business enterprises has been tried.

A Task Force on Education and Training for Minority Business Enterprise[2] published a final report in January 1974. Their basic findings after 18 months of effort are listed as follows:

1. The alarmingly high failure rate of minority-owned businesses is attributed primarily to poor management and business skills of the owners and managers of these enterprises.
2. There is a chronic shortage of trained minority talent available to meet the pressing need for owners, managers, and business technicians in the growing number of new and expanding minority business firms.
3. Management and business skills are critical elements in the survival and successful growth of minority business enterprises.
4. Education and training programs designed to provide needed management and business skills must become an integral part of the national strategy to expand minority business ownership.
5. Entrepreneurship as a career opportunity for minority youth is given inadequate attention within the total educational system.
6. There is a wide range of existing national, state, and local resources which can be enlisted to support or conduct minority business enterprise education and training programs for existing, potential and future entrepreneurs.

The task force report further states that as of the date of their report no single federal agency had the ultimate responsibility for minority business education and training development. It stresses further that the need is urgent and that steps should be taken without delay to correct the existing deficiencies.

The two tables that follow illustrate the employment and income patterns of minority persons. Among the minority groups the number of self-employed persons is a very small percent of the total employed, and family income levels for certain minority groups is very low in comparison to the average family income in the United States.

## Office of Minority Business Enterprise

The federal government provides most of the technical assistance to minority groups through the Office of Minority Business Enterprise. These efforts are primarily devoted to such things as local business development organizations, business resource centers, minority businessmen's and trade associations and other joint programs with state and local government

---

[2] See *Report of the Task Force on Education and Training for Minority Business Enterprise* (Department of Health, Education, and Welfare, January 1974). The Executive Committee of this group represented the Department of Commerce, the Department of Health, Education and Welfare, and the Department of Labor.

**TABLE 3-1**
**Minority persons 16 years of age and over (by class of worker, 1970)**

| Class | Black | | Spanish-speaking | | Japanese | | American Indian | | Chinese | | Filipino | |
|---|---|---|---|---|---|---|---|---|---|---|---|---|
| | Number | Per-cent | Number | Per-cent | Number | Per-cent | Number | Per-cent | Number | Per-cent | Number | Per-cent |
| Total employed | 7,361,143 | 100 | 2,893,630 | 100 | 263,972 | 100 | 190,233 | 100 | 183,562 | 100 | 131,555 | 100 |
| Private salary & wage workers | 5,545,534 | 76 | 2,389,487 | 83 | 180,790 | 69 | 133,113 | 70 | 128,304 | 70 | 102,707 | 78 |
| Government workers | 1,560,020 | 21 | 366,459 | 13 | 53,980 | 20 | 46,483 | 24 | 34,705 | 19 | 24,154 | 18 |
| Self-employed workers | 243,460 | 3 | 128,509 | 4 | 26,672 | 10 | 9,732 | 5 | 17,797 | 10 | 4,442 | 4 |
| Unpaid family workers | 12,129 | 0 | 9,175 | 0 | 2,530 | 1 | 901 | 1 | 2,756 | 1 | 252 | 0 |

Source: U.S. Department of Commerce, Bureau of the Census, Census of Population, 1970.

TABLE 3-2
Median income of families

| Group | Median income | Percent of white income |
|---|---|---|
| Total United States. . . . . . . . . | $ 9,616 | 96 |
| White. . . . . . . . . . . . . . . . . | 9,977 | 100 |
| Black . . . . . . . . . . . . . . . . . | 6,063 | 61 |
| Spanish-speaking . . . . . . . . . . | 7,348 | 74 |
| Mexican . . . . . . . . . . . . . . | 6,962 | 70 |
| Puerto Rican . . . . . . . . . . . | 6,165 | 62 |
| Cuban . . . . . . . . . . . . . . | 8,529 | 85 |
| American Indian . . . . . . . . . . | 5,832 | 58 |
| Japanese . . . . . . . . . . . . . . | 12,215 | 126 |
| Chinese. . . . . . . . . . . . . . . | 10,610 | 107 |
| Filipino. . . . . . . . . . . . . . | 9,318 | 93 |
| Hawaiian* | | |
| Female. . . . . . . . . . . . . . | 2,931 | |
| Male . . . . . . . . . . . . . . . | 6,485 | |

* Family data are not available for Hawaiians. These figures represent median individual incomes.
Source: U.S. Department of Commerce, Bureau of the Census, Census of Population, 1970.

agencies. The activities conducted through 1972 included the counseling of 16,000 minority businesspersons, packaging of 1,500 loan applications, and providing management and technical assistance to over 5,000 minority firms.[3] In spite of these efforts much more is needed, and it seems reasonable that the programs of OMBE will continue to provide help.

## Limited SBICs

Limited SBICs are Small Business Investment Companies which specialize in providing equity loans, long-term loans, and management assistance to small business concerns owned by socially or economically disadvantaged persons. To qualify as disadvantaged, the business must be at least 50 percent owned and managed by individuals from disadvantaged groups.

Amendments to the Small Business Investment Act of 1972 increased the potential operating conditions for the Limited SBICs. By the end of 1972 there were 53 licensed Limited SBICs, with private capitalization of $18.4 million. So far the effort is limited in terms of potential minority business effort. Progress, however, is being made and undoubtedly will continue.

[3] U.S. Department of Commerce, Progress Report, the Minority Business Enterprise program, January 1972, p. 99.

## SMALL BUSINESS INVESTMENT COMPANIES

One form of venture capital investment firm is the Small Business Investment Company (SBIC). This form was generated by the Small Business Investment Act of 1958, and as of 1974 there were about 700 licensed companies. Of these, about 450 are active, and include not only companies with small groups of local investors but also firms that are quite large and publicly traded. About 80 of the total are owned by commercial banks.

An SBIC may invest up to 20 percent of its capital in a single small business, based on the original minimum private investment of at least $150,000. If the firm specializes in venture capital financing and is capitalized at more than $500,000, it may qualify for SBA-direct or SBA-guaranteed loans aggregating up to $20 million.

The loans made by these firms are usually in excess of $75,000 and financing must be made for at least a five-year period. Many of the investments have been made in companies that are engaged in scientific or technological development and innovations.

The SBICs are permitted to make long-term loans, purchase stock in the company, acquire debt securities, or combine equity and loan financing. Companies which wish to obtain loans cannot have assets over $7.5 million, net worth of $2.5 million, or annual profits (two-year average) of over $250,000.

As is apparent from the foregoing, SBICs are sources of financing for the "larger small business." The SBICs are also interested in companies which have a definite growth potential, not the firm that is in a conventional industry or business with a stabilized business activity. Some proven "track record," with an established profit pattern and growth potential, is usually necessary before an SBIC will consider a loan to an enterprise.

## VENTURE CAPITAL FIRMS

The term *venture capital* has been used in discussing SBIC activity in the previous section. The indication is that those firms are venture capital sources and do provide capital under somewhat more risky circumstances than conventional financiers do.

There are, however, many other venture capital firms, or private groups, that do provide help to the new or growing small firm. As explained previously, venture capital is nearly always placed in a business situation that represents short-term stability and substantial long-term growth potential.

Entrepreneurs, prospective business operators, and promoters of suitable firms and potential business propositions should not overlook venture capital sources. These may only exist locally, or they may have to be discovered by the entrepreneur. In a sense, substantial investors in a newly formed corporation are venture capitalists, but they invest only if the odds are right.

A newly formed business, or one to be expanded, can be used to solicit support. Depending on the nature of the idea or proposed activity, the venture capitalist will base his judgment and decision on the elements of risk versus the potential of payoff. Venture capitalists do take sizable risks, but not without commensurate possibilities of substantial rewards.

In securing aid for the small business, the owners and operators must make sure they do not relinquish too much for the support received. Combinations of high interest rates, a share of the profits, having seats on the board of directors, and take-over agreements are all a part of the bargaining used by venture capitalists. The reason for the entrepreneur or owner to have his own business must not be lost to the venture capital firm as a condition of getting into or furthering the business.

Bankers, SBIC managers, and others in financing institutions are all potential sources who can suggest possible venture capital sources.

## FRANCHISING

The subject of franchising is included here because, if properly administered, franchising can be a real supporting basis on which a business can be started. This is notwithstanding the fact that franchising is under considerable attack for practices that are not in the best interests of the franchisee.

It is important to recognize that the principles on which franchises are based are fundamentally sound. Growth in the past 25 years is substantial testimony to the fact that the franchise industry has been a "growth industry" and in the period of rapid growth and expansion it developed many opportunities which were exploited by the franchisees. The franchisor provides the knowledge of business in accounting, standards and performance, merchandising, and product or service quality and performance. In addition, they add expertise and economies of scale in purchasing, promotion and advertising, financing, and other elements necessary to a streamlined, efficient program. The franchisee provides cash flow to the parent organization, investment of his own money into the franchise and fixed capital items, and works hard as his or her own boss in making the business a success. With these inputs from both sides the franchise is supposed to be an "unbeatable" combination.

Franchising has failed in many instances for several reasons. These can be summarized for both sides as follows:

### Where franchisors failed

1. Selling franchises only, with little thought given to the actual businesses to be created. Often a fraudulent practice which has been difficult to control.
2. Too rapid an expansion of franchised outlets in order to generate

cash from franchise sales. This left many franchises with very little guidance and direction.

3. Saddling the franchisee with too restrictive a set of operating controls and conditions. These are often stringent and abusive and defeat the teamwork needed for success.

4. A lack of "follow-through" once the franchise is established.

## Where franchisees failed

1. Assuming that the franchise system makes up for a lack of business training and managerial ability. The unscrupulous franchisor may sell the franchise and worry about his franchisee later.

2. A blind belief in numbers and multipliers. Many franchisees have been willing to accept facts and figures which are encouraging and perhaps inflated. The man who runs the business must always remain a realist.

3. A failure to seek competent legal and business advice regarding the franchise agreement and its operating conditions. While many franchisees have had legal advice, it has not always been given or accompanied by sound business evaluation. These things go hand in hand.

4. A lack of understanding of the nature of business and the elements of planning, organizational development, controls, and financing. Many franchisees have little understanding of basic cost accounting, budgeting, and adjustment to fluctuating cash flows.

Based on what has been said, why even consider that a franchise is a supporting element for small business? The answer is that a great many small businesses are now being conducted in a successful manner under the franchise system. Reputable and ethical franchisors such as *McDonald's* hamburgers, *Ben Franklin* variety stores, and *True Value* hardware stores are examples of firm names that support a large number of franchisees, who for the most part are satisfied with the franchise conditions. Firms such as these, and others, go to great lengths to make sure that their franchisees succeed. They know that they make money only if their retail and service outlets succeed. Otherwise, profits and reputations go downhill.

## Franchising systems

The basic form of the franchise system is a franchise organization which is formed to do business through firms that deliver the end product or service. In doing this the franchisor sets up the organization and develops the plan and format, which is then provided to the franchisee for a fee. The more common franchise arrangements are in distributorships, auto dealerships, service stations, retail stores, food service businesses, and manufacturing.

The "fast food" type of operation is probably the best known, particularly in the rapid growth period of the past 20 years. Somewhere around 40,000 fast-food outlets were in existence in 1970, with sales in excess of $5 million. The Holiday Inn chain is a good example of excellence in the service field, and the General Motors auto dealerships were, on the whole, very successful prior to the economic downturn and high gasoline prices that came in the early part of the 1970s.

A great deal can be learned from a careful study of the ethical systems enumerated earlier, along with a particular concentration on an individual company. At this point of time in the maturing cycle of the franchise industry, there seems little reason to move quickly into any franchise venture. Franchising may typically come on strong in the energy and environmental fields, particularly the development of various applications of solar energy. Even so, careful, thoughtful investigation is necessary before making any commitments. Recently, the federal government and state governments have tightened up their control over franchising arrangements to help protect potential franchisees. In 1971 California made effective the California Franchise Investment Law. This law requires that franchisors provide extensive information to the potential franchisee at least 48 hours prior to the signing of the franchise agreement.

### Franchise agreement analysis

The analysis process should be thorough and complete. The things of primary importance are suggested by the following summary list:

1. The history of the franchisor and franchisees as to success and profitability.
2. Cost analysis and financial requirements. Initially, for the franchise, for the royalty or percentage on volume, and *all* other financial commitments such as requirements to buy products and services.
3. A willingness for the franchisor to permit interviews of present and past franchise operators and an examination of pertinent operating data.
4. A full disclosure by the franchisor of the results of site studies, real estate agreements, "lease-backs," and how and under what conditions these will be applied.
5. Positive evidence of the training to be given the franchisee. Where, when, by whom, and the names of individuals who can be contacted who have received such training. Also evidence of continuing training or periodic retraining.

6. A complete and thorough review of the franchise agreement with the potential franchisee, with copies furnished for careful review by the franchisee's attorney.
7. A willingness by the franchisor to compromise potentially "abrasive" conditions in the franchise agreement. This may be contrary to the franchisor's policies, but some conditions are *potentially dangerous* to the position of the franchisee.

The above list could be extended with each new subject or sub-subject carrying its own word of warning. In spite of the fact that franchisors in the past have been rather arbitrary in dictating their terms, the inquiry and investigation conducted by the interested party should reveal whether the possible consequences have actually been used against the franchisee.

Entering into a franchise agreement is something which requires careful investigation and analysis—far beyond what can be included here. Useful information for the prospective franchise holder can be gained from the following list of reference books and pamphlets:

*Franchising reference sources:*

1. *1971 Directory of Franchising Organizations.* New York: Pilot Industries Inc., 347 Fifth Avenue, 64 pp. $2.00. Directory and guideline information for over 700 franchise firms.
2. Kursh, Harry. *The Franchise Boom.* Englewood Cliffs, N.J.: Prentice-Hall, 1969, 477 pp. A revised edition of a thorough treatment of the franchising field. Contains information useful to women and minority enterprises.
3. *The Annual: A Franchise Directory.* 1970 ed. New York: International Franchise Opportunity, 288 pp. A listing of over 1,450 American, Canadian, and overseas franchisors.
4. *The Franchise Guide.* Princeton, N.J.: Resource Publications, 1969, 458 pp. A comprehensive analysis of over 400 different franchises. A good cross section of different types.
5. Dias, Robert M., and Gurnick, Stanley I. *Franchising: The Investors Complete Handbook.* New York: Hastings House, 1969, 123 pp. A text that deals with the pros and cons of franchising. Information is valuable as a guide and checklist for the prospective franchisee.
6. Metz, Robert. *Franchising: How to Select a Business of Your Own.* New York: Hawthorne Books, 1969. 344 pp. A very good analytical book that outlines the steps to be taken in selecting a worthwhile franchise.

## TRADE ASSOCIATIONS

Nearly every segment of small business activity is a part of some identifiable related business activity. These might be hardware stores, variety stores, retail sporting goods stores, food wholesalers, florists, and many, many others. Most of these identified groups are represented by trade associations, which in turn may have an assortment of helpful materials for their membership.

Quite often the association publishes a newsletter or monthly magazine. These tend to run heavily to advertising, but at the same time do contain feature articles and information from the constituent membership which is useful to the operating manager or owner. Some associations have training programs and educational materials, but in general their published materials tend to run heavily to pragmatic how-to-do-it materials. In addition, meetings, workshops, and other get-together efforts are used to disseminate ideas and workable examples to the membership.

The principal value of the trade association and its efforts would be to expose the entrepreneurs to the kinds of owners and managers that represent his industry, plus the manner and methods that are used by these people in operating these businesses.

In running his or her business a prospective small businessperson should take advantage of the trade association and its efforts. Initially the dues may be more than one can afford, but in all probability the benefits from the membership are well worth the cost.

There are so many trade associations that it is impossible to give space to even a small number of them within this chapter. The entrepreneur or manager should consult a directory of trade associations to find out which ones he or she might wish to join.

## BUREAUS OF BUSINESS RESEARCH

It is customary for each senior state university to maintain a bureau of business research. These may also be existing in other state schools and in private schools as well.

The research materials developed by bureaus of business research are quite often the ideal thing for the small business owner or operator. Many reports and studies are generated on a regional or industry basis without regard for direct economic benefit to the bureau. In addition, the majority of publications are by law or policy available to the public. The cost is often very low, a fraction of what would be charged by a private agency. In addition, specific questions will often be answered if the knowledge has application to a group, rather than a single business. As an example, the Bureau Research at the University of Colorado publishes a *Directory of Manufacturers in Colorado*. This has been sold to the public in recent years for $15.00. As a source of company names, principal executives by name, and number of employees, no other publication can duplicate it. As a reference and mailing list it is invaluable and as such has a steady sale each year.

Again, as in the case of trade associations, it is impossible to enumerate the listing of these business bureaus. A prospective entrepreneur or manager should write to the leading business bureau in his state and ask for the list of available publications on state economic activity. It is also a good time to inquire about the possibility of special studies which would be useful and which might be financed by federal or state agencies or the particular trade association.

## ECONOMIC DEVELOPMENT ASSOCIATIONS

This category of helpful supporters of small businesses includes a "mixed bag" of organizations. These may be land development companies that are building and promoting industrial parks, railroad land development companies which wish to develop plant sites, and perhaps municipally financed industrial development districts, promoted by the local community or county.

A wide range of possibilities exist through these development associations. They provide useful building or operating sites, building and lease-back of factories, warehouses, etc., and in some cases arrangements for financing and employee help.

These kinds of associations are well enough established and available on a broad enough scale that they warrant investigation by a new or perhaps established entrepreneur or owner. The average person is unaware of the extent to which these associations exist and the kinds of help they provide.

In Colorado, the Colorado Economic Development Association is one of the largest, best known, and most successful organizations of this type which is primarily devoted to the cause of minority businessmen and women. Other associations throughout the United States are also working in behalf of certain types of businesses or groups of individuals. The prospective small businessman or woman should find out if an economic development firm or association has services available to help the business venture. If such an opportunity exists, it is very likely that the total services available through the association will include guidance, counseling, and management assistance. What is available probably goes much farther than what is provided by many other supporting organizations.

## COMMERCIAL BANKS

A number of the larger commercial banks, particularly those which have a number of branches, are engaged in certain programs for the smaller business. The best known of these is the *Small Business Reporter,* a publication series of the Bank of America in San Francisco, California. The *Reporter* is divided into Business Profiles which relate to particular

**FIGURE 3-1**
**Banks provide useful data for their customers**

# EMPLOYMENT PROFILES OF EACH STATE

Analysis of this chart shows the economic compositions of the labor force in each state. In this way, an accurate picture of the economic forces at work within each state emerges for use in your planning.

You will note, for instance, that 13% of Wyoming's labor force is employed in mining – nearly double the percentage of any other mountain state. 5% of Nevada's workers find jobs in manufacturing – ¼ the rate for the Rocky Mountain Region as a whole.

Colorado's employment composition is diverse but with heaviest emphasis on manufacturing, trades, and services.

**PERCENT DISTRIBUTION OF TOTAL EMPLOYMENT IN EACH STATE: 1970 – 1971**

| | Colorado | | Arizona | | Idaho | | Montana | | Nevada | | New Mexico | | Utah | | Wyoming | | Total Mountain States | |
|---|---|---|---|---|---|---|---|---|---|---|---|---|---|---|---|---|---|---|
| | 1970 | 1971 | 1970 | 1971 | 1970 | 1971 | 1970 | 1971 | 1970 | 1971 | 1970 | 1971 | 1970 | 1971 | 1970 | 1971 | 1970 | 1971 |
| CONSTRUCTION | 7.0% | 7.6% | 8.5% | 9.3% | 6.2% | 6.2% | 5.8% | 6.0% | 11.8% | 10.9% | 8.3% | 8.5% | 5.8% | 6.0% | 7.3% | 7.6% | 7.6% | 7.9% |
| FINANCE, INSURANCE, REAL ESTATE | 7.3 | 7.3 | 7.3 | 7.6 | 5.5 | 5.5 | 6.1 | 6.3 | 5.0 | 5.2 | 6.1 | 6.2 | 6.2 | 6.4 | 5.3 | 5.1 | 6.6 | 6.7 |
| MANUFACTURING | 21.2 | 20.3 | 21.2 | 19.2 | 25.9 | 25.6 | 17.4 | 17.0 | 5.3 | 5.3 | 11.4 | 10.8 | 21.3 | 20.7 | 9.9 | 9.7 | 18.6 | 17.8 |
| MINING | 2.6 | 2.4 | 4.2 | 4.4 | 2.1 | 1.9 | 4.2 | 4.1 | 2.4 | 2.2 | 8.1 | 7.9 | 5.1 | 5.0 | 14.6 | 13.2 | 4.3 | 4.2 |
| MISCELLANEOUS NON-MANUFACTURING | 1.4 | 1.5 | 2.0 | 1.9 | 1.9 | 2.1 | 1.7 | 1.7 | 1.4 | 1.4 | 1.4 | 1.7 | 1.5 | 1.4 | 2.1 | 1.9 | 1.6 | 1.7 |
| RETAIL TRADE | 23.2 | 23.2 | 23.4 | 23.6 | 24.8 | 24.5 | 27.5 | 27.4 | 19.6 | 19.6 | 25.8 | 26.1 | 23.3 | 23.5 | 26.9 | 27.2 | 23.8 | 23.8 |
| SERVICES | 21.8 | 22.4 | 21.5 | 22.2 | 18.0 | 18.8 | 21.9 | 22.2 | 43.4 | 44.1 | 24.9 | 25.0 | 21.0 | 21.8 | 18.9 | 19.9 | 23.3 | 23.9 |
| TRANSPORTATION AND PUBLIC UTILITIES | 7.6 | 7.4 | 5.5 | 5.6 | 6.6 | 6.7 | 7.9 | 7.8 | 7.0 | 7.1 | 7.9 | 7.7 | 7.1 | 6.9 | 9.3 | 9.3 | 7.0 | 7.0 |
| WHOLESALE TRADE | 7.9 | 7.9 | 6.4 | 6.2 | 9.0 | 8.7 | 7.5 | 7.5 | 4.1 | 4.2 | 6.1 | 6.1 | 8.7 | 8.3 | 5.7 | 6.1 | 7.2 | 7.0 |
| TOTAL | 100.0 | 100.0 | 100.0 | 100.0 | 100.0 | 100.0 | 100.0 | 100.0 | 100.0 | 100.0 | 100.0 | 100.0 | 100.0 | 100.0 | 100.0 | 100.0 | 100.0 | 100.0 |

This table provides a comparison among the eight states and a comparison of employment categories within each state. In six of the eight states, manufacturing, retail trade and services are the three largest employment sectors. From 1970 to 1971, the number of jobs in Colorado increased by 3 percent. Construction, service industries and retail trade were the most rapidly growing employment sectors in Colorado in 1971.

Source: *Jobs/Colorado;* Colorado National Bank; Denver, Colorado.

kinds of business; Business Operations, which analyze functional segments of a business; and Professional Management, devoted to the professions.

The publication of the *Small Business Reporter* series are made available from time to time and can be obtained on a subscription or single order basis.

Other banks and banking chains publish information or newsletters which are helpful in preparing the businessman or woman who is seeking loans. They also deal with subjects such as accounting statements, budgeting, and general management topics. The newsletter and bulletin materials are more general in nature but are often free and provide a good economic analysis of business activity and results in selected areas of business such as agriculture, retail sales, manufacturing, and the tourist industries.

## OTHER SUPPORTING ORGANIZATIONS

As mentioned early in this chapter, there are many sources of help and information which are provided by federal, state, and local governmental

**FIGURE 3–2**
Statewide business activity shows small business vitality (Idaho, 1975)

---

## NEW DEVELOPMENT REVIEW

**BOISE:** The J. R. Simplot Company is negotiating with officials of the Soviet Union for the sale of a potato processing plant to be located in Russia . . . Ground breaking ceremonies took place in January for a $12.5 million addition to St. Luke's Hospital . . . A second Keystone Pizza opened at 4091 W. State . . . Bank of Idaho will build a new 4,240 sq. ft. branch on Bogus Basin Road . . . Safeway has opened a new 25,000 sq. ft. store in the Cole Village Shopping Center . . . Continental Air Conditioning, distributor of the Carrier Line, will open a 10,000 sq. ft. warehouse and branch office . . . Topping out ceremonies were held at One Capitol Center, Idaho's tallest building . . . C. Anthony opened a new 12,000 sq. ft. store at Cole and Ustick Roads . . . Smiths' Food King announced opening its fourth store in Boise, a 27,000 sq. ft. structure at Overland and Cole Roads . . . Morrison-Knudsen is constructing a 75,000 sq. ft. office building to house its engineering and mining staffs.

**CALDWELL:** A new family restaurant, Fiesta Time Cafe, has opened at 114 S. 7th . . . Mr. C's, specializing in floor coverings, is a new retail facility at Kimball and Arthur Streets.

**COTTONWOOD:** The Cottonwood Saleyard, owned by Urban "Shorty" J. Arnzen, serves Idaho livestock men between Council on the south to St. Marie on the north, as well as some from southeastern Washington state.

It takes four full-time employees and 18 part-time employees to service the average 250 stockmen and buyers at each weekly sale.

Sales volume for the Cottonwood enterprise exceeds $500,000 on large sales. In 1973, a total yearly volume was in excess of $12 million.

This livestock auction yard has been in operation since 1943 and previously it was a shipping point on the railroad to Camas Prairie.

**DUBOIS:** Construction has begun on a new courthouse.

**IDAHO FALLS:** DeMott Tractor Company moved into its new 16,000 sq. ft. facility . . . A new Shakey's Pizza Parlor is completed at 475 E. Elva . . . Spencer Opal Mines has opened the Opal House at 685 N. Gatemile, specializing in Idaho opals . . . A new $120,000 Country Kitchen Restaurant is now in operation.

**MERIDIAN:** Bob and Denise Casper opened Bob's Sew and Vac Center . . . Dana Welker established Beyond Repair, a ski equipment sales and repair shop.

**MOSCOW:** The Orogrande Lodge of Orogrande, Idaho is now owned by the Orogrande Company of Moscow. Purchase price was $250,000. The lodge will provide year-round recreation services and plans are under way for an additional 30 units.

FIGURE 3–2 (*continued*)

---

**MURTAUGH:** The A. E. Staley Manufacturing Company has its potato starch plant in operation.

**OROFINO:** Orofino Industries, Inc. is open and manufacturing sport coats.

**POCATELLO:** Idaho's first Ernst Home Center is scheduled to open in March. The 44,000 sq. ft. home improvement center will carry more than 45,000 items geared for the do-it-yourselfer . . . $200,000 has been made available to a seven county southeastern Idaho area to hire unemployed persons in local government under the Comprehensive Employment Training Act . . . Howard Carlson has opened Carl's Steak House . . . Dellart Floral moved to its new location at Third and Center . . . Checker Auto Parts at 655 Yellowstone is a new business . . . Hilton Inn will build a new 15-unit motel on a 14-acre site on Pocatello Creek Road.

**POST FALLS:** Clare-Pendar has been awarded a contract by Western Electric Company to construct a new line of modern telephone operator push-button switches.

**PRIEST LAKE:** Mrs. Jane A. Rea has founded Jarae's of Idaho, a shop specializing in all kinds of crafts and do-it-yourself projects . . . The Northern Light Craft Company, opened by Brian Conley, features handmade items by local artists.

**REXBURG:** A new 24,180 sq. ft. Safeway store is now open for business.

**RUPERT:** Three units of the planned nine unit Minidoka Medical Clinic have been completed.

**SALMON:** Cook's Silver Spur, specializing in sports equipment, is in its new $50,000 facility . . . A 12-unit, $185,000 apartment complex has been completed.

**SANDPOINT:** Mr. and Mrs. Bill Greenwood have opened Greenwood Sales and Service, an appliance store.

---

Source: *Idaho Image*, January–February 1975; Idaho Division of Tourism and Industrial Development, Boise, Idaho.

agencies. In addition, there are private organizations which are specifically operated for business ventures on a smaller scale.

It is not possible to review and analyze even a small portion of these organizations within the scope of this chapter, but their existence and services should be investigated by anyone who might use their help. The last chapter of this textbook provides many useful references for this purpose.

Typical of some of these organizations are state departments of Commerce and Industry or Industrial Development. Municipalities have local

Development Commissions and Chambers of Commerce. At the federal level, cabinet-level organizations publish a great deal of material relating to the business operations that are affected by their activities and actions.

In the past several years much has been done in the area of help and guidance for minority groups. Special agencies can be found which are helpful and which can often provide direct financial help to the smaller business. These are in addition to the better-known activities referred to earlier in this chapter.

## SUMMARY

There are many supporters of small business activity who are ready and willing to provide help, guidance, training, and financial assistance. They must, however, be located, and then approached in the right way and within their operating "ground rules." The small businessperson *must take the responsibility of finding out what is available, where to obtain it, and the relative value to a particular business venture.*

Initiative, resourcefulness, and perseverance are three traits that are mandatory for success in acquiring benefits from the supporting firms and agencies throughout the United States.

## QUESTIONS

1. What kinds of personal contacts should a prospective entrepreneur make before establishing a business in an unfamiliar community or shopping area?

2. Should the Small Business Administration be limited to much smaller businesses for the lending or participation loan programs? Why?

3. In view of economic conditions in the mid-1970s should the SBA be allowed to expand its operations substantially and to operate at higher levels for several years?

4. Is giving preference to small business suppliers and contractors a desirable form of subsidy?

5. Small Business Investment Companies make very few loans under the $50,000 to $75,000 range. Should they be required to make a number of loans for less than this?

6. What approach and position as to ownership and management should a small businessman or woman take in negotiating for financing with a venture capitalist?

7. Why should franchisors write such tight contracts and expect to exercise such tight control over franchisees?

8. In what areas might an independent business be able to do a better job than a franchised organization?

9. What are the most useful kinds of published information that are available from trade associations?

10. What kinds of published bulletins or studies are available from schools or colleges in your own state?

## PROBLEMS

1. Secure a franchise agreement from one of the established franchise companies that represents a type of business in which you are interested. Review and analyze provisions that relate to the following:

   a. The *"Right of Inheritance"* clause—if there is one, may it allow the franchise to be passed on to the holder's heirs?

   b. *Termination Penalties*—what is the dollar penalty for terminating the franchise agreement?

   c. The *No Goodwill Clause*—which may state that the franchisor owes nothing for goodwill if the franchise is bought back.

   d. *Accelerated Depreciation*—a clause that permits the franchisor to buy back the franchisee's equipment, at a figure based on accelerated depreciation. This may be a condition of terminating the franchise.

2. Write for or pick up a list of publications that are available from your state university *Bureau of Business Research* (these organizations are variously titled). Review the list and determine if the following information is given for each county and community of over 2500 population in the state:

   a. Retail trade in dollars and by type of business.

   b. Building permits and contract construction.

   c. Employment by trade or skill; and likewise, unemployment data.

   d. Occupancy rates for housing and commercial space.

   e. Transportation data—highway traffic counts, airline passenger counts, and data as to origins and destinations.

   After looking at these, determine if some of this data along with additional text material might be useful to small business operators.

## BIBLIOGRAPHY

Baumback, Clifford M., and Mancuso, Joseph R. *Entrepreneurship and Venture Management*, Englewood Cliffs, N.J.: Prentice-Hall, 1975. A readings book with limited text comments. Valuable as a "framework" reference book which follows the stages of a business through start-up, growth, stability, and decline.

Dible, Donald M. *Up Your Own Organization*, Santa Clara, Calif.: Entrepreneur Press, 1971. An invaluable source book for the kinds of information dealt with in this chapter. Contains an extensive bibliography.

Office of Economic Opportunity. *Catalog of Federal Domestic Assistance.* Washington, D.C., 1970. A description of the federal government's domestic programs which assist the American people in furthering their social and economic progress.

Schabacker, Joseph. *Strengthening Small Business Management.* Washington, D.C.: Small Administration, 1972. The edited papers of the late L. T. White, former Vice President and Director of Research and Education of Cities Service Petroleum Company. A very useful informative guide to the problems of management and marketing in the small business.

Schreier, James W., and Komives, John L. *The Entrepreneur and New Enterprise Formation.* Milwaukee, Wis.: Center for Venture Management, 1974. The most thorough and complete reference available on sources of information relative to small business activity. This resource guide has to be the one complete indispensable publication for anyone who needs some quantity of reference materials.

# 4

# The appropriate
# form of ownership

Every business activity is conducted within a legal framework which is specifically established, or exists by operation of law. If established, it might be a partnership or corporate form created to accomplish a limited purpose or possibility a broad range of activities. If no action was taken by the business operators to create a legal form then the law would establish that a proprietorship or some form of partnership exists.

Before the planning of a venture can proceed very far the appropriate legal form and operating structure must be considered. Legal form is a key feature in initiating a new venture as well as an important step when new owners assume the continuation of a going business.

## THE INFORMATION BASE—FACTS AND JUDGMENTS

Before actual consideration of a legal form is undertaken, the prospective entrepreneurs must produce answers to questions such as those that follow below. Variations will develop, but in general the total list provides the base on which the actual choice of the legal form is made.

1. Ownership—Will there be one or more owners? Will their ownership be equal?
2. Management—Is management one or more persons who may or may not be the same individuals as the owners?
3. Financing—How much money is needed for the enterprise and what sources will most likely provide it?
4. Liability—Is it desirable to separate the assets of the business from the personal assets of the business operators?
5. Incentives—Will the business be able to provide the incentive necessary to acquire needed managerial talent for growth and success?
6. Taxation—Will the legal form permit the minimizing of the total overall tax load imposed on the business?

7. Retention of income—Which form will provide the maximum ultimate income to the principals, consistent with other major operating conditions?
8. Protection—Will the values developed in the business be preserved if key persons are no longer available due to illness or death?

The above is a list of the more typical items that are the main basis for the selection of the legal business form. Variations, or changes in direction or emphasis, will depend on the particular needs of the entrepreneurs.

## SEARCHING FOR THE RIGHT LEGAL FORM

Prior to the selection of the legal form, the prospective businessmen or women should study the anticipated operational patterns of the proposed business. They should be particularly concerned with the geographical areas to be covered, particularly across state boundaries; security and financing arrangements; labor contracts; and other circumstances of these kinds. After this review the details involving the internal operations can be examined. Investigations should attempt to assess *the importance of the following to the particular enterprise being considered.*

### Ownership, management, and financing

The owners and managers will want to utilize a legal form that best protects their interests and allows maximum flexibility in operating the business. Proprietorships and partnerships are potentially well suited for this purpose, but may have shortcomings as far as financiers and supporters are concerned. Outsiders supporting the business must have safeguards; they will not necessarily reject the proprietorship or partnership, but will demand extra safeguards to protect their interests.

### Liability

The corporate form is most often promoted as providing protection against the loss of nonbusiness assets by the principals involved. It is fine for the purpose, but does little to protect the investor or minority stockholder. The protection afforded is beneficial to the principals, but runs into opposition when support is requested from supportors who require adequate safeguards for their investments.

### Incentives

An incentive program for the growth and development of an expanding managerial nucleus is difficult with the proprietorship or partnership form of organization. The corporate form is much better in terms of more easily divisible shares and the liquidation or sale of interests among the parties involved.

## Taxation—retention of income and protection of assets

The above items are quite personal and selfish in nature. The particular legal form that is best suited for an individual or group will vary a great deal. In general, the principals would like to develop the business in such a way that capital gains can be achieved instead of ordinary income. If, as an example, the corporate form were used for these purposes, then there may be disadvantages that develop in other operations areas that might make the partnership form more attractive.

What is *Right?* The foregoing brief comments are not intended to establish any particular guidelines to the actual selection of the legal form. Rather they are included at this point to establish the fact that the selection is not a "one way street." What is *right* for entrepreneurs may not be acceptable to bankers and other supporters. Self-serving personal advantages of one form may not be realistic when considering other aspects of an enterprise. Many trade-offs must be considered. A more detailed analysis is provided in the remaining portions of this chapter.

## COMPARING THE LEGAL STRUCTURE—PROPRIETORSHIPS, PARTNERSHIPS, AND CORPORATIONS

Another logical step in the process of selecting the legal form for operating a business, is to proceed to the "pro and con" stage of inquiry. Advantages and disadvantages are examined and related to the proposed operations and the persons involved. This is a customary and useful part of any analysis. *However, only the interests and viewpoint of the entrepreneurs is considered, without considering the unique operating characteristics of any particular business.*

## Sole proprietorship

### Advantages

1. *Easily created and terminated.* Some restrictions and licensing will be necessary, but the sole proprietorship can be brought into existence without many formalities and is easily terminated.
2. *Direct, undiluted action.* With ownership control and management in one person, the action taken by business is direct and coordinated in the mind and action of one individual.
3. *All rewards to the owner.* No other persons or business share in the profits ultimately available to the owner. He works for himself and determines his own destiny.

4. *Flexibility.* The owner is able to react quickly and positively regarding necessary changes in the business. This also provides the opportunity to develop a very efficient operation.
5. *Minimum regulation and taxation.* A proprietorship is generally small and lacking in economic power. It has not been the subject of much regulation or special treatment as a source of tax revenue.

### Disadvantages

1. *Unlimited liability.* The owner must be ready to satisfy business debts with his own personal assets if the business is unable to meet its obligations.
2. *Ownership and management limitations.* The business cannot assume additional ownership without becoming a partnership or corporation; management personnel are thus excluded from the incentive of position of ownership.
3. *Capital limitations.* Equity capital is generally limited to assets of the owner. This can be a serious restriction on the growth and expansion of a small business. It is almost a foregone conclusion that a small business is usually short of capital, regardless of its opportunities and past record.
4. *Perils of the individual.* If the owner dies, becomes seriously ill, or encounters serious personal problems, his business is immediately affected. Under tragic circumstances, the value of his operation is likely to disappear very quickly—in the case of death, perhaps overnight.

## General partnership

### Advantages

1. *Pooling of resources.* The partnership is frequently useful in *conveniently* bringing together two or more persons who as a group have more business potential than as individuals. Ideas, managerial talent, money, and fixed assets are frequently combined to produce a successful business.
2. *Ability to obtain capital.* The combined financial resources of all the general partners stand behind the negotiations for business capital. While the amount of money solicited may seem small in comparison to many corporations, the total partnership liability, along with the intimate relationships of the partnership, provides strong support for capital acquisition.
3. *Simplicity and incentive.* The concepts of the ordinary partnership are simple—equality. Each member is motivated by knowing that the success of the partnership is in part due to his efforts, and that as the business prospers he will be rewarded as agreed upon earlier in the partnership agreement. This encourages the partnership members to

place the success of the business above their own self-interest. Inducements to employees can include the chance to become a partner.

4. *Limited regulation and taxation.* A partnership, much like a proprietorship, is subjected to a minimum amount of regulation, and its partners are taxed on their own individual incomes. Under certain conditions a partnership of ten or fewer persons can incorporate to achieve corporate benefits and still retain the right to divide partnership income among the partners.

### Disadvantages

1. *Unlimited liability.* All the partners are ordinarily liable for the actions of each other. This will probably be a joint and several liability which applies even though one or more partners are unaware of the acts of another.
2. *Tenuous existence.* The partnership is subject to many eventualities which may terminate or disrupt its operation. It may be terminated voluntarily or legally; it may be involuntarily terminated by the death, insanity, or incapacity of a partner. A serious disagreement among partners may affect the proper conduct of the business even though the disagreement does not result in dissolution of the partnership.
3. *Proper management harmony and coordination.* The equality of the partners is simple in theory and somewhat more difficult in practice. Partners may not agree, leading to power politics. Division of work assignment may prove awkward, and necessary duties can be neglected. A strong leader needs followers, and a condition of equality among partners will require compromise.
4. *Problems in share liquidation.* A partner's share is not easily disposed of except by agreement with the other partners, and then most likely to one or more of the remaining partners. Attempting to dispose of a share to an outsider without proper valuation can meet with opposition.

## Corporation

### Advantages

1. *Limited liability.* The owner of stock in a corporation has a limitation of liability to the amount of stock owned.
2. *Legal entity.* The corporation is an entity separate and distinct under law, with ownership represented by shares of stock. It may own property, is not affected by the death or withdrawal of its stockholders, and is protected as a person as to "due process and equal protection" covered in the Fourteenth Amendment of the U.S. Constitution.
3. *Ready transferability of ownership.* The shares of stock can be sold

or transferred without difficulty. Some problems may be encountered in finding a market, but this is typical in many small businesses.

4. *Obtaining capital.* Forming a new corporation with a "saleable" idea can provide opportunities to sell stock to a variety of investors. Later, a corporation which has achieved some stability can usually bargain more effectively for a substantial amount of capital than either a proprietorship or partnership.

5. *Employee benefits.* The corporation has a better chance to create incentives for employees and minor stockholders. Stock ownership and bonuses, pension plans, insurance programs, and other "fringe" benefits can be created more readily and possess tax advantages when borne by the corporation. In some cases these advantages can also benefit the ownership of the family or "closely held" corporation.

### Disadvantages

1. *Legal formality and cost.* Creating a corporation may require considerable time, effort, and expense. In addition, the corporation is subject to considerably more control and more exacting compliance with regulations than the proprietorship or partnership. This continuing, exacting legal compliance by the board of directors and management requires formal records covering many of the actions of these two groups.

2. *Doing business in other states.* Before a corporation can transact business in another state, it will ordinarily have to file a copy of its charter with that state. In addition, it will probably have to designate an agent to represent it in the event it is sued in that state.

3. *Possible division of ownership and management.* Through stock sale, the majority ownership of the corporation may be divided among absentees. The board of directors may wisely control management, or through apathy or neglect it may allow the business to be managed by those who are ineffective and lacking in motivation.

4. *Protection of minority interests.* One or more stockholders holding the  majority of stock will control the corporation. Minority stockholders are without recourse against the group except in cases of unlawful acts or violation of the fiduciary relationship. Even where legal recourse is available, it may be difficult to pursue and too late to protect the minority stockholders' interests.

## OTHER LEGAL FORMS OF BUSINESS ORGANIZATION

The three forms of business organization discussed above are those most commonly used by the small businessperson. Other legal forms may be used from time to time, although their nature and application is much more limited.

## Limited partnership

As the name implies, the limited partnership is a partnership with certain limitations. In most respects the limited partnership is very similar to the general partnership, but it provides an opportunity for one or more partners to be designated as special or limited partners, as opposed to the general partners of the business. *It is not possible to create a limited partnership without both general and limited partners.* The purpose of the limitation is to permit certain partners to invest in the business and to be given the protection of limited liability to the extent of their investment. Such protection, however, is only available if the limited partner does not take an active part in the management; and if he does, he runs a risk of losing his status as a limited partner.

Before considering a limited partnership, the various partners should consult an attorney and discuss in detail with him the possibility of utilizing such form. In addition, the various provisions of the Uniform Limited Partnership Act, which has been adopted in many states, should be carefully studied to determine whether or not a limited partnership is more appropriate than one of the other legal forms.

## Joint venture

The joint venture can be considered a form of partnership that is created for the express purpose of bringing together several partners to engage in a business activity which is normally very specialized and exists for a limited, specific purpose. In most cases a joint venture is formed for the purpose of producing a play, engaging in oil exploration, constructing a major project such as a dam or airfield, or perhaps certain speculative ventures. The joint venture operates very much as a partnership, although a number of states have by statute limited the acts of the various adventurers and their ability to bind each other.

## The business trust

A business trust is a form of legal organization in which there is a trustee appointed who will manage the business and its operations through a trust relationship. The control of the business is exercised by the trustee who operates it for the benefit of those who have transferred their property for this purpose. The ownership of the principals is represented by trust certificates which entitle these people to participate in the profits of the operation, with liability transferred to the trustee. A business trust was much more prevalent in the past at a time when it was used extensively for the purposes of avoiding regulation and taxation. At the present time such advantages have largely been eliminated, and the business trust is ordinarily regulated like a corporation.

## SUB-CHAPTER "S" CORPORATIONS

A business may elect to be classified as a corporation but be taxed as a partnership. In this way the advantages of limited liability and other corporate circumstances can be achieved, but the burden of double taxation can be avoided. See sections 1371 to 1379, Internal Revenue Code of 1954.

This election is only possible if certain conditions are met. These are that it must be a domestic corporation; have only one class of stock outstanding; have ten or fewer shareholders who are not aliens, all of whom consent to this election; and not more than 20 percent of the gross income is from interest, dividends, rents, royalties, annuities, or gains from the sale or exchange of securities.

This option is often a very desirable variation for a small business, as the provisions fit most small firms operated in the traditional fashion.

## FACTORS AFFECTING CHOICE OF LEGAL FORM

Prospective business operators start out by making most decisions that affect the internal operations of their business according to their own wishes. In many areas of operations this is permissible; in the case of the legal form it is more difficult. There are many conditions from outside the business that are important and will cause the prospective entrepreneurs to shift their choice from one form to another.

*1. Initial capital and financing plans.* Virtually no businesses are financed entirely from internal sources. Both equity capital and conventional loan sources will impose on the business conditions which protect their interests. It is not hard to visualize that equity holders normally like the possibility of rapid growth and a liquid position afforded by the corporate structure, with its stock shares. Loan sources may prefer the partnership form backed up by the personal commitment of all the partners. Timely, unique, and promotable ideas encourage the use of the corporate form and a heavy reliance on stock sales.

The above examples could be continued, but would only serve to further establish the point that financial investment interests may force a change of legal form. This one thing is so critical in most businesses that it may change the choice when all other factors indicate that another form would be preferred.

*2. Changing benefits and obligations of owner-managers.* Prior to the final selection of a legal form all business partners and joint owners will have to think long and hard about their future life together. Attempts will and should be made to look ahead and anticipate how and in what manner the personal destinies of each member of the group will be affected. Serious and thoughtful discussions will take place. Problems that once appeared to be of little concern are now much bigger. At this point the legal structure and its impact on the prospective owners is reassessed. Very likely the legal form selected may change, along with many of the operating conditions that govern the managers' tenure and performance.

*3. Taxation and government regulations.* Managers are generally aware of the impact of government on their business in a general sort of way. The initial choice for the small business may not be influenced greatly by problems included under this category. Before long, however, taxation and regulations begin to loom larger. Owners begin to search for relief, some even exhibit irrational judgment where taxes are concerned. Finally hard choices are made, often accompanied by a change in form.

*4. Exploitation.* People, time, money, and products can all be exploited under the right circumstances. Variation in legal form are very useful for this purpose, along with internal variations for particular conditions. Incentive ownership, agreements, franchises, market positions, and many other operating techniques will often convince the management of a need for a different legal form for their operation.

*5. Growth, expansion, merger, and sale.* Each of these may demand a shift to another legal form. They may be a considerable distance "downstream" from the time the business started, but each may be an adequate reason for a business to need to change. In fact, a change is often mandatory to achieve the full value of the proposed course of action.

## SUMMARY GUIDELINES FOR SELECTION OF LEGAL FORM

### Sole proprietorships

1. Easily formed—few legal requirements.
2. A minimum of special operating requirements—usually very little more than for the individual himself.
3. No limitation on personal liability.
4. Ownership or partial interests can be easily transferred.
5. Capital acquisition depends on the personal ability of owner. All assets—personal and business—are one and the same.
6. The business is terminated at the death of the owner.
7. Proprietor and the business taxed as a single entity.

### General partnerships

1. Easily formed with little required formality. A partnership agreement is recommended to safeguard individual interests.

2. Characterized by the "concerted action" of all partners. This applies to all activities as well as ultimate dissolution.
3. All partners have unlimited liability.
4. Capital acquisitions depend on the composite financial standing of the partners.
5. Death of any partner brings dissolution.
6. All partners taxed on each person's individual income.

## Limited partnerships

1. Probably requires a formal agreement indicating the role of both general and limited partners.
2. Limited partners must not assume a management role in the business; otherwise they may be held to be general partners. Limited partners are investors.
3. Continuity and liability of the general partners are the same as for general partnerships. Limited partners' activities are separate and do not change an otherwise general partnership.
4. No special tax liabilities.

## Corporations

1. Require formal processes of formation and operation. Start-up costs probably begin at around $300.
2. Provides easily divisible ownership, limited liability and continuity of existence—all of benefit to entrepreneurs.
3. The only viable form where substantial equity financing is needed. Very attractive to use in exploiting unknown situations.
4. Corporate taxation imposed along with subsequent tax on stockholders' income. Not always bad, but usually not a desirable condition.
5. Advantages of Sub-Chapter "S" are available anytime corporate status is contemplated by any small business venture.

## Joint ventures and trusts

These are not used nearly as often as the previous forms outlined. Consult with an attorney if special requirements indicate the possible use of these.

## FOLLOW-UP ACTION AND DETAILS

It is not possible in a textbook of this kind to adequately explain all the various operating provisions of the various legal forms available for use. Any prospective entrepreneur who plans to engage in an enterprise should allot some time to a review and study of typical operating conditions and format. In most business law textbooks containing the Uniform Commercial Code there are references to the Uniform Partnership Act, the Uniform Limited Partnership Act, and the Model Business Corporate Act. In some texts, these will be included in complete form. They should be examined rather carefully.

A competent attorney who understands the proposed venture and its participants is a requisite whenever involved relationships are being created. This should not be just *any attorney*, but rather an individual who is sufficiently informed and interested so that he can provide answers and explanations that give the participants insight into what may transpire under varying sets of circumstances.

Special conditions exist that relate to a particular legal form in a given state. Restrictions may be even more stringent within a county or city. These are numerous and variable. They do not change the basic legal forms, but add to them. Such provisions will have to be identified and accepted as a part of the total legal format to be used.

## Comparison of operational features

A very brief comparison of operational features is provided in Table 4–1. This table is very brief and is not intended to reflect the exact circumstances in any particular state. It summarizes the prevailing conditions that exist in most jurisdictions, but should only be used to get a quick "feel" for the differences among the three principal legal forms. Details and specific requirements must be established for each business within each home state and in any other states where business activity is conducted.

## SUMMARY

The legal entity chosen for an operating enterprise is one of the most significant steps in the ultimate successful operation of the business. The selection of the form to be used depends on the ability of the entrepreneurs to understand the advantages and disadvantages of any forms, from the standpoint of both the business owners and those who support it from the outside. Often the goals of each of these groups is in conflict with the others.

The process of investigation and evaluation is related to the future. Selection of the legal form along with particular operating details can only be judged over some period of time. In general, the prospective entrepreneurs should attempt to be astute and perceptive. They are attempting to relate a present choice to a set of "downstream" circumstances. If they

54

**TABLE 4–1**
Legal form comparison summary

| | *Proprietorship* | *Partnership* | *Corporation* |
|---|---|---|---|
| Creating the business | Simple acts of any business activity. May require a business license. | By acts of doing business or written formal agreement and business license. | Requires formal process and filing of documents. |
| Ownership | Sole control. | By agreement, or equally among each partner. | By amount of stock ownership. |
| Duration of existence | Lifetime of owner. | For duration of partners' lives. Partners may be replaced and substituted. | Continuous, in compliance with law of state incorporation. |
| Business names | A Christian name, or filing a *doing business as* (dba) statement. | Christian names or filing a *doing business as* statement. | Registration required of the trade name and trade marks. |
| Fees required | No standard fees. May require a *retailer's* or similar license, or personal certification. | No formal fees. May require a license and registration for out-of-county or state operations. | Fees for registration and stock issued. Fees and registration for out-of-state operations. |
| Annual requirements | Renewal of licenses and registrations. | Renewal of license and registrations. | Annual reports and franchise taxes, as to all states of registration. |
| Taxation | Based on taxable income generated in each state for state taxes. Federal tax on net total income. | Taxable income by states for state-generated income. Federal tax on each partner's taxable income. | Corporation tax on state-generated income. Federal and state taxes on shareholders' salary and dividend income. |
| Termination of business | At will of proprietor—no formality. | No particular formality. Partners should publicize termination to avoid further liability. | Should be terminated by formal declaration. Shareholders' rights are protected until formal "winding-up" is accomplished. |

Note: Individual states may vary the circumstances of ownership.

analyze, choose, and implement their choice wisely the enterprise will have a strong framework to support the operations that follow.

## QUESTIONS

1. How are the interests of management and outsiders resolved when legal forms are being considered?

2. How can the successful operation of a business be converted to capital gains?

3. How can the legal form of business affect the success with which employers capitalize on employee talent and performance?

4. What legal form would be most useful in providing incentives for employees who are integrated into the managerial group?

5. Considering the many potential difficulties associated with a partnership, why are a considerable number of businesses started and operated with this legal form?

6. What are the principal potential dangers that constantly threaten a proprietorship from a management and ownership standpoint?

7. How is a partnership able to increase its bargaining power for capital as compared to the opportunities available to a proprietorship?

8. What particular caution must be exercised by a limited partner in a limited partnership?

9. What things are of such importance to a partnership that they should be recorded in some minimum form of written agreement?

10. *a.* What might be the consequence of management of not complying with the legal formalities required by state incorporation laws?
    *b.* What rights would stockholders and creditors have if legal formalities were not complied with?

## PROBLEMS

1. Obtain a copy of the Uniform Partnership Act and read it with some degree of care. Analyze in particular Part IV, "Relations of Partners to One Another."

    Answer the following questions which involve circumstances which are covered by the act in one or more sections:
    *a.* What obligations are assumed by a partner who joins an existing partnership?
    *b.* How is it possible to determine what benefit is due a partnership involving the actions of one partner who has other personal activities in addition to partnership matters?
    *c.* Why is it particularly important to distinguish between partnership investment and loans made to the partnership by one or more partners?
    *d.* What action might be taken by the beneficiary of a deceased partner to insure that the benefit of the partnership interest is fully realized?

2. Purchase a copy of the *Tax Guide for Small Business* issued yearly by the Internal Revenue Service of the U.S. Treasury Department. Review carefully Chapter 1, Sections 1, 2, 3, and 4. Observe that these sections are primarily provided to assist the taxpayer in properly meeting his income tax liability.

    Examine carefully the provisions that apply to each of the legal forms in regard to the following:

56

a. How income is determined for an individual within each of the three legal structures.

b. What determines the way in which various items are valued and what establishes the "basis" for a given interest?

c. Gains or losses arising from transactions outside the normal business operations of the enterprise.

d. The determination of values assigned to an individual at the time a business is divided, liquidated, changed to a different legal form, or changed in some significant way from what existed before.

## BIBLIOGRAPHY

Dible, Donald M. *Up Your Own Organization.* Santa Clara, Calif.: Entrepreneur Press, 1971. A book that deals with a number of important points to be investigated before starting a business. Oriented primarily to financing and financial sources, with comments about their relationship to the prospective entrepreneur.

Internal Revenue Service. *Tax Guide for Small Business.* Washington, D.C.: U.S. Treasury Department—Yearly. A must for the prospective entrepreneur. A comparison study should be made of the various sections which relate to Sole Proprietorships, Partnerships, and Corporations. Tax consequences can be compared along with regulations pertaining to each form of business.

J. K. Lasser Tax Institute. *How to Run a Small Business.* 4th ed. New York: McGraw-Hill, 1974. A detailed analysis of the various aspects of establishing and operating a business. Written in a form which tends to eliminate excessive detail, the emphasis instead is on the essentials to be analyzed and resolved.

Rubel, Stanley M., and Novotny, Edward G. *How to Raise and Invest Venture Capital.* New York: Presidents Publishing House, 1971. A variety of business situations requiring financing are reviewed. The importance of legal form is not discussed directly, but the importance of owner-financier relationships are discussed in a number of independent articles. Excellent background for an understanding of legal relationships.

# 5

# Laws, regulations, and taxes affecting small business

Wherever a business is operated it will be subject to an assortment of legal restrictions and controls. In the United States the federal government exercises control through its power to regulate those activities which are "Federal in character." The most prominent of these is the control exercised over interstate commerce. Control of interstate commerce extends to a wide variety of activities, such as transportation, radio and television broadcasting, product shipments across state lines, and other forms of business that in some way are interstate in character. Other business activity is also specifically controlled at the federal level, but is of lesser importance to the average independent entrepreneur.

At each level of government, a mixed pattern of laws, regulations, controls, and taxation is applied to all forms of business. Controls continue at state levels, then by counties, and ultimately within the smallest political unit, usually a municipality. Considerable inquiry and investigation of the applicable laws is mandatory prior to the actual launching of an enterprise.

## LAWS, STATUTES, AND ADMINISTRATIVE REGULATIONS

The legal framework controlling business is based on federal and state laws, statutes, and administrative actions.

*Laws* are based on the old English common law or updated versions adopted since the colonial days of the 1700s. Laws may thus be based on the precedent of the various case decisions making up the common law, or on statutes enacted by the U.S. Congress or state legislatures.

*Statutes* are laws that are the result of formal action by a properly constituted governmental body. Characteristically, many federal and state

57

laws, including much of the common law, will be codified and included within the U.S. Code or the official statutes of the various states.

*Administrative regulations* are issued by administrative agencies at federal and state levels. These agencies are created by legislative action, and operating within the statutes that created them, they administer and control business by issuing rules, regulations, and directives. As lawfully established extensions of the more formal legal bodies, they can exercise a wide range of control over their particular segments of business activity.

## ADMINISTRATIVE AGENCIES

A number of well-known agencies govern business activity at the federal level. The following are typical administrative agencies, and a brief indication of their control areas in interstate commerce is given.

*Federal Power Commission.* Production and distribution of energy materials used for power applications: Controls are applied to development, transportation, pricing, etc.

*Securities and Exchange Commission.* Regulation of the creation and sale of securities used to finance business enterprises. Very exacting controls are imposed to prevent fraudulent activity.

*Interstate Commerce Commission.* Regulation of railroads and trucking; including rates, equipment standards, safety, and many other aspects of surface transport.

*National Labor Relations Board.* Jurisdiction over wages, hours, and conditions of work, and of the rights of workers to engage in collective bargaining.

Many other federal agencies do exist which will have some impact on the operation of certain businesses. Anyone contemplating the operation of a business will need legal advice regarding the areas in which federal government regulations may affect the operation of the business.

## ADMINISTRATIVE COVERAGE AT STATE LEVELS

Administrative regulation and control is far more extensive at state levels than at the federal level. The following is a partial list of the typical kind of agencies that govern at state levels. (The list is compiled from agencies existing in the state of Colorado.)

Division of Air Pollution Control  (Department of Health)
Bond and Securities Division  (Department of Treasury)
Coal Mine Inspection Division  (Department of Natural Resources)
Colorado Land Use Commission  (Executive Branch)
Division of Employment  (Department of Labor and Employment)
Division of Water Resources  (Administered by the State Engineer)
Department of Health

Industrial Commission of Colorado　(Department of Labor and Employment)

Public Utility Commission

Sales Tax Division　(Department of Revenue)

Unemployment Compensation　(Department of Labor and Employment)

Water Pollution Control Commission　(Department of Natural Resources)

Workmen's Compensation Claims　(Department of Labor)

Agencies at state level govern a wide variety of businesses and also control the qualifications of persons who engage in certain business activity. The following *partial listing* of occupational categories from the state of Colorado is again typical of the control exercised by state administrative agencies.

| | |
|---|---|
| Abstractors | Land surveyors |
| Accountants | Nursing home attendants |
| Architects | Outdoor advertisers |
| Attorneys | Pesticide applicators |
| Bankers | Physical Therapists |
| Barbers | Plumbers |
| Cemetery workers | Practical nurses |
| Chiropractors | Professional sanitarians |
| Cosmetologists | Real estate salespersons and brokers |
| Detectives | Shorthand reporters |
| Electricians | Theatrical agents |
| Insurance brokers | |

Regulation at the county and municipal levels is very similar to that applied at state levels. Typical areas of coverage are building codes, land use and zoning, public health and safety, taxation, licensing and franchising certain kinds of business, and a wide variety of other activities which are similar in scope.

## ADMINISTRATIVE INVESTIGATION AND CONTROL

Administrative bodies through their various officials will conduct investigations and hearings. Some of these will involve an actual issue or complaint which has been brought by an individual or business. In other cases the investigation will be instituted at the option of the administrator and will be done for the purpose of investigating a particular practice or issue. It is interesting to note that various court actions through the years brought against administrative bodies have tended to confirm a pattern of rather broad powers on the part of these agencies. As an example, outside of actions conducted by the National Labor Relations Board, administrative agencies can solicit expert testimony without the necessity of abiding by the strict rules of courtroom procedure.

If a particular business is affected by some direct action on the part of an administrative agency, the owner is entitled to notice of hearing and an opportunity to appear and to properly present his views. If, on the other hand, his is merely one of a class of businesses which is being investigated, the owner may not be given the opportunity to present his case, although some hearings are frequently quite broad in scope. The administrative body desires a good cross section of opinion and wants to avoid the criticism that it has taken action on incomplete information or lack of sufficient testimony by interested parties.

## CHALLENGING ADMINISTRATIVE ACTION

There are two principal areas in which administrative action has been challenged. The first of these occurs when legislation sets up the agency and prescribes the duties and particular specific regulations for which the agency will be responsible. Much of the difficulty is a lack of clarity and definiteness in the legislation so that a particular business or businessperson may know exactly what rules and regulations he must follow. This has been particularly troublesome in the qualification of certain professional and semiprofessional people. Occasionally it is the indirect aim of a state legislature to restrict entrance into a given activity and to attempt to implement this through the establishment of control exercised by the administrative body. Individuals have successfully challenged nebulous and indefinite restrictions.

A second group of problems involves the exercise of discretion on the part of the administrative organization. Where the action of the particular administrative individual or group has been arbitrary or capricious or has been done without proper regard to the facts, then the individual or business who is the subject of this action has a legitimate basis for complaint. However, if the action of the administrative body has been properly conducted, with proper notice, hearing, consideration, and investigation, the businessperson normally has very little chance to attack the process.

## LICENSES, PERMITS, FRANCHISES, AND CERTIFICATES

Lawful business activity is predicated on permission granted by one or more levels of government. Quite frequently this takes the form of a license, permit, franchise, or certificate that grants the privilege of conducting a business. While these terms have somewhat different meanings, in essence they will produce the same end result. Licenses and permits are generally thought to be rather freely granted, whereas the terms franchise and certificate may be reserved for activities which are much more limited in scope, restricted to a limited number of establishments, and based on certain lawful discretionary determinations exercised by those granting the privilege. Thus, a city may grant a franchise for the operation of taxicab service or a garbage hauling service.

Where personal qualifications are involved, society has seen fit to empower its lawmakers with the objective that licensing and permits will achieve some degree of control over the standards of performance of different groups of people. Professional people must meet rather extensive requirements involving training and education, and they must take an examination before they are qualified to be licensed. The reasoning here is that they are engaged by the public to perform services which are critical and must be accomplished with a considerable degree of intelligence and knowledge. Furthermore, the activities of professional people have significant consequences, which are determined by knowledge very rarely possessed by the individual to whom the service is rendered. The client or customer is entitled to some reasonable level of competence.

## LEGISLATIVE "OVERKILL"

Controlling business activity through the licensing of individuals provides a very interesting insight into the conduct of business and the effect of the legislative process. Every state legislative session will produce a surprising number of new bills related to business licensing as well as business control. Although it may appear that much of this legislation is proposed as a means of raising standards in certain areas of business activity, in reality the main purpose may be nothing but restriction on the number of persons engaged in such activity and holding back the number of the new competitors to be licensed. Quite often, arbitrary and unreasonable legislative action aimed at personal licensing and control has been found to be unconstitutional.

## THE UNIFORM COMMERCIAL CODE

Over a long period of time, commercial transactions developed particular characteristics which tended to segregate them into categories depending on their function. The more common of these were sales, negotiable instruments, and contracts. Eventually business transactions became well established and were classified under uniform act titles such as the Uniform Negotiable Instruments Act and the Uniform Sales Act. Many states did adopt the uniform acts.

Ultimately it became apparent that more equitable and consistent results would be reached if the majority of commercial transactions were included in one master uniform act. Through the efforts of the American

Law Institute and the National Conference of Commissioners on Uniform State Laws, a comprehensive body of law was formulated. Adoption by the states began in the early 1950s and is now complete as to all states.

In Article 1 of the official text the following purposes of the act are stated:

1. To simplify, clarify, and modernize the law governing commercial transactions.
2. To permit the continued expansion of commercial practices through custom, usage, and agreement of the parties.
3. To make uniform laws among the various jurisdictions. The code contains 10 sections, 2 of which, the first and last, deal with general matter, and the other 8 being devoted to the various areas of commercial transactions. These areas of coverage are classified as follows:
   a. Sales.
   b. Commercial paper.
   c. Bank deposits and collections.
   d. Letters of credit.
   e. Bulk transfers.
   f. Warehouse receipts, bills of lading, and other documents of title.
   g. Investment security.
   h. Secured transactions, sales of account, contract rights, and chattel paper.

Anyone who is considering a business venture should secure a copy of the Code and read it over carefully. A "Business Law" textbook will often contain the Code and is a good reference to use along with the Code to obtain legal information about typical business documents and transactions.

## PERSONAL RIGHTS AND DUTIES

Small business operations are concerned with many activities in which personal considerations are of primary importance. Legal relationships of a personal nature will be tempered by the personality of the owner and reaction to this by other individuals who deal with him.

### Leases, franchises, and license agreements

A lease will ordinarily involve an interest in real property, whereas franchises and license agreements are negotiated with other business organizations for the purpose of establishing certain rights and duties under which business is to be conducted.

Businesspersons considering the lease of a building or other business property should consider very carefully what duties and obligations are involved under the lease agreement. Lessors will be interested in provisions which will protect their property, develop an adequate rate of return, and protect them from actions of lessees which might place them in a position of liability. Lessees are interested in getting a lease which will permit flexibility of operations, compensation terms which are consistent with the business operation, rights of sublease or relinquishment as conditions warrant, and allowances for improvements to the premises which are necessary from time to time. The lessees as business operators should understand that a lease, being an interest in land, will allow a rather broad privilege in the use of the property. Conditions of the lease must be very carefully complied with, and any substantial violation may allow the lessor to regain possession. Lease payments, agreement to comply with certain duties such as the payment of taxes, renewal of licenses, and compliance with municipal restrictions should be carefully observed.

Franchises and license agreements should be studied to determine what is being furnished by the franchisor and what is included in the price being paid under the agreement. Important considerations are the kinds of controls the franchisor will exercise and the restrictions that are placed on the business. Other considerations will involve the amount of assistance provided to the business, the cost of such assistance and whether or not it is mandatory, the quantity of products or materials to be maintained, and what sales volume is necessary to maintain the franchise. The businessman should know what options are available to him if the operation does not prove successful.

## Ownership of real property

Property ownership may be a desirable condition for the operation of a business. If property is bought or sold, the legal steps necessary in the transaction should be handled by the firm's legal representative.

Ownership under a proprietorship should provide no legal complications; however, in the case of a partnership or corporation, care should be taken not to assume obligations which will commit too much of the firm's resources to property ownership, or create complications at the time of liquidation or sale of the property.

Opportunities to use and develop property are broader when the property is owned, as opposed to most privileges under a lease. Many small businessmen are not as efficient in property management as a professional who specializes in this activity. Frequently, it is possible to arrange a lease or rental agreement which is more advantageous for a beginning or even a continuing business, leaving the owner time to plan and to devote the majority of his or her energy to other phases of the business operation.

## Patents, trademarks, and copyrights

The benefits of a patent are available through various arrangements. A businessperson may patent something on his or her own, which will require the services of a patent attorney, preparation of appropriate exhibits and reference material, and some period of time for research and perfection of the patent.

Patents are often made available to businesspersons on a royalty basis with negotiations conducted directly with the patent holder. Patent rights to a particular product or process may be acquired by purchase or used on a royalty basis, with payment on a percentage of dollar volume or quantity of output.

A trademark is issued for the purpose of identifying the marks and symbols that are used by a particular manufacturer or producer. Protection is afforded by registration, and is perfected by actually using a mark or symbol in conjunction with a particular product. The combination of trademark and product must not resemble or duplicate those used by another firm.

A copyright is issued to an author, composer, or artist granting an exclusive right to the use of a written, drawn, painted, composed, or photographed work. The copyright is issued for a period of 28 years with the privilege of renewal for an additional 28 years. Regulations governing the securing of a copyright are outlined in a pamphlet entitled *Copyright Law of the United States of America*. Regulations of the copyright office are issued by the Library of Congress, which controls the copyright process. In some cases, the long, extended use of a name in conjunction with a particular product will establish some proprietary interest in that name, although this is not something which can be predicted with any degree of accuracy.

## Bankruptcy

Bankruptcy is a process of resolving certain financial difficulties involving debtors and creditors. It is administered by the federal government. The business may be liquidated or reorganized; and if liquidated, the available assets are applied against the debts of a business in some equitable fashion according to the bankruptcy laws and under the control of the bankruptcy court. An individual or business reaching an impossible financial condition can file a petition in bankruptcy on a voluntary basis. Certain conduct on the part of one or more officials of the business, which is contrary to the interests of creditors, allows the creditors to file a petition in bankruptcy asking that their claims be honored to the extent of the business assets. Other options available to the creditors are the creditors composition and the corporate reorganization.[1] These arrangements

---

[1] The details of a particular course of action under the Bankruptcy Act are quite complex. Consult the Bankruptcy Act, *United States Code*, Title II; or William M. Collier, *The Collier Bankruptcy Manual*, 2d ed., ed. William T. Laube (New York: Matthew Bender & Co., 1965).

are available to creditors because a full liquidation in bankruptcy often destroys any possible chance of financial recovery. If the business is allowed to continue, there is at least a possibility the creditors will achieve more than if the business were liquidated.

## TRANSACTIONS WITH THE PUBLIC

Business dealings involving possible difficulty are often transactions which are conducted with individuals and businesses outside the firm. Relationships with these groups of people are continuous and amount to considerable volume over time. The more important of these are analyzed briefly.

### Agency

Persons conducting business transactions through individuals employed by them or working under their control are utilizing agents. Agency relationships pose a considerable threat to the principal and his or her organization because legally an agent is acting in behalf of the principal. Without indications to the contrary, the agent is empowered to engage in a number of different activities which will obligate the principal. The principal is well advised to choose agents carefully to make sure they properly understand what their agency powers are, the areas where they must exercise care in their negotiations, and when to refer negotiations back to the principal. Circumstances will require that third persons be informed of agency powers, who possesses what specific types of power, and the time at which an agency relationship is altered or terminated. Major responsibility is placed on the principal because he or she is the one who has created the agency relationship and is in the best position to control and regulate it. The consequences of agency dealing should be determined ahead of time and steps taken to avoid independent action by an agent.

### Contracts

All business activity is accompanied by contractual obligations. Business difficulties arising from contractual relationships usually involve a misunderstanding, a failure to perform because of inability or controversy, or unhappiness with subsequent events not contemplated at the time the contract was negotiated.

The most common type of contract negotiations carried on by the average business involves the sending of a purchase order, as an offer, which is then accepted by the seller and becomes a contract. In recent years it has become customary for the buyer to use a basic contract form which is then supplemented with special provisions pertaining to the particular contract. This somewhat tailored contract is then submitted to the seller, and if he or she wishes to make changes or alterations the buyer is notified and an amendment to the basic contract is prepared and submitted to the seller.

The seller negotiating with the buyer through a salesman will use a sales order or sales memorandum as evidence of the negotiations between the seller's representative and the buyer. This is usually submitted to the seller's home office for review and preparation of the final contract.

## Secured transactions

A security transaction is used by a creditor when he or she needs to establish protection to cover financial risk associated with a sale. Conditional sales, installment sales, and chattel mortgages are typically used for personal property sales, allowing the seller to retain some degree of protection to insure payment. Frequently the best protection is for the creditor to take back a note from the buyer to insure payment of the obligation.

One variety of security arrangement is "field warehousing." This three-party transaction includes a lender, a borrower, and some kind of warehouse agent. Certain business operations develop sizable quantities of materials or finished goods which are not subject to the protection given by model and serial number identification and the use of chattel. mortgages. Field warehousing ideally applies to these circumstances.

An area is set aside on the business premises; the property is placed there and marked to indicate that it is under a security arrangement with some lender, administered by a warehouse agent. Goods or inventory can then be added or subtracted from the storage area, but only under the control of the warehouse company. This avoids the risk to the lender that the particular business will pass a good title to unidentifiable goods. Lenders are protected and borrowers accommodated without the risk that goes with open-account loans where the lender assumes the risk without security.

## Sales

Sales transactions involve a sale, delivery of the product, passing title to the product, and possibly deferred payment. Evidence of a cash sale should be given the buyer, such as a sales slip or ticket. If an installment or time payment sale is made, then a more formal record should be prepared. In many states before merchants engage in installment selling, they must register with state authorities indicating their intention of doing so. When personal property is sold that can be identified in a specific fashion, such as a manufactured item with a serial number and model number, a chattel mortgage can be prepared and filed at the courthouse in the jurisdiction where the sale is made. This is a way of establishing a security interest in the product to insure payment or repossession at a later date. Many merchants will take a note or a chattel mortgage from a buyer at the time of a sale but will not use it against the buyer unless he or she becomes delinquent.

## Warranties

Warranties are either expressed or implied. If expressed, they are statements made by the seller; if implied, they are attached to the transaction by law. Public policy has extended the obligation to buyers under implied warranty, and they are normally protected by what is known as "merchantable quality" or "fitness for a purpose." The businessperson should determine to what extent he or she is obligated under implied warranties, what he or she wishes to do with express warranties, and be prepared to support the position taken. Liabilities under warranty are probably best handled by insurance, and the insurance carrier will suggest ways to reduce potential liability. Negotiations conducted with suppliers should outline the obligations of both parties and what methods of protection and repayment are to be provided by the supplier.

## Documents of title

Documents of title to some kinds of personal property facilitate handling, storage, financing, and sale. *The two principal forms for business use are the order bill of lading and the negotiable warehouse receipt.* Both of these documents of title establish title in personal property which is evidenced by the document. The advantages are obvious. The title to the goods can be sold, transferred, or pledged without the necessity of moving the goods themselves.

The order bill of lading is ordinarily used by the seller in conjunction with a bank draft. He or she will ship goods on a common carrier, using an order bill, and forward the original copy, along with the bank draft, through his or her bank, to a correspondent bank at the terminal point of delivery. Payment for the goods must be accomplished in order to get the original copy of the order bill and secure delivery of the goods. Sellers can thus insure payment prior to the time that the consignee is able to obtain the goods. The negotiable warehouse receipt is issued against goods in storage and facilitates the process of sale, loan, or security arrangement. It is frequently used in connection with agricultural products and other types of materials stored in warehouses where some time will elapse before movement and use. Both instruments have rather specialized use, but in their appropriate place are very worthwhile.

## Advertising

With care and judgment there is no need for the advertising program of a small business to generate any legal retaliation. Obviously, advertising must not be false or deliberately misleading, and it must not be defamatory in character. Advertised prices should be fairly stated and adhered to. Flagrant violations and various "bait and switch"[2] tactics will sooner or later lead to reprisals by the Better Business Bureau or legal action by the local district attorney.

The federal government has increasingly taken a more strict attitude in regard to advertising. Some questions still remain unanswered, but in general there must be a reasonable relationship between the product itself, the quantity or contents of the container, the size of the package and the use of the advertising that promotes the product. Many more advertising claims and their represented products are being reviewed by the Federal Trade Commission to determine if there is "truth in advertising." Stricter standards and more regulations are foreseen in the future.

## Pricing

Legal problems relative to pricing are associated with so-called "fair-trade pricing," selling below cost, and discriminatory pricing governed by the Robinson-Patman Act. Occasionally small businesspersons will become involved in situations where their prices are questioned or perhaps threatened. They will usually know about fair-trade pricing because of stipulation laid down to them by the manufacturer or distributor who attempts to control the prices of products, and will be advised by their attorney or accountant as to applicable state and federal laws. Many violations undoubtedly occur without knowledge on the part of the businessperson, or for such a short period of time that there are no repercussions.

Interstate commerce and federal regulations affect the prices of some products and labor services. Individuals must be careful not to engage in price-fixing agreements, any conspiracy to fix prices, or use price as a means of destroying a competitor. Pricing of services is frequently accomplished by establishing schedules which are accepted by businesspersons within a particular area. In a number of states, prices of certain services will be controlled by state boards or in some cases a federal board; a businessperson has little discretion to change this. Regulated prices apply to things such as milk, haircuts, and taxicab transportation.

---

[2] "Bait and switch" is the technique of advertising a product at an attractive price and then refusing to provide the item to the responding customer. Instead, the customer is subjected to a deliberate plan aimed at selling a different, more highly priced item.

## RELATIONSHIPS WITH EMPLOYEES

The obligations and duties which an employer must assume in dealing with employees has changed substantially over the past 40 years. Conditions of employment, minimum wage rates, and safety standards have all been subject to substantial changes, for the most part in favor of the employee. Even though employers are not engaged in interstate commerce, they will likely be subject to state regulations which are not very different from those imposed by the federal government.

### Federal Civil Rights Act of 1964

This act made it unlawful as a condition of employment to discriminate on the basis of race, religion, age, or sex. A number of states, beginning with New York had previously enacted such laws, which set the pattern of protecting employees from such arbitrary discrimination. The provisions of the act are administered by an Equal Employment Opportunity Commission.

### Fair Labor Standards Act of 1938

The basic Fair Labor Standards Act, with later amendments, established minimum wages, overtime regulations, and child labor standards for employees engaged in interstate commerce or the production of goods for interstate commerce. The act was modified by changes in 1949, 1961, 1963, and 1966. The 1963 amendment forbade wage differentials based solely on sex and took effect in 1964.

### Occupational Safety and Health Act of 1970

This is one of the most far reaching and comprehensive acts passed in recent years, affecting many areas of labor-management relations. Its coverage extends to over 60 million employees—all those whose activities affect interstate commerce. It requires that employers and employees comply with safety and health standards that are promulgated by the U.S. Department of Labor.

A provision in the act allows individual states to operate their own "approved" plans. There were as of late 1974, 24 states operating their own "approved" plans which under federal law must be at least as effective as the federal program. The degree of surveillance and control under the Act is increasing with additional numbers of compliance officers assigned to the tasks of enforcing the provisions of the federal act or a subordinate state plan.

Certain industries and substances are considered critical and are subject to particularly stringent controls. These are listed as follows:

| Critical industries | Critical substances |
|---|---|
| Transportation equipment manufacturing | Asbestos |
| | Pesticides and chemicals |
| Roofing and sheet metal | Silica |
| Food and kindred products | Carbon monoxide |
| Lumber and wood products | Lead |
| Heavy construction | |

## Workmen's compensation

Plans which are now established by statutes in every state provide that an employee, or certain specified relatives of a deceased employee, are entitled to recover damages for the injury or death of the employee. Recovery is possible whenever the injury arose within the course of the employee's work from a risk involved in that work. Recovery may be denied for a willfully, self-inflicted injury or harm sustained while intoxicated.

There has been a widening of the coverage of these various statutes, which now tend to include occupational diseases such as lead poisoning, silicosis, injury from radioactivity, and "black lung," which is brought on by years of exposure to coal dust in underground mining.

Employers who are subject to the act may, through variations in state laws, comply with their state provisions in one of three ways. They may post a bond consistent with the coverage required for their type of employment and number of employees; they can buy insurance from a private carrier; or they may enroll in a state-administered compensation fund.

## Unemployment compensation

All states provide in some form a method of payment to employees who are severed from their employment, through the action of the employer, a shared responsibility, or the sole action of the employee. Compensation is highest for a severance by the employer, less where there is a shared responsibility, and least where the fault is entirely that of the employee. Where the employee is at fault, there will normally be some period of time such as 20 weeks, as a penalty, before benefits will begin.

The employee, to be eligible for benefits must meet a number of requirements, such as a previous period of employment with a "covered" employer and have been paid wages in some multiple of the weekly benefit applied for. In addition, he or she must be able and available to accept a job and make a proper effort to comply with the rules of the agency which handle the unemployment benefits program.

## REGULATION OF COMPETITION, PRODUCTS, AND CREDIT

The brief descriptions that follow are provided as a means of alerting the entrepreneur to some areas of regulation which are rather critical. The basic pattern of laws and control are often established first at the federal level. Following that, state laws are often enacted which tend to extend the pattern of control over business which is intrastate in character.

### Competition

The areas of regulation are primarily concerned with unfair competition, such as price cutting to destroy competition, kickbacks, false advertising, discriminatory selling, reciprocity, and other similar devious activities. The Federal Trade Commission is involved with enforcement of the federal laws under the Clayton Act and the Federal Trade Commission Act.

At state levels, many states have experimented with laws similar to the federal regulations. They attempt to similarly control the unfair aspects of competition, selling below cost (resale price maintenance laws), and activities in restraint of trade.

### Products

The regulation of product standards is a rapidly expanding field of regulations. The Food and Drug Administration is charged with controlling the interstate shipment and sale of articles which may pose a hazard to the health and safety of consumers. Items such as cancer-producing substances, flammable articles, paints containing lead, and potentially hazardous toys are included among those that are so controlled.

At state levels the regulation and control is probably under the state board of health. Particular control is exercised over foods, water, meats, solid wastes, noise, etc. The extent of control is quite broad and necessitates that any potential business operator exercise care in searching out areas of regulation that may apply to his or her business. A corresponding level of regulations will also follow at municipal levels. These must also be determined and complied with.

### Credit

The Truth in Lending Act was the direct result of efforts by the Board of Governors of the Federal Reserve System. It became effective on July 1, 1969, and was passed to regulate the conditions under which credit was extended to buyers. Controlled under the designation of "Regulation

Z," by the Federal Reserve System, the act applies to businesses, professional people, and tradespeople. In fact, the act applies to any individual or organization that extends or arranges credit for which a finance charge is or may be payable, or which is repayable in more than four installments. The act further concerns itself with finance charges and the annual percentage rate; open end credit such as that extended by credit cards and revolving charge accounts; and real estate credit. The act does not set the maximum interest rates, leaving that to the individual states.

The two following sample forms (Figures 5–1 and 5–2) are shown to illustrate what is acceptable for an open end charge account and for a

**FIGURE 5–1**
An approved "open end" charge account form

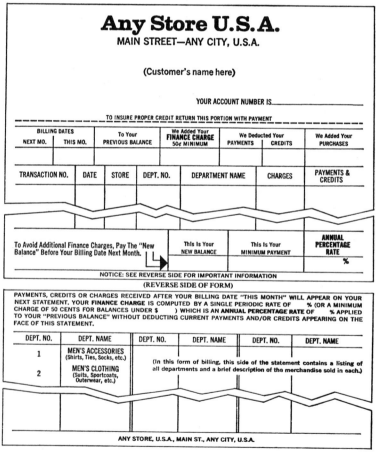

Source: Board of Governors, Federal Reserve System, *What You Ought to Know About Federal Reserve Regulation Z—Truth in Lending*. Washington, D.C., Government Printing Office, 1969.

**FIGURE 5–2**

An approved retail installment contract form

Seller's Name: _____     Contract #_____

**RETAIL INSTALLMENT CONTRACT AND SECURITY AGREEMENT**

The undersigned (herein called Purchaser, whether one or more) purchases from _____(seller) and grants to _____ a security interest in, subject to the terms and conditions hereof, the following described property.

PURCHASER'S NAME_____
PURCHASER'S ADDRESS_____
CITY_____STATE_____ZIP_____

| QUANTITY | DESCRIPTION | AMOUNT |
|---|---|---|
|  |  |  |
|  |  |  |
|  |  |  |
|  |  |  |
|  |  |  |
|  |  |  |
|  |  |  |

Description of Trade-in:

| | |
|---|---|
| Sales Tax | |
| Total | |

1. CASH PRICE                                    $_____
2. LESS: CASH DOWN PAYMENT  $_____
3.      TRADE-IN                            _____
4.      TOTAL DOWN PAYMENT  _____$_____
5. UNPAID BALANCE OF CASH PRICE   $_____
6. OTHER CHARGES:

   _____          $_____
   _____          $_____

7. AMOUNT FINANCED                 $_____
8. **FINANCE CHARGE**                 $_____
9. TOTAL OF PAYMENTS               $_____
10. DEFERRED PAYMENT PRICE (1+6+8)  $_____
11. **ANNUAL PERCENTAGE RATE**        _____%

**Insurance Agreement**

The purchase of insurance coverage is voluntary and not required for credit. ___(Type of Ins.)___ insurance coverage is available at a cost of $_____ for the term of credit.

I desire insurance coverage

Signed_____ Date_____

I do not desire insurance coverage

Signed_____ Date_____

Purchaser hereby agrees to pay to_____ _____ at their offices shown above the "TOTAL OF PAYMENTS" shown above in _____ monthly installments of $_____(final payment to be $_____) the first installment being payable _____ 19____, and all subsequent installments on the same day of each consecutive month until paid in full. The finance charge applies from ___(Date)___

Signed_____

Notice to Buyer: You are entitled to a copy of the contract you sign. You have the right to pay in advance the unpaid balance of this contract and obtain a partial refund of the finance charge based on the "Actuarial Method." [Any other method of computation may be so identified, for example, "Rule of 78's," "Sum of the Digits," etc.]

Source: Board of Governors, Federal Reserve System, *What You Ought to Know About Federal Reserve Regulation Z—Truth in Lending.* Washington, D.C., Government Printing Office, 1969.

retail installment contract. Anyone who is involved with credit and installment selling with accompanying interest charges should be familiar with Regulation Z and should obtain the official text, or obtain the text and the manual[3] published by the Federal Reserve System's Board of Governors (for samples of approved forms). Particular applicable details can be reviewed with the company accountant or the firm's CPA.

_____

[3] See source note in Figure 5–1.

## TAXATION—PERSONAL AND BUSINESS

The success of any business will result in profits which are then subject to taxation. Taxes are collected in a variety of ways, but the principal levy is through the federal and state income taxes. Tax planning to avoid unnecessary taxation, primarily the federal income tax, will probably require the services of a good accountant as well as the advice of the firm's lawyer.

Minimizing or avoiding the tax burden is generally accomplished by some of the following means:

1. Keeping net income as low as possible to avoid the increasing percent levied in each higher tax bracket.
2. Avoiding "double" taxation (first against corporation income and then against shareholder's income), which occurs in the corporate form of business.
3. Legitimately diverting business income into the expenses of salaries or fees that may accrue to the benefit of the taxpayer. Family partnerships may accomplish this.
4. Converting ordinary income into capital gains which will be taxed at 50 percent of the rate applied to ordinary income.
5. Combining the choice of legal form and the firm's operational pattern to permit some discretion as to when income is taken out of the business.

### Tax liability according to legal form

Different rates of income will produce different total tax liability, depending on the form of business from which the income is derived. The following summaries are based on the Federal Tax Regulations for 1975.

*1. Proprietorship.* Rate of Net Taxable Income determines the tax. From a low of 14 percent on $1,000 to a high of 70 percent on $100,000.

*2. Partnership.* Same as the proprietorship, but the partner only pays on his or her portion of partnership income when the income is received.

*3. Sub-Chapter "S" corporation.* Same as the partnership, but may be based on a fiscal year which varies from the calendar year. Income can be taken as dividends in the most advantageous of two consecutive years.

*4. Corporation.* Taxation of income to the corporation and again on the dividends to the stockholder. (Up to $25,000 (Corporation) 22 percent; above $25,000 (Corporation) 48 percent.) Stockholder then pays the proprietorship rate on his own personal dividends.

There are many specialized facts and circumstances which will alter the tax liability of a business or individual. It is not possible in a text of this type to explore these even briefly. To do so would only lead to a series of questions which when answered would lead to others. The U.S. Tax Code is a testament to this.

One thing that may be of help in regard to taxes is to suggest that the small business owner consult periodically with his accountant, attorney, and estate planner to determine if he or she needs to adjust his or her net worth placements. Thus, if the net worth is vulnerable to tax it may be advisable to shift it to a protected position or perhaps donate gifts to children or charities.

The 1974 Pension Reform Act changed substantially a great many features of group and self-employed retirement plans. For the self-employed small entrepreneur the provisions of this act provide opportunities for the creation of a self-financed retirement plan.

Self-employed persons may contribute per year the lesser of two rates, $7,500 or 15 percent of earned income. Additional provisions and conditions make this an attractive arrangement for a person who wishes to set up his own self-financed retirement plan. The act also provides for a method of cash payments for "retirement savings" in addition to the basic plan. The provisions of the Pension Reform Act, which went into effect in 1974, should be reviewed with an accountant, attorney, or estate planner who is familiar with its coverage.

## QUESTIONS

1.  What factor is nearly always involved when it becomes necessary to decide whether a business is subject to control by a federal law?
2.  What are the particular advantages of administrative agencies in controlling and regulating business activity?
3.  Why are administrative agencies often accused of promoting the interests of the businesses that they regulate?
4.  Why might a municipality place a very high license or franchise fee on a particular form of business?
5.  When might it be reasonable to challenge an administrative ruling that was detrimental to the conduct of a particular established business enterprise?
6.  How would you decide which provisions of a business contract should almost always be reduced to writing?
7.  What has been the effect of Ralph Nader's activities in terms of the product liability that must now be assumed by the producers and sellers of consumer products?
8.  What are the most frequent criticisms levied against advertising methods? Are there valid reasons for such criticism?
9.  How are the rates of interest determined under the Truth in Lending Act?
10. Why would an individual who had income from a corporation along with other outside income be particularly concerned about the proportions of income generated from each source?

## PROBLEMS

1.  Secure a copy of a business-related state administrative agency ruling, a state statute to be enforced by an administrative agency, or a municipal ordinance:
    Analyze and comment on the provisions of the particular ruling, statute, or ordinance, from the following standpoints:
    A.  Does the action outlined restrict some lawful business activity?
    B.  Is the particular document an effort to correct an injustice, protect the public, or restrict competition?
    C.  Why was such action taken and what forces brought about the document in question?

2.  Contact the Better Business Bureau or the Chamber of Commerce in your area. Inquire as to the kinds of complaints that are presented to these organizations regarding false and/or misleading advertising, and related unfair trade practices. Try to determine if certain firms are responsible for the majority of customer complaints.

3.  Visit a local manufacturer and determine whether or not his business has been affected to any extent by the Occupational Safety and Health Act. Inquire about the following:
    A.  The increased cost or investment in his business to comply with the provisions of the act.
    B.  How often he is visited by "compliance officers" and his feeling generally about their efforts in enforcing the act.

## BIBLIOGRAPHY

Anderson, Ronald A. *Government and Business.* Cincinnati, Ohio: Southwestern Publishing Co., 1966. This book is valuable in giving an understanding and perspective as to the relationship of the federal government to business activity.

Beckman, Gail McKnight; Berdal, Walter F; and Brainard, David G. *Law for Business and Management.* New York: McGraw-Hill, 1975. A book which deals with the kinds of transactions that are involved in starting and operating a business. Certain materials dealing with coverage of the Uniform Commercial Code are useful.

Liles, Patrick R. *New Business Ventures and the Entrepreneur.* Homewood, Ill. Richard D. Irwin, 1974. Some very good basic materials on financing and taxation which are particularly relevant to the small businessperson. Case materials illustrate situations involving legal complications and include supplementary text comments.

Smith, Len Y. and Roberson, G. Gale. *Business Law.* St. Paul, Minn.: West Publishing Co., 1971. A comprehensive business law textbook which covers many types of transactions dealing with various aspects of the Uniform Commercial Code.

# 6

# Buying or selling a business

Everyday, across the United States and throughout the world, businesses are started, bought, sold, merged, inherited, or liquidated. Each of these events, plus others, have an impact on the total structure of the small business "scene." For any one person or a group of individuals, whose interests are small business management, these changing patterns provide valuable data for study and review. More particularly, what kinds of businesses are being bought and sold, and for what reasons. Within the changing framework, are there genuine opportunities to acquire a viable operating business; or to successfully sell a business at a realistic price?

This chapter is oriented to the idea that successfully buying or selling a business are possible management alternatives that should be included as managerial responsibilities of all small business managers. Failing to explore a purchase possibility, or selling out at less than full value are serious management errors. Realistic efforts should be made to prevent either event.

## DEVELOPING THE INFORMATION BASE

Prior to buying or selling a business, some effort should be made to acquire and analyze information which supports the contemplated transaction. Unless a concerted effort is made, there may be a tendency to overlook something which is vital to the contemplated purchase or sale. The emphasis here is on factors different from those which are involved when a business is started from scratch. Furthermore, other portions of this textbook do not deal specifically with the sale of a business. Properly compiled, the information base can be used both ways—as a source on which to rely prior to purchase and, conversely, what the seller should know when approaching those who are potential buyers.

*Economic census.*[1] The U.S. Bureau of the Census publishes a wide assortment of economic census information. The 1973 series were developed on information gathered in 1972 and are the latest series now available. They are being repeated at 5-year intervals for the years ending in "2" and "7," so the next full series will probably be available in late 1978. Individual censuses are available on the following subjects:

| | |
|---|---|
| Retail trade | Mineral industries |
| Wholesale trade | Transportation |
| Selected service industries | Outlying areas |
| Construction industries | Enterprise statistics |
| Manufactures | |

The census data will not give directly related information to any particular buy or sell situation. *Rather, these business and economic censuses should be used to examine aggregate data and to identify trends, gauge potential markets, and forecast certain economic changes. These are valuable references, and can provide a wealth of valuable base data.*

*Key business operating ratios.* The most available source of operating ratios on a national basis are the publications of Dun and Bradstreet, Inc., 99 Church Street, New York, N.Y. Operating data are published yearly and are available for periods within two or three years of the current time period. The data are included in pamphlets under the following titles:

1. Key Business Ratios (retailing, wholesaling, manufacturing, and construction)
2. Cost of Doing Business
   (corporations)
   (partnerships and proprietorships)
3. Terms of Sale (manufacturing and wholesale lines)
4. The Business Failure Record (yearly)

The particular value of the Dun and Bradstreet material is to provide basic operating information on a nationwide basis. Like the census information, the data are broad in scope but valuable as a basic reference to establish guidelines for specific review and comparison.

*Industry, agency, and geographical studies.* A wide range of these are available from sources too numerous to list. In general, the entrepreneur or manager should contact a state university Bureau of Business Research (titles vary), trade associations, regional planning commissions, and other similar organizations. The objective is to obtain data which re-

---

[1] See *Mini—Guide to the 1972 Economic Censuses;* U.S. Department of Commerce, Bureau of the Census, 1973. Price $1.00. For availability and ordering, contact the Publications Distribution Section, Social & Economic Statistics Administration, Washington, D.C., 20233.

late to the selected enterprise, so that valid judgments about "going value" can be established.

The foregoing is not intended as a substitute for information described in a later chapter dealing with research on a much broader scale. The emphasis here is on sources and data which are related and important to making a judgment on the going value of a particular business. Recorded industry and economic data are helpful for this purpose.

## FRAMEWORK OF OPPORTUNITIES

When the entrepreneurs or owner-managers start into the job of buying or selling a business it is mandatory that they identify several factors which support whichever position they happen to occupy. In this effort it is necessary to look beyond the more conventional analysis and probe deeply into less well-recognized circumstances which are very significant in the ultimate transaction. The following ideas are offered to indicate how this investigation might proceed.

### Customers

Customers are more than a certain number, living in particular places, with an average level of income. Why does a particular business have an opportunity to sell a customer something? What is it that provides the motive to buy? It is a well-known fact that people's wants are varied, with some products and services being in high demand, while others are scarcely noticed. There may be more than one principal reason, creating difficulty in making a clear identification. Possibly this is a combination of function and desire; function being the performance characteristics of the product or service, and desire being a group of intangibles which provide a sense of satisfaction and well-being.

Assuming that the functional aspects of products and services are readily understood, the following psychological relationships are offered as examples of another form of customer-oriented opportunities for small businesses.

1. *Status or prestige.* If a product or service is thought to have quality, scarcity, uniqueness, or the proper endorsement, it will encourage status- or prestige-buying.
2. *Discounts and bargains.* Persuasion to buy is enhanced if the item is offered at a bargain price, or is thought to be a bargain.
3. *Health and vigor.* The emphasis that contemporary society places on vigorous, energetic lifestyles encourages the purchase of a vast assortment of things.

4. *Service and accommodation.* Providing the "extras" has enabled many a small business to succeed. The use of stamps, prizes, delivery, and gift-wrapping services are typical examples.
5. *Protection and security.* Warranties, money-back offers, free service, and liberal exchange policies are all within the area of assurances which may encourage a buyer to select something that provides security or protection.

The smaller business is uniquely oriented to satisfy the combined needs of function and psychological desires. An alert entrepreneur can analyze and respond to situations which are difficult for a large impersonal organization.

## Market opportunities

The buyer or seller of a business will want to analyze the particular business from the standpoint of how market opportunities are being met. This is more than the conventional analysis of past success and the obvious satisfaction of easily identified needs. A more penetrating and broader analysis should reveal some form of latent untapped potential. The following suggestions are offered as being useful for this purpose:

1. Providing a brand new product or service, based on technology, needs, and desires.
2. The creation of unique or innovative forms of merchandising or the provision of services.
3. Doing an existing job better and more efficiently than the present industry or direct competitors.
4. Capitalizing on social and economic changes. Inflation, unemployment, scarcity, and customer attitudes create problems for many businesses but create opportunities for others.
5. Finding a niche in an expanding market not presently being served.
6. Using newer technology to make a previously uneconomical product or service.
7. Catering to consumers' desires that change and develop more rapidly now than in the past.

The way to think about these market opportunities is in terms of what can the small business do better than other larger organizations.

## Thrust

The use of the word *thrust* is to identify the one or more characteristics of the particular business which are vital to its success. In dealing with thrust it is well to understand that it is not necessarily a conventional feature or a combination of such things as location, layout, and good management. It is often one or more intangibles which really carry the business forward and with success.

When a business is being bought, care should be taken to identify the thrust forces and make sure that they are not lost in the exchange. Likewise, if the business is being sold and a strong thrust element can be maintained, this fact should be highlighted to enhance the sale.

## Reputation

Most businesses which are seriously being considered for purchase or sale have been around for a while. If so, they will have a reputation among some number of existing or potential customers. If the reputation is based on existing customers, this will be reflected in past sales and is properly carried as goodwill. This is discussed in another part of this chapter. If, however, a good reputation exists, but has not been exploited, the latent potential for increased business is a strong plus factor. A good reputation is very possibly something that can be capitalized on under new management or circumstances. If it is identifiable, the buyer and seller should attempt to assess its value and importance.

### BUYER'S AND SELLER'S GOALS

When one or more prospective entrepreneurs consider going into a business, the initial idea is often to start a new business from "scratch." There is nothing wrong with this, but an effort should be made to determine whether or not a business can be purchased and provide advantages that are more attractive than the creation of a new enterprise. Sellers should also recognize that many potential entrepreneurs are not thinking about buying; that they need to be contacted and presented with an attractive proposition.

## Buyer's goals

Buyers will have to go through a lot of thought and "soul searching" before they can make up their mind about getting into small business. At some point their attention should be focused on the purchase possibilities of a business that will fit their plans. Prior to considering possible choices, buyers should apply thought and effort to a determination of their goals. If done ahead of time and with some deliberation, the chances are these goals will be more realistic and valid than if considered under pressure.

*Timing.* Starting a business is often a fairly long time process. Entrepreneurs may plan, save money, and work to gain experience before actually starting. There is no reason why the process needs to be much different for a purchase. Preparation can still involve many of the same things, plus a decision to acquire what is "right" whenever it is found. The prospective owner may decide to look around casually or intently, depending on his own judgments. The idea might be to catch a money market or a particular business when the buyer had a definite advantage in bargaining. Another aspect of timing is to trade money for a business that is some years ahead in development versus starting from the beginning with a lesser investment.

*Exploitation.* Opportunities are often exploited from an established base point or position. The prospective buyer may wish to exploit something, but cannot do so starting from scratch. He searches and finds a going business where he can pursue his goal as a partner or stockholder. The goal of exploitation is met without having to wait to put together an entirely new venture.

*Environment.* The prospective buyer may desire a combination of geographical features, a community of a particular size, or a particular kind of a business of a certain size. Circumstances may be such that these things together are out of the question for a new business. However, they might exist in one or more businesses which may be available for purchase. Even though they are not known to be for sale, that does not preclude inquiry to find out if acquisition is possible.

## Seller's goals

The seller may never think of selling, but should not forget how fragile a small business is and the importance of working toward goals which will maximize his or her life's work.

*Motivation.* A single business may be a life's work for many entrepreneurs. For others the stimulus of putting together something which grows and becomes successful is really what counts. The eventual large size and its heavy administration work load is not enjoyed. When the business reaches the point that it "possesses" the owner, it may be time to quit. The important point is that businesses do change. If goals can no longer be realized it is time to sell.

*Capital gains.* A proprietor's goal may be to achieve financial independence. Once this is reached a going successful business can probably be sold to realize substantial capital gains. Additional time may produce minimal increases and there is always the risk that the owner will die, or other events may reduce the value of the business. Many a small manufacturer who could finance with a public stock sale in the middle 1960s would have no chance at all in the mid 1970s. The time to sell is when things are right and substantial capital gains can be realized.

*Governmental intervention.* A great many small business operators are highly independent. They selected a small business because they could do things as they saw fit and in their own style. Considerable freedom still exists for the small business because exemptions from control are made to firms of small size with few employees and to those not engaged in interstate commerce. As the business grows, more and more government regulation and control applies. A reasonable goal is to sell and let someone else battle the bureaucracy.

*Personal estate.* Most businesspersons try to develop a personal estate plan. For the smaller businesspersons a desirable goal could be to leave their heirs the proceeds of their efforts rather than the business itself. This may be similar to the capital gains route, but more long range. Plans may be to transfer the ownership over time to an employee. Portions may be given yearly to the children. A sale may be made with a long-term payout. These possibilities often support the idea that businesspersons should pick their own time to sell, and not have it forced on them by circumstances beyond their control.

## PATHS TO OWNERSHIP

The way to get to be an owner of a business does not have to based on an outright purchase. There are ways in which it can be accomplished over time or through an arrangement which will include advantages for both buyer and seller.

*The hired manager.* The hired manager may be an employee who is hired for the specific purpose of being the future owner. Under this arrangement the buyer works and gets a chance to find out more about the business, and the seller has the benefit of a serious employee who will view the job somewhat differently from the average employee.

It is important to understand the purpose of each party. The buyer is probably entitled to a period of time in which to firmly decide on plans to purchase the business. Being of potential ownership caliber, he or she has the right to expect some premium in compensation if his or her options are not exercised. Once the options are exercised, the employee then has a self-interest and can move forward as he or she sees fit. The seller must realize the position of the prospective owner and the fact that the seller is best served if he or she avoids penalties or a strictness that will discourage a good prospective buyer.

*Investors.* Investors are often looking for talent that they can tap to enhance their investments. One good way is to "bankroll" promising people who have ability but are short on cash. The statement is often made that an investment in people is the best of investments, because people possess potentials that go far beyond the investment in nonhuman resources.

The prospective small business owner may search out such investors and bargain for their services. Single or small group investors who place sizable sums at the disposal of one or more individuals may extract a high price for their investment. On the other hand they recognize the value of good talent and the unwillingness of a capable individual to surrender too much for their assistance. Under the right circumstances, the investor-buyer combination is a very valid alternative.

*Long-term buyers.* Many businesses, such as drugstores, insurance agencies, mortuaries, and abstract offices, are sold on time to an operating partner or stockholder. The owner can sell while the business is alive and well and the buyer can spread out his commitments over several years. The owner can continue to work, train the new owner, receive income over time for tax advantages, and keep an eye on his or her remaining interest to make sure the enterprise is properly handled so that the final pay-out is not lost.

*The option.* An option may include a variety of arrangements that permit the buyer to extend the period of review and consideration until a later date. The option may include an employment contract for the buyer or perhaps a performance contract by the seller proving the worth of the business to the buyer. The sale might be predicted on the ability of the buyer to develop reasonable competence and to feel assured that the proposition is sound.

As in all options, the buyer must pay something for the privilege of having the right to buy, while still retaining the right to drop the option if things do not look right before the option expires.

*Consultant.* A consulting service provides many opportunities for the consultant to learn the inner workings of businesses that employ this kind of outside adviser. Considerable work with a firm may reveal latent opportunity that can be exploited best by the consultant. An element of trust and confidence is expected in such dealings, but this need not prevent the consultant from making a valid reasonable offer to buy the business. The talents added may save a bad situation for the previous owner, and provide a true opportunity for the buyer to prove that his or her advice is sound when put to the true test of his or her own direction and control.

*Partnerships.* Most partnerships start from the beginning with partners that contemplate an indefinite time for the duration of their association. If a partnership continues, even though it may be converted to a Sub-Chapter "S" corporation, the time will come when ownership changes are necessary. Prospective buyers may only want a partial interest initially and can decide later if a regular partnership is agreeable to them. On the other hand, they might propose a Sub-Chapter "S" to allow them to buy in and perhaps increase their interest over time.

Many different possibilities for a buyer are presented under the various legal forms; a minority investor, on the other hand, accepts the management structure and has little chance to influence or change the operation of the business.

## SUMMARY—MOTIVES OF BUYERS AND SELLERS

Buyers should buy when they establish the fact that the purchase is clearly advantageous over starting a new business. Buyers can determine that businesses are for sale, that a particular business needs the right person to take it over, and that business is only valuable when provided with the right talent. What the buyer visualizes in the business is a potential to achieve results with new talent that outweighs the potential in starting something new.

Sellers sell to protect, perpetuate, revitalize, solidify, or liquidate. Sale is inevitable, but is timed to achieve maximum value ahead of decline, adversity, or failure. Superior buyers are attracted to a viable business, rewarding the owner for having foresight in selling when he or she can furnish and receive good value. Most businesses are not sold on the upside of the growth and vitality curve, but prudent appraisal suggests that selling at this time may be a wise move, showing foresight and good judgment.

## BUYING AN EXISTING BUSINESS

At some point in time the serious would-be entrepreneur decides that the period of review and investigation is over. It is time to really get busy and acquire the business which meets his or her needs and goals. Many things must be done before the obligation is assumed and the capital investment begins.

The buyer should divide the acquisition process into two parts. The first relates to the personal situation and objectives. He or she is interested in achieving a satisfactory position in each of the following:

1. To buy at the right price.
2. Minimizing of present and future taxation—perhaps a balance as to short and long run.
3. Financial terms which are reasonable and within an ability to pay.
4. Maintaining the momentum and vitality developed by the seller.
5. Eliminating or minimizing any liabilities or latent difficulties that might carry over from the previous owner.
6. A sales contract, which protects the buyer's interests in the business, from the seller or others, for a reasonable period of time.

If the buyer cannot buy and achieve a satisfactory position on the first five items, he or she may have second thoughts about going ahead with

**FIGURE 6–1**
Classified ads help to locate buying and selling opportunities

BUSINESS
BROKERAGE
DIVISION OF:

Heller-Mark
Realtors

**NITE CLUB**
Lakewood lounge—grossing over $20,000 monthly on bar! Min. food! Has lge. 7% loan which can be assumed. This is a winner! For appt. to see call Bill Lapin. 388-6306.

**COCKTAIL LOUNGE**
Brighton! Illness forces sale. Priced right with great terms—Long term lease with low-low rent. Better hurry. This will go fast! For more info. call Bill Lapin. 388-6306.

**BEAUTY SHOP**
Make offer on this beautifully decorated, spotless shop. Owner must sell fast. Mr. Berman. 388-6306.

**LIQUOR STORE**
7 years of highly profitable ownership to present owner. 1,300 sq. ft. shop near Cinderella City. Liberal terms, price and buy. Mr. Berman. 388-6306.

**MEN'S AND WOMEN'S HAIRSTYLING**
FANTASTIC price on this well established shop! Invest under $7 M and get 5 times return the first year. 12 stations. Mr. Berman. 388-6306.

**2 SKI SHOPS**
Buy 1 or both. Owner wishes to retire and will give liberal price and terms. 8 years same S.E. Shopping center location. Mr. Berman. 388-6306.

**WELL KNOWN BAKERY**
25M plus inventory will make you the owner of this fine bakery. Established 26 years. $300,000. In busy East Denver Shopping area. Mr. Berman. 388-6306.

**DRY CLEANING PLANT**
Large volume store. Established customers. Equip. in exc. condition, good lease. Terms. Call Mr. Boslow or Mr. Zelson. 388-6306.

**VENDING ROUTE**
Juke Box, Game Mach., etc. Growing established area. Low oper. costs. Big profits. $40M net in 1974. Call Mr. Zelson or Mr. Boslow. 388-6306.

**COLORADO'S LARGEST BUSINESS BROKERS**

**AUTHENTIC FRENCH CUISINE**
Located in scenic Colo. Rockies. Only 100% Authentic French restaurant in Colo. Netted over $40,000.00. Included in selling price is 1 1/2 acres of mtn. land plus business. Owner willing to finance with small down payment. Priced below market value. Mr. Friedman or Mr. Goodman, 388-6306.

**SURGICAL & ORTHOPEDIC SUPPLIES**
Man and wife opportunity. Owner will train or free schooling available. Great hospital location. Call Mr. Goodman or Mr. Friedman, 388-6306.

**ELECTRO PLATING**
Old established firm doing good volume—centrally located—over $200,000 in inventory and fixtures. Excellent opportunity for a chemical engineer—Call Mr. Goodman or Mr. Friedman, 388-6306.

**PKG. LIQUOR**
**S.W. SHOPPING CENTER**
Close to $600,000.00 volume. Beautiful store. Long lease. Unlimited parking. 29% down, owner will carry balance. Call Mr. Friedman or Mr. Goodman, 388-6306.

**LOUNGE & PROPERTY**
Small down, owner will carry at low interest. Lge. off street parking area. Owner leaving town and must sell. Chance of a lifetime. Call Mr. Friedman or Mr. Goodman, 388-6306.

**A & W DRIVE IN**
Best in Denver area. Only 29% down. Net shows more than down payment. Exceptional terms and owner will carry. Call Mr. Friedman or Mr. Goodman, 388-6306.

**RESTAURANT & LOUNGE**
So. Denver's finest. Seating for 220. All new and beautiful. Pride of ownership. Plenty off street parking. Owner will help financing. Call Mr. Goodman, or Mr. Friedman, 388-6306.

**IF I HAD A BROTHER...**
And felt his life goals could best be achieved through owning and operating his own business I'd recommend he enter the personnel placement field. In 17 years our organization — international in scope — has grown to almost 200 offices all of whom follow the same success pattern of operation. If your forte is people and if you're in a position to make an investment of approximately $25,000, then talking to us may be one of the most significant acts of your life. Call Bob Angell, Director of Franchise Marketing toll free at (800) 321-2309. (In Ohio call him collect at (216) 696-1122.) Or write requesting our complete franchise kit.

*Management Recruiters®* 1015 Euclid Avenue Cleveland, Ohio 44115

**OWN YOUR OWN BUSINESS!**

**WANTED**
WHITE AUTO STORE DEALERS for progressive towns in ARIZONA, NEW MEXICO, COLORADO, TEXAS, OKLAHOMA, ARKANSAS, MISSOURI, LOUISIANA and other states throughout the south and southeast. Over 700 stores are now operating successfully.

If you are an energetic person, a moderate investment will start you on the road to success with a WHITE AUTO STORE.

We have 6 full line distribution centers to supply our dealer stores.

**ACT TODAY!**
**WRITE FOR FREE BROCHURE**

**J. B. PARRISH**
**WHITE AUTO STORES**
3910 CALL FIELD RD.
WICHITA FALLS, TEXAS
76308
PH. (817) 692-3410

**Milex TUNE UP**

**SUDDENLY... MILEX TUNE-UP CENTERS ARE A VERY IMPORTANT BUSINESS**

● FUEL CRISIS . . .
increase gas mileage with a TUNE-UP
● INFLATION CRISIS . . .
Cut gas costs with a TUNE-UP
● ECOLOGY CRISIS . . .
Decrease pollution with a TUNE-UP
● INCOME CRISIS . . .
Increase earnings with a MILEX TUNE-UP CENTER

Milex Tune-up grows with each crisis. Over 100-million cars will need tune-ups to add gas mileage, cut pollution. JOIN MILEX . . . $27,500 cash investment required. No automotive or technical experience required. Milex provides comprehensive training and support programs. CALL (312) 298-3424 COLLECT Ask for Mr. Canon or Mail Coupon for Free Facts.

**SPECIAL-PRIME LOCATION AVAILABLE**
Attend our training school and be in business immediately

MILEX INC        DP0316
Suite 206, 2600 River Road
Des Plaines, Illinois 60018
NAME . . . . . . . . . . . . . . .
ADDRESS . . . . . . . . . . . . . .
CITY . . . . . . . . . . . . . . . .
STATE . . . . . ZIP . . . . . . . .
TELEPHONE . . . . . . . . . . . . .

the purchase. It is also possible that the second stage of inquiry would not need to be completed if the five items mentioned could not be satisfactorily resolved. Considerable time and effort must be put forth on the analysis of the particulars of the business. However, before too much time and effort is expended the buyer should approach the seller to determine whether satisfactory sale terms can be arranged. The buyer can then continue the detailed investigation, knowing that the efforts are not being wasted.

## Appraising the business

Some points in the following list will have been considered by the buyer initially, before approaching the seller with a proposal. The buyer needs to know enough about this possible purchase to decide whether he or she is interested at all. If so, he or she proceeds, and at the appropriate time decides with the seller whether the sale is a good possibility. If things look right the buyer proceeds with the total assortment of analyses which are necessary before the deal is consummated.

No attempt has been made to divide the list into which inquiries should be made before and which after the contract terms are determined. Each purchase is unique and provides its own particular sequence and timing. Much depends on the nature of each party and the complexity of the transaction.

1. What is the past history as to the profits of the business year by year, going back at least five years?
2. Has the business gained or lost market position in the past five years?
3. What competitive changes have taken place, and has the business withstood these changes?
4. Is the location good? Is it decreasing or increasing in value?
5. If the lease and physical premises are good, can the location be retained?
6. Does cost analysis reveal proper balance in terms of expenditures, income, and return on investment?
7. Are the physical features of the business up-to-date and appropriate?
8. What products and product lines are represented?
9. Can favorable relationships be maintained with suppliers?
10. Are banking sources appropriate and adequate, and can they be maintained?
11. Does the business have strong management and supporting personnel, and can these be retained after the departure of the owner?
12. What community or trading area changes might possibly threaten the business?
13. Does the business have a strong affinity with customers or clients, and can this be retained under new management?
14. Has the company been progressive in terms of meeting competitive demands regarding wage rates, pensions, bonuses, hospitalization plans, and the general well-being of the organization?
15. What prospects does the business have for increasing its share of the market and remaining competitive in the years ahead?
16. Why is the present management selling out?
17. Does the business have a strong support staff such as a lawyer, CPA, and consulting firm which can be retained if desired?

## Financial analysis

Initially, financial analysis will be necessary to get a good grasp of what has happened to the business in the past. If the inquirer is lacking in the ability to properly analyze financial statements, then he should get professional help, preferably someone locally who has no conflict of interests and who can add information of an explanatory nature to the facts appearing in the statements.

*Profitability.* Nothing will be so important to the consideration of the prospective buyer as the profit pattern of the business. Profitability will form the basis of much of the subsequent negotiations that may be conducted. If profits are relatively high, based on investment, then goodwill assumes a considerable portion of the inquiry. If, on the other hand, profits have been low, consistent, and stable, then perhaps different factors assume greater importance.

Financial statement analysis requires comparisons over time, and any single period even up to one year may not be too meaningful. As suggested earlier, three years may be an appropriate period; however, if statements are available for a longer period of time they should undoubtedly be reviewed. Sales trends, ability to withstand adverse conditions, growth, improved profit position, economies of scale, and general evidence of aggressiveness as shown in the statements are all items of vital concern. Much of the inquiry might well be done in the presence of the present ownership, with frequent questions to explain the reasons for variances that appear.

In analyzing statements it is also important to consult related industry reference materials. Averages compiled by such businesses as Dun & Bradstreet, Eli Lilly, National Cash Register, and the trade associations related to them may provide background material with which individual line items can be compared by ratio and percentages, and various accounting ratios applied.

*Return on investment.* Some part of profit is allocated to rate of return on investment. In spite of the prime importance which is attached to profitability, the investment return figure, even though it be encouraging based on the general assessment of the business, is of no consequence unless compared to the asking price for the business. The rate of return calculation must include a reasonable valuation of all assets so that a proper relationship is established between the factors of investment and rate of return.

Analysis of past records should contemplate such things as follows:

1. What was the rate of investment return, and did it properly include allowance for ownership effort, time, and energy in addition to tangible fixed investment?
2. Were the past profits due to capable management or because the busi-

ness was fortunate enough to have a good location and the supporting effort of successful nearby establishments?
3. Were profits increased by paying substandard wages, minimum withdrawals by the ownership, and an unrealistic lack of adjustments in the accounting system such as a failure to write off bad debts?

Computations for the future should examine:
1. Losses due to the departure of the previous owner.
2. The time lag involved in the start-up under new management.
3. Higher prices that may have to be paid for goods and services until reputation and momentum are established.

### Guidelines for analysis

1. Valuation and rate of return are always related. If valuation is too high, rate of return will be reduced, with the opposite result if valuation is low. Start first with all tangible assets and determine the stated or book value which should appear on the balance sheet. Physically inspect all such assets and write down if justified to the true or representative value. Value all intangibles at as true a value as possible. Total up and relate to the investment and proprietorship interest. Rate of return from business operations is expressed as a percent achieved for a given investment. Comparison to industry averages for similar businesses will point out whether rate of return is higher or lower than average.

2. Where a service business is concerned, intangible factors will frequently comprise a bigger portion of the total than the tangible assets. In such case great care must be exercised in establishing valuations, because the purchase relates to intangible values created by the previous ownership. After the business is purchased the values will decrease, at least temporarily. Substantial devaluation may thus be justified if the previous ownership is removed.

3. Tax considerations will probably require the services of a lawyer or tax accountant. The buyer wishes to achieve the goal of paying for high-valued expense items and low-valued capital items, which will produce a higher proportion of ultimate capital gains. The seller also wants capital gains, but requires the reverse applicable of values to achieve them. Some negotiation and compromise will be needed to fairly accommodate both interests.

*Note:* Consult Chapters on Finance and Accounting and a *Federal Income Tax Manual* regarding problems of "basis" and capital gains.

## Asset valuation

It is highly unlikely that the assets of any business are completely current and that they will fit exactly into the "fresh look" desired by the new management. The appraiser must then take the seller's sale schedule, examine it in detail, and apply a figure which should be discounted as much as 10, 15, or perhaps 20 percent.

*Inventory and equipment.* Extremely careful analysis must be applied to all aspects of the inventory including its age, condition, quantity, balance, and, lastly, its potential for sale. Quite likely the method of analysis will start with goods ready for sale. "Potential for sale" analysis should be made as late as possible in the purchase negotiations, otherwise the evaluation made at an early date may not reflect a decline in quality of the merchandise inventory which the present owner has allowed to take place in contemplation of the potential sale.

In wholesaling operations, similar analysis must be made of the inventory for sale, with particular attention given to sales potential, which requires review of recent sales to customer accounts. An examination of the sales records may reveal that recent sales have been secured on the basis of special inducements so that present ownership could present a favorable picture to the prospective buyer.

Manfacturing and service businesses have different aspects regarding inventory, each of which is important to that type of operation. Manufacturing analysis will necessarily include an item-by-item check and evaluation of every part number in the inventory starting with basic raw materials and working through to final finished products. Rate of use, bad stock, obsolete items, and quantities held for repeat orders and spare parts will all be a part of this check. The inventory of service businesses is often difficult to value accurately because it is made up of a variety of things such as tools, equipment, franchised products, and spare parts whose value to a new owner is uncertain. Specialized tools and equipment can be extremely important and should be examined very carefully for condition and their appropriateness to the contemplated service activity.

In addition to this, other equipment related to any individual business operation should be carefully examined and compared as to its *current value* to the new owner. If this equipment will not be utilized in the new business operation and it has little sale value, it should be substantially discounted. Specialized equipment is particularly vulnerable to a loss of value, and even though the equipment is relatively new it may not be disposed of at a figure approaching book value.

## Competition

Modern small businesses may seldom enjoy a position of monopoly. Even though they are located in a community where they are the sole provider of certain products or services, it is unlikely that the population is willing to accept their product or service as the only one of its kind without considering competitive alternatives of, say, another community.

The business buyer is thus obliged to look carefully at the competition, whether it be a directly competing store in the area or the nearby mail-order catalog store operated by one of the major merchandising concerns. Records of the existing business will show very little regarding the extent of competition. When studying the competition of a prospective business, the buyer should determine first the number and location of the competitive businesses. Then he should ask himself the following questions: How aggressive are these businesses? What has been their past growth? Will these same businesses be competitive in the future? Are other competitors likely to be established?

### Contracts, leases, and franchises

Any contractual arrangement should be carefully reviewed, preferably with an attorney. Careful study should be made to determine whether or not such arrangements have been properly drawn and what provisions have been made for the assumption of business by the new management. A final check should be made just prior to the contract signing to make sure that all involved parties understand their privileges and obligations.

### Mailing and customer lists

Many small businesses today involve mail-order operations as a part of their business even though they operate a retail establishment. These mail-order name and address listings have value, and if bought on the open market they may command a price from a few cents up to 20 cents or more, depending on the degree of specialization. Valuation will depend on how difficult it was to acquire these listings, how much they are worth to the business, and the apparent use that has been made of them in the past.

### Credit records

Most businesses will involve selling goods and services on credit, at least to some extent. Credit reports, credit records, and the historical analysis of experience with various accounts are important and may be considered a valuable asset to the business. They should be reviewed as to age and completeness and their appropriateness to the operation to be conducted in the future.

### Confirmations

Many items involved with past operating records of business need to be confirmed with outside people. Examples are such things as invoices, sales records, accounts and payments to suppliers, and the state of title or lease arrangements regarding equipment, machinery, and inventory. Confirmation may be best handled by professionals such as a CPA or a business consulting service. Confirmation, in essence, should substantiate all things represented by the records, and any deviations should be presented to the owner for review and possible explanation.

## Management and ownership

The existing management and ownership are always a plus factor in a successful business. There are times when they are so important that their removal from the business may cause serious problems for the new owner or manager.

It is probably desirable for the prospective buyer to assess the importance of the managers and/or owners and to think about how best to handle the transition with a minimum of difficulty. It may be possible to persuade some or all of the managerial staff to stay on with the new owner. The previous owner may stay through some period of time after sale, but it is usually better for the new owner or owners to plan to become self-sufficient as quickly as possible. Two top men in any organization is not something which should continue beyond a few months.

The buyer must be very thorough in all the negotiations with the seller, insist on a reasonable noncompetition clause in the sales contract, and should check out carefully the following personal aspects of the seller:

1. All tax statements and contracts that the owner filed or signed in the past five years.
2. A request to secure a confidential character report and evaluation.
3. A review of the credit rating of the business by a professional reporting organization such as Dun & Bradstreet. This should probably include the past three to five years.
4. A record of all real estate transactions in the past three to five years, and the present ownership of all personal and company property.
5. A schedule of the assets of the business, from whom acquired, when, and their present ownership.

## Goodwill

One of the most troublesome factors to deal with in buying a business is goodwill. The difficultly with goodwill is that it is a very difficult feature to evaluate properly.

Goodwill is usually computed on the basis of the extra earning power of the business over and above a reasonable return on investment for that particular type of business. This may extend into the future from one to five years depending on the stability and established position of the firm.

## Computing the selling price

The determination of the selling price for the business will vary from one situation to the next, but in general follows the outline set out in Figure 6–2.

**FIGURE 6–2**
**A formula for computing the selling price of a business**

The following is a suggested formula for arriving at a price for a business. It is approached from the point of view of the buyer but should also be of help to the seller. Since all businesses are different, this cannot cover all types. It can only be a rough guideline to point up some of the key considerations.

**Step 1.** Determine the adjusted tangible net worth of the business. (The total value of all current and long-term assets less liabilities.)

**Step 2.** Estimate how much the buyer could earn with an amount equal to the value of the tangible net worth if it were invested elsewhere.

**Step 3.** Add to this a salary normal for an owner-operator of the business. This combined figure provides a reasonable estimate of the income the buyer can earn elsewhere with the investment and effort involved in working in the business.

**Step 4.** Determine the average annual net earnings of the business (net profit before subtracting owner's salary) over the past few years. This is before income taxes, to make it comparable with earnings from other sources or by individuals in different tax brackets. (The tax implications of alternate investments should be carefully considered.)
The trend of earnings is a key factor. Have they been rising steadily, falling steadily, remaining constant, or fluctuating widely? The earnings figure should be adjusted to reflect these trends.

**Step 5.** Subtract the total of earning power (2) and reasonable salary (3) from this average net earnings figure (4). This gives the extra earning power of the business.

**Step 6.** Use this extra, or excess, earning figure to estimate the value of the intangibles. This is done by multiplying the extra earnings by what is termed the "years of profit" figure.
This "years of profit" multiplier pivots on these points. How unique are the intangibles offered by the firm? How long would it take to set up a similar business and bring it to this stage of development? What expenses and risks would be involved?

FIGURE 6–2 (*continued*)

---

What is the price of goodwill in similar firms? Will the seller be signing a noncompetitive agreement?

If the business is well-established, a factor of five or more might be used, especially if the firm has a valuable name, patent or location. A multiplier of three might be reasonable for a moderately seasoned firm. A younger, but profitable, firm might merely have a one-year profit figure.

**Step 7.** Final price = Adjusted Tangible Net Worth + Value of Intangibles. (Extra earnings × "years of profit.")

Here is how the formula described above might work in evaluating two businesses for sale:

| | | Business A° | Business B† |
|---|---|---|---|
| 1. | Adjusted value of tangible net worth (assets less liabilities) .................. | $50,000 | $50,000 |
| 2. | Earning power—at 10%‡—of an amount equal to the adjusted tangible net worth if invested in a comparable-risk business, security, etc. ...................... | 5,000 | 5,000 |
| 3. | Reasonable salary for owner-operator in the business ...................... | 12,000 | 12,000 |
| 4. | Net earnings of the business over recent years—this means net profit before subtracting owner's salary .............. | 20,000 | 15,000 |
| 5. | Extra earning power of the business (line 4 minus lines 2 and 3) .............. | 3,000 | − 1,500 |
| 6. | Value of intangibles—using three-year profit figure for moderately well-established firm (3 times line 5) .......... | 9,000 | None |
| 7. | Final Price—(lines 1 and 6) .......... | $59,000 | $50,000 (or less) |

---

Source: Reprinted with permission from "How to Buy or Sell a Business," *Small Business Reporter*, vol. 8, no. 11, Bank of America, San Francisco, copyright 1969.

° **In example A,** the seller gets a substantial value for intangibles (goodwill) because the business is moderately well-established and is earning more than the buyer could earn elsewhere with similar risks and effort. Within three years the buyer should have recovered the amount paid for goodwill in this example.

† **In example B,** the seller gets no value for goodwill because the business, even though it may have existed for a considerable time, is not earning as much as the buyer could through outside investment and effort. In fact, the buyer may feel that even an investment of $50,000—the current appraised value of net assets—is too much because he or she cannot earn sufficient return.

‡ This is just an arbitrary figure, used for illustration. A reasonable figure depends on the stability and relative risks of the business and the investment picture generally. The rate should be similar to that which could be earned elsewhere with the same approximate risk.

The buyer would generally prefer to purchase assets rather than stock or merchandise because of tax advantages. Increases in assets over time are subject to capital gain whereas stock or merchandise develops ordinary income. A higher valuation of assets at the beginning results in a lower spread and eventual tax payment at the time the business is sold if at the time asset value can be held down.

As inferred above, sellers want the opposite results from the sale transaction. They would prefer to sell off the assets at a lower figure and reduce their tax liability, and shift buyers' payments to the stock or merchandise account, where no tax liability occurs. There are obviously limits to what can be done, but an attorney or accountant will need to advise what is proper under a particular set of circumstances.

Some difficulty may arise between buyer and seller in this area of valuations. The parties should plan to discuss the matter some time ahead of the final negotiations of sale.

## Final negotiations

At the time of sale buyers must make sure that they are protected against subsequent action by the seller, creditors of the business, and the taxing and regulatory authorities. To ensure protection, the buyers must make sure that the following things have been done:

1. *Bulk transfers.* Comply with the Uniform Commercial Code provisions which require the filing of a notice of intent to purchase, and publication of such fact in an authorized newspaper.

2. *Release of liens.* An investigation with the proper state office of the extent of security interests of the seller and creditors of the business. A release of lien rights may be asked from the creditors, to be obtained and furnished by the seller. If there is any doubt, the buyer should have an attorney handle this part of the transaction.

3. *Tax obligations.* All possible tax obligations should be checked out and releases furnished indicating that sales and use taxes, income tax, withholding tax, unemployment taxes, and workmen's compensation payments have all been paid. These obligations can result in an attachment against the business, and may not show up until long after the seller is gone.

A number of others things are necessary in the final Buy-Sell Contract. The buyer and seller will be represented by their own attorneys who will work out the details of the final agreement. Much of what is necessary has been covered in various parts of this chapter.

## Buying through a broker

The search for an appropriate business to purchase may be conducted through a broker. The broker should be able to provide advice, suggest possible businesses for sale, and give some help on analysis and evaluation. It is difficult, however, to assess clearly the basic motives and integrity of the broker.

If the broker represents the sellers, he or she looks to the seller for a commission and is obviously interested in making the sale. Great care must be exercised in dealing with brokers and no money paid or any agreement signed without consulting a competent attorney.

## SELLING A BUSINESS

Throughout this chapter the principal emphasis has been on the problems associated with buying a business. The reasons are based on the fact that this text is devoted to small business management, and management starts with ownership. In the sections dealing with buyer's and seller's goals, some ideas were presented which outlined differences in what buyers and sellers hope to achieve. Elsewhere reference is made to particular circumstances that are important to the seller. Most of the items of major concern for both parties have at least been mentioned and discussed.

Sellers should relate their situation to that of the buyer. Referring back through the chapter they can identify subjects in which the buyer's position is made known. Taking the opposite position, they can ask why the buyer is concerned about something and then decide what the seller should be prepared to do to meet this concern.

In most cases the seller will hope to achieve the following:

1. To sell when the business is sound and successful, and without pressure or duress.
2. The achievement of maximum capital gains and a minimum of tax liability.
3. A sale which stays sold. A sale to a buyer who has a good chance of success and ample financial resources.
4. A sale without complications. A minimum of loose ends such as second mortgages, carry-over obligations, and delayed settlements.
5. A sale which is a source of pride and pleasure for the seller.

## QUESTIONS

1. What kinds of information should the prospective buyer be looking for when reviewing the information base?
2. How is it possible to know when you have found a "genuine business opportunity"?
3. How can you identify and measure a buyer's motives that lead to a purchase?

4. Is the factor of timing the purchase or sale of a business more critical for a small business than for a large one?

5. In what areas of business activity is a smaller business able to do a job superior to that of a larger competitor?

6. What are the ways to measure the "thrust" that propels a successful small business?

7. What are the hazards in acquiring a business over an extended period of time?

8. What precautions are necessary in analyzing the profitability of the smaller business?

9. How much investigation should be done before a prospective buyer makes known his or her intentions to the owner of the business being considered?

10. How should the prospective buyer handle the negotiations leading up to a price on the value of goodwill?

## PROBLEM

The mid-1970s is a developing period of increasing problems in business operations and an increased number of business bankruptcies and failures.

Review the financial notices in a metropolitan newspaper or a financial reporting paper that is published in most cities of 100,000 or over. Pick out the foreclosure sales, liquidations, and bankruptcy proceedings. Study these and then do one or more of the following:

1. Attend a foreclosure sale.
2. Investigate why a particular business failed.
3. The extent of the losses suffered by the creditors of the business that failed.
4. The success or failure record of the owner-manager of the business that failed.

## BIBLIOGRAPHY

Arthur Anderson and Co. *Tax and Trade Guide—United States*. Chicago, Ill.: 1972. A comprehensive fact book on doing business in the United States. Information that is included deals with business organizations, banking and finance, taxes and taxation, and other related data. Particularly good as a reference manual.

Buchele, Robert B. *Business Policy in Growing Firms*. San Francisco: Chandler Publishing Co., 1967. A series of functional approaches to business operations along with many short case examples. An invaluable source of ideas and techniques for learning what to do and what not to do in your own small business.

Bunn, Verne A. *Buying and Selling a Small Business*. Washington, D.C.: Small Business Administration, 1969. A paperback that contains extensive information on the things to know and what should be done in buying or selling a small business. An absolute "must" for anyone who has not been through a previous purchase or sale.

Dible, Donald M. *Up Your Own Organization.* Santa Clara, Calif.: Entrepreneur Press, 1971. A book which contains an extensive assortment of ideas and possible ways to start, finance, and grow in your own business. Has a very valuable bibliography.

Hansen, James M. *Guide to Buying or Selling a Business.* Englewood Cliffs, N.J.: Prentice-Hall, 1975. A new and very excellent book on the buying or selling of a business. This text works from a real estate base, but is not restricted to that industry. A valuable resource tool for any buyer or seller.

Liles, Patrick R. *New Business Ventures and the Entrepreneur.* Homewood, Ill.: Richard D. Irwin, 1974. A book of cases and text material that provides valuable insights into the operation of typical smaller ventures. Is particularly good in highlighting the importance of real success potential, instead of being in a business which has a limited future.

# 7

# Preparing and using a prospectus

Every prospective business venture will require the help of a number of individuals and organizations to succeed. If the venture is the initial launching of the enterprise, then a fully developed plan for support is necessary. Subsequent major activities requiring outside help will also need their own special master plan—tailored to the particular needs of the situation.

The prospectus is the entrepreneur's own "moment of truth"—the time at which the master plan is made known and support is sought from those who can help. Whatever planning or preparation has taken place previously—it is of no consequence unless the plan can be implemented. A prospectus is the instrument to accomplish the necessary end results.

A prospectus may vary widely as to style and format, but in general must include all things that are related and necessary to convince those whose aid is solicited. A complete and comprehensive document is needed to launch the business initially. Subsequent major business changes will also require their own special treatment. The complete effort should include the following:

1. A brief and concise description of the business and the reasons that it is needed.
2. An emphasis on the one or more major "thrust elements" of the proposal. The entrepreneur must explain how a particular opportunity will be exploited—successfully.
3. The owner/manager's relationship to the business—skills, experience, time, effort, and commitment.
4. A sequential analysis and explanation of the manner in which success for the proposal will be achieved.
5. A candid analysis of the risks involved and how such risks or uncertainties will be dealt with, i.e., competition, unforeseen events, etc.
6. Sufficient pro forma statements and financial data to support the proposed plan for a reasonable initial period.

### ANALYSIS LEADING TO THE PROSPECTUS

Considerable work must be done before the actual prospectus is begun. For most individuals, this is their first effort in assembling and presenting information calculated to convince an assortment of individuals that the proposition deserves support. To do this successfully, a number of factors must be analyzed and evaluated in terms of their importance to the final prospectus.

*A self-serving sequence checklist.* To get started with the total project it is necessary for the businessperson to arrange the effort in a logical manner. Initially, it is desirable to have a "dry run" through the total sequence required but in a manner which will give maximum results for the effort expended. A suggested format for that purpose is outlined in Table 7–1. Using this, the inquiry can proceed in sequence, until all topics have been covered. If during the process, the investigation reveals that a particular item is a serious stumbling block, additional time can be spent on that item before proceeding. If no resolution seems possible, a new approach can be taken, or the matter set aside until a new opinion or judgment can be applied, using different values and assumptions.

It is important to recognize that Table 7–1 has purposely been designed to maximize the entrepreneur's effort. Section I, Personal Factors, can be adjusted to apply to a variety of business situations and is preliminary to all other effort. Section II, Factual Data, encompasses an analysis of existing data pertaining to a given business. The information exists and may be obtained with reasonable effort. In general, such data is firm and reliable. In Section III, Judgment Decisions, businesspersons must force themselves to produce realistic answers to tough questions. Even so, it is desirable to work through the list without too much delay. Further investigation and inquiry should properly await the actual creation of the formal document. At this stage the checklist is the initial "once-over" that provides a perspective for later efforts.

*The importance of sequence.* The sequence used in presenting the facts in the prospectus is important. For example:

1. Personal goals, attitudes, and commitments must be dealt with first. While this information is subjective, no further inquiry is valid without a strong conclusion that the one or more entrepreneurs can personally apply themselves to the needs of the proposed enterprise.

2. Inquiry should proceed from "at hand" information, through objective data, to items which require the most in terms of time, money, and effort. Thus in Table 7–1, items 1 through 9 are rather quickly dealt with, while 10 through 17 need be used only if a strong "go-ahead" is indicated.

3. A series of investigations should have overlapping value. Thus, if personal inquiry indicates a strong pattern for success in one type of business, relationship to other business types is a fairly easy process. Likewise,

TABLE 7-1
Sequence checklist for prospectus preparation

| Initial inquiry | *I. Personal factors*<br><br>1. Ability needed for the particular business venture.<br>2. Experience—in the proposed business or related business activity.<br>3. Dedication—to the demands of a business operation.<br>4. Self-discipline required to live within the limits imposed by financiers, competitors, and customers. |
|---|---|
| Summary | |
| Second stage inquiry | *II. Factual data*<br><br>5. Zoning laws.<br>6. Licenses, franchises, and permits.<br>7. State and federal laws.<br>8. Administrative regulations.<br>9. Professional certification (personal licenses, etc.). |
| Summary | |
| In-depth analysis | *III. Judgment decisions*<br><br>10. Appropriate legal form.<br>11. Basic formula for success.<br>12. Initial capital needs.<br>13. Projected income and expense budgets.<br>14. Competition—amount and vitality.<br>15. Physical features of operation.<br>16. Commitments by investors.<br>17. Your professional team—lawyer, accountant, banker. |
| Final conclusion | |

investigation into factual data will ordinarily furnish information applicable to a number of business situations. Where operational features of a business require analysis which is very difficult and the information obtained demands subjective interpretation, there is less chance of applying the information to another business opportunity.

4. Each factor, condition, and subjective judgment should be resolved and accepted before moving on to the next. Some one of these may remain in doubt for a time, but clear grounds for failure of any critical condition affecting the ultimate success of the proposed business is a warning to proceed cautiously. A different approach with some new ideas may develop answers which will provide added confidence and enable the analysts to continue with enthusiasm.

## The three steps of analysis

Each stage of analysis will require its own special emphasis and concentration. Strength in the final prospectus will reflect the care that must accompany all stages of work from start to finish.

*Personal factors.* All persons who have a direct bearing on the ownership and management of the business must be included in the analysis of personal factors. Strengths and weaknesses must be dealt with—the strong points emphasized and the weak points reinforced to the extent they will not damage the overall result.

Lenders and suppliers may be doubtful as to certain claims made for the abilities of the principals. Possible doubts should be discussed and efforts made to provide answers for the obvious questions that will come up.

*Factual data.* The factual data dealt with in Section II provides a chance for prospective businessmen and women to establish a real advantage. Within this analysis area there is a wide range of characteristics that have a bearing on the business being considered. If the prospectus is "thin" in other aspects a strong case should be formulated from the factual base. There is virtually no limit to things which could be shown to have a bearing on a business in some form or other under certain conditions. The section can be exploited by applying some imaginative thinking.

*Judgment decisions.* The final section of analysis is related to subjects requiring careful evaluation and ultimately judgmental decisions. Being highly subjective, these decisions will be questioned by those who are approached to support the prospectus. Often, the proponents will need considerable help in formulating this section so that it is plausible and convincing.

It is advisable to seek help in support of the subjects dealt with at this stage of analysis. It is here that the banker will be able to advise on what a bank needs and wants from a prospective borrower. The accountant will advise as to the form and presentation of data in a manner which is acceptable to the total business community. An insurance agent will discuss and advise as to the needs of the business in the casualty field, along with the hazards of business interruption or the loss of key personnel through accident or death. Other advisers might be a knowledgeable real estate broker, a management consultant, or a market research adviser. These and others might be well worth the expense of their services at this stage of the evolving business.

It may be argued that the contact with outside individuals at this stage of business development is premature. There is some logic in this and the risk of disclosure at this point is a real possibility. The counter-argument is that if no previous outside contacts have been made it is none too soon to start, and that some feedback from experts is needed to properly deal with the kinds of information that are typically Section III items.

## Varying emphasis by type of business

Business operations will vary widely, depending on the characteristics of the business and the individuals involved. These differences must be reflected in the prospectus in relation to their importance to the ultimate business objective. A theoretical proposal would proceed by presenting each functional activity with adequate coverage and convincing conclusions, without balancing or adjustment. Unfortunately, real-life situations do not provide these opportunities.

Business activity can be divided rather logically into retailing, service, manufacturing, and wholesaling. Further subclassifications will include local versus broad markets, combinations of each of the main classes, and individual business characteristics such as seasonal operations, unique merchandising, franchise operations, and a host of other variances.

In a retailing organization, it would be very important to outline in considerable detail the amount of work and investigation done regarding such things as the location of the business, traffic patterns, particular product lines available to the business, and the presentation of anticipated business activity by each department, along with inventory variations.

In contrast, a manufacturing concern might tend to emphasize the design and unique applications of its products, the plans to be followed in penetrating the market, adequate production capability, and adjustment to varying competitive changes.

Operation characteristics of wholesaling tend to be built around volume and service conducted at minimal cost combinations, while service businesses are heavily identified with management. Wholesaling has diminished in importance in the field of small business while the small service businesses are now the faster growing segment of small business activity.

*Developing the right emphasis mix.* To highlight the importance of what to emphasize and why, the editorial stages of the prospectus will require some careful thought and selection. In Table 7–2 a format is outlined which should help in identifying how to examine the various factors of concern and their relative importance.

Care should be exercised in using Table 7–2. It is furnished as a guide to the process of selection and emphasis—not as a rule-of-thumb outline. The creators of the prospectus will struggle mightily at this point in the task, particularly if they do the job that should be done. It may take five drafts to get started and ten rewrites. Whatever it takes, it must be well done. Sloppy thought and careless treatment of operational matters will

TABLE 7–2
Characteristics of operational importance by type of business

| Type of business | Degree of importance | | |
|---|---|---|---|
| | First | Second | Third |
| Retailing | Product lines<br>Location<br>Traffic density<br>Drawing power<br>Layout<br>Parking<br>Leases<br>Franchises | Physical facilities<br>Labor restrictions<br>Consumer credit<br>Goodwill | Transportation<br>facilities |
| Service | Franchises<br>Liability<br>Goodwill | Location<br>Product lines<br>Parking<br>Environment | Layout<br>Zoning<br>Consumer credit |
| Service–Retail | Location<br>Liability<br>Product lines<br>Goodwill | Labor restrictions<br>Zoning<br>Traffic density<br>Drawing power<br>Environment<br>Layout | Zoning<br>Consumer credit |
| Manufacturing | Transportation<br>services<br>Zoning<br>Layout<br>Patents<br>Labor restrictions | Location<br>Parking<br>Warranties<br>Customer credit<br>Liability | Traffic density<br>Drawing power<br>Layout<br>Environment |
| Wholesaling | Low-cost facilities<br>Layout<br>Customer credit<br>Product lines | Leases<br>Zoning | Labor restrictions<br>Locations<br>Drawing power<br>Environment |

quickly expose a prospective entrepreneur as lacking in an understanding of the basics. Don't let it happen.

## Timing

One of the essential talents of a "winner" is timing. In the case of the prospectus, timing is an integral part of the job.

In general, two aspects of timing are important. The first is the recognition of factors that are timely, such as the high interest rates and the ravages of inflation in the mid-1970s. The other has to do with the actual timing of the prospectus itself. At what point in time will it be presented and considered? Is it appropriate at that point in time, and if not, can it be reworked so that it is timely?

Understandable difficulties with timing are associated with such things as when to approach a given market or institution for money, meeting a change in a zoning deadline, or a change in the balance of power of a regulatory board—such as a county planning agency.

It is particularly disturbing in the mid-1970s to realize that "times are different." Small businesses are suffering from a lack of "muscle" and bargaining power, materials and fuel shortages, and ill-advised municipal and governmental actions. At the same time, one person's plight may be another's opportunity. Timing decisions should stay high on the list of late-action modification to the basic plan and format.

## Exploitation

Each and every prospectus must propose to exploit something. Exploitation in this sense is not to be thought of as something bad but rather the process of capitalizing on opportunities. In general, these can include ability, people, products, time, knowledge, and wisdom, as well as opportunities of a more subtle nature.

As the prospectus takes shape, the goal of exploitation can serve to guide the planning and organizing around this underlying themes. Without it, the final prospectus may wander aimlessly and be lacking in strong dedication to a given objective.

In pursuing any given exploitation goal, analysis should proceed step by step. It is important to provide answers to anticipated questions. What is the product or service good for? What unique application is available? How does this or that factor fit with the other factors? The thread of inquiry follows logically to develop the strongest case possible for the proposition. What you know is one thing; your proposed results must be conclusive in the minds of your supporters.

*One cautious note:* Sometimes the proposition may do the job so well that those exposed to it wind up using it for themselves. Be careful in areas where there is limited protection. Try to deal with reputable organizations, and if necessary withhold certain vital data until it is appropriate to reveal it. Reasonable persons will understand this concern for protecting vital information. This can be discussed in an honest and forthright manner.

## Competition

Few business activities are free from competition. In theory, business without competition will adopt practices which are nonaggressive and will wind up the victim of its own greed and/or lack of aggressiveness. At any point in time competition might be described as aggressive, passive, low level, dormant, and so on. The important thing is to realize that any threat or potential threat may generate action on the part of established competitors. The prospective businessperson should be careful not to misread the competitive signals, yet it is surprising how many business ventures are proposed on the assumption that competition is either decadent or nonexistent.

Potential supporters approached by the prospective small businessman will weigh the element of competition very strongly, usually more so than the proposer himself. Because of this, much time and effort must be taken to develop and analyze the competitive climate. Considerable interviewing, personal observation, and inquiry will be required to develop good fundamental data. Following this will be the application of good thinking and judgment. Much of the latter will be concerned with the probabilities of human behavior, something which is difficult to predict.

A comparison of the various factors of competition by use of a matrix is illustrated in Table 7–3. This method requires the assignment of numerical values and is useful in developing a graphic display. Such a method helps to provide a summary overview rather than one which is segmented or detached.

## NEW VERSUS EXISTING BUSINESS

The format and emphasis adopted for the prospectus will be somewhat different for an existing business than for a newly formed one. Primary emphasis in this chapter is devoted to the new business. However, analysis should include comparison of the possible new business against the opportunities in an existing business. Generally the importance or worth of each functional portion of a business will differ from another business, so that the final judgment is based on a total evaluation rather than an item-by-item matching.

The total evaluation will make it possible to establish a price that the prospective buyer is willing to pay. The total composite will probably include something for goodwill; i.e., the amount of income in excess of a reasonable investment return. Values will be reduced where a business is unsuccessful or in financial difficulty.

Special attention should be given to items such as goodwill, valuation of assets, removal of successful or failing management, subsequent activity by the former owner, and subtle and obscure reasons for the business being offered for sale. Occasionally a business might be acquired at a bargain, but this is a rare circumstance. An apparent bargain is perhaps the most dangerous condition with which to deal. It may encourage hasty or snap judgments instead of careful logic and analysis.

TABLE 7–3
New-entry competitor comparison table
(arbitrary rating scale 0–100)

| Value factors for comparison to proposed business | Established competitors* | | | | |
|---|---|---|---|---|---|
| | A | B | C | D | E |
| Location | 90% | 75% | 50% | 60% | 20% |
| Facility size | Large | Medium | Medium | Large | Small |
| Percent of existing potential market for new enterprise now served | 20% | 10% | 12% | 17% | 5% |
| Total or partial competitor | Total | Noncritical lines and/or services | Total | Only critical lines and/or services | Partial and of no consequence |
| Managerial abilities | Strong | Strong | Average | Improving | Weak |
| Aggressiveness | 80% | 60% | 15% | 10% | 5% |
| Momentum | Strong | Increasing | Declining | Unknown | Weak |
| Financial strength | Strong | Limited | Average | Vulnerable | Weak |

* One or more of these may be mail-order or other nonresident firms.

# THE PRETESTING PROCESS

It is reasonable to assume that the prospectus will be prepared, reworked, and edited by the principals in the business venture. In addition, it will be reviewed by friends, relatives, and others who are friendly to the cause. This, however, is not enough, as it is important that the prospectus be seasoned. The famous football coach, Jock Sutherland, of Pittsburgh University, once said, "The time to play sophomores is when they're juniors." The same can be said for a given proposal.

Again, it may be prudent to secure professional advice—that of a CPA, attorney, and others. If properly used, these experts are well worth the cost. Another approach is to pretest the prospectus with people who will not be asked to support the business. The pretesting process will be especially valuable in the following areas:

1. The master plan—is it good or bad? If bad, what needs to be corrected?
2. What is wrong with the format, content, age of the information, and graphic materials? *Lenders are particularly critical of outdated financial data.*
3. Possible realignment and adjustment—does there need to be a change in objective or direction? Are sequence and logical development lacking? The first two pages are critical and should probably be a short, hard-hitting convincing résumé.
4. Does the prospectus answer questions like these?
   a. What makes you think you can do this?
   b. Why should we risk our money on this enterprise?
   c. Where did you get this figure and that data?
   d. Why do you think your budgets are realistic?

It is easy at this stage to become discouraged, but to do so is to lose the battle. Instead, review the criticisms and analyze them for valid objections. Avoid the assumption that these things are a direct attack on your ability or integrity.

## SEQUENCE AND FORMAT

Time spent on sequence, readability, and format may be as rewarding as any other phase of preparing the prospectus; thus, the tendency to relax at this point should be avoided. In general, a good small business prospectus will proceed along the following lines:

1. Title page—including the proposed name, date, and name and affiliation of the principal officers.
2. Table of contents—if such is needed because of length or complexity.
3. Introduction—to outline briefly and concisely the proposed operation. This is very critical. Two or three well-written pages will encourage and stimulate the reviewer. A poor job may establish a mental image that defeats an otherwise sound proposal.
4. Functional analysis—step by step and in depth.
5. Summary and conclusions.
6. Supporting data—bibliography, exhibits, supporting data, etc. While the outline is simple, it will enhance the chances of acceptance if it follows a sequence which is familiar to the business world.

Style of writing and readability are also important, along with proper word usage and correct spelling. This is not to suggest that the writer assume any particular style or method but rather that the chosen style be consistent and well done. If necessary, it would be well to solicit editorial help from people who are familiar with businesspersons and their methods of communication.

The format used should consider the judgment of the people preparing the final document. Printing and photographic techniques are available which can accomplish whatever is desirable considering the audience. Certain subtle limitations exist which should be observed. For instance, a formal proposal by a consulting firm for a continuing governmental contract will be entirely different from a proposal to a private risk capital source for funds to finance a new business producing complex manufactured products.

## THE BARGAINING AND SELLING PROCESS

Before presenting the prospectus, a final step is to determine what limitations will govern the bargaining process. Initially, there will be no statements regarding what the proponents expect. They will be asking for support, without any accurate idea as to the kinds of answers they will receive. They must, however, decide the conditions under which they will accept outside support.

## Ownership, profit, and interest rates

The most common features of bargaining are related to what degree of ownership the owners are willing to relinquish, whether they will be willing to surrender part of the profits, and what rates of interest they are willing to pay. One or more of these areas in various degrees will probably be involved in the negotiations. *The important thing is to know the value of the proposition and whether these features are being settled in favor of the solicitors or those being asked for support.* If too much is given up, the net effect is to reduce those who think they are small businesspersons to the status of low-cost management being exploited for someone else's benefit and profit. Unless the prospectus is valued before the negotiations begin, commitments may be agreed to which are more liberal than necessary or inconsistent with the anticipated operations.

In most cases total support for a business venture will not come from one source. As each portion of the operations is committed there will be a change of conditions for those who follow, with adjustments to be made by the owners in their own master plan. Master plan changes will also come about through negotiations which do not result in any agreement but point up circumstances which are objectionable. In such cases it will be necessary to reevaluate the prospectus and decide what changes in conditions are necessary.

## Competition for support

Applying for support for a business venture is always a competitive process. This competition extends to a variety of financial arrangements, product lines, franchises, locations, and a number of other conditions. Support sources may drive a hard bargain, or simply not show interest. The reasons may be personal, but most often they are competitive. As an example, one company in the loan and finance field stated that it would review, to some extent, an average of 80 business proposals for each loan that was ultimately completed. Many of these applicants had not prepared a prospectus, or if they had, it was inadequate. The majority failed because they could not compete effectively for the available funds. When the state of competition is known, the prospectus will reflect it originally, but changes will be required as long as negotiations continue.

## Planning for the sales effort

The following ideas should prove helpful to persons who have never tried to organize a small business venture and to those who have tried but failed.

1. *Do not be fooled by the ease of getting into business.* Legal restrictions may be very easy to meet and opportunities seemingly available in almost any activity of interest. A personal decision and commitment are not enough; they must be supported by other people who will be involved in the proposed enterprise. An appreciation of the ways of the business world will enable an individual to approach the negotiations with the right mental attitude.

2. *If your negotiations reveal that you have an impossible proposition, discard it.* There are times when an individual becomes so personally involved that he fails to properly analyze and apply good judgment. It is much better to realize an impossible situation and to avoid it than to pursue it under doubtful circumstances. Later the idea can be reviewed; if it still possesses merit it can be tried again with a fresh approach.

3. *Prepare to expect skepticism and rebuffs from the business world.* Statistics confirm the high failure rate of beginning small businesses. As such, any business will be classified as a "loser" until such time as it can be proven that the proposition deserves support. Such support will seldom come easily or quickly.

4. *Resolve all internal differences before making any presentations.* This applies to the partnership or corporation where there is more than one person involved. In addition, develop consistent data and answers to be used in personal interviews supporting the prospectus.

5. *Attempt to read the pulse of the business world before approaching*

*anyone with a proposal.* The combinations of money supply, business attitude, state of the business cycle, and the condition of the local economy will all have an effect on your chances for success. Knowing something about these circumstances will enhance the ability to negotiate.

6. *When making a presentation, do not undervalue anything which will support your cause.* This applies to time, effort, ability, personal investment, dedication, and anything else that is related. Confidence and assurance in the prospectus are absolutely necessary to obtain the aid of outsiders. Point out the fact that the anticipated enterprise will provide the conditions of success. This in turn should provide incentive and motivation for the owners. Supporters recognize that a successful management is the most important ingredient for their own protection and success.

7. *Show an appreciation for the importance of investment values and an adequate rate of return.* For some reason, small business operators are not very realistic, particularly in regard to the return on their own investment and the value of their time. It is important to indicate a willingness to do whatever is necessary to make the business a success, but realistic monetary rewards should not be overlooked. Investors will be persuaded if the total proposed financial operation will produce income which is consistent with every facet of investment.

## QUESTIONS

1.  If prospective businesspersons are able to provide their own financing in the beginning, should they still prepare a prospectus? Why?
2.  What circumstances would call for the preparation of more than one prospectus?
3.  What should be emphasized when a business changes from a proprietorship to a partnership or corporation?
4.  Are there business circumstances that would encourage a firm to discard the corporate form?
5.  How would you establish monetary values for various intangibles dealt with in the prospectus?
6.  What is the purpose in identifying the one or more "thrust" elements that will be exploited by the alert entrepreneur?
7.  What are the most frequent criticisms that are raised by people who are asked for help via the prospectus?
8.  How does a lack of financial capital and inflation influence the preparation of a prospectus?
9.  How would you ensure that a prospectus had an adequate pretest?
10. Why would weighting factors be assigned to each major section of the master plan leading to the prospectus?

## PROBLEM

### What financiers look for

The checklist below is used by a sizable organization that finances a wide variety of business enterprises. This particular series of questions is used in connection with interviewing the principal operating official of a going enterprise.

Read each numbered item carefully and try to decide what is important about each one.

Answer the questions posed at the end of the summary.

### Lender's base data checklist

1. Exact name of applicant:
   Address:
   Telephone No.:
2. Officers and directors or other principals and their percentage of ownership of the company:
3. Who referred you to us?
4. Form of organization: corporation _____ partnership _____ proprietorship _____ or other _____ (Explain)
5. Date of incorporation or organization:
6. State of incorporation:
7. Number of stockholders:
8. Description of principal products or services or other business:
9. Number of employees:
10. Name any subsidiary of applicant and describe their business.
11. Was amount of loan determined by formal projection of capital?
12. Amount of financing requested: $_____.
13. Equity _____ or mortgage loan _____.
14. Proposed repayment schedule.
15. How many additional personnel will be employed if loan is made?
16. Are you willing to personally endorse a loan?
17. Who are your auditors?
18. Are you audited annually?
19. Who is your attorney?
20. Where do you bank?
21. Does your company owe any past-due federal or state income, personal property real estate, or withholding taxes?
22. Set forth the consideration for the capital stock of your company, including shares issued for cash (C), fixed assets (F), services (S), or other (O).
    In what proportions?
23. Describe any material legal proceedings (courts or administrative agencies) in which the company has been or is involved, other than routine litigation incident to the business.
24. Itemize amounts which officers, directors, and owners of more than 10 per-

cent of the business have withdrawn for salary, dividends, or other in the past year.

25. Approximate net worth of company: $_____.
26. Description of principal plant and other property and approximate costs thereof:
27. Have your assets ever been appraised? Yes _____ No _____.
28. What was the company's gross income for the last years? 19_____, $_____; 19_____, $_____; 19_____, $_____.
29. What was the company's net income for the last three years? 19_____, $_____; 19_____, $_____; 19_____, $_____.
30. Who are your major competitors?
31. Who are your major customers?
32. Through what channel will your product be marketed?
33. Have you applied to any other financial institution for financing? If so, who?
34. Specific purpose of financing and manner in which proceeds will be used:

## Advise applicant of following

*If financing is approved . . .*

1. Closing costs, including legal and accounting fees, will be borne by applicant.
2. Annual audits will be required.
3. Mortgage loan average interest rate.
4. Equity loan average interest rate.
5. Appraisal of assets, if required, would be at applicant's cost.
6. If equity loan, incorporation of business will be required.
7. We will be represented on board of directors.

## QUESTIONS

1. What is the relationship of the checklist and the prospectus as to content and detail?
2. With a change of wording, nearly all the numbered items could be stated so that they would apply to a beginning business. Would it be reasonable to expect that the prospective businessperson would have to provide reasonable answers to all the above applicable items?

## BIBLIOGRAPHY

Bank of America National Trust and Savings Association. "Opening Your Own Business: A Personal Appraisal." *Small Business Reporter*, vol. 7, no. 7 (1971); "Steps to Starting a Business." *Small Business Reporter*, vol. 10, no. 10 (1972). Available by mail from the Small Business Reporter, Dept. 3120, Bank of America National Trust and Savings Association, San Francisco, Calif. 94120. $1.00 each. Valuable pamphlets outlining needed details that supporters want before they will commit funds or assistance.

Baty, Gordon B. *Entrepreneurship—Playing to Win.* Reston, Va.: Reston Publishing Co., 1974. A valuable source document for the preparation of the prospectus. Works from the viewpoint of the individual and what he or she should and must do to run a successful enterprise.

Buchele, Robert B. *Business Policy in Growing Firms.* San Francisco: Chandler Publishing Co., 1967. A very thorough detailed analysis of many aspects of planning and their relationship to success in small business.

Dible, Donald M. *Up Your Own Organization.* Santa Clara, Calif.: Entrepreneur Press, 1971. A valuable reference book for anyone who is interested in getting started in his own business. Has an extensive and valuable bibliography.

Hollander, Edward D. et al. *The Future of Small Business,* prepared by Robert R. Nathan Associates, Inc. New York: Frederick A. Praeger, Inc., 1967. A very worthwhile book regarding the realities of small business operations, particularly as divided into manufacturing, retail trade, services, and construction.

# 8

# Management— a team approach

As was pointed out in the preceding chapters, the basic process of management is to be concerned with planning, organizing, directing, and controlling the work environment. That is, the manager must be able to conceive the total operation in order to plan what and when things will be done; the manager must be able to organize employees, machinery, and material around these plans; the manager must be able to direct the performance of the plans through organization; and he or she must be able to maintain adequate control over the entire operation.

The traditional approach to the process of management is, without question, entirely logical and valid. However, in many cases, this approach sounds and looks a good deal simpler than the small business practitioners' problems. Therefore, this chapter will deviate slightly from the standard approaches to the management process by highlighting some of the more common problems confronting the practicing small businessperson and by suggesting what he or she might do in trying to develop a winning combination of subordinates, managerial practices, and resource allocation in the firm.

## REQUIREMENTS FOR GOOD MANAGEMENT

To be successful as a small business manager, one must instill in one's subordinates a degree of entrepreneurial spirit and feeling. This first of all means that the small business manager must understand what is meant by "entrepreneurial spirit" or personality. Although these factors are discussed in greater detail in Chapter 2, basically the successful entrepreneur is one who possesses a hardworking, middle-class set of social values with little desire to move up the social ladder or to become socially prominent. This is, in turn, coupled with an unremitting, unyielding desire to achieve and accomplish certain objectives.

Developing such a spirit in a subordinate is not a simple task, particularly since the small businessperson many times may personally display little respect for lines of authority and control, and is sometimes accused of being unable to achieve satisfactory relationships with subordinates except on a patriarchal or patronly basis. Thus a dilemma arises: Although instilling entrepreneurial spirit in one's subordinates is essential to developing a winning combination of people, material, machines, and money in the business world, the very personality pattern which will foster success in small business management sometimes tends to run in conflict with achieving such success. How, then, does one solve this dilemma and create a strong management team?

## HOW GOOD MANAGERS DO IT

The foregoing highlights the fact that small business managers have their work cut out for them if they are to develop a winning combination among subordinates. This is true whether the small business organization is composed of two persons or two hundred. The fact remains that the manager is responsible for developing the people in the organization. Fortunately, there are some guidelines which can be used by the small business manager in making things happen in the manner and way in which he or she desires. These guidelines are concerned with a way of thinking about managing and, therefore, cannot be compiled like a grocery list. Thus, each will be discussed in turn rather than merely listed.

*The good manager makes things happen.* Nicholas Murray Butler, former president of Columbia University, once said that there were three kinds of people: people who make things happen; those who watch things happen; and those who don't know what has happened. Effective small business managers not only know what is happening but also make things happen. They make their own decisions to increase sales, to develop a new product, to cut costs, to improve quality, to tap new markets, or to expand plant or facilities. Further, once these managers have determined what they intend to make happen, they will put all of their brains, leadership, and drive into making it happen. The manager who engages in making things happen is, of necessity, a dynamic, driving individual, one who is unyielding and unremitting in the pursuit of shaping not only the company but the total business environment.

*The vital shift from doer to manager.* A second guideline for the effective small business manager is that he or she must be a manager rather than a doer. This requirement is becoming even more necessary today than it was several years ago.

A manager is an expert in analyzing total situations, in classifying problems, seeing cause and effect relationships, and in identifying and pursuing the proper course of action. This, of course, requires that the successful small business manager be a creative thinker who can predict and foresee unfortunate or troublesome circumstances before they arise. Such creative thinking requires that the small business manager work *smarter* rather than *harder* and that he or she think along broad gauge lines rather than along lines of specialized, limited procedures. Thus, in anticipating future problems and in attempting to develop a course of happenings which will be beneficial, the successful small business manager must focus his or her attention on shaping and directing events, not spending longer or harder hours in the shop, plant, office, or warehouse trying to turn out more work in an effort merely to keep up with a competitor.

**People and management success.** The third requirement for successful small business managers is that they do not go out of their way to be a "nice," or a friendly competitor, a swell boss, or otherwise popular individual. This doesn't mean the small business person should have Scrooge as a model (although, financially, it could be said that Scrooge *was* a successful small business manager). It does mean, however, that it is not essential to be the most popular boss in three counties to be a successful manager of a small business.

The principle behind this requirement is that no one person will be liked by all people, and that persons who attempt to or endeavor to be liked by all people will necessarily alienate some people. The effect of such actions tends to be circuitous, and ultimately friend-seekers are reduced to a level of trying to ingratiate themselves with everyone, which is impossible in a superior-subordinate relationship. One expert on the management of people described his own experiences in this regard in the following manner:

> I once believed that a leader could operate successfully as a kind of adviser to his organization and could avoid being a "boss." In doing so, I suspect I hoped to duck the unpleasant necessity of making difficult decisions and taking the responsibility for one course of action among many uncertain alternatives. I couldn't have been more wrong, but it took a couple of years to realize that a leader cannot avoid the exercise of authority any more than he or she can avoid responsibility for what happens to the organization.

Perhaps this approach can be more concisely stated in the famous quotation, "Nice guys finish last."

**Being results-oriented.** A fourth guideline for successful small business management is that the small business manager in managing his or her organization must be results- and responsibility-oriented. This means that the small business manager must know precisely what results he or she can expect from the plans which he or she has made. This also means that small business managers will be responsible for their actions in achieving these results. The ends do not necessarily justify the means, but the end result does have to be clearly defined. Take, for example, the commonly sought results of profits and growth of the firm. These results cannot be accomplished without full regard of the rights of all individuals affected in the organization. Extracting profits and developing a growing organization based on unethical conduct or shady means will not result in a well-founded and firmly established, continuing enterprise, or one that has a strong team. Yet, by the same token, if the organization *is* composed of subordinates who are aware of the ordinary standards of fair play and good conduct and who are *also* clearly results-oriented, the ethical small business manager will likely attain the desired results.

*The effective small business manager works through the organization.* The final guideline which the small business manager can use in developing an effective and winning combination is to work through the organization and efforts from that organization rather than by himself or herself. This maxim should be obvious, yet it is an often-ignored principle. The fact is simply this: *Once a small business gets of sufficient size, one person can no longer operate that business.* This means that the manager must develop subordinates, and as the organization continues to grow, he or she must develop large numbers of subordinates.

The development of subordinates requires that the manager be effective at delegating responsibility and authority for various tasks. This requires that the manager relinquish direct control over the performance of the job. Unfortunately many managers seem unable to comply with this final maxim. The problem is that they seem to feel that they, personally, are the only ones who can do the job correctly, effectively, or in the manner in which it must be done. Thus they fail to relinquish the obligation to actually perform the work, and they end up in the ridiculous situation of paying people to watch them (the boss) work. Obviously such a situation is to the distinct detriment of the small business manager. The only purpose it serves is that of running up costs and working hours on the part of the manager; it contributes nothing to profit.

## WHY SMALL BUSINESS MANAGERS FAIL AT MANAGING

The preceding section has served to point out the need for managerial expertise in building a strong team on the part of the small business manager. Although it is recognized that each business has unique problems of its own, there are several common pitfalls with which many small business managers are often confronted and which often result in poor managerial practices. The following sections of this chapter will discuss these pitfalls and how they can be avoided.

*Wasting time.* Wasting time is one of the most common hazards to good management. It is often difficult if not impossible for the small business manager to determine for himself or herself how he or she wastes time. In fact, many times the manager will not even know that he or she is wasting time. Most often managers will feel that everything which they do is absolutely essential and a definite requirement for satisfactory management of the business.

Despite this attitude, more often than not, many of the "essential" tasks which managers feel they must accomplish are not only unessential but they are totally and completely superfluous. Although such a statement is likely to be laughed off by the manager (or cause downright indignation that such an accusation might be made) the truth of the matter is that laughing it off or becoming indignant doesn't diminish the pathetic consequences which result from the unknowing and unwilling waste of time. Much like many of the Rube Goldberg inventions that didn't do much of anything but cause wheels to spin, many of the activities of small business managers do not amount to anything functional; they are just wheel-spinning and muscle-flexing activities.

Many managers of small businesses waste more time than they should. For example, Clark C. Caskey, a noted managerial consultant, found that the reasons managers don't get things done is because they put off, postpone, or otherwise procrastinate in doing things they dislike, find difficult to do, have experienced failure at, do not see as being critical, or feel a lack of opportunity or capability to perform. On the other hand, he found that the things managers spend their time doing are things they like to do, do well, have experienced success at, or have perceived as being absolutely critical. Unfortunately, however, those things that the manager likes to do and is good at do not necessarily carry top priority in *needing* to be done. Thus managers do things that don't need doing and put off doing things that need to be done. The interpretation which must be given this phenomenon is that, like the teen-ager who "doesn't have time" to clean his room but does have time to talk on the telephone for hours on end, many small business managers are working hard from the standpoint of putting in time, but they often are wasting time—doing unessential and unnecessary tasks which they like to do, when they should be using that time to perform the unappealing parts of the job which are beneficial if accomplished.

*Avoidance of certain duties.* It becomes obvious that the nemesis of many managers is their inability to differentiate between what functions *have* to be performed and what functions are pleasant, fun, or otherwise nice to perform if they have time. Overcoming this pitfall is not easy for small business managers, but it can be done if they will first recognize that many of the activities which take their time do so because they are not effective disciplinarians of their time. Second, they must make an effort to reconstruct their personal performance priority scale. Of course, restructuring one's personal performance priority scale is, in many cases, easier said than done. For example, it may be very difficult for Jack, the TV repairman, to stop spending 30 minutes a day across the street with the proprietor of a restaurant over a cup of coffee, even though he realizes that if he devoted that time to work it would promote better customer relations, sales, profits, and growth of the firm. The problem for Jack is not only that a friend may feel rebuffed, but that he feels he needs a break from the daily work routine. Difficult as it may be, however, the task of good management is to recognize activities for what they are—necessities or nonessentials.

To help the small business manager analyze his or her own activities and their relative usefulness to the goals and objectives of the business, the following questions need to be asked:

1. Can this activity be *eliminated* or *delegated?*
2. Can this activity be *combined* with others?
3. Can the time required to perform the activity be *reduced?*
4. Can the sequence of activities be *changed?*

The answers to these questions should provide the small business manager with a great deal of insight as to whether or not his or her activities are "fun things" or essential, productive, profit-contributing activities.

*Inability to assign work.* Inability to make effective work assignments is another failing of many small business managers. Such inability can be extremely detrimental because it not only serves as a bad example to the subordinates but it also gives them license to fail in performing their jobs. Delegating work effectively permits the supervisor to devote his or her time and attention to other, more critical tasks. Furthermore, it is often an important training device for developing subordinates and also increases morale of subordinates.

Basically, the reasons that managers fail to delegate work fall into one of the following categories:

1. They are little Napoleons who must satisfy their own ego by keeping all authority.
2. They feel that they can do it better themselves, and they refuse to permit others to do it in a "substandard" manner.
3. They are unable to communicate to their subordinates precisely what it is that they want done, when, where, and how much.
4. They lack confidence in their subordinates' abilities to do the work which should be delegated to them, because:
   *a.* They are afraid the subordinate will miss the main point.
   *b.* They are not sure of the subordinate's judgment in the unusual or uncommon situation.

    *c.* They feel the subordinate does not follow through on ideas which are given him.

    *d.* They feel that the subordinate is too young to command the respect of other employees, customers, or clients with whom he or she will be working.

5. They feel that they lack feedback or other control mechanisms by which the subordinate can be "checked up on."
6. They are afraid that their subordinates will "outshine" them or otherwise prove that they know as much or more about the job than the boss.
7. They are afraid to trust anyone besides themselves.
8. They suffer from a martyr complex—because they desire to have people feel sorry for them, they refuse to delegate work which logically could be done by other people.
9. They are possessed by a "guilt drive"—they feel guilty if they have nothing to do, and delegating work to others leaves them in that "awkward" position.
10. They fear they will be criticized for being too much of a taskmaster.
11. They want to do the job themselves.
12. They don't know what to delegate.

The above reasons are basically shortcomings on the part of the small business manager and are easily corrected once they are recognized.

The ability to delegate work effectively as a small business manager requires effective planning. The manager must know what he wants done, when, where, how much, and by whom. Once the overall plans have been set for the operations of the business, then specific actions can be taken to alleviate the stumbling block to effective delegation. These specific actions include:

1. *You must delegate.* Managers must recognize that even though all their subordinates look up to them because they control all the puppet strings in the organization, they will not *continue* to control the organizational strings if they do not delegate work to their subordinates. The only small business which can survive as a one-man operation is the small business that is so small it employes only one man.

2. *Don't do the job too well.* It must be recognized that the "I can do it better myself" fallacy is, in fact, a fallacy. Even if a manager can do a job better than subordinates (which research shows is less often true than the boss usually believes), he or she must nevertheless delegate it to someone who can do the job *well enough.* In other words, he or she must look at the benefits of the total operation which will arise from spending time supervising the overall operations of the firm. It is possible to do some jobs too well, thus jeopardizing the entire operation.

3. *Communicate.* Inability to communicate to subordinates is a block to effective delegation that can be easily overcome. All that is required is that the boss learn to make a concerted effort to apprise subordinates of plans and objectives and assign responsibilities to them. This can best be done by using a system of "management by objectives," which is discussed in the next chapter.

4. *Choose intelligent subordinates.* If the manager lacks confidence in his or her subordinates he or she should actually determine whether or not the subordinates are so ignorant that they often miss the main point of ideas, whether they display poor judgment in crises situations, and whether they have the ability to follow through on ideas. Any subordinate that fails to pass these tests should be summarily discharged. However, if the problem is the fact that the person is considered too young to command the respect of clients, customers, or co-workers, this mental block should be viewed as precisely that—a mental block. Experience shows that young, knowledgeable, competent people quickly gain the respect of others because of their knowledge and ideas.

5. *Use the management-by-exceptions principle.* The solution to the problem of control is relatively simple. Control means feedback, and feedback can be gained through written or oral reports, periodic observations, or the employment of the management-by-exceptions principle whereby the manager prescribes rules to cover all usual situations so that subordinates can decide all routine cases by applying these rules. Exceptions—nonroutine—situations are not decided by subordinates but are taken to the manager for resolution.

6. *Recognize your weaknesses.* Fear of being shown up should not be a reason for inability or reluctance upon the part of a manager to delegate work. The sign of a good manager is one who recognizes that his or her abilities lie in certain areas and that there are some areas in which others can do a more effective job. For example, a good manager might be a lousy bookkeeper. Recognizing this, he or she would do well to hire the best bookkeeper available and take pride in the ability to hire good people and use their talents. Thus, effective managers will capitalize upon having subordinates who can do some jobs better than they can do them themselves.

7. *Take a chance on subordinates.* Fear of taking a chance can be a very real detriment to a manager when it comes to delegating work. Certainly the manager would not want to entrust his or her business to a subordinate if a decision might be made which could totally ruin the business firm. However, this is not the kind of fear which tends to make managers reluctant to delegate. More commonly, it is a simple mental aversion to taking any kind of a chance. This can be overcome, perhaps, by the recognition that operating a business in and of itself requires a certain degree

of risk-taking. If the manager is unable to take any risks, he or she should not be trying to operate a business.

8. *Don't be a martyr.* Those managers who enjoy playing the role of the martyr must recognize that the sympathy they enjoy is usually short-lived and seldom results in admiration. Since recognition is their true goal, they can overcome the martyr complex once they realize they will receive more recognition through a job well done—in this case, the successful management of their business.

9. *Overcome the guilt drive.* The guilt drive, like the martyr complex, can easily be overcome once the manager accepts it for what it is—an obstacle to the successful operation of the business. Leisure time is a perfectly ordinary, legitimate, and common goal for which most people work. Furthermore, it is not only a legitimate goal but also a necessary one in terms of physical health. In trying to overcome this obstacle, the manager would do well to consider the consequence to the business if he or she were to end up in the hospital for a couple of months as a result of a heart attack, ulcer, or other mental or physical breakdown resulting from over-work.

10. *Recognize that real respect comes from being well organized.* No one who knows what must be done in a business will be accused of being too much of a taskmaster. People who are disorganized—and therefore end up demanding things be done when there is insufficient leadtime or unrealistic time constraints—are those who are accused of being taskmasters. Managers who are well organized practically always are respected and have the reputation of being astute executives.

11. *Recognize that there is seldom sufficient time to do by oneself all the jobs that one wants to do.* Any person running a small, dynamic business will find that there are many things he or she might want to do. But endeavoring to do them all is seldom possible. Thus, priorities must be established and some of the "fun to do" things must be assigned to others.

12. *Understand the difference between managing and doing.* Anyone pretending to own, operate, and manage a small business must be fully cognizant of his or her obligation to *manage,* leaving the technical *doing* dimensions to his or her subordinates. A manager must plan, organize, direct, control, motivate, communicate, and delegate. He or she has only secondary responsibilities to lift, carry, sort, wrap, disassemble, etc.

The above 12 reasons explain why many managers in small businesses are ineffectual at making work assignments. However, studies show that some employees fail to shoulder responsibility, even if the boss is a good delegator. Let us look at some of those problems.

**Letting subordinates avoid tasks.** Another primary reason some managers of small businesses have difficulty in building a strong management team is because they permit their subordinates to avoid duties that are assigned to them. One authority in the area of small business management has indicated that the following are reasons why many subordinates manage to escape duties that otherwise should be shouldered by them:

1. They "delegate back" to the boss—by playing dumb, they take the work back to the boss to "show them how" or "get them started." Often the boss ends up doing it.
2. They slow down, claiming they have too much to do. The boss thus must do it if it is to be done.
3. They "know" the boss will probably not be happy with what they have done so they just won't do it, waiting for the boss to "do it right in the first place."

*Self-pity versus luck.* Self-pity is another hazard which can serve to the detriment of the small business manager and the effort to develop a winning combination in a profitable firm. If things don't go right, it's so much easier to say "the other guy had all the breaks" rather than look for the real reasons for failure.

There is little question that luck has something to do with a person's success in the business world. Luck is always an element in every situation, and this includes the environment in which the effective manager works. However, the part which luck plays in business success seems to have one amazing feature which is usually not recognized—it seems that luck is something which is always on the side of the other guy. But those who are considered lucky usually accredit their "success" to pure hard work. One successful entrepreneur in California even published his motto in that regard saying "The harder I work, the luckier I get."

The concept of luck would tend to raise a question: Just how much is success a function of luck and how much is it a function of hard work? Obviously, if success is always a result of luck, then the unlucky ones have every right to engage in self-pity. However, if success is a result of hard work, then self-pity upon the part of the unsuccessful is not justified.

According to much which has been written on the subject of success, self-pity is probably not justified. George S. Odiorne, Dean of the College of Business at the University of Massachusetts, in writing about the factor of luck and the role it plays in the lives of various individuals, once made the following comments:

> The concept of luck is a vast, face-saving device for many of us, for it prevents us from having to confront our own personal shortcomings and inadequacies.

In short, "luck" provides a wonderful excuse for failure, a rationale for not working hard, and an alibi for poor performance.

While it is probably impossible for a small businessperson to eliminate all element of luck, there are ways in which he or she can become a "lucky" executive and make his or her company one of the "lucky" few which succeed to grow. To do this, the small businessperson must be a leader rather than a follower.

*Being a leader, not a follower.* The lucky manager is the manager who makes things happen. One executive who has given advice as to how managers can make themselves "lucky" says that the key ingredient is a long-range frame of mind. This frame of mind is based on: (1) application of knowledge, (2) study of all angles which must be considered, (3) brain power directed toward the qualitative and quantitative aspects of directing effort, (4) the will to plan, and (5) communications ability. Put in more functional terms, this means that managers who are endeavoring to create luck will (1) possess know-how; (2) be alert to changes in taste of consumers, trends, locations, competitive products, and services which are being produced, and trade connections which they can develop to enhance their position; and (3) will map a strategy toward ameliorating any undesirable developments which occur. If such activities are undertaken by small business managers, there is no reason for them to be beset with misfortune or bad luck, for they will then be "lucky" small business managers who do not need to engage in self-pity. Further, the small business manager who is not constantly lamenting life will necessarily be setting a better example for his or her subordinates. If subordinates do not have to observe a self-sympathizing boss who blames poor business conditions on anything from the weather report to a visit of the in-laws, they will be much more apt to think in terms of responsible workmanship. They will know that failure to perform will be recognized for what it is—failure to perform and not bad luck.

*Belief in the "better mousetrap" as a truism.* The last very common error of thought which tends to prevent small business managers from developing an effective work team is found in the idealistic beliefs of many small business managers. It is literally true that thousands of small businesses have been started by people who have felt that they, and they alone, possess a particular product or ability to provide a service which could not be produced or provided by others. This belief is commonly held in our folklore by the saying that "he who builds a better mousetrap will have a path beaten to his door."

There is, of course, some truth to the "better mousetrap" philosophy. But most of the successful businesses which have been started have been based not on a single good idea but on an idea which synthesizes or combines several good ideas of many other people. Often these ideas are easily copied, and if popular, they are soon faced with competition. While patents and copyrights offer some protection, it is more common to see the success of a Henry Ford, who takes the ideas of numerous other people and combines them into a not wholly differentiated product but one which provides the basis for a continuing, growing enterprise. The small businesspersons who are providing a unique product or service which people "can't resist buying" are nonexistent or very few in number. The pragmatic small business manager will instantly admit that he or she is not and never was selling a unique product or service, but only a slightly differentiated product or service. Typically, such a person will also be quick to advise anyone who thinks they do have a unique product or service to forget it if they think that that product or service is all that is needed to assure success in a small business venture.

Selling a highly unique product or service is not an easy task; in fact, selling any product requires extremely hard work upon the part of the small business manager. Unfortunately, few prospective small businesspersons recognize this fact; nor do they realize that their personal attitude determines the tone and attitude with which their subordinates approach their work. If the boss continuously proclaims that there is no explanation for why people are so stupid and fail to buy their product or service, a similar attitude will be assumed by the salesclerks, production employees, and service staff. This attitude can only result in lower sales, as few customers will tolerate indifferent, aloof sales personnel who don't seem to care whether a purchase is made or not. Although the old cliché of "the customer is always right" has long been overworked, it still holds the key to many a small business success. Those who pamper their customers are often those who succeed; those who sit back and wonder how people can be so stupid account for a large share of those who fail.

## PROVIDING LEADERSHIP—KEY TO MANAGEMENT'S SUCCESS

*Managing personnel.* One common failing of small business managers is their general lack of ability at managing their personnel—at providing leadership for their people. Small business managers tend to fail in this respect even though today there is a wealth of knowledge which exists in respect to the management of one's subordinates. It is often as near as the closest public library, and a great deal of it is available in a very readable and entertaining style. Yet many small business managers fail to avail themselves of such information—particularly those who have not extended their formal education or whose education has been primarily in scientific or technical fields.

Not only has such education by means of self-study been avoided but other even easier ways of learning have also been ignored by small business managers. For example, throughout the country any number of executive development and training programs are offered which are conducted with the sole intent and purpose of training managers to handle employees. But statistically, most of the people who attend such training sessions come from the giant corporations. Presently a few of the trade associations are beginning to awaken to the need for small business management training and are doing a commendable job of sponsoring such training programs for their members. Also Management Research Corporation and High Yield Management, Inc., have been offering such courses for the past few years. But, by and large, such groups are in the minority, and the problem seems to be of a self-feeding nature, wherein the manager who doesn't need it responds, while the manager who does need it doesn't know it, and fails to avail himself or herself of the material through such firms.

Many times the reason an effective small business operation is not developed to its full potential is because the manager lacks the information and knowledge to do it. It is not a lack of ability to learn on the part of either the small business manager or the employees; the simple fact is that small business managers have not made available to themselves the knowledge which they need and can use in developing an effective work team.

Knowledge of the need, however, should indicate to the small business manager the need for conscious effort in this direction. Further, it should make the manager aware of several steps which can be taken toward making himself or herself a more effective manager. Thus, only one other essential is lacking: knowing whether or not he or she possesses the requisite leadership characteristics and ability to do the job.

*Knowing one's leadership characteristics.* Anyone can be a leader. Everyone who owns a small business (or is considering starting one) possesses the requisite leadership characteristics and abilities for successful management, even though they have different personalities, traits, quirks, and idiosyncrasies. It is entirely possible for the small business manager to make a success of his or her operation irrespective of his or her own personal quirks and idiosyncrasies because there is no one best style or technique of leadership; rather there is an infinite variety of managerial or leadership techniques which can be successfully utilized by the right individual. Furthermore, it is often difficult to emulate a certain leadership style, for what works for one person may not be suitable for another. Therefore, the real problem which confronts the small business manager in determining whether or not he or she is capable of providing the kind of leadership or managerial style necessary for success is whether or not he or she understands his or her own leadership characteristics.

In recent years there have been many different authors who have written about leadership effectiveness. William Reddin and Fred Fiedler are two such men of recent times who have made quite a point of the fact that one's leadership effectiveness is really dependent upon many things. In fact, the "Contingency Theory" of leadership has developed from the work of many recent authors who say that not only is there not one best style of leadership, but that any particular style could be bad or ineffective if used in the wrong situation.

Essentially, today it is argued that primarily three interlocking variables enter into determining how successful one will be as a leader in a small business. One of these factors is the personality and charisma of the small business manager himself or herself; one is the attitude, personality, and charisma of the people the manager is bossing; and one is the situation itself. For example, one small businessperson might be a thorough, firm, demanding person and be successful, while another might be just as successful by being soft-spoken, even bashful—but they must have the right kind of person working for them. While it is true that some approaches to leadership have a more pleasant appeal than others (especially in terms of a nice-person approach) it is not true that the best results are always attained from such strategies. Today's modern theories thus argue that all people *can be* effective leaders if they work at it. Just so, however, all can fail at being effective, too.

The problem of leadership, therefore, is not which leadership style is the best and must be used; rather, it is a question of identifying and being aware of one's own style and finding subordinate employees who will respond effectively to the style which one happens to possess. In other words, it is more important for the small business manager to find subordinates who will respond to his or her native, intuitive methods of management than it is for the small business manager to attempt to reorient his or her own personality, attitudes, and self-image along the lines of what someone might claim the "right" or best leadership style or technique for a manager to use. It is unquestionably true that there are good and bad leaders, but it is just as unquestionably true that identifying good and bad leaders is a function of the subordinates who evaluate the leader. Thus, being a good, effective, *and successful* leader is a function of picking followers who will work well with the leader; poor leadership and failure are associated with incompatible followers.

## SUMMARY

While the world is full of successful and unsuccessful small business managers, a small businessperson's success will largely be a function of his or her ability to develop a winning combination. It is, for the most part, not the result of luck, a better product or service, or other good fortunes of a windfall nature. The success which many small business managers have achieved has been the result of some good fortune, but it is also a product of a lot of hard work in implementing sound managerial practices. Much of the hard work has, therefore, been focused on the development of a winning work combination: primarily one which has found the small business manager making adequate use of his or her personal time, delegating work to subordinates, failing to engage in self-pity or day-dreams of building a better mousetrap, and providing realistic leadership for the employees who are working for him or her.

It was pointed out that providing realistic leadership for one's sub-ordinates is not only a function of avoiding the problems which are com-mon to most, if not all, unsuccessful small business managers but it also requires the would-be successful small business manager to have a su-perior understanding of his or her own personality. Managers must recog-nize themselves for what they are—their own strengths and limitations—and build organizations which will function effectively within those limits. In short, truly successful small business managers who have developed the winning combination will have made themselves managers of their own individual, separate, and distinct work situations. They will have become leaders who can and are willing to stand on their own merits. They are not concerned about winning popularity contests or what their subordinates might think of their decisions, goals, objectives, or opinions, but they are results-oriented and will accept nothing less than 100-percent performance from themselves and their subordinates.

## QUESTIONS

1. Describe what is meant by "entrepreneurial spirit." Can the small busi-nessman instill such spirit in his subordinates? How?

2. What is meant when it is stated in the text that a good manager is a gen-eralist rather than a specialist? Do you agree with this statement? Why or why not?

3. Can small business managers expect to be both successful and popular with their employees? If so, explain how it is possible; if not, explain why not.

4. What is meant by being "results- and responsibility-oriented?" Should small businessmen be results-oriented, or should they be people who are willing to "wait and see" what happens? Why?

5. The text states that many managers seem unable to effectively delegate work to subordinates? Do you agree? Why or why not?

6. One problem for many small businesspersons is the fact that they waste their time on "essential" tasks? Can this be possible? Why? Explain in detail.

7. Explain what is meant by the text in respect to the manager's performance priority scale.

8. If you were a small businessperson, what questions would you ask your-self to determine whether or not you were wasting your time?

9. Describe the role and phenomenon of "luck" in the success of small busi-ness management. Do you feel "luck" is an element of small business suc-cess? Why or why not?

10. Explain the small business manager's role as a leader in his or her organization. Can leadership be developed by just any small businessperson? What is the best style of leadership for a small businessperson?

## PROBLEMS

1. Five years ago your company opened a small store in a distant city. Mary White, one of the women first hired to work in the store showed supervisory ability and was soon put in charge of a rapidly expanding department. She was very successful. Sales and morale were high in her group.

   Since the branch store had limited chances for advancement and the main store had greater opportunities, you moved Mary to the main store and placed her in a supervisory position in a department similar to the one she had been handling so successfully. However, in the large, well-established main store things are run differently than in the small branch store. Six months have passed, and Mary is trying hard but she hasn't gotten her new job under control.

   1. List and give the reasons for differences between running a department in a large well-established store and a small branch store.
   2. Can a person be a success in one and a failure in the other? Why? Why not?
   3. How should Mary have been inducted into and trained for her new job?

2. The production in your small operation has been steadily decreasing, and you strongly suspect that the men have deliberately organized a slowdown. You question several of your good workers, and they admit that they are being pressured into holding back production, but they refuse to incriminate any of their fellow workers by naming the ringleaders of the slowdown. When you ask the cause of the slowdown, they tell you that the cost of living is increasing and that they need to make more money by working more overtime.

   You believe that right now there is no justification for more overtime. In addition, you feel that if you submit to this type of pressure, you will lose control over your group.

   1. What are the possible solutions to this problem?
   2. What are some of the possible consequences of the above solution?
   3. How can the situation be prevented from recurring?
   4. What leadership characteristics do you need to develop? Explain.

3. Don Trickle had long wanted to start his own photography business. He was an avid amateur photographer and felt sure he knew all it took to run a business.

   After rounding up a grubstake of $10,000 he had started his own business. It was a success from the start and now Don has ten people working for him. Four of these people are part-time employees—a secretary, a bookkeeper, a janitor, and carpenter (who makes props and other special equipment for photographic jobs). The rest are all photographers.

Until recently Don had felt he was a good manager. He treated his people well—almost as if they were his children. Today, however, after a big scene, all Don's photographers quit—or at least said they were quitting—and left.

Reflecting on the material in Chapter 8:

1. Why might these photographers have quit Don?
2. What could Don have done (not done) to avoid this problem?
3. If you were Don, what would you do to prevent this kind of a problem from occurring?

## BIBLIOGRAPHY

Anyon, G. Jay. *Entrepreneurial Dimension of Management.* Wynnewood, Pa.: Livingston Publishing Co., 1973, 217 pp. Discusses the nature of entrepreneurial behavior.

Collins, Orvis, and Moore, David G. *The Organization Makers.* New York: Appleton-Century-Crofts, 1970, 232 pp. Revised edition of *The Enterprising Man.* Compares different kinds of entrepreneurs.

Dailey, Charles A. *Entrepreneurial Management.* New York: McGraw-Hill, 1971, 208 pp. This book explains the risk-taking dimensions of entrepreneurial management. Assesses how entrepreneurs solve management problems.

Swayne, Charles, and Tucker, William. *The Effective Entrepreneur.* Morristown, N.J.: General Learning Press, 1973, 173 pp. An analytical treatment of what is characteristic of successful owner-managers of smaller, entrepreneurial businesses.

# 9

# Planning for managing

By definition, to plan means to make a detailed program of action, involving the selection of objectives, policies, and procedures. There is little confusion as to what is meant by planning and there are seldom any doubts in the small businessperson's mind about the importance of planning. Planning is needed for successful operation of the business, and the ability to plan is therefore one of the essential elements of small business leadership.

Unfortunately, even though there is much statistical evidence which supports the fact that planning should, and does, pay off in successful operations, lip service is often all that is paid to that need by small business people. Therefore the importance of planning to the success of the small business manager cannot be overemphasized. Planning is necessary at all levels of management, particularly the top level.

## MANAGING FOR RESULTS

In recent years the concept of management known as "management by objectives" or "management for results" has emerged as a useful tool for the small businessperson in trying to plan for and establish performance goals and objectives for his or her business operation. The concept of management by objectives was originally coined as a phrase by Peter Drucker in his book *The Practice of Management*. Since that time it has become a well-known managerial concept.

Although the managerial concept of management by objectives or managing for results is relatively well known, many people who own and/or manage small businesses are not aware of what the concept truly means. It is one thing to say that one should establish performance objectives as an integral process of making and managing business plans. It is something else for someone to genuinely understand what establishing these performance goals and objectives means. Management by objectives does not mean such things as writing out job descriptions for employees; nor does it mean a technique to use in measuring a subordinate's performance at performance appraisal and salary review time. Management by objectives concerns itself with establishing specific performance goals and objectives for various parts of the organization of the small business. If the business is truly small—say five people or less—the management by objectives statements might be one simple policy statement which specifies what the business expects to do in terms of growth, developing its share of the market and business volume, marketing plans and strategies, return on investment, and other overall operating strategies. If the business is of larger size, however, the management by objectives statements assume a different proportion. In a larger business that has various operating departments or units, objectives statements will be made for the overall corporation from a policy stance, but there will also be objectives statements established for performance goals and objectives of each department or major subunit of the business firm.

## Establishing objectives

Establishing performance goals and objectives for a going small business is not easily accomplished. However, there is a rather common sequence or routine which can be followed in establishing performance goals and objectives. The sequence includes the following steps:

*Step 1.* Set up a corporate policy committee establishing who will serve on the committee (this might be the Board of Directors, or merely the owner if the business is extremely small); define their duties; determine the times and the completion date for the statement of corporate objectives.

*Step 2.* Assign members of the policy-making group their various duties in developing their ideas and/or outlining what the corporate policies and objectives ought to be with respect to specific functions within the organization.

*Step 3.* Have the policy maker(s) review the total policy statements outlined by the various individuals and assess the effect of the individual policies on mutually dependent functions.

*Step 4.* Agree to the corporate policy which is to be established and reduce that policy to written form for all to utilize.

*Step 5.* Assign individuals within the separate functions of the organization to outline detailed operating plans and objectives which they will use in implementing and accomplishing the general corporate policies as stated in the policies objectives.

*Step 6.* As a committee, review the overall policy manual, by function, to correct any errors of omission or commission which may have occurred.

*Step 7.* Implement the corporate policy and objectives statement.

The procedures involved in establishing the corporate policy manual should be carried out methodically. Common sense, of course, prevails, for it is a simple planning function that is to be done: making sure that the plans are thorough and concise and then implementing the plan. However, one thing must be pointed out clearly. All of the various functional areas within the business must be considered in establishing the plan. Thoroughness is probably more important than any other factor in establishing corporate goals and objectives.

## What goes into corporate objectives

Corporate objectives can encompass many things. However, the following items are usually considered in establishing overall corporate objectives by most small businesses in the United States. They include:

1. Financial objectives
2. Personnel objectives
3. Customer and public relations objectives
4. Advertising objectives
5. Accounting objectives
6. Production objectives
7. Credit and collection objectives
8. Purchasing and inventory control objectives
9. Sales objectives
10. Profit objectives
11. Legal objectives
12. Security objectives for the organization

It should be noted that in very small businesses many of the above functions cannot be clearly separated from each other. Furthermore, it is common for many of these areas to overlap. This is even true in large corporate structures of the $100,000,000 plus variety. Nevertheless, it is incumbent upon the small business manager to establish operating goals and objectives in each of these specific areas.

## How one plans and manages by objectives

In a functioning system of management by objectives, the senior operating executive must necessarily establish overall corporate goals and objectives. He or she should do this through a committee of the more responsible people who know what is going on in the operation.

Many small business people have found that there is a cycle to the establishment of *performance* goals and objectives. Essentially the cycle— Phase 1—begins when the overall corporate policies and objectives are established for the business. Then, in Phase 2, the small businessperson allocates the portions of the total corporate goals and objectives to responsible subordinates who actually have the job of implementing those goals and objectives. These subodinates are then set free in Phase 3 to take appropriate action in their departments to obtain the desired goals or objectives. Naturally, of course, the manager must be supportive of and cooperative with subordinates in facilitating their accomplishment of the goals and objectives. Necessarily, he or she does not actually perform the job for them, but does make sure that all problems which may come up can be coped with or otherwise contended with by the responsible subordinate.

Phase 4 in the cycle of management-by-objectives is accomplished when, after the subordinate has had sufficient time to implement the assigned policies and objectives, a review is made to compare the results with the original goals and objectives. At this stage, a formal assessment is made of progress concerning the accomplishment of the operating goals and objectives of the business, and then the cycle starts all over again. Thus, Phase 5 is simply a repeat of Phase 1 (in which the manager of the business establishes new goals and objectives to be obtained by the organization). Necessarily, of course, these new goals and objectives are the outcome of what has been happening to business during this time and the degree of success or failure which subordinates have had in implementing the original performance goals and objectives. Thus Phase 5, when the second round of goals is established, might include the continuation of some of the original goals and objectives of Phase 1 if they were not realized. However, it must be noted that there will be a great number of questions concerning why or why not a subordinate was able to accomplish the goals or objectives which he or she had been assigned.

## REQUIREMENTS FOR PLANNING

The fine art of managing any small business necessarily requires that the small business manager be adept at planning. But what kinds of planning does a small business manager engage in? Does one actually differentiate in the types of plans that one makes? Exactly what are the requirements for effective planning on a comprehensive scale in a small business?

These, and other questions asked above, must be answered if one is to become an effective manager of a small business. There are certain capabilities required for good planning in any small business and these essentials include:

### See the situation as a whole

A primary ingredient of effective planning in the small business is that the small businessperson see the overall situation as a whole. This is why it was emphasized in the first portion of this chapter that overall corporate goals and objectives must be established. This is true whether the business is very small or quite large. The overall corporate goals and objectives must necessarily be seen before the subordinates' goals and objectives can be established for each operating department or unit in the small business.

### Divide the whole into workable parts

Once small business managers have taken an overall view of corporate goals and objectives as they see them, they must be able to break the whole situation into workable parts. This is why it is so important that the various categories of objectives be so clearly developed in the overall corporate policy statements. Each of these statements then can be broken down into parts for production operations, financial control, advertising plans and strategies, and other purposes.

### Use constructive imagination

Many people feel that they are not imaginative. Therefore they do not use imagination constructively in trying to establish performance goals and objectives. Wishing something so does not make it so, but trying to define where one wishes to go with one's business is not wishful thinking if it is based upon realistic, concrete, obtainable, and measurable performance objectives. Thus it is imperative that the small businessperson try to define what the performance goals of the business will be, in terms of the quantity of business expected, the quality of work expected, when the various goals are expected to be realized, and within what budgetry or other financial constraints these goals are to be accomplished. In fact, these four parameters—quantity, quality, time, and cost—are the four parameters which any small businessperson should use in trying to be constructively imaginative in determining future goals and objectives for each major operating unit within his or her business organization.

### Be objectively analytical

Any effective small business manager will be ineffective at planning if he or she is unrealistic in establishing performance goals and objectives for the organization. Necessarily, therefore, effective small business managers are objectively analytical in assessing what they intend to do in the forthcoming planning period. They do not expect to reach the unreachable or obtain the unobtainable. However, they do necessarily attempt to "stretch" their organizations and perform up to their capability. This requires a very realistic and honest assessment of what the expectations for the business can actually be.

### Measure the effect of the plan

Yet another dimension essential to planning at the small business level is a capability to measure what is happening when the plan is being implemented. It must be recognized it is possible to both overplan and underplan for any business. Just so, it is also possible to overcontrol and undercontrol the implementation of that plan. Many small businesspersons plan but they fail to set up ways to measure or assess the implementation of the plan. Others set up excessive control devices that are a hindrance to thorough and accurate implementation of the plans. Realism again becomes the key. In this case, however, the key to success concerns realism in the measurement of the performance of the plan as it is being implemented and not the realism of the plan itself.

### Avoid getting bogged down in details

Some people seemingly cannot avoid the need to become emotionally attached to the irrelevant. Many small business managers, in attempting to establish operating plans for their organization, get bogged down in detail and never truly put into effect the overall statement of plans for the business, let alone the various portions of the business. Getting bogged down in the details of exact procedures which will be used to implement each plan necessarily is an indicator of poor planning capabilities on the part of the small businessperson. It is imperative that they realize that the primary purpose is to establish the plan. Implementation of the plan comes when one has the time to nitpick about various details concerning the plan.

### Work with large quantities of unknowns

Another essential requirement for effective planning upon the part of the small businessperson is the ability to operate in the face of uncertainty and the unknown. More attention will be devoted to this later in the chapter but it must be realized that this ability to face uncertainty—and to operate effectively within that air of uncertainty—is indispensable to effective planning.

## ESTABLISHING PLANS OF OPERATION

The first section of this chapter was designed to explain the use of the concept of management by objectives in planning for the overall operation of the small business. Now that the reader has a firm grasp of what is meant by utilizing the concept of management by objectives, and what is required to put it into practice, it is necessary to probe into some refinements of the planning function. This and the following sections will be devoted to that task.

One of the primary jobs of the small business manager is the establishment of a master or long-run plan of operation for his or her firm. Master planning should, ideally, be engaged in even before the actual small business is made into a going, operating concern. Unfortunately, many small businesses are started without benefit of a master plan of operation. Thus, many small business managers may find that even though they have going concerns, they need to rethink or establish from scratch some basic master or long-run plan of operation. Whether or not the small businessperson is planning to start a business or has a going concern which he or she wants to perpetuate, the principles of establishing such plans are the same.

## The time to dream and the time to be conservative and realistic

One of the fundamental principles of establishing master plans of operation is recognition that there is a difference between dreaming and realistic planning of a challenging nature. Plans very definitely should not be wishful thinking about things that can never be accomplished. By way of example, General Motors will not be replaced in the near future, no matter how carefully the plans are made by anyone now starting his or her own automobile manufacturing firm. The same thing can be said for any of the enviable firms which rank among the 100 largest in the United States.

The foregoing is obviously a truism, and no small business manager is going to conceive any notions of displacing one or more of the corporate giants existing in the United States today, at least not overnight. However, the time does come when the development of business plans that are realistic nevertheless appear to be approaching the impossible, while at the same time are realistic. This time comes when business plans are established which effectively push and stretch the company's abilities, but only within reasonable limits. This is considered a desirable goal by many. Although small business managers are wasting their time and money when they are making plans which obviously overreach their capacity and abilities, they are being realistic and striving for success if they are designing plans which will stretch their capabilities to their limits. As has been stated, "You need to know the capacities and capabilities of your company. You need to know whether your people will be able to produce or sell according to plan. You need to know your resources, and how much money you can spend. If you don't have much uncommitted money, you can make few choices and don't have much planning freedom."

## Strategies and tactics of master planning

The strategies and tactics of making a master plan of operation for a small business firm is as much an art as it is a science. In developing such a plan of operation, the small business manager is formulating and directing his or her own future. But, as was pointed out above, he or she is possibly limited by two serious factors. One is the element of uncertainty; the other is limited imagination.

*Uncertainty.* Planning, by its very nature, deals with the future and therefore is always filled with uncertainty and the possibility of change. This limits one's ability to plan. However, it will be recognized that the mere existence of uncertainty is not always a disadvantage for the small business planner. The reason is that uncertainty also exists for the small business's competitors. Although the small businessperson cannot perdict his or her own future, neither can competitors. Further, it should be recognized that the small businessperson can capitalize on the fact that uncertainty does exist. There is little question but that those companies which forecast and plan well for the future are better prepared than those which do not plan and are caught by surprise. Thus, the planning small business manager can work the negative features of uncertainty to his or her advantage simply by facing the issue squarely.

*Limited imagination.* Planning requires imagination, and the problem is that while everyone possesses some imagination, most people don't possess a lot of imagination. Thus, limited imagination can pose a problem for the small business planner, since it is necessary if one is to predict where he or she will be 5, 10, or 15 years hence. By way of illustration, for example, few people could have predicted five years ago where they would be today; nor could they have predicted five years ago what today's business conditions would look like. Furthermore, the problem compounds as the time period is increased.

The really successful small business planner is the one who possesses the right kind of imagination to permit him or her to foresee the future with some (small) degree of accuracy. Naturally, some people are more adept at this task than others. However, limited imagination should not be used as an excuse for lack of planning. At stated before, everyone possesses some imagination, and this imagination, however limited, should be put to use in speculating about the future. Often a person has more imagination than he or she thought; but as with many other things, if it is not used, such ability becomes defunct. A well-oiled machine is much more efficient than one which has been allowed to rust and gather dust.

## Benefits and advantages to long-run and master planning

There are some positive aspects to the art of master planning. One of these positive aspects is that the planning centers on a subject with which the small business is familiar. This lightens the task considerably, for it is much easier to plan the future when one knows the market in which one is dealing.

A second advantage to small businesspersons in practicing the art of master planning is that they are making plans which will affect themselves. This means that the small businessperson has the opportunity to reject committing the business to those things which he or she does not want to do or does not feel capable of doing. At the same time, the manager can attempt to commit his or her business to things which are felt to be desirable. This is not always possible for the professional manager hired by a large corporation.

Normally, when one plans, certain courses of action are established while others are precluded. Precluding certain courses of action takes away much flexibility which would be available were the plans not made, and thus the plans can become a disadvantage if the future turns out differently than anticipated. This does not have to be the case in master planning, however, because the strategy of the master planner can be designed along the lines of making plans that can be changed at reasonable cost and in reasonable time should the situation require it. In other words, the small businessperson can plan to avoid crisis situations and the high costs that are incurred when unanticipated crises arise for the small corporation. This sometimes requires that the small business manager lay two sets of plans: one to be followed when things go right; and the other to be used if things go wrong.

### Formalizing the plan

Once a master plan of operation has been decided upon, the plan should be formalized. Formal plans are usually accomplished; informal ones are not. For example, the difference between the following two proposals is apparent: "I really need to start an investment program; I think I'll buy some property" and "I made a bid on the corner lot of Broadway and Pearl consistent with my overall investment plans of buying one acre of commercial property this year." Obviously, the person who has investment plans in the first situation really has nothing more than wishful thoughts, perhaps a good idea, and probably little likelihood of ever investing in real estate. The second person, however, has taken formal action with respect to a definite plan which he or she has put together. Obviously the second person is more apt (1) to invest in real estate and (2) to be more successful at it.

Analogous to the foregoing example, the small business manager who formulates clear, concise plans and spells them out in detail is much more apt to develop better plans along a master scale than is the individual who simply speculates from the comfort of a rocking chair. Put simply, so long as a plan is nothing more than a vague idea, it is not much of a plan; formalized plans that have been put down in writing are much more likely to be carried out, and the desired-for results are much more likely to be obtained.

In short, then, there are numerous advantages to long-run or master planning, and these advantages are so great that to be without them is foolish for any small business manager. In operational terms, these advantages include the following:

1. They help direct the efforts of the organization into new growth areas, thus avoiding stagnant and/or low profit areas.
2. They not only show the areas of operations which the firm should go into in the future but they also disclose when action must be taken to get into those specific business areas.
3. They help the manager take stock of his or her operations and identify the sources of strength and weaknesses which exist in the organization.
4. They highlight various future needs such as additional manpower, subordinate managers, machinery, new facilities, and new locations. They help give some stability to the firm, particularly in the short run, because they serve as a source of perspective as to how particular short-run plans fit into the overall scheme of operations.

## OTHER PLANNING METHODS

### Short-run planning

Master and long-run planning can be said to be concerned with the infinite and barely foreseeable future; short-run planning applies to the more immediate time period of three to six months, or, at most, a year. Thus, although short-run planning deals with the future (1) it does not permit total reshaping and redirection of the firm, and (2) it therefore requires much more careful and specific formulation.

Short-run planning is essential to the day-to-day success of the small business because it allows the small businessperson to deal with specific problems and issues which cannot always be anticipated in long-run planning. By way of example, one small business manager failed to recognize in her long-run planning that property which she held had some commercial value. However, due to the rerouting of a particular road the commercial value of this same property increased considerably, and in the short run the small businessperson had ample time to capitalize on the increased value of her land holdings.

Thus, the nature of short-run planning emerges. It gives the small businessperson the opportunity to work within the framework of long-run and master plans, but it also allows the implementation of long-run and master plans in the most efficient and effective way possible. Short-run planning permits the vague, ambiguous areas of the long-run plan to jell into shape. In the short run, small business managers are better able to see the situation which is developing as a whole; can be more objective and analytical in evaluating the situation, can avoid getting bogged down in details which are meaningless; and have more rapid feedback on the efficacy of their plans and how they might change the situation to promote effectiveness.

## Planning for special events

Another kind of planning in which the small businessperson will frequently find himself or herself engaged is planning for a special event. This is often called task-force management or project management. It is no different from any of the other types of planning other than it is concerned only with a specific project, program, or other special event. However, the importance of integrating the special events plans with the long- and short-run plans of the firm cannot be overemphasized. The problem is that many times small business managers find themselves in the position of not seeing the forest for the trees. They fail to recognize the ramifications and implications of following a particular course of activity in implementing a special project, and as a result, they end up encumbering—if not destroying—the operations of the rest of their firm.

One example of this problem which comes to mind is the case of the once-small business operated by Henry Ford:

> Henry Ford made a relatively inexpensive automobile available to the American public through his production genius—and made barrels of money in the process. Yet, because of his disregard for the marketing function, company dealers, competition and customers, he succeeded in piloting his company from an undisputed and unchallenged first place in the auto industry in 1927 to a miserable and challenged second place in 1928. He did this by closing shop for six months to introduce his Model A, and because of his short-sighted plan succeeded in pushing his company from the class of one of the greatest money makers to one of the greatest money losers of that time.[1]

Thus, by becoming engrossed in the changeover from producing the Model T to producing the Model A, and by forgetting the operation of the rest of his firm, Ford nearly destroyed his whole enterprise. He became so engrossed in one tree that he forgot it belonged to a forest.

## Crisis planning

The final kind of planning situation which the typical small businessperson is faced with is planning during a crisis situation. As mentioned above, planning helps avoid crisis situations and the concomitant crisis

---

[1] From an unpublished paper by Lawrence L. Steinmetz on the Ford Motor Company.

decisions that are made. However, it must be recognized that some crisis situations will arise no matter how well plans have been formulated. Thus, some ability at reformulating plans must be possessed by the small businessperson. If a decision must be made in the face of a crisis, the following guidelines should be used:

1. The manager should get into a relaxed frame of mind. He or she should try not to decide under stress or without sufficient time. He or she should also concentrate on the problem at hand and exclude other things for the time being.
2. He or she should not try to anticipate all eventualities. Not only are there entirely too many things which could happen, but such an effort may prevent him or her from focusing on the logically predictable effects of his or her decisions.
3. He or she should not expect to be right all of the time. In the crisis situation the successful manager is probably only right a little more often than he or she is wrong.
4. He or she should not be afraid of failure. Fear of failure is one of the biggest causes of failure and creates additional mental tension which tends to muddle one's thoughts.
5. He or she should act decisively. Indecision itself creates tension, but, more specifically, tenacity of purpose and forceful implementation of plans will make up for several minor shortcomings in the plans formulated.
6. When the crisis situation is truly upon the manager, he or she should decide how to act and not put off making the decision. Procrastination will only increase the difficulties encountered in the crisis situation.
7. He or she should try to develop alternative solutions if conditions warrant, but by the same token the manager must be willing to stick by the original decision rather than continually mulling over it and trying to modify it. The manager must recognize that it is more important to be decisive than to have the right plan—that alternative plans are only functional in light of total impracticality of the original plans.

## MANPOWER PLANNING—AN EXAMPLE OF THE PROBLEMS ENCOUNTERED IN PLANNING FOR THE DAILY OPERATIONS OF THE SMALL BUSINESS

### Indivisibility of employees

Manpower planning is one of the most trying situations which a typical small business manager will encounter. The major problem with manpower planning is that, unlike many other things, people are not divisible. That is, the typical small business manager can buy things, build things, and otherwise establish things pretty much in units of a size which will best fit his or her needs. However, in the case of manpower, this is not possible to the same degree, particularly in the very small firm. People are people, and they must be hired, one whole person at a time. Of course it is possible for a small business person to hire people part-time, but only in exceptional circumstances are highly qualified, valuable employees obtained in this way. Most quality people who are serious about working want full-time employment. The only exception to this is the occasional individual, who because of health, family, or other reasons, desires a limited work load. Such situations, although permitting the hiring of a part of a person, usually are not satisfactory, because they often end up with the small businessperson creating work which is not really necessary for the part-time employee during slack periods—an expensive proposition. The problem of indivisibility of people complicates the small business planner's efforts even more when the problem is considered in respect to managerial personnel. Most small businesses have one, two, or three subordinate managers who control the various functions of the operation. Many times, such a firm is large enough to hire the exact amount of rank-and-file help needed, but they are not big enough in all cases to hire the exact amount of high-level managerial talent needed. This problem is more severe than the problem of indivisibility of rank-and-file employees because of the higher salaries commanded by managers and because of the absolute scarcity of qualified part-time managerial help. For example, as can be seen in Figure 9–1, it might be possible for the Kis Company to hire as many rank and filers as needed in each of their three plants, but they must hire a whole manager for each plant—even though the operations at Plant No. 3 amount to only half the magnitude of the work at Plants 1 and 2 and require only half as many employees. The ideal solution to this situation is to hire half a manager, which is impossible. What

FIGURE 9–1
Kis Company organizational chart

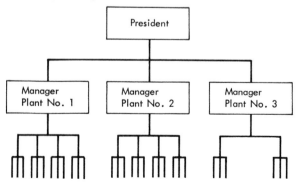

does happen is either the hiring of excessive managerial talent or the stretching of limited managerial talent. In both cases the result is an expensive misuse of managerial ability.

## Lack of facilities for developing managers

The indivisibility aspect of human beings is further compounded by the lack of facilities possessed by the typical small business for properly recruiting, selecting, developing, and training its personnel. The problem is one of both general lack of funding and of indivisibility. Usually the small business firm has limited funds and is reluctant to devote said funds to recruiting, selecting, developing, and training personnel. But even if money is not a problem, there is still the indivisibility problem which shows up in two counts. First is the indivisibility of the employees being recruited, selected, developed, and trained; second is the indivisibility of the people who are actually performing the personnel function. Thus, General Motors can have several personnel departments, but the Kis Company can logically have only one. This means that the Kis Company will be greatly hampered in its personnel functions because of the need to spread the personnel manager's efforts around to three different plants.

## Lack of economies of scale

The third problem which complicates the personnel planning aspect for the small business firm is lack of the usual economies of scale which other, larger business firms can capitalize on in dealing with their people. One such diseconomy comes from the compensation aspect of employing people. That is, the bookwork required is the same, whether 25 or 2,500 people are paid. Though the process is repeated several additional times in the larger corporation, still the same number of books, the same number of financial manipulations, the same kinds of records must all be kept. Whether the records are many or few, they incur certain fixed costs which necessarily mean a relative diseconomy for the small business.

Another problem which results in a lack of economy of scale arises in the administration of fringe benefits to small business employees. For instance, both small and large corporations like to provide some form of accident, sickness, hospitalization, or other insurance coverage for their employees. However, large corporations get breaks on their expenses for these fringe benefits because they can enroll their employees in company group plans. Unfortunately, the small business often is not large enough to compose a "group" and therefore must enroll in one of the many commercial group plans, sometimes paying a higher rate. These rates are higher partly for statistical reasons, but also because the large corporations can often minimize their premiums by keeping a staff nurse, and in many cases a staff physician, on the corporate payroll to minimize the extremely expensive "first-dollar" claims experienced by commercial group plans. Obviously a small business the size of the Kis Corporation cannot hire a physician to be in residence at its plants. Therefore, the costs of any insurance plan would be higher for the Kis Corporation, per number of employees, than for the large business firm.

## Personality complications

Another problem in personnel planning is that of the possible conflict of personalities which can be anticipated but cannot be predicted by a small business manager. The problem is that in the small business everybody knows everyone else. This can create a situation involving a great degree of harmony and unison of action with complete accord on the part of all employees. However, it can just as easily cause a great deal of discord, and more often than not, such is the case. This disharmony will quite obviously work to the detriment of the small business firm because one disgruntled person represents such a much larger percentage of the total work force in the small business firm than in the larger firm.

## The chore of planning

The foregoing was designed to highlight the fact that personnel planning can be one of the most trying of all small business planning efforts because of the nature of people. Not only are people indivisible, they also tend to talk back, and often have opinions of their own. Thus, any small business manager who fails to plan in terms of staffing his or her establishment will likely fail in operating the firm. It is extremely essential that the small business manager think in terms not only of the short-run "who will be my fry cook today" situation but also in the long-run "who will be my maître d' five years from now when I've hit it big"—and even in the longer run, "who will ultimately replace me as president and general manager of my restaurant chain?"

People-planning problems are not the only sticky problems which the small business must face. Many other planning problems are just as critical and difficult. Therefore, it is necessary for the small business manager to learn to plan. He or she must plan in the long run and in the short run, must be prepared to plan in the crisis situation, and must be able to plan to meet special events. Logically, this can all be accomplished by incorporating the concept of management by objectives which not only gives completeness to the planning but also gives timely and accurate feedback, as required, particularly for short-run plans.

## PLANS THAT FAIL

Before we leave the topic of planning, one other element must be considered. Planning for success does not guarantee success; sometimes plans fail. The most common reasons for failure include miss-guessing or failing to properly assess the public's reaction, failing to foresee certain events as being probabilities, or failing because the planning itself was inadequate.

Thus, the small business manager should reconcile himself or herself to the fact that he or she may likely fail at some time or other in attaining the goals which have been established through careful planning. However, such a result should not cause a great deal of concern. To begin with, this is not an uncommon phenomenon; but more importantly, to have plans go awry does not mean complete failure, nor that the small business planner is worse off than had he or she not planned at all. Planning, whether the plans are realized or not, will help shape the direction, goal, and ultimate destiny of the firm. If that firm is anywhere near being well conceived and well founded, the plans should have helped it realize better results. It might be well to keep in mind the advice of the Cheshire Cat in Lewis Carroll's *Alice's Adventures in Wonderland:* If you don't know where you're going, any path will take you there.[2]

## QUESTIONS

1. Explain the concept of management by objectives.
2. Can the concept of management by objectives be used in evaluating the efficiency of a small business? Of a part of a small business? How?
3. Explain how to establish objectives in a going concern, being careful to trace through the whole process.
4. What is meant by a master plan of operation? Must all small business-people concern themselves with such plans? Why?
5. Explain the role of uncertainty in the function of planning. Can uncertainty be used to the advantage of the small business?
6. What are the advantages to long-run planning? Any disadvantages?
7. What is the difference between long-run and short-run planning? Are both important? Why?
8. When is crisis planning appropriate? How should it be done by the small business if it is to be successful?
9. Develop some of the unique planning problems you think are common to small business operations.
10. What should the small business planner do if he or she fails in carrying out his or her plans?

---

[2] Lewis Carroll, *Alice's Adventures in Wonderland* (London: Macmillan and Company Ltd., 1865).

## PROBLEM

Dick Tutton picked up his cup of coffee, took a big gulp, and told Fred Rose that he "had to get back to work." Fred said, "You're always strung out, Dick. You need to get better organized."

Leaving the coffee shop on his way back to his Office Supply Company, Dick reflected on Fred's comments. "I know my work seems disorganized, but what could I do differently?" he thought. "I tell people what to do and then watch them mess it up. I was told it was bad management strategy to just do what one's subordinates can't do. But what other way is there? It certainly seems that there ought to be a better way of doing things. But I sure don't know what it is. I wonder if Mr. Byte, the banker, could help me?"

You are Mr. Byte:

1. What would you tell Dick?
2. Are there any systems of management that Dick should know about? What are they? How do they work?
3. What three important management tips might you apprise Dick of?

## BIBLIOGRAPHY

Cohn, Theodore, and Lindberg, Roy A. *How Management Is Different in Small Companies.* New York: American Management Association, 1972, 48 pp. An AMA publication assessing the "differences" in managing small and large companies.

Drucker, Peter F. *Managing for Results.* New York: Harper & Row, 1964, 240 pp. One of Drucker's earlier works—analyses how management develops opportunities with a results-oriented approach to running a business.

Odiorne, George S. *Management by Objectives.* New York: Pittman, 1965. A witty look at the system of management by objectives as applied in U.S. business and industry.

Wayne, William. *How to Succeed in Business When the Chips Are Down.* New York: McGraw-Hill, 1971, 178 pp. An excellent presentation on the everyday problems encountered by small businesses which determine the success or failure of the business. Shows how to avoid the bankruptcy court.

# 10

# Organizing, assembling resources, supervising/ directing, and controlling

The job of the manager is to plan, organize, direct, and control a business operation. The previous chapter was concerned with the process of small business planning. Therefore this chapter will address the concept of organizing, directing, and controlling organizational efforts from the small business manager's point of view.

## ORGANIZING AND ASSEMBLING RESOURCES IN THE BUSINESS

In the field of business management, it is axiomatic that nothing will get done until there is management, that organizations must be designed to accomplish the goals or objectives for which they are established. But the goals or objectives of any organization are never stagnant, and they do not lend themselves to any definitive listing. They are always changing, and therefore designing the proper kind of an organization for the small business is an ever changing part of the process of management. Fortunately, however, there are some guidelines which can be developed for meeting these ever changing requirements.

## How size of business relates to organizational form

It can be said that very few small business managers have mere existence as their goal. In fact, simple existence is a stagnant philosophy. Rather, the typical small businessperson usually has desires for his/her company to grow from a small operation into a large operation, if not into a giant in the field. Therefore, one of the problems that the small businessperson has is developing an organization which will do the desired things for the firm. Essentially there are four stages of growth for the typical organization, with the organizational structure differing at each stage. The stages are:

1. The direct supervision stage.
2. The supervised supervisors stage.
3. The indirect control stage.
4. The divisional organization stage.

These stages of growth are correlated with the success of the small business. Success is always desired, but achieving the required growth in the small business necessitates development of the different organizational structures which will facilitate the expanded operations.

The company which is in Stage 1 of its successful career is at the direct supervision stage. This stage is typified by an owner-manager who directly supervises almost all the work done by his (almost) 25 or 30 employees. Any reports, communication of plans, and/or other control measures are few in number and are handled on a firsthand observation basis. However, with more than 25 to 30 employees the company moves into the second stage—the supervised supervisors stage—and a different organizational form becomes important.

Once a company has grown to the supervised supervisors size, the lowest level work done in the organization is generally supervised by a foreman or supervisor who reports to the owner-manager. The owner-manager no longer supervises operative employees directly; rather he or she supervises them through the capacities of other people. This means the manager must learn to delegate authority, to give orders, and to analyze the results being obtained from the work unit through indirect reports and controls rather than by actual observation. Therefore it should be understood that at its inception a small business is usually easily run with direct control and supervision by the owner-manager, but if that owner-manager is successful—even to only a moderate degree—he or she may likely expand beyond the 25- or 30-employee cutoff point, and continued success from that stage on will depend on his ability to manage supervisors, rather than to manage operative employees.

Once the small business manager has developed a company large enough to be at the supervision-of-supervisors size, he or she can relax for awhile, for at this stage the business will be relatively immune to any additional requirements to alter managerial practices, styles, and techniques until the company progresses to the indirect control stage in its growth. The indirect control stage is arrived at when the company acquires between 250 and 300 employees. At this point the small businessperson will probably need to supervise supervisors who, in turn, supervise foremen who supervise or direct operative employees. In other words, the small businessperson will now find it necessary to supervise at a tertiary, or third, level of supervision.

The difficulty for the small businessperson at this stage is that he or she is two steps removed from the actual business operations and seldom will have direct contact with people who are actually making the product or providing the company's service. Furthermore, at this point the small business manager will find it necessary to have people in advisory capacities to help with esoteric matters, such as personnel problems, public relations problems, etc. Further, the small businessperson will find that he or she is becoming increasingly dependent upon ability to use reports to review the work accomplished by subordinate managers who are in charge of large segments of the business. Thus the small businessperson will be increasingly less able to rely on personal, direct contact and supervision of employees. Therefore, at this stage in the organization's growth, the manager becomes very dependent on reports, and necessarily will have to learn to operate by establishing policies, systems, and procedures rather than relying on intuition, instinct, and hunch as a technique for coping with the workaday problems.

It might be said that in the stage of indirect control, the small business manager is in a position of truly learning how to manage people rather than how to manage *the work* of people. However, if the small business continues to grow the small businessperson will find that he or she still has "not learned it all" in having learned how to be a successful manager at the indirect level. When the small company begins to crowd the large company category—say around 1,000 employees or so—the organizational problems again change for the small business manager. That is, when small companies begin to approach substantial size they will frequently begin to find it necessary to operate on a divisional nature. Operation on a divisional basis is, at least today, the fundamental basis on which all the giant corporations in the United States are managed. In a divisional organization structure, various people (e.g., vice presidents) are in charge of certain product lines rather than limited functions or operations. For example, whereas in the indirect control stage the small businessperson might find it expedient to have a vice president in charge of sales, a vice president of production, a vice president for industrial relations, and others, in the divisional stage of organization he will find that the various vice presidents in charge of functions must be replaced by vice presidents in charge of making and selling particular product lines or services. In other words, once a company is big enough to be concerned about the divisional organization structure, it basically is a conglomerate company, that is making and selling several distinct products or services.

By now it should be obvious that any growing small business must pass through several different stages in its organizational growth. These stages will require differing managerial skills and ability. For this reason, the small businessperson must be familiar with the various principles and fundamentals of organizing and operating a business.

## Principles of organization

In managing a small business, there are many elements of good management required for success. One is well-organized work. Well-organized work is a result of (1) getting the work divided and grouped into individual jobs and (2) defining the interrelationships between these jobs.

There are innumerable rules which have been established with respect to the principles of developing an effective and appropriate organization. A very condensed list of such principles would include the following:

1. A good organization is designed to accomplish specific purposes.
2. There should be unity of command, with only one person responsible for any given activity.
3. Authority must be clearly spelled out.
4. Decision-making should be accomplished at the lowest level possible.
5. Communication is, desirably, a two-way street, working both from the top man down and from the bottom man up.
6. Employee performance in the organization is monitored and controlled.
7. The limits of control of any individual within the organization must be made clear.

The foregoing principles of effectively organized work are essential guidelines for the manager of the small business. Good managers instinctively develop such ideas. However, assuming that most users of this text are (or will be) small businesspeople who are still in the formulation stage of their businesses, some elaboration on the above principles is probably desirable. Therefore, each will be briefly discussed below.

*1. Organizations are designed to accomplish their goals.* One of the fundamentals of good organization is that the organization is designed to accomplish specific goals. There is no such thing as a single best kind of organizational structure. Some companies are designed to manufacture products, other companies are designed to sell merchandise, while other companies are designed to service machinery, appliances, etc. The kind of organization which is most effective is therefore a situational phenomenon, depending upon the objective of the firm. An automobile manufacturing firm, for example, would have an organization strongly geared to expedite production, whereas a used-car dealership would have little design for production and would be concerned instead with having salesmen on the lot.

*2. One boss at the top.* The principle of one person being responsible for the operation of the organization is ancient and therefore needs little elaboration. Basically, this principle is known as unity of command. The idea is that one person must be responsible for getting the job done: a single head must coordinate the work of the many and varied people who are the contributing parts to the whole. For the same reason that a bridge cannot be built with one engineer designing the west side of a bridge while another designs its east side, a small business cannot operate with more than one person making the controlling decisions concerning the operation of the business.

3. *Authority is clearly defined.* This principle can be thought of as the requirement to clearly assign work responsibility to others. Many times the small business manager will make a subordinate responsible for a job but will fail to give him the authority to accomplish the job. Invariably, trouble will result from such action. A person cannot be held responsible for stopping the sun from shining when he doesn't have the authority to do so; similarly, an employee cannot be held responsible for failing to perform work if he does not have the requisite authority to perform that work.

*Delegating enough authority to allow employees to do their job*

4. *Decisions should be made at the lowest possible level.* The principle behind the requirement for the small businessperson to permit subordinates to make decisions wherever possible is twofold in nature. It frees up the time of the manager of the small business and it permits the person who has the most knowledge of a situation to make the decision quickly and resolve the issue. The point is, decisions concerning minor details should be made at a level that will best conserve on top-level management's time. The person in the company who has enough knowledge, information, and ability to make an intelligent decision should make that decision. Requiring a higher level manager to make the decision wastes the time of the subordinate, who must take the problem to the higher manager, and wastes the time of the higher manager, who must then make a decision that could have been made by the subordinate.

*Allow subordinates to make decisions*

5. *Communication must be a two-way street.* Another principle of effectively organized work is that the boss should consult with subordinates as to any ideas they might have about their job, particularly about problems which they must face. The point behind this principle is that, in addition to the fact that asking subordinates for suggestions will make them feel important, occasionally subordinates can produce some good solutions simply because they look at a given problem from a different viewpoint than the manager does. If the subordinate has a good idea there is no reason that the small business manager should not use it. However, the manager won't know that the idea exists unless he or she asks the subordinate for help.

*Ask subordinates for suggestions re their job*

6. *Employee performance is monitored and controlled.* Most experts on small business management agree that work which is checked up on will likely be done, while that which is not checked up on likely will not get done. This principle is sometimes thought of as the principle of accountability, where a person is required to account for what he has done on the job. However, more important than the name given to this principle

*Require subordinates to Check up on sub. work*

ple is what it is driving at: Work should not be demanded which is not required and work should not be assigned which is not desired. After all, no one will do work which is neither required, desired, and, therefore, not "checked up on."

**7. The small businessperson must give each subordinate a finite span of control.** Principle No. 7 of effectively organized work is that each subordinate must have a limited or finite span of control over a specified area of responsibility. This is particularly true in respect to the small business which has progressed to or beyond the supervision of supervisors stage. That is, the small businessperson must give all his or her subordinate supervisors definite limits to their areas of responsibility. Not to do so violates the principle of one person being in charge of one job. This principle is fundamental; and, in fact, it can be found in the Bible, stated as "No man can serve two masters." The reason for this principle is that no matter how well two superiors get along, check, consult, and coordinate their activities, *the time is bound to come,* when together they will either ask their subordinates to do more than they can do, not require enough of them, or worse yet, issue conflicting orders. Therefore, for an effectively organized operation, the small businessman should have established specific zones of control which are inviolate insofar as other supervisor's ability to invade these zones of control is concerned. Formal organization charts (see below) will help facilitate this matter.

### Kinds of formal organization

So far, the various stages of growth of organizations and some fundamental principles of effectively organized work have been discussed. Now it will be beneficial to discuss the various forms which formal organizations might take. These various forms are: *functional, line,* or *line and staff.* Organization charts are presented to help visualize these ideas.

*Functional organizations.* The functional form of organization (see Figure 10–1) is an extremely old concept, albeit having little popularity today. However, the small businessperson must understand the principle of the functional organization because most small businesses *start* as functional organizations and *then grow into* organizations which are either line, or line and staff. What is meant by the functional organization, at least in the traditional sense, is that each supervisor is in charge of a specific function, rather than in charge of specific workers. For example, assuming that there might be eight functions which are being performed in a smaller business, there might be one supervisor in charge of each function. Therefore, you might find a supervisor who is in charge of all operations having to do with inspection, another who is in charge of all operations concerning rework, and another who is in charge of all opera-

FIGURE 10–1
Taylor's functional organization

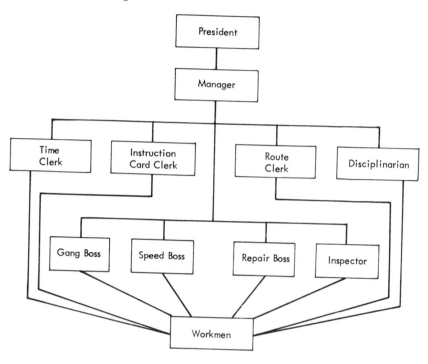

tions concerning the order or sequencing of work. Each of these supervisors would have the final say in respect *to the function that they boss.*

Normally, the business that is just starting will have only a few people working in it, thus only a few people will be in charge of all functions. However, when the organization grows just a little bit—perhaps into the supervision of supervisors stage—a business then must add one, then another, and finally a third, or more, level of managers or supervisors who go between the owner and the actual operative employees. Each of these go-betweens at first will be in charge of one specific function of the work which is done. Obviously this means that as any one employee moves from function to function he or she works for a different supervisor. And this is the source of trouble with the functional form of organization. People become confused when they work on more than one function and therefore are working for more than one boss. Not only do job responsibilities get extremely confusing but it becomes very difficult for a supervisor to observe the performance of the function when there are large numbers of people to supervise—say 100 or more. Therefore, the func-

FIGURE 10–2
Simple line organzation concept applied to small retail
store

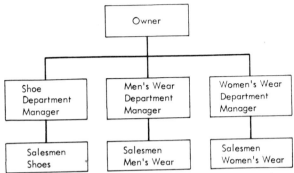

Note: Salesmen report to departmental managers who, in
turn, report to the owner.

tional form of organization is only amenable to the very small organization. However, because small businesses tend to start small, the small
businessperson should be aware that in all likelihood, the first kind of organization which will be utilized will be the functional organization.

*The line organization.* The pure line organization (see Figure 10-2)
is the second form of organization, but it, too, is not in great use today.
The line organization should be thought of as one primarily concerned
with the company's main product or service. In the line organization there
is limited use of such things as staff specialists and/or staff departments.
There may be departments that do different things, but in each department one person is directly in charge of another who is directly in charge
of yet other people who are providing the company's main products or
services. The line organization differs from the functional organization in
that each supervisor, rather than being in charge of a specific function,
no matter who it is done by, is in charge of a specific operational unit and
the people who are assigned to work in that operational unit. For example,
in the military a platoon sergeant is in charge of the men in his platoon,
no matter what their assigned objective. Similarly, in a small business
which makes tents and awnings the owner or manager is in charge of all
the people who perform the various jobs of making tents and awnings.
When the tent and awning manufacturer becomes big enough there will
be a supervisor of tent makers and a supervisor of awning makers, the
same as when there are enough platoons to make a company each platoon
leader will supervise his platoon in accomplishing a specific job. The difference boils down to this: whereas under the functional organization
there would be a supervisor of stitching, a supervisor of sewing, a super-

visor of cutting, etc., in the tent and awning shop, in the line organization one person would be in charge of bossing all the specific operations necessary to make the product.

*The line and staff organizations.* The line and staff form of organization (see Figure 10–3) is really the most feasible organization today, at least for companies which have grown beyond the direct supervision size. The line and staff differs from the straight line organization in that there is a staff organization *in addition* to the line elements of the organization. That, is, in respect to the line *operations,* the line and staff organization is designed and operates just like the line organization. However, there is also an additional element—the staff—which is established to advise and *assist* the line managers in being effective at getting the line work accomplished. For example, it might be said that the line organization does the work and the staff organization advises the line organization on how to do it. Line managers say: "Do." Staff officers say: "If and when you do, do it this way." For example, a line manager might tell an employee to sew two pieces of canvas together and that he will be paid $3.10 an hour for performing this operation. A staff employee would advise the line manager that if he does tell the employee to sew two pieces of canvas together and that he will pay him $3.10 an hour, he should inform him that coffee breaks will be authorized only at such and such a time, and any grievances which he might have will be filed through the personnel department, etc. In other words, the line and staff organization is really nothing more than the extension of the line organization with staff advisers whose

**FIGURE 10–3**

Classical line and staff organization concept applied to small manufacturing firm

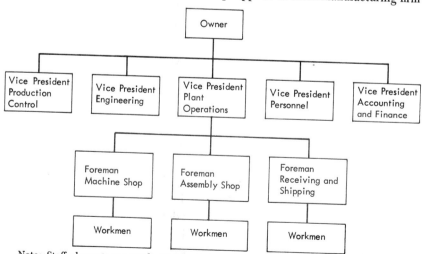

Note: Staff elements are production control, engineering, personnel, and accounting and finance. Line element is plant operations.

job it is to advise, control, serve, and coordinate the efforts of the line people.

It should be obvious from the above discussion that there might be a parallel in the kinds of formal organization which one would find in any given company depending upon the stage of growth of the firm. That is, the extremely small business starting out might start as a functional organization. However, it might evolve into the line kind of organization and once it gets any real size at all, it may readily become a line and staff organization because of the exigencies of the physical size and the number of employees of the firm. Therefore, the small businessperson should be aware of all three of these forms of business organization.

## The informal organization

No textbook discussing the formal organizations of business would be complete without at least passing mention of the phenomenon called the informal organization. The informal organization cannot be seen, but it certainly can be felt by the small businessperson. Unfortunately, the small businessperson can do little or nothing about the informal organization other than recognize the fact that everyone is a part of it, and that it can work both to his advantage and to his disadvantage.

The informal organization is nothing more than the informal "system" of employees and employee interactions which develop in any work environment. Whereas the formal organization is something which can be charted on a graph showing direct lines of authority and responsibility between superiors and subordinates, the informal organization cannot be charted nor can any direct lines of authority be established. Rather, the informal organization is a myriad of interpersonal relationships which are formulated on the job between people who must work together. These relationships arise as a result of friendship and other associations which develop both on and off the job and represent the fact that employees affect each other informally as well as formally. The informal organization is frequently "lead" by the "natural born leaders," who may either benevolently or maliciously try to influence employee behavior on the job. The job of the small business manager is to recognize the fact that the informal organization does exist, that natural-born leaders will emerge in any situation, and that the leader of the informal organization can work either to the small business's advantage or detriment, depending upon the attitude and aspirations of the informal leaders. Therefore, the small businessperson should not ignore the existence of the informal organization but should rather recognize that it does exist, try to find out who its leaders are, and use these leaders' abilities to positively orient his employee's efforts.

## SUPERVISING AND DIRECTING ORGANIZATIONAL EFFORTS

The job of the small business manager is not only to plan what actions will be taken by his organization and to design an organization which is capable of enacting these plans, he must also direct the enactment of the plans which he has established for his organization. This means that the small businessman must be adept at communicating with, counseling, motivating, and disciplining the efforts of his men, as well as organizing the use of material, machines, and money.

### Communicating with subordinates

Communication, like the weather, is very much discussed but very little is ever done about it. Most managers recognize the need for effective communication; however, very few recognize the fact that they are poor communicators.

The very essence of directing employees at their job is the ability to communicate. But there is a great disparity between what should be done and what is done. For example, studies have shown that in the average business, the typical worker only understands and comprehends about 20 percent of what top management thinks they understand, and the general foremen may only grasp about 30 percent or so. Further, not only does the typical worker only understand about 20 percent of what his top level management thinks and hopes he understands, but because of this lack of understanding, the typical worker is not equipped to be an effective subordinate who can accomplish the job. Therefore, it is of the utmost importance to the small businessperson, in attempting to make a success of his or her operation, to know how to better communicate with employees.

*Communication—a two-way street.* At the outset of any discussion of communications as a tool in effectively directing work, it should be recognized that communication is a two-way street: that is, effective communication requires that the small businessperson be able to communicate ideas to a subordinate, but by the same token, it also means that the subordinate should be able to communicate ideas to the boss. Therefore, any small businessperson who is effective not only knows how to communicate *to* subordinates, but also *with* subordinates.

In communicating with one's subordinates, it is essential that the small businessperson understand the principles of effective communication. They can be put into practice in these ways:

1.  Have a precise idea in mind of what the message is which is to be communicated to the subordinate.

2. Have a plan as to how the message can be most effectively communicated to the subordinate; i.e., what mode of communication will best "reach" a subordinate.
3. Understand the subordinate's background and experience and what might best help the subordinate to effectively understand the information which is being communicated to him or her.
4. Understand the personal values of the employee and what personal appeals might be used in making the communication more effective and meaningful.
5. Be aware of the mental and physical state of the subordinate when he receives the message.
6. Understand what the subordinate expects and hopes from the small business manager as a result of the communication.
7. Understand what his or her *own* personal motives and goals are and what he or she intends to gain from communicating to the employee in the manner elected.
8. Think through a proper timing, sequence of thoughts, locale, and style of delivering the message.
9. Follow up promptly with whatever action must be taken if any action was indicated in the communication.
10. Check on whether or not the subordinate indicates that he or she clearly understood the message, either by asking questions or observing the subordinate's immediate and subsequent performance on the job.

Compliance with the above rules for effective communication should help the small businessperson in conveying messages to subordinates. However, that is only half the battle. The other half is the question of whether or not the small businessperson permits subordinates to communicate with him or her—i.e., the problem of whether or not the small businessperson effectively listens to subordinates. The essence of this problem primarily resides in the fact that it is altogether too possible for people to "listen" without hearing what they are being told. Ten bad habits which are typical of small businesspeople and preclude them from being effective listeners are:

1. Not being interested in the subject.
2. Criticizing the manner of delivery (rather than what is being said).
3. Getting overstimulated because of emotional bias at things which the subordinate says.
4. Listening for facts rather than ideas.
5. Insisting on logic instead of ideas.
6. Faking attention to the subordinate and thinking about other things.
7. Tolerating (and/or creating) distractions while the subordinate is talking.

8. Evading or avoiding anything difficult or complex which the subordinate has to say.
9. Submitting to emotional words or phrases used by the subordinate rather than concentrating on the message.
10. Wasting thought power by failing to utilize the capacity of the mind to think faster than a human being typically speaks, thereby not trying to integrate the message with the overall situation.

The above enumerated bad listening habits obviously apply to the small businessperson in his or her workaday life not only in managing subordinates but also in relation to customers, clients, salesmen, etc. That is, people are either good listeners or bad listeners; and people who are bad listeners tend to be bad listeners all the time, not just part of the time. Obviously the bad listener and the unorganized or disorganized speaker cannot be effective managers of subordinates. They will not be able to communicate orders, nor will they be able to understand why various jobs are left undone and why many things which are done are done wrong.

## Counseling with subordinates

Just as the small businessman who does not talk or listen effectively cannot direct employees effectively on the job, he or she cannot counsel effectively with them. To be able to effectively counsel with subordinates —and therefore be able to effectively direct their efforts on the job—the small businessperson must have the following information: what his or her subordinates are doing; what their unsolved work problems are; do they have suggestions for improvements; and how do they feel and think about their jobs, their associates, and their company. Finding out such information can be an extremely difficult task, particularly if the small businessperson does not recognize the fact that he or she needs such information before they can effectively counsel with subordinates in the direction of improving their efforts on the job. Obviously, finding out such information is a problem of effective communication and the ability to direct the job.

## Maintaining discipline

One of the remaining subjects which needs to be discussed under the heading of directing the efforts of small business employees is the maintenance of discipline among employees. Invariably, some employees will create disciplinary problems on the job. This will be true no matter how carefully employees are screened before they are hired and it will become an increasing problem with the small businessperson if he or she does not know how to cope effectively with disciplinary problems.

By conservative estimate, probably 95 percent of the employees of any given business organization conduct themselves in a normal and reasonable manner, rarely causing any problems, certainly causing few problems requiring discipline. However, the remaining five percent of the employees may at some time or other create disciplinary problems, and possibly one percent may create serious disciplinary problems. They will create disciplinary problems because they resent authority, have little or no respect for other people, and are defiant of the usual rules of good conduct. Curiously enough, if the small businessperson does not deal effectively with those very few who do violate the rules, for whatever reason, the employees' disrespect will very likely spread and infect the many. Therefore, in directing the efforts of one's employees, it is essential for the small businessperson to know how to effectively deal with disciplinary problems.

*The objectives of discipline.* Effective discipline has three main objectives: (1) fostering a feeling of mutual respect between people; (2) keeping employees satisfied, while at the same time getting them to conduct themselves in accordance with established rules of conduct; (3) insuring that employees can perform their duties safely and efficiently. In order to accomplish this, the small businessperson should:

1. Keep instructions clear and simple.
2. Follow the rules himself/herself.
3. Never tolerate violations.
4. Gather all relevant facts when problems come up.
5. Permit the employee who has violated a rule an opportunity to explain his or her position.
6. Take appropriate and timely action.

The foregoing list of strategies which can be used by the small businessperson in attempting to maintain discipline on the job are relatively self-explanatory. However, really knowing the principles of effective disciplinary action does not insure that the small businessperson will be able to maintain discipline the way he or she should unless the principles behind discipline are understood. For example, the small businessperson should know that, philosophically speaking, the purpose of discipline is both compliance with established rules of conduct and be able to invoke *corrective* actions in the event of someone violating these rules. This means that the small businessperson should never attempt to be punitive, vindictive, or try to "get even" with an employee for violating a rule. No discipline is maintained if malicious activity is engaged in by the "boss"; rather all that is accomplished is that each side becomes hardened in its attitude.

Another fundamental requirement of effective discipline is that the small businessperson be able to clearly distinguish between major and lesser offenses. Unfortunately, entirely too many small businesspeople interpret the degree of an offense largely with respect to how *they* feel on a particular day rather than with respect to the actual circumstances of the offense itself. Furthermore, not only do they tend to fail to differentiate between major and minor offenses, but many small businesspeople also just as consistently fail to consider other basic factors which are important in the maintenance of discipline. That is, many times if the small businessperson feels bad, he or she will not try to determine the real cause, will not consider the prior performance record of the employee concerned, will not consider the length of service of the employee, will not consider how long it has been since the last time the employee caused a problem, and may ignore or not even look for mitigating or aggravating circumstances. Obviously, the small businessperson who ignores such factors is in no position to discipline an employee. If he or she does not consider all the preceding factors he may, on the one hand, ignore a serious violation and issue only a minor oral reprimand, and on the other hand, he might fire an employee who committed a very minor offense. Obviously, the small business manager who is not adept at considering the basic elements required to maintain discipline and the basic philosophy behind disciplinary activity will be an ineffective director of the efforts of employees, particularly those very few employees who create disciplinary problems.

## CONTROLLING THE ORGANIZATION

The word control has a variety of meanings. Therefore, it is absolutely essential to have a clear understanding of what is meant by the concept of control in respect to a small business operation. Control, as defined, means the force which guides a business to a predetermined objective by means of implementing predetermined policies and decisions. Thus defined, control means that the small businessperson guides the interests of the business along an established path toward an objective. Having control does not mean steering the path, but it does mean informing operating management of any significant deviation from the course. Control likewise does not take action, but it frequently compels the small business manager to instigate action by turning a spotlight on the pertinent facts of any circumstance. It might be said, therefore, that control of the small business is a three-stage process: the first stage is the adoption of the plan; the second is the reporting of *actual* performance of the small business as compared with the *plan* for performance; and the third is making decisions and taking any required corrective action.

## Kinds of control

There are various kinds of "control" which can be observed in running a small business. Control of one nature is that "control" enjoyed by the owner of a business—i.e., he or she is free to do what they please to, with, or about the business. However, control of another nature might refer to that bailiwick of operations centered in a board of directors to the small business, particularly where they have the authority for making or carrying out policy or operating decisions. Therefore, the various aspects which the concept of control can take sometimes leads the small business manager to a confused position with respect to what is meant by control. Thus, the remaining portion of this chapter will be devoted to elaborating upon various concepts of control and what they mean to the small businessperson.

*Directorial control.* One form of control found in many small businesses is the control exercised by the board of directors. Literally speaking, such control is basically of broad scope, and it is usually of an advisory nature. One of the reasons that directorial control is of such an ambiguous nature is that small business managers customarily consider a board of directors to be merely a legal requirement. They name boards of directors because their state laws (and their bankers) require them to, but there is little, if anything, expected of the board members by way of formal involvement in the conduct of the business.

Some small businesspeople, however, find that the board of directors can provide a great amount of benefit and assistance to the corporation, if requested. For example, most members of small corporation boards are in a position to have the interest of the corporation at heart and to offer some degree of experience and skill in making operating plans and decisions for the corporation. Furthermore, even if ideas are not solicited from board members, the board itself can be used to review major operating policy decisions and other plans which will affect the future course and direction of the business. Therefore, it goes without saying that the small businessperson should do more than perfunctorily select board members. There are many sources of qualified board members, and the problems of the small businessperson concerned with directorial control is finding properly qualified individuals who have the time and are willing to serve as members of the corporate board.

*Daily operating control.* The second form of control which might be invoked in the successful small business is that of the workaday operating control required. That is, it is necessary for a small businessperson to establish, coordinate, and maintain an integrated plan for the conduct of operations in the small business. This plan must provide cost standards, expense budgets, sales forecasts, profit planning, programs for capital investment and financing, and any other necessary procedures to implement the operating plans. Establishing such plans however, does not insure that the small businessperson will necessarily have adequate control of operations. In controlling a small business there is a duty not only to establish operating plans but also to measure performance against those plans and to take corrective action when it is determined that results are not in compliance with the plans.

Fortunately, the manager of the extremely small business will not have as much difficulty in maintaining control of operations as will the person in the larger small business. The extremely small business is subject to direct control (as discussed above) and will pose fewer serious problems for the small businessperson. He or she has daily contact with all aspects of the operations and with what progress is being made compared to the plans. However, when the small business grows to the second and particularly the third and fourth stages of company growth—when indirect control in the supervision of supervisors is all the time that the small business manager has to devote to controlling operations—then the small businessperson must be able to recognize that what is required by way of the control function of management will be far different than what was required when he or she was the manager of a much smaller business. For example, under the direct supervision stage of growth, the small businessperson can take immediate corrective action to remedy troublesome situations. However, in the supervision of supervisors stage of size, the small businessperson must have some way in which he or she might be apprised of (1) the fact that things are getting out of control and (2) what is being done (as opposed to what he or she should do) to get them "back in control." Therefore, the small businessperson must recognize that the larger and more successful the business becomes, the more necessary it becomes to be able to control the organization from a remote position. *This means, in essence, that the manager must be able to maintain control of operations by the use of reports which subordinate managers submit rather than by direct observation.*

**Use of reports to maintain control.** Control becomes an increasing problem for the small businessperson as the firm grows and becomes more successful. Control is maintained by the establishment of some system by which feedback is given the manager as to how subordinates are carrying out the plans which are established for them. This type of feedback can be oral reports, written reports, or any other form of communication which is designed to apprise the small businessperson of what is happening. But whatever the method used, reports are made about the conditions and circumstances existing in the small business. Therefore, it can be said that control can be attained by the small businessperson through the use of reports. The following rules, although general in nature, are guidelines for the small businessperson in using reports to maintain operating control of the organization:

1. Reports must cover separate organizational units (i.e., reports must cover only separate organizational units; all other reports are unacceptable). It is undesirable and, in fact, useless to lump the performance of several operating units together in one report. Such a report will not permit the manager to isolate and understand which units are performing up to snuff and which are not.

2. Reports must be designed to update the manager's information, and under no circumstances should late reports be tolerated. This is a simple matter, yet it is often ignored. Any report which highlights a bad situation six months after that bad situation began is entirely worthless in today's dynamic business world. Reports must be prompt and up-to-date if the manager is to have any control over the work which is being done, particularly if he or she intends to take remedial action. The manager must know when a bad situation arises or when a bad situation is getting worse in order to take the required action in time to alleviate matters.

3. Reports must not be designed to make anyone look good. The fundamental principle of reporting is the reporting of facts—not the mechanical process of trying to make everybody look good. The small businessperson should recognize that many subordinate managers, because they want to look good to the boss, oftentimes permit their subordinates (or themselves) to make reports which tend to hide or otherwise modify bad or poor performance on their part. Reports which are designed to hide (or which enable the subordinate manager to hide) or otherwise gloss over poor performance are worse than useless. They are, in fact, a detriment to the effective management of the small business.

4. Reports must always be designed to include notes with respect to actions which are taken and/or which are planned to be taken. If the manager intends to have sufficient and adequate control over the organization, he or she must design reporting procedures which not only highlight the fact that things are getting out of control or that bad situations are developing but which also give some idea of what is being done to remedy these situations. Knowing what, if any, action has been taken by the subordinate manager will permit the small businessperson to determine whether or not he or she personally needs to take any action or if the subordinate's actions are sufficient. If a subordinate manager recognized a bad situation, assumed some initiative, and engaged in some remedial activity, the small business manager may not need to act. On the other hand, if the small businessperson deems the remedial activity taken by his or her subordinate as insufficient or incorrect, he or she may want to act. Therefore, the small business manager should never permit himself or herself because of poor reports to get in a position of deciding to do something when somebody else has already taken some action to remedy the given situation. The consequences of such a situation are practically always chaos. Thus, any small business manager worth his salt will demand re-

ports which not only tell what has happened but also what is going to happen in order to obviate future problems and/or to remedy past problems.

5. A final rule to use in designing a good reporting system is that reports must be designed to highlight comparisons of performance between various organization units and/or individuals within the organization. The small business manager who hopes to evaluate the performance of subordinates individually or in units must have reports which obviously highlight critical elements in each individual's or unit's performance. Thus reports must be designed to underscore those elements of performance which can be compared and which are meaningful. They should not be designed to hide, cover up, or otherwise embellish poor performance or force the small businessperson to compare apples with bananas.

The foregoing points highlight what a small businessperson might do by way of using reports to maintain control over operations of the small business. However, simply knowing how to use the various reports which a small businessperson must demand of subordinates does not insure that the small businessperson will necessarily maintain adequate control. Sometimes even though a small businessperson is using reporting techniques to the best of his or her capacity, there is a failure to maintain control because he or she does not have the proper attitude toward the control function. In short, some small businesspeople commit grave errors of attitude in attempting to maintain control of their operation. Some of these errors include:

1. The small businessperson runs hot and cold on particular items, sometimes demanding a report while at other times acting as if the subordinate is an idiot for submitting the report.

2. The small businessperson talks in terms of overall objectives which he or she expects the subordinate to accomplish but neglects to state how the subordinate should accomplish the objective.

3. The small businessperson fails to establish targets for the improvement of activities which are found out of control, thus doing in essence nothing more than telling the subordinate he or she is not doing a satisfactory job but failing to offer any helpful suggestions.

4. The small businessperson sometimes indicates (either by word or action) to subordinates that he or she is not interested in details of any particular operation, therefore instilling apathy and indifference in subordinates toward job performance.

5. The small businessperson may make subordinates feel as if they are informing on themselves when things get out of control. The small businessperson, in effect, may stymie any initiative upon the part of the subordinates to volunteer information that things are getting out of control if he or she makes a big scene when things have not progressed as they should have and says things such as "why didn't you tell me this before?"

Although they may not appear serious at any given time for the typical small businessperson, the above errors can destroy managerial control. The small businessperson must always be on guard not to work against himself by committing such errors when attempting to establish control of operations. Control is required in all levels of activity of the business. In establishing and maintaining control, the manager must remember to take action which fits the situation, which is corrective in nature, and which will not destroy the morale of subordinate managers and/or employees.

## QUESTIONS

1. Discuss the various stages of growth experienced by most successful small businesses.
2. Discuss what you believe to be the five most important principles of organization listed in the text.
3. What is the essence of the statement "one person—one boss"? Explain.
4. What is a functional form of organization? How does it work?
5. What is a line form of organization? How does it differ from a line and staff organization? Explain.
6. What is the informal organization? Why is it important to the small business manager?
7. Write an essay on the general subject of "The Communication Problems of the Small Businessperson."
8. Write an essay on "Discipline and the Small Businessperson."
9. What is meant by control? How is it obtained by the small businessperson?
10. How can a person running a small business use reports to insure effective managerial control?

## PROBLEM

1973 was the start. Bill's business then was only an idea. He wanted his own business—his own furniture business. Not a retail store. He wanted to manufacture special items, create unique designs, form built-ins, etc.

Bill's business boomed at first. Then, two years ago, something happened. Things slackened off. The energy crisis and the "economic times" might have contributed to the problem. Then, too, his more recent problems with his family might have affected him personally. His ex-wife, Trudy, always said he was disorganized.

Another contributing problem might have been the way he worked with people. George Morgan seemed lazy, but Bill had tried to work with George. Employees complained all the time about their working conditions, too. But Bill had not thought much about that until some people got hurt running a saw.

Bill felt he needed organization. But he didn't know what—or how.

1. What advice would you give Bill?
2. If you were Bill, how would you change your behavior—list the specific things you would do?
3. How does one maintain discipline at work in a situation like Bill's?

## BIBLIOGRAPHY

Ianni, Francis A. J. *A Family Business*. New York: Russell Sage Foundation, 1972, 198 pp. This book takes the reader through an in-depth assessment of one family's activities in running a small business.

Mancuso, Joseph. *Fun and Guts—The Entrepreneur's Philosophy*. Reading, Mass.: Addison-Wesley Publishing Co., 1973, 208 pp. Just plain interesting reading on the trials and tribulations of small business managers. An excellent book.

Swayne, Charles, and Tucker, William. *The Effective Entrepreneur*. Morristown, N.J.: General Learning Press, 1973, 173 pp. An analytical treatment of what is characteristic of successful owner/managers of smaller, entrepreneurial businesses.

# 11

# Personnel and employee relations

For the small business manager an important area of involvement is the field referred to as employee relations or personnel management. Most people today instinctively know what is meant by personnel management, but many small businesspeople minimize or completely neglect employee relations as part of their job.

The job of personnel management is basically to recruit, select, develop, train, and maintain a stable work force. But this checklist is meaningless unless the small businessperson understands the importance of personnel management.

## THE PERSONNEL FUNCTION

The need for the personnel manager—or at least for someone to perform the job duties of the personnel manager—arises from what is called the "black box" phenomenon. That is, of all the factors of production employed by the small businessperson, only one has an impenetrable, unpredictable control device which the small businessperson cannot see into, take apart, rewire, reprogram, or otherwise alter to always and irrevocably do his or her bidding. That "black box" is the human mind, made up of a few ounces of gray matter and almost as perfectly unpredictable as it is similar in design, size, weight, and shape.

The personnel function results from the unpredictability and seeming irrationality of the black box, or what might more clearly be called the difference in the ways that various people act. For example, it was stated above that personnel management's function is to recruit, select, develop, train and maintain a stable work force. Such seems a simple requirement at first, but it is not so simple if one considers the black box and the fact that what may be an effective recruiting device for one employee ( e.g., an offer of a good position, responsibility, and the possibility of advancement) may not appeal at all to another individual who is interested in

170

pay, working conditions, and liberal company benefits. The job of the personnel manager is to know these differences in the acting and reacting of black boxes and to use the appropriate appeal in recruiting employees. But once this is done (which is not as easy as said), there is the problem of selecting the right person from among those black boxes which have been recruited. Now the following questions occur: Which one is a hothead? Which one will come to work regularly and on time? Which one will be a know-it-all? Which one drinks too much? Which one has severe problems at home? *Which one will, all things considered, be the best employee?*

Once the "best" employee is selected, he or she must then be developed into a qualified employee, must be trained to do th jobs expected, and finally, must (one hopes) be enticed to remain with the company. However, remaining with the company involves the satisfactory—both from the company's viewpoint *and* the employee's viewpoint—resolution of problems involving absenteeism, sickness, vacations, safety issues, suggestions, grievances, and other items. In short, the function of the personnel manager is a never ending, yet essential, job if the small business is to prosper and grow. This does not mean that a personnel manager per se must be on the payroll, but it does mean that the small business manager will have to be personally adept at handling employee relations until his or her organization becomes large enough to hire a personnel manager.

Unfortunately, many small businesspeople are not proficient in handling employee problems for a variety of reasons: they simply don't know what is involved; they feel that they are "protected" because they are "too small" to have any real personnel problems; they feel that because their business operation is small they can have personal, daily contact with their employees and "keep their fingers on the pulse of the employee"; they feel that their informal, "open door" policy will alert them to any serious personnel problems before they begin; and they think they possess all the requisite insight needed to hire the kind of employee who won't pose any personnel problems.

In short, it might be said that gullibility, ignorance, and simple naiveté in hiring and managing employees is a common source of difficulty for small business managers. They often believe that all people are honest and straightforward or that, as shrewd businesspeople, they can tell who will be (or is) a good or bad employee. Unfortunately, too often just the opposite is true. Although the large majority of people in the world will do an honest, capable day's work for their employer, some people either will not or cannot. This occurs in both large and small businesses, but the problem is more acute for the small business manager. If a large business with 10,000 employees has 10 incompetent workers, these employees only account for 1/1000 of the total, but a small business with 25 employees can't afford to have even one incompetent employee on the payroll because it would mean that 1/25 of the labor force was ineffective.

## FINDING EMPLOYEES

One of the first steps the small businessman must learn as a personnel manager is the effective recruiting of employees. The only thing more pathetic than a person who wants a job and can't find it is a job that needs a person to fill it. Many owners of small businesses, unfortunately, often have jobs but don't know how to go about finding qualified people to fill them. The problem is complicated not only by the fact that they may not know where to go to find someone to fill the job but many times they feel they can't afford some of the more commonly used devices to recruit employees. Furthermore, people seldom just "drop in" to see if, perchance, any help is needed—the way that many large organizations get their employees.

Therefore, it is a difficult job for the small business manager to know how and where to recruit employees. Fortunately, there are really only two fundamental sources of manpower: internal and external, and a study of these sources should help the small business executive in solving these problems.

### Internal recruiting methods

Internal recruitment of required employees is by far the simplest and best way to find a person to fill a job. Promoting a person from within carries the advantages of knowing how the person works, his or her reliability, strengths, and weaknesses, and other characteristics. Furthermore, it is good for the morale of the employees, who see a policy of promotion from within as offering them *all* the possibility of advancement. In fact, there are no real disadvantages to promoting from within, with the exception, perhaps, of jealousy upon the part of someone not promoted or "passed over," and the possible drawback that many times there is no one already in the employ of the company who is capable of filling the vacant job (or who is willing to take on the new job with its increased responsibilities).

It must be recognized that all employees must be new employees at some time. Therefore, even though internal recruiting is probably best, it is necessary also to consider some of the outside or external sources which can be used in finding employees.

### External recruiting sources

There are a variety of external sources which many small business managers use in finding needed employees. Basically they include:

1. Newspaper advertising.
2. Trade paper advertising.

3.  Radio advertising.
4.  Telephone solicitation of "leads" given by other employees.
5.  Display window signs.
6.  Checks with personnel managers of other companies.
7.  Employment agencies, both public and private.
8.  Rehabilitation centers.
9.  Draft boards and veterans bureaus.
10.  Customers and suppliers.
11.  High school, college, and university placement and counseling offices.
12.  Trade schools, business colleges, and night schools.
13.  Labor unions.
14.  Churches and social groups.
15.  Businessmen's clubs.

It should be recognized that each of the above sources may be more or less effective, depending upon the kind of employee being sought. For example, college and university placement offices are excellent sources for managerial trainees, but a labor union hiring hall generally is not, nor are trade schools, window signs, or circular advertisements. Thus, it is up to the small businessperson to first decide what kind of talent he or she is looking for and then choose the sources most likely to produce leads to such talent.

It should also be recognized that some of the above methods are expensive, while others are free; but more important, cost and results are not always commensurate. That is, public employment agencies are free and often are excellent sources for finding employees for lower level jobs, while newspaper advertisements cost money and may not be effective if poorly written. Furthermore, some thought should be given to getting broad coverage of job openings to avoid possible claims of discrimination in hiring practices. Thus use of many sources of finding applicants is, as a general rule, most desirable. Free sources are often productive and should not be ignored for reasons of integrity and economy.

## SELECTING EMPLOYEES

Once the manager of the small business has determined how he or she intends to recruit the required manpower, then attention must be devoted to the question of how to select one applicant among those who apply for the job. The personnel selection devices available to the small business manager to help make this selection commonly fall into four groups: (1) the application blank (used at the time the person applies for the job—it may include a physical examination); (2) the interview (used to get a reading on the applicant's abilities, personality, and attitudes toward working); (3) various tests and examinations (to determine the applicant's proficiency, skills, aptitude, vocational interests, and other job-related capabilities); and (4) reference checks of the individual's prior work record and work history.

Even though the above techniques have been available to small business managers for several decades, statistically they are very seldom used. Perhaps that is because they are not well understood. While whole books can be devoted to explaining these devices, the following brief explanations are presented to give the reader an idea of their simplicity, ease, and inexpensiveness.

## Application blanks

Anyone who has applied for a job in his lifetime has probably had occasion to complete an employment application form. One study found that 70 percent of the companies with more than ten employees utilized some such device. However, there is a considerable difference in employment application forms. They can be of a variety of sizes and shapes, but they all should at least ask questions which will provide the employer with a summary autobiography of the candidate—an interview on paper—and a sample of the applicant's neatness, thoroughness, and ability to answer questions. The form can go further and give a complete history of the person, a full physical report, and perhaps a full rundown on the applicant's family.

It can be seen in Figure 11–1 that there is a variety of information which can be obtained by using an application blank. However, job candidates should not be asked to fill out such forms if the information obtained is not to be used in assessing the applicant's suitability for the job.

## Interviews

Interviews may vary in style and design, but virtually all managers will at some time interview potential job applicants, whether they think of it consciously or not. Quite possibly more use has been made of the employment interview than any other screening device and this is as it should be. The interview is easily the single best screening device. The traditional purposes of the employment (screening) interview are normally stated as:

1. Evaluating the applicant's appearance, speech, mannerisms, etc.
2. Gathering factual information about the applicant, his or her background, and experience.
3. Providing the applicant with information about the company and the job.
4. Sizing up the applicant's attitudes, personality traits, goals and expectations.

FIGURE 11-1

| Name<br>Last | | First | | | Middle | Describe the type of work you want: | | |
|---|---|---|---|---|---|---|---|---|

KIS CORPORATION
EMPLOYMENT APPLICATION FORM

INSTRUCTIONS
1. Type or print CLEARLY in INK.
2. Answer each question FULLY and ACCURATELY. Use additional sheet if necessary.
3. Do not include information regarding race, color, age, creed, or national origin.
4. Sign and date application on reverse side.

| Address | Number | Street | City | State | Zip | Telephone | Social Security No. |
|---|---|---|---|---|---|---|---|

| ( ) Single ( ) Divorced<br>( ) Married ( ) Widow(er) | No. of dependents (include yourself) | Ages of children | If married woman, give maiden name. |
|---|---|---|---|

| U.S. citizen?<br>( ) Yes ( ) No | Health<br>( ) Excellent ( ) Good ( ) Fair ( ) Poor | Height | Weight | |
|---|---|---|---|---|

| Minimum rate expected:<br>$ per | What shift do you prefer? | List handicaps, chronic ailments, serious illnesses, operations: |
|---|---|---|
| Do you object to working nights? ( ) Yes ( ) No | | |

Have you ever received workmen's compensation payments?
( ) Yes ( ) No If yes, explain.

| In case of emergency, notify: | Name (last, first, middle) | | | Telephone | | |
|---|---|---|---|---|---|---|
| | Address | Number | Street | City | State | Zip |

EDUCATION (include all U.S. Military Service Schools)

| | Name and Address | From | To | Course | Graduated |
|---|---|---|---|---|---|
| Elementary | | | | | |
| High School | | | | | |
| Other | | | | | |

EXPERIENCE (include all U.S. Military Service, summer and part-time jobs—AND ALL PREVIOUS KIS EMPLOYMENT)

| Employer's name and address<br>(list last employer first) | From<br>mo.,yr. | To<br>mo.,yr. | Salary per wk.<br>or wage per hr. | Occupation | Brief description<br>of duties | Specific reason<br>for leaving |
|---|---|---|---|---|---|---|
| | | | | | | |
| | | | | | | |
| | | | | | | |
| | | | | | | |

5. Securing sufficient information from the applicant so that an intelligent investigation of the applicant's background and capabilities for the position can be made.

It can be seen that the stated purposes of the employment interview coincide with many of the needs of the employment situation, particularly Point 4. To the extent that it is desirable to get a reading on a person's ethics, standards, emotional stability, or ability to adjust to a new job, the facility of the screening interview cannot be denied.

## Tests and examinations

The use of tests and examinations have long been a device considered of some value in the selection process. However, there is some question as to how valuable these techniques are and in what situations they should be used as well as to the legality of the use of certain tests. The area of psychological testing is a sensitive area with supporters on both sides of the issue. Essentially, however, personality tests are of dubious legality and therefore should be avoided.

### Reference checks and similar reports

A final technique used in screening applicants is that of the reference check. This technique is often misused because people who use it tend to think of it primarily as a way to check on the honesty of the individual. Actually, the reference check has a threefold purpose:

1. It will help to verify the truth of what the applicant has said in his or her résumé, application blank, or interviews.
2. It will help in checking on possible omissions of information supplied by the candidate, as well as serving to clarify unclear points.
3. It will help determine some estimate of the applicant's ability to handle the job for which he or she is considered—by answering questions as to whether the candidate has exhibited the necessary skills, frame of mind, attitudes, etc., on previous jobs.

The reference check is, therefore, a good device for gleaning additional information about the candidate which might be significant to successful functioning on the job. In fact, some people consider this to be the basic purpose of the reference check.

## TRAINING AND DEVELOPING EMPLOYEES

Once a person is selected for employment by the small business manager there is still the problem of training the person to do the job which is required. Many small business executives tend to overlook this requirement—frequently thinking that a stock clerk should just "know" how to stock shelves, how to keep the supply bins neat and orderly, and how to reorder merchandise. But such is not the case, and sometimes the problem is far more complicated (for example, the manager of the small manufacturing business usually must train people to do certain specific actions in sequence). Therefore, it is very seldom that a new employee arrives on the job with complete knowledge of the duties and obligations required. He or she may need additional skills, knowledge, or other information.

This skill, knowledge, and other information is imparted to the employee through the process of training and development. Training and developing an employee should, however, be distinguished from "educating" an employee. Education is knowledge which the individual should have gleaned while in grade school, high school, or even college, such as how to add, subtract, read, and write. On the other hand, the purpose of *training* is to improve the employee's abilities in on-the-job skills and requirements. Education, therefore, is normally of little *direct* use so far as the job is concerned, while training is specifically designed to facilitate the employee in performing the job. The overall objective, then, of a good training program (be it formal or informal) is to make the worker equal to the job to be performed.

## How much to train

Training is an investment in one's ability to do a job, but like any investment, there is necessarily a cost involved in training. The training costs can be inconsequential or they can be a matter of great importance. Training an employee to be a janitor usually does not involve a great deal of cost, but training a person to be an efficient forklift operator in a warehouse is an entirely different matter. It is going to take more time to train the employee and it is going to cost a good deal more. Therefore, it will frequently be as much a question of the businesses' ability to afford the requisite training as it will be the recognition of the need to train the employee. But it should go without saying that an employee who is not well trained will be probably a much more costly employee than the individual who is adequately trained even though it costs more for the training.

## DEVELOPING A STRONG WORK FORCE

### Promoting employees

The question of promoting employees was touched on previously in this chapter under the general topic of recruiting from within. However, it should be recognized that although recruiting from within is a good policy, not all people want to be recruited from within. That is, many people are not anxious to become higher level personnel in any given organization, and some even staunchly avoid or refuse to accept a promotion with the attendant additional responsibility. Therefore, it might be said under the general heading of promoting employees that the wise small business manager should categorize personnel into three different groups: those who are not interested in any kind of advancement or promotion, those who are interested in rising only "so far" and then staying there, and those who are interested in fighting their way to the top, to include becoming a partner or shareholder in the small business. In any well-balanced organization there is obviously room for all three kinds of employees, although it should be recognized that in the very smallest business such will probably not be the case.

Promoting an employee has an extraordinarily large number of advantages. It instills a certain feeling of pride and feeling of accomplishment in the person receiving the promotion, it may stimulate the employee to greater effort, it may encourage the employee to develop to greater capacities, it may keep the employee from seeking other employment opportunities, it usually builds morale upon the part of all employees, it gives an employee a feeling of accomplishment, it develops a feeling of closeness and kinship to the organization. However, promoting an employee from within carries with it some disadvantages. Because an incumbent is promoted from within, no real "new blood" is introduced into the organization; no fresh viewpoints or ideas are engendered; the possibility exists that the employee will not work out when promoted, thus creating a serious personnel problem if he or she must later be discharged or demoted; a certain amount of disappointment, jealousy, and charges of favoritism may be generated by the people who were "passed over"; and there may be just a general loss of morale within the organization if "the boss's pet" is promoted.

## How to pay people

In addition to the question of promoting an employee, another problem for the small business manager is how much to pay employees, whether to pay them all the same, to pay them differently on the basis of unequal work, and to pay them increments on the basis of length of service, cost-of-living adjustments, etc. Therefore the whole question of remuneration is as important in the small business as it is in the large corporation.

The question of how much to pay an employee is more than a simple dollars-and-cents problem. There are essentially two forms of compensation that people look for in a job; monetary and nonmonetary. The nonmonetary compensations (sometimes referred to as psychic income) are things such as advancement, recognition, responsibility, a feeling of achievement, pleasure of doing the work, and other intangibles. These factors must be supplied on the job by the small business, but they have little relationship to the hard facts of paying an employee. That is, recognition and responsibility can be obtained by the employee whether or not he or she is given any specific amount of monetary compensation. Therefore, the aspects of "psychic income" will not be considered here, for they more rightly belong under the heading of "employee motivation." What will be considered here, however, are the two aspects of monetary compensation which must be considered by the small business owners—absolute and relative.

### INSURING FAIR PAY FOR QUALITY WORK

#### Absolute income

In determining how to compensate employees it is necessary that the small business manager consider first the absolute amounts of money that he or she intends to pay employees and then consider how to divide this absolute amount of money in a fashion that it will be acceptable, relatively, to those employees. The basic issues which must be considered under the heading of absolute income for employees include the following:

1. *The effort factor.* All people like to think that they are being paid directly in proportion to the physical and mental expenditures they make on the job. Therefore, people like to feel that there is some correlation between the physical or mental effort they expend on the job and the size of their paycheck. Thus, in establishing the absolute amounts of money to be paid to an employee, the small business must think in terms of the cold, cruel facts of how much is being demanded of an employee by way of physical or mental work and what that employee will expect to receive for this work.

2. *Time.* A second factor which people like to feel has some direct relationship to the amount they are paid is the time that they spend on the job. This is particularly true of rank-and-file employees who feel that they should be paid for their time whether or not it is productive time; "down time" is considered just "tough luck" for the employer. Being paid for one's time is ingrained in our economic history. This is not only a standardized assumption behind the principle of wages from the employee's viewpoint but employers themselves think in terms of billing for time spent. For example, employers make bids and estimates on time bases. Therefore, in determining the absolute amounts of pay which a person will likely expect to receive, the small business manager must think in terms of the time demanded of the employee on the job.

3. *Ability of the firm to pay.* A third factor which looms important in determining the absolute amount of monies that a small business must pay employees is the *ability* of the small business to pay. That is, some businesses certainly have more "ability" to pay than do other businesses, for some firms are far more profitable than are others. It should be recognized that the ability of a person to pay many times is the overriding factor in determining the amount of pay which is offered by the small business. However, paying on the basis of ability to pay is inconsistent with sound wage theory. The small business owner who pays on an "ability-to-pay factor" must recognize that if all employers paid on this basis and if there is any large degree of mobility upon the part of employees, there will be a constant turnover with the best employees going to the most profitable firms, thus eroding away the profit incentive for the small business. However, many small businesses get away with an "ability-to-pay" policy if they don't feel profits are that essential and/or because many employees will stick with an employer because of inertia, if for no other reason.

4. *The cost of living.* Another factor in determining the absolute

amount of money to be allocated to employees is the absolute cost of living in the specific area in which the employee works. That is, to some extent all people work for income which they can spend to provide a living for their family. If the cost of living in the area of the small business operation is extraordinarily high, the business will necessarily have to expect to pay employees more than if it is in a low cost-of-living area. Furthermore, many employees are more than aware of the cost-of-living index because the government is continuingly announcing changes in the index, and unions are constantly trying to tie the level of wages in their contracts to the cost-of-living indexes published by the government.

5. *Legislation.* Another factor which must be considered in determining the absolute amount of wages which a business must pay is the factor of legislation. There are laws which establish minimum wages to be paid employees, the hours for which overtime must be paid, etc. The small business must necessarily comply with this legislation to the extent that it covers employment. Thus federal and state laws (and possibly city laws) may help determine the absolute level of wages paid by the small business.

6. *Role of the union.* Another extremely important factor in determining the absolute level of wages to be paid employees is the impact of labor unions. No business is immune from having its employees organized into labor unions, and to the extent that the small business is either unionized *or is threatened* to be unionized, the "union wage scale" may have a bearing in determining the absolute amount of wages to be paid employees.

7. *Supply and demand.* The final factor which must be considered by the small business in determining the absolute amount of wages to pay employees is the old economic principle of "supply and demand." To most small businessmen generally and to the bulk of the population specifically, this concept is nebulous at best, yet it is in very real operation in the labor market. The fact is, the absolute supply of labor available in an area compared to the amount of demand for such labor will influence the amount of money which this labor receives. For example, it is a commonly observed factor that common laborers consider themselves underpaid. One of the reasons they are underpaid is because, in relation to their demand, they are in overabundant supply. That is, even though construction firms and other employers of unskilled labor say they need more laborers, they tend to find enough at the low wages they offer to fill their jobs. If they increase the amount of wages (as do some of the companies in the larger cities), they always discover that they have more than enough people who will work at the higher wages. Therefore, because the demand for laborers is relatively fixed in number (by the number of available jobs at any given time), as a group, the supply of laborers deter-

mines the price (which equates supply with demand) that will be paid for their services because in essence they bid down their wages to that level. The principle of supply and demand works in the same way for the business which must determine how much it must—or is willing—to pay employees. If there is an inordinate supply of employees and very little demand for their services (similar to the situation concerning laborers), the small businessperson can establish a low absolute wage (demand) and find sufficient employees (supply) to work; likewise if there is a low supply and a high demand for employees, then the small business will have to pay a high wage to attract employees.

We have now concluded the discussion of the factors important in determining the absolute amount of wage that a small business must pay employees to keep them on the job. However, as was pointed out above, it is also important that employees be paid fairly, relatively. The following section of this chapter will be devoted to discussing how the small business might make sure that it is paying employees sufficiently on a relative basis.

## Relative income

In reflecting on the general reliance on individualism, it might be fairly said that all people are not so much interested in being paid equal income as they are interested in being paid *unequally* for *unequal* work. That is, most people recognize that some jobs are harder to do, require more skill, and demand more of the employee by way of responsibility than do other jobs. Therefore, most people will agree (for example, all labor unions agree) that the question of equal pay for equal work is more a question of making sure that people are paid unequally for unequal work on a fair, equitable, pro rata basis. This, in short, is the requirement which must be met by the small business if it is to succeed in paying people on an acceptable relative basis. Fortunately, some guidelines have been established to help a business manager insure that he or she is paying unequally for unequal work, on a fair and equitable basis. This system is called job evaluation and will be explained below.

*The importance of job evaluation.* Job evaluation determines the value of one job *as compared* to other jobs being performed by employees. A job evaluation alone is not a completely satisfactory answer to all questions of employee remuneration because it does not help determine the *absolute* pay level for employees. However, it does provide a sound basis upon which to make decisions and to formulate wage policies so that different employees are paid *relatively* for the work they perform on the job.

Job evaluation does this by seeing to it that people are paid on the basis of the total contribution they make to the product of the business. Job evaluation does this by insuring that a laborer will not be paid more than a supervisor just because the laborer does more physical exertion; that is, it insures that all the factors entering into accomplishing a given job are considered in determining the wages for that job, including skill, educational requirements, and mental effort, along with physical requirements of the job.

Conducting a job evaluation for a small business necessarily involves the collection of the details involved in doing all jobs. Collecting these facts can not only help the employer in determining how much to pay employees but can also prove an economic benefit to the employer by showing how to (1) simplify work methods; (2) assign tasks to jobs; (3) train new workers; (4) select, promote, and transfer employees; and (5) improve working conditions and prevent accidents. Therefore, any job evaluation program gives a sound foundation on which to base wages, to help cut down wage inequalities, to facilitate cutting out the arbitrary and haphazard setting of wages, and to help the small businessperson make the difficult decisions of selecting, promoting, or transferring employees within the organization. It does so by forcing a thorough evaluation of all jobs performed in the small business and specifying the requirements for successful performance of these jobs, rather than guessing who can do what job, who should do what job, and how much each person should be paid for the job done.

Other advantages also arise from the use of a job evaluation technique by the small businessperson. Many times labor turnover can be reduced because employee morale is heightened as a result of job evaluations and the fact that employees believe they are paid fairly (albeit unequally) for unequal work. Further, a job evaluation program will facilitate recruiting new workers because the employer now knows exactly what to look for in a person recruited for a given job. Furthermore, training is facilitated because, again, the requirements of the job are known and written down. Another important aspect of the job evaluation program is the aid that it gives employers in dealing with unions. Not all unions subscribe to job evaluation as a cure-all, but because it gives a factual base for establishing wage rates, many unions use the findings from a job evaluation study as a groundwork on which to discuss major and fundamental wage issues during negotiations and collective bargaining proceedings.

Therefore, a job evaluation program is exceedingly important to the small business manager, particularly once the business becomes of sufficient size to have experienced real difficulty in determining how much to pay whom, and when. Although the cost of a job evaluation program may seem high when first thought of, in the long run it generally will pay for itself many times over in decreased costs and other efficiencies.

## The assignment of absolute relative wages

Once the job evaluation process is complete, then the small business-person will know precisely which jobs are worth more, which jobs are worth less, and which jobs are "in between" so far as their value to the business is concerned. Once the small businessperson has ascertained this information on a relative basis, then he or she can look at the absolute pay scale and determine how much to pay for a given job—that is, how much he or she can pay for a given job and be reasonably sure that rate will be reasonable both absolutely and relatively. However, anyone who knows the intricacies of operating a business will quickly testify that a business-person rarely, if ever, has a free hand in establishing wage levels. For example, wages cannot be established unilaterally by the small business-person if he or she is unionized, no matter how accurate the job evaluation system and regardless of the ability to pay. Furthermore, as mentioned above, there are laws and other constraints and restraints which operate to force the small businessperson to pay more or less money for specific jobs. Also, the manner in which he or she will pay his employees must be considered. That is, the small businessperson must decide whether to pay employees a wage or salary, and to what extent to pay them in the form of fringe benefits such as hospital and surgery insurance, sickness and accident insurance, life insurance, vacation or holiday pay, paid rest periods, severance pay, supplemental unemployment benefits, company paid pension plans, shift differential, tools and clothes compensation, profit sharing, and even possibly stock purchase plans. All of these benefits are forms of "other kinds" of employee remuneration and must be resolved by the small businessperson. However, when faced with making these decisions, a small businessperson should avail himself or herself of the good books available in public libraries on the general subject of wage and salary administration.

## UNION-MANAGEMENT RELATIONS

For the most part, small businesses are less unionized than are large businesses. There are a variety of reasons for the lesser amount of unionization in small business operations. One reason is that there is a limited amount of protection from unions for small businesses under federal labor law, that is, federal laws do not apply to any small businessperson working solely in intrastate commerce. More important, however, small businesses of genuinely small size are not particularly appealing to union organizers: It would appear that the size of the catch isn't worth all the effort. The point is, the union organizer would much prefer to spend five days of his or her time trying to organize the employees in a 10,000-employee plant than he or she would to organize the members in a 10-

employee plant. The amount of dues and the feeling of great satisfaction, for example, is simply the more appealing result of organizing the large plant rather than the small. However, even though there is a certain amount of shelter in being "pint-sized" the fact that a business is small certainly offers no immunity from unionization. In fact, there are some unions that specialize to some extent in organizing small businesses, particularly small manufacturers, service industries, printing and trucking industries, and construction crews.

Unfortunately, most small businesspeople who have developed their own businesses have rather strong personal (anti-union) feelings. Part of the reason is that they feel they have "made it on their own" and that their employees only want to unionize to "take it away" from them. Further, the union itself, by definition, means that an employee is willing to rely on the strength and muscle of others, which would seem the very antithesis of the owner's attitude. For the most part, the small businessperson will feel that it is only honorable and respectable to rely on one's own drive and initiative rather than on a group drive or initiative. Employees do join unions, however; and the small businessperson must be prepared to face up to this fact. This is true especially if he or she is a "large" small businessperson or if he or she trades in interstate commerce, because it would appear that unions are making more and more inroads into this heretofore relatively unorganized area.

Unionization of one's small business, of course, need not be regarded as a tragedy. Many employers operate successfully for years dealing with labor organizations. Furthermore, many small businesspersons—a good example is a man who starts his own construction crew—not only have been unionized the entire time that they have been small businesspersons, but they were union card carriers themselves before they set up their own business and they still retain their membership in the union.

Therefore, the threat of the union is not necessarily the harbinger of doomsday for the small businessperson. However, the small businessperson must be aware of the role of the union, and he or she should be familiar with the labor laws and other legislation which govern our society.

## QUESTIONS

1. Why must the small businessperson be adept as a personnel manager?
2. What are the various sources a small businessperson might use in recruiting personnel? Which are the best? Worst? Why do you think so?
3. Critically analyze the use of the interview technique in screening potential employees.
4. Discuss the various forms of tests which the small businessperson might use in screening job applicants.

5.  Describe the various forms of training which the small businessperson might use to train rank-and-file employees; to train managerial employees.
6.  Discuss the problem of paying employees.
7.  What is a job evaluation program?
8.  Do you feel people want to be paid unequally? Why?
9.  Do small business people need to worry about unions? Why?
10. Outline a comprehensive personnel program for a small business hiring 40 employees.

## PROBLEM

Del had a problem—an intriguing problem. At work, everything seemed fine. Everyone was friendly with each other, no one really seemed to take himself or herself too seriously, and things went along smoothly.

Things off the job weren't all that good, however. Del knew that four of his best employees were members of a union. Further, he knew that they were always talking about "the union" and what it could do for the other employees. In addition, there were grumblings about pay and other working conditions.

Del didn't really know what to do about all the complaints. He did know that he was paying as much in wages to some of his best employees as he was actually paying to himself.

1.  Does it sound like Del has a potential problem?
2.  What would you do, if you were Del, about their prospective problems?
3.  What actions would you expect of Del's prospective union organizers?

## BIBLIOGRAPHY

Dailey, Charles A. *Entrepreneurial Management.* New York: McGraw-Hill, 1971, 208 pp. This book explores the risk-taking dimensions of entrepreneurial management. Assesses how entrepreneurs solve management problems.

Hosmer, A. Arnold; Tucker, Frank L.; and Cooper, Arnold C. *Small Business Management.* Homewood, Ill.: Richard D. Irwin, 1966, 605 pp. A good book of cases on small business management. Reading it will help in developing a feel for what it takes to manage a small business.

Shivers, Allan. "Motivations and Risks of Private Business." Michigan State University, *Business Topics,* no. 17 (Winter 1969), pp. 7–10. An insightful article on the motivation of small business managers.

Tamarkin, Robert, ed. *The Young Executive Today.* Chicago, Ill.: Allen-Bennett, 1972, 417 pp. If you are young and in a hurry to build your own business this is the inspirational book you will want to read.

# 12

# Capital:
# Needs and sources

Once the appropriate legal form of organization has been selected, the manager of a new business venture must identify the firm's needs for capital, and the best sources of capital. The problem involves estimating those funds necessary to promote and organize the business, as well as those funds necessary for the going concern.

For purposes of this discussion, the word *capital* refers to the total funds employed in the firm; the owners' contributions, *equity;* and those funds provided by creditors, *debt.* As indicated above, the new business needs capital for several purposes: to cover promotional expenses, to provide working capital, and acquire fixed assets. In the going concern the problem is determining if working capital and fixed assets are adequate and provided by the best possible sources. The importance of these decisions is demonstrated by the fact that inadequate capital is one of the most common causes of small business failure.

## Promotional expense capital

Promotional expense capital includes payments to individuals for their services as promoters. The payments may be a cash fee or an ownership interest in the firm. In addition to financial and legal planning, promotional expenses include such things as utility company deposits; options to purchase or lease land or buildings; attorneys' fees; and in the case of a corporation, state organization taxes and franchise taxes. There may also be costs associated with locating initial sources of equity capital and in finding a suitable business location.

## Working capital

For investment purposes, working capital should be defined as total current assets. Generally speaking, working capital consists of the dollars invested in *cash, inventories,* and *accounts receivable.* Through the normal operations of the firm, these dollars represent "circulating capital." As inventories are built up, sales volume generated, and receivables collected dollars move through the circulating capital cycle. The problems associated with managing working capital are discussed in Chapter 15. The objective here is to provide an approach to determining working capital needs.

Every business must provide a cash reservoir to handle its day-to-day operations because inflows and outflows of cash are rarely, if ever, synchronized. On certain business days outflows will exceed inflows and the cash reservoir will have to be drawn down. On other days inflows will exceed outflows, and excess cash will be available.

The amount of cash required in the cash reservoir will be dependent upon a number of factors unique to the particular type of business. These factors include sales volume, whether sales are cash or credit or both, the credit terms, the paying habits of customers, and any other expected or possible unexpected cash outlays that could involve substantial amounts of cash. In estimating the amount of cash required in a particular situation, the relationship between out-of-pocket expenses and the generation of sales revenue is important.

Determining the length of time the expenses are due before cash receipts will be adequate to cover them provides an estimate of the amount of cash required. In a new business, however, cash reserves must be provided to handle unexpected contingencies; thus a considerable amount of subjective judgment is involved in arriving at the desired cash balance.

The amount of working capital invested in inventories in the small business usually represents a major part of working capital. Factors affecting the inventory investment include the seasonality of sales and (in the case of the manufacturing firm) the seasonality and length of the production cycle. In estimating inventory investment in a new firm, the ratio of net sales to inventory (for the particular line of business) published by Dun & Bradstreet, or the appropriate trade association, may be helpful. For example, if net sales of a small retailer in the clothing business is typically six times inventory, $100,000 of inventory would be required to support sales volume of $600,000. The amount of inventory required can also be determined by considering inventory as a percent of current liabilities or inventory as a percent of net working capital.

The third working-capital use consists of an investment in receivables if credit is offered. Factors affecting the amount of investment required to support a credit program include the proportion of cash sales and credit sales and the terms of payment offered to credit customers. The seasonality of sales and changes in general business conditions which might affect the payment pattern of customers are also important.

In estimating the investment necessary in accounts receivable, published ratios may again be helpful. If the average collection period and the amount of credit sales are known the average amount tied up in accounts receivable can be determined. For example, an average collection period of 40 days means that 40 days' sales (one ninth of annual sales) are in the form of accounts receivable at any given time. Thus, if annual sales are $450,000, the investment in accounts receivable is $50,000 at any given time.

## Capital for fixed assets

Fixed assets are defined as assets of a permanent nature that are used in the business to produce a product or offer a service. Typical fixed assets are buildings, machinery, equipment, and land. Obviously the particular type of business operation has a great deal to do with the size of the fixed asset investment required. A small retail firm may be able to lease a building and only require fixed assets in the form of furniture and fixtures. On the other hand, a motel business may require thousands of dollars of fixed assets to get the operation under way.

A word of caution is necessary at this point. In any particular type of business there is some minimum quantity of fixed assets necessary for profitable and efficient operation. For example, a one-unit or two-unit motel or a filling station with one gas pump would be grossly inadequate in terms of fixed asset investment. The result would be inefficiency, with little or no profit.

It is also important to recognize that a firm's flexibility is inversely related to its investment in fixed assets. Dollars invested in land, buildings, and equipment involve long-term commitments. Furthermore, the equipment may be of a technically specialized nature, and substantial losses and delays could occur if liquidation was necessary. These inherent inflexibilities in fixed asset investment serve to emphasize the importance of a thorough investigation of fixed asset needs before the commitment of dollars.

## AN OBJECTIVE APPROACH TO ESTIMATING CAPITAL NEEDS

Although the standard ratios and data produced by various organizations may prove helpful in estimating capital needs, it is hazardous to rely exclusively on such indicators. Therefore the manager should also make his own estimates based on his experience and knowledge of conditions in the line of business, and the particular market area where the firm is going to operate.

## Cash needs

In attempting to determine a minimum required cash balance, the amount of cash outflow that will be needed before cash inflows begin coming in can be estimated. This involves anticipating payments necessary for such items as labor, rent, supplies, utilities, and other expenses that will occur as soon as the business is open. To be on the safe side, a cash balance necessary to pay two or three months' expenses without figuring on any cash inflows during that period might be appropriate— because the time required to achieve a satisfactory sales volume may be considerable. In addition, there is always the possibility of unexpected or hidden expenses. Both of these factors suggest that the cash balance in the initial period should be a generous one.

## Investment in accounts receivable

A similar type of investigation is used to determine the investment requirement in accounts receivable. The problem is to anticipate the relationship between cash sales and credit sales, formulate the credit terms that are to be offered to customers, anticipate the paying habits of credit customers, and consider all the costs associated with administering the credit program.

Additionally, the manager must realize that once a credit sale is made, the account receivable may not turn over before inventory must be replenished. Small businesses frequently get into trouble by not adequately capitalizing the volume of credit sales they provide customers. They tend to think only in terms of sales volume; thus, as credit sales increase, the amount of working capital available to replenish inventory decreases and inventory levels decline. Then, as a result of inadequate inventory, sales volume eventually declines.

## Investment in inventory

In estimating the investment necessary in inventories, the types and quantities of products to be stocked must be considered. For the new business this presents the problem of first determining what is a reasonable and attractive selection of items to offer and then estimating sales for each item. In some cases suppliers will offer advice concerning reasonable inventory stocks to their customers. Turning customers away because of out-of-stock situations really hurts. On the other hand, the manager cannot expect to handle an infinite variety of items for selection in order to avoid lost sales. Another factor important in determining appropriate inventory levels is the location of suppliers and the time required to replenish supplies.

In manufacturing, the problem is more complex. The level of inventory must be estimated for raw materials as well as for work in process and finished goods. Also such problems as the lead time for delivery and production and the cost of labor and materials going into the production process must be considered.

As a general rule, the manager should err on the high side in estimating working capital requirements. A common weakness in many small businesses is inadequate working capital and a disproportionate investment in current assets relative to fixed assets. Too much capital is tied up in assets that are difficult to convert to cash. The real danger arises if the business must depend on daily receipts to meet obligations coming due on a daily basis. Then, when a slump in sales or unexpected expenses occur, the firm may be in serious financial trouble.

## Investment in fixed assets

In calculating the amount of investment required in fixed assets, price quotations on machinery, equipment, tools, and furniture and fixtures are available from suppliers. Land and building cost estimates may be based on prices asked by the sellers. The manager must realize the lack of flexibility associated with the purchase of fixed assets. As a general rule it is desirable to minimize fixed asset investment when possible.

Frequently there will be a choice between leasing and buying fixed assets. For most small, new firms leasing arrangements are attractive. They not only reduce the capital requirement in fixed assets, but provide a flexibility that is helpful if the business is more successful or less successful than originally anticipated.

The foregoing discussion has been concerned with determining the needs for funds in the new business venture. However, the same questions must be answered in situations in which the entrepreneur buys the going concern. Additionally, it must be determined if the purchase price of the going concern is reasonable, a problem considered in Chapter 6.

## SOURCES OF CAPITAL AND CREDIT FOR SMALL BUSINESS

There are four basic means of generating funds for small business: trade credit, loans, equity financing, and reinvestment of profits.[1] Trade

---

[1] The discussion in this section was based in part on information provided by the Bank of America in its *Small Business Reporter* publication entitled "Financing Small Business." Inquiries regarding this and other *Small Business Reporters* available should be directed to *Small Business Reporter*, Bank of America NT & SA, San Francisco, Calif., 94120.

credit involves the purchase of goods, supplies, and equipment on credit from suppliers. The principal sources of small business loans are commercial banks, other financial institutions, and interested individuals. Equity financing involves selling ownership interest in the firm to someone as a partner or stockholder. The reinvestment of equity simply involves plowing some part of the profits back into the business.

## Fund sources and risk

All fund sources involve some degree of risk. From a control point of view, the plowing back of profits is the least risky because only the owners are concerned. Risk increases considerably, however, when the owners ask another party (creditor) to provide borrowed funds. The trust and good faith the creditor has in the owners usually must be backed by something of value. Thus, credit normally involves tangible security or collateral that the lender can claim if the borrower fails to repay the debt.

The highest degree of risk is assumed by the investor who is interested in providing additional equity financing. The only security is a voice in management. For the existing owners the risk is that additional equity financing may jeopardize control.

The various sources of funds can be categorized according to the level or degree of risk. The risk inherent in the transaction will determine the terms of the agreement and the cost.

### EQUITY FINANCING

When the organizers of a small business cannot provide at least 50 to 60 percent of the total capital required, equity financing is called for. Recall that equity represents ownership, and shows up on the financial statement as net worth. Most of the funds to start up a business will be obtained from equity sources.

As indicated, the provider of equity will usually demand some control over the management function. The source of equity funds will in part be determined by the legal form of organization. There are six potential sources of equity financing.

## Sole proprietorship

The sole owner of a business maintains exclusive control over the management function, and because of this, equity sources are limited to personal savings, securities or real estate owned, other personal property of high value, or funds which are supplied informally by friends, relatives, or customers.

## Partnership

When two or more persons share the ownership and liabilities of a business, their sources of equity are much the same as in the single owner-ship situation. Frequently, the person with a good idea (or experience and skill in management) and inadequate funds will join another individ-ual who can provide the required capital.

## The corporation

The corporation is formed by three or more individuals who apply to a particular state for a corporate charter. Ownership interest is represented by the number of shares of stock each person holds. A unique and attrac-tive feature of the corporation is that each person's liability for the obliga-tions of the firm is limited by his or her extent of ownership. The source of equity capital for the corporation simply involves the sale of capital stock to friends, relatives, stockbrokers, or any other interested parties. If the stockholders have a voice in management by being able to vote the shares (which is usually the case), raising equity through the sale of stock can jeopardize control.

## Small Business Investment Companies

A number of companies have been licensed by the Small Business Administration to provide equity capital to small businesses and in some cases make long-term loans. A Small Business Investment Company (SBIC) will supply equity financing to sole proprietorships and partner-ships that can qualify. In corporate organizations they will buy the capi-tal stock outright. Some SBICs are also interested in the convertible de-bentures of small corporations. A convertible debenture represents an unsecured debt of the firm, convertible into common stock at some future date at agreed-upon terms. On the debt side, an SBIC will either grant outright loans of 5 to 20 years; or guarantee loans made to the business by a commercial bank.

## Venture capital groups

It is not uncommon for groups of investors to form "venture capital" associations to provide equity capital to promising small businesses. They typically prefer to deal with corporate organizations and either buy stock outright or invest in convertible debentures.

## Local or business development corporations

These organizations are similar in many respects to the SBICs. Associations of private businesses and citizens form to promote business ownership, employment, and income in their respective communities. They may raise funds through strictly private sources or through public subscription. They generally provide equity financing, but have been known to make long-term loans (5 to 20 years) and guarantee commercial bank loans.

### DEBT FINANCING

When the organizers are able to provide at least half of the capital needed through their own equity funds they generally seek the remainder from one or more debt sources. The creditors are not able to exercise any control over the management function as long as the debt agreement is adhered to. The loan contract, however, usually stipulates certain conditions the borrowers must observe. Borrowed capital is indicated in the financial statement as "liabilities." It is repaid, along with interest, out of profits and/or the sale of assets.

The sources of borrowed capital can be grouped, in terms of risk, into four classes. There are eight institutions in the four classes, that provide some 21 different types of financing.

### Class I sources: Low risk, lowest cost

The Class I sources include commercial banks, life insurance companies, and savings and loan associations. They deal principally in short-term debt (less than one-year maturity) and intermediate-term debt (three- to five-year maturity). However, in some cases, long-term debt is possible (beyond a five-year maturity).

*Commercial banks.* The commercial bank is the most economical source of borrowed capital available to the small business. It provides more debt to small business than any other source, either directly, or through other sources (finance companies and trade suppliers) which borrow from the bank. Loanable funds come from customers' demand and time deposits, and loan policies are influenced by management decision as well as by government regulation. If at all possible, the small business manager should establish and maintain a good relationship with a commercial bank. The following list indicates the types of financing banks normally provide.

1. *Commercial loans.* This is the most common type of loan that banks make to small business. A commercial loan is for short-term seasonal

needs; maturity is 90 to 180 days; and collateral may or may not be required.

2. *Term loans.* This bank loan arrangement normally provides funds for up to five years, on a secured or unsecured basis. The principal is paid down by periodic installments, and typically the business must adhere to certain conditions spelled out in a term loan agreement.

3. *Bank credit cards.* A retailer is able to offer credit to customers without financing the sale or assuming any credit risk through acceptance of bank credit cards. BankAmericard and Master Charge are the two nationwide plans of prominence. The cost to the retailer is normally five or six percent of the sale price.

4. *Equipment financing and leasing.* Commercial banks will loan on equipment as collateral, and can also arrange for the small business to lease equipment for negotiated periods of time.

5. *Real estate loans.* Banks make real estate loans to purchase, construct, or improve buildings; or to acquire land. These obligations are always secured by the asset financed, under strict agreement.

6. *Inventory distribution financing.* These bank loan arrangements permit manufacturers to distribute inventories to customers at times or in quantities most consistent with production schedules and capacities. The goods are produced and shipped to seasonal businesses long before the season starts. The manufacturers use "extended dating" in granting the customers credit, which means the invoice is not due until well into the season. The benefits to the manufacturer are a reduction in inventory storage costs and the savings of level production over seasonal production.

7. *Accounts receivable financing.* Commercial banks will loan money on accounts receivable pledged as collateral. However, such arrangements are only done on a recourse basis, which means that if accounts pledged become slow paying or bad, they must be replaced with good ones. Thus, the small business manager is left with all the problems and costs of collection.

8. *Factoring.* Several commercial banks maintain factoring departments which will buy accounts receivable outright; on a nonrecourse basis. This arrangement has the advantage of eliminating the costs of the credit and collections function in the firm, but may cut back on sales if particular customers are not acceptable credit risks to the bank.

9. *Secured and unsecured "other" loans.* These loans are made with or without something of value being pledged. Most often the real basis of the loan is the borrower's honor and financial strength, and the firm's potential for success. In other cases, high-value personal items, or the savings deposits of an individual or business, serve as security.

10. *Commodity or inventory loans.* Bank loans are made to manufacturers or wholesalers to purchase commodities (inventories) that are readily marketable, nonperishable staples. The goods serve as collateral.

11. *Floor planning.* This is a form of inventory loan that banks make to retailers on large consumer durables, such as automobiles and appliances. Title remains with the bank, but possession is given to the seller. As the individual items are sold, the loan balance is reduced.

12. *Indirect collection financing.* This arrangement is used when a retailer generates a large volume of consumer sales contracts but prefers to retain the control and collection of the accounts. The commercial bank discounts the contracts (receivables), but permits the firm to administer the credit program.

**Life insurance companies.** These institutions may provide debt financing, on a secured basis, to low-risk business firms that are well established. Their other function as a source of funds is to make long-term, low-interest loans to their policyholders, based on the cash value of the individual policyholder's contracts.

**Savings and loan associations.** These institutions accept savings deposits from the public and use these funds to specialize in real estate loans. They are chartered and regulated by the state and/or federal governments. As a source of debt capital to small business, savings and loans provide two possibilities. First, the small business owner may obtain funds from a savings and loan by mortgaging or refinancing the family home. Second, all associations can make real estate improvement loans to small businesses.

## Class II sources: Moderate to low risk, low cost

The only institution considered to be in Class II is the Small Business Administration (SBA). This federal agency administers funds appropriated by Congress and controlled by the Bureau of the Budget, to assist small businesses. The SBA was established in 1953 to fill an apparent need of small businesses for intermediate- and long-term funds (the average loan maturity is near five years).[2]

As a prerequisite to obtaining a SBA loan, the firm must be unable to qualify for private commercial financing. As indicated, the SBA will service moderate to low risk needs at a relatively low cost. SBA loans are of five types and may be "direct" or in "participation" with a commercial bank.

**Direct loans.** An amount up to $100,000 can be provided directly to qualified small businesses if adequate collateral is available.

**Bank participation loans.** The SBA supplies up to 75 percent of the loan required or $150,000 (whichever is less); and the commercial bank puts up the remaining 25 percent.

---

[2] A more complete discussion of the services and functions of the Small Business Administration is provided in Chapter 3.

*Displaced business loans.* These are SBA loans made to businesses displaced by federally-funded programs such as urban renewal. The loan limit is 133 percent of the value of the business displaced or $350,000 (whichever is less).

*Economic opportunity loans.* Physically handicapped individuals and members of minority groups can acquire SBA funds for establishing a small business under the economic opportunity program.

*Guaranteed loans.* The SBA can provide guarantees up to 90 percent or $350,000 (whichever is less) on business loans from commercial banks, at the lenders' standard interest rates.

## Class III sources: Moderate risk, moderate cost

The Class III sources of funds include leasing companies, inventory and equipment suppliers (known as trade credit), and commercial finance companies. The inventory suppliers and commercial finance companies deal exclusively in short-term credit. The equipment suppliers and leasing companies provide intermediate-term credit (one to five years).

*Leasing companies.* These concerns lease buildings and/or equipment to small businesses at fixed rentals for negotiated periods of time. The principal advantage is to reduce initial capital requirements.

*Inventory and equipment suppliers.* One of the most important sources of funds to small business is the trade supplier. Since their customers' success contributes to their own, trade suppliers permit small businesses to buy inventory on credit, or equipment on an installment basis. Certain manufacturers may also lend money to individuals or groups to establish dealerships for the manufacturers' products or to finance expansion. Inventory is normally financed for 30, 60, or 90 days; with discounts for prompt payment. Equipment is usually financed for a period up to five years with a 20 to 30 percent down payment required.

*Commercial finance companies.* These companies provide small business with funds for several purposes; and under a variety of arrangements. They generally deal at the retail level. Inventory or equipment can be used as collateral. Additionally, they will finance accounts receivable on a recourse basis or will factor receivables (buy outright) on a nonrecourse basis. Secured or unsecured commercial loans are also made to meet seasonal or short-term money needs for periods of 90 to 180 days.

## Class IV sources: High risk, high cost

Only one source of funds falls in the high risk, high cost group: the personal finance company. Because of the cost, it should be considered as a last resort. Personal finance companies loan relatively small amounts to individuals on a secured basis. All are short-term installment loans running from 3 to 36 months. The unique feature of personal finance companies is that they will take risks and accept types of collateral that commercial banks and other institutions will not.

## SUMMARY

There are a wide variety of sources of funds for small business. Initially, it is suggested that 50 to 60 percent of the funds be raised through equity channels. The use of the funds will dictate the source.

One of the most widely used sources of funds is credit from inventory suppliers. If discounts are taken, trade credit can be very economical.

Commercial bank loans are typically used to supply short-term funds; but term loans running up to five years are also available in some cases. Such loans are normally secured and require collateral in the form of inventory, equipment, or real estate. Commercial bank credit is normally the most economical; thus it is important that the small business manager establish and maintain a good bank relationship.

It may be possible for the small business to finance the purchase of equipment on an installment basis through the equipment supplier, or to arrange for equipment leasing through the supplier.

The Small Business Administration and the Small Business Investment Companies should also be considered as sources of long-term funds.

If the business firm is large enough, and if the corporate form of organization is being employed, the manager may want to consider the sale of capital stock or bonds to raise funds.

Retained earnings constitutes a major source of funds for financing the expansion of small businesses. Although reliance upon internally generated funds may limit the rate of expansion, it does provide a conservative approach.

Other sources of capital for the new or expanding firm include business development corporations, venture capital groups, commercial finance companies, life insurance companies, savings and loan associations, personal finance companies, and loans from officers, friends, relatives, and customers.

## QUESTIONS

1. Describe the three basic types of capital required in initiating a new business firm.
2. What are the three primary uses of working capital? How would the small businessman proceed in determining the amount of working capital needed in each of the primary uses?
3. What factors must be considered in calculating the amount of investment necessary in fixed assets?

4. What are the eight major sources of borrowed funds available to small business?
5. What are the alternative possibilities for financing the purchase of equipment?
6. Why is a good relationship with a commercial bank so important to the small business?
7. What are the five types of loans available through the Small Business Administration?
8. What kind of debt arrangement is unique to the financing of large inventory items, such as automobiles and appliances? How does it work?
9. What miscellaneous informal sources of funds may be available to the small business?

## PROBLEMS

1. Visit a local bank and discuss the financing of small business with one of the commercial loan officers. Does the bank make a point of providing some amount of "venture capital" to promising small businesses in the area? Ask for a copy of the loan application to see what types of information the bank requires of small business loan applicants.

2. Contact the nearest office of the Small Business Administration and discuss its role in financing small business in the community. Ask for the various application forms for an SBA loan and compare them with the information and data the local banker requests from loan applicants.

3. Examine the role of any venture capital groups or business development corporations that exist in the community to finance small business. Is there a Small Business Investment Company in the area? If so, examine its role in financing small business in the area.

## BIBLIOGRAPHY

Engler, George N. *Business Financial Management,* chaps. 16, 17, 18, 19, and 20. Dallas, Tex.: Business Publications, 1975.

Hunt, P.; Williams, C. M.; and Donaldson, G. *Basic Business Finance,* chaps. 11, 12, 13, 14, 15, 16, 17, 18, 19, 22, and 27. Homewood, Ill.: Richard D. Irwin, 1974.

Johnson, Robert W. *Financial Management,* chaps. 12, 13, 14, 17, 18, 19, 20, and 21. 4th ed. Boston: Allyn and Bacon, 1971.

Prather, Charles L., and Wert, James E. *Financing Business Firms,* chaps. 10, 11, 12, 13, 14, 15, 16, 17, and 18, 4th ed. Homewood, Ill.: Richard D. Irwin, 1971.

# 13

# Accounting and financial control

The experienced entrepreneur knows there is a close relationship between good accounting practices and business success. To keep in touch with financial conditions on a day-to-day basis requires accounting information that is accurate, properly organized, and continually up to date. From another view, a good accounting system must be comprehensive enough to satisfy the purpose of financial control, yet easy to understand and interpret. Financial decisions based upon inadequate, unreliable, or confusing accounting information often lead to financial disaster.

An effective system of accounting and financial control has three fundamental objectives. The first is to accurately inform the small business manager of his or her current financial status. Current accounting records expose potential problem areas and permit the necessary corrective action before too much damage results. Current financial records are also necessary to properly analyze the firm's performance through time, and to provide the necessary information for the prompt and accurate filing of tax returns. Finally, up-to-date business records provide the information necessary to periodically prepare certain financial statements and reports required or requested by interested outsiders. For instance, the banker will require that complete and accurate financial statements accompany a bank credit application, and suppliers often request financial statement information to assist them in making credit decisions.

The second objective of a good accounting system is to maintain effective control of the firm's assets. If the investment of time and effort in a business enterprise is to return a profit, the entrepreneur must manage rather than be managed. Effective control is only possible through an accurate record of the availability and use of assets. There is no place for carelessness or error in effective financial management. Furthermore, complete and accurate accounting records will serve to protect the small business owner against the possibility of fraud, theft, or waste on the part of employees and other associated with the business venture.

199

The third objective of an effective accounting system is to serve as a basis for business planning. A lack of good planning and direction keeps small businesses small, and prevents them from ever realizing their full profit potential. Good accounting records are an indispensable tool in the decision-making process. Only after the manager knows the past, can he or she have any success in determining the future.

The remainder of this chapter begins with a general discussion of basis accounting theory and terminology, followed by a general description of the accounting records basic to any accounting system. Finally, there are sections on methods of handling the record-keeping function and on how the entrepreneur may use the computer in the accounting function. Although some of the discussion is in terms of a retail business, the fundamentals and principles introduced are basic to any business firm, be it involved in retailing, wholesaling, or manufacturing.

## BASIC ACCOUNTING THEORY AND TERMINOLOGY

*Assets* are what the business owns; *liabilities* are what a business owes. Cash, accounts receivable, supplies, furniture and fixtures, building, land and equipment are typical assets. Typical liabilities include accounts payable, notes payable, wages, and taxes that have not been paid. The capital of the business is the owner's contribution and represents the difference between total assets and total liabilities. This is the concept upon which all accounting systems are based:

$$\text{Assets} = \text{Liabilities} + \text{Capital.}$$

To further clarify, there are two claims against the total assets of a business: liabilities represent the creditors' claims, and capital represents the owner's claim. It follows, therefore, that regardless of the transaction involved, total liabilities plus capital always equal total assets. For example, if the manager buys a delivery truck for $4500 and pays cash, the cash account is reduced by $4500, but the value of another asset (equipment) is increased by $4500, and total assets remain unchanged. In another example, if a bank loan of $1500 is paid, the asset cash is reduced by $1500, but so is the liability bank-notes-payable reduced by $1500, and the equation remains in balance.

### Double entry accounting

The two examples cited above indicate that every business transaction affects the accounting equation in two ways because every transaction is simply an exchange of one item for another. This is the basic idea behind double entry accounting, which records the twofold effect of every transaction.

In accounting terminology every business transaction represents a debit entry in one account and a credit entry in another account; thus total debits always equal total credits. Of course any particular account may have both debit and credit entries. Whether a particular entry is a debit or a credit will depend on the type of account and on whether the transaction to be recorded increases or decreases the account. For example, when the manager bought the truck for cash, the amount paid for the truck was entered as a debit to the equipment account and as a credit to the cash account. And when the bank note was retired, the transaction was recorded as a debit to notes payable and as a credit to the cash account. Figure 13–1 shows the effects of the various debit and credit entries on

**FIGURE 13–1**
**Debit and credit entries**

| Type of account | If the transaction *increases* the account, enter it as a | If the transaction *decreases* the account, enter it as a | Typical balance |
|---|---|---|---|
| Asset | Debit | Credit | Debit |
| Liability | Credit | Debit | Credit |
| Capital | Credit | Debit | Credit |
| Income | Credit | Debit | Credit |
| Expense | Debit | Credit | Debit |

the basic accounts and indicates what is likely to be the typical balance in each of the accounts. All records of an accounting system are based on this double entry concept.

## THE BASIC FINANCIAL RECORDS

The financial records of a business begin with the documents that indicate the business transactions *as they take place*. These include such things as sales receipts, cash register tapes, petty cash slips, purchase orders, checkbook stubs, invoices, and monthly statements from suppliers. Thus, every financial transaction, regardless of how informal, should produce some sort of written record.

This information about the various transactions is first brought together in one or more *journals,* which are called *books of original entry.* When regular entries are made, a journal provides a permanent chronological record of financial transactions. Transferring information into the journals is not complicated, and the time spent will pay off when it becomes necessary to trace information on a particular transaction.

To make the information recorded in the journals more usable, each item is periodically totaled and transferred to a *ledger account.* A ledger account is a record of the increases and decreases of one particular type of asset, liability, capital item, income, or expense. A business will use as many ledger accounts as it needs to keep track of its operations. For example, a small business with little equipment will only have one equipment account, whereas a larger business with several types of equipment will have numerous equipment accounts.

Finally, the journal information is periodically compiled into the financial statements. The two basic financial statements are the *balance sheet* and the *income statement.* Although the journals yield the basic data for the income statement, preparations of the balance sheet requires that financial transactions also be posted in a general ledger of asset and liability accounts. Each transaction is entered in the general ledger as both a credit and a debit, according to the principle of double entry bookkeeping. In most small businesses, an accountant or bookkeeper is responsible for posting to the general ledger and preparing the financial statements.

The financial statements serve as the basis for analyzing the firm's performance over a period of time as well as for determining the financial condition of the firm at a point in time. The income statement and balance sheet are the two documents that individuals outside the firm usually request in analyzing the firm's performance.

The balance sheet indicates the financial condition of the business on a particular date by summarizing the various asset, liability, and capital accounts. The statement is referred to as a balance sheet because it represents the accounting equation. The assets (on the left-hand side) always equal liabilities plus capital (on the right-hand side). Thus, the balance sheet tells the business owner, as well as all others, the relationship between creditors' claims on the assets and the owner's claims on the assets.

The income statement represents a summary of business operations over a period of time. The various sources of income and expenses during the period are recorded, and the profit or loss that results is indicated.

Figures 13–2 through 13–5 present examples of the records that have been briefly discussed above. Figure 13–2 illustrates a typical sales and cash receipts journal; and a cash disbursements, purchases, and expense journal. Figure 13–3 lists the general ledger accounts that would typically be used in a retail business. Finally, Figure 13–4 presents an illustration of a typical income statement, and Figure 13–5 a typical balance sheet.

**FIGURE 13-2**
**Sales and cash receipts journal**

| Date 19— | Description and/or Account | Total sales (Credit) | Charge to Customers (Debit) | Collections on Accounts (Credit) | Miscellaneous Income and Expense Entries | | General Ledger Entries | |
|---|---|---|---|---|---|---|---|---|
| | | | | | (Debit) | (Credit) | (Debit) | (Credit) |
| | | | | | | | | |

**Cash disbursements, purchases, and expense journal**

| Date 19— | Payee and/or Account | Check No. | Amount of Check (Credit) | Merchandise Purchases (Debit) | Payroll Deductions | | Miscellaneous Income and Expense Entries | | General Ledger Entries | |
|---|---|---|---|---|---|---|---|---|---|---|
| | | | | | Income Tax (Credit) | Social Security (Credit) | (Debit) | (Credit) | (Debit) | (Credit) |
| | | | | | | | | | | |

**FIGURE 13–3**
**Chart of general ledger accounts**

ASSETS

(All asset accounts normally have debit balances except those marked credit.)

*Current Assets:*
Cash in bank
Petty cash
Accounts receivable
Allowance for bad debts (*credit*)
Merchandise inventories

*Fixed Assets:*
Land
Buildings
Allowance for depreciation–buildings (*credit*)
Delivery equipment
Allowance for depreciation–delivery equipment (*credit*)
Furniture and fixtures
Allowance for depreciation–furniture and fixtures (*credit*)

LIABILITIES*

(All liability accounts normally have credit balances.)

*Current Liabilities:*
Accounts payable
Notes payable–current
Income taxes withheld–federal
Income taxes withheld–state
Social security tax payable
Sales tax payable

*Long-Term Liabilities:*
Notes payable–long term

CAPITAL†

(All capital accounts normally have credit balances except those marked *debit.*)

Proprietor's capital
Proprietor's drawings (*debit*)
Profit and loss (*credit* if profit; *debit* if loss)

\* If the business is a corporation, the liability accounts will also include the following:
federal income tax payable and state income tax payable.

† The capital accounts listed here are for a single proprietorship. If the business is a partnership, capital and drawing accounts are provided for each partner. If the business is incorporated, the capital accounts are as follows:
Capital stock
Retained earnings
Dividends paid (*debit*)
Profit and loss (*credit* if profit; *debit* if loss)

## The sales and cash receipts journal

The information in the sales and cash receipts journal is normally entered on a daily basis. Each column is marked debit or credit to indicate the typical entry. If it is necessary to make a credit entry in a debit column, or a debit entry in a credit column, the entry is circled. Total sales, charge sales, collections on accounts, and total cash receipts can all be entered on the same line of the journal.

Items to be included in the Miscellaneous Income and Expense column, or in the General Ledger column, are identified in the description column. Miscellaneous receipts that represent either refunds on expense items, or income not due to sales, are entered in the credit column of Miscellaneous Income and Expense. These would include receipts from such sources as rent collections, interest, and refunds from suppliers. Miscellaneous receipts that do not represent income or expense items are entered in the credit column under General Ledger. These would include such receipts as additional investment of capital in the business, or loans from banks. In most small business operations the general ledger column of the sales and cash receipts journal is seldom used.

After the entries for the day have been made, the work should be carefully checked to see that the total of all entries in the debit columns equals the total of all entries in the credit columns. Then at the end of the month, each column of the journal is totaled, and again a check is made to see that the debit column totals equal the credit column totals.

The miscellaneous income and expense entries should finally be summarized to provide a single figure for each account or type of expense appearing in the columns. The information can then be used to construct the balance sheet and income statement.

## The cash disbursements, purchases, and expense journal

All checks written for whatever purpose should be entered in the cash disbursements, purchases, and expense journal on a daily basis. Entries in the merchandise purchases column and payroll deductions column need no explanation. The general ledger columns of the cash disbursements journal are used only for the entries that directly affect the assets, liabilities, and capital of the business as recorded in the general ledger. Typical examples are purchases of furniture or equipment, payment of bank loans, and withdrawals of the proprietor or partners.

As in the sales and cash receipts journal, a daily check is made to see that debits equal credits. Then at the end of each month each column of the journal is totaled and another debit-credit comparison is made. All items appearing in the Miscellaneous Income and Expense and General

Ledger columns should be summarized so that only one total is shown for each account.

## The income statement

The income statement is normally constructed monthly. It shows the results of operations for the month, and may also include columns to show operating results for the year to date. It is useful to express the figures in the income statement as a percentage of net sales. A comparison of these percentages (commonly known as operating ratios) on a month-to-month basis is a valuable means of analyzing performance.

The first entry in the income statement is net sales, which equals gross sales in dollars less any returns and allowances and sales taxes (see Figure 13–4). The next entry is beginning inventory, which is taken from the previous month's inventory account in the general ledger. This figure plus merchandise purchased during the month equals goods available for sale. The ending inventory is then substracted from the total of goods that were available for sale and the result is the cost of goods sold for the month. Net sales less cost of goods sold equals *gross profit*, also commonly called *gross margin*.

**FIGURE 13–4**
**Income statement**

(Month of _____ 19___ )

| | Amount | Percent of sales |
|---|---|---|
| Net sales . . . . . . . . . . . . . . . . . . . . . . . . . . . . . | $ _____ | 100 |
| Less cost of goods sold: | | |
|   Beginning inventory . . . . . . . . . . . . . . . . . . . . . | $ _____ | |
|   Merchandise purchases . . . . . . . . . . . . . . . . . . . | _____ | |
|   Merchandise available for sale . . . . . . . . . . . . . . . | _____ | |
|   Less ending inventory . . . . . . . . . . . . . . . . . . . . | _____ | |
|     Cost of goods sold . . . . . . . . . . . . . . . . . . . . | $ _____ | |
| Gross margin. . . . . . . . . . . . . . . . . . . . . . . . . . . | $ _____ | _____ |
| Less expenses: | | |
|   Salaries and wages . . . . . . . . . . . . . . . . . . . . . | $ _____ | _____ |
|   Rent . . . . . . . . . . . . . . . . . . . . . . . . . . . . . | _____ | _____ |
|   Utilities . . . . . . . . . . . . . . . . . . . . . . . . . . . | _____ | _____ |
|   Supplies . . . . . . . . . . . . . . . . . . . . . . . . . . . | _____ | _____ |
|   Advertising . . . . . . . . . . . . . . . . . . . . . . . . . | _____ | _____ |
|   Depreciation. . . . . . . . . . . . . . . . . . . . . . . . . | _____ | _____ |
|   Taxes. . . . . . . . . . . . . . . . . . . . . . . . . . . . . | _____ | _____ |
|   Insurance . . . . . . . . . . . . . . . . . . . . . . . . . . | _____ | _____ |
|   Interest. . . . . . . . . . . . . . . . . . . . . . . . . . . . | _____ | _____ |
|   Delivery expense . . . . . . . . . . . . . . . . . . . . . . | _____ | _____ |
|   Bad debts . . . . . . . . . . . . . . . . . . . . . . . . . . | _____ | _____ |
|   Other expenses . . . . . . . . . . . . . . . . . . . . . . . | _____ | _____ |
|     Total expenses . . . . . . . . . . . . . . . . . . . . . | $ _____ | _____ |
| Operating profit (loss) before: | | |
| Owner's withdrawals and | | |
| Income taxes . . . . . . . . . . . . . . . . . . . . . . . . . | $ _____ | _____ |

Then the expenses of operations are totaled, and the gross profit (or margin) less total expenses equals *operating profit* or *loss* before owner's withdrawals and income taxes. This is the figure on which the owner will determine his or her income tax liability and represents both compensation for his or her efforts and a return on investment. The income statement is now complete.

The net profit or loss result derived in the income statement can be checked by balancing the general ledger. After all the entries have been made in the general ledger for the month, the debit balances should be totaled and the credit balances should be totaled. The difference between these two results should equal the *bottom line* figure on the income statement.

## The balance sheet

The small business owner should also prepare a monthly balance sheet. Recall that the balance sheet is simply a summary of general ledger accounts, and in contrast to the income statement, shows conditions in the business as of a specific date.

The first entry on the asset side of the balance sheet is *current assets* (see Figure 13–5). Current assets include cash and those assets that will be converted to cash during the normal course of the business, within a year. The cash account includes both petty cash and cash on deposit in a bank.

Accounts receivable include amounts due for merchandise or services purchased but not yet paid for by customers. At this point an allowance is made for that portion of accounts receivable that is estimated to be uncollectible. The allowance is usually estimated as a percent of the average balance of accounts receivable, or as a percent of net credit sales for a period, based on previous years' experience.

The final entry in current assets is inventory. In a retail business, inventory consists of merchandise owned by the company, either on the shelves or in storage, and listed at cost or market value, whichever is lower. In a manufacturing concern, the inventory account is broken down into raw materials, goods in process, and finished goods. At this point, a figure for total current assets appears on the balance sheet.

The next general grouping of balance sheet accounts is *fixed assets*. Fixed assets are those items used in the business operation that are not intended to be resold. Typical fixed assets include land, buildings, machinery, trucks, automobiles, and furniture and fixtures. In contrast to accounts receivable and inventories, which produce income by being converted into cash, fixed assets produce income indirectly through their use in operations.

The final entry in this section of the balance sheet is allowance for

**FIGURE 13–5**
**The balance sheet**

### ASSETS

*Current Assets:*
Cash
  Cash in bank . . . . . . . . . . . . . . . . . $_____
  Petty cash . . . . . . . . . . . . . . . . . . . . _____   $ _____
Accounts receivable . . . . . . . . . . . . . . $_____
  Less: Allowance for doubtful accounts . . _____   _____
Inventories. . . . . . . . . . . . . . . . . . . . _____
      Total Current Assets. . . . . . . . . .   $ _____
*Fixed Assets:*
Land . . . . . . . . . . . . . . . . . . . . . . . $_____
Buildings. . . . . . . . . . . . . . . . . . . . . _____
Delivery equipment. . . . . . . . . . . . . . . _____
Furniture and fixtures . . . . . . . . . . . . . _____   $ _____
  Less: Allowance for depreciation. . . . . . _____
      Total Fixed Assets. . . . . . . . . . .   $ _____
      Total Assets . . . . . . . . . . . . . .   $ _____

### LIABILITIES AND CAPITAL*

*Current Liabilities:*
Notes payable, due within one year . . . . . $_____
Accounts payable. . . . . . . . . . . . . . . . _____
Accrued expenses. . . . . . . . . . . . . . . . _____
      Total Current Liabilities. . . . . . . . .   $ _____
*Long-Term Liabilities:*
Notes payable, due after one year . . . . . . _____
      Total Liabilities . . . . . . . . . . .   $ _____
*Capital:*
Proprietor's capital, beginning of period. . .   $ _____
Net profit for the period. . . . . . . . . . . . $_____
Less proprietor's drawings† . . . . . . . . . . _____
Increase in capital. . . . . . . . . . . . . . . _____
    Capital, End of Period. . . . . . . . . .   $ _____
      Total Liabilities and Capital . . .   $ _____

° For partnership or corporation, see footnotes to Figure 13–3.
† If the business suffers a loss, the proprietor's drawings will be added to the net loss to give the total decrease in capital.

depreciation. All the fixed assets but land will eventually wear out. In recognition of this fact the owner periodically makes an allowance for depreciation, thereby reducing the stated value of the assets. At this point current and fixed assets are totaled and the asset side of the balance sheet is complete.

The first entry on the liability side of the balance sheet is *current liabilities*. Current liabilities include all debts due within one year. Typical current liability accounts include notes payable, accounts payable, and accrued expenses. A typical note payable is the sum of principal payments on a bank loan that falls due within one year. Accounts payable include those monies the company owes to suppliers and other business creditors for such things as materials, merchandise, and insurance. And finally, accrued expenses indicate such things as wages, interest, and other amounts owed but not yet paid by the business as of the date of the balance sheet ( and for which bills or invoices will not be received ).

The *long-term liabilities* include those debts or parts of debts that are not due to be paid within a year. Most common entries in this category are long-term mortgages on property owned, long-term loans, and long-term purchase contracts. The loan account shown in Figure 13–5, notes payable, would typically represent principal payments on a bank loan due after one year. Current liabilities plus long-term liabilities equal total liabilities, and the second major grouping of accounts on the balance sheet is complete.

The last major section of the balance sheet is the *capital account.* If one assumes that the balance sheet represents a single proprietorship, the proprietor's capital at the beginning of the period is entered; net profit for the period is added; any withdrawings are subtracted; and the result is capital at the end of the period. On the other hand, in a corporate organization, the capital section of the balance sheet will include such entries as common stock, preferred stock, earned surplus, capital surplus, and possibly one or two reserve accounts representing earned surplus that is earmarked for a particular purpose.

The foregoing brief review gives some idea of the format for the various financial records that serve as the basis for any accounting system. The description provided is not intended to provide a workable accounting system, for in any particular case the small business owner must decide the best way of handling the accounting function. Specific guidelines for the selection of an appropriate accounting system will be provided at the end of this chapter. In addition, several ready-made accounting systems designed for use in any retail or service establishment are listed. At this point, however, brief mention is made of accounting information that may demand summarization in more detail than that provided by the journals. This does not mean that the journals can be eliminated, but only that there are certain types of records that may have to be kept in addition to the journals to make certain kinds of accounting information more useful.

## SPECIAL TYPES OF ACCOUNTING RECORDS

The first of a number of special accounts that may prove useful is a detailed record of accounts receivable. Two important benefits of such a record are: more accurate billing procedures and ready information for evaluating the firm's credit collection policies. For example, if receivable turnover is declining and the average collection period is increasing, an accurate, detailed accounts receivable record should indicate the particular customer accounts causing the problem.

Most managers find that a separate and detailed inventory record is also helpful. Accurate inventory records are not only essential to the control and security of inventory stocks but also provide information necessary for purchasing decisions and for the evaluation of inventory policies.

It may also prove valuable to organize accounts payable information in a separate set of records. Such detail can protect the credit standing of the firm by indicating such things as available cash discounts, and final payment due dates.

Detailed records may also pay off in production. The successful production process is one properly controlled. Production controls provide the basis for product costing, and permit the detection of costs resulting from idle machines or idle manpower.

A fifth possibility is a detailed sales record that will aid in the analysis of such things as the effectiveness of advertising, market coverage, and the profit derived from certain customers. Furthermore, sales records are needed to provide the basis for compensation of salespeople.

Finally, detailed tax records are a necessity and can save hours of time in filling out the various tax forms that must be periodically submitted to state and federal authorities.

In summation, the number and types of accounting records necessary in any particular business will of course depend on the nature of the operation. It is important, however, to keep in mind that the main objective of any accounting system is to provide the most accurate and complete information possible.

## MANAGING THE RECORD-KEEPING FUNCTION

An accounting system is only as useful as it is up-to-date and accurate. To prevent errors and to safeguard the assets of the business, the accounting system must provide for certain internal checks. A standard method for protecting against errors or employee fraud is to have two or more individuals involved in the record-keeping function.

An alternative approach to ensuring accuracy is to employ the services of a public accountant or a bookkeeping service that caters to small business. Data are normally submitted by mail, and periodically the service provides financial reports by mail. Assistance will also be provided by a bookkeeping service agency in filling out tax returns and in making periodic audits.

Still another approach to handling the accounting function is to purchase one of a number of simplified bookkeeping systems that have been prepared for use by small businesses. Such systems are ideal for the business owner who knows little about accounting, or finds the services of a bookkeeping service expensive.

Several commercial agencies produce simplified bookkeeping systems that may be purchased in most office supply stores. An appendix at the end of this chapter provides specific information on the names, prices, and sources of specific systems designed for use in any retail or service establishment. The Small Business Administration can also be helpful in locating the source of a record-keeping system for a particular type of business.

Of course, the obvious approach if the small business owner is familiar with general accounting practice and theory is for him or her to design an accounting system. In doing this, however, care should be taken to avoid oversimplifying the system by failing to provide adequate checks and balances to protect against error.

## Use of the computer in small business record-keeping

The use of electronic data processing is rapidly becoming feasible for the small business. At present, a retailer with annual gross sales of $100,000 or more who is willing to spend around half of one percent of gross sales in processing fees can acquire much of the accurate up-to-date information that would take many hours or even days to assemble.

Two major problem areas in which use of the computer proves valuable are in inventory control and accounts receivable management. The following comments indicate the types of service that are presently available for these two purposes.

*Coding on cash register tapes.* Information on inventory and accounts receivable can be recorded as a code on cash register tape at the point of sale. Cash registers designed to record information on computer-readable tape as daily transactions are rung up can be leased for $50 a month and up, or purchased for $2,000 to $5,000. Usually on a weekly basis, the tape is removed from the machine and mailed to a data processing center. A few days later, the manager gets back a computer printout with as much detailed information as he or she needs, desires, or can afford.

*Coding on adding machine tapes.* Computer-readable tapes can also be used in conjunction with an adding machine instead of a cash register. The machine is similar to a regular adding machine but has a device attached which punches a paper tape as entries are made. Operation of the machine requires no special training and it is available at costs between $600 and $2,200.

The following example illustrates how a punch tape accounting system works. The small business owner identifies all checks and deposits by assigning general account numbers and enters the cash items and necessary adjusting journal entries on the tape adding machine. Each entry includes a reference number, general ledger account number, and a dollar amount. The average tape machine operator can enter 250–300 transactions an hour, which represents a great savings over the time required to make such records by hand.

The punch tape is then mailed to a service center where the information is transferred to punched cards used to produce the necessary records. Within a few days the service center produces and returns printed journals, a general ledger, and financial statements. Thus, the function of making journal entries, posting to a general ledger, and constructing the financial statements is accomplished efficiently with a high degree of accuracy.

*Packaged programs.* Computer service bureaus or data processing centers can usually provide packaged programs for both accounts receivable and inventory management. Because these ready-made programs are easily adapted to any small business, the initial conversion fee may be as low as $200. The monthly processing fee is generally based on the number of items processed and lines printed on each report.

*Computer consultants.* Many accountants and management consultants are familiar with computer programming techniques. These individuals can assist in setting up retail programs, but will generally refer the actual processing to a computer service bureau. Normal consulting fees for such services start at about $20 an hour.

*The banker's computer.* Commercial banks throughout the country own or have access to computer facilities. The ones that maintain their own equipment are usually willing to assist small business in a widening range of record-keeping functions, including the management of accounts payable and accounts receivable, as well as payroll and inventory management.

## CONCLUDING REMARKS

The basic accounting records are designed to supply accurate and complete information on the assets, liabilities, net worth, sales, expenses, and profits of the business venture. Furthermore, the various accounting records provide the information necessary to construct the financial statements which summarize the firm's operating results. Finally, it is the analysis of these financial statements that provides the necessary guidance so important to rational decision-making.

Good accounting practices are an essential ingredient in the success of any small business. One of the most frequent causes of business failure is the ineffective control and analysis of operating results. Thus, it is extremely important that the small business owner find an accounting system that will function effectively at a reasonable cost. In this regard, the dollars spent in the establishing of an appropriate accounting system represent one of the most productive investments the entrepreneur will ever make.

# Appendix

## Accounting systems designed for use in any retail or service firm

Most of the record-keeping systems listed below are available from local stationery stores. If a particular system is not available from your local retail store, you may contact the publisher at the address given with each entry.

*All-Facts Bookkeeping System.* Wilson Jones Company, 270 Madison Ave., New York, N.Y. 10016; 6150 W. Touhy Ave., Chicago, Ill. 60648. Bound book style (Stock No. S–4) $12.05. Contains the following forms: 50 double-page cash journal forms; also forms for summaries; profit-and-loss statement; balance sheet; asset and depreciation record; mortgage and loan record; and employees' earnings record for 16 employees. Includes directions and filled-in specimen sheets. Loose-leaf style contains 100 double-page cash journal forms and includes all other forms mentioned above.

*Dome Simplified Monthly Bookkeeping Record, #612; Dome Simplified Weekly Bookkeeping Record #600.* Price $4.50. Dome Publishing Company, Dome Building, Providence, R.I. 02903. Available in stationery stores and chain stores. Contains the following forms sufficient for recording the results of 1 year's business: monthly record of income and expenses; annual summary sheet of income and expenditures; weekly payroll records covering 15 employees; individual employee compensation records. Also contains general instructions, specimen filled-in monthly record of income and expenses and list of 276 expenses which are "legal deductions" for Federal Income Tax purposes. This record was designed by a CPA and fits every type and kind of business.

*General Business System.* General Business Services, Inc., 7401 Wisconsin Ave., Washington, D.C. 20014. Complete, easy-to-maintain, preprinted record-keeping system; custom designed for sole proprietors, partnerships, and corporations; provides a monthly *profit and loss statement* and proof of accuracy, meeting requirements of Internal Revenue Service. Through their local authorized field directors, service includes: review and analysis of particular record-keeping requirements; furnishing a complete set of records installed on business premises; personal instructions on use and maintenance of records; guidance throughout the year by trained local counselor; preparation of Federal and State income tax returns, both business and personal, with guarantee of accuracy by professional staff at national office; tax advisory service by tax specialists for research and answers to income tax questions; monthly tax bulletin with money-saving ideas; and supplementary services by local field directors as required. Also offers on an optional basis: computerized monthly billing, computerized bookkeeping, collection system for delinquent accounts, and tax preparation service for employed individuals.

*Greenwood's Approved Business and Income Tax Record.* The Greenwood Company, 710 South Federal St., Chicago, Ill. 60605. System No. 212. Permanently bound book $8.75; looseleaf style $16.25. Contains the following forms: daily record for month; record of daily cash receipts; bank deposits; record of cash payments for month; monthly totals; yearly balance sheet; yearly profit-and-loss statements. Also includes filled-in specimen sheets. Users are offered free advisory bookkeeping service. Individual and weekly payroll records are also available.

*Ideal System: General Bookkeeping and Tax Record.* The Ideal System Company, Post Office Box 1030, Berkeley, Calif. 94701. Available in three sizes: $4.50, $6.50, and $9.95. Contains the following forms sufficient for recording the results of one year's business: receipts and expenses; summary statement; employee's payroll record; payroll summary; depreciation; contributions; proprietor's account form; fixtures and equipment; loan and note record; insurance record; special forms.

*Ideal System: Merchants Bookkeeping and Tax Record.* The Ideal System Company, Post Office Box 1030, Berkeley, Calif. 94701. Contains the following forms sufficient for recording the results of 1 or 2 years' business: sales and cash receipts; purchases; payments; distribution of expenses; bad debts; depreciation; monthly summary and statement of income; employee records; payroll summary; furniture, fixture and equipment record.

*Key-Rec Receiving Systems.* Moss Key-Rec Systems, Inc., 2224 Benton Ave., Dayton, Ohio 45406, or branch offices of SCM Allied/Egry Business Systems licensee. This firm specializes in solving business systems problems through survey, analysis and application of a paper work simplification system. Key-Rec has over 50 record-keeping and control systems to handle such problem areas as customer and vendor returns and inquiries, special orders, returns-to-vendors, "bad" checks, ombudsmen, etc. for all types of businesses. A prime area of concentration is in the control over receipt and distribution of merchandise and payment of invoices for the retail and service industries. Stock "off-the-shelf" forms are available to suit individual customer needs. All Key-Rec forms carry a Performance Guarantee. Many free helpful bulletins, including KEY-REC IDEAS, are available.

*Kolor-Key.* Moore Business Forms, Inc. Post Office Box 5250, Oakland, Calif. 94605 (Eastman Station). May be ordered through local Moore Business Forms representatives. System includes basic business forms (sales slip, invoice, statement, voucher check, purchase order, daily cash control, duplicate deposit slip); instructions for preparations and filing of forms; record-keeping aids. The System is adaptable to a wide range of businesses and can be easily modified as the business grows and forms need change.

*Modern Merchant Simplified Bookkeeping.* The Johnson Systems, 828 North Broadway, Milwaukee, Wis. 53202, $4.95. Contains the following forms sufficient for recording the results of 2 years' business: daily sales; expenses.

*Simplified Master System.* Simplified Business Services, Inc., 901 Barclay Bldg., Bala Cynwyd, Pa. 19004. Includes personalized business consultation services and preparation of Federal and State Income Tax Returns by accounts, also Business Advisory and Tax Questioning and Answering Service. Available through authorized local distributors. Contains the following forms sufficient for record-keeping: current business expenses; total employees' weekly salaries; cash withdrawn for personal use by the owners or partners; daily cash receipts; summary of current business expenses; payment for notes, fixtures, and equipment; summary of monthly cash payments; payments for merchandise on everything bought to resell; summary of daily sales including charge sales; work sheets; income tax information sheet; balance sheet and statement of net worth on a comparative basis; monthly and accumulated profit and loss statements; stock and bond records; record of sales of business real estate or personal property, etc. Record of income from estates; record of real estate and property expenses and income; personal deduction records; real estate mortgage records; equipment and property inventory and depreciation records; inventory; notes payable; notes receivable; insurance records, work sheet. Available in different editions for individuals, partnerships, and corporations. Includes (in addition to both forms and services) a Business Advisory Service; business bulletins and instructions; business improvement ideas; management techniques and ideas and instructions on their use; free membership in the Security Small Business Association providing opportunity (in most States) to purchase low-cost Group Life Insurance without any medical examination.

Numerous accounting systems are also available for use in specific retail and service trades. A listing of these appears in Small Business Bibliography No. 15 which may be obtained from the Superintendent of Documents, U.S. Government Printing Office, Washington, D.C.

In addition to the systems listed, some trade associations, manufacturers, and wholesalers offer specially designed record-keeping systems to their dealer customers. These systems are prepared to meet the general record-keeping needs of a large variety of retail and service trade establishments. On the other hand, the owner of a small business may find it advantageous to have a system adapted to his or her special requirements by a trained public accountant.

The installation of accounting systems and the preparation of tax returns is a service commonly rendered by public accountants. These professional men are listed under appropriate headings in the yellow pages of any local telephone directory. For complete listings, you may request membership rosters from the American Institute of Certified Public Accountants, 666 Fifth Ave., New York, N.Y. 10019, and the National Society of Public Accountants, 1717 Pennsylvania Ave., N.W., Washington, D.C. 20006.

Public accountants also render many accounting services, such as auditing, preparation of reports for government agencies, tax planning, analysis of financial reports, and a variety of specialized management advisory services.

Many of the Small Business Administration's management publications discuss the necessity for keeping adequate records and the services available from public accountants. Most of these publications are slanted toward a certain phase of business operation or a specific kind of small business. Examples are:

1. *A Handbook of Small Business Finance,* Small Business Management Series No. 15. 95 cents.
2. *Financial Recordkeeping for Small Stores,* Small Business Management Series No. 32. $1.30.

These two booklets may be ordered from the Superintendent of Documents, U.S. Government Printing Office, Washington, D.C. 20402. Send check or money order made payable to the Superintendent of Documents.

## QUESTIONS

1. What are the three basic objectives of a workable system of accounting and financial controls?
2. Define the terms *asset, liability,* and *capital,* and identify the *accounting equation.*
3. Discuss the financial records that serve as a basis for any good accounting system.
4. Differentiate between the balance sheet and the income statement.
5. On the income statement, what is the difference between gross profit and operating profit?
6. What types of information are entered in the sales and cash receipts journal?
7. Discuss three situations in which some particular special type of accounting record may be useful and necessary.

8. What suggestions would you have for the small businessperson that would protect against errors in the accounting records and safeguard the assets of the business?

9. Discuss the uses of electronic data processing in performing the accounting function.

10. How can integrated data processing be used by a small business without heavy investment in physical facilities?

## PROBLEMS

1. Contact a public accounting firm in the community and discuss the services it provides to small businesspersons as well as the fees for such services.

2. Obtain a copy of one of the many bookkeeping systems that have been prepared for small businesses and analyze it in terms of its advantages and disadvantages.

3. Interview a number of the more successful small businesspersons in the community regarding the use of integrated data processing and prepare a report on its feasibility and acceptance.

4. The ABC Company has provided you with the following information:

| | |
|---|---|
| Real estate. . . . . . . . . . . . . . . | $ 12,000 |
| Accounts payable. . . . . . . . . . . | 60,000 |
| Accounts receivable. . . . . . . . . | 56,000 |
| Buildings. . . . . . . . . . . . . . . | 100,000 |
| Earned surplus. . . . . . . . . . . . | 180,000 |
| Prepaid expenses . . . . . . . . . . | 8,000 |
| Cash . . . . . . . . . . . . . . . . | 36,000 |
| Inventories. . . . . . . . . . . . . . | 100,000 |
| Capital stock. . . . . . . . . . . . . | 200,000 |
| Equipment. . . . . . . . . . . . . . | 128,000 |

Construct a balance sheet for the ABC Company.

5. You have obtained the following information about the XYZ Firm:

| | |
|---|---|
| Bond interest payable . . . . . . . . | $ 4,600 |
| Rent expense . . . . . . . . . . . . | 2,000 |
| Cost of goods sold . . . . . . . . . | 70,000 |
| Wages. . . . . . . . . . . . . . . . | 19,000 |
| Net sales . . . . . . . . . . . . . . | 220,000 |
| Selling costs . . . . . . . . . . . . . | 24,400 |

Construct the income statement for the XYZ Firm, and assuming an income tax rate of 47 percent, indicate the earnings after taxes and interest.

## BIBLIOGRAPHY

Horngren, Charles T. *Accounting for Management Control, an Introduction.* 3d ed. Englewood Cliffs, N.J.: Prentice-Hall, 1974, 619 pp.

Pyle, William W., and John Arch White. *Fundamental Accounting Principles.* 7th ed. Homewood, Ill.: Richard D. Irwin, 1975, 850 pp.

Tracy, John A. *Fundamentals of Financial Accounting*. New York: John
Wiley & Sons, 1974, 619 pp.

All three of the above cited textbooks provide an excellent and comprehensive
presentation of basic accounting theory and practice. They are recommended
for those who may choose to establish their own accounting system, and for
those who simply desire to gain additional insight into the values of good accounting practice.

# 14

# Financial management in the small business—Part 1

Once the funds have been raised to properly capitalize the small business, the owner is faced with the problems of financial management. Managing the operation from the financial point of view involves two basic objectives. The first is to insure that an adequate flow of cash is available to pay bills as they come due. The second objective is to make the business as profitable as possible.

At first glance the objectives may appear to be inconsistent. One could argue that any dollar held in cash or liquid form represents a sacrifice of earnings the dollar could produce. Thus, holding cash reduces the profitability of the business. Although this view is valid, it is shortsighted. Making the business as profitable as possible requires that some liquid assets (cash) be available at all times. The failure to have adequate cash on hand when needed to meet current liabilities would eventually affect such factors as the credit rating of the firm, its ability to take cash discounts when favorable, its relationship with suppliers, and the cost of borrowing money. Therefore an adequate level of cash is consistent with the objective of making the business as profitable as possible.

It is important that the small business manager recognize the dynamic aspects of accomplishing the liquidity and profitability objectives. In the going concern the objectives are really never reached; they simply represent a day-to-day problem.

In terms of managerial functions, achieving the objectives can be expressed as a three-step process. The first step involves the careful planning of future needs for funds, both short-term and long-term, through the maintenance of an efficient budgeting system. The second step involves acquiring the needed funds from the most economical mix of sources. And the third step is to use the acquired funds in the most efficient manner. This third step is often referred to as the control function and, if properly conducted, provides insights from past experience that may improve future performance.

219

## THE DUAL OBJECTIVES OF FINANCIAL MANAGEMENT: A CLOSER LOOK

### The liquidity objective

A conception of cash flow within a business is vital to an understanding of the liquidity objective. The concept of cash flow involves the timing of cash receipts and cash disbursements. In the typical small business sales are seasonal to some degree; thus at times cash inflows exceed outflows, but at other times cash outflows exceed inflows. As a result cash on hand will sometimes be excessive and sometimes inadequate. The timing problem in cash flow management can be visualized by imagining a situation in which cash inflows are always precisely equal to cash outflows. That is, every time an outflow of cash is called for, an inflow of cash is available. Under such conditions the need for cash on hand would be zero. Unfortunately, few if any businesses enjoy such a position. A typical cash flow cycle is illustrated in Figure 14–1.

Because cash is the common denominator of all transactions, the focus of attention in the cash flow cycle is on the cash account, or the cash reservoir. Cash flows into the cash reservoir on an intermittent basis as

FIGURE 14–1
The flow of cash in the business firm

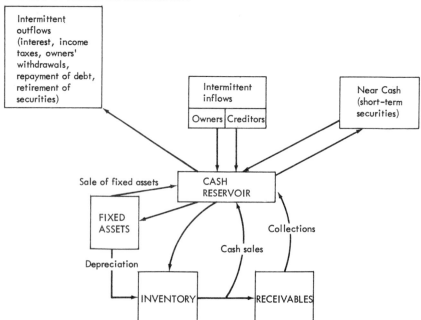

Note: Such expenses as supplies, wages, and selling and administrative expenses are paid in the general circulation of cash.

needed from two sources: owners and creditors. Cash may also flow into the cash reservoir, when needed, from the liquidation of short-term securities. These near cash investments represent the temporary employment of cash that is forecasted to be needed at some future date. (Of course, when cash is excessive the flow may be from the cash reservoir into near cash investments.)

The most regular flow in the cash flow cycle involves working capital. Working capital is defined for purposes of this discussion as total short-term assets. Thus, as shown in Figure 14–1, there is a regular ongoing flow of cash from the cash reservoir into inventories, from inventories into receivables, and from receivables back into cash. To the extent that *cash* sales are generated, cash flows directly from the inventory reservoir into the cash reservoir.

Two basic outflows occur. At various intervals a business will give up cash in return for fixed assets, such as a cash register or display cases. Over time it expects to recover these costs through the sale of merchandise, just as it expects to recover the cost of inventory that is purchased for resale. Since the fixed assets are not immediately used up in the same way that inventory turns over, it is necessary to allocate a portion of the fixed asset cost to each item of inventory sold. This is most frequently done by spreading the original cost of the fixed asset over its estimated service life, and then charging the estimated cost of each year's service to the inventory sold during the period. Thus, in pricing and selling inventory the small business manager is seeking to recapture not only immediate and out-of-pocket costs, such as cost of goods sold, wages, and utilities; but also other costs that were out-of-pocket some time ago. This latter group of costs is represented by the fixed assets; and the portion of their original cost that the manager charges to current year's sales is termed *depreciation*. Therefore, as shown in Figure 14–1, cash flows into fixed assets and is "recovered" through the sale of inventory. So it can be said that depreciation generates cash to the extent that revenues from sales exceed current expenses.

The second major outflow that occurs involves cash payments made intermittently to parties outside the business for such things as interest on debt, income taxes, the repayment of debt, and owner's withdrawals. In summary, then, Figure 14–1 depicts the flow of cash in the firm and reflects the nature of the liquidity objective; that is, to provide as nearly as possible for the synchronization of cash inflows and outflows.

## The profit objective

As previously noted, the liquidity objective is linked to the profit objective in that profitability is only maximized if every dollar is put to its most efficient use. In terms of the cash flow cycle, the profit objective involves

**FIGURE 14–2**

The relationships that determine the earning power of the firm

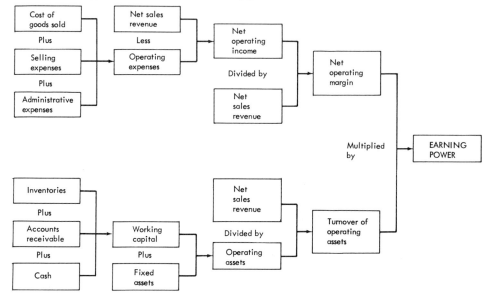

the concepts of margin and turnover. In other words, the return per dollar of operating assets each time it goes through the cycle, coupled with the number of times it completes the cycle in some period of time, constitutes what is termed *earning power.* To clarify the profit objective, the factors that influence earning power are illustrated in Figure 14–2.

In more precise terms, the earning power of the business depends on the operating margin multiplied by the turnover of operating assets. The margin equals net operating income divided by sales, with operating income defined as net sales revenue minus operating expenses. The turnover of operating assets is determined by dividing operating assets into sales, with operating assets defined as all those assets that are necessary in the operation of the business (i.e., working capital as well as fixed assets).[1]

---

[1] A simple example will help clarify the earning power calculation. Assume net sales income of $600, operating assets of $200, and net operating income of $60. In such a case, the net operating margin is $60/$600, or 10 percent, and the turnover of operating assets is $600/200, or 3. Therefore, the earning power of the firm is 3 times 10 percent, or 30 percent. Remember that net sales represent gross sales minus returns and allowances; net operating income equals gross sales minus operating expenses; and operating assets include the total investment in working capital and fixed assets. Another way to define operating assets is to simply include the value of all assets necessary in conducting the business operation. This would include everything from display cases and inventory, to a typewriter and delivery truck.

The close relationship between the liquidity, or cash flow objective and the profit objective is now apparent. For example (as Figure 14–2 will show), if the cash balance is higher than necessary, operating assets are higher than they need be, turnover is less than possible and earning power is reduced. Obsolete inventory and accounts receivable that are uncollectible produce the same result. In terms of margin, if trade discounts are not taken, operating expenses are increased, and operating income, margin, and earning power are reduced.

It should be evident that the objective of the small business owner is to find that combination of margin and turnover that maximizes the earning power of the firm. This is not an easy task, for margin and turnover tend to move inversely. For example, an increase in the margin can be accomplished by increasing the selling price. But as price (margin) increases, sales (and turnover) may decline. And if the decline in turnover is more than proportional to the increase in margin, earning power will decline. On the other hand, the small business owner may think he/she can increase turnover by reducing the selling price. However, if the decrease in the margin resulting from the price cut is more than proportional to the increase in turnover, earning power will decline.

## Summary of the objectives

The objectives of good financial management should now be clear. First, cash flow must be adequate to meet bills as they come due. There is for every situation some best amount of cash necessary to meet this objective—based on the timing of cash inflows and outflows for some selected period of time. Second, the relationship between margin and turnover must be such that the earning power of the business is as high as possible.

Given the objectives, the functions of the manager from a financial point of view become evident. The responsibilities involve planning the needs for funds consistent with the objectives; acquiring the needed funds at minimum cost consistent with the objectives; and managing the use of the acquired funds consistent with the objectives. The remainder of this chapter is concerned with the planning function. The following chapter considers the acquisition and management of funds.

## THE PLANNING FUNCTION

Of the three principal functions of the financial manager, the planning function is the most challenging in terms of foresight and good judgment. Planning future needs for funds requires consideration of the long-run course of the business venture as well as the short-run goals. In other words, the demands for funds will range from short-run temporary needs for the seasonal build up of inventory, to the replacement or expansion of fixed assets.

The following discussion of the planning function differentiates between planning the needs for funds in the next or forthcoming period and consideration of long-run expenditures. Generally speaking, the planning function must include a familiarity with financial analysis, cash budgeting, a means of planning for profits, and a reasonably reliable method of determining the desirability of long-term investment opportunities in the business.

## RATIO ANALYSIS AND THE PLANNING FUNCTION

The entrepreneur invests time, effort, and capital in the business venture and is interested in obtaining an adequate profit in return. With this as the objective, does the firm measure up to expectations? Some means for determining the operating efficiency of the firm must be devised.

One of the most helpful approaches to this problem is the examination of certain ratios and relationships evident in the balance sheet and income statement. If properly done, the quality of the firm's management can be revealed through an effective analysis and interpretation of its financial statements.

Ratio analysis is not only useful as a tool in appraising the current position and past performance of the firm for the owner but is frequently employed by outsiders who wish to appraise the firm's financial position. For example, the banker wants to make a careful analysis of the prospective borrower's position before lending money. Trade creditors will also be interested in the financial position of the business in making a credit decision. Thus, whether or not the entrepreneur considers ratio analysis valuable as a tool for internal use, he or she is often asked to provide the information that ratio analysis affords to others.

### Use caution in ratio analysis

The basic problem in using ratio analysis as an aid in performing the planning function, and in providing information for others, is understanding that ratios are of little value as an end in themselves. Ratio analysis may suggest a problem, but ratios cannot explain the causes or seriousness of the situation. Thus, ratio analysis provides guides, not precise measurements, with which the manager can analyze the business operations.

The objective here is to suggest a few ratios and relationships that are most commonly used to measure small business performance. It is suggested that these ratios be calculated and examined either monthly or quarterly and that emphasis be put on significant changes over time.

## Standards for comparison

The small business manager may compare ratios within the firm on a historical basis and outside the firm with certain selected industrial standards. If the firm has operated for some time, historical standards can be easily established. In setting up these internal guides the manager must decide what level of performance is reasonably attainable in his or her particular situation. If there is a desire to supplement the historical guidelines with industrial indicators, they can be obtained from such sources as the Small Business Administration, Robert Morris Associates, Dun & Bradstreet, Inc., and the Department of Commerce.

## Suggested framework for ratio analysis

There are two basic types of financial ratios: operating ratios and structural ratios. Operating ratios express relationships among various items in the income statement. The dollar figures in the income statement are converted to percentages that compare individual statement items to total net sales for the period. Net sales equal 100 percent and the other percentages are obtained by dividing each item's dollar amount by the net sales figure. These ratios reveal what part of each sales dollar is gross profit after inventory is paid for, and how the various expenses reduce this profit. Thus, operating ratios provide a closer examination of the expenses incurred in producing income and can be used as tools to lower costs, improve efficiency, and increase profiability.

In review, the following basic elements should be included in an income statement, and are used to compute the operating ratios. First, the business manager must determine a net sales figure for the period. Net sales are defined as gross sales less returns and allowances, cash discounts, and estimated uncollectibles. Next, cost of goods sold is calculated. Cost of goods sold is defined as beginning inventory at cost, plus net purchases, less ending inventory at cost. This provides a gross profit figure (or gross margin), which equals net sales less cost of goods sold.

Operating expenses are next, grouped usually into selling, administrative, and general. They include all cash and noncash expenses incurred in the business operation, such as salaries, rent, utilities, supplies, insurance, taxes, bad debts, owner's withdrawals, advertising, and depreciation. Gross profit less total operating expenses equals net profit, less interest expense equals net income before taxes. Finally, taxes are accounted for. Figure 14–3 presents a typical income statement.

The operating ratios reveal the relationship of cost of sales to sales, total expenses to gross profit, and net profit to net sales. In addition, ratios for individual expense items will indicate the relative importance of each.

**FIGURE 14-3**
**Income statement (year ending December 31, 1975)**

Gross sales
  Less: Returns and allowances
        Cash discounts
        Estimated uncollectables
Net sales
Cost of goods sold:
  Inventory, January 1, 1975
  Cost of goods purchased
  Total goods available
    Less: Inventory, December 31, 1975
  Cost of goods sold
Gross profit (i.e., net sales minus cost of goods sold)
Operating expenses:
  General and administrative expenses
  Selling expenses
    Total operating expenses
  Net operating income (i.e., gross profit minus total operating expenses)
    Less: Interest expense
Equals net income before income taxes
  Less: Income taxes
Equals net income after income taxes

Also important are changes in the relationship of each component of the income statement to changes in sales from period to period. Thus, a comparative analysis of operating ratios over a period of time affords a valuable analysis of internal trends with reference to cost of sales and expenses.

The second approach to ratio analysis involves the use of structural ratios. Structural ratios are those that show the relationships between various balance sheet items; and those that compare an item on the balance sheet with one on the income statement.

As in the case of operating ratios, the relationships are expressed as percentages or ratios, and provide the basis for comparisons historically within the firm, or with the experience of other businesses in the same industry. The structural ratios presented below are suggested as the most meaningful and useful in most cases.

## Structural ratios pertaining to the working capital position

It has been established that working capital must be both adequate in amount and liquid in nature to accomplish the liquidity and profitability objectives. It follows that an analysis of the firm's cash flow cycle reflects the overall efficiency of management. Furthermore, an analysis of the cash flow cycle through the use of various structural ratios will point up such things as the impact of the scale of operations on cash requirements, the need to arrange additional financing before cash is exhausted, and the danger of overbuying and overexpansion. The following ratios are suggested to analyze the working capital position.

   *Current ratio.* The current ratio relates current assets to current liabilities and is intended to give some indication of the firm's solvency; the ability to pay bills as they come due. On the current asset side, the principal items are cash, accounts receivable, and inventories; the current liabilities include accounts payable and notes payable.

   Unfortunately, the current ratio alone can be very misleading as an indication of bill-paying ability. The reason is that inventories are included as a current asset, and certain portions of inventory may not be very liquid in a current sense. In fact, an inventory problem resulting from overbuying or obsolete items would not be indicated by the current ratio.

   Many financial management textbooks state that a two-to-one current ratio, or better, is considered good. Reliance on "rules of thumb," however, can be dangerous, and a current ratio of two-to-one is a good example. A cash-poor firm unable to pay its bills on time or unable to take advantage of trade discounts can have a current ratio of two-to-one or better. In fact, firms have been known to go bankrupt with a current ratio of two-to-one.

   Obviously, if the current ratio is low, the firm may encounter difficulty in paying bills. On the other hand, a current ratio that is too high reduces profitability. The difficulty arises out of the timing of cash flows (discussed earlier). A high current ratio may represent excessive cash balances, excessive inventories, or some questionable accounts receivable. Thus, all one can conclude is that a current ratio that appears to be too high or too low demands further analysis.

   *Quick ratio.* A second ratio that is helpful in evaluating past performance and the present position is the quick ratio. The quick ratio relates current assets to current liabilities just as the current ratio, but on the asset side inventories are omitted. Thus, it is the quick ratio which gives a truer indication of the firm's ability to pay bills.

   Cash is the most liquid asset. Accounts receivable represent sales that have been made, but until these accounts are collected they represent dollars that are one step removed from cash. Inventories, on the other hand, are stocked in anticipation of future sales that may or may not materialize. Thus, in terms of liquidity inventories are two steps removed from cash.

   It follows that a more valid test of the ability of a firm to produce cash flow to meet current liabilities is the test that excludes inventories. The firm that has a good deal of obsolete and slow-moving inventory as a result of overbuying will not see the problem in the current ratio; but it will certainly be evident in the quick ratio.

   *Percentage composition of current assets.* The third suggested aid in an analysis of the working capital or current position is to take each of the current asset items as a percentage of total current assets. Such a breakdown of cash, receivables, and inventories provides insight into the liquidity position that cannot be provided by either the current ratio or the quick ratio. Significant variation from what is expected in the percent composition of current assets at any particular time should be examined closely.

*Average collection period.* One of the most important indicators of current conditions in a business that sells on credit is the average collection period. The average collection period indicates how liquid the receivables are by indicating the average number of days each dollar of credit sales is outstanding. The calculation involves dividing the annual credit sales figure by 360 to determine the credit sales per day. Then the daily credit sales figure is divided into accounts receivable. The result is the average collection period expressed in days.

The average collection period proves most useful when watched over time. An average collection period that is increasing may indicate poor collection policies or an increase in slow-paying accounts. On the other hand, an average collection period that is too short may indicate credit policies that are too strict. Customers that are potentially profitable are being turned away.

An important relationship to note is that between the average collection period and the firm's credit terms. Credit terms of 30 days and an average collection period of 42 days may call for an analysis of individual accounts. A lax credit policy can be dangerous and costly, for the continued congestion of funds in receivables cuts down the flow of funds for reinvestment in inventories.

*Inventory turnover.* This ratio is the cost of goods sold divided by average inventory at cost. It tells the manager how rapidly dollars are flowing through inventory, and how current is the inventory.[2]

An inventory turnover that appears too low may indicate overbuying or a hard core of obsolete or slow-moving merchandise. An inventory turnover that is too high may indicate incomplete stocks and a frequent sacrifice of sales. Many of the financial problems of small business can be traced to poor inventory management. It is the inventory turnover ratio that will be indicative of such problems.

*Net sales to working capital.* Known also as turnover of working capital, this ratio measures how actively the firm's cash is being put to work in terms of sales. Net working capital is defined as current assets minus current liabilities.

---

[2] Inventory turnover may also be calculated by dividing sales by average inventory at market price. The important point is to recognize that, regardless of the formula used, cost of goods sold cannot be related to the market value of inventory; nor can sales be used with inventory at cost.

If the ratio of net sales to working capital is low, the manager should either reduce working capital or increase sales. On the other hand, a business with a high turnover of working capital is attempting to support too large a volume of business with its present level of working capital investment. Such a business may appear very profitable, but sales supported by a thin working capital position establish a balance of cash inflows and outflows so delicate that it may be easily upset—by such things as a sudden loss of sales, or a deterioration in accounts receivable turnover. The obvious solution in such a case is additional working capital, or a reduction in sales through price increases or tighter credit terms.

## Structural ratios pertaining to the net worth position

The second set of structural ratios useful to the small business manager deals with net worth. Recall that net worth is the excess of total assets over total liabilities. It represents the owner's equity in the business.

Net worth ratios are valuable in comparing equity interests to creditor interests, in evaluating profitability, and in analyzing investment in fixed assets. It is important that net worth in the net worth ratios is defined as tangible net worth. Intangible assets such as goodwill, patents, and copyrights should be ignored.

*Debt-to-net-worth ratio.* One of the most important of the net worth ratios is the debt-to-net-worth relationship. It relates total debt to tangible net worth, which compares the dollars that creditors have contributed in financing the business to the dollars the owners have contributed. Creditors use this relationship to get some indication of the risk involved in lending to the firm. For instance, if the debt-to-net-worth ratio is one to one, the assets can decline 50 percent in value before threatening the solvency of the business. On the other hand, if there are two dollars of debt per dollar of equity, the assets can decline only 33 percent in value.

If the debt-to-net-worth ratio is too high, the manager will find it difficult to borrow additional funds. On the other hand, if the debt-to-net-worth relationship is too low, profits are probably being sacrificed.

Many small business managers maintain the idea that they should finance as much as possible from equity sources to lend stability to their financial position. Such stability may be very costly, however, in terms of profit. For instance, the financing of seasonal inventory out of equity means that in the off-season these funds will be idle and virtually nonproductive. In such a case, the more profitable decision is to borrow, and creditors would assume this to be a legitimate demand for credit.

Thus, the debt-to-net-worth relationship must be such that the manager is using credit in the most efficient manner in terms of profit. This means there is some level of debt appropriate at any given time for a particular business. In terms of flexibility and growth, the small business manager should not overborrow; in terms of profitability, the manager should not underborrow.

*Fixed assets to net worth.* Some small business owners have the tendency to overinvest in fixed assets. Particularly after a period of very profitable operations the urge is to modernize and expand, often in excess. The ratio of fixed assets to net worth monitors a firm's position in this respect.

*Net profit to net worth.* Finally, it is important to analyze profit in terms of net worth. Net profit expressed as a percent of net worth indicates the return on the owner's equity in the business. The value of such a figure is apparent, but it should not be confused with the earning power of the firm.

Earning power, as previously explained, refers to the return to the operating assets of the business. Earning power indicates the efficiency with which the total assets of the firm are being utilized. The net-profit-to-net-worth relationship indicates the efficiency with which the owner's funds are being utilized. Whether or not a particular return to net worth is acceptable depends on the owner's individual appraisal of risk and a personal judgment as to what is adequate. Of course, guidelines on profitability are also available from the various sources of industrial information mentioned above.

### Summary and conclusions on financial analysis

The foregoing discussion cites the more important financial ratios and relationships that should be periodically calculated, recorded, and analyzed to provide insight into the financial position of the firm.

In using ratios, one must keep in mind the significance and limitations of each. Furthermore, in any type of analysis such as this, the manager must keep in mind the overall position of the firm.

The first step is to take particular care in selecting the standards for comparison, both historical and industrial. Then any variation from the norms demands explanation. Furthermore, marked differences that occur over time also require explanation.

As for historical standards, it is suggested that the ratios be recorded on a monthly basis over a two-year moving period. An analysis of such records should then establish distinct patterns which will be helpful in establishing guidelines for performance. Historical comparisons beyond two years are probably of little relevance and can be ignored.

Despite the fact that rules of thumb and standards quoted by outside sources are available, such guidelines must be used with caution. Each business venture is unique, and despite many apparent similarities between two firms, they may be different enough to make a comparison on a financial or operating basis of limited value.

The small business manager must be concerned with the most efficient use of funds, and the simple tools of ratio analysis provide a means for evaluating management policies. Despite its shortcomings, ratio analysis aids the financial manager in planning the needs for funds. Furthermore, ratio analysis can indicate when funds management policies should be altered to afford a more efficient and profitable utilization of the firm's financial resources.

## CASH BUDGETING AND THE PLANNING FUNCTION

Another principal tool in the planning function is the cash budget. A cash budget represents the manager's plans for the future expressed in dollars and cents. The management of day-to-day operations from a financial point of view involves anticipating the timing of cash receipts and disbursements. The cash budget is a prediction of future cash flows based on an expected level of sales volume.

A good cash budget is important because it charts the course of the business in reaching its liquidity objective and, thus, in maximizing profits. Furthermore, the comparison of actual experience with budgeted experience (once the operating results are in) provides a basis for improving future performance. The cash budget is concerned with short-term needs only. Consideration of long-term needs for funds is treated in the following chapter.

The first problem in constructing a cash budget is selecting the time period. The budget period must be long enough to permit effective planning. If it is too short, significant cash flows just beyond the period may be overlooked. On the other hand, if the period is too long, the chance of errors in forecasting is increased.

Once the budget is completed, it is reviewed on a regular basis throughout the period and adjustments in the various estimates are made as warranted. The review interval may be monthly, or even more frequent if desired.

In general, there are no hard-and-fast rules for good cash budgeting. However, it is important that the budgeting procedures be tailored to the unique characteristics of the firm.

### Preparation of the cash budget

The cash budget records the movement of cash into inventories, receivables, and back into cash. It anticipates cash inflows and outflows over some future period of time. Thus, the cash budget indicates future needs for short-term funds by showing when (in the period) cash outflows will exceed cash inflows and additional funds will be needed; and when (in the period) cash inflows will exceed cash outflows and cash will

232

build up. Given some cash balance going into the period, cash inflows and outflows are matched to indicate a net increase or net decrease in the cash balance by the end of the budgetary period.

As previously noted, the first step is to select the budget time period. In a seasonal business it is suggested the budget cover the season and be reviewed at least monthly. In a nonseasonal business, with sales reasonably constant, a budget period of six months is usually appropriate.

The second step in preparing the cash budget is to estimate sales. In predicting sales, the manager must consider internal factors as well as external factors. From an internal point of view, historical information on past sales in particular product lines is usually helpful. From an external point of view, a number of factors should be considered. For instance, what would be the effect on sales of a change in price? What would be the effect on sales of additional advertising; or changes in quality and styling? What would be the effect on sales of adding a product line? What would be the competitor reaction to any action the manager takes to affect sales?

Having considered both the internal and the external factors, the sales forecast itself requires a great deal of experience and good judgment if it is to be reliable. And, remember, the cash budget is only as good as the sales forecast.

The following example is provided to demonstrate the preparation of a cash budget for a small retail firm. The IKC Gift Shop is an exclusive gift shop that has peak sales during the Christmas season. The objective is to prepare a cash budget for IKC for the period August 1 to January 31. The purpose is to examine cash flows in the period and expose any problems the firm may encounter in meeting its liquidity objective.

Conditions in the IKC Gift Shop are as follows:

1.  The gift shop caters to the wealthy class in a small Chicago suburb and thus offers credit to its customers. As a result, only 40 percent of total sales is for cash. The other 60 percent of sales is on an open-book account basis.
2.  Of the credit sales, an average of 75 percent is collected in the first month following the sale and 25 percent is collected in the second month following the sale.
3.  The gross profit margin on sales averages 30 percent; thus the cost of goods sold equals 70 percent of sales.
4.  All inventory purchases are paid for during the month of purchase.
5.  A basic inventory of $15,000 (cost) is always maintained, and the store policy is to purchase adequate inventory each month to cover the following month's sales.
6.  A minimum cash balance of $5,000 must be maintained.
7.  Accrued wages and salaries and other liabilities remain unchanged.
8.  Additional financing necessary will be in multiples of $1,000.

The IKC balance sheet dated August 1 appears as follows:

| | | | |
|---|---|---|---|
| Cash | $11,200 | Accrued wages and salaries | $ 1,000 |
| Accounts receivable | 15,900 | Other liabilities | 1,720 |
| Inventory | 29,700 | Capital | 67,680 |
| Furniture and fixtures | 13,600 | | |
| | $70,400 | | $70,400 |

Past sales amounted to $19,000 in June and $17,000 in July, and the sales forecast through February is available as follows:

| | |
|---|---|
| August | $21,000 |
| September | 33,000 |
| October | 29,000 |
| November | 45,000 |
| December | 55,000 |
| January | 25,000 |
| February | 23,000 |

Monthly expense information available is as follows:

*Wages and salaries*

| | |
|---|---|
| August | $2,000 |
| September | 2,200 |
| October | 2,200 |
| November | 2,400 |
| December | 2,400 |
| January | 2,000 |

*Rent:* $600 per month.
*Other expenses:* 2 percent of monthly sales.

Given the above information, it is now possible to start preparing a cash budget for the period. The record of monthly cash inflows and outflows will indicate those months in which additional cash will be needed, and those months when surplus cash will be available. In other words, the cash budget will indicate when borrowing will be needed during the season; in what amount; and when it will be possible for IKC to repay the loan.

The first step is to prepare a work sheet that will give total receipt figures month by month. Figure 14–4 shows the work sheet for the IKC Gift Shop. As indicated, the receipt figures are based on the relationship between credit sales and cash sales, and the collection pattern of credit sales.

Given the total receipt figures, the cash budget can now be prepared. The cash budget is divided into two types of transactions. The operating transactions record the effect of the monthly cash inflows and outflows on the cash position. The financial transactions follow the operating transactions and record the adjustments necessary in the monthly cash balance to provide the funds to carry the firm through the budgeted period. The operating transactions for the IKC Gift Shop are shown in Figure 14–5.

As apparent in Figure 14–5, during the months of August through

FIGURE 14–4
IKC Gift Shop work sheet

| | June | July | August | September | October | November | December | January |
|---|---|---|---|---|---|---|---|---|
| Sales (forecasted) . . | $19,000 | $17,000 | $21,000 | $33,000 | $29,000 | $45,000 | $55,000 | $25,000 |
| Credit sales (60% of monthly sales) . . . | 11,400 | 10,200 | 12,600 | 19,800 | 17,400 | 27,000 | 33,000 | 15,000 |
| Collections: (75% of previous month's credit sales) . . | | $ 8,550 | $ 7,650 | $ 9,450 | $14,850 | $13,050 | $20,250 | $24,750 |
| (25% of credit sales two months hence) | | | 2,850 | 2,550 | 3,150 | 4,950 | 4,350 | 6,750 |
| Cash sales (40% of monthly sales) . . | | | 8,400 | 13,200 | 11,600 | 18,000 | 22,000 | 10,000 |
| Total Monthly Cash Receipts | | | $18,900 | $25,200 | $29,600 | $36,000 | $46,600 | $41,500 |

November (except for September) the relationship between cash inflows and outflows is such that it is impossible for IKC to maintain its minimum cash balance requirement without making temporary additions to the cash balance. Thus, the questions are: how much cash will be needed; when is it needed; and when can IKC be expected to pay it back? These questions are based on the assumption that for a seasonal increase in inventory IKC will use debt of some sort, either trade credit from suppliers or a self-liquidating inventory loan from a commercial bank.

The answers to the how much, when, and how long questions are provided in the financial transactions section of the cash budget. The financial transactions for the IKC Gift Shop are recorded in Figure 14–6.

Figure 14–6 provides all the information necessary to plan IKC's need for short-term funds. Based on the assumption that the sales forecast is valid, IKC will have to borrow up to $12,000 over a five-month period, beginning in August. Furthermore, if it is assumed the best source of such funds is a short-term bank note, the loan can easily be retired in late December and a handsome profit realized.

**FIGURE 14-7**

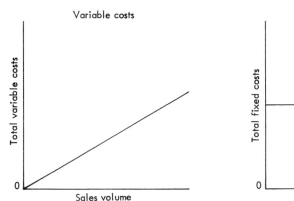
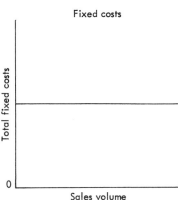

reaction of revenue (and profits) to various sales volumes under existing pricing policies. The following illustration demonstrates the application of break-even analysis.

Cloverleaf Bottlers, Incorporated, produces and bottles soft drinks. The productive capacity is 500 cases a day. Fixed costs are $100 a day and variable costs are 60 cents per case. The soft drinks sell for $1 a case.

Given this information, the level of output (i.e., the volume of sales) necessary for Cloverleaf to produce a profit can be determined. Figure 14-8 graphically gives the solution.

The fixed costs of Cloverleaf are represented in Figure 14-8 as a straight line at the level of $100, consistent with the definition of a fixed cost. The variable cost line represents variable costs of zero at zero volume, and total variable costs of $300 at capacity. Superimposed on the fixed cost line, the variable cost line also represents the total cost line; total costs being $100 at zero output (all fixed costs), and $400 at capacity ($100 fixed plus $300 variable). The revenue or price line in Figure 14-8 has its origin at zero and extends upward to $500 at capacity, which represents the price of $1 per case.

The break-even level of sales volume is represented by the intersection of the total revenue line with the total cost line; and is defined as that sales volume where total costs just equal total revenue. Notice that in Figure 14-8, the break-even level of sales volume for Cloverleaf is 250 cases.[3] This can be checked by the following simple computation.

---

[3] The algebraic solution for the break-even point is obviously much more reliable than reference to a graphic presentation. The formula $f + vx = sx$, where $f$ equals fixed cost, $v$ equals variable costs per unit, and $s$ equals selling price per unit gives the correct result. For example, in the case above:

$$\$100 + 0.60x = \$1.00x$$
$$0.40x = \$100$$
$$x = \$250$$

FIGURE 14–8
Cloverleaf Bottlers, Incorporated break-even analysis

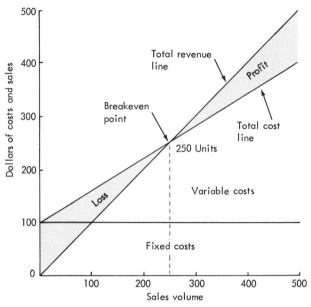

Total Income: 250 × $1     = $250
Total Expenses: Fixed costs = $100
                Variable costs = 250 × 0.60 = $150
                $100 + $150 = $250

This means that every day Cloverleaf can experience a sales volume of 250 cases or more, the operation is profitable. On the other hand, a daily sales volume of less than 250 cases fails to cover total costs.

The value of break-even analysis is now apparent. The difference between the total cost line and the revenue line indicates profit or loss at any level of sales. The higher the break-even point, the less chance the business has of operating at a profit over the long run. The lower the break-even point, the more likely is profit over the long run.

The application of break-even analysis involves two important elements. First, the break-even level of sales volume must be related to the firm's normal level of operations, and what are considered normal variations in sales. For instance, in terms of the Cloverleaf example and a break-even level of sales volume of 250 cases, the important questions are: what is considered to be the normal or average daily sales volume, and what is the expected range of sales volume over time? In a seasonal business such as soft drinks, it may be that during certain times of the year a level of operation below the break-even point is expected. If, however, operations were to continue for an extended period of time below the break-even point, due to a loss of sales or an increase in costs, steps must be taken to shift the break-even level of sales volume, or increase the average daily sales if the business is to be continued on a profitable basis. In other words, with a break-even level of 250 cases, the firm is faced with answering the question; what is the probability that the firm will ever have to operate below the 250-case level? Furthermore, if operations for a time are below the 250-case level, how long is such a condition expected to continue, and what are the reasons for such a condition? Finally, if the break-even level appears to be too high relative to what is considered to be a normal level of sales volume, what steps can be taken to shift the break-even point? The answers to these questions are important, for the relationship between the break-even level of operation and the normal level of sales volume can have an important influence on the ability of the firm to borrow funds.

The second important element to consider in the application of break-even analysis is the relationship between changes in profit and changes in sales volume. This relationship is defined as the degree of operating leverage, and equals the percent increase in net operating income divided by the percent increase in output.[4] In general terms, the degree of operating leverage reveals the probable effect on profits of expansion or contraction of sales volume starting from any given point.

For instance, at a volume of 300 cases in the Cloverleaf example, a 10 percent increase in sales volume results in a 60 percent increase in net operating income. Under such conditions the degree of operating leverage is six. Furthermore, because break-even analysis assumes straight-line relationships between changes in costs, output, and revenues, the degree of operating leverage at a sales volume of 300 cases remains constant. In other words, given the present level of sales volume of 300 cases and a degree of operating leverage of six, a one percent increase in sales volume will result in a six percent increase in operating income; a two percent increase in sales volume will increase income by twelve percent; and so on in the ratio of one to six.

What actually happens to produce a degree of operating leverage is

---

[4] The degree of operating leverage can be determined algebraically with the following formula

$$x = \frac{x(p - v)}{x(p - v) - F}$$

where $x$ equals the sales volume at which the degree of operating leverage is being determined, $p$ equals the price, $v$ equals the variable cost, and $F$ equals the fixed cost. Using the figures assumed above in the formula produces a degree of operating leverage of 6 at a level of output of 300 cases. That is,

$$300 = \frac{300(1.00 - 60)}{300(1.00 - 60) - 100} = \frac{300(0.40)}{300(0.40) - 100} = \frac{120}{20} = 6.$$

easily explained. Below the break-even level of sales the difference between sales revenue and variable costs is needed to cover fixed costs. However, once sales exceed the break-even volume and all fixed costs are covered, sales revenue less variable cost equals profit. Thus, a relatively small increase in sales volume above the break-even point may produce a sharp increase in profits.

It should be apparent at this point that the level of fixed costs is an important determinate of both the break-even point and the degree of operating leverage. The higher the level of fixed costs to total costs, the higher will be the break-even point, i.e., the higher sales volume must be to cover total fixed costs. On the other hand, the higher the level of fixed costs, the higher will be the degree of operating leverage above the break-even point; that is, the larger will be the contribution to profit per sales dollar once the fixed costs are covered.

This presents somewhat of a dilemma for the small business manager. If the firm is operating above the break-even point, a higher level of fixed costs (a higher operating leverage) is preferred. However, increasing fixed costs to increase operating leverage raises the break-even point, which increase the possibility that the firm may, on occasion, produce below the break-even point (unprofitably). Thus, the manager must strike a compromise by attempting to attain as high a degree of operating leverage as possible, consistent with a break-even point that is comfortably attainable.

In concluding this discussion of break-even analysis, brief consideration is given to those factors that could shift the break-even level of sales, and to limitations of the analysis. First, any change in pricing policy (in graphic terms) affects the slope of the total revenue line. Price increases lower the break-even point; while price decreases raise the break-even level of sales. Second, any changes in the variable cost per unit (in graphic terms) affect the slope of the total cost line. Increases in variable costs raise the break-even level of sales; while decreases lower the break-even point. Finally, any changes in fixed costs affect the height of the total cost line. If fixed costs are increased, break-even will be higher; while decreases in fixed costs lower the break-even level of sales.

There are three principal limitations of break-even analysis. First, the analysis represents a short-run static relationship of costs to sales volume. The data used are historical, and any variation in conditions that affect costs will quickly change the relationship. Second, the relationships indicated in the graphic presentation are represented as straight-line functions, which may or may not hold true for all levels of operation. For instance, variable costs may increase as sales volume increases to high levels and approaches capacity. Finally, the graphic analysis assumes that regardless of sales volume, the price is constant. This may not hold true if price decreases are necessary to increase volume; or if a firm reduces price to maintain sales volume when business is slow.

Despite its shortcomings, break-even analysis provides the small business manager with insight into the relationship between costs, revenue, and sales—insight into the ability of the business to produce a profit.

## SUMMARY ON THE PLANNING FUNCTION

The role of the small business owner as financial manager involves planning the needs for funds, acquiring the needed funds, and managing the acquired funds. The planning function is the basis of this chapter.

An important aspect of the planning function is to examine the present financial position and the past performance of the firm. This chapter presented a framework of financial ratios that help satisfy this need and give insight into the potential of the firm. The ratios also expose problems of a financial nature that demand attention.

An indispensable part of the planning function is the cash budget. The cash budget represents a projection of cash inflows and cash outflows. It indicates those periods when borrowing may be necessary, what amount of borrowing may be necessary, and when funds will be available to retire the debt. Reliability of the cash budget depends on the accuracy of the sales forecast.

The cash budget is only concerned with the short-term needs for funds. The need for additions to or replacement of fixed assets involves capital budgeting, which is treated in the following chapter.

Finally, break-even analysis provides a valuable tool in planning for profits. It indicates the relationship between costs, revenues, and sales volume, and thus the relationship between sales volume and profits. Furthermore, given some level of sales, break-even analysis shows the effect on profits of increasing or decreasing sales volume.

## QUESTIONS

1.  What are the two basic objectives of the small business owner as financial manager?
2.  Discuss five important uses of cash buildup resulting from a profitable sales period.
3.  What is the typical relationship between margin and turnover? Apply the concept in a brief discussion·of two or three small businesses in your community.
4.  Discuss the financial ratios that are helpful in examining the working capital position of a small business.
5.  Why is the current ratio a poor indicator of the firm's liquidity position?

6. Why is the debt-to-net worth ratio one of the more important relationships to be considered in assessing the position of the firm?

7. Define a cash budget. What are the two important steps in preparation of a cash budget?

8. Define the break-even point and the degree of operating leverage. Discuss the means of shifting the break-even point.

9. What are the three principal limitations of break-even analysis?

10. What is the basic characteristic of those decisions that would result in an increase in the degree of operating leverage?

## PROBLEMS

1. You are the financial manager of ABC Company. The earning power of your company has shown a considerable change in the last 10 years and you want to find out why. So you proceed to make an analysis of the following:

| STATEMENT OF EARNINGS (000s omitted) | *Year* 1965 | 1975 |
|---|---|---|
| Sales | $100 | $200 |
| Cost of goods sold | ( ? ) | ( ? ) |
| Gross profit | ( ? ) | ( ? ) |
| Operating expenses | ( ? ) | ( ? ) |
| Net operating income* | $ 20 | $ 80 |
| Interest expenses | ( ? ) | ( ? ) |
| Taxable income | ( ? ) | ( ? ) |
| Taxes 50% | ( ? ) | ( ? ) |
| Income after taxes | ( ? ) | ( ? ) |
| Preferred dividends | ( ? ) | ( ? ) |
| Net income available to residual owners | ( ? ) | ( ? ) |

\* The company has no nonoperating assets or nonoperating income.

| BALANCE SHEET ITEMS (000s omitted) | *Year* 1965 | 1975 |
|---|---|---|
| Net operating assets* | $200 | $300 |
| All noninterest bearing liabilities | 130 | 50 |
| 5% bonds | 40 | 160 |
| 4% preferred stock | 0 | 50 |
| Common stock capital account | 10 | 10 |
| Capital in excess of par value | 10 | 10 |
| Earned surplus | 5 | 15 |
| Reserve for corporate expansion | 5 | 5 |

\* The company has no nonoperating assets or nonoperating income.

You computed the following ratios for the years 1965 and 1975:

| | *1965* | *1975* |
|---|---|---|
| Operating ratio | 80% | 60% |
| Gross margin | 40% | 55% |

Based on the information given above write on a piece of notepaper:

a. The unsupplied figures for the statement of earnings for the years 1965 and 1975.

b. Answers to the following questions:

| | | |
|---|---|---|
| The operating margin in 1965 | ? | % |
| The operating margin in 1975 | ? | % |
| Assets turnover in 1965 | ? | times |
| Assets turnover in 1975 | ? | times |
| Earning power in 1965 | ? | % |
| Earning power in 1975 | ? | % |

c. Words to complete the following sentences:
1. The change in the operating margin from 1965 to 1975 could be accounted for by—
2. The change in turnover from 1965 to 1975 could be accounted for by—
3. The change in earning power from 1965 to 1975 could be accounted for by—

2. We have the following information available for Company A:

| | |
|---|---|
| Selling price per unit | $2.00 |
| Variable cost per unit | $1.20 |
| Fixed costs | $40,000 |
| Units produced and sold | $60,000 |

## Questions

1. Compute the break-even point in units for Company A.
2. What is the degree of operating leverage at 60,000 units?
3. Using the information shown below in the balance sheet, calculate the following:
   Turnover of operating assets.
   Average collection period (based on 360 days).
   Gross profit percentage.
   Inventory turnover (based on year-end inventory).
   Debt to net worth.
   Acid test ratio.

### BALANCE SHEET

| ASSETS | | LIABILITIES AND CAPITAL | |
|---|---|---|---|
| Cash | $ 62,500 | Notes and accounts payable | $250,000 |
| Accounts receivable | 125,000 | Common stock | 200,000 |
| Inventory | 262,500 | Retained earnings | 300,000 |
| Plant and equipment | 300,000 | | |
| | $750,000 | | $750,000 |

4. Following is certain information relative to the position and business of American Stores Company:

*Current assets* as of September 30:

| | |
|---|---|
| Cash on deposit | $12,000 |
| Inventory | 30,000 |
| Accounts receivable | 10,000 |

*Current liabilities* as of September 30:

Accounts payable. . . . . . . . . . . . . . . . . . . . . . . . . . . . . . . . . . 10,000

*Recent and anticipated sales:*

September. . . . . . . . . . . . . . . . . . . . . . . . . . . . . . . . . . . . . . . 40,000
October . . . . . . . . . . . . . . . . . . . . . . . . . . . . . . . . . . . . . . . . 48,000
November . . . . . . . . . . . . . . . . . . . . . . . . . . . . . . . . . . . . . . . 60,000
December . . . . . . . . . . . . . . . . . . . . . . . . . . . . . . . . . . . . . . . 80,000
January . . . . . . . . . . . . . . . . . . . . . . . . . . . . . . . . . . . . . . . . 36,000

*Credit sales.* Sales are 75 percent for cash, and 25 percent on credit. Assume that credit accounts are all collected within 30 days from sale. The accounts receivable on September 30 represent the credit sales for September (25 percent of $40,000).

*Markup.* Gross profit averages 30 percent of sales.

*Expenses.* Salaries and wages average 15 percent of sales, rent 5 percent, depreciation (a noncash expense) 1 percent, all other expenses 4 percent. Assume that these expenses are disbursed each month.

*Net operating profit.* 5 percent.

*Purchases.* There is a basic inventory of $30,000. The policy is to purchase each month additional inventory in the amount necessary to provide for the following month's sales. Terms on purchases are 2 percent, 10 days; net 30 days. Assume payments are made in month of purchase, and all discounts are taken.

*Fixtures.* In October $600 is spent for fixtures, and in November $400 is to be expended for this purpose.

On the basis of the facts as given above, complete the following schedules on a separate piece of notepaper.

1. Complete Schedule A.

### SCHEDULE A—ESTIMATED MONTHLY DOLLAR RECEIPTS

| Item | September | October | November | December |
|---|---|---|---|---|
| Total sales . . . . . . | $40,000 | $48,000 | $60,000 | $80,000 |
| Credit sales. . . . . . | 10,000 | 12,000 | ? | ? |

| Receipts | October | November | December |
|---|---|---|---|
| Cash sales . . . . . . . . . . . . . . . | $36,000 | ? | ? |
| Collections on accounts receivable . . | 10,000 | ? | ? |

2. Complete Schedule B.

### SCHEDULE B—ESTIMATED MONTHLY CASH DISBURSEMENTS FOR PURCHASES

| Item | October | November | December |
|---|---|---|---|
| Purchases. . . . . . . . . . . . . . . . | $42,000 | ? | ? |
| Less 2 percent cash discount. . . . . . | 840 | ? | ? |
| Disbursements. . . . . . . . . . . . . . | $41,160 | ? | ? |

3. Complete Schedule C.

### SCHEDULE C—ESTIMATED MONTHLY CASH DISBURSEMENTS FOR OPERATING EXPENSES

| Item | October | November | December |
|---|---|---|---|
| Salaries and wages. . . . . . . . . . . | $ 7,200 | ? | ? |
| Rent . . . . . . . . . . . . . . . . . . | 2,400 | ? | ? |
| Other expenses . . . . . . . . . . . . . | 1,920 | ? | ? |
| Total. . . . . . . . . . . . . . . | $11,520 | ? | ? |

4. Complete Schedule D.

SCHEDULE D–ESTIMATED TOTAL MONTHLY DISBURSEMENTS

| Item | October | November | December |
|---|---|---|---|
| Purchases. | $41,160 | ? | ? |
| Operating expenses | 11,520 | ? | ? |
| Fixtures | 600 | ? | ? |
| Total | $53,280 | ? | ? |

5. Complete Schedule E.

SCHEDULE E–ESTIMATED CASH RECEIPTS AND DISBURSEMENTS

| Item | October | November | December |
|---|---|---|---|
| Receipts | $46,000 | ? | ? |
| Disbursements. | 53,280 | ? | ? |
| Net cash increase | ? | ? | ? |
| Net cash decrease | $ 7,280 | ? | ? |

6. Complete Schedule F. Include in the schedule the amount (in round thousands of dollars) necessary to keep the Cash account above a minimum of $8,000 desired at the end of each month.

SCHEDULE F–FINANCING REQUIRED BY AMERICAN STORES COMPANY

| Item | October | November | December |
|---|---|---|---|
| Opening cash | $12,000 | ? | ? |
| Net cash increase | ? | ? | ? |
| Net cash decrease | 7,280 | ? | ? |
| Cash position before financing | $ 4,720 | ? | ? |
| Financing required | 4,000 | ? | ? |
| Financing retired | ? | ? | ? |
| Closing balance | 8,720 | ? | ? |
| | ? | ? | ? |

# BIBLIOGRAPHY

Engler, George N. *Business Financial Management,* chaps. 1, 3, 4, 8, and 12. Dallas, Tex.: Business Publications, 1975.

Helfert, Erich A. *Techniques of Financial Analysis,* chaps. 1, 2, and 3. 3d ed. Homewood, Ill.: Richard D. Irwin, 1972. Helfert gives a concise treatment of the basic fundamentals of finance. This is a good quick-reference manual.

Hunt, Pearson; Williams, Charles M.; and Donaldson, Gordon. *Basic Business Finance,* chaps 1, 6, and 7. Homewood, Ill.: Richard D. Irwin, 1974. This is a good basic finance book.

Johnson, Robert W. *Financial Management,* chaps. 1, 3, 4, and 9. 4th ed. Boston, Mass.: Allyn & Bacon, 1971. A good, easy-to-read treatment of financial management.

# 15

# Financial management in the small business—Part 2

The preceding chapter discussed planning the needs for funds. The purpose of this chapter is to consider the acquisition and management of funds. Also included in this chapter is a section on capital budgeting—the techniques for determining when additional long-term investment opportunities are desirable.

## FACTORS TO CONSIDER IN THE ACQUISITION OF FUNDS

Chapter 12 was concerned with a description of the various sources of funds available to the small business. Now it is time to look at the factors that must be considered in determining the particular source of funds that is appropriate for a particular use. First, it is important that the source of funds be consistent with the use. For example, if the cash budget indicates a temporary need for increases in current assets (inventory, accounts receivable, and cash), short-term sources should be used. On the other hand, if additions to fixed assets are needed, long-term funds should be used. Thus, the small business manager must distinguish between permanent and temporary needs to determine the type of funds he or she is to seek in financing those needs. Generally speaking, it is desirable to finance fixed assets and permanent current assets with long-term debt and equity. The particular mix of debt and equity in any situation will depend upon a number of other factors to be considered below.

### Matching the source of funds with the use

The reason for financing a fixed or permanent asset with permanent funds is related to the cash flows obtained from the asset. Through the sale of a product or the performance of a service, the small business manager obtains a cash inflow which covers the direct costs of operation, the recovery of a portion of the investment in the fixed assets, and profit. However, because fixed assets are normally used for a number of years, the recovery of such an investment is a slow process. In such a case it would be unwise to promise to repay a creditor who has financed a fixed asset at a rate faster than cash inflows can be generated from the use of the asset.

Looking at the problem from the short-term side, the higher the proportion of temporary current assets employed, the greater the need for short-term debt. The argument against using long-term debt or equity to finance temporary current assets is related to the profit objective of the firm. That is, as inventories are sold and accounts receivable turn into cash the excess cash should be used to reduce debt, for it would be unprofitable to pay interest on a loan when the borrowed funds were not being utilized. Furthermore, if temporary current asset needs were financed with equity funds, the use of this money in the off-season in cash or short-term securities would represent an unprofitable investment of owners' capital.

In summary, a principal objective of the manager in determining the appropriate source of funds is to finance temporary current asset needs with flexible short-term debt that will expand and contract with corresponding fluctuations in the assets. On the other hand, in financing fixed assets, long-term debt and equity are required because of the extended period involved in recovering the investment. However, matching the source of funds with the use of the funds is not the only factor that should be considered in solving the acquisition problem.

## The use of financial leverage in selecting a source of funds

Another factor to consider in selecting a source of funds is the possibility that the return on ownership capital can be improved through the use of financial leverage. The typical small business owner invests his savings, time, and effort in the business. Thus, everything should be done to maximize the return to the ownership investment. Consistent with the objective of maximizing the return to ownership capital, the manager must arrange the sources of funds to obtain as high a rate of return as possible without assuming undue risks. Stated in a more practical way, on the strength of the equity investment, some amount of debt funds can be raised outside the firm. Furthermore, it is highly probable that these funds can be employed in the firm at a return in excess of their cost. Any time this is possible, the return per dollar of ownership capital will exceed the average return per invested dollar; and this is favorable financial leverage. For purposes of definition, financial leverage is being used any time a portion of the assets are financed with funds bearing a limited return. It must be noted, however, that financial leverage in any particular case may be favorable, unfavorable, or neutral, depending on the level of income. The following examples provide a better understanding of financial leverage.

Assume in Situation A that the small business manager invests $1,000 in the firm, represented by ten ownership shares worth $100 each. Now assume that the $1,000 investment produces an income stream before taxes of $60. With a corporate income tax rate of 48 percent, the tax liability equals $28.80, and earnings after taxes are $31.20, or $3.12 per ownership share. In this situation no financial leverage is being employed.

Now compare this with Situation B, where a portion of the assets are financed with debt, which requires a fixed return. Assume that the small business owner finances the $1,000 of investment through the use of $800 in equity (represented by eight $100 ownership shares) and $200 of debt at an interest cost of 5 percent. If we assume that the $60 income stream produced by the $1,000 investment remains constant, we now subtract the $10 interest charge as a before-tax expense, and come up with an earnings before taxes figure of $50. Applying the 48 percent corporate income tax rate, the tax liability is $24 and earnings after taxes equal $26, or $3.25 per ownership share. In this example, favorable financial leverage has been employed. The manager has financed a portion of the assets with funds bearing a limited return, and has been able to earn on those assets an amount in excess of the cost of the borrowed funds. Hence, the return per ownership share exceeds that available under the all-equity situation.

As previously noted, the desirability of using financial leverage is largely dependent upon the level of income. The next example illustrates this important point. With the capital structure assumed above of $800 equity (eight ownership shares), and $200 of debt at a cost of 5 percent, notice what happens when the income stream produced by the $1,000 investment drops from $60 to $30. The interest charge on the debt remains at $10; hence before-tax earnings equals $20. Applying the 48 percent corporate income tax rate, the tax liability equals $9.60 and after-tax income equals $10.40, or $1.30 per share.

In order to prove that financial leverage is not favorable in this particular situation, compare the return per ownership share of $1.30 with the return per share under an all-equity capital structure and an income stream of $30. In such a case, a 48 percent tax rate would produce an income tax liability of $14.40 and thus, after-tax income would equal $15.60, or $1.56 a share. Thus, with an income stream before taxes of $30 financial leverage is unfavorable; because the return per ownership share is greater with the all-equity capital structure than with the debt and equity mix.

Realizing the importance of the income stream in determining whether financial leverage is favorable or unfavorable, it is apparent there is a break-even level of income at which (in terms of return to ownership shares) it is a matter of indifference what debt-equity mix is used. For example, in the illustration above, assume an income stream of $50. In the levered situation, before-tax income equals $40, the tax liability equals $19.20 and the after-tax income available to equity equals $20.80, or $2.60 per share. Furthermore, with the all-equity structure and a $50 income stream, the tax liability equals $24, the after-tax income equals $26, and the return per ownership share is also $2.60. Thus, at income-before-interest-and-taxes of $50 it is a matter of indifference what the capital structure is. For further proof, assume debt of $400 and equity of only $600. With income of $50 in this case, the interest charge has increased to $20; hence income before taxes equals $30. Applying the 48 percent corporate income tax rate, the tax liability equals $14.40, after-tax income equals $15.60, and the return per share, as expected, is $2.60.

In conclusion, the decision to use financial leverage is largely dependent upon the expected level of income. In deciding on the use of leverage, the break-even level of income should be compared with the expected level of income.[1] If it appears the chances are better than 50–50 that earnings before interest and taxes will exceed the break-even level, the manager might decide to use some financial leverage. However, the comparison does not tell how much financial leverage to use. The amount of financial leverage that should be used in any particular situation is directly related to the probability that earnings before interest and taxes will exceed the break-even level and the amount by which they are expected to exceed that level.

## Other factors to be considered in selecting the source of funds

In addition to suitability and income considerations in selecting the appropriate source of funds there are the factors of risk, control, flexibility, and timing. The factor of risk is directly related to the financial leverage decision. Any time debt is used the manager must relinquish a prior claim on income and the firm's assets to the creditor. This means if the business firm gets into financial difficulty, the equity contributors will be the first

---

[1] The break-even level of earnings before interest and taxes may be computed by use of the following formula. If $X$ equals earnings before interest and taxes at the break-even level, $K^1$ equals the number of ownership shares outstanding when debt financing is not used, $K^2$ = the number of ownership shares outstanding when both debt and equity are used, $I$ = the dollar amount of interest on the debt, and $T$ = the corporate income tax rate, then the break-even level of income before interest and taxes may be computed as follows:

$$\frac{X(1-T)}{K^1} = \frac{(X-I)(1-T)}{K^2}$$

Applying this formula to the examples used above:

$$\frac{0.52X}{10} = \frac{0.52(X-20)}{6}, X = \$50.$$

to sacrifice their claims on income and the assets. Thus, the decision to use financial leverage involves a comparison of the possible benefits with the risks that are inherent in the use of debt in the capital structure.

Another important consideration in selecting the source of funds is the desire of the small business owner to maintain control of the firm. In the sole proprietorship, the owner has complete freedom of control. However, an unwillingness to bring in outsiders to share control may also limit the ability to raise additional funds.

In the partnership, all partner-owners normally have an equal voice in management; whereas in the corporation each common shareholder is entitled to vote in proportion to the number of shares owned. If the primary objective of the owner or owners is to maintain control, it would appear best to raise funds from creditor sources. But the employment of this policy could prove to be a paradox, for if the owners borrow more than they can service or repay, the creditors may seize the assets of the firm to satisfy their claims. In an attempt to keep control all control is lost. Therefore, it may be safer to sacrifice a measure of control by increasing equity than to run the risk of losing control to creditors by using too much debt.

Flexibility means having as many alternative sources of funds open as possible. Such a position enhances the manager's bargaining power when dealing with a prospective supplier of funds. If the manager is already overextended in terms of debt a serious limitation is imposed on the availability of additional funds. Although debt funds may be generally available at attractive rates, it may be impossible to borrow. Prospective lenders are much interested in the debt-equity relationship. Thus, the small business manager must recognize the need for balance in the sources of funds, for it is this balance that provides flexibility.

The last factor to consider in selecting the source of funds is timing. Timing is closely related to flexibility, for an important consequence of flexibility is that it enables the manager to seize opportunities that minimize the cost of borrowing. Of course, in certain instances, funds will be needed and must be obtained even if they are relatively costly. But any time the manager is in the market for funds, the present costs of raising capital should be compared with future expected costs. It may be wise to delay a particular investment for three to six months if the cost savings from lower interest rates is significant.

In conclusion, determining the particular source of funds to be used in financing the business should be based on the factors of suitability, income, risk, control, flexibility, and timing. There is no simple, clear-cut method of assessing the relative importance of these factors in any particular situation. Human judgment based on experience and knowledge is a necessary ingredient in planning the types of funds to be sought.

## ASSET MANAGEMENT

Once the small business manager has planned the need for funds and selected the particular sources of funds that are most appropriate to finance those needs, there remains the continuing job of ensuring that the funds are employed efficiently.

As far as cash management is concerned, the problem is predicting discrepancies between inflows and outflows. The basic tool used to forecast these discrepancies is the cash budget, discussed in Chapter 14.

In addition to the predictable cash flow discrepancies revealed in the cash budget, there is also the possibility of unpredictable discrepancies. Such discrepancies could result from such factors as a labor strike, bad weather, or the financial problems of certain customers. Because any of these events could either interrupt cash inflow or cause a sudden cash outflow, the manager should maintain a certain portion of the cash balance to meet these situations. Cash maintained for these purposes should be considered as a type of insurance. The amount of cash necessary to allow for such discrepancies is a matter of judgment, based on experience.

The size of the cash balance maintained to meet cash outflows will depend somewhat upon the availability of funds. As a general rule, the better the firm's credit standing, the smaller the amount of cash necessary to keep on hand. With an excellent credit rating, sources of funds will normally be available to supply the cash necessary to cover an unforeseen drain. Thus, good cash management involves the establishment and maintenance of a good credit standing.

In addition to having external sources of funds available to supply needed cash there are also means of producing funds internally to meet unexpected or unusually large drains of cash, other than from the owner's own cash reserve. For example, a small business manager might sell and lease back machinery and equipment. Another possibility is the sale of accounts receivable.

In addition to the problems involved in controlling the outflow of cash, another problem is making certain incoming cash actually ends up in the bank account or in the cash drawer; not in the pockets of some employee. This is not uncommon because very few small firms are able to adopt the elaborate precautions available to a larger company. Incoming cash can be fraudulently diverted in a number of ways. Payments on accounts receivable may be "pocketed" and an entry made in the customer's account to show that it was written off as a bad debt, or that merchandise was returned and the appropriate credit was given. Probably the best solution to this problem is to organize the handling of incoming cash into several steps, each step handled by a different employee. Then a cash leakage would require the collusion of a number of people.

Opportunities for fraud are also present in cash flowing out of the business. Payment may be made to nonexistent suppliers or funds may be withdrawn for fictitious purposes. Once again, probably the best control device is simply to divide the payment process into various steps so that several employees are involved.

It should be mentioned at this point that the small business manager may want to consider bonding those employees that frequently handle relatively large sums of money or handle cash on a day-to-day basis. The bonding of employees is discussed in Chapter 19.

Discount terms will have some effect on the inflow of cash. The objective of discount terms is to persuade the customer to pay his account during the discount period.

On the other hand, the small business manager should delay cash disbursements for purchases as long as possible. If materials are purchased on terms of 2/10 net 30, payment should be made by the 10th day to obtain the 2 percent cash discount, but there is no advantage in paying the account on the first or second day. By delaying payment until the last day, the funds can be usefully employed for an additional eight or nine days.

Another problem in cash management is the use of excess cash. If cash is only idle temporarily, soon to be reemployed in the firm, the manager should earn some small return on these funds. The reason the return will be small is obvious; the principal concern is to invest the funds so they can be quickly converted into cash when needed.

Probably the best investment for this purpose is U.S. Treasury bills or high-grade commercial paper. Since these securities will be redeemed at their face value, the manager does not need to be concerned about intervening fluctuations in their market value. If the period during which the funds will be idle is highly predictable and relatively long, a savings account or certificates of deposit at a commercial bank may prove useful. The problem associated with the savings account, however, is that advance notice of withdrawals could be necessary, and the funds may have to be on deposit for a certain minimum number of days in order to draw any interest.

In summarizing the management of cash, recognition must be given to the timing problem that results from certain predictable and unpredictable discrepancies in cash flows. It is much more difficult to judge whether cash is inadequate than if it is excessive, because failure to maintain adequate cash balances is much less apparent. Probably the best approach is to compare cash balances over time within the firm itself and with other firms in the industry, if this is possible. Useful bases for comparisons are the percentages of cash to sales, cash to current assets, and cash to current liabilities. If the percentages vary considerably over time within the firm, or if they vary from those typical for other firms in the industry, indications are that cash management policies need improvement.

## Management of accounts receivable

The management of accounts receivable involves controlling the level, acquisition, and collection of receivables. The level of receivables is controlled by setting credit terms. Once the manager has established the credit terms, the market to which the firm appeals has been defined. Within this market, there remains the task of selecting and rejecting individual credit applicants from among all who are attracted by the credit terms. Of course in most cases, the manager must establish credit terms consistent with the terms of his competitors to be successful. Thus, in establishing the credit sales program, the credit terms customary in the industry must be taken into consideration.

Once the credit terms and standards have been set, the manager will have little impact on the level of receivables. The level of credit sales will vary with the general level of business activity. Although the level of receivables may be affected by rejecting certain credit applications, and by adopting aggressive collection policies; these activities have a smaller effect on the level of receivables than the initial and fundamental decisions concerning the terms on which credit will be offered, and the overall credit standards to be applied.

Once the manager has some idea of the quality of credit applicant to accept, some investigative procedures for examining credit applicants must be developed. Additionally, controlling the collections of receivables involves establishing a systematic and efficient collections program.

In administering a credit program a credit policy that is too restrictive may involve a sacrifice of sales and also increase the cost of the program. On the other hand, too lenient a credit policy may increase bad debts to unacceptable levels.

Any evaluation of the credit sales program is difficult. One valuable tool of analysis is the average collection period. As discussed in Chapter 14, it measures: the efficiency of granting credit and collecting past-due accounts.

Another possible measure of credit program performance is to compare the number of orders rejected to the number of credit sales. If the manager is rejecting an unusually high percentage of orders, terms may be too tight. The percentage of monthly collections on past-due accounts can also be compared to the accounts past due at the beginning of each month, to gain insight into the efficiency of collection activity. A more complete treatment of credit management is provided in Chapter 25.

## Management of inventory

The management of funds invested in inventory is important because in many cases inventory is the largest single asset, particularly on the current side. Equally important is the fact that inventory is the least liquid current asset; hence errors in management are not readily remedied.

As in the management of cash, the manager has the problem of reaching a compromise between too much inventory and too little inventory. Determining the right level requires a balancing of the costs and risks of carrying inventory against the benefits derived from having the inventory available. As inventory levels are increased, a point is eventually reached where the additional costs outweigh the additional benefits.

There are a number of costs associated with carrying inventory. First, there is the cost of funds invested in inventory and equipment to handle the inventory. Next, there is the cost associated with the space occupied by the inventory, which may include depreciation charges, maintenance charges, rental charges, taxes, heating and utility costs, and janitorial labor costs. Then there may be certain inventory service costs, such as taxes and insurance, the labor costs of receiving and stocking, inventory record and bookkeeping costs, pilferage costs, and deterioration costs. Finally, there may be the costs associated with the risk of a price decline, the risk of a style change, or other causes of obsolescence.

In considering the cost question, it is important to recognize those that will vary with the level of the inventory carried, and those which are fixed. For example, costs related to the space occupied usually remain fixed in the short run. On the other hand, the cost of funds tied up in inventory will vary with the level of the inventory.

The small business manager faces a number of problems in determining the best inventory level. First he must determine what quantities are most economical to buy. Is it profitable to buy in large lot sizes and incur the costs of storing the inventory, or is it more reasonable to buy in smaller lot sizes? Closely related to this is the question of safety stocks to absorb unexpected fluctuations in inventory availability or sales. Here the manager has to weigh the cost of being out of stock against the cost of maintaining the safety stock.

Also important is the lead time necessary in ordering inventory, that is, the time period involved in ordering and receiving delivery. When the lead time is long and the season is short, there may be no opportunity to replenish stocks if sales run higher than originally estimated. In such a case, sales lost are lost forever. On the other hand, if inventories are overstocked, price reductions may be necessary to clear out inventory after the seasonal peak. This of course, reduces the profit margin. If excess inventory is carried over until the next season, all the costs of storing and handling the excess are incurred.

In evaluating the effectiveness of inventory policy, calculation of inventory turnover is useful. This tool for analysis is discussed in Chapter 14. Also important is a regular check on the control of stockouts, obsolescence, and spoilage of inventory. For instance, what items are most frequently out of stock and for how long? Is there a frequent problem with inventory becoming obsolete? What percent of inventory, if any, normally represents spoilage?

Finally, the small business manager should compare actual performance with planned performance. This check of past estimates of sales with actual sales will help to improve sales forecasts in the future. One of the most frequently neglected areas in small business management is effective inventory control. A more complete discussion of inventory management is provided in Chapter 20.

## Management of fixed assets

The investment of funds in fixed assets involves the commitment of dollars over an extended period of time, usually several years. Fixed asset investment is a form of deferred expense. A cash outlay is made at one point in time, but the cost of the outlay is charged to those periods in which the use of the assets is realized.

As in inventory management, there are certain costs to consider in determining the appropriate fixed asset investment. First, there is the cost of funds to purchase the fixed assets, as well as any tools or equipment needed to service the assets. Next, the cost of space occupied by the fixed assets includes depreciation charges, maintenance charges, rental costs, taxes, and utility costs. Some fixed assets, such as machinery, have certain service costs associated with their purchase. Typical machinery service costs include property taxes, insurance costs, maintenance costs, and depreciation. Finally, there is always the risk of obsolescence. In making the fixed asset decision, the small business manager is again involved in balancing all the costs associated with buying the fixed asset with the benefits from its use.

In deciding upon a particular level of fixed asset investment, the small business manager may have to consider the problem of safety stocks. For example, a department store must be built and stocked with furniture and fixtures in order to handle peak sales periods, but during slack periods much of the furniture and fixtures remain idle. There are several ways of minimizing this safety stock of fixed assets. The department store may have special sales at particularly slow times to attract customers, or may encourage consumers to shop early and avoid the seasonal rush.

The fixed asset investment decision, whether it involves the replacement of old equipment or the purchase of new equipment, is a capital budgeting decision, and the manager must relate the net investment outlay to the net benefits the outlay will produce over time.

In evaluating the management of both inventory and fixed assets, the manager should realize there may be idle stocks that should not be reduced to zero. Some stocks of inventories and fixed assets may be needed to allow for unpredictable changes such as a sudden increase in demand, or the breakdown of a machine.

Because inventory levels can usually be adjusted quickly, anticipation stocks are accumulated largely to meet seasonal increases in demand. Stocks of fixed assets, on the other hand, cannot be readily changed and often must be accumulated well in advance of expected long-run increases in sales.

## CAPITAL BUDGETING

Capital expenditures involve relatively large sums of money invested over relatively long periods of time; hence errors in evaluating fixed asset investment opportunities can cause serious consequences. Most firms, at any point in time, have several investment opportunities that could be undertaken. Capital budgeting is the means for evaluating investment opportunities in terms of profitability.

Capital budgeting is based on the assumption that capital should be employed in such a way as to provide the most profitable return. Accepting the proposition that capital may not be adequate at any given time to finance all the possible projects that appear feasible, the manager must have some means of ranking opportunities in order of priority.

For example, suppose in a small manufacturing firm, the existing long-run investment opportunities include the development and introduction of a new product; the purchase of new data processing equipment to aid in administering the credit program; the replacement of the company's delivery trucks; expansion of sales promotion into a new territory; construction of a new office building; or the employment of several additional salespeople for a more intensive selling program in the existing market. In most cases it is unlikely that capital is available in amounts adequate to finance all six investments regardless of their profitability. Therefore, some technique must be used to rank the proposals in terms of their desirability.

The remainder of this chapter establishes certain techniques for evaluating alternative investment opportunities.

### Setting up the problem

The three capital budgeting techniques to be developed include the payback method, the average-rate-of-return on average investment method, and the present value method. Regardless of the technique employed, however, there are two basic steps necessary in setting up the problem. The first is to determine the net initial outflow of cash required by the new investment, that is, the initial cash outlay. The second is to determine the net annual inflows of cash as a result of the new investment. In other words, the objective is to determine the amount of funds initially required to make the investment and the stream of cash benefits that will accrue over the investment period.

Assume the manager of a small manufacturing firm is considering the possibility of replacing an old machine presently in use. It is obsolete, but could be used for another three years if necessary. In determining the initial investment required, all possible cash receipts and the necessary expenditures associated with the purchase of the new machine must be considered. These would include not only the cost of the new machine, but also shipping costs, installation costs, and any additional working capital required as a result of the purchase.

For purposes of example, assume the cost of the new machine is $8,000, freight charges amount to $500, and installation costs are $500. If these are the only cash expenditures required, the initial investment would be $9,000, minus any cash receipts resulting from the investment decision.

The most likely cash receipt in the replacement decision is the salvage value of the old machine. It is important to note, however, that the only concern in determining the initial cash investment is with cash flow. Thus, certain costs are ignored. For instance, the old machine could be used for three more years; hence, it is likely to have a book value. It is unlikely, however, that the salvage value will be precisely equal to the book value. If the resale market is good, the old machine may sell at a price in excess of the book value. On the other hand, the resale value in the secondhand market may be considerably below the book value. Whatever the case, the only concern is with the cash inflow from the sale, regardless of the difference between the cash inflow and the book value. If the old machine sells for an amount less than book value the book loss should not be charged against the purchase of the new machine, for the loss involves no cash outflow.

The reasoning behind this procedure is simple. The loss (equal to the difference between the actual salvage value and the book value) has no relationship to the decision to buy the new machine. Whether the cost of the old machine has been recovered over the period it has been used is a matter of history. To charge this loss to the potential of the new machine is not good logic. The present decision should not be burdened with losses resulting from past decisions.

Getting back to the example, assume the old machine sells for $1,000; thus we have a cash receipt of $1,000 associated with the investment decision and it is to be subtracted from total cash expenditures. Step one is now complete; it has been determined that the decision to replace the old machine involves an initial cash investment of $8,000.

Now for the second step: calculating the future net change in cash inflows resulting from the initial cash outlay. The old machine produces some cash flow; so in step two the only concern is with the change in this cash flow, produced by the new machine. Assume the new machine will increase sales revenue annually by $18,000 and has an estimated life of three years. In order to produce the $18,000 of additional annual sales, however, advertising expenditures must be increased by $2,000 a year and an additional salesperson must be hired at a salary of $8,000 a year. So from the additional sales revenue of $18,000, additional expenditures of $10,000 a year are subtracted to arrive at a net change in cash inflow before taxes of $8,000.[2]

In determining the profitability of the replacement decision, an after-tax figure is preferred, thus the differential flows of cash must be adjusted for taxes. This is not as simple as it may sound; unless the depreciation rate on both the old machine and the new machine are identical. If the old and new depreciation are the same and an income tax rate of 50 percent is assumed, the net annual cash benefit after taxes would be $4,000. But if there is a difference in the old depreciation rate and the new depreciation rate, the $8,000 before-tax figure must be adjusted for this difference prior to calculating the income tax liability.

For example, assume that the old machine was being depreciated $2,500 a year, and that the new machine is to be depreciated on a straight line basis at $3,000 a year ($9,000 ÷ 3); thus there is an additional depreciation charge of $500.[3] This reduces the addition to taxable income from $8,000 to $7,500, and applying the 50 percent income tax rate, it produces a tax liability of $3,750.

Step two is complete and produces the following conclusions: the new machine will produce a net addition to profit after taxes of $3,750 a year, and a net annual cash benefit after taxes of $4,250 a year as shown in the summary below. This is the first time that the net profit after taxes figure has been mentioned. It is used in one of the capital budgeting techniques to be described.

---

[2] In determining the annual net change in cash inflow, the manager must be very careful to consider *all* net changes in expenses. For example, the purchase of a new machine to replace a machine currently being used may involve a difference in maintenance costs. If so, the annual net additions to maintenance costs or the annual maintenance cost savings should be treated in the same manner as the added sales expense is handled.

[3] The new machine can be depreciated for tax purposes before considering the benefit of old machine salvage. In the example this means that the depreciable amount is $9,000.

|                                              | *Books*  | *Cash flow* |
| -------------------------------------------- | -------- | ----------- |
| Net added cash inflow, years 1–3............ | $8,000   | $8,000      |
| Annual depreciation on old machine, $2,500   |          |             |
| Annual depreciation on new machine, $3,000   |          |             |
| Net change in depreciation................ | 500      |             |
| Taxable income....................... | $7,500   |             |
| Taxes at 50 percent................... | 3,750    | 3,750       |
| Net profit after taxes................. | $3,750   |             |
| Cash flow after taxes.................. |          | $4,250      |

## The payback method

The first of three methods available to evaluate investment opportunities is called the payback method. It involves simply determining the length of time necessary for the sum of the net cash benefits to equal the initial outlay. In other words, the payback period is calculated by dividing the initial cash outlay by the annual cash benefits. In the example, with an initial cash outlay of $8,000 and an annual cash benefit after taxes of $4,250; the length of time necessary to recover the initial investment is 1.88 years, or about 1 year and 11 months.

The payback method is useful in two situations. First, if the firm is cash poor it may be most important that the initial investment be recovered as soon as possible. Second, if the firm is subject to rapid technological change the manager may be interested in recovering the initial investment as soon as possible.

There are two major deficiencies in the payback method. First, it ignores variation in the rate at which net cash savings are realized. For instance, assume that two investment opportunities requiring an initial cash outlay of $12,000 have the following income streams: Machine A produces $2,000 the first year, $4,000 the second year, and $6,000 the third year; whereas Machine B produces $6,000 the first year, $4,000 the second, and $2,000 the third year. Although both Machine A and Machine B are paid for in three years the investments are not equally desirable. Based on the premise that money has a time value, and when recovered can be employed elsewhere, the machine that provides the larger sums in the earlier years is more profitable.

The second deficiency is that the payback method ignores any stream of income extending beyond the payback period. For example, assume that two investment opportunities both require an initial outlay of $9,000. In Case A the net cash benefit is $3,000 a year for a five-year period, whereas in Case B the net cash benefit is $3,000 a year for a three-year period. Although both investments are paid for in three years, the investment in Case A is more profitable because of the longer income stream.

**TABLE 15–1**
**Present value of $1.**

| Years hence | 4% | 6% | 8% | 10% | 12% | 14% | 15% | 16% |
|---|---|---|---|---|---|---|---|---|
| 1 | 0.962 | 0.943 | 0.926 | 0.909 | 0.893 | 0.877 | 0.870 | 0.862 |
| 2 | 0.925 | 0.890 | 0.857 | 0.826 | 0.797 | 0.769 | 0.756 | 0.743 |
| 3 | 0.889 | 0.840 | 0.794 | 0.751 | 0.712 | 0.675 | 0.658 | 0.641 |
| 4 | 0.855 | 0.792 | 0.735 | 0.683 | 0.636 | 0.592 | 0.572 | 0.552 |
| 5 | 0.822 | 0.747 | 0.681 | 0.621 | 0.567 | 0.519 | 0.497 | 0.476 |
| 6 | 0.790 | 0.705 | 0.630 | 0.564 | 0.507 | 0.456 | 0.432 | 0.410 |
| 7 | 0.760 | 0.665 | 0.583 | 0.513 | 0.452 | 0.400 | 0.376 | 0.354 |
| 8 | 0.731 | 0.627 | 0.540 | 0.467 | 0.404 | 0.351 | 0.327 | 0.305 |
| 9 | 0.703 | 0.592 | 0.500 | 0.424 | 0.361 | 0.308 | 0.284 | 0.263 |
| 10 | 0.676 | 0.558 | 0.463 | 0.386 | 0.322 | 0.270 | 0.247 | 0.227 |

## The average rate of return

The average rate of return method is the percentage of average annual net income after taxes to average investment over the life of the project. This method is based on the reported accounting income figure.

In applying this method in the example the average net profit after taxes of $3,750 per year represents the income stream. And assuming straight line depreciation, average investment is $4,500, or one half of $9,000. Thus, the average rate of return method produces a rate of return of about 83 percent.

There are three deficiencies in the use of the average rate of return method. First, because we average the annual income figure, the method ignores any differences in the flows on a year-to-year basis. Second, the duration of the income flow is ignored. And third, the method ignores the time value of money (explained below).

## The net present value method

The most reliable method of evaluating alternative investment opportunities is the net present value method because it considers the time value of money. The time value of money concept recognizes that a dollar to be received a year from today (or anytime in the future) is less valuable than a dollar possessed today. This is true for three reasons: immediate pleasure is preferable to postponed pleasure; there is always the risk that the future dollar will not be received; and dollars possessed today can earn a return. Thus, the rational person would not ordinarily relinquish today's dollar in exchange for a promise that it will be returned in the future, unless some payment is to be received for its use in the form of interest. If the individual felt that foregoing immediate pleasure, plus accepting the risk that the dollar will never be returned, requires an

| 18% | 20% | 22% | 24% | 25% | 26% | 28% | 30% |
|---|---|---|---|---|---|---|---|
| 0.847 | 0.833 | 0.820 | 0.806 | 0.800 | 0.794 | 0.781 | 0.769 |
| 0.718 | 0.694 | 0.672 | 0.650 | 0.640 | 0.630 | 0.610 | 0.592 |
| 0.609 | 0.579 | 0.551 | 0.524 | 0.512 | 0.500 | 0.477 | 0.455 |
| 0.516 | 0.482 | 0.451 | 0.423 | 0.410 | 0.397 | 0.373 | 0.350 |
| 0.437 | 0.402 | 0.370 | 0.341 | 0.328 | 0.315 | 0.291 | 0.269 |
| 0.370 | 0.335 | 0.303 | 0.275 | 0.262 | 0.250 | 0.227 | 0.207 |
| 0.314 | 0.279 | 0.249 | 0.222 | 0.210 | 0.198 | 0.178 | 0.159 |
| 0.266 | 0.233 | 0.204 | 0.179 | 0.168 | 0.157 | 0.139 | 0.123 |
| 0.225 | 0.194 | 0.167 | 0.144 | 0.134 | 0.124 | 0.108 | 0.094 |
| 0.191 | 0.162 | 0.137 | 0.116 | 0.107 | 0.099 | 0.085 | 0.073 |

interest charge of 20 percent, then today's dollar should be returned one year from now with 20 cents interest, for a total of $1.20. To put it another way, the present value of $1.20 to be received a year from now discounted at 20 percent is $1.

This introduces the problem to be solved in using the net present value method of capital budgeting. Initial cash outlays represent dollars that must be spent today. The income stream, on the other hand, represents dollars to be received at some time in the future. Therefore, in order to compare the two (and arrive at a valid conclusion as to the profitability of the investment opportunity), we must compare the present value of the dollars to be received in the future with the present value of the initial cash outlay.

In figuring the time value of money, a present value table such as Table 15–1 can be used. It indicates the present value of $1 to be received at the end of N years; discounted at a rate of discount X. For instance, assume we want to know what amount invested at 20 percent will return $1 a year from today. Find the 20-percent column in Table 15–1 and go down to the line representing year 1. The present value of $1 to be received a year from now discounted at 20 percent is $0.833.

Similarly, $1 to be received at the end of two years, discounted at 20 percent, has a present value of $0.694. Taking this one step further, we can now determine the present value of a stream of cash benefits represented by $1 to be received at the end of year 1 and $1 to be received at the end of year 2 discounted at 20 percent. The answer is simply $0.833 plus $0.694, or approximately $1.53.

The net present value method of capital budgeting simply involves discounting the stream of future cash benefits to be received over time at a selected rate of discount and comparing the present value of the future benefits with the initial cash outlay.

The application of the net present value method is relatively simple.

All the manager does is select a minimum acceptable rate of return; set the problem up by completing steps one and two (described above); then discount the stream of net cash benefits at the selected rate of discount.

The next step is to subtract the initial cash outlay from the present value of future cash benefits. If the answer is zero, the rate of return is exactly equal to the selected rate of discount; if the answer is negative, the rate of return is less than the selected rate of discount; and if the answer is positive, the return exceeds the minimum required.

Applying the present value method to the example used in the explanation of the payback and the average rate of return method, assume that a minimum return on the replacement machine of 30 percent is required. Thus, we go to the 30-percent column in the present value table and make the following calculations: the present value of the $4,250 cash inflow in the first year is 0.769 ($4,250), or $3,268; the present value of the $4,250 to be received in the second year is 0.592 ($4,250), or $2,516; and, the present value of the $4,250 to be received in the third year is 0.455 ($4,250), or $1,934. Thus, the total present value of the income stream is $7,718. Subtracting the initial cash outlay ($8,000) from this figure gives a negative result, which indicates the rate of return is less than 30 percent. The investment decision does not satisfy the return required and, on the basis of profitability, should be rejected.

## Ranking the investment proposals, considering risk, and evaluating the nonmonetary aspects of the investment decision

If a number of investment opportunities are available and capital is limited, the various opportunities can be ranked according to their net present values. The opportunity providing the highest net present value would be ranked number one; the second best, number two; and so on. Both the payback and average rate of return methods are simple to apply, but involve the noted deficiencies.

One of the problems associated with capital budgeting and the ranking of alternative investment opportunities, is that the probability of realizing the anticipated income stream is not considered in the net present value method. Two projects with equal net present values may have different degrees of risk, and evaluation of this risk factor involves an estimation of the range of error that may be present in estimating the future income stream. That is to say, even though the net present value figures are the same in two cases, the probability of receiving the anticipated income stream may be different, and one proposal may be preferred over another on this basis.

It must also be recognized that none of the methods take into consideration the nonmonetary aspects of the investment decision. There may be investments that are necessary, even though it is difficult to determine their net present values; or despite the fact they do not rank high among the various alternative opportunities. For instance, it may be that buying a new machine would be very profitable, but a parking lot for employees is necessary. So the machine purchase may have to be postponed and the parking lot built. In another case, it may be that additional advertising appears necessary to maintain the firm's share of the market, even though it is difficult to determine the effect of the additional expenditures on cash inflows.

Thus, the final selection process involves consideration of both monetary and nonmonetary aspects. Even though there may be considerable error in applying the capital budgeting techniques, the manager knows the investment decisions were based on the best available information, not just intuition.

In concluding, the small business manager's success will depend somewhat on the experience gained from past investment decisions. Thus, once the investment decision is made, it should be evaluated through time by comparing actual costs with anticipated costs, and actual benefits with anticipated benefits. Experience and good judgment play such an important role in the capital budgeting decision that a thorough evaluation of past investment decisions is essential to improve the decision-making process in the future.

## QUESTIONS

1. What are the advantages and disadvantages of employing financial leverage in the small business?
2. Discuss the factors of risk, control, flexibility, and timing as they relate to selecting a source of funds.
3. What is the principal problem associated with managing the cash account and what tool can be used in solving the problem?
4. Distinguish between controlling the level of receivables and controlling the acquisition of receivables.
5. What costs are associated with determining the appropriate inventory investment?
6. Discuss the two steps in setting up a capital budgeting problem.
7. Define the three capital budgeting techniques discussed in the chapter.
8. Explain what is meant by the statement "money has a time value."
9. What are the disadvantages or deficiencies in using the average rate of return method and the payback method in capital budgeting?
10. What is meant by the "nonmonetary aspects" of the investment decision? Give examples of some typical nonmonetary considerations.

## PROBLEMS

1. Compute the following:
   a. The present value of $4,000 to be received at the end of five years, discounted at 8 percent.
   b. The present value of $2,000 to be received at the end of each year for five years, discounted at 10 percent.
   c. The present value of $3,000 to be received at the end of years 1 and 2, and $4,000 to be received at the end of years 3 and 4; discounted at 6 percent.

2. The information below pertains to three alternative investment opportunities:

|  | Investment A | Investment B | Investment C |
|---|---|---|---|
| Initial cash outlay. | $5,400 | $9,000 | $12,000 |
| Estimated economic life | 3 years | 6 years | 6 years |
| Salvage value. | 0 | 0 | 0 |
| Differential cash benefit before depreciation and taxes |  |  |  |
| 1–3 years | $2,400 | $4,500 | $ 4,600 |
| 4–6 years | 0 | $3,500 | $ 7,200 |
| Annual straight line depreciation charge | $1,800 | $1,500 | $ 2,000 |

Assume the corporate income tax rate is 50 percent and rank the three proposals by using the payback method, the average rate of return on average investment, and the net present value method. How do you explain the differences in the rankings?

## BIBLIOGRAPHY

Engler, George N.  *Business Financial Management,* chaps. 5, 6, 13, 14, and 15. Dallas, Tex.: Business Publications, 1975.

Helfert, Erich A.  *Techniques of Financial Analysis,* chap. 5. 3d ed. Homewood, Ill.: Richard D. Irwin, 1972.

Hunt, Pearson; Williams, Charles M.; and Donaldson, Gordon.  *Basic Business Finance,* chaps. 2, 3, 4, 5, 8, and 9. Homewood, Ill.: Richard D. Irwin, 1974.

Johnson, Robert W.  *Financial Management,* chaps. 5, 6, 7, 8, and 10. 4th ed. Boston, Mass.: Allyn and Bacon, 1971.

# 16

# The company image—
# build it or buy it?

In promoting his or her firm, the small businessperson must recognize that it is essential that he or she be concerned with the business image. What is meant by developing a small business image, however, should be clarified because of the variety of meanings which have been applied to the terms "company image" or "business image."

It is true, for example, that many critics of Western society, and particularly critics of the U.S. economy, think of it as a materialistic society. That is, it is not uncommon for Asian, African, South American—and in some cases European—nations to think of the typical businessperson in the United States as a waste-maker, a pyramid climber, and a status seeker. Perhaps this "image" which foreigners have of the typical U.S. small businessperson has been perpetuated by movies and certain books designed as exposés which emphasize the extremes and minimize the normal. Nevertheless, this is the "image" held by outsiders.

Such a conception of the *typical* business manager in the United States is not only erroneous but it is harmful to the day-in-day-out, hardworking business executive, whether he or she is working in the small or large organization. Obviously, the swashbuckling image of today's corporation executive is not the kind of image which is desirable under any circumstances, be it correct or erroneous. Thus, the discussion that follows will concern itself with the practical, day-in-day-out illusion which the average citizen in the average town has of the typical small business—an illusion which by design, intent, and purpose is promoted by the small business manager in an effort to enhance both the efficiency of his or her operation and the marketability of his or her product or service.

## Why worry about the company's image?

In order for a firm to *promote* a certain image, it is obviously necessary for the small business manager to first *establish* the desired image. The small business manager must know consciously what image he or she desires to portray to the public and his or her own personnel. This requires, in turn, an understanding of how important an image is to the people involved. Generally, it is accepted that the image conveyed to the public is all-important. Since the image conveyed is so important, it must be recognized that a conscious, deliberate effort should be made by the business to sharpen or highlight the desired image to the public and the business personnel. It is not sufficient, as one writer has put it, merely to ". . . utter statements in somber tones about the need for better images." But it is, of course, asinine to try to develop an image which does not exist—e.g., the cut-rate firm that advertises in exclusive magazines in an endeavor to create a false impression. In short, a firm's image is all-important, but to be effective, this image must be within the realm of reason and practicality.

## What images are made of

There are, of course, a variety of images which small businesspersons can attempt to develop for their businesses. They can develop an image of being "exclusive"—that is, being the sellers or providers of nothing but the best. They can develop an image of being "inexpensive," perhaps appealing to people in the lower income brackets or people who feel that they do not need the durable features of "the best." They can develop an image of being innovative, providing the latest in fashions, styles, or designs, or they can develop the opposite image of being quite reserved and conservative, thereby appealing to a different clientele.

The objective of the whole image-building game is not necessarily to develop the *best* company image. Rather, it is that the small business-person determine the *right* image—i.e., the image it is he or she wishes his or her business to convey, and to whom. He or she can then endeavor to establish such an image to the *appropriate* group. Thus, the small business might also attempt to establish different images for different groups of people if it can successfully isolate its market or clients with separate advertising campaigns or, more practically, by having different branch stores or service facilities.

Determining the image desired and conveying this image to the appropriate persons is very difficult. However, there are some characteristics of successful company images that the practical business manager can strive to achieve.

1. To begin with, an image is *synthetic*. That is, any image which is developed by a small business is deliberately planned and created to give a certain impression to particular people for a definite reason. Thus, almost any image desired can be *created,* and by the same token any image created can also be *changed* by deliberate effort.

2. An image must be *believable*. That is, images should be within the realm of the realistic. They should not be designed to convey something totally impossible or irrelevant. For example, it usually is futile for a small business in a small country community to convey the impression that the store carries the latest Paris fashions. Most of the people in small, rural communities simply are too realistic to accept such a delusion, even if they would like to think that the designs of the top Paris couturiers are available to them.

3. An image is a vehicle or *means toward an end*, it is not an end in itself. In this sense the image is passive rather than active. In other words, image building is the development of "a likeness" of the organization; but in final analysis the organization is the "likeness" of the image. Thus, an image is constructed from actual circumstances which exist and which are brought into existence for purposes of image building. However, after a certain amount of time, people will identify themselves in some relationship with the image constructed; then, actual circumstances begin to adapt to the image developed. Thus, when a business hires a public relations firm to develop a desired image, the firm is initially putting itself in the position of determining what image the business wants to develop, but once the image is built the business will necessarily have to comply with the image developed by the public relations firm.

4. Although passive, an image must be *alive* and *concrete*. That is, any image that is developed must be a vivid, almost tangible thought, feeling, or emotion. For example, consder the TV commercials for food or beverages in which taste or flavor is almost brought alive by the product which is portrayed—or the impression of elegance and good taste suggested by a particular automobile ad. Similarly, the small business can make its image vivid—something which can be "felt" by employees, customers, and clients alike.

5. An image should be *simple*. Developing a corporate image requires the ability to simplify very complex, meaningful thoughts. Just as the football coach knows that he must keep his game plans extremely simple so that all his players can understand and comply with them, so should the small business manager recognize that simple thoughts and actions should be used to convey an image to others. The small business can convey its image by simple, provocative slogans, advertisements, or jingles; by the thoughtful, quiet, and unassuming decor of an office; or by a method of answering a telephone call.

6. An image should be *ambiguous*. In final analysis it must be recognized that although image building requires several specific, deliberate steps to be taken by the image builder, it must above all still be vague and ambiguous. To be successful an image must be something which can be perceived and accepted by a large number of observers. Such commonality of application for the corporate image necessarily requires that

the image be vague or ambiguous enough so that each individual can see in it something with a special personal meaning. A wide range of people and personalities will be exposed to the specific stimulus of the image, and they will receive this stimulus in widely divergent lights and viewpoints. Sufficient ambiguity is therefore required for all people to receive the image in the *best* light. Thus, an image designed to be conservatively interpreted, should still be ambiguous enough to avoid conveying the notion of a "stuffed-shirt" organization to large segments of the population.

## Building your company image through your own image

The foregoing discussion was designed to highlight the factors which must be considered in building the image which a small business wants to convey. An additional aspect, however, must be considered by the owner of the small business and that is the factor of his or her own personality. The small businessperson is always viewed as an extension of his or her business, and no matter what he or she does, the firm will always be associated with the image of the owner/manager held by the general public.

The importance of this factor is probably best summarized in the old cliché "you can take the boy out of the country, but you can't take the country out of the boy." Likewise, the small business manager cannot effectively change his or her personality to suit any image, and because the image he or she conveys will tend to permeate the entire organization, it must be recognized that to a large extent the owner/manager's personal image will determine the image of the company.

## Knowing what image your small business projects

The question therefore arises: "How can one determine what one's own image is and develop a suitable image that serves the business well and will permit the maximizing of profit and growth for the firm?"

To answer this question, the small business manager should analyze himself or herself by self-questioning, and thus determine the image to be conveyed. Basically these questions require a recognition of one's own self-driving needs.

Once the small business manager determines the image he or she wishes to project through the business, then the question is how to establish this image and perpetuate it through at least the foreseeable future, until such time that circumstances change and it is deemed advisable to establish a different image. This last is an extremely difficult proposition—to determine when to change an image so that one will keep in tune with the times.

## WORKING TOWARD THE DESIRED IMAGE

### Do's and don't's of developing the desired image

Success in developing the desired image would appear to rest primarily on how well one understands people rather than on how hard one works at it. That is, developing the desired image is more a question of going about it in the right way than of how much effort is devoted to the task. In order to establish an image, it is imperative that the individual understands what it is he or she is trying to do.

The word *image*, as defined in most dictionaries, means a reproduction or imitation of the form of a person or a thing (fame, renown, etc.). Thus, a small business establishing an image must first form the framework in which the consumers of its product or service view the firm. In order to create this framework it is critical that the small business manager know why and on what grounds people form their opinions and attitudes about companies. Let us look at a few fundamental principles.

### People are not always rational

The small business operator should realize that developing an image is not clearly and distinctly a function of "informing people" or otherwise advising customers and clients of the "facts," because people are not always rational. For example, if a corner druggist informs customers in a matter-of-fact manner that the discounters are selling certain items below invoice price, the customers are not going to continue to buy in the drug store at the higher price. In fact, such "truth in advertising" would probably drive away customers rather than win them over. Studies show that people may often openly deplore big business and the "unethical" practices of big business. At the same time, however, they may buy practically all of their groceries, drugs, incidental garments, and other items from the large chains and discounters. Further, they may knowingly pay a higher price for some items of merchandise which they buy at the same time that they purchase a loss leader which they know is featured to entice them into the discounter's store. In other words, although the public is often aware of the "tricks" used by business, they still fall for them time and time again. Thus, one of the preliminary "do's" of developing a desired reputation is to understand that people will formulate opinions as to the merits or demerits of a particular firm on the basis of hunch or feeling, as much as on the basis of a logical test.

### Most people identify their image with the company they deal with

The second principle which small business managers must be aware of in developing the desired image is that people respond to other people, institutions, and companies in ways which will help them to protect their own self-image. This means that many times people will have a built-in bias about specific companies and stores which has developed as a result of the enhancement of their own self-image or self-respect. This principle explains why, for example, buyers of some inexpensive products will avidly argue that their product is "economical" rather than "cheap," or that their expensive purchase was "essential" rather than ostentatious. In short, people are responding to the images that businesses develop for their products. These businesses build the images in their advertising campaigns in a way which will help customers enhance their own self-esteem—people like to be "economical," but not "cheap." The small business manager, in building a company image, therefore, is advised to present logical, plausible reasons which will enhance the self-image or self-esteem of the customer or client.

## Preconceived ideas help build images

The third principle of image building is that people tend to use as references thoughts or attitudes already in their minds in forming a basis for accepting new products or companies. On the one hand, this maxim states that a person going into a type of business which is not held as particularly reputable is doomed to have a bad reputation regardless of his or her activities. An example might be a very honest, legitimate businessperson going into the real estate field. Many people feel that all real estate people are out to get the best of them, even though that is not true. Therefore, no matter how honest an individual may be, if he or she is dealing in real estate, he or she may be regarded with suspicion. On the other hand, the maxim also states that a small business might capitalize in reputation building because the general public holds a particular line of work in high regard. Numerous examples of this vicarious reputation-formation come to mind. One is the peddler of yesteryear who assumed the title of "doctor" or "professor" to enhance sales of his magic elixir; another, more practical, example is the "aura" surrounding work in the electronics or computer fields or space technology. These industries are highly romanticized and most people associate them with brilliant, dynamic, dashing young executives. Such a common attitude on the part of the public has been capitalized on by some unscrupulous people who have started their own small business in the garage with a fancy letterhead and the knowledge of the melting point of solder. Therefore, another "do" emerges for the small businessperson interested in developing a reputation. That "do" is to capitalize, if possible, on the commonly held conceptions and *mis*conceptions of the general public in respect to his or her line of business.

## Established images are difficult to change

A fourth principle of image building is that if a particular firm or industry has a *commonly* held reputation which people have accepted, a change in that image will be resisted by most people for a long time. This principle differs from the third principle in that it states that if a firm has a certain reputation, people will be slow to accept a new reputation, whereas the third principle states that a firm can most easily develop reputations consistent with preconceived notions about that field of endeavor. Therefore, the fourth principle dictates that in attempting to develop a reputation or image for the firm the small businessperson should (1) determine what (if any) reputation his or her firm has and (2) reinforce or otherwise support the public's opinion along these lines if the image is a desirable one. Basically, this principle states that it is far easier to convince a person of the truth about something if that is what the person already believes than it is to change the person's belief. A person who is basically a Democrat is more easily convinced to vote a straight Democratic ticket than is one who is a Republican. People tend to gravitate toward confirming their preconceived notions. The small business which has what is considered a desirable reputation should make efforts to maintain that opinion in the minds of its supporters.

## Images must overcome doubts

If the doubts or anxieties of customers and clients have given a company an undesirable reputation, that "bad" image may be hard to change. The best way to improve a bad company image is to take immediate action to dispel any uncertainty or doubts which the customers have. Thus, if a small businessperson thinks his or her firm is suffering from a poor or otherwise undesired reputation, the only way to alter this undesirable image is by taking careful, considered action designed to dispel or alleviate the doubts and uncertainty in the customers' minds which are causing them to hold the firm in ill repute. For example, it is a commonly voiced criticism of the firms which provide house repairs and services, such as plumbing, painting, or pest control, that they are unreliable, disreputable, and out to "fleece the public." Faced with such a general reputation, the business which genuinely intends to do an honest job in performing such services should recognize that it is operating in a field characterized this way, and should make efforts to offset the doubts or concerns in the minds of their customers. Many people desiring to do a good job and operating under such handicaps have found it expedient to register with such organizations as the local Chamber of Commerce and

Better Business Bureau. They then offer these signs of stability and honesty to prospective customers before attempting to sell their services or products.

## Images must be palatable

Another principle of image building is that new or altered reputations are more easily accepted by customers and clients if they are phrased in terms already acceptable to the customers and clients. Thus, in attempting to develop a unique or different reputation for the firm, the small business-person should recognize the social values held sacred by certain groups of people and make their appeals in keeping with these values. Therefore, the small business that wants to establish a reputation for high-quality merchandise at low prices should direct its sales pitch to low and middle income classes who are more concerned with low prices for the quality received than with quality per se. In contrast to this, the small business that wants to appeal to clientele with elegant tastes will direct its sales pitch along the lines of quality only and will likely avoid the element of price.

## Impressing many people is required for image building

The final consideration in developing the desired image is that reputations are based on large numbers of people rather than small numbers. This is another way of saying "the squeaking wheel gets the grease." The point is that a firm's reputation is largely the result of what and how much is being said about it. Therefore, the small business which will succeed in developing the desired reputation is the one which impresses great numbers of people with its honesty, integrity, quality, fashion, or whatever it wishes to emphasize. Thus, the automobile dealer who wants to develop a reputation for selling at low prices must constantly feature the low-price theme in company advertisements. In this way the dealer will get the largest possible number of people discussing the dealership as a low-price dealer rather than a shoddy repair dealer or a poor service dealer.

## THE ECONOMICS OF DEVELOPING A GOOD IMAGE

It should be clear by now that in attempting to develop the desired reputation for a firm, the small business has a variety of things to contend with. For example, in order to build an image a small businessperson might take certain steps, such as decorating his or her store in an unusual way. The steps one takes—influenced of course by the type of business one is in—and how well one carries them out will determine how successful one is in building a company image. The secret is to choose the correct steps and those that one can afford financially. Thus a small business which is intent upon developing a particular reputation must know how to determine economically which of these decisions or steps can be justified, and therefore be considered. Actually, by use of a simple schematic device the small business can determine with relative ease the value, relevance, and importance of any of the decisions or steps to take. This method is presented in Figure 16–1. It should be obvious that any small business can generate a schema similar to this figure, based on information relevant to the particular business.

In devising and utilizing such a figure, it can be seen that in determining what reputation-developing activity one intends to engage in, the small businessperson must recognize two facts: (1) there is a dollar cost which will be incurred for any reputation-developing activity; and (2) the dollar cost will increase at a progressive rate for the more complex, the more out-of-the-ordinary, the more bizarre reputation-developing activities. By charting these particular activities along a cost curve, the small businessperson can determine which activities are economically feasible for the firm and which are not. By way of general experience, it

**FIGURE 16–1**
**Image/cost curve**

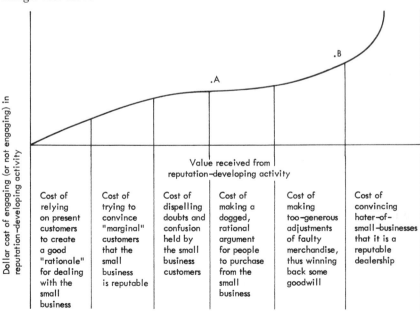

would appear that the financially uneconomical area is located somewhere between Point A and Point B on Figure 16–1 where the cost curve becomes progressively more skewed. Beyond Point B the incremental increase in cost far outweighs the incremental increase in favorable reputation which is promoted by the reputation-developing activity, while before Point A the return far outweighs the expenditure. Therefore, as a matter of policy, the small business which has this figure for its image/cost curve should be reasonably considerate in dealings with customers, and should neither sidestep nor appear to sidestep responsibilities to inform the public in general of the advantages resulting from dealing with that firm. However, there would appear to be little sense in attempting to win over a potential customer who is already antagonistic toward the small business or the area of activity in which the small business is engaged.

## BUYING A COMPANY IMAGE

No chapter on image and reputation building would be complete without some mention of the phenomenon of buying an image. Images can be bought in two ways: by buying out a going concern or by buying a franchise from a large franchisor. Both these methods of buying a business image have some advantages and disadvantages. These are discussed below.

### Buying out a concern

Buying a going concern offers several advantages to the small business-person, as mentioned in Chapter 6. One of the most significant of these opportunities is the image which comes with the purchase, *providing* the buyer is able to both *receive* and *use* the image. Unfortunately, sometimes it is difficult to find a going concern for sale which has a desirable image that the new buyer can use.

Most small businesspeople who are interested in selling out their businesses do so for one of two reasons: they either want to get out of business altogether, or they want to get rid of *that* business. A buyer is much more apt to receive a desirable image from a seller who wants to leave the business world than from a seller who wants to "unload" a particular business.

If the seller of the business is selling because he or she wants to go completely out of business, then he or she will probably be willing to sell the use of the company name (and possibly, the use of his or her own name). In this case, the buyer then at least is getting some of the makings of the image that the seller has developed. However, if the seller has as his or her intention the mere selling of one business to be free to start another, then he or she probably will not be willing to sell the use of the company's name, and certainly not the use of the personal name. Therefore, in the second circumstance, there is little or no advantage to buying an image, because one would get little or nothing.[1] In the first instance the buyer at least will be assured of receiving the company name, even if he or she does not continue its use; but this is not true when the seller intends to start another business and will not sell the personal name.

Even if the seller intends to go completely out of business, there is still some question about the feasibility of using the image which has been bought. Since the seller *may have been the image* of the firm he or she is selling, even if he or she retires or moves out of the city and is *never heard from again,* the image may go too.

Thus, it is conceivable that it is impossible to buy the image of a going concern. Therefore, the prospective small business operater should be aware of the limited success he or she may have in trying to "buy" the image of a going concern. The only hedge is to be reasonably sure that the company name which one is buying is *the* essence of the image of the business.

## Buying a franchise

A second way to buy an image is to buy a franchise. In its commonly used form, franchising is basically a system of licensing whereby an individual derives the benefits of a well-known name, national advertising, and a prescribed territory. Names such as Western Auto; Chicken Delight, Incorporated; The Hertz Corporation; Holiday Inns of America, Incorporated; Arthur Murray, Incorporated; McDonald's Systems, Incorporated; Howard Johnson Company; and Culligan, Incorporated, are all franchised organizations with which the average person is familiar.

*Advantages to franchising.* Numerous advantages exist for the small businessperson who purchases a franchise, which is one of the reasons that franchise relationships are so popular. One of the primary reasons that franchise operations appeal to prospective small businesspeople is that it gives one a chance to fight effectively against large corporations; they provide the "little man" with a chance to get into a nationally advertised business with nominal capital.

Among the several functional advantages to franchise operations, over and above being in business for oneself, are the following: national and local advertising, technical support, merchandising and purchasing assistance, credits and collection assistance, marketing aids, and administrative assistance. But most important, the small businessperson who purchases a

---

[1] It should be noted that some people will sell their name just to get out of the business, but in doing so, they will sell as little as possible, will limit or constrain the use of the name, and generally will try to minimize the image they are selling to the buyer.

franchise knows that as a result of holding that franchise he or she can expect to "buy an image."

David B. Slater, as president of Mr. DoNut of America, Incorporated, elaborated on some of the advantages of buying an image via a franchise by stating that a franchisee can expect the following to accrue from his or her franchise relationship: First, he or she will have an established brand name which will in and of itself carry an image; second, he or she will be assured of quality in both the image and product because of the quality control restrictions the parent company will place on operations; third, the small business operator will have locational analysis and financial development aid, all of which will contribute to the image of a well-run business; fourth, the operator will receive managerial training in general supervision, again enhancing his or her image as a shrewd businessperson; and fifth, he or she will receive the advantages of national advertising and merchandising campaigns, which will add to the visibility and thus the enhanced image of the franchisee.

Therefore, the franchise operation offers many of the advantages of both big and small business, particularly the image of bigness. However, before the small businessperson goes off the deep end and runs out to buy the first franchise he or she can find, he or she should also be apprised of the numerous disadvantages which occur under a franchise operation.

*Disadvantages to franchising.* The primary disadvantage with a franchise operation is that the franchisee can never divorce himself or herself from the franchisor and therefore will tend to lose his or own identity. That is, the very advantage of the franchise operation also carries with it the disadvantage of anonymity upon the part of the franchisee. For example, one might ask oneself how many franchisees he or she knows by name. The answer will probably be few, if any. The point is that the very advantage of being connected with a "large, national chain" carries with it the threatened disadvantage of being considered only as part of a large national chain and not as an individual. Thus, a price must be paid for buying a "big business" image.

Anonymity is not the only disadvantage to national franchising. Another is that of standardization. That is, the franchisee is not entirely free to operate his or her business as he or she sees fit. Rather, he must frequently subscribe to numerous sets of established standards, requirements, and procedures. These not only concern the performance on the job—the making of the product or providing of service—but also reporting procedures. There is, of course, a reason for this required standardization. As the saying goes: "A weak cup of coffee served in one shop can lose a customer for the other; a day-old product served as fresh reflects badly on the management of all." In franchising, the customer does not view the shop he or she patronizes as one entity; if a customer is dissatisfied with one shop, he or she is apt to blame the entire chain.

The third disadvantage to franchise operations is the sizable cost. Nobody gets something for nothing, and the franchisor is not going to give away a name, idea, and the benefits of experience for nothing. In return, the franchisor is going to demand one or all of the following: a percentage of the franchisee's profits, a fee at the outset of the relationship, a markup on supplies sold to the franchisee, a markup on the rent paid for the location of the franchisee, or a markup on the initial equipment package which the franchisee purchases from the franchisor. Therefore, franchises are not obtained cost-free, and the franchisee who wants to capitalize on the franchisor's name must be willing to pay for it.

A fourth disadvantage to the franchise operation lies in the control of the operation. Much in the same manner that a parent corporation looks at a division, the franchisor views the franchisee. The franchisor has a certain vested interest in the activities and particularly the success of the franchisee and has a right to attempt to control the franchisee to the extent of looking after its own interests. However, the franchisee—particularly the person who goes into business to be his or her own boss—will frequently view this as being excessively restrictive control; something at which one first balks and later perhaps even openly resists. Such resistance cannot be avoided, and it is a logical outcome of the control required by the franchisor.

A fifth disadvantage which often crops up under the franchise operation is disenchantment with the franchise. Such disenchantment does not necessarily arise because a franchisor failed to hold to its obligations. Most often it means that the original financial goals of the franchisees were pitched too low and they find that they are no longer satisfied with the deal negotiated with the franchisor. When such a circumstance arises the franchisee usually wants out because of a feeling that the franchise is a dead end. However, wanting out and getting out are two different things. Once committed to the franchise it becomes very difficult to get out, both legally and financially.

A final disadvantage to the franchise operation is the possibility that the small business will "go down with the ship." Under franchise operations if the national franchisor goes bankrupt because it gets too greedy or suffers from mismanagement or the numerous other misfortunes which can befall franchising chains, the franchisees may also face bankruptcy. One well-known franchisor—Tastee-Freez—was forced to file bankruptcy, which resulted in damage to the image and health of the various franchisees associated with the chain. Other franchise operations have experienced similar happenings.

The bankruptcy of the national franchisor, however, is not the only problem related to "going down with the ship." Another problem is that in many cases national franchisors have exhibited an inability to adapt to changing market conditions, changing consumer buying patterns, tastes, and habits. Inability to meet changing conditions can hurt any business, and franchise operations seems to have a history of being slow to adapt to change. This factor seems to be a paradox at best, because most franchises which have developed have done so because they have offered a product or service which caught the whim or fancy of large numbers of people almost overnight. Yet, by the same token, they die out because they seem to be unable to adapt to new changes—new whims, habits, tastes, and patterns—on the part of consumers. The reason for this lack of empathy probably resides in the nature of the franchise operation itself. The parent franchise company has extreme difficulty in moving its many "independent partners"—its franchisees. That is, the parent company can only boss the franchisees around to the extent that they have contractual agreements giving them such authority. Many, if not most, franchise operations provide very limited authority to the parent company when it comes to significant changes in operational procedures.

## Making the decision to buy an image or develop an image

The foregoing sections on the advantages and disadvantages of building an image by developing one's own, buying a going concern, or franchising are meant to give the reader some idea of what can and cannot be accomplished by the small businessperson hoping to build or buy an image. The advantages are many, but so are the disadvantages. Therefore persons who are contemplating starting their own business must face the decision of whether to buy that image or develop it on their own. There is no clear-cut guide to help the small businessperson make this decision. The possibilities of receiving an image are dim when a prospective small business operator buys a person out, but they are only slightly better when one buys a franchise. Therefore, two further aspects of buying a franchise need be considered to give the reader a total picture on the prospects of successfully buying a business image. These include: (1) how well suited is the small businessperson for franchising and (2) how well suited is the prospective franchisor for the small businessperson.

*Is the small businessperson suited for franchise operations?* The first question which the small businessperson must answer is whether or not he or she is suited to work under a franchise agreement. The following kinds of questions must have positive answers before the small businessperson can logically entertain notions of seeking a franchise. They include:

1. Do I have sufficient capital to meet the requirements of the franchisor *and* for living expenses until the business is profitable?
2. Do I have evidence that the franchisor is reputable?
3. Will I receive sufficient training and merchandising aids?

4. Will affiliation with the franchisor be superior to going into business for myself with no outside affiliation?
5. Am I willing to sacrifice the independence of action I would get from not being aligned with a franchisor?
6. Is the contract fair?
7. Does the contract guarantee a protected territory?
8. Are the provisions for termination of the contract satisfactory?
9. Has the franchisor been in business long enough to demonstrate the likelihood of profitability of the system?

If all answers to the above are in the affirmative, the small business-person can then consider himself or herself a logical candidate for a franchise operation. On the other hand, if any answers are negative, or if there has been hesitation in answering some questions positively, it is quite likely that the individual will eventually become dissatisfied with a franchise agreement.

**Checking out the prospective franchisor.** If the small businessperson is still interested in the possibilities of going into a franchise operation, he or she must also determine that the franchisor is someone with whom he or she wishes to deal. It is not enough merely to think that it would be nice to be a Howard Johnson Motel operator or a Western Auto supplier. If an individual wants to operate in a specific chain or with a particular franchisor, he or she must *know* that they will be able to get along effectively with the franchisor. To determine whether or not this is possible, the small businessperson must check out the prospective franchisor. In so doing, there are many questions that need answers. These include:

1. A clear-cut definition of the kind of business the franchisor is in: is the franchisor a partnership or a publicly or privately owned corporation, or is it affiliated with any other business?
2. Has the franchisor been in business long? If so, what is its Dun & Bradstreet rating?
3. Is the franchisor a member of the Chamber of Commerce, the Better Business Bureau, etc.? What is its record with these organizations?
4. What are the names and addresses of the banks with which the franchisor deals? What is the franchisor's credit rating?
5. What has been the approximate gross volume for the franchisor in each of the past several years of operation? Has it fluctuated? What are the trends of its performance?
6. What are competing or similar products or services provided by the franchisor?
7. What kind of reports do other franchisees make on the franchise?
8. Is the franchisor's product or service being currently marketed on other than a franchise-only basis?

9. How many franchises or distributors are there at present?
10. What does the company provide by the way of (*a*) prospects for selling franchises or distributorships, (*b*) franchisee contracts, (*c*) sales manuals or operation manuals, (*d*) promotional materials or kits?
11. Are any of the franchisor's management personnel distinguished in their field in some way? How?
12. Does the franchisor provide trainee and other schooling for franchisees? What does such training cost?
13. Does the franchisor provide assistance by way of handling franchising activities, orders, problems, trouble-shooting, etc.?
14. Has the franchisor ever been bankrupt or have any of the franchisor's officers been employed by any business organization which has gone bankrupt?
15. Have there ever been any Better Business Bureau, Federal Trade Commission, or other complaints, or cease-and-desist orders against the franchisor?
16. What minimum investment is required if franchises are being sold?

Obviously, several of the above questions must be asked and answered to the satisfaction of the small businessperson thinking of going into a franchise operation before he or she commits funds. To ignore these questions leaves the success of the franchise operation up to pure luck, and going ahead with the franchise operation when several of the answers to the above questions point in a negative direction would demonstrate fool-hardiness upon the part of the small business manager. If the franchisor cannot stand the above tests, the small businessperson would probably be much better advised to go into business and develop his or her own image. In contrast, however, if the franchisor checks out on all of the above, then the small businessperson might be well advised to buy the company image.

## SUMMARY

This chapter highlighted the fact that small business images don't just happen; small businesspersons must work for them. More importantly, however, it also pointed out the fact that when working for an image, the small businessperson must do so intelligently, deliberately, and with knowledge of the principles of image building. It was pointed out that the degree of effort involved in image building is no substitute for the application of knowledge. Finally, the foregoing chapter also highlighted many of the advantages and disadvantages of "buying" an image, either by buying out a going concern or by buying a franchise.

## QUESTIONS

1. Why is the fine art of image building necessary for the small company? Explain in detail.

2. Support the statement that "it is *not* necessary for a small businessperson to develop the best company image he or she *can*." Explain in detail why you support this statement!

3. Characterize what you feel is the essence of a company image. How would you use these characteristics to build an image? Explain in detail.

4. It is sometimes stated that the image which any small business has is really just an extension of the image that the company's clientele hold of the owner of the business. Is this true? Why or why not?

5. How can small businesspersons ascertain what image they and/or their business project? Explain in detail.

6. The text lists some do's and don't's for developing an image. Critically analyze the advice behind any three of these points.

7. Write an essay on "The Economics of Developing a Good Image."

8. What would be your advice to a friend who asked what you thought of his or her buying an image? Explain in detail when your advice might be favorable and when it might not be favorable.

9. What advantages do you see to buying an image by way of a franchise? What disadvantages? Explain in detail.

10. How would you evaluate a prospective franchise, assuming you were seriously considering going into business for yourself? Explain in detail the steps you would go through, the questions you would ask, etc?

## PROBLEM

Margaret Snyder was considered a "nut" by many people's standards. As owner-manager of a pool hall (Meg's Billiard Parlor) she was looked at as being "unprincipled." No one was really supposed to run a pool hall and bar unless they had "little or no class."

Meg didn't mind the lack of respect she felt in the eyes of others in her community. After all, profits were high. What she really resented was the fact that her customers—or really anybody—who was interested in the leisure activities of the "pool room" variety were looked down upon—whether they were men or women.

1. What could Meg do about her problem?
2. Was Meg realistic in thinking that anything she could do would change the community's attitude?
3. What would you advise Meg to do?

## BIBLIOGRAPHY

Mindenhort, David. "The Entrepreneur's Use of Language." *Sociolinguistics in Cross-Cultural Analysis*. Washington, D.C.: Georgetown University,

1972, pp. 57–66. This brief work looks at the way entrepreneurs use language.

"Organizational Characteristics of Growing Companies." *Journal of Management Studies,* vol. 4, no. 2 (May 1967), pp. 204–19. Study of growth of small firms, mostly in the printing industry.

Pollack, Irwin W., et al. "Social Classes and the Subjective Sense of Time." *Archives and General Psychiatry,* vol. 21, no. 1 (July 1969), pp. 1–14. Interesting analysis of how time and class consciousness affect the entrepreneur's business acumen.

Sadler, P. J., and Barry, B. A. "Action Research in a Small Firm." *Journal of Management Studies,* vol. 5, no. 3 (October 1968), pp. 316–17. An analysis of organization and communication in a small printing firm.

# 17

# Business locations—
# analysis and selection

A suitable business location is one of the more critical factors in the ultimate success of any given enterprise. The actual building, or premises, along with the necessary supporting features, will place susbtantial financial demands on the business. Frequently it is the principal feature of operation, requiring long-term obligations and commitment, and considerable investigation is necessary to determine if a location can really provide what is needed, within the financial limits of the chosen enterprise. The total configuration of location, building features, and environment is thus dealt with first as a subject for analysis and judgment. The building and its facilities are discussed more specifically in Chapter 18.

## ANALYSIS PROCESS AND SEQUENCE

Considerable effort is needed to properly analyze all the things that are important to the selection of a location. In general the overall task is divided into two major parts. These are identified as follows:

1. *Process.* In setting up the process the prospective entrepreneur must decide how he wishes to ultimately find a location. Should the individual define his own personal desires and needs and then proceed to find what fits? Or, would it be more appropriate to decide what the business really needs, and then be willing to search for the conditions that really meet that need. The process thus becomes significant because the conditions can be "stacked" in such a way that the process is different each time the criteria and circumstances are reoriented.

2. *Sequence.* The sequence of analysis, like the process employed, can vary from one situation to another. The basic difference is that sequence moves, through the data inquiry and review, from that which is obtainable, apparent, and measurable, to that which is vague, obscure, and requiring subjective judgment.

Process is what you do and why; sequence is the order in which you examine and evaluate.

Assuming that the prospective entrepreneur has an idea in mind, he or she will set up a working format. Limits, goals, environment, life-style, and other similar conditions will be set. The prospective manager then begins to narrow down the assorted patterns that exist. Data will be reviewed as to population, income patterns, employment data, and other broad types of data. Rather quickly the inquiry moves to circumstances involving a town, community area, or perhaps one or more shopping centers. As the inquiry proceeds, it becomes more difficult and subjective. Alternatives will develop and several possible choices will probably develop. Final, detailed and thorough analysis should reveal that location which is the best, given the input circumstances.

## PERSONAL VALUES AND GOALS

Most prospective business operators would do well to try to resolve their own personal relationships to a business venture before doing any amount of serious inquiry. If this is done, then the selection process can continue with the expectation that personal problems will not interfere with the selection of the right business location.

*Geographical or community preferences.* Some people have strong personal reasons for wanting to live in an area possessing certain geographical conditions or, more specifically, in a particular community. An individual might choose an area possessing high altitude, mild climate, ample sunshine, and low rainfall. Within these limits a variety of communities might be satisfactory. On the other hand, the individual may decide that only one particular community possesses all the features which are important to him or her personally. Such might be the individual's hometown, which for one or more reasons he or she is reluctant to leave. So the person decides on the area and/or community first and then looks for a possible business opportunity.

*Business-oriented preferences.* Other types of individuals may have a strong desire to engage in a particular kind of activity. They know such businesses must be located in particular places due to their nature and relationship with suppliers, markets, customers, and perhaps other conditions. Realistically they examine a variety of possibilities wherever they occur, having decided that the business activity itself is the principal factor governing his choice.

*Environmental setting.* People differ as to the pattern of living they hope to achieve. For some, the large metropolitan areas possess attractions which are important, while others prefer the small town and its substantially different pattern of business and social relationships. When the environmental conditions are a particularly sensitive factor they should not be ignored. This may be particularly true of the desires of a wife as well as of a husband, and this can include many things such as school facilities, cultural activities, and just plain "elbowroom."

*Relocation potential.* Starting a new business or the acquisition of an existing one may provide the opportunity for the entrepreneur to relocate in circumstances which are more to his or her liking. One may wish to leave the hometown and needs a good reason for doing so. Perhaps the business being considered has outgrown its potential where it is and needs a change. Frequently new people in new surroundings have a better chance of success than where they or their business are well known.

## MARKET VALUE AND VALUE-IN-USE

Locations possess two kinds of value. The first and broadest is market value—the value which the location has if it is allowed to seek and find in the market that value which is "highest and best" for the particular location. Unfortunately, the prospective small business operator must operate within the realm of market value.

Value-in-use is not the same as market value. It is the value that a particular business will place on the location (land and/or building) for a given use. The smaller business must accept the broad impact of market value for a given location; its owners hopefully search for a location in which market value and value-in-use are equal, or at least very close. Many times this is not true; a business must pay a premium because its value-in-use is not equal to the going market value.

## VALUE-IN-USE AND PRICE

From the previous section, the point was made that a location has a going market value and a more restricted, particular use value. Locational values are measured in dollars; thus the need to match up correctly price, value, and location for a particular business.

The enterpreneur must find a location in which the value-price relationship is right for his or her business. Within the variations available there will be something which is right. It may not be perfect, but it will provide what is needed to accomplish the necessary results. It is never permissible to select a location which is barely acceptable, or to buy, rent, or lease on price alone. Every business operation requires a minimum as to location, which must be recognized for every situation. In general the business operator will be looking for a location described by one of the following situations:

1. A business not requiring any particular kind of location. This might be started in a minimum acceptable place, if the price is right and there are indications that the location will improve within a reasonable time.

2. The value-in-use to a given business may be in excess of the market value. In such a case the selected business is able to gain an advantage because its operation is different and more appropriate than what is generated by the market.

3. Many businesses, other than retail or retail-service combinations, have considerable latitude as to their locations. Other buildings, particularly in areas just outside the main shopping districts are often available. These may be appropriate and provide a low-priced entry location for a new enterprise.

4. Value-in-use is personal to the enterpreneur. As such, he or she can negotiate on the basis of personal needs. If the market is weak, the prospective entrepreneur has the upper hand because his or her selection may be made from among a number of possibilities.

## KEY FACTORS IN LOCATION SELECTION

Operators of small businesses, business consultants, financiers, and land use specialists have all expressed opinions about locations for the operation of business enterprises. For the most part their ideas are sound and should be used as conservative guidelines. Surprisingly, many businesses have succeeded, even though they have defied the proven and acceptable criteria. For the most part, however, the poor location will not contribute to a successful enterprise.

The importance of key factors is that as a group they are not the same from one location to the next. A comparison of locations will require that the analyst provide a way in which an assortment of factors can be consolidated, evaluated, and compared. Usually the process involves an assignment of values on a scale or index which are then converted to dollar amount for comparison.

When the prospective enterpreneur has decided what his personal criteria will be and understands the value-price analysis process, it is time to move on to actual locational analysis. The process involved is probably best divided into three main categories. These are:

1. Location and site analysis
2. Supporting features
3. Intangibles

Items in the first category are physically related to the actual location. Those in the second category are related, but not in a direct relationship. Those in the third category have a relationship, but one which is somewhat detached and difficult to determine. Each of these will be examined in the order given.

## Location and site analysis

The actual location requires an examination of the following specific features:

1. Land (if vacant)—Size, shape, and elevations.
2. Land and buildings—Placement, frontage, exposure, access, etc.
3. Services and access—Streets, utilities, alleys, sidewalks, and parking.
4. Transportation facilities—Rail, truck, bus, and air.
5. Zoning and site use—Limited, controlled, nonconforming, etc.
6. Supporting services—Fire and police protection, garbage disposal, sprinkler systems, street lighting, security patrols.
7. Costs—Lease, rental, improvements, upgrading, and financing.
8. Carrying charges—Taxes, licenses, fees, maintenance, etc.

As indicated by the above listing, the examination of the location or specific site is a fairly involved process. It is beyond the scope of this textbook to examine these features in any detail; the entrepreneur, however, will want to conduct his own thorough inquiry.

The land itself can be observed, and if necessary, experts can be asked for necessary specific opinions. Soil conditions, underground water, and elevation changes can all be computed by competent engineering firms. Re-surveys may also be necessary. Land and building combinations can also be studied and estimates made as to necessary changes.

Other physical features can likewise be examined and evaluated. Streets, utilities, transportation access, and zoning regulations require "digging and assembling" but may not require expert opinions or judgments as to their relationship to the business.

Costs and carrying charges require computation and comparison. Some professional help from an accountant or other professional may be needed.

## Supporting features

A number of features which are not actually a part of the location or site are still important items of consideration. These may support or detract from the location but the supporting factors must obviously outweigh the undesirable ones.

*1. Community characteristics.* A community will possess a number of unique characteristics. Even within a community there may be substantial differences from one part of the town to another. Chamber of Commerce data will reveal the economic characteristics that are important. These are typically such things as per capita income, the employment base, population growth, and trade orientations. Visual inspection indicates evidence of prosperity or decay, vitality or despair, etc.

*2. Environment.* A potentially successful small business needs a good environment in which to operate. Such is revealed by the age and appearance of buildings, condition of streets, apparent vitality of the surrounding and supporting businesses, and the "thrust" of business generated in the total supporting business community.

*3. Competition.* Very few businesspersons today are able to operate without competition. If no local competitors exist, it is likely that mail-order houses have penetrated the market. Mass media, particularly television, and good transportation have tended to give consumers considerable product knowledge and the ability to search for and find the products which they desire.

Market research aimed at competitors and products will show where competitors are located, what they sell, their size, and the nature of their operation. Much can be learned by small businesspersons on their own without too much expenditure of time and effort.

Working with a community map and the "Yellow Pages" of the telephone book will reveal locations which can then be pinpointed on a map. Comparison with trading area studies which are available for many localities will give insight into the market structure and the possibilities for a new or existing business.

Close proximity is not always bad as indicated by the clustering that often occurs of businesses such as automobile dealers, shoe stores, and restaurants.

Competitive factors presented by the total array of competitors must be evaluated individually and then weighed as to their total impact. A typical competitive "inquiry list" might proceed as follows:

1. Who are direct competitors?
   *a.* Products offered.
   *b.* Customers served.
   *c.* Impact within trading area.
2. What competitors have what portion of your contemplated market?
3. What proportion of the available market is served by nonresident competitors, i.e., direct sellers, mail-order firms, and regional department stores?
4. How do you secure an initial foothold and subsequent increases in sales to reasonable volume levels?
5. Are your estimates realistically based on the past experience of other small businesses similar to your own?

*4. Trading area.* Small businesspersons must apprise themselves of the geographical extent of their trading area. If a customer shops a community on a repeat basis, he or she is part of the trade area. By its nature, wholesaling may include a much larger area than a retail store, and manufacturing might serve customers throughout the United States. Products, stores, communities, and services all have their trading areas, and each or all of these in various combinations should be evaluated in terms of a particular location.

Initially, it may be quite difficult to estimate a trade area, except for studies that have previously been done, with resulting analyses and conclusions. Inferences and relationships can be established where justified. Most such studies are by inquiry, questionnaire, bank check source analysis, and other types of identification. Frequently other, noncompetitive merchants can be of help as can bankers and Chamber of Commerce officials.

Competitive division of the local market and penetration by outside sources should be examined, but they will be difficult to pin down. Some help should be available from suppliers, wholesalers, and perhaps a management or marketing consultant if other sources are inadequate.

*5. Transportation costs and services.* The cost of transportation and the service levels provided have been a source of increasing frustration for a number of small businesses. In many cases transportation costs have been increasing faster than other costs of doing business, while the level of services has deteriorated. Table 17–1 gives a quick summary of some typical transportation data assembled in 1973.

Other kinds of supporting features can be visualized for a variety of business situations. In each case they should be examined if they seem pertinent to a given business situation.

## Intangibles

As the name implies, intangibles are difficult to identify and assess. Personal preferences of a pragmatic nature have been discussed previously. They are important and readily identified as one class of intangibles. Some of the more unique intangibles are quite different. A given individual may become obsessed with the notion that taxation be avoided, even at costs which outweigh the actual taxes themselves.

In recent years, there have been developing trends in the areas of consumer product protection, environmental protection standards, and tightening land use laws. These are typical examples of intangibles that must be assessed as to their impact on a business, but they are difficult to measure with any degree of accuracy.

## COMPARISON OF POSSIBLE LOCATIONS

So far an attempt has been made to outline how a prospective businessperson would engage in any typical location analysis. No decision can be

**TABLE 17-1**
**Transport service and cost comparisons**

**PART A: SERVICE**

| | Parcel Post | United Parcel | Bus | REA express | Surface express | Air express | Truck line |
|---|---|---|---|---|---|---|---|
| Pickup and delivery | No | Yes | No | Yes. Within a designated service area | Yes. Corporate city limits | No. Extra charge by separate carriers | Yes. Within a liberal service area |
| Minimum charges | No | No. 1 lb. and up | Yes. 0–10 lb. $1.75 | Yes. 1–5 lb. $3.35 | Yes. 1–5 lb. $1.30 | Yes. 0–5 lb. $7.50 | Yes. 100 lb. $3.75 |
| Quantity limits per customer | No | Yes. 100 lb. to one consignee per day | No | No | Yes. 200 lb. to one consignee per day | No | No |
| Size and weight restrictions | Yes. 70 lb. and size limits | Yes. 50 lb. 108 total inches length-width-girth | Yes. 100 lb. 141 total inches length-width-girth | No. Restrictions not applicable to small shipments | 100 lb. per package. 200 lb. to one consignee per day | Not restrictive. Shipper must observe weight-cube ratio | Not restrictive on small shipments |
| Service area | All postoffices | Expanding service areas. Some restrictions | Restricted to points on business routes | Good | Limited. Listed terminal points | Limited. Listed terminal points | Broad. Through connecting carriers |
| Service time | Medium. Some areas slow | Expedited | Medium | Expedited | Expedited | Fast | Medium to fast |
| Expediting and tracing | Difficult | Good to excellent. Through district offices | Sometimes difficult. Depends on terminal efficiency | Varies. Based on efficiency of terminal operations | Generally good. Through district offices | Fast | Good. Will vary some between carriers and terminals |

**PART B: SHIPPING COSTS**

| | Parcel Post | United Parcel | Bus | REA express | Surface express | Air express | Truck line |
|---|---|---|---|---|---|---|---|
| 5 lb.–100 mi. (for min. chg.) | $ .85 | $ .85 | $ 1.40 to 2.45 | $3.90 | $1.55 | $ 7.50 | $ 4.15 |
| 10 lb.–200 mi. | 1.30 | 1.45 | 2.90 | 3.90 | 2.05 | 13.99 | 4.15 |
| 30 lb.–500 mi. | 3.10 | 3.35 | 3.65 | 4.25 | 5.35 | 16.90 | 10.50 |
| 50 lb.–500 mi. | 4.60 | 5.25 | 5.90 | 6.40 | 5.35 | 19.12 | 10.50 |
| 100 lb.–500 mi. | Not available | Not available | 10.80 | 6.40 | 6.65 | 22.55 | 10.50 |
| 100 lb.–1,000 mi. | Not available | Not available | 15.00 | 8.50 | 6.65 | 28.25 | 11.33 |

* Typical rates listed are for a general miscellaneous class of articles.
Source: John B. Kline and Martin F. Schmidt, "Development Options for Small Shipments," *Colorado Business Review* (Boulder, Colo.: College of Business and Administration, April 1973), p. 3.

made on the strength of a single situational analysis. Alternative locations will develop, with strengths and weaknesses of features, values, and price which require some further form of analysis.

## Comparison analysis

It is unlikely that a given location can be properly analyzed and priced without comparison with other possible locations. No two locations will have the same advantages and disadvantages. Value and the asking price will likewise be a measurement based on a total of different characteristics for each locational site.

Theoretical evaluation is possible as a bench mark, but it does not reflect conditions as to local demand and pricing. In addition, theoretical data are frequently compared to industry averages which are composites of widely varying data. In budgeting and cost allocation analysis these averages will be helpful and will be applied by financial sources. For the individual, however, it will be necessary to develop data on comparable features of various locations and then apply weighting factors which provide the measure of ultimate worth.

Weighting factors may be hard to establish, but they are generally applied within a framework which includes: (1) the specific type of business, (2) the different functional divisions of the business, and (3) the relationship and importance of the location. For each different business, functional feature, and location, the weight assigned will change. Even though such assignments are based on judgment, if they are applied with consistency by the same person, they will show differences even though the magnitude might be questionable. If honestly done they are of considerable value, particularly to develop information for the financial sources who will be asked to support the operation. Table 17–2 shows a location comparison rating sheet.

## LOCATIONS FOR DIFFERENT KINDS OF BUSINESS

### Retailing

Nearly all forms of retailing require locations which are suitable for the particular business involved. For many retailers location is so important that it may be the one principal factor between success and failure. No one particular advantageous feature is usually enough by itself to guarantee success to the new entrepreneur. A good location, however, may give the business operator an initial period of success, which provides the "breathing time" that is needed to overcome certain shortcomings that develop in the initial period of operation.

*Drawing power.* Retailing depends on drawing power—either from

**TABLE 17-2**
Location comparison rating sheet

---

## I. PRIMARY ACCEPTANCE OR REJECTION FACTORS

|  | | *Locations under consideration* | | |
|---|---|---|---|---|
| *Answer Yes or No* | A | B | C | D |
| 1. Is this location available? | | | | |
| 2. Will zoning allow your proposed business? | | | | |
| 3. Does this site meet minimum business needs? | | | | |
| 4. Do existing structures meet minimum initial needs? | | | | |
| 5. Is the price of this location within your operating budget? | | | | |
| 6. Is the location with or without buildings, fairly priced for your needs? | | | | |

A "no" answer may be sufficient reason not to proceed with further investigation unless correction or modification can be achieved.

## II. SITE VALUATIONS

|  | | | | |
|---|---|---|---|---|
| *Use percent scale 0 to 100* | A | B | C | D |
| 7. How does this location compare with the best possible location available? | | | | |
| 8. What rating would you give the present buildings on the site? | | | | |
| 9. How would you rate your locational environment compared with the best environment existing within your trading area? | | | | |
| 10. How would you rate the adequacy of available parking for automobiles? | | | | |
| 11. What rating would be given to the nature and quantity of combined foot and auto traffic passing your location? | | | | |
| 12. What is the improvement potential of this location? | — | — | — | — |
| Total . . . . . . . . . . . . . . . . . | | | | |

TABLE 17–2 (*continued*)

## III. TREND ANALYSIS

*Brief answer as to conclusions*

| | A | B | C | D |
|---|---|---|---|---|
| 13. Has the location shown improvement through the years? | | | | |
| 14. Is the owner and/or landlord progressive and cooperative? | | | | |
| 15. What major patterns of change are affecting this location: | | | | |
|    *a.* Streets—speed limits—paving. | | | | |
|    *b.* Shopping centers. | | | | |
|    *c.* Zoning. | | | | |
|    *d.* Financial investment. | | | | |
|    *e.* Dynamic leadership and action. | | | | |
| 16. What businesses have occupied this location over the past 10 years? | | | | |
| 17. Have the businesses identified in 16 (above) been successful? | | | | |
| 18. Why is this location now available? | | | | |
| 19. Are a number of other suitable locations available? | | | | |
| Compare the answer for each business and rank each by number from among those reviewed (1–2–3–4). | (1) | (2) | (3) | (4) |

## IV. PRICE-VALUE DETERMINATION

| | A | B | C | D |
|---|---|---|---|---|
| 20. What is the asking price of each location? | | | | |
| 21. What numerical total for each site is developed through questions 7 to 12? | | | | |
| 22. Is there a "no" answer to any question 1 through 6? | | | | |
| 23. Do the answers to questions 13 through 19 develop a pattern which is: | | | | |
|    *a.* Highly favorable. | | | | |
|    *b.* Average. | | | | |
|    *c.* Minimal. | | | | |
|    *d.* Questionable. | | | | |
|    *e.* Not acceptable. | | | | |
| Ranking position of each location based on numerical totals and preferences as to subjective items in III and IV. | (3) | (2) | (4) | (1) |

the particular business itself, or from that provided by other businesses. There may be several ways to provide drawing power. One technique would be to mount a substantial advertising campaign and so convince potential customers that they would seek out the particular firm. This and other related forms of stimulus are probably not too appropriate in most cases. A better approach is built along the lines of selecting a location which provides the right exposure to enough customers in the right frame of mind to trigger some initial inquiry or transaction. Power will develop as reputation and success develop. Combined locations such as shopping centers, the drawing power of a large store in the vicinity, a crucial establishment such as a bank or U.S. Post office, are all examples of features which provide drawing power that can be capitalized on by the neighboring small business. It makes no difference whether the small business is in the customer path or in the vicinity of the customer's destination—chances are good that he or she has an opportunity for some business activity.

*Access.* The automobile has imposed serious limits on many locations. The propensity of the average American to drive an automobile has led to the rise of the shopping center and the deterioration of many "downtown" shopping districts. A lack of parking at the destination point may be just as serious as the unwillingness of a customer to walk any reasonable distance.

One-way streets, upstairs locations, poor sidewalks, and other related conditions all have an impact on access. Proximity may be misjudged; merely being close is not always sufficient for the business. In fact, there are in many places locations that are avoided by people, for reasons that are not well understood. This in part may be a carry-over from the days when many residents of a given community did not want to be seen "on the wrong side of the tracks."

If a location, or the surrounding area, has a history of a succession of unsuccessful businesses it should be avoided. Logic may not condemn it, but the small business had better not attempt to overcome that kind of situation.

*Environment.* The environment dealt with here is the area surrounding the business or in close enough proximity that it affects the location in some fashion. If access draws customers in, the environment should not drive them away.

The environmental relationship is built around the idea that psychologically the customer is influenced by what the senses and experience tell him or her. If the environment is "right" or complimentary, the small business will benefit because the potential customer or client finds what he is looking for in the place where he expects it. Surprises are fine, but a business may not exist long enough to overcome environmental disadvantages.

The prospective business operator should view the environment of his location very carefully. Usually the new business needs the following:

1. Businesses which are compatible—this implies that other businesses should appeal to the same kind of customers in terms of their income, desires, intelligence, etc.
2. Evidences of vitality and prosperity—an environment that is alive and stimulated by capable and energetic business operators.
3. Good zoning regulations and land use controls—protection against objectionable business practices. Often this is tightly controlled in well-managed shopping centers.
4. Municipal and community support—enlightened city officials who support and work for the betterment of resident businesses.

In general, an area in which the existing businesses are obviously well managed and successful is the place to locate the right kind of new business. Much can be learned from careful observation and evaluation.

*Competition.* It is unlikely that any form of retailer is free from some fairly effective competition. If there are not competitors within the nearby geographical area served, then competition may develop from mail-order firms or adjacent communities.

A very major purpose of a location is to develop competition advantages. As explained under the earlier section on access, the automobile developed particular patterns of competition, notably the shopping center and its particular characteristics. With the energy crisis and recession of the middle 1970s, a good bit of this may change. People will probably restrict the use of their automobiles, and locational analysis will need to be restructured.

Competition can be examined and data gathered by any prospective business operator. Some professional help may be needed to interpret some kinds of data, but this should not be a substitute for the entrepreneur's own education and understanding. Information is needed on who are the competitors, where are they located, which ones have what share of the market, where potential customers now shop, etc. Analysis methods can be obtained from a basic textbook in marketing or retailing. Often local advertising agencies or Chamber of Commerce managers can provide useful data and opinions.

## Services

Service businesses were the fastest growing segment of small business activity in the 1950s and 60s. As per capita and disposable income increased, consumers shifted more and more of their needs to the service specialist.

The growth of service enterprises was often not well planned nor based on very sound logic. As a result, many could not exist on service alone. To complement the service operations, many expanded into service-retail combinations. If the location did not support retailing, then a move was necessary.

With today's changing conditions, the prospective owner of a service enterprise should think carefully about location. Many existing self-sufficient service businesses do not need any particular kind of location. On the other hand, times may change, requiring something different. Services rely heavily on labor. With substantially increasing labor costs, some services may become more competitive. If so, then location becomes much more critical.

Within the total framework of operations, the service business should be located in the best location it can afford. A main street gives exposure, even though the business, such as a plumbing shop, is seldom patronized directly. Quick access to customers and low costs for service calls dictate a centralized location. Copy-making firms are the prime example of the need for centralized, convenient, accessible locations.

Some ingenuity may pay off in how the operator chooses a location. If operating from home, the owner may be prevented by zoning from having a sign to identify the location. He or she may, however, advertise on a service truck and park it in front of the establishment. One highly regarded television repair shop located close to a major retail-service competitor. The repair shop flourished on overflow from the retail-service competitor.

## Industrial locations

Most of the comparisons made previously between different forms of business have compared retail, service, manufacturing, and wholesaling businesses. In considering location, manufacturing here is described as industrial. The reason for this is that in recent years a large number of smaller businesses have been created which do engage in manufacturing, but are normally described as "light, clean industries." Many such enterprises are required to be located in industrial zones, but are not thought of as manufacturing in the traditional sense. Such industrial zones include a wide variety of activities, such as printing and publishing, warehouses, research and development firms, and small-scale versions of traditional manufacturing.

The industrial location for the smaller business is usually not a difficult problem. Many trade-offs are possible and the smaller enterprise is often located in the home community of the original founders, because of certain advantages that can be developed in a familiar locality. Many smaller industrial enterprises start out in older buildings, where space and versatility are possible—if no special building features are required.

Analysis for the industrial location should concentrate on a combination of the following:

1. Community features—Labor supply, utilities, land values, taxes, climate and zoning.
2. Markets and transportation—Market distances, transport costs, service times, warehousing, and distribution.
3. Trade-off analysis—What can be traded off—labor, input materials, transportation, taxation, etc.
4. Intangibles—Key employees' satisfaction and motivation. Attractive surroundings and appealing cultural advantages in the community or nearby.

*Location appraisal.* If the selection of the industrial location is very critical in terms of long-range commitment and/or substantial investment, the small business operator may wish to secure professional help. Industrial development organizations and companies such as the Fantus Corporation specialize in industrial locations. Their professional help is backed by specialists who can pass judgment on circumstances which may be beyond the competence of many small business operators.

## Wholesaling

Traditional wholesaling operations have declined substantially, in the years since World War II. There are still some smaller wholesalers in business, but many of the wholesale functions have been absorbed into the activities of franchisors, manufacturers, and cooperative merchandising organizations.

The criteria for a wholesale location revolve around efficiency of operations. Wholesalers will frequently locate in the older commercial district to capitalize on a centralized location which is conveniently served by railroad sidings, truck loading platforms, main highways, and overflow warehousing space. These operations are almost always oriented to a high volume at low unit cost. Low overhead and fast customer service are also important in such operations.

Locations for wholesaling can probably be assembled best by real estate brokers and commercial property management firms. Some firms such as USCO and Trammel Crow Distribution Corporation lease space which is specially designed for efficent handling of wholesale materials and merchandise. In any case, the selection of a warehouse location is usually an easier proposition than for other forms of small business.

## SPECIALIZED LOCATIONS

A number of developments have taken place over the past 25 years which have changed substantially the environment for business locations.

Most of these changes resulting in specialized locations are based on a desire to achieve integrated shopping areas, revitalize deteriorated districts, and combat rapidly rising land and building costs.

These specialized locations are usually located in one of the following arranged areas.

1. Shopping centers
2. Urban renewal centers
3. Downtown malls
4. Specialty clusters
5. Internal leased space
6. Industrial districts

A brief discussion of each of the above may be helpful in the choice of a location for a given enterprise.

*Shopping centers.* These are familiar to everyone and come in a wide variety as to the "mix" of businesses, drawing power, size, and decor. Larger shopping centers have usually been based on the presence of one or more sizable firms such as a J. C. Penney store, along with a major grocery supermarket, plus a variety of other smaller businesses. In more recent years, a number of such centers have been built without the dominant tenant, although these have tended to be of smaller size.

In general the shopping center is inclined to be a desirable location for many kinds of business. The principal difficulty for most smaller businesses is in negotiating a lease or rental which the business can afford to pay. The tenant may pay on a percent of gross volume of sales, a flat monthly sum plus a percent over a certain volume of sales, a sum per square foot of space, or perhaps a flat sum with a renegotiation after a fairly short period of time. The principal difficulty for the smaller tenants is that their location cost is often quite high. Major tenants usually drive a hard bargain; the center managers attempt to develop a considerable portion of their net income from the smaller tenants who need the viable location, but have little bargaining power as to price.

Any prospective tenant for a shopping center must analyze carefully his investment, duration of commitment, break-even figures, and cash flow before making such a choice. Such a center can be good, in fact very good, but it may also burden the business with a cash outlay which the business can't handle. Be very cautious about restrictions on signs and advertising-limiting covenants.

*Urban renewal centers.* The mid 1970s is a little early to tell just what are the prospects for locations in urban renewal centers. Evidence so far would indicate that many of these areas will prove attractive and viable over some period of time.

A careful assessment of the renewal center should indicate the relative stage of renewal, what is the nature of the development, and what the plans are for the future. Frequently, renewal areas, in part, were converted to commercial parking lots prior to rebuilding. Rebuilt portions are provided with parking, and if the price is reasonable, the center may be an attractive place to locate.

One crucial factor is the length of time since the area has been a vital business locale. If other areas have become established, this may be a real question mark for the revitalized center.

*Downtown malls.* These ordinarily do not displace the established businesses. For a new business a decision on location is primarily based on the length of time since the mall was established, and the state of business activity now and before the mall was established.

Mall areas where the streets are not critical in moving substantial quantities of traffic, or if they are equipped with alternate parking, stand the best chance of maintaining or enhancing their business potential.

Comments relative to shopping centers and urban renewal centers are also applicable to this category.

*Specialty clusters.* These are frequently "mini-shopping centers." The specialty shops may be highly variable but are probably retailers that need some identity and exposure. In many instances, these clusters are located to provide access or at least advertising exposure to main arterials. Others are on the periphery of established shopping centers.

A prospective tenant should be cautious about a specialty cluster until solid evidence is available that the cluster rental or lease fee is appropriate to the particular location.

Rental or lease costs should be in line with appropriate criteria and normally somewhat below main shopping centers. One good possibility is for several tenants to arrange with a financier to build a building with lease-back arrangements.

*Internal leased space.* Major stores, particularly a number of small "chains" frequently lease out space for specialty operations such as shoes or film and photo services. This may also be an open space rental or lease on adjacent property owned by a high-volume business. Many of these locations are very attractive and of interest to small business operators.

The principal drawbacks to the internal space are its normally high cost and control by the landlord or primary tenant. Such arrangements are usually only made if the owner figures that the leasing tenant can do a better job than the principal, or return more money than can be generated by that space for a different purpose. If conditions change, the tenant or subtenant may find his arrangement is made untenable or perhaps terminated. Good legal advice is a must in such two- and three-party arrangements, with the strong recommendation that business be done with reputable people. A small business is seldom in a financial position to engage in a lawsuit involving property rights.

*Industrial districts.* Industrial districts are planned areas set aside for various types of industrial activity. Some are quite restricted as to type of business and the control and placement of buildings and their physical features. Others have very few restrictions.

The following resumé for the year 1974 is typical of an industrial district for light industry.

**TABLE 17–3**
**Industrial park data sheet**

---

ATLAS INDUSTRIAL PARK                    BOULDER COUNTY

*Location*—West Midway Boulevard, Broomfield, Colorado

*Area*—50 acres. PLANNED INDUSTRIAL DISTRICT. 60 percent leased or sold. Owned by Commander Leasing Company. Cost of sites is $0.75–$1.25 per square foot. Lease price negotiable.

*Improvements on Site*—Eight buildings occupied with 400,000 square feet of space

*Topography*—Level          *Adjacent Land Use*—Industrial and Commercial

*Transportation*—
   Highway: Paved street on site and U.S. Highways 36 and 287 adjacent to site.
   Railroad: Colorado, Burlington, and Quincy Railroad on site.
   Airport: Stapleton International Airport 20 miles from site.

*Utilities*—
   Electric power and Natural gas: Public Service Company of Colorado on site.
   Water and Sewer: City of Broomfield on site.
   Telephone: Mountain Bell on site.

*Covenants*—Building setbacks, landscaping, parking, water control.

*Contract*—Richard A. Rogers, 305 West 56th Avenue, Denver, Colorado 80216 (Telephone—303-222-6925)

---

Source: Denver Chamber of Commerce, Denver, Colo., 1974.

Industrial parks and districts are normally very attractive locations. In many areas, they will control the major portion of land on which locations are feasible. Such locations should be investigated before a decision is made.

## WHEN TO CHANGE YOUR LOCATION

1.  Growth in population and trading area is not benefiting the business at the present site.

2. Business operations show that the enterprise is now established and capable of growth beyond the opportunities at the present site.

3. Other site development and available locations provide opportunities not previously available.

4. Upgrading of the present site by sizable capital expenditures to achieve proper operating environment may be better accomplished elsewhere.

5. Relocation may preclude or eliminate the possibility of competition's gaining increased advantages for the available market.

6. Locational change may be a stimulus to accomplish a variety of improvements in business operations that would otherwise be delayed awaiting such an event.

## QUESTIONS

1. Why is the price asked for a certain location not always consistent with the needs of a particular business?

2. What will determine the minimum conditions of a location which are necessary for a particular type of business activity?

3. Why must personal preferences be resolved first, before an active search is conducted to obtain a suitable location?

4. How can a prospective entrepreneur find out what the possible trading area is for a given business in a particular location?

5. How does the environment surrounding a particular location vary in its effect as to different kinds of businesses?

6. Why should a service business consider a location that has reasonable access and exposure to the public?

7. What pattern of location is most prevalent among small manufacturers?

8. Why should a number of possible locations be considered simultaneously and compared with each other before a choice is made?

9. Why is a certain sequence of analysis followed when a location is being investigated?

10. Should a possible change of location be considered on a regular schedule? Why?

## PROBLEMS

1. Visit a fairly sizable diversified shopping center with at least one major retail store and a total of at least 15 different establishments. Analyze the following:

   a. The preferred parking areas.
   b. Foot traffic density at various points.

c. The location of various kinds of enterprises.

d. The size of the various establishments.

Following this analysis, contact the shopping center manager and inquire about the following features:

a. The rental price per square foot or whatever other method is used.

b. Degree of control over each tenant which is exercised by the management.

c. The length of time that the tenants have been in operation.

d. How often a location is likely to be available.

Then answer this question: Does your analysis indicate that the shopping center management has fairly and correctly priced the available space based on the factors affecting the value-in-use of a location?

2. Contact the office of the city planning director (or other appropriate official) in a community which is subject to city planning and zoning. Find out what major zoning changes, annexations, and variances have taken place in the past two years. Visit one or more areas which have been rezoned for business purposes and attempt to answer the following questions:

a. Why was business zoning established?

b. Have businesses been established and if so what kind?

c. Are the best locations being developed first?

d. What kinds of business activity would be appropriate to the newly rezoned areas?

## BIBLIOGRAPHY

Bank of America. *Small Business Reporter* (Business Profiles, and Business Operations). Jenepher Walker, Managing Editor; Bank of America, San Francisco, Calif. A continuing series of summary advisory pamphlets. The Business Profiles deal with particular kinds of businesses, while Business Operations relate to functional areas of operation. These are very well written, concise, and yet meaningful to a layman or someone more experienced.

Hartley, Robert F. *Retailing.* Boston: Houghton Mifflin Co., 1975. A textbook which has much of value regarding locations and the elements that relate to good merchandizing sites. Contains a good assortment of resource materials.

"Problems of Location and Real Estate." *Journal of Small Business Management.* (Theme of this issue). National Council for Small Business Management Development, Bureau of Business Research, West Virginia University, Morgantown, W. Va., January 1972.

Klatt, Lawrence A. *Small Business Management—Essentials of Entrepreneurship.* Belmont, Calif.: Wadsworth Publishing Co., 1973. A very good treatment of many aspects of small business management. Chapter 7 deals with locations and provides a good list of references. Has good related information, particularly for retailers.

Price, Waterhouse, and Co. *Information Guides for Doing Business Outside the United States.* New York: Price, Waterhouse, and Co. A series of pamphlets identified by countries, outlining what is necessary to conduct a business in that country. Not specific as to a particular location but invaluable to the prospective entrepreneur interested in a particular country.

# 18

# The building—and operating facilities

Choosing a location is often tied to the combined choice of location plus the building and its operating features. The problem of location is always of first priority—nothing can ordinarily be done to change the basic character of a location. The building, however, can be changed, along with its facilities. Practically, there are limits to what can be done, but every prospective business owner needs to examine combinations of locations, buildings, and facilities in order to know what is available and at what price.

The majority of small enterprises are started in existing buildings, which will be adapted to the particular business. Beginning entrepreneurs usually start with several limitations, particularly in operating capital. Prime locations, new buildings, and the most modern of facilities are beyond their initial capabilities. Modifications and "scaled down" criteria frequently dictate that the operating location and its facilities be adequate, but not much more.

Entrepreneurs initially tend to rent or lease for limited periods because they are uncertain about the possible success of their business and because of the lack of capital for fixed capital commitments. Many locations are adequate, but do not include buildings and facilities which are suitable for the larger, better established, and more secure enterprise. These more modest locations are what the new business operator is looking for. Money spent on an "upgrading" here may produce results which are quite adequate and at a cost much less than that of a better location with a better building which is more in demand by a variety of businesses.

## THE BUILDING'S PHYSICAL FEATURES

The actual building to be used for the proposed enterprise must be examined as to its main physical features. These are characteristics of the

305

actual structure which are relatively fixed and cannot be altered or changed without considerable effort and expense. These principal features are:

1. Space
2. Configuration
3. Frontage
4. Access
5. Layout
6. Compatibility

*Space.* The actual space, generally floor space, is the basis on which the value of most buildings is calculated. Not all floor space is of equal value, but given a number of related characteristics, it is floor space that is acquired and used.

The floor space is good, average, or negative, depending on certain features that bear directly on its usefulness. Open space allows the space to be divided or partitioned. Columns, doorways, windows and stairways restrict what can be done with the space available. If properly placed they enhance the space; if not, they detract from its usefulness. Physical proportions are also important. These are considered on the basis of size of rooms, their width, depth, ceiling heights, location of doorways and windows, and the appropriateness of these to each other.

*Configuration.* Elements of configuration are related to the basic design and appropriateness of the building to a given purpose. As in the case of space, the physical features are very significant and are in total very instrumental in the usefulness of the building to the tenant. Configuration would go much further than the features mentioned in regard to space. All systems would be included, along with the adaptability of the building to a given purpose, or for meeting a particular group of objectives. Another aspect of configuration is related to style and appearance —features that may have considerable importance in certain retail operations and at times for a service business.

*Frontage.* Frontage provides exposure and contact with customers and clients, and, it is hoped, some lasting impression on those who will become customers in the future. Some amount of lineal footage along the street, mall, highway, or other artery is necessary. How much, in what place, and of what kind is not an easy question to answer. For some businesses, in a very congested shopping area, 10 or 12 feet may be all that is needed. For another business, 100 feet might be inadequate.

Adequate and fairly priced frontage probably depends on the ability of the prospective business operator and his or her advisers to assess correctly the impact of frontage and its contribution to the proposed business.

Frontage which is too little, bracketed between substantially larger businesses, or ineffective because of bad design and/or door placement is always questionable and should probably be rejected. A corner, with frontage on two sides, is not necessarily better. In general it should be, but a higher asking price is not necessarily an indication that the corner is definitely better.

*Access.* Access, as a building feature, is a much more subtle element than access to a location as discussed in the previous chapter. Obviously, the customer or client must be able to reach the building physically without difficulty and in a manner which does not vary too much from accepted standards of customer convenience.

Access in total includes the entire premises and accessibility in all respects. Elevators, stairways, partitions, doorway sizes, traffic flow patterns, and zoning controls are all a part of access. Even the lighting and color schemes may have a positive or negative effect on the willingness of individuals to travel a certain corridor or seek out an obscure part of a building.

Access problems require careful analysis and an understanding of the fact that some traits of human nature are not easily understood. It is best not to be overly optimistic in predicting how access for customers will actually be accomplished until some evidence develops that the access provision is succeeding.

*Layout.* The considerations of layout for a basic structure are not ordinarily too difficult. Unless the floor space is badly arranged with doorways in awkward places and poor placement of stairways and other serious defects, an adequate layout should be possible. Sometimes an older structure cannot be altered to any extent without bringing the entire building into compliance with current building codes. If changes in plumbing, heating, wiring, or fire controls are needed for good layout, it may be more prudent to look elsewhere for a suitable building.

*Compatibility.* If a building does not fit into its environment and provide what the entrepreneur needs at that location, it is not compatible. Differences in style and appearance are readily apparent, but they are not necessarily incompatible.

More serious problems arise from differences in elevation between the chosen site and adjacent or nearby buildings. Too much or too little setback is always a question mark. A poorly planned lighting system (interior and/or exterior) can create impressions that are wrong or misleading.

Occasionally the extreme design or appearance is advantageous, but it is questionable as an approach by an unproven entrepreneur. Novelty is not the same as incompatibility. Incompatibility is deep-seated and tends to defy any easy solutions.

Oftentimes first impressions of a situation are important. The prospective new businessperson should attempt to record some basic first impressions for later review. These should not replace logical analysis, or be disregarded because of more importance being given to other aspects of the new enterprise.

## ZONING AND LAND USE CONTROLS

The past 25 years has been a period in which zoning has become firmly established in the majority of business and residential areas across the United States. The past 10 years has seen a variation of zoning develop which is described generally as land use regulation and control. Whereas zoning applies in the more heavily used areas, land use is more generally applied to rural areas. Neither is exclusive in this—but this is commonly how these are thought of in connection with controls over the way in which property may be used.

The trends in zoning and land use in most cases are probably contrary to the long-range interests of small business owners and operators. Zoning and controls tend to require compliance with a variety of conditions and circumstances. Higher standards and more restrictions tend to raise the price of land, restrict the amount of land available for use, and to increase the costs of buildings.

If a business is allowed to continue as an existing business under a "grandfather clause,"[1] this may provide an advantage over new ventures which are denied these privileges. Over the course of time, all businesses will be brought into compliance.

Buildings and other structures are affected in a variety of ways. The most important of these are described briefly under the following categories:

1. Building controls—Buildings for any use (business or otherwise) are controlled as to the amount of land needed for a given type of structure; height, setback, utility and street access, fire protection, construction features, and many other related conditions.

2. Designated uses—Building and locations for business are subject to tight controls. Certain business operations may only be conducted in certain properly zoned areas. Some businesses such as liquor stores, pawn shops, and even professional offices may be controlled by administration boards. Such boards may control a location and in addition the actual premises occupied. A typical example is a state law that prohibits a dispensing optician from occupying any premises where the operation is conducted jointly with another business.

3. Prohibited uses—Standards adopted by zoning boards and land use agencies have become increasingly more restrictive. As an extension of designated uses, many business activities are now prohibited in many

---

[1] A *grandfather clause* is a provision in a law or statute which permits the continuation of a condition or business practice which is contrary to the law. The privilege may extend to a structure, an individual, or a particular business practice.

land use areas, or are subject to tight controls where they are permitted. Typically, gasoline may not be transported or stored within municipal corporate limits in containers of over 1,500 gallons. No vehicles can be operated whose noise level exceeds a certain limit. The generation of smoke fumes, dust, and water pollution beyond certain limits are prohibited—effectively the business is either prohibited or severely restricted.

Many activities are so designated that the total business operation must be wholly confined to the premises of the lot on which the business is conducted. Signs, such as revolving beacons or flashing signs are often prohibited. Accessory buildings may not be allowed. Buildings may be restricted or prohibited in a "floodplain" area, or where unstable soil conditions exist. It is quite common to deny a number of business uses for a building unless adequate off-street parking is provided. What is adequate depends on the community and its particular needs.

An example of business zoning classification is shown in Figure 18–1. This particular illustration is very typical of zoning provisions for business where business activity is divided into several categories. Businesses covered in Figure 18–1 are of a nonindustrial nature and represent typical retailing and service establishments.

**FIGURE 18–1**
**Typical zoning provisions for restricted business areas**

---

B–BUSINESS DISTRICT
(RESTRICTED BUSINESS AREAS)

11.1   USES PERMITTED

1.   Uses numbered (1) through (9) as permitted in T–Transitional District;

2.   Places for the conduct of any restricted business, not limited to the following: antique shops and art shops; banks; barber shops and beauty parlors; book and stationery stores; clothing shops; department stores; dry goods and variety stores; eating and drinking places; electrical and household appliance stores; florists; furniture stores; gasoline stations; gift shops; grocery stores; hardware stores; jewelry and craft shops; music, radio and television stores; newsstands; office supply stores; offices for business and governmental use; optometrist shops; package liquor stores; photographic studios, equipment and supply stores; public utility collection offices; shoe stores; sporting and athletic goods stores; indoor theaters; toy stores; travel bureaus; and watch repairing.

3.   Public utility mains, and underground facilities; and

4.   Accessory buildings and uses.

11.2 MINIMUM LOT AREA

   1. on land where the principal building is *not* connected to *both* public water and public sewer facilities . . . 15,000 sq. ft.;
   2. on land where the principal building *is* connected to *both* public water and public sewer facilities . . . no minimum requirement.

11.3 MINIMUM LOT WIDTH

   1. on land where the principal building is *not* connected to *both* public water and public sewer facilities . . . 120 ft.;
   2. on land where the principal building *is* connected to *both* public water and public sewer facilities . . . no minimum requirement.

11.4 MINIMUM LOT FRONTAGE . . . 40 ft. (minimum front lot line)

11.5 MINIMUM FRONT YARD . . . 60 ft.

   (minimum distance of any building from the centerline of a street or highway, except as specified in Section XVIII)

11.6 MINIMUM SIDE YARD . . . 10 or 12 ft. (as amended Feb. 24, 1969)

   (minimum distance of buildings from each side lot line or one half the distance between detached buildings on the same lot)

11.7 MINIMUM REAR YARD . . . 20 ft.

   (minimum distance of any building from the rear lot line or from the centerline of an alley where one exists)

11.8 MAXIMUM BUILDING HEIGHT . . . 50 ft.

Any prospective small business owner should review carefully all relevant regulations dealing with zoning and land use. Locations and buildings are coming under increasingly more restrictive measures and controls. This affects the number of available building and site combinations and the price of those that qualify for permitted use.

## COVENANTS AND SOCIAL STANDARDS

Many business properties are not owned and controlled by those that use and occupy them. This is quite often the case for many small businesses. The control of an owner or property manager may be quite restrictive and contrary to what the small business operator would like to do with the building and surrounding land area.

Property owners and agents exert control in ways which they think will best maximize their capital investment. If the market for commercial properties is tight, tenants and lessees can expect restrictions which favor the owner. If a single property or one-tenant building is involved, the restrictions may be arbitrary and overly restrictive. If the market is weak, the owner will be inclined to be more reasonable in the negotiations. In a multiple-business use area, such as a shopping center, owners and property managers tend to adopt measures which they feel are consistent for the entire group of businesses. In general, they will favor the larger tenants over the smaller ones. Typically, signs and advertising on the actual building site are strictly controlled. This may not be a problem for a large major retail store, but it is a serious handicap for a small business.

## CONSTRUCTION FEATURES

Construction features of a building should be investigated quite thoroughly because in most instances a building's major characteristics cannot be changed without considerable expenditure. Items to be investigated are:

1. **Basic building materials and the method of construction.** Newer buildings often use trusses for roof support to eliminate interior columns or load-bearing partitions. Combinations of concrete masonry materials and structural steel may provide a very good building, particularly from the standpoint of maintenance, fire protection, remodeling, and ultimate expansion. Older buildings usually do not have the advantages resulting from modern construction.

2. **Service and equipment characteristics.** Items in this category include the provision of an adequate electrical system, including many outlets, three-wire service for 220-volt or higher voltage service, adequate modernistic lighting fixtures, air-conditioning equipment, a good heating system, rest room facilities, circulation and exhaust fans, and any other equipment which may be pertinent to the business operation.

3. **Interior criteria.** Consideration will vary widely from one type of business to another, particularly from an operation such as retailing to that of manufacturing; but it must include, within reason, a proper wall, ceiling, and floor arrangement which is needed for appearance, utility, and maintenance. The amount of floor loading that can be applied in a building with suspended floors must be computed to determine whether or not limitations are imposed by such construction on the storing of merchandise or the placing of machinery in particular places. Older buildings may have basements, balconies, or second stories which can be used,

but they may be limited as to their usefulness. More modern buildings may be built on one floor and have the advantage of a solid concrete floor, movable partitions, and limited window space. A building with these characteristics can be adapted to a variety of internal arrangements.

**4.** *Appropriate design.* Often undesirable design elements in a building are not particularly important to the business operation if through remodeling they can be concealed to present the desired appearance. Small factories, offices, restaurants, and specialty mercantile establishments have been located in existing buildings where the unusual elements of design and construction have given a uniqueness and drawing power to an otherwise very ordinary business operation.

## BUILDING IMPROVEMENT AND UPGRADING

If the building is new, having been built for the upcoming tenant, most major building and site features have been planned and implemented. In an older building, the tenant will probably want to change a number of features, both inside and out.

*Additions to the realty.* Permanent additions to the realty, which become an inherent part of a structure are "attachments" and ordinarily cannot be removed by the tenant. These additions should be discussed with and negotiated for with the owner, inasmuch as they usually benefit the property. Movable items, such as certain fixtures and equipment, that are not attached, are normally the property of the tenant and may be removed at the end of the occupancy.

*Exterior changes.* Many older buildings need exterior changes, but often no more than a "facelift." This may be accomplished by building a false front, putting in new windows, doors, and trim, or perhaps a new paint job. Surface treatment is often low cost and rather dramatic in terms of changed appearance. A number of experienced people regard a changed exterior appearance as mandatory for a new tenant. This may not be necessary for a highly successful business which is being acquired, but entirely justified where a new business is starting. Contemporary and modernistic appearances may be highly desirable; in other cases they are not appropriate. Careful study as to expenditure and payoff potential will prove to be worthwhile.

*Interior changes.* Changes in the interior of a building are usually divided into two major categories:

1. Structural changes
2. Decorative changes

If the basic structure is being altered, substantial problems may develop. Many building codes specify that basic structural changes require that the building be brought up to the standards of the existing building code. This can pose substantial problems in terms of electrical wiring, plumbing, heating, fire protection, etc. Minor changes, such as moving a partition may be allowed as will redecorating, painting etc. Frequently, the ingenuity of the new tenant can accomplish a substantial improvement without a great deal of expense. Floors, ceilings, doorways, and windows are subject to a variety of changes. Often the difference between an adequate interior and something much better is very small. This can be the guideline for measuring what is needed and the time when it is right to go ahead with the project.

## INVESTMENT PLANNING FOR THE BUILDING

The total program involving the building and its facilities is a substantial long-term commitment for any business. The smaller business is faced with the same kinds of decisions as the large business, but on a reduced scale.

Both a new and older building and its facilities will require a good comprehensive long-range investment plan. Initially the business needs are a good building in which to get off to a good start. A conservative investment is prudent until the business proves that it can succeed.

If the business survives for the first year and is reasonably healthy at that point, serious long-range plans are necessary. The planning is usually predicated on normal healthy growth and the improvement of the building and facilities to keep pace with society and the trends of the times. Provision should be made to expand, move to a new location, build a new building, remodel, redecorate, and anything else that is important.

At least once a year the capital investment program should be reviewed, including the investment in the building and its facilities. Depreciation rates, rates of inflation, and other economic data should be studied. Methods of financial analysis such as payback and discounted cash flow should be examined to determine the economic feasibility of alternative courses of action. Consult the chapters on financial management for details on this. The important thing is *not to put off decisions in this area of investment until it is too late to maintain the right environment that is needed.*

## EFFECTIVE LAYOUT

Layout is concerned with the proper utilization of floor space according to the needs of a particular business. Retailing, service, manufacturing, and wholesaling are all different and require specialized layouts within the internal restrictions of the building structure. In a retailing operation, the layout of a store is primarily concerned with promoting sales activity; to achieve this the needs and accommodations of customers are considered

314

very carefully. In a manufacturing enterprise, layout is concerned with the effective support of production and efficiency regarding the movement of materials, manufacturing sequences, and varying levels of product output and product mix. Service businesses and wholesalers likewise have individual problems requiring special consideration as to layout.

## Retailing

Business operations conducted for the customer and in his or her presence are the subject of an analysis by hundreds of thousands of businesspersons every day. Builders of retail stores, architects, manufacturers, wholesalers, department store chains, and other merchants are constantly considering layout in order to determine the most effective way to merchandise products.

*1. External features.* The entrance to the store must be attractive and well placed in regard to the amount of frontage available. Many businesses have chosen to remodel so as to achieve offset type entrances which provide more window display space and help to develop a traffic pattern which will encourage customers to pass by a number of merchandise displays. Some people like to have the outside display windows open to the interior of the store, whereas others prefer closed back windows which use only the immediate area behind the window for display. Such arrangement will provide shelf and storage space within the store, behind the front display windows.

*2. Internal features.* Aisles should be designed so that customers will be inclined to pass by a variety of merchandise, and yet enable the management to serve the customers conveniently with adequate checkout points and credit and customer service offices. Aisleways that run parallel to the main store entrance rather than at right angles will aid in visual observation of merchandise and have a tendency to draw customers farther into the store. Cash registers or service centers can then be located at strategic points to aid employees in observing the needs of customers and to provide surveillance over shoplifting, a condition which has become an increasing problem in connection with self-service merchandising.

In addition to basic layout, shelf and display areas have been continuously studied by merchandisers. Shelf space generally is rated in terms of its position within the store, aisle location, distance from the floor, and its association with other products. Floor space within a store is generally rated as being most attractive at the front and to the right, based on 100 percent exposure close to the main entrance and the phenomenon known as the "right-hand reflex." This reflex is due to the fact that the majority of people are right-handed, and as a result, they habitually keep to the right and probably go through a store in a counterclockwise pattern. Merchandise that is located near the front and to right of the main entrance will have the greatest potential for the sale. A business conducted in a building with more than one floor must allow for the lesser value of floor space located in basement and upper-story areas, as well as locations remote from main store entrances or internal aisleways.

## Service businesses

The layout for a service business should be oriented around a combination of service and sales. No one will know before the business is created just what proportion of sales and service may eventually develop. It is best to anticipate that some customer contact may be necessary, or that the business may need to expand into some form of sales to complement the service activity. If so, layout is important.

*Layout analysis.* The service business owner will need to think through what he or she will do, the way it will be done and the efficiency of his or her layout. Labor, machinery, equipment, and time must be maximized. The internal layout is studied to achieve a smooth flow of orders and paper work; fast and easy handling of parts and supplies; convenient placement of telephones, catalogs, inventory and equipment, and fast service for the business being provided.

Scale drawings of physical features, time studies and job standards, and flowchart analysis will help in improving service effort and efficiency.

*On-site customer service.* If the business conducts business with the public at the service site it is important to make sure that such service makes money for the business. Inventory must be safeguarded. Jobs must be set up so that service personnel can handle customers along with their service work. A study of the total customer profile of work generated will show how the layout can best accommodate the total work load. Walk-in trade, telephone orders, service truck scheduling and dispatch, and other similar aspects of the business can all be worked into an efficient layout plan.

## Manufacturing

By its nature, manufacturing lends itself to a fairly thorough type of analysis based on manufacturing methods and procedures. This has resulted in a considerable amount of study of the problems of factory layout. Even with such knowledge available, a great number of small manufacturers have not followed through to develop good, effective factory layout.

Factory layout analysis generally begins with a study of the amount and shape of the available floor space and the existing openings such as windows and doors, as well as the loading docks, ceiling heights, and permissible floor loadings. A base floor plan can be drawn up including all physical characteristics of the building, and templates constructed representing the floor space of the equipment to be installed. After experimenting with the placing of the templates the best layout can be determined. In some cases wooden or paper three-dimensional models can be constructed which will not only give floor placement but also height and space relationships which may be important to some kinds of operations.

### Manufacturing layout checklist

1. The products to be manufactured, with attention given to quantity, variation, value, and so forth.
2. The consistency of the operation.
3. The equipment to be used.
4. The relationship of equipment, personnel, materials, aisle space, and rate of operation.
5. Product flow through the plant.
6. Provision for changes in product and equipment, and expansion plans for future operations.

*Environmental considerations.* Lighting is a principal environmental feature, and all plant layouts must take into account either the present placement of lights and their type and kind, or the possibility of providing a lighting pattern which is appropriate to a revised plant layout. Lighting has many implications such as the amount of light, placement of lights, the creation of shadows, the contrast present, and the type of light sources used from a technical standpoint. Color is another aspect of plant design which may affect the layout to be achieved; for example, certain color combinations may be desirable in one area and perhaps not in another. Layout should also include considerations of physical characteristics such as noise, the availability of circulation, and air conditioning—all of which have an effect on the workers' environment and ultimately their degree of effectiveness.

*Services support.* Service characteristics of importance in manufacturing will include provision of adequate electrical service, the use of in-plant transportation equipment such as lift trucks, the efficiency of access to storage service areas, and everything connected with moving materials through the manufacturing area. In-transit plant storage of raw materials and finished goods will create a need for space, and reasonable allowances for them must be built into the layout plan.

The warehousing function in manufacturing demands special considerations in layout. These include the type of warehouse, necessary storage, kind of equipment used to move material, space needed for such movement, frequency of movement, possibility of congestion, need for protection of certain materials, and overall support of the manufacturing operation in an efficient manner.

# Wholesaling

Wholesaling is generally characterized by an operation which must be highly efficient and conducted on a volume basis. The layout plan for such operation is made similar to that of manufacturing, with a floor plan which is carefully examined for maximum efficiency. By necessity, many warehousing operations are frequently conducted in older premises which may not be perfectly appropriate to the most efficient kind of operation. Ordinarily warehousing for a wholesaler will take into consideration the following major items:

1. Ample low-cost space.
2. Access to the facilities needed to conduct the operation, such as a railroad spur, loading dock, truck access, and reasonable proximity to all these services and all customers served.
3. The utilization of material-handling equipment.
4. Utilization of the techniques of automation to whatever degree is appropriate, such as automatic conveyors, closed-circuit television, intercommunication systems, and remote control devices.
5. The safeguarding of all goods in terms of climatic features such as proper combinations of heat, moisture, clean air, adequate circulation, prevention of contamination, and other characteristics of storage.
6. Physical protection and control.

Heavy volume operations in wholesaling frequently create opportunities for loss, breakage, and theft. The operation must include adequate methods of protecting the stock from employee theft, minimizing damage and loss, and providing for a ready accountability and verification of all quantities on hand and available at any time.

## SITE AND ENVIRONMENT

The features which are directly connected with the building and surround its exterior are generally considered as *site* factors. Environmental features tend to include those things which surround the building. The environmental features may extend for some distance, and are usually under the control of other landowners. Environmental features are important as long as they have an impact, even though they are some distance away. ( See Figure 18–2. )

## Street, sidewalk, and service areas

Basic customer access was discussed in the chapter on locations. Analysis in regard to the building are somewhat more sophisticated. The entire

318

FIGURE 18–2
America's Main Streets are changing with the times—A view of Main Street in Grand Junction, Colorado, showing the results of "Operation Foresight."

Photo: Courtesy Grand Junction Chamber of Commerce.

site must be analyzed to determine if the building not only can be served, but if there are also real plus factors that encourage customers and service people to willingly visit the building.

Streets and sidewalks may not be well lighted, or they may be frequented by loitering "hippies," who discourage potential patrons. Delivery services may be very awkward or difficult, causing deliveries to be held up. A location on the left side of a one-way street may be bad because of the natural tendency for drivers to stay on the right-hand side.

Some attempt should be made to find out what standards and norms are expected by persons who visit the building.

### Setback and frontage

In most business communities, businesses located along any particular street will have a uniform setback from the street. Each individual business should effect some degree of individuality in regard to setback, the design of the store front, and the entrance. A particular theme or motif for the building front may do a great deal to enhance the actual site. This may include the use of modernistic materials such as redwood, glass, plastic, corrugated metal, wood shakes, and other materials used in one or more combinations to create a unique appearance. In addition, an illuminated sign can be designed which is complementary to the theme followed on the store front. The height of a building may not be a problem, but if the building is either higher of lower than the premises on either side, or located on a corner, it may be desirable to alter the building to conform with the adjacent buildings. On the other hand, a building of greater height may be advantageous for advertising purposes or the use of particular combinations of color and decoration as an added drawing power.

## Complementary construction and appearance

Not all buildings and sites need to be complementary with the surrounding buildings and shopping areas; however, there may be good reason to conform. In recent years a large number of buildings suitable for occupancy by small business have been built in downtown areas as well as outlying locations. Many of these buildings are quite different and in some cases extreme; however, they may be perfectly appropriate to support a particular business activity. The mere fact that a building is different need not be reason to reject it, but rather to examine it carefully and to determine if its uniqueness will have persuasive effect. Some communities have created a central theme, which has been followed by a majority of businesses. These are exemplified in the "western town" such as Scottsdale, Arizona, or the colonial theme as followed in some New England areas.

## Parking

The customer of today is a mobile customer and as such will not walk more than a certain distance from his automobile. It may be difficult to determine this distance, but ordinarily the point of contact will probably have to be within one or two blocks. It is a matter of record that many businesses have flourished in remote locations if they are accessible to an automobile, whereas others have suffered substantially when they relied on foot traffic because they were located too far from the place of departure from an automobile. Parking developments in recent years have included the joint efforts of merchants to buy and maintain parking lots, which are either free or metered. Other inducements to get customers into the store are outlying parking lots with free transportation to shopping areas and the removal of parking meters on downtown streets. In any event, parking is a complementary feature of business operations which is absolutely necessary to a successful operation and must be so considered in connection with any building to be utilized.

### Environment improvement

Anytime a building and site is being examined for possible selection, it is important to examine the surrounding environment and determine what are its chances for improvement.

The prospective entrepreneur will be interested in whether or not the building site has a chance to improve, and to what extent surrounding businesses and landowners will participate in such effort. Property improvement is usually accomplished by a willingness and ambition on the part of the businesspersons in the area. Frequently a certain amount of leadership exercised by some members of a group will generate action on the part of others. This leads to an upgrading of the area, making it more attractive to customers and eventually building up persuasive business factors which accrue to all the businesses in the vicinity.

### Building and site ratings

A good way to conduct an analysis of the building and its basic features is to determine what factors are important for a certain type of enterprise and then make comparisons between available possibilities.

In Table 18–1, the relative importance of certain factors to given businesses is shown. This will enable the prospective business operator to assign values to different features of a building and its site and environment. If combinations of retailing, service, manufacturing, and wholesaling are contemplated, an integrated checklist can be devised from this table.

### THE NEW BUILDING

At some point in the selection of a location and a building it may be prudent to consider a new building. It may be that several tenants can join together for a building, or space can be found in a building being constructed by others. In any event, the possibility should be kept open and perhaps pursued.

*Construction.* Construction features in newer buildings include many newer materials and techniques that can be quite attractive. Better lighting, heating, air conditioning, and other elements of comfort and style can be incorporated. Good design as to communications and traffic patterns can be set up in the beginning. Features that tend to detract from the basic appearance and form can be skillfully hidden or concealed. Movable partitions and modular furniture and operating fixtures can be designed which allow great flexibility.

*Site planning.* If a site possesses certain drawbacks, these can often

**TABLE 18–1**
**Business building and site-rating table (by importance and type of business)**

| Factors | Retailing | Service | Manu-facturing | Wholesaling |
|---|---|---|---|---|
| *Building features:* | | | | |
| Age | 1 | 4 | 3 | 4 |
| Space | 1 | 3 | 1 | 4 |
| Configuration | 1 | 4 | 4 | 3 |
| Appearance | 1 | 3 | 3 | 4 |
| Frontage | 1 | 4 | 4 | 4 |
| Access | 1 | 2 | 1 | 1 |
| *Interior utilization:* | | | | |
| Floor space | 2 | 3 | 1 | 1 |
| Room dimensions | 1 | 3 | 1 | 4 |
| Ceiling heights | 2 | 2 | 2 | 4 |
| Stairways, elevators | 3 | 3 | 1 | 1 |
| Window space | 1 | 3 | 4 | 4 |
| Utility services | 3 | 1 | 1 | 3 |
| *Improvement potential:* | | | | |
| Building exterior | 1 | 3 | 4 | 4 |
| Building interior | 1 | 3 | 2 | 2 |
| Site | 1 | 2 | 3 | 4 |
| Surrounding area | 2 | 2 | 3 | 4 |
| Streets and walks | 2 | 1 | 3 | 3 |
| Access | 1 | 1 | 2 | 1 |
| Expansion | 2 | 2 | 1 | 1 |
| *Site and environment:* | | | | |
| Streets and service areas | 1 | 2 | 2 | 3 |
| Setback and frontage | 1 | 3 | 4 | 4 |
| Parking | 1 | 2 | 2 | 3 |
| Surrounding businesses | 2 | 3 | 4 | 4 |
| Area environment | 2 | 3 | 4 | 4 |

*Key to ratings:* 1 = critical, 2 = very important, 3 = not ordinarily important, and 4 = minimum importance.

be minimized at the time of construction. Screening, retaining walls, court-yards, and other methods can help to upgrade a site and make a new building even more attractive.

**Services.** All forms of services are today very important to most businesses and can be planned for in the new building. Standby power and fuel sources may be critical for a manufacturer. Adequate pure water is also necessary—perhaps from a special location. Delivery, trash service, burglary patrols, and police protection may also be of considerable importance. Adequate fire protection is often of prime importance.

**Parking.** The use of the automobile as a means of access to the vast majority of businesses has created problems for large as well as small businesses. If a building is located where there are a number of businesses, which provides a combined "drawing power," then parking may be a problem. The large shopping center will have its parking area; the smaller business located elsewhere will have to rely on some different combination.

So many possibilities exist that it is impossible to adequately cover them. The important thing for the beginning businessperson is to recognize the importance of adequate parking (usually off-street), and to make sure it exists to support the business.

## WHEN TO REMODEL, EXPAND, OR MOVE

The factor of change is always present and will eventually bring about conditions which will require modification in the business operation. Examination of change affecting business would reveal that in a majority of cases businesses are slow to recognize change and to react to it in a positive way. In many communities throughout the United States, established businesses have been left out of the new business growth taking place in other locations within their community; they have allowed their premises to remain static and thus go out of style. Often they will be eliminated or put under severe handicap by changes in business operations which they fail to perceive.

It is very difficult to establish any key criteria or method of measurement which will indicate to the businessperson when he or she should remodel, expand, or move. The problems presented by remodeling, expanding, or moving are unique to each business and each area. However, the following discussion will provide some guidelines for the businessperson who sooner or later will probably have to consider each of the three possibilities.

*Remodeling.* A decision to remodel may in many cases be more of an act of faith than anything else. Even though a business continues to prosper, and return on investment seems to be holding up well, it may be that periodic remodeling and renovation is necessary to keep the business in a competitive position. Enterprisers should use a checklist similar to that developed at the time they established or acquired their business, and with this prepare a rather detailed and honest appraisal of their own situation. Such appraisal would proceed item by item and should probably be done on a yearly basis, with particular emphasis on factors of appearance, competitive loss or gain, available funds, and a dedication to stay in business.

*Expansion.* Expansion of a business operation may be a decision that is easy to come by. The needs for expansion are generally apparent and fairly well delineated. If a factory needs more room for machines, inventory, and finished goods, this is readily apparent; and likewise the decision to expand may be reached by a retail store if it cannot adequately service customers and is obviously losing business because of a lack of facilities.

In studying expansion, the examination of the business will probably proceed more in the area of financial analysis, including an appraisal of what the volume of business will be in the future, consequences of expansion, and the prospective financial obligations. A final comparison of "opportunity costs" will indicate the expected rate of return for the expansion investment. If other opportunities are more promising, they may delay expansion; however, proper value must be assigned to the factor of additional potential that the expanded business will possess.

**Moving the business.** At some point in time opportunities in the area of remodeling or expansion are no longer a feasible proposition. Sometime prior to this point, possibly as much as five years, the businessperson may have decided that he or she will move and begin making preparations for this event. A decision to move is a very critical one, and it generally involves a great deal more risk and expenditure than either remodeling or expansion. However, many businesses have not prepared adequately for their moves: they have either delayed until such action is too late, or they undertook to move at a time when they could ill afford to do so. Much of the analysis regarding a move is similar to that of remodeling or expansion with further emphasis given to certain subjective comparisons such as what is the value of a new building site over the old one, and what is lost by moving which will have to be made up, over time, at the new site? Merchandising has traditionally had longer tenure in locations than most other types of business; however, the time span for a given location seems to be getting shorter. Persons in service or manufacturing operations should consider short-term leases in recognition of the need to perhaps expand or contract operations rather quickly and substantially.

## QUESTIONS

1. Why is an older building often selected for starting a new enterprise?
2. How would you estimate the value of the investment in a *new appearance* for a beginning business?
3. Do building codes place a burden on an entrepreneur who would like to utilize an older building?
4. Based on the architecture of the "fast food" chains such as McDonald's, is it reasonable to assume that a small business may successfully utilize a building that is *different?*
5. How would you attempt to measure the impact of the surrounding environment on a beginning business?
6. Why is floor space alone a poor criteria in evaluating a building for a particular purpose?

7. How do you measure the relative value of a building located among many others along a "business strip," such as an older highway or main street.

8. What precautions do you take in signing up to be a tenant in a new building with a number of other tenants, who are as yet unknown?

9. How would you analyze the problem of how long to commit a business in a lease or rental of a building?

10. Why are businesses often not moved as soon as they should be?

## PROBLEMS

1. Review the "Yellow Pages" of a phone book for a city or combined marketing area of some size. Pick out a business which by description and listing is *obviously small and also different or unique* as a business enterprise. In making your selection pick out a business with an intent to find out the following:

   *a.* What is your *initial reaction* to the surrounding environment and the building itself? (Before entering the structure.)

   *b.* Is the impression created by the visual inspection of the exterior consistent with what actually is conducted inside?

   *c.* Does the interior appearance and layout seem appropriate to the business being conducted?

   *d.* What about the combination of the building and facilities strike you as being *particularly good or bad?*

   Record your observations as quickly as you can after the actual observations take place.

2. Select a particular type of small business which is a conventional retail store, service shop, manufacturer, or wholesaler.

   Identify at least five actual firms which are in the same business, within reasonable geographical proximity, and of about the same size.

   Prepare your own checklist of things you would like to observe in the business activity selected. Visit each firm in turn and record what you have seen and any particular comments about each feature.

   Identify what you think are the strong and weak points of each operation.

## BIBLIOGRAPHY

Bunn, Verne A. *Buying and Selling a Small Business.* Washington, D.C.: Small Business Administration, 1969. The text has some very good material on analyzing a company, including the site evaluation and the analysis of various capital portions of the balance sheet.

Marquardt, Raymond A.; Makens, James C.; and Roe, Robert G. *Retail Management.* Hinsdale, Ill.: The Dryden Press, 1975. A retailing text with some very excellent material on store layout, locations, and site evaluations. Concentration is in retailing, but applies to other businesses that deal with the public.

Moore, Franklin G. *Production Management.* 6th ed. Homewood, Ill.: Richard D. Irwin, 1973. A book that deals primarily with production, but has much that applies to buildings and layout. Very readable and valuable as a reference for capital investment decisions and utilizations of resource inputs.

Trade Marketing Information Guide Inc. *The Marketing Information Guide.* (monthly). Washington, D.C. A monthly publication that carries information sources relating to marketing. A valuable reference for materials relating to the building and its facilities along with other aspects of marketing management.

# 19

# Insurance and
# the small business

The individual who starts a small business creates risk by placing himself in a situation in which the outcome is uncertain. And although the desired outcome is to profit, business statistics indicate that business failure is also a very real possibility.

The type of risk created when a business is started is basic to the free enterprise system and is termed *speculative,* or *dynamic,* risk. There are three possible outcomes in speculative risk situations: profit, status quo, or loss. It is the hope for a profitable outcome that motivates the small business owner to accept the uncertainty of speculative risk. If the motivation is not present, or if the outcome in a speculative risk venture proves unprofitable, the individual may seek a more secure position by working for someone else.

In addition to the creation of speculative risk, the small business venture also exposes the owner to what may be termed *pure,* or *static,* risk. Pure risk situations are those in which there are only two possible outcomes: loss or no loss. Although pure risks are often difficult to avoid, they may be assumed or transferred. Insurance is a social device for the *transfer* of certain pure risks, whereas speculative risks are, generally speaking, not insurable.

The purpose of this chapter is to provide the small business owner with a basic understanding of insurance and the management of pure risk.

## CLASSIFICATIONS OF PURE RISKS

There are three types or classes of pure risk: property, liability, and personal. *Property* risks include the loss of tangible property because of such perils as fire, lightning, windstorm, hail, theft, and a multitude of others. In addition, loss of use, or added expense because of the loss of tangible property are also property risks.

*Liability* risks involve the loss of existing assets or future income because the business owner is declared legally liable for actions that result in bodily injury or property damage to others. The possibility of legal liability covers a wide range of situations including such things as the distribution of a defective product, the maintenance of the business premises in a condition unsafe to the public, and actions of employees in dealing with customers.

Finally, *personal* risks include the loss of a person's income-producing ability through premature death, disability, sickness, accident, or retirement.

## RULES OF RISK MANAGEMENT

Robert I. Mehr and Bob A. Hedges in their book *Risk Management in the Business Enterprise* cite what they consider to be the "rules of risk management." Although their guidelines for the management of pure risk may appear quite simple and perhaps intuitive, they do provide a useful framework within which risk management decisions can be made.

The *first* and probably most important of the three rules is "don't risk more than you can afford to lose." The treatment of pure risk involves determining how each individual exposure to pure risk should be handled. As a practical matter pure risk will either be assumed or transferred through insurance, and in deciding whether to assume or transfer the risk, the small business owner must estimate the maximum size of the potential loss. If the best estimate indicates a maximum potential loss so large that its occurrence would result in bankruptcy or serious financial impairment, risk assumption is not feasible. In other words, relating the maximum potential loss to the resources of the loss bearer will determine the importance of the risk exposure. Of course the maximum sustainable loss, as well as the resource base, will vary from firm to firm and from time to time in a particular firm.

The *second* rule of risk management is "don't risk a lot for a little." From the individual's point of view, insurance involves the exchange of a certain small loss (the premium) for the elimination (actually the transfer) of a potentially large loss. In implementing the second rule, the premium should be related to the potential loss and treated as a savings or cost. For example, if comprehensive physical damage insurance on a $4,000 automobile costs $35 a year, the savings or return if the insurance is not purchased and the risk is assumed equals $35/$4,000 or .875 percent. The owner is exposing a $4,000 investment to possible loss or damage for less than a 1 percent return and that's "risking a lot for a little." On the other hand, a driver who pays $40 a year for auto collision coverage with a $50 deductible, when the same coverage with a $100 deductible would cost only $12 a year, is paying a cost of $28/$50 or 56 percent for the second $50 of coverage. Here, from a cost point of view, the car owner is paying dearly for a small return. In the first case, the purchase of insurance is consistent with the rule and in the second case it is not.[1]

The *third* rule of risk management is simply to "consider the odds." This general rule can be more specifically expressed in terms of three types of judgmental errors common to most amateur risk managers. First, there is the tendency to underestimate the chance of loss in connection with "long shot" situations. This is particularly true if an individual is asked to risk a little for the possibility of a large return. However, as the amount of dollars risked increases, the possibility of loss becomes more important. For example, one might accept risking $1 in a gambling situation where the chances are only 1 in 50 of winning $100. On the other hand, the same person may reject risking $1,000 in a gambling situation where the chances are 1 in 5 of winning $5,000.

The second judgmental error is allowing the smallness of chance of loss to overshadow the largeness of the potential loss. When the risk taker senses that the chance of loss is very remote, there is a tendency to ignore the possibility of loss, even in those cases where the potential loss is large. An example of this would be the retailer who considers the possibility of a product liability suit so remote that he ignores the fact that judgments in such cases are very large.

Finally, the third error in judgment is somewhat the reverse of number two, that is, the case where the near-sureness of an apparent gain causes the size of the potential loss to be underestimated. People who insist on driving in excess of the speed limit violate this rule, as do jaywalkers, and people who, because they haven't had an automobile insurance claim in some time, rationalize that they would be saving money by not buying insurance.

## PROBLEMS IN APPLYING THE RULES OF RISK MANAGEMENT

Despite the apparent common-sense nature of the rules of risk management, there are six potential problems one must consciously avoid in applying the rules. Unfortunately, the evidence shows that small business managers as a group are highly susceptible to these difficulties of application.

1. *The problem of objectivity.* It is human nature for most individuals to be conceited in various degrees regarding their own abilities. This seems to be particularly true of those who seek the independence of own-

---

[1] The cost of 56 percent implicitly assumes that the insured has an average of one collision claim a year in excess of $100, which of course is unlikely. If one assumes the insured averages less than one collision a year, the cost of the second $50 of coverage is even greater than 56 percent.

ing their own business. This type of person tends to overvalue gains and undervalue losses, which leads to a violation of all three rules.

2. *The problem of inadequate information.* Making decisions from a position of ignorance is dangerous; yet it is always easy to overlook the facts because of the time normally involved in gathering and interpreting information. A good example of this is the small retailer who does not realize the exposure to legal liability in not maintaining safe premises for customers. Furthermore, time is not taken to find out. A little effort in this direction can be well worth while. Trade associations, lawyers, the Small Business Administration, and several other sources of information exist that could prevent some sleepless nights.

3. *The problem of psychic income.* This problem evolves from the universal human tendency to overestimate potential gains and underestimate potential losses. It is "the dream of great things." Business failure statistics are in large part empirical proof of the urge for psychic income, that is, income that never is produced beyond the imagination. From an insurance point of view, the individual who gets involved in the psychic income problem is the same type of individual who tends to generally ignore static risks.

4. *The problem of oversight.* The person who has the problem of oversight maintains the idea that "it can't happen to me." More specifically, this takes two forms. Either the potential costs in any particular decision involving risk never appear as real as the benefits, or the risk-taker believes that the costs are not even associated with the gains. For example, the person who only drives his automobile within the speed limit when the police are sighted, does so because he may be caught and receive a speeding ticket; yet he ignores the high costs of disability or accidental death.

5. *The problem of risk aversion.* This problem is in a sense the opposite of the attitude represented in the first four instances. In this case, the individual is so sensitive to risk situations that decisions involving risk are all aimed at risk avoidance, the minimization of risk. The maintenance of such an attitude is costly for two reasons. First, opportunities that are basically sound may be rejected; and second, unnecessary costs may be incurred to transfer risk when such a decision is not warranted. In this regard, an important thought comes to mind—that is, the good businessperson doesn't seek to avoid risk, but only to intelligently control it.

6. *The problem of the inevitable error.* Finally, the small business owner must recognize that regardless of the time, effort, and money spent on risk control, the improbable will sometimes happen. Risk involves the possibility that some future event will occur no matter how remote that possibility may seem. Of course, the most rational approach to this reality is to simply follow the rules of risk management.

## METHODS OF HANDLING RISK

At this point it is appropriate to discuss the methods for handling static risk situations in the small business. They include risk avoidance, risk assumption, risk reduction, the shifting of risk, and risk transfer.

The avoidance of static risk is only a possibility when there is a choice available, and in most instances this is not the case. For example, the possibility of fire or windstorm loss to a business building may be minimized, but cannot be avoided. On the other hand, an example of a situation involving a choice is when the loss of large sums of money by theft can be avoided by management policy regarding the handling and transfer of funds.

Risk assumption is a second possibility and may be voluntary or involuntary. Involuntary risk assumption can result from ignorance, stubbornness, irrational reasoning, or lack of funds. Voluntary risk assumption, on the other hand, may be the best decision in a particular situation, or may be necessary because appropriate insurance coverage is simply not available.

Although the small businessperson rarely has the opportunity to self-insure, it is a means of risk assumption. Self-insurance involves the establishment of a fund within the business to handle the possibility of financial loss as a result of a particular peril or hazard. It is different from simple risk assumption, however, in that it involves estimating the potential loss for the period and earmarking funds intended to absorb the estimated losses. The problem in self-insuring is, of course, estimating the potential loss in some scientific manner, which requires a large enough number of units exposed to loss that the law of large numbers applies.[2] For this reason, it is not a feasible tool for risk assumption in most cases.

The reduction of risk involves taking steps to affect both loss frequency and loss severity. Reducing loss frequency involves an awareness on the part of the small businessperson and his or her employees that good housekeeping and proper safety precautions are beneficial in the prevention of loss. On the other hand, it is also important to take those steps that

---

[2] The law of large numbers is a concept in probability theory which says that the larger the number of trials of a specific event, the more nearly the actual outcome will approach the expected outcome. The expected outcome may be expected based on opinion or theory (called "a priori"), as in flipping a coin; or may be based on actual observation or experience (called "a posteriori"), as in the frequency of household fires in a particular city. For example, in flipping a coin, the chance of it coming up heads is .5 and the more times you flip the coin the more nearly heads will result 50 percent of the time. In house fires, empirical evidence will indicate expected losses and also an expected variation from expected. As you increase the observations, however, the variation between expected and actual will narrow. From this brief explanation, it should be apparent that most business managers are not in the position to apply the law of large numbers, because their groups of units or exposures are not large enough to provide a reliable estimate of expected loss.

will minimize the amount of loss once the loss begins. In any case, it is important to remember that efforts to reduce risk are important, with or without insurance. With insurance, risk reduction programs may mean premium reductions; in other cases good risk reduction may eliminate the need for insurance altogether.

The most common way to shift risk is by contract. Such arrangements as subcontracting, surety bonds, and hedging are typical examples of shifting risk. Through subcontracting the person or persons contracted to perform a particular task will be responsible for adequate performance. In the case of surety bonds, the bonding company guarantees that a particular individual will perform in a prescribed manner. Hedging is accomplished by buying and selling goods for future delivery in such a way as to protect against a fluctuation in the market price.

Finally, risk transfer is accomplished by the purchase of insurance. It is important to not look at insurance as a substitute means of handling risk if some other method is more appropriate. More will be said of this in a section on buying insurance.

## PRINCIPAL TYPES OF INSURANCE COVERAGE

After small businesspersons have carefully examined their exposure to static risk, they must determine their basic insurance needs. Those insurance needs common to most small business organizations are briefly described below.

### Property

A standard *fire insurance policy* is a must in any circumstance. It covers losses to goods and premises resulting from fire and lightning, and also losses caused by the removal of goods from the premises endangered by fire. In addition, most business owners consider it necessary to purchase an *extended coverage endorsement* which extends the standard fire policy to include the perils of explosion, riot, vehicle damage, windstorm, hail, and smoke damage.

If the business operation is conducted on leased premises the owner must determine the extent of the owner's insurance coverage. Usually that policy does not include coverage for the tenant's inventory and equipment.

In the case of burglary or robbery, burglary insurance is available and will compensate the business owner for stolen property in cases of forced entry. (The major coverage excluded is the theft of business accounts.) Robbery insurance, on the other hand, will pay for losses of property if force or threat of violence were involved. Loss of payroll and securities can also be added to the robbery contract if desired. In the case of small retailers, a combination policy called the *storekeeper's burglary and robbery policy* is tailored to cover small losses due to both perils at a premium that is considerably less than that for the more comprehensive crime policies assembled by an insurance agent.

One additional property contract that the small business owner may want to consider is *business interruption insurance,* which pays net profits and expenses in cases where a business is partially or totally shut down because of a fire or other insured cause. The total claim is based on an estimate of what the business would have normally earned or incurred, but lost during the term of closure.

### Casualty

One of the most important insurance coverages the small business owner must obtain is *general liability insurance,* which covers the costs of defense and judgments brought against the company because of bodily injury and/or damage to the property of others. In addition, under most circumstances this policy should probably include *product liability* coverage. The small business failure statistics are full of instances in which a legal liability lawsuit forced bankruptcy.

In addition to the general liability policy, all company-owned cars and trucks and their drivers should be covered by *automobile liability insurance,* and liability insurance should be carried on employees who use their own cars for company business.

### Life

The use of *life insurance* can benefit the business operation, as well as the heirs of a covered individual. To assure a measure of continuity and financial stability to the venture, the following options are available. In the sole proprietorship life insurance can be used to provide cash for the survivors of the deceased owner and used to continue or dispose of the business. On the other hand, in the partnership or corporation the proceeds of a life insurance policy can be used to fund a buy-sell agreement in the event of the death of a partner or stockholder. Finally, in certain instances, life insurance can be used to reimburse the firm for financial loss resulting from the death of a key man in the business, or to build up a sinking fund to be available upon the key man's retirement.

### Workmen's compensation

Most states make workmen's compensation programs mandatory. Such plans provide benefits to employees injured at their place of work, regardless of the legal liability of the company. The schedule of benefits is defined by state law and thus vary from state to state. Normally, however, they include medical care and income payments for a disabled worker and his or her dependents. Certain classes of employees are often excluded, particularly those in agricultural or domestic jobs. Premiums are based on the employee's salary or wage level and the type of work involved. Hazardous jobs will carry a rate as high as ten percent of salary whereas low-risk occupations may cost as little as one percent of salary.

## Bonding

The small businessperson can use various types of bonding arrangements to shift the financial responsibility for an employee or a job to a third party. The third party is known as a surety, and is either a licensed bonding company or an insurance company. A fidelity bond placed on an employee will reimburse the employer if the employee steals company funds. As a general rule, any personnel having access to company funds should be bonded, without exception. A surety bond guarantees the performance of a job. For example, a general contractor in the construction industry is reimbursed if a bonded subcontractor fails to complete a job according to the terms of the agreement that was made.

### THE NONPROFESSIONAL RISK MANAGER

The proper management of static risk is a tough job for the untrained. In a typical situation, the small business owner is concerned with the allocation of some limited number of premium dollars in some optimal manner. He or she must select among the risk management tools of assumption, reduction, and transfer to achieve the maximum protection against static losses. In more specific terms, the task involves answering the following three questions:

1. What kind of insurance should be purchased?
2. How much insurance should be purchased?
3. From whom should the insurance be purchased?

A major problem encountered in developing appropriate answers to these questions stems from the small business manager's need for help and the fact that the insurance adviser is usually also the insurance salesperson. The insurance agent works on a commission basis, which means the more insurance he or she sells the more income he or she makes. Thus, the unscrupulous salesperson would tend to recommend the purchase of insurance in instances where the risk may be more appropriately handled in some other way. In other cases, the agent who puts a priority on sales volume rather than satisfied clients, may not be a good adviser simply because he or she has never taken the time to gain the knowledge required to properly analyze static risk situations.

It is fortunate that although such conditions do exist in the insurance industry, they are not widespread. The majority of insurance agents are competent, intelligent, and knowledgeable in their jobs. Such conditions do, however, suggest that the small business owner must treat the selection of an insurance adviser as a serious matter. This task is more clearly stated by saying the small business owner should know enough about insurance to:

1. Know when advice is needed.
2. Recognize if the adviser is good.
3. Know when the advice is good.

### General principles of buying insurance

An insurance contract is a complex document which the layman finds difficult to understand. Furthermore, given the large number of contracts available and the scores of modifications that can be added, there are literally hundreds of combinations from which to choose. This can make buying insurance a perplexing problem if certain general principles are not adhered to.

As a general principle, the small business manager should buy insurance only when it is the most appropriate and least expensive means of achieving the financial security which is desired in the face of uncertain losses. Therefore, under what circumstances is insurance the most appropriate and least expensive means available? Two important rules must be applied in answering this question.

*Rule 1: The large loss principle.* Insurance should be used on the premise that the probability of loss is less important than the possible size of the loss. In other words, if a situation exists where the potential loss could be large, the fact that the loss is highly improbable should be ignored. Since the small business owner must assume some risks and transfer others, it is rational to transfer those he or she cannot afford to bear. This is commonly known as the large loss principle.

Often times the complaint is voiced that those who need insurance the most are those who can least afford it. To some extent this is true, because the need for insurance is based on the inability to withstand the possible loss if insurance is not purchased. So while those who need it can least afford it, they are the very ones that can least afford to be without it. Any potential loss that could lead to severe financial stress or bankruptcy requires insurance. Thus, in deciding whether to buy insurance the question is not, "can I afford it?", but "can I afford to be without it?" This, of course, is closely related to the first rule of risk management cited earlier: "Don't risk more than you can afford to lose."

**Rule 2: Insurance is a last resort.** The transfer of risk through insurance should only be done when absolutely necessary—because it is costly. Insurance always costs more than the expected value of a loss (i.e., the probability of loss times the potential loss) because the premium must also include administrative and selling costs, plus profit. Thus insurance is economically feasible only when the probability of loss is low and potential loss severity high. If the probability of loss is high and potential loss severity low, the use of insurance is a poor decision.

Unfortunately, people tend to want insurance in situations in which the probability of loss is high and loss severity relatively low. Such people fail to appreciate the true function of insurance, which is to guard against the catastrophic economic loss. A good example of this error in judgment is the person who prefers full coverage when deductibles are available.

Unfortunately, it is easy to find cases in which the insurance industry has violated the large loss principle. The most common is the offering of full coverage in instances where deductibles should be used. Although there is nothing morally wrong with full coverage, it is certainly not the way to spend the limited number of premium dollars that the small business manager typically has available.

## Selecting the agent and the company

The first step in deciding where to buy insurance is to focus on the agent, not the company. As previously indicated, the careful selection of an insurance adviser (agent) is a fundamental part of insurance buying.

A good agent has two primary qualifications: a thorough knowledge of insurance and a genuine interest in the needs of his client. Fortunately, one will find that the better agents usually represent the better companies.

Some agents are "independent," which means they represent several companies. Others, particularly in life and health insurance, represent only one company. Then there are insurance brokers who can help in setting up an insurance program and acquire the coverage through any number of companies. The distinction between the agent and broker is that the agent represents and works for the company, whereas the broker represents and works for his or her client.

In choosing the company, there are four factors to consider: financial stability, claims service, company policy on cancellation, and premiums. As for financial stability, the layman should consult the evaluations of the Alfred M. Best Company which can be found in most university, college, and public libraries. In the property and liability areas, *Best's Insurance Reports* and *Best's Key Rating Guide* are published annually. In addition to financial strength, the Best reports also rate efficiency of operations and caliber of management. The rating key is explained in each of the publications and can be easily understood.

As for life insurance, Best publishes *Life Reports* and the *Spectator Life Insurance Yearbook* annually. Both contain detailed financial and historical data on most life companies, and each company is rated. Again, a clear explanation of the ratings is provided.

In examining a company's claim services, there are two sources of information. Talk to the agent about claim-settlement procedures and, if possible, contact some of the company's policyholders who you know have recently had claims.

Finally, a knowledgeable and understanding agent is the best source of information on the company's cancellation policy and premiums.

### Tip on insurance prices

In buying insurance, the small business manager must realize there are no bargains. Saving a few dollars in premiums may mean the difference between good service and average or poor service. The old adage applies in insurance as in most anything else, "you get what you pay for."

There is hardly an insurance policy in existence that some company cannot make a little broader for a higher premium. On the other hand, the same company can trim the coverage and reduce the premium. Keep in mind, however—this does not mean that the cheapest insurance is always the poorest; nor the most expensive always the best. All it really indicates is that the broadness of coverage is an important determinant of the premium. In comparing price, be sure to consider the advice and service needed and whether these are adequately provided by the company selected.

### QUESTIONS

1. Distinguish between speculative and pure risk. What are the three classes of pure risk?
2. What are the "rules of risk management?" Think of several examples in your own recent experiences when you have violated the "rules."
3. What do you consider the most important problem you face in applying the rules of risk management?
4. Discuss the methods of handling risk and for each method give two examples of its proper application.
5. Review the principal types of insurance coverage a small business owner must consider buying.
6. What are the three basic problems the nonprofessional risk manager faces in managing static risk?

7. What is the "large loss principle?"
8. Why should insurance always be considered as a last resort?
9. What four factors are most important in selecting a company?
10. How should one compare premium rates in deciding what insurance company to buy from?

## PROBLEMS

1. Contact a local fire and casualty insurance agent and discuss with him the problems most frequently encountered in satisfying the insurance needs of small businesses in the community.

2. Contact two or three successful small businesses in your community and review their insurance programs. Ask the managers questions regarding why they do or do not have particular types of coverage.

## BIBLIOGRAPHY

Elliott, Curtis M., and Vaughan, Emmett J. *Fundamentals of Risk and Insurance.* New York: John Wiley & Sons, 1972.

Greene, Mark R. *Risk and Insurance.* 3d ed. Cincinnati, Ohio: South-Western Publishing Company, 1973.

Mehr, Robert I., and Cammack, Emerson. *Principles of Insurance.* 5th ed. Homewood, Ill.: Richard D. Irwin, 1972.

Mehr, Robert I., and Hedges, Bob A. *Risk Management: Concepts and Application.* Homewood, Ill.: Richard D. Irwin, 1974.

All of these books provide supplemental reading to the material presented in this chapter.

# 20

# Inventory control

Inventory control is a critical factor in the operation of a small business. To be sure, in some businesses, particularly those concerned with service functions, inventory may be a negligible factor. However, in many small businesses, such as manufacturing, retail store, and wholesale operations, inventory costs can be a sizable element in the success or failure of the operation. Therefore, any small business which has sizable investment in inventory should be aware of the mechanics of good inventory control.

## DIMENSIONS OF INVENTORY CONTROL

Because of the importance of inventory control to the small business, it is necessary to develop the specific purposes and objectives of inventory control. This will enable the prospective small business manager to understand the benefits gained from effective inventory control and help avoid the pitfalls of poor inventory management.

### Physical protection

Physical protection of the items of inventory is one of the fundamental objectives of inventory control. Inventory and materials, just like cash, machinery, or equipment, are valuable business assets and must be protected from the ravages of theft, shrinkage, and deterioration.

To help insure the physical protection of inventory and material, it is recommended that a physical inventory be taken at least once a year and preferably quarterly or semiannually. Such physical inventory should not only include the counting of case lots or boxes but should include a spot check of the merchandise which is packed in the boxes or bins. The key to physical inventory control is the recognition that physical protection not only means that the goods are on hand (be they raw materials, goods in process, or finished products) and protected from physical deterioration but that they are also protected from theft by both customers and employees. Constant observance of materials is necessary. If losses

338

through pilferage or errors in handling stock by inexperienced or careless employees are to be avoided, some kind of consistent control over inventories must be exerted.

The importance of physical protection of inventory cannot be overemphasized in high-inventory operations which require a great deal of physical handling. The more times an article is physically handled the more apt the item is to suffer physical damage. For example, the merchandise is often brought into the storeroom, taken out of the shipping case, stored in a reserve bin, then brought to the sales counter and inspected by three or four prospective buyers before it is finally purchased. It is then wrapped by the salesclerk and carried home by the customer. The process becomes even more involved if the item is to be delivered. When the merchandise is of a highly perishable nature, physical handling becomes increasingly important. Items commonly found in grocery stores like fresh fruits and vegetables, fresh meats, and frozen products can rapidly deteriorate because of heat, breakage, evaporation, sunlight, or any other physical changes which can affect the product. Customers shopping in the store are a threat to merchandise—consider the havoc which can be created in a card and stationery shop by one gummy-fingered child whose mother and father are preoccupied with their own purchases.

Not only is protection from theft and deterioration an important element in the control of merchandise but items such as tools and small machines also need physical protection. For example, many manufacturers have to provide tools such as wrenches, electric drills, and so forth for their employees. The loss, theft, or breakage of these tools can be very costly and must certainly be considered in the physical protection of inventory items.

## Investment control

Investment control can be a very significant objective for small businesspeople who engage in a rigid inventory control process. Control of inventory and material mean the control of the investment of money by the small business. Indeed inventory is *money*. It may be held temporarily in the form of a barrel of flour, a sheet of steel, an iron casting, or a bag of chemicals, a bolt of cloth, or a spare grinding wheel. But that is where the similarity ends. Beyond that, it represents money on which you *pay* interest instead of earn interest. After a year, $100 in the bank may be worth $110. After a year on the shelf, $100 worth of inventory is worth nearer to $80 *and* it has cost you $20 expense to carry it, in addition to the foregone interest.

Therefore, it should be obvious that one of the major objectives of inventory control is to reduce the investment tied up in inventory to the barest practical minimum. This objective not only reduces the investment of funds in inventory but it has the corollary advantages of providing more working capital to the small business, decreasing the amount of storage space required for the inventory, reducing insurance premiums and taxes, and lessening the loss to inventory items because of deterioration, obsolescence, shrinkage, or breakage.

While the desirability of minimizing the investment tied up in inventory becomes blatantly obvious, one word of caution must be made. Although the small business is well advised to minimize the amount of funds tied up in inventory, caution must be taken not to keep too little inventory. Also one should consider the advantages of any special prices or deals which one might get by buying in quantity and receiving quantity, or other, discounts. The objective of investment control in inventory management is not one of merely minimizing costs. Rather, it is one of optimizing the expenditure of funds. Too little inventory may mean lost sales, while too high inventories may mean lost capital funds.

## Material and product flow control

The third objective of inventory control is to have perpetual or continuous control of material or product flow as required. This objective of inventory control is particularly crucial to the small business. Continuous operations are essential to economic operations, be it in a warehouse, a manufacturing plant, a retail store, or a service operation. Any delay in operations because of lack of materials or parts can be a serious matter. Business may be lost, and profits unrealized. This is always an undesirable situation, but for the small business which depends so often on the return business of a satisfied customer, it can result in success or failure of the business.

Therefore, it is imperative that in endeavoring to maximize profits, the small business manager has some idea of the whereabouts and amounts of various inventory and material which is on hand, in process, or on order. Anyone who has experienced looking for a form which cannot be found or who is expecting raw materials which do not arrive—or even a payment on an account receivable which is not received—knows the importance of such fingertip control over various items. In short, the continuous successful operation of any small business depends to some degree on its having the necessary material when it is needed and where it is needed. The only way to assure that needed material is in the proper place, in the proper amounts, and at the proper time is by some effort of inventory control which is designed to tickle memories or otherwise give some physical stimulus to the small business manager, apprising him or her of the fact that stocks are low, parts have not arrived, merchandise is missing, and so on.

## Cost control

The fourth objective of inventory control is that of cost analysis. Having an adequate control system over inventory can provide a wealth of useful information for cost and administrative control purposes. For example, keeping adequate control over all materials purchased, material in process, finished products on hand, and amount of scrappage or wastage can be extremely important to the small manufacturer in determining costs of manufacturing. Likewise, records of what is in the stockroom, what is on the shelf, and what has been sold can be immensely useful to the small retailer in determining how much of what to reorder, rather than just "guessing" that he or she should reorder some of this and some of that. Further, like the manufacturer, the small retailer can use such records to determine how much it costs to handle each particular item of merchandise.

There are, of course, several other advantages to inventory control and its use in making cost analyses. For example, accurate records of the value of inventory can be very beneficial to the small business operator in approaching the local bank for a loan or an insurance agent for an adjustment of fire or theft loss. By the same token, accurate records of value of merchandise which has been sold (and which therefore must be replaced from working capital if future sales are to be made) can deter a small business operator from making unwarranted cash withdrawals from the business because of an apparent, but misleading, solid cash position.

Another advantage of accurate inventory records is that it provides cost information which enables the small business manager to price services more accurately. For example, take the instance of a glass blower who very carefully charged for (1) his time in blowing glass and (2) all the raw materials which went into the glass products, but failed to keep record of the time (and therefore failed to charge for his time) spent ordering materials, breaking bulk, and storing the materials. It wasn't until it was pointed out to him that such activities were part and parcel of the costs of maintaining inventory that he realized he was underpricing his services.

## Promoting sales

Another primary objective of accurate inventory control techniques is that of promoting sales. Although this objective is not always apparent, it is extremely important to the small business manager and his or her success. The fact is that greater sales are achieved if goods are available when they are demanded. A customer comes into a store and wants to buy a product today, not two weeks from now; a purchasing agent orders merchandise from a company salesman for delivery on a specific day, not "sometime in the future." Lack of merchandise can, in short, result in lost sales. More important than the lost sale may be a lost customer, which in turn will ultimately reduce future sales. Therefore, accurate inventory records can ensure that the manufacturer has the right product produced at the time it is needed, or that the retailer has the demanded product in stock.

This objective means the small business manager should optimize inventory in order to maximize sales, rather than minimize inventories in an effort to reduce costs. However, there is a danger here: many retailers can be led down the primrose path of believing that they should never be out of any product; manufacturers can be led to believe that they must always have the product ready to ship; wholesalers may think that they must have the requested product in stock; and service people may believe that they must be able to instantaneously provide any and all kinds of services demanded. These notions are, of course, fallacious. There are numerous times when the cost of shortage is less than the cost of over-stocking.

What is required is that the small business operator determine what items are important enough to always have on hand and what items do not warrant constant supply. In short, the small business operator should arrange stocks and supplies so that the business is never out of high-demand items, is only occasionally out of often-demanded items, but seldom stocks low-demand items. Here again, it becomes obvious that inventory control records are required to determine the demand on inventory. That is, the manager should know for an average week which items are sold in large amount, which are sold in moderation, and which items have not sold at all. If such records are kept, the manager will be able to maximize sales by always having the high-demand items on hand, while at the same time inventory costs will be reduced because the business will not have working capital tied up in seldom-demanded items.

## RULES FOR GOOD INVENTORY CONTROL

Now that the various objectives of inventory control have been explored in some detail, it is important that the fundamental rules behind inventory control be enumerated. These ideas are called rules rather than principles because, unlike principles, they are not always true; however, they are grounded on solid experience. Basically, these rules include:

1. The proverb of the vital few and the trivial many.
2. The proverb that uncontrolled inventory is too much inventory.
3. The proverb that the aim of inventory control is perfection.
4. The proverb that one fourth of any inventory is waste.

## The vital few and the trivial many

The law of the vital few and the trivial many states that there is a maldistribution of importance of all items of inventory—that some items are vital while others are trivial. This idea originates from the philosopher Wilfredo Pareto. While this reference has been directed to many generalities, its relevance has long been recognized in respect to inventory control. Business managers in general have come to consider their inventory items to be of two different types: some inventory is of a vital nature on which records must be kept; while other inventory is of a trivial nature on which the cost of the record-keeping is more expensive than the cost of any pilfered, broken, or otherwise deteriorated merchandise.

In current practice, the principle of the vital few and the trivial many has evolved to what is frequently called ABC inventory control. Under this method, all inventory items are designated as either A, B, or C items.

A items are those vital few items which are very expensive, hard to come by, or vital by way of perpetuating sales. Therefore A items receive the full treatment of record-keeping, costing, and protection from the elements. Further, the need for these items is calculated ahead of time, thus providing ample lead time for reordering. Because of their high cost, these stocks are always held at a bare minimum, but frequent reorder points are established.

C items, at the other end of the pole, are classed as the trivial many which are the waste items. C items get little attention in planning and record-keeping because they are low in value and are not of particular importance. Items of the C variety tend to be paper clips, staples, paper bags, postage stamps, letterheads, etc. About the only control which should be devoted to these items is that when the supply is obviously low, this fact is brought to the attention of whoever is responsible for replacing them. To help keep a sufficient inventory of these items on hand, a good suggestion is to have one bin as the "last container" or to have a minimum supply tied in a sack or boxed, and once that sack or box is broken into, a reorder is made. No calculation is made for future need for C items, and usually they are so trivial they are charged to an overhead account rather than priced individually to products.

It should be obvious that because C items are not strictly controlled, they will boost up inventory cost. However, because these items are so trivial in cost or will not cause lost sales of any consequence, it is generally felt that just keeping them on hand in a loose fashion will minimize the expense of control, record-keeping, and frequent reordering to the point that these reduced expenses will more than offset increased expenses because of the lack of control.

B items, of course, are far less important than the A items but more important than C items. These items, for example, might have moderate costs applied to them or they may create lost sales if stocks were depleted. Therefore keeping adequate tabs on these items is not quite as important as keeping tabs on A items but more important than keeping tabs on C items. B items are therefore controlled routinely and mechanically. Many times all that need be done with B items is to determine a minimum stock limit and a standard reorder quantity on the basis of past sales and use. Then whenever the stock of an item gets down to this minimum limit, a standard quantity is reordered. Thus if there is a big run on B items, it might be possible to experience an outage, but by this system the business will normally never be out of these items for a very long period of time. Furthermore, even if an outage occurs, more are coming in very shortly, and probably the sale or two lost because of the shortage will not be of any significance.

### An uncontrolled inventory is too much inventory

The second maxim of inventory control is that any inventory which is uncontrolled is bound to be too much inventory. Elementary as this saying may be, it is often ignored because at first glance it appears to contradict the idea behind C items in ABC inventory control. However, in actuality the deliberate lack of control is some control, and therefore even C items cannot be called uncontrolled inventory items. More important than the academic argument, however, is the principle behind this adage on uncontrolled inventories.

Not only are truly (not deliberately) uncontrolled inventories extremely expensive because they tie up money and space as well as cost money in insurance and taxes, they also represent a hidden danger simply because they have a built-in attraction to small business managers. That is, an uncontrolled inventory situation is a comfortable (if not desirable) position to be in and one toward which the typical small business operator will gravitate. Perhaps this principle can be more succinctly stated as "most people are pack rats." Most people—small business operators included—have the built-in desire to "store a little away" for the future. Because of this they will often stock more items than they need, or order ridiculous quantities because of some appealing but unrealistic quantity discount. One is reminded of the story about the small-town grocer who bought a carload of catsup from a salesman, only to be queried by his son later as to why he bought so much catsup. His reply to his son was that he knew that he didn't need the catsup, but he felt that the salesman had a "pretty good pitch."

The point is that when inventories are not controlled, they will practically always be too large. Salesmen are always interested in taking orders, and having too much inventory is always more appealing to the small business operator than too little, even though it is expensive. Ample inventory eliminates the worry caused when new supplies don't come in on time; production can always proceed on schedule; and customers never have to wait for a finished product. Everyone is happy, but the money tied up in inventory is enormous. Therefore, the second maxim of inventory control states that if there is no control over inventory, the assumption can probably be made that the inventory is too high.

### The aim of inventory control is perfection

The third adage of inventory control is that perfection in the supply of inventory items is the aim of inventory control. In order to have a perfect supply of an item, the business should never run out of anything and at the same time never have anything on hand and never have to pay high prices because of buying in small quantities.

Of course, it should be obvious to anyone that such perfection—as in anything else—is, for the most part, unattainable. However, realistic appraisal of the inventory process dictates that this perfection must be a continuous goal if anywhere near perfection is to be attained. This statement takes the form of an adage because many people throw up their hands in despair and quit trying when they recognize the fact that perfection can never be attained. They will not even try to achieve perfection unless there is some easy, mechanical way to attain the objective. Therefore, this maxim is necessary because it gives a vote of confidence in maxim Number 1—the law of the vital few and trivial many. What it really states is that the small business (1) should try to attain perfection, but (2) if it does not attain perfection it should not be discouraged. There is, after all, a mechanical means of formalizing inventory techniques which can be conducted on a nonthinking, rote basis.

### One fourth of any inventory is waste

The fourth adage of inventory control is that it can be assumed that one fourth, or 25 percent, of the value of inventories is eroded by the various costs of carrying the inventory for a year. This feature of inventory control is altogether too commonly misunderstood or ignored by small business operators. In general, the problem is that inventory costs continue whether merchandise is sold or not. Usually small businesspersons overlook inventory costs because they do not pay them all at once. For example, they pay their taxes on inventory on one day; they pay their rent for space occupied by inventory on another day; and they seem never to recognize that they are short of money and must borrow from the bank because of pre-purchased, unneeded inventory. Frequently small business operators will argue that while they are cognizant of these costs, they can justify carrying a seasonal item of inventory from one year to the next because they already have the space and the item has already been purchased. They rationalize away this need to move the merchandise, saying that those costs to be incurred have already been paid. The truth, however, is that some costs have been incurred, but not all. When next year's season rolls around, those items of merchandise which are stored may be so deteriorated because of dust, sunlight, and careless handling that they will be worthless. Statistically, the business would be as well off to sell an item of merchandise at 25 percent off cost than to store the item for one year. Thus, the small business, be it a manufacturer, retailer, wholesaler, or service business, is better advised  to sell off seasonal or other items which will be stocked for periods upwards of a year at cost or even 25 percent below cost rather than store the item. Conversely, the business can figure it is breaking even or getting ahead if it can sell the item for more than 75 percent of cost rather than store it for 9–12 months.

The fourth maxim—that one fourth of any inventory carried is waste— is not a very scientific figure. However, it is a very pragmatic, workable idea which the small business manager should continuously carry in the back of his or her mind when it comes to inventory decisions.

## INVENTORY CONTROL IN YOUR KIND OF BUSINESS

Basically, the methods of inventory control are the same in all businesses. However, the needs of the various types of business dictate differences in the techniques of inventory control methods. Therefore, the following is designed to highlight some of the basic differences in techniques used in retailing, service, manufacturing, and wholesaling operations.

### Retailing

It can safely be said that the key to inventory control for the small retailer is to keep inventory well balanced at all times. The first requirement for keeping a well-balanced inventory is that the retailer stock only the proper sizes, colors, styles, and price lines. The second requirement is that all high-turnover items never be out of stock; and thirdly, stock turnover should be as rapid as possible. Therefore, the typical retailer is faced with the problem of having a myriad of facts and figures with which to comply. For example, it is not sufficient to have sports jackets which are in high demand if they are all of the wrong size or wrong color; rather, there must be sufficient numbers of the highly demanded sports jackets in the commonly demanded sizes and colors.

In order to be able to meet all specifications in the myriad of items (which sometimes will run up to 15 or 20 thousand) carried by the typical retail store, the retailer must be able to accurately predict needs in high-demand items from the standpoint of size, shape, color, and texture and stock this merchandise accordingly. Therefore, the retailer's inventory problem basically centers on the ability to keep accurate records of what is sold. For this reason, there are a variety of techniques which are designed to eliminate the guesswork and memory element of inventory control for the retailer. These techniques of inventory control include: (1) personal observation, (2) physical counts, (3) the on hand–on order–sold record, and (4) the perpetual inventory.

Each of the above methods of inventory control used by small retailers can be very effective in the proper circumstance and thus merit some elaboration.

*1. Personal observation.* As the name implies, personal observation is the personal inspection of inventory by the retailer. The manager inspects stock to see what is moving slowly, what is moving fast, what he or she is out of, and what is on order. Obviously, this technique is not very scientific nor accurate unless pencil and paper are used, which limits it to a small store with a small variety of merchandise. Of course, if the retailer of a small store has a relatively constant rate of sale and the owner or manager is always on the premises, the accuracy of the technique will be increased. However, the personal observation technique is not recommended for the usual retail establishment.

*2. Physical check.* The second basic technique used by retailers to control inventory is the physical check. Similar to the personal observation technique, the physical check consists of a personal investigation on the part of the small business manager as to the varieties of merchandise on hand. However, in the physical check technique a deliberate count is made of all items of merchandise on hand and on order instead of simply observing the inventory situation. Technically, a physical count is conducted by two people going from item to item (usually over a weekend or sometime when the store is not open for business) with one person calling off the name of the item, the number of items on hand, and the value of the item while another person records this information. The purpose behind two people working in tandem is that accuracy, honesty, and completeness are more assured under this technique.

Of course when a physical count is made by the small business manager (and an assistant), he or she is apprised in one formal report of the precise conditions, status, and value of all the inventory on hand. By comparing one physical audit with its preceding audit and the amounts of merchandise ordered during the period, a precise profile of what merchandise is selling and what is not can be developed.

*3. On hand–on order–sold record.* The third technique commonly used by retailers in inventory control is what is commonly called the

FIGURE 20–1
On hand–on order–sold record

| ITEM: ALP SHOES<br>Name of supplier: Jones, Inc.<br>Street address: 1419 Pine<br>City and state: Uptown | | ON HAND–ON ORDER–SOLD RECORD | | | | | | |
|---|---|---|---|---|---|---|---|---|
| | Size | 2-13<br>On<br>hand | Rec'd<br>2-16<br>On<br>order | Sold | 2-27<br>On<br>hand | Rec'd<br>3-4<br>On<br>order | Sold | 3-13<br>On<br>hand |
| White Arctic | 8 | 3 | 5 | 2 | 6 | 0 | 2 | 4 |
| | 8½ | 1 | 4 | 2 | 3 | 1 | 2 | 2 |
| | 9 | 6 | 0 | 2 | 4 | 0 | 1 | 3 |
| | 9½ | 2 | 1 | 0 | 3 | 0 | 1 | 2 |
| Brown Arctic | 8 | 4 | 6 | 3 | 7 | 0 | 3 | 4 |
| | 8½ | 2 | 4 | 2 | 4 | 1 | 3 | 2 |
| | 9 | 5 | 1 | 2 | 4 | 1 | 1 | 4 |

Explanation: On hand—goods on hand on that date; On order—goods on order; Rec'd—date merchandise on order received; Sold—inventory on hand on first date, plus goods on order which were received, minus number on hand on next date.

on hand–on order–sold record. This record is a device which, although time-consuming to keep, is extremely helpful to the retailer in determining what sizes, colors, and styles are being purchased. Figure 20–1 illustrates how the on hand–on order–sold record shows precisely and instantaneously the amount, size, color, and style of merchandise on hand, on order, and recently sold.

Obviously this type of record is very flexible and adaptable to all types of goods handled. However, such records rapidly become bulky and hard to maintain. Therefore, unless keeping such a record is imperative, careful consideration should be given to its relative merits and demerits before any retailer decides to use such a technique.

4. Perpetual inventories. Perpetual inventories are very similar to the on hand–on order–sold record. However, in the perpetual inventory, records are kept of each item of merchandise as it is brought into the store, stocked, and sold. Obviously, it is hard to justify the time and expense in keeping perpetual inventories, and they rapidly lose their enchantment to the harried business manager. Thus, usually the perpetual inventory technique is limited to only very high-value, important lines of goods which warrant very strict control. "A" items of inventory are of this nature. The advantages of the perpetual inventory method are that the retailer knows at all times the amount of goods that he or she has on hand and their dollar value, as well as the style, size, shape, color, and texture.

## Service industries

The nature of service industries permits small business operators engaged in providing services to maintain much more accurate records of inventory while at the same time spending much less time at record-keeping. This is because the service industry usually must keep record only of materials and supplies purchased which are expended by way of providing the service. Therefore, a TV repairman need only account for parts which he purchases for repairing TV sets, while a seamstress needs to account only for materials which she purchases for her sewing, and the woodworker need account only for parts used in manufacturing the products. The service person's job is simplified by the fact that practically all the parts which he or she buys will be of common, ordinary bulk sizes and quantities and can be easily recorded simply by costing out items which are used on a job basis once the job is finished.

Therefore, because of the nature of the service industry, the only record-keeping necessary is general control over inventory received for stock, and accurate records showing when stock items are "drawn" for use in providing the service. Thus, it should be obvious that in the service industry, ample record-keeping involves use of the principle of ABC inventory control, supplemented by job costing of parts. Thus, most items purchased for stock can be rated as either A, B, or C items and reordered accordingly, while as the various jobs occur, items used can be simply noted on an attached job ticket. In this way inventory items are reordered as needed, while particular customers are billed for items used in servicing their apparatus. ( See Figure 20–2 for a sample job ticket. )

## Manufacturing industry

Manufacturing concerns face problems unlike retail and service industries simply because of the nature of their business. Manufacturers transform raw materials and parts into finished products; retail, wholesale, and, for the most part, service industries simply act as middlemen. Therefore, the manufacturing manager is concerned with four inventory problems: (1) ample raw materials and supplies to keep the manufacturing process going; (2) the control of work in process in an effort to eliminate theft, pilferage, and deterioration; (3) the control of finished goods until such time as they are shipped to retailers, wholesalers, or service establishments; and (4) the purchase of new and up-to-date raw materials.

Since an outage of an important production part could make it necessary for a manufacturer to shut down operations, it is essential that the manufacturer either engage in some kind of perpetual inventory control or some basic reorder-point strategem which signals ( $a$ ) the need to re-

**FIGURE 20–2**
Job ticket

|  |  |  | Order No. 00630 |
| --- | --- | --- | --- |

Customer Name:   Sam Jones
Address:   496 Grape
City, state:   Uptown        Zip Code:_____
Nature of repair:   TV is blurry

| Quantity | Article |  | Price |
| --- | --- | --- | --- |
| 1 | X3294 |  | 4.50 |
| 1 | X3295 |  | 2.19 |
| 1 | ZG solenoid |  | .15 |
|  | Labor |  | 21.00 |
|  |  |  |  |
|  | Subtotal |  | 29.84 |
|  | Tax |  | 1.40 |
|  | Total |  | 29.24 |
|  |  |  |  |

order stock and ($b$) the fact that if more is not reordered an outage can occur. Maintaining a perpetual inventory has already been discussed and therefore does not need further elaboration here. However, the use of reorder points does need more explanation because it is the more commonly used device by small (and large) manufacturing enterprises, and it is probably the safest and least expensive and least time-consuming technique to use.

Using this technique is not at all difficult for the small business manager once he or she has an understanding of the principle behind reorder points. This can most easily be shown graphically as illustrated in Figure 20–3.

In the diagram of reorder-point inventory control in Figure 20–3, it can be seen that the quantity of stock on hand is plotted along the vertical

**FIGURE 20–3**
Diagram of reorder point inventory control

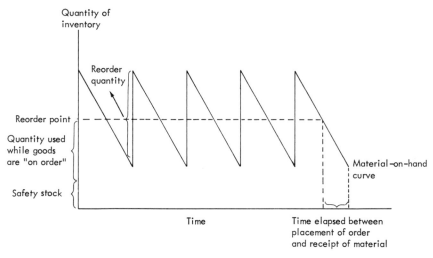

axis and a curve is drawn which represents the increase and decrease in materials on hand as stock is used and replenished. It will be noted that as time progresses, the material-on-hand curve goes down, indicating the gradual use of this raw material in the manufacturing process. If no additional goods are reordered, ultimately the material on hand will be depleted to zero. However, the material-on-hand curve takes on a sawtooth appearance because when new stock which has been ordered is received, the material-on-hand curve will instantly jump up, displaying the increase in stock on hand. Thus, the height of the sawtooth will represent the quantity reordered. The reorder point occurs when the manufacturing manager knows that if material is not reordered the business will likely run out because of the time that will elapse between the placement of the order and the receipt of the material.

Ideally, of course, the reorder point should be established at that point in time where the manufacturer is just running out of material on hand as the new order is received. Practically speaking, however, this is impossible because of delays which can occur in placing an order or transporting the material from the supplier. Therefore most manufacturers also include a buffer, cushion, or "safety stock," which they always retain on hand just in case their reorder-point calculations or delivery-time calculations are slightly off. Therefore, this "safety stock" is not considered in planning when to reorder a particular raw material; rather it is just assumed that this material is always on hand as a safety supply to prevent a production-crippling "outage" from occurring.

In using the reorder-point inventory control device, the small business manager should (1) calculate how long it takes to order raw materials and have them delivered, (2) calculate how much material will be used during this elapsed-time process, (3) add in what he or she considers to be a safety-stock factor, and (4) thus determine the minimum quantity of inventory which the company can have on hand before that particular merchandise must be reordered.

The quantity of merchandise which the manufacturer reorders when the reorder point is reached, of course, must be sufficient to replenish the stock back to the reorder-point level. However, most managers find it expedient to reorder amounts greater than are needed to restore stock to the reorder point, because otherwise they would be perpetually reordering when raw materials are received. Just how much more to order than is needed to replace stock to the reorder point is not always an easy decision to make. However, the *economic lot* concept is a device which many small business manufacturers find useful in determining how much to reorder at a specific time.

Basically, the *economic lot* concept states that the amount of material reordered is that quantity which gives the manufacturer the lowest cost per unit for that merchandise. That is, the economic lot concept recognizes the following facts: (1) processing frequent orders costs money, (2) carrying excessive inventory is also expensive, and (3) buying in large quantities tends to enable the manufacturer to purchase raw materials at some quantity discount. Therefore, the economic lot concept basically means that because the costs of processing paper work and ordering too frequently in too small amounts will raise the cost of merchandise, while ordering infrequently in gigantic lot sizes (although reducing paper work costs and price per unit of merchandise) runs up such costs as inventory taxes, storage costs, shelf wear, bin costs, and interest on investment, it follows that the optimum quantity which can be reordered must be computed to the point where the paper work expense, shelf wear, and inventory-carrying costs are reduced to a minimum while the quantity discounts are maximized. This optimum number is the economic lot quantity which should be reordered. Graphically the idea is presented in Figure 20–4. There it can be seen that the per-unit costs of goods purchased (typically) goes down the larger the quantities purchased (and thus the more infrequent the orders placed), but at some point this per-unit cost reaches a minimum and then begins to rise because of the increasing inventory-carrying costs. At the bottom of this curve is the economic lot or the optimum number of units to reorder. Of course, practically speaking, it should be recognized that although the economic lot can be computed to a fairly accurate quantity, the unit-cost curve will be relatively flat over a range of 25 percent above and 25 percent below the economic lot quantity, not to mention the fact that suppliers will rarely

FIGURE 20-4
Economic lot diagram

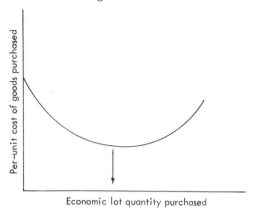

be interested in supplying odd lots. Therefore, this figure need not be a precise number but a convenient number somewhere around the economic lot size.

Because of the nature of the manufacturing process it should be clear that the inventory control problem of the manufacturer differs from that of the retail, service, or wholesale fields because the manager must schedule work designed to transform raw materials into products. However, the tranformation problem is not the only problem which the small business manufacturer faces. He or she also has an inventory problem much like that of the retailer, wholesaler, or service business since the manufacturer must have finished products on hand for resale when demanded by wholesalers, retailers, or service industries, and must protect this inventory from the ravishes of time, wear, and theft. Therefore, it might be stated that the small manufacturer's inventory control problem is twice that of other industries because it is also faced with the same problems which confront the others.

## Wholesaling industry

The wholesale industry inventory control problem is not altogether different from those of the retailing and service industries. Fundamentally, the difference is that, typically, wholesalers buy in larger lots and carry heavier inventories than do retail and service industries. In fact, it is not uncommon for some wholesalers to carry half or more of their total assets as investments in inventory. Because such a large percentage of the wholesaler's operating capital is tied up in inventory, it might be said that although the wholesaler's inventory problem differs little from those of retail or service establishments, it is more critical toward the success or failure of the business. Any mistake made in inventory handling will represent a much more serious problem. Therefore, accurate records are imperative for the wholesaler. The techniques are the same as those used by the retail and service industries; the emphasis is merely greater.

It is heartening to note that most small wholesalers are becoming increasingly aware of this phenomenon and are attempting to avoid the problem. There appears to be a widespread acceptance among wholesalers today of the principle of low gross margin and high turnover as a way of operation. To remain in business the wholesaler must be able to compete with low-margin competitors, and it merely stands to reason that the only way to make a satisfactory profit from low-margin items is by selling in high volume.

## INVENTORY CONTROL SYSTEMS

No chapter on inventory would be complete without mention of the various kinds of mechanical inventory control systems which are being used. The following, therefore, is designed to highlight some of the more commonly used procedural techniques for keeping control over inventory. However, it must be recognized that the varieties of techniques seem almost endless, and they are mainly designed to facilitate the general techniques of personal observation, physical counts, on hand–on order–sold, and perpetual records.

### Manual inventory control systems

The most commonly used manual inventory control systems are essentially paper transfer techniques. The paper transfer technique means essentially the following or routing of inventory items on paper. Figures 20–1 and 20–2 are examples of paper transfer inventory control systems. However, the varieties of paper transfer systems are endless because they are so simple and readily applicable to almost any problem. Basically all that need be recalled about the paper transfer system is that when an item of inventory is bought, sold, moved, or transferred, a notation is made on some record to that effect. The record itself is kept at a specific spot and is designed to apprise the small business operator, at a glance, of the location of inventory or material.

### Visual inventory control systems

Visual inventory control systems are very similar to the manual control systems except that they are better designed to disclose the progress of material or equipment. Visual inventory control systems are particularly useful to manufacturing operations because they do show the status of work in process.

One of the fundamental visual control systems which has been long in use is called the Gantt Chart. Actually, the Gantt Chart itself is not in common use today, but there are several kinds of commercial variations of Gantt Charts on the market which are being utilized. Basically, the Gantt Chart, designed by Henry Gantt almost 70 years ago, is a graphic presentation of the status of machine use and material use. The three most commonly used variations of the Gantt Chart today are the Produc-Trol® boards, Sched-U-Graphs®, and Boardmasters®. All of these techniques use a time scale across the top, and all use lines down the side to show what is being visually portrayed, whether machines, orders, or material. They are pratically always kept in central production control offices, not out in the shop.

All of the above techniques have as their primary advantage the ability to highlight trouble spots when they are occurring and sometimes before they occur. The main drawback is that they are extras: they all require extra work because the same records of inventory must be kept in writing. Further, unless they are currently posted—and this could mean daily, hourly, or even to the minute—they are always a little bit out of date, and thereby somewhat misleading. Nevertheless, they are nice refinements if the small business manufacturer can afford them, particularly if he is working on a production schedule which is extremely tight and in which all machines and material must be used to the optimum advantage.

## Mechanical and automated inventory control systems

In addition to the manual and visual inventory control systems, there have been other mechanical and automated techniques developed with the onset of automatic data processing. Unfortunately, in many cases small businesses cannot avail themselves of the advantages of these systems because of cost. All mechanical and all automated inventory control systems require the use of electronic memory units or computers. Their main advantage is that they provide instantaneous information on the status of any inventory of material, as well as other information as to how much has been ordered, when it was ordered, and whether or not more should be ordered at the present time. The problem, of course, is that having such information is costly, particularly if memory units and computers are involved. Thus, most small business operators find that they do not have adequate funds to mechanize or automate their inventory control systems; and many discover that even if the funds were available, the need for mechanization and automation would be limited because of the small size of their establishments. Nevertheless, it should be recognized that when a firm becomes of sufficient size and has sufficient prosperity, it may be desirable to convert to a mechanical, punched-card record of inventory, or to use computers. It should also be pointed out that when the small business reaches the size that warrants investment in mechanized or automated inventory control systems, any of the large manufacturers of data processing equipment stand ready to advise the small business manager specifically on the type of equipment available and the job it will do for the specific operations of that small business.

## PRINCIPLES OF INVENTORY MANAGEMENT

There are several principles of inventory management which, although employed in the above analysis, have not been mentioned specifically. Since they are fundamental to good inventory management, they merit some consideration by the prospective small business manager and will serve as a basic review of the foregoing material.

### Least-cost balancing

One principle of inventory management which must always be employed is the principle of least-cost balancing or optimization. That is, as developed in much of the foregoing, the basic problem of inventory management is not to minimize cost or to maximize supply, rather it is to optimize both cost and supply. The principle is that there is some optimal position for holding and ordering inventory which recognizes the fact that while ordering large quantities might make the cost of materials cheaper, the cost of carrying the inventory ultimately will become greater. There is a delicate balance between the two which represents the optimum. Achieving this optimum cost is referred to as least-cost balancing.

### Utilizing suppliers and customers

The second principle of inventory management is that the effective inventory manager will utilize suppliers and customers in passing off costs of inventory to any extent which is possible. That is, the small business manager will endeavor to avoid any and all inventory costs by (a) having a supplier stock the item rather than bearing the burden of carrying the inventory or (b) charging the customer enough to cover the cost of having borne a required inventory.

As simple as this principle sounds, it is often ignored by small business managers. Many of these managers find themselves in the situation of having stocked entirely too many items. Therefore they not only tie up their funds by stocking the inventory but have incurred unnecessary costs because the stocked merchandise was not needed or wanted for some time. At other times, the small business operator fails to charge customers a fair price for their product or service because they fail to recognize all of the elemental costs of carrying inventory. Needless to say, either circumstance is to be avoided if at all possible. If items are only occasionally called for or if even when called for they are not needed immediately, the effective inventory manager will not stock such items and will therefore pass on the expense of carrying a full inventory to the supplier. When that is not possible, then the manager will charge sufficiently to cover the costs involved. This principle—often called the "living off the other guy" principle—is extremely valuable and the usual practice of people who are considered effective inventory managers.

## Effective purchasing

The third principle of effective inventory management is that effective purchasing policies should be pursued. Perhaps the old stock market adage of "buy low and sell high" represents the gist of this principle. The small business manager who has engaged in effective inventory management will only purchase for stock those items which are needed and in optimal quantities rather than stocking items which might be needed in quantities which supply the lowest price. Not only must the effective inventory manager buy low and sell high, he or she must buy something which he needs and only in the quantities which are needed. The housewife who is often laughed at because she may purchase a hat or dress which she didn't need or particularly want because "It was such a bargain that I couldn't afford to pass it up" is a classical joke. But the fact is that many small business managers—both men and women—fall victim to the same line of thought when they stock a 20-year supply of letterheads. They apparently never considered that even if they are still in business 20 years hence, the letterhead might be a little out of date by that time.

## Financing arrangements

A fourth principle of effective inventory management is that when one finds oneself in a bad inventory situation, he or she does his or her best through financial arrangements to escape these difficulties.

One of the frequently used techniques to financially alleviate an overstocked inventory position is called *field warehousing*. This technique is usually employed in those circumstances where, because of ignorance, avarice, or order error, the small business operator finds himself or herself in an overstocked position with entirely too much working capital tied up in dead stock. By employing the technique of field warehousing through financial arrangements with a bank or broker the small business operator is often able to make a loan on the value of the excess inventory. That is, many banks and other financial institutions are willing to lend small business operators up to 75 percent of the value of excess inventory if the small business operator is willing to "field warehouse" this merchandise. This involves storing the excess merchandise in a warehouse or in some other identifiable and controllable storage area (which many times can be found on the premises of the small business). What is required is that the financial institution have control over the release of the field warehoused merchandise for sale. Obviously they will not release any part of it for sale until such time as the loan is paid or at least partly repaid. It should be clear that the field warehousing kind of financial arrangement is a real boon to the small business operator, particularly those in the manufacturing business. Thus, the small business manufacturer who is governed by a seasonal market (for example, the manufacture of ski jackets) will in the early spring be manufacturing hot and heavy for the fall and winter market, but will not be selling the product at that time. Therefore, by "field warehousing" the operator can finance this advance production in an effort to get operating cash for continuing operations until such time as sales start picking up in the fall.

### Transportation analysis

A final principle of effective inventory control management is that ample attention be devoted to transportation problems and transportation costs. Many times apparently "good" buys are deceptive because although the price is cheap, the buyer sees this low price advantage eroded away by increasing transportation costs or other problems such as unforeseen delays in delivery of the merchandise. This usually occurs because in the haste to take advantage of an apparent "sale," the small business operator fails to realize that the price was quoted for delivery at the factory rather than at the shop door. Problems can also crop up if delivery is undependable, late, or even impossible because of unsolvable packaging and crating problems.

The consequences of ignoring transportation costs and other problems should be obvious to any small business manager. However, because such problems are frequently overlooked by the small business operator, this problem has to be mentioned in any listing of principles of inventory management.

### SUMMARY

The objectives of inventory control are physical protection of the merchandise; control of investment, material, or product flow information; cost analyses; and the securing of maximum sales for the firm. These objectives can be attained in a variety of ways, and indeed they must be pursued in a somewhat differing fashion by retailers, service operations, manufacturers and wholesalers.

Although the nature of the business does have a bearing on the type of inventory problem which a small business happens to have, there are several guidelines that can be utilized in solving these problems. Some of these guidelines take the form of rules which are not always true but tend to be true often enough to serve as guidlines to effective inventory control. In addition to these rules there are also principles of effective inventory management which must be complied with by the small business manager, not to mention the various physical control systems which have been devised to help the small business manager in controlling inventory.

In the final analysis, however, it is up to the individual small business operator to determine how he or she intends to control inventory and manage material. If he or she is on top of inventory at all times, he or she will be well down the road to a successful operation. However, if the manager is unconcerned about inventory and does not effectively control it, he or she will without a doubt be doomed to failure. This is particularly so if the business has a large amount of operating assets tied up in inventory. Especially vulnerable to inventory difficulties therefore are wholesalers and manufacturers of seasonal products.

## QUESTIONS

1. What are the objectives of inventory control? Explain why each of these are important to the small business operator.
2. What is the "law of the vital few and the trivial many?" Of what usefulness is this law to anyone concerned with inventory control?
3. Can you support the statement that "an uncontrolled inventory is too much inventory?" How? How is it possible to have too much inventory?
4. The text states that one fourth of any inventory is waste. Is this true? Why? Explain in detail.
5. What is the special inventory problem of the typical retailer? Why is it generally unique to retailing? Explain in detail.
6. How does the service industry inventory problem differ from retailing? From wholesaling? From manufacturing?
7. What is meant by reorder-point inventory control? How does it work?
8. What is safety stock? Is the safety stock concept relevant to the economic lot concept? How? Explain in detail.
9. What are manual inventory control systems? How do they work? How do they differ from visual inventory control systems?
10. What is least-cost balancing? What is field warehousing? Explain both concepts in detail.

## PROBLEM

Jack "Spider" Webb, in his day, was one of the best downhill racers in the country. Many a cup he had won—he even had had the privilege of having one of the major ski manufacturers name one of their better lines of skis after him.

Unfortunately, Spider wasn't quite as good a businessman as he was a skier. When he finally broke his leg in a freak accident (he slipped and fell in his living room testing the release tension on a ski binding he was planning to test for the manufacturer the next day) he had to quit skiing. That was when he decided to take his winnings from the races he had won on the pro circuit and open his own ski shop at one of Colorado's newest (and best) areas.

It seemed that all was a disaster for Spider. He had sunk all his money, plus all he could borrow from family and friends into a loser. Spider's bookkeeping service had just informed him that he had lost another $3,000 last month (October) during a time when sales should have easily caused a monthly profit, if not offsetting some of the earlier month losses (May, June, July, August, and September) which are normal in the off season. His bookkeeper told him that his losses were due to "inventory shrinkage," whatever that meant.

1. What might Spider's bookkeeping service have meant by "inventory shrinkage"?
2. What might be the cause of Spider's "inventory shrinkage"? List at least five logical causes.
3. What might Spider do about the five causes enumerated in answer to the second question to eliminate future "shrinkage"? Explain in detail.

## BIBLIOGRAPHY

Burkhalter, Louis D., and Flaherty, Catherine L. *It's Only Money*. New York: Carlton Press, 1971. An interesting presentation of what can go wrong in financing and the financial management of a small business.

Rakstis, Ted J. "How to Fail in Business without Really Trying." *The Kiwanis Magazine*, vol. 51 (February 1966), pp. 41–44. Good study on the usual reasons for small business failure.

Rutberg, Sidney. *Ten Cents on the Dollar on the Bankruptcy Game*. New York: Simon and Schuster, 1973. This book could be called a primer for anyone facing the prospect of having a failing business on their hands.

Shelton, William A. "Small Merchants Need Help." *The National Public Accountant*, September 1971, pp. 8–11. Brief assessment of financial (mis)-management of small businesses.

# 21

# Production operations and controls

Production operations are a necessary and important part of every business activity. Every business must produce the products or services which are the end result of its particular reason for being in business. Products are easily identified and related to specific methods and processes, while services are somewhat more variable and in some cases intangible. Regardless of what is done and how it is done, the business must produce whatever specialty it is equipped to do, and do it in an organized and efficient way.

Production operations include manufacturing, which is often used in this text as one of the four major divisions of small business activity. It is the intent of this chapter to cover all forms of production operations and controls, relating specifically to manufacturing where it is appropriate.

## PLANNING PRODUCTION OPERATIONS

All forms of production activity should first be analyzed and planned so that the work can be done in the best possible way. Initial planning can be examined within the following categories:

1. Production layout (product, process, or some combination)
2. Production work load (units, time schedules, consistency)
3. Production capability and versatility (men, machines, experience, extra resources)
4. Production standards (labor, machines, costs, and time)
5. Production systems and procedures (manual, closed loop, computer-assisted, rigid, or flexible.

*Production layout.* A good layout helps the business to produce whatever product or service is desired. Job activities should be studied to know what has to be done, where it has to be done, and with what kinds of layout. Manufacturing relates heavily to work flow, and resulting machine placement, and efficiency in moving the product from one operation to the next. A *process* layout groups men and machines doing similar work. These are often classified as shops, such as the machine shop, forge shop, paint shop, etc. A *product* layout is used where the product dominates, and the product movement controls where the machines are placed and the work carried out.

In a service industry business, layout is concerned with a layout which facilitates the orderly handling of customer orders and the efficient flow of service parts, paper work, and service personnel.

*Production work load.* Balancing and adjusting the work load is a constant process for the production and operations manager. The actual physical product or the service delivered is often a multi-stage activity involving a whole series of events and activities. Many of these follow each other; others are performed simultaneously.

One real advantage of many smaller enterprises is the ability to develop alternative talents and experience, and for management to use these to the best advantage—when and where needed. Real ingenuity in planning and carrying out the production work load is the mark of a good small business manager. It can pay very big dividends in the lower costs of the end products delivered. The higher the proportion of labor that is involved in a given form of production, the better the chance is that a small business can compete with a larger one. This is particularly true when job assignments are flexible and personnel are adept and willing to perform where needed.

*Production capability and versatility.* Many small businesses exist because they can perform production activities or perform services which are difficult for larger business. The economies of scale usually require considerable specialization of machines and job duties to achieve low cost end results. There are numerous kinds of production operations which are ideal for the smaller business. These are of several kinds:

a.  Production of a line of products which are similar, but variable as to quantities per order and the number sold to any one customer. An example might be a company that makes specialized medical instruments. The total market is small, but ample for a few smaller firms. Products can be altered to meet individual customer demands.
b.  Production of the one-time product—one after another. No one can beat the versatile small manufacturer who really knows how to do this well.
c.  Versatile subcontracting to produce short-runs of products which larger businesses cannot handle on their own equipment efficiently. Small business subcontractors also exist because they have low overhead and can produce more cheaply than a larger business.

Numerous other variations exist. It is important to realize that many small businesses are provided with opportunities because they do possess the ability to achieve efficient production operations which cannot be matched by a larger, less flexible organization.

*Production standards.* Small business operators must review and be familiar with work and performance standards. Standards are important because they replace outdated rules of thumb, or conjecture and opinions, which are often just not valid. Standards that are developed in an industry, or certain data that has been valid elsewhere, give a good base from which to work. In general, standards are work standards, time standards, job standards, and cost standards.

*Production systems and procedures.* All forms of production effort benefit by repetition and experience. Considerable benefit can be gained by a careful analysis of the systems and procedures used to schedule and accomplish the various production tasks. Manual methods are acceptable if the activity is on a small scale and employees are voluntarily responsive to flaws or shortcomings in the work patterns and procedures. As the total production mix becomes more complex and expensive, it is necessary to develop more sophisticated systems and procedures.

The small business has a decided advantage in the area of systems and procedure if the management is informed and able to utilize some of the newer and more sophisticated techniques that are available. The production effort should be helped by the systems and procedures that are adopted, rather than create an "empire of record keepers" whose goal is the process, and not the end result. The small business operator can assess the situation and use what is beneficial to him.

## THE NATURE OF SMALL MANUFACTURING

Activities classified as manufacturing are of major concern to anyone who is involved with production operations. This is because for many people manufacturing is synonymous with production operations. Actually this is not strictly the case, as has been explained earlier in this chapter, but manufacturing does contain a high proportion of production operations, in terms of end products produced.

Manufacturing includes by various definitions traditional factory processes, but also laundries, bakeries, printing establishments, dairies, and other business forms, not normally considered as manufacturing.

Another way to classify manufacturing is by the orientation of the business in terms of its raw material inputs or the utilization of its end products. In this system, manufacturers might be classified as follows:

*a.* Resource-oriented
*b.* Local market manufacturers

*c.* Subcontractors

*d.* Broad market suppliers

*e.* Servicing manufacturers

Nothing is very logical or precise about such a classification; it is merely a way to think about how manufacturers come into existence and are supported within the economic system.

The importance of manufacturing and production operations is this: *Manufacturing is heavily oriented to physical activities. This includes the acquisition and movement of materials, the employment of machines and energy, the utilization of technical and human skills, and a high reliance on the ability to integrate many complex activities, both in sequence and concurrently.*

Manufacturing depends on effective operations and controls. What is said in this entire chapter always has a substantial input into manufacturing; every business, however, must analyze and develop its own efficient production operations and controls. Much can be learned from the manufacturing industries. Study their methods and procedures for ideas and practices.

The remainder of this chapter is concerned with specific aspects of small business which are related to the operation and control of the requisite production functions.

## PRODUCTION ECONOMICS

The nature of production operations is most generally characterized by a series of operations that must be organized and implemented so that an efficient end result is obtained. For any given company the combinations will be different from another company, even though the products are identical. Within a company, the combinations are different, based on the time involved, available machines, quantities scheduled, and other factors bearing on the work to be done.

*Trade-off analysis.* A number of informed individuals are of the opinion that production management might also be called "trade-off management." The reason for this is the extensive number of alternatives that are available when production activities are being considered. Typically, management may plan to use lower skill workers in greater numbers because of the same total costs as a fewer number of higher skilled workers. Subcontracting may be substituted for the firm's own production of a given item. The alternatives are almost endless—one thing exchanged for another.

Typically trade-offs should be investigated, particularly to provide an alternative in case the first choice fails, and as a matter of good managerial homework. Don't accept the first viable choice; others may exist which are better. But who knows of this until comparisons are made?

*Facilities mix.* Since the end of World War II technological development has been quite rapid. Considerable technology has been incorporated into machinery, factory equipment, and support units such as computer installations. Much of this technological advancement provides opportunity for much higher levels of output in equivalent time periods, or at the same cost. However, this is not always the case. Frequently, *portions* of the technology can be utilized, at levels which are about right for small business operations.

Facilities combinations should be investigated in areas of full or semi-automation, numerical controlled machines, materials handling equipment, and closed loop control systems. Details about these applications are available through reference books in manufacturing management.

*Optimum lot sizes.* Many production processes are broken into units of output, even though the production may be constant, involving continuous output. Any economic analysis should attempt to determine what are the optimum lot sizes for efficiency in the production runs—along with other related costs. Lot size analysis is made up of set-up costs, continuity in the production runs, service to the end customers, and carrying costs on excess quantities produced.

*Opportunity costs.* With the many possibilities available for alternative production methods, some recognition is given to the cost differential of various courses of action. This comparison and assessment in dollars is the determination of opportunity costs.

Actually the measurement can be in either direction from a base, although the method is thought of as opportunity cost analysis. If an opportunity to achieve a greater return is given up, there is a cost associated with the higher priced alternative chosen. On the other hand, several alternatives may have equivalent pay-offs at different levels of output. Direct results may vary, be equivalent in the short run, and not the same in the long run.

Small business should think in terms of opportunity costs because of the need to maximize a number of production features which are not standardized and can be used to good advantage through skillful management.

*Learning curves.* Experience developed in shipbuilding and the aircraft industries during World War II was later translated into a technique known as the learning curve. This production planning tool is useful when the identical job or product is produced over time in some substantial quantity. Direct labor costs can be predicted to decline at some measurable rate as each successive quantity of production is doubled. From 2, 4, 8, 16, 32, and on up, the quantity and cost of direct labor will drop—at a predictable rate.

Perhaps the majority of small businesses do not deal in quantities and uniformity of production that produces a declining direct labor cost pattern. Nevertheless, the idea is sound and should be applied even though the results are uneven. Every job has its learning and improvement patterns which improve with increasing experience.

*Capital investment analysis.* This subject is a part of production economics, but is not dealt with here. Refer to Chapter 15 which explains such things as payback analysis, discounted cash flow and rate of return analysis.

Most of the capital investment analysis connected to production activities is used to determine the feasibility of machinery and equipment acquisitions and investments in raw materials and other input inventories.

## PHYSICAL PRODUCTION FACILITIES

The physical production facilities that are needed by the small business can often be made up of many more variables than a large business. This is true for several reasons. Frequently the small business manager can accomplish the necessary production tasks with equipment which is outmoded for higher levels of output. A number of managers of small businesses, particularly manufacturing, are quite resourceful and can equip machines with "home-made" tooling which does an adequate job. In the smaller business, the building and its features are often not really important to the individual who has a personal mission in life—to create something which is all his or her own.

### Plant facilities

The small manufacturer has certain conditions working in his favor regarding his plant facilities. Manufacturing frequently does not demand a particular kind of location, especially when it is being conducted on a small scale. This permits the utilization of many different kinds of buildings and many different kinds of locations. An older factory building which has been vacated or an old warehouse building is often suitable for manufacturing, but for nothing else. Under these conditions it can be acquired at a low rental or lease figure or perhaps purchased at an attractive price. A new facility is an attractive proposition if a landowner has some land which is primarily suitable for small manufacturing and he is desirous of realizing some income from the vacant site.

### Equipment

Investment in equipment for manufacturing is subject to considerable discretionary choice on the part of the manufacturer. A small manufacturer may utilize equipment which has been downgraded from a higher output use somewhere else. Often he or she can obtain this equipment by making it known what type of used equipment is wanted. With such information the manufacturer or distributor can perhaps work out a three-party transaction.

Equipment may also be secured under various financial arrangements which have come into widespread use in the last 20 years. Essentially these involve various types of lease and rental agreements, as opposed to purchase. Leases and rentals are attractive because they establish the cost of such equipment as a current business expense to be charged off against current operations. If the equipment is purchased, it must be capitalized and depreciated over a period of time. Purchase and depreciation write-off will probably be cheaper than either lease or rental; however, many businesspersons as well as larger manufacturers do not know how long they can expect to use a particular piece of producing machinery. They are uncertain about productive life and hesitate to invest on a long-term basis. Under lease or rental, higher cost will be necessary; but at the same time the commitment period can be reduced to one or two years, or perhaps less, and if at the end of this period the equipment is no longer needed it can be returned to the lessor or renter.

## PRODUCT DESIGN, DEVELOPMENT, AND RESEARCH

One of the most dramatic features of many kinds of manufacturing is the rapidity with which new products replace older ones. Products, materials, and processes in all forms of production are constantly being changed and replacement is much faster than most people realize.

In a large manufacturer of many diversified products, such as Minnesota Mining and Manufacturing, a 20-year time span there may develop replacement of as much as 65 to 70 percent of the original product line.

The particular importance of product innovation and replacement to the small producer is that:

1. New opportunities will always be developing.
2. Many new ideas, products, and processes will be developed initially by the smaller firm.
3. Innovation in design, development, and research is just as possible in a small business as a large one.
4. A fragmenting of input materials, as well as finished goods, develops opportunities for smaller businesses.
5. Subcontracting and specialty product manufacturing is a big area that is ideal for many small firms.
6. Technology tends to develop specialization, often to very narrow product specialties. Many of these are so limited that only small businesses can provide the quantity needed.

## PURCHASING FOR PRODUCTION

All production is supported by the acquisition of some combination of raw materials, components, equipment, and services, along with other specially designated inputs which are needed for the production effort.

*Sources.* The smaller company will seldom have a full-time purchasing manager. This job will be done by someone who probably has a number of different activities to administer. Sources have always been important because any acquisition from outside sources is no better than the firm providing it. In the period since World War II the purchasing function has been blessed with the development of many new specialized products, improved supply sources throughout the world, and the availability of many options that did not previously exist. Beginning in 1972 the total situation regarding sources began to change quite dramatically. Vendors and suppliers were faced with shortages of materials, unstable prices, and inflation. The relatively long period of stability in source performance had come to an end.

Dependence on sources as of 1975 may be on different terms than pre-1972. Inflation and higher financing costs will cause producers to reduce product lines and various aspects of service.

*Prices.* Many of the same comments on sources can be applied to prices. Many commodities and raw materials had long-term price stability and lesser increases than other products up until about 1965. In the mid-1970s, prices are very unstable. Many prices are rising in the face of declining production demands. The small purchaser must learn and educate himself or herself in the dynamics of the marketplace. Even then, one must take considerable risks. One is pretty much on one's own in a topsy-turvy world of prices that are not very rational, based on previous rules of thumb and sophisticated measures.

In addition to enlightenment, the purchasing manager will need skill in relating prices to such things as inventory-carrying costs, availability of funds, and inventory valuation methods.

*Value analysis.* In the strict sense, value analysis is an economic measure. However, it is used a great deal by purchasing managers to develop improvements in the purchase programs. In a way it is a method of thinking how purchasing should be accomplished.

The basis of value analysis is to assume that nothing is bought unless it contributes value. Products, processes, materials, systems, time, and effort are all subject to review. Value is what it is worth to the buyer and no one else. Rigorous inquiry is applied to every conceivable part of a product or total purchase, to determine if the personal value is really there. As said before, the mid-1970s are difficult times. Value analysis should be applied continuously to make sure the purchasing program is *lean and effective.*

In Figure 21–1 a sample form is shown which could be used as a preliminary checklist to determine the difference in value between competing materials or components used in the production process. Analysis with Figure 21–1 is not detailed, but rather a way to assemble important costs and judgments to see if further, more detailed, analysis is justified.

## MATERIALS HANDLING

Materials handling in small manufacturing should be just as efficient as materials handling for big companies. It may involve small quantities,

FIGURE 21–1
Value analysis preliminary checklist

| *Items* | A | B | C |
|---|---|---|---|
| 1. Purchase price<br>2. Interest on investment<br>3. Transportation charges<br>  *a.* Packaging costs<br>  *b.* Loss or damage—average costs<br>4. Storage charges<br>5. Purchasing costs<br>6. Inventory carrying costs (direct)<br>  *a.* Taxes<br>  *b.* Insurance<br>  *c.* Loss or damage estimates<br>  *d.* Obsolescence and deterioration<br>    estimates | | | |
| Dollar Totals ($) | | | |
| 1. Quality rating  (Experience and<br>  *a.* Materials    Reputation)<br>  *b.* Design<br>  *c.* Functional potential<br>  *d.* Workmanship<br><br>2. Vendor performance  (Experience and<br>  *a.* Ability        Reputation)<br>  *b.* Reliability<br>  *c.* Integrity<br>  *d.* Services provided | | | |
| Opinion and judgment totals<br>(Good-Average-Poor) | | | |
| Final rating ($'s and Opinions) | (3) | (2) | (1) |

less mechanized equipment, and less frequent movement; however, many materials handling techniques are well within the capital resources of the small company because many small-scale materials handling systems do not require elaborate or expensive equipment. In general, the less materials are handled the better. Every movement involves an order, receipt, and possible damage. Small-scale manufacturing may utilize a single individual who handles both incoming components and outgoing finished goods. As an example, he or she would be responsible for maintaining the inventory utilizing techniques and information presented in Chapter 20 and would likewise be in charge of shipping and distribution. At all times he or she would know not only the status of manufacturing but also the status of supply to manufacturing and the withdrawals of finished stock requiring subsequent manufacturing replacement.

## MAINTENANCE

Maintenance of the factory and its production facilities is often ignored or not properly understood by the small manufacturer. Recognition must be made of the right kinds of maintenance, the scheduling of maintenance activities, and the protection of the production process through maintenance. Most equipment manufacturers will provide maintenance manuals and instructions regarding their own equipment. In addition, many of these manufacturers offer maintenance contracts which provide various services over time for a stated contract price. A small manufacturer may be reluctant to follow instructions or to purchase a maintenance contract on the basis that it is too expensive or unnecessary. Such, however, may be a false economy in the sense that many of the problems which are the results of lack of maintenance or poor maintenance are very insidious and build up over a period of time without being easily recognizable.

Maintenance is often scheduled even though the need has not been definitely established. In this way possible machine failures and resulting downtime can be avoided, and as experience is gained the scheduling can be brought in line with indicated needs. Maintenance is generally described as remedial or preventive.

## STANDARDS, INSPECTION, AND MEASUREMENT CONTROLS

All manufacturing must constantly adhere to certain standards. In general, these standards are determined on an overall basis when the product is designed, knowing the capability of the manufacturing operation. When the design for the product is formulated, it will be designed so that all operating components will mesh and produce the ultimate standardized result that is necessary. In this regard, equipment, material, manufacturing methods, and employee capability along with inspection processes will play a role.

Inspection is a confirmation process to determine whether or not a particular result is being achieved as planned. Some inspection will provide the opportunity to redesign and improve that which is being done; in other cases it will be used merely as a check on performance and a determination that the quality levels are being maintained within reasonable tolerances.

## Statistical quality control

Statistical quality control has come into widespread use for the purpose of controlling manufacturing processes. Its purpose is to hold to a minimum the amount of production which is unacceptable, to provide a means of separating acceptable from unacceptable lots of production, and to establish consistent inspection processes under a variety of conditions.

With the use of charts and statistical analysis it is possible to predict with a fair degree of accuracy what can be achieved in a particular production process, what are reasonable control limits, how to analyze in-phase or out-of-phase production, and how to institute corrective measures quickly so as to limit nonstandard production runs.

*Normal distribution.* The main statistical tool of quality control is the normal distribution curve. This is the curve that will result if a process is subjected to chance variation only. If a normal distribution curve is assumed, it can be said that by chance the following percentage of products will fall within the following ranges:

68.27 percent of the products will fall within $\pm 1\sigma$ from the mean.
95.45 percent of the products will fall within $\pm 2\sigma$ from the mean.
99.73 percent of the products will fall within $\pm 3\sigma$ from the mean.

For further explanation of the meaning of $\sigma$ (standard deviation) and normal distribution, consult a textbook on statistics or quality control. The same reference should also be consulted for a more detailed explanation of the remaining material in this section. It is not possible in this text to examine at length the background supporting a statistical quality control program; however, the illustrations that follow are the most common methods of statistical analysis used in controlling production quality.[1]

*Quality control charts.* The most important statistical quality charts are the mean ($X$) chart, the range ($R$) chart, the number of defects per unit ($D$) chart, and the percent defective ($p$) chart. In each of the charts a mean or average figure ($X$, $R$, $D$, or $\bar{p}$) is computed from samples, and an

---

[1] See Franklin G. Moore, *Production Management*, 6th ed. (Homewood, Ill.: Richard D. Irwin, 1973); or Acheson J. Duncan, *Quality Control and Industrial Statistics*, 4th ed. (Homewood, Ill.: Richard D. Irwin, 1974).

372

FIGURE 21–2
Mean control chart

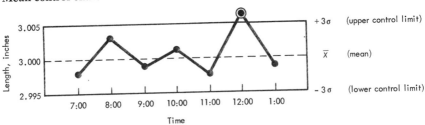

upper and lower control limit (usually $\pm 3\sigma$) is determined by using statistical formulas or by using statistical quality control tables and certain statistical measures. Additional samples are then taken and plotted on the charts. Plottings outside the control limits indicate an operation or process out of control, and specific action can be taken to correct the operation or process. Also, certain patterns such as consecutive plottings near the outer control limits or consecutive plottings moving toward the outer control limits could indicate a process or operation that is going out of control, and steps to correct it should be initiated. Specific examples and illustrations of the main types of statistical quality control charts are discussed in the following paragraphs:

*Mean* ($\overline{X}$) *charts.* A typical mean chart is shown in Figure 21–2. This chart was constructed for a particular item whose length was 3.000±.005 inches. It is obvious that in plotting the samples it can be determined that production is within limits, is running to the high or low limits, or is extremely variable within the $\pm 3\sigma$ limits. When the upper or lower limits are exceeded, some corrective action must be taken (circled sample).

*Range* ($R$) *charts.* The R chart shows variations in the ranges of samples. The mean of the sample ranges is shown as the dotted line ($\overline{R}$) in Figure 21–3. When additional samples are taken and the range of the samples are plotted, those that exceed the upper or lower control limits indicate a process or operation that is out of control, and corrective action should be initiated.

FIGURE 21–3
Range chart

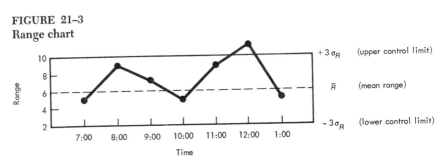

**FIGURE 21-4**
Number of defects per unit chart

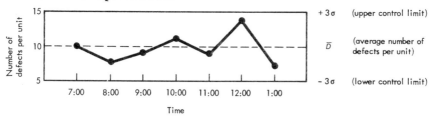

*Number of defects per unit (D) charts.* These charts are used in cases where the number of defects per unit are important. They can be used to control the number of defects on the printed circuit boards produced in a radio or television assembly line. Three $\sigma$ control limits can be set on these charts. See Figure 21-4.

*Percent defective (p) charts.* The p chart is used to control the percentage of defective units. The average percentage defective ($\bar{p}$) is computed from samples, and the upper and lower control limits ($\pm 3\sigma$) are computed from either statistical formulas or by using statistical tables and measures. When additional samples are taken and the percentage defective in each sample exceeds the $\pm 3\sigma$ limits when plotted on the chart, corrective action should be initiated. A typical p chart is shown in Figure 21-5.

## Inspection sampling

A variety of inspections are necessary before a product can be produced and sold as a finished unit. As stated previously, standards must be established first, based on the nature of the product, the quality level desired, and manufacturing capability.

Purchased components and raw materials will be bought to a standard. When received they must stand inspections to confirm condition, count, and quality. The first two relate to transportation: whether the goods are

**FIGURE 21-5**
Percent defective chart

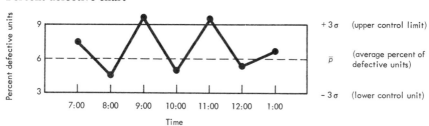

received without damage and if the amounts received agree with the shipping papers, such as the bill of lading and invoice. Sampling will ordinarily not be applicable to this process. The confirmation of quality requires an appropriate technique which assures the buyer that the goods or materials conform to the specifications. A sample is used where it is representative of the total lot or shipment. A sample from a homogeneous mass such as a barrel of paint or a melt of steel should be a true representation of the total mass. On the other hand, a sample from a lot of similar individual items must utilize statistical methods as to sample size, variance, and predictability. Properly done, the samples inspected will develop a pattern of defects which the buyer should be aware of. He can then adjust his procedure of inspection to reveal whatever combinations of defect information he is willing to pay for.

Inspections throughout production are conducted at appropriate points in the manufacturing cycle. The point and nature of such inspections will be governed by the need to know certain facts before additional work is done on the product and reasonable alternatives such as a final inspection only. As experience is developed, the amount of inspection may change, utilizing smaller or larger samples, a change in the point of inspection, and perhaps the consolidation of several inspections into one overall test of performance. Experience should consistently reduce total inspection costs for additional production of identical items.

## METHODS ENGINEERING

All kinds of production processes require constant review and assessment to make sure that the work is being done efficiently. Improvement in production activities is often within the jurisdiction of an industrial engineer. The small company, however, will apply its own methods engineering, and do the job with a nonprofessional.

*Work simplification.* Simplifying a job may not take the talents of any particular type of individual, but rather the application of an alert mind. In general, it involves investigating time, space, distance, weight, and other factors related to the production process. If any of these things can be improved, eliminated, or streamlined, work simplification has been accomplished.

Analysis should also include the determination of what talents employees possess and matching these to jobs that utilize such talents.

*Time study.* Following the job analysis it will be necessary to set certain job limits or quotas. In terms of work this may be achieved by conducting time studies; that is, a timing of work sequences under appropriate conditions to determine what is the proper job time standard. In general, time standards are set on operations which are repetitive and have a short time cycle. The small manufacturer can develop this on his or her own, although there may be no wish to establish piece rates as a result of the time study but rather to assign job time standards. One aspect of time study is the use of MTM (Methods Time Measurement), a technique of using previously established standards for job or work segments which are then applied in whatever combination they occur in some other job.

*Work sampling.* Some jobs are of such long duration and variable patterns that they would be very difficult to examine, utlizing ordinary time study. In these cases it may be desirable to utilize the work sampling technique. This proceeds by assigning a sequence in which certain observations are made of a particular job and worker over a period of time, with a sufficient number of observations to determine the work pattern. The size of the sample, the duration of observations, and the results obtained will be governed by statistical criteria.

If professional help is not available, the manager of a small company should acquire certain books and reference materials involving time study and work measurement and then go to work on his or her own to study, analyze, and establish job standards. Considerable improvement can ordinarily be achieved in productive activities, and over a period of time knowledge can be gained as to how certain techniques can be applied to other operations.

## SYSTEMS DESIGN AND APPLICATION

At some point the small business manager must examine a number of interrelated activities that support and facilitate the production processes. In this regard he or she must check the following items:

1. What kind of performance factors is he or she getting from various employees?
2. Does he or she have an effective system of delegation of authority through orders, commands, directives, and memorandums?
3. What is the "feedback" system, and is it accurate, dependable, and rapid?
4. Is the company showing a constant improvement in productive output, better planning, lower costs, and a reduction in the time and effort involved in doing a job?
5. Is he or she learning more about the products, the competitor's products, markets, supply sources, and other factors dealing with the operation which are outside and beyond control?
6. What utilization is being made of improving technology and support equipment to the manufacturing processes?

In systems design and analysis a manufacturer must keep up to date, employ knowledgeable people, and constantly analyze what he or she is doing and the results obtained. Constant inquiry and evaluation will improve the ability to design the supporting network of forms, records, procedures, and reports, and various other types of control devices and mechanisms which are applicable.

## PERT AND CPM

Two techniques, Production Evaluation and Review Technique and the Critical Path Method, have been developed to aid in the planning, scheduling, and control of complex one-time projects. An installation, such as a large building, chemical plant, dam or power plant are typically controlled under PERT or CPM. The small business can use it also—on a scale which fits its own operations. Work that is done in sequence, where each step is critical, is the area where these techniques are very helpful.

The work to be done is outlined on a network diagram, drawn to visually illustrate each event and activity. *Events* are represented by numbered circles in sequence. They are considered to be points in a time sequence. *Activities* are the jobs or work which must be performed between each stated event. Time estimates are assigned and measured in any appropriate unit such as days or weeks.

A rather simple example of laying an underground conduit is shown in Figure 21–6. This example uses a PERT diagram which is quite similar to the CPM diagram.

Path D is the *critical path* because it is the longest sequence of events that must be done *in order* to complete the project. If any activity in this sequence is held up, the project time period is extended. *Slack* is computed by using the formula shown in the illustration. Slack is not cumulative through the alternate paths.

Considerable space would be necessary to explain additional details of these two techniques. What is shown and explained here will give some ideas which can be used by anyone who might wish to experiment with these techniques.

## COST CONTROLS

Production processes and sequences are designed to be highly efficient when operated at optimum levels. Output other than optimum tends to develop costs that are probably hard to control and difficult to predict ahead of time. Serious efforts should be made to set up methods of cost controls which provide prompt feedback and ways to anticipate cost changes as production rates vary.

*Estimating, costing, and pricing.* Any producer of product lines, particularly the typical small manufacturer, must know costs in order to set company prices. Initially there is concern with estimates and bids on alternatives in the total production system. From there the analysis moves to

# FIGURE 21-6
## PERT network diagram (conduit project illustration)

T  Earliest possible event time $(T_E)$

Ⓣ  Latest allowable event time $(T_L)$

△  Slack $(T_L - T_E = t')$ [activities which have zero slack (△) form the critical path]

Criticality (days slack)

⊶⊶⊶  0 Days (critical path)
━━━  1 Day
━━━  2 Days
───  11 Days

| Path | Event numbers in sequence | Days to complete | Days slack |
|------|---------------------------|------------------|------------|
| A | 1–2–3–4–7–10 | 49 | 1 |
| B | 1–2–3–4–6–7–10 | 48 | 2 |
| C | 1–2–3–4–6–8–9–10 | 48 | 2 |
| D | 1–2–3–4–5–8–9–10 | 50 | 0 |
| E | 1–2–5–8–9–10 | 59 | 1 |
| F | 1–2–9–10 | 39 | 11 |

a concern with varying quantities of production, break-even analysis, value analysis, improvement curves and yields with different types of trade-offs. Activities are converted to dollars as a common denominator of measurement and considerable time is spent in determining how costs develop and why.

Cost centers must be established where costs are accumulated. Knowing the amount of cost in a product up to a certain point will give a reading as to the state of efficiency and the "in-phase" condition of a production run. Over a period of time, information will reveal whether or not some part of production is "slipping," or whether losses or deficiencies elsewhere are being made up. Cost control centers are located at critical points so that changing quantities of production can be isolated and cost-analyzed.

*Production runs, lots, time blocks.* Discretionary options within the control of the manufacturer often relate to the length of production runs, the size of certain lots, and the assignment of time. Thus, in a particular instance a production run of one week is efficient and should develop costs up to a certain point; but a run of twice that long will spread setup costs over a greater number of products and result in lower unit cost. The application of production run and time lots is very much like any economic analysis and can be useful if proper cost information is known in order to arrive at such judgments. Here again, it is very important to know all costs and to know these under varying conditions before a proper decision can be made.

*Modification, rescheduling, and cost adjustment.* Manufacturing does not ordinarily run smoothly for long periods of time. In fact it is apt to be quite erratic for the majority of small manufacturers. Cost analysis over time should permit the small businessperson to estimate with some degree of accuracy the implications of product changeover, substitution within schedules, rescheduling, various types of overlap runs, the impact of overtime, and anything else which is at variance with the normal production schedule. While this may be difficult to do, it is a necessary aspect of production and manufacturing industries, and no one can long survive in this type of business without an intuitive feeling for the cost implication of these various consequences.

## SUMMARY

The activities related to production processes have a great deal of importance to any kind of small business. The manufacturing industries may be more heavily dependent on production activities than either retailing or service, but all businesses must do a reasonably good job in the production area.

To excel in the production areas requires a combination of thorough groundwork in understanding operations and processes, plus an ability to excel in predicting what will happen under a given set of circumstances. The small producer, of his or her own specialty, must think constantly of conversion processes. He or she considers efficient design, material yield, break-even points, product mix, long versus short product runs, direct versus nondirect labor ratios, and many other complex relationships. The individual who can do this will have a good production operation—furthermore he or she should have no trouble producing products or services in an efficient manner.

## QUESTIONS

1. How might a prospective entrepreneur analyze a production-oriented business to decide whether his or her talents would fit the situation?

2. Is it possible for a small business with versatile productive capability to compete with much larger enterprises? Why?

3. How can a smaller productive enterprise compete if using equipment that is outmoded for use in larger businesses?

4. How does leasing and rental of equipment provide opportunities for the small business?

5. Why does the production manager strive constantly for standard components, long production runs, and a minimum of product variation?

6. How should a production manager select the activities under his or her control which are most promising as to cost and performance improvement?

7. Is it reasonable to expect a small business to have fewer machine breakdowns and failures than a large business? Why?

8. What chance does a smaller business have to achieve more consistent product quality standards than a large business?

9. Should a small business make use of time studies and performance ratings?

10. How would you suggest that unlike production activities be compared to develop comparable cost data?

## PROBLEM

Ron Hurtt and George Flambeau are presently employed as design and development engineers by the Westing Corp. They are in their late 20s, married but without children, and have been employed by Westing since graduating from college. Neither one has any formal or informal education or experience in business.

Both Ron and George feel that the economic situation of the middle 70s will create unfavorable conditions for Westing and perhaps mean that they will lose their jobs. They have seriously discussed forming their own firm and feel that they should do so before too much more time passes.

One intriguing idea that they have thought of is the possibility of getting into some phase of solar energy. They have done some inquiry and investigation and now realize that they must conduct a feasibility study of the particular aspect of this potential industry that they might wish to enter.

## Questions

Answer the following questions which are important in a study of this kind:

1. Is it wise to launch a new technical production enterprise when general economic conditions are not very stable?
2. How do you go about selecting a niche in an embryonic undeveloped industry?
3. What criteria determines the areas in which a small business can participate?
4. How would you assemble data which would indicate how fast the industry would develop?
5. What is significant about the fact that the sun's energy is freely available and not subject to control by any one firm or industry?
6. How would an assessment be made of the possibility of competition from other small firms that might be encouraged to tackle the same project?

## BIBLIOGRAPHY

Ammer, Dean S. *Materials Management.* 3d ed. Homewood, Ill.: Richard D. Irwin, 1974. A thorough analysis of materials management and its importance to the manufacturing process. This material is not usually understood or available to many business people. A good reference to develop ideas about managing materials.

Johnson, Richard A.; Newell, William T.; and Vergin, Roger C. *Production and Operations Management.* Boston: Houghton Mifflin Co., 1974. A very good basic book on production and manufacturing management. Has good illustrations and basic diagrams that help to explain useful concepts and applications.

Klatt, Lawrence A. *Small Business Management: Essentials of Entrepreneurship.* Belmont, Calif.: Wadsworth Publishing Co., 1973. A very well done up-to-date book on management and entrepreneurship. Particularly good in the subject areas of retail management, finance, and the basics of production management.

Moore, Franklin G. *Manufacturing Management.* 6th ed. Homewood, Ill.: Richard D. Irwin, 1973. A basic text on production management that has some coverage on virtually every area relating to production and manufacturing.

# 22

# Advertising— waste or wisdom?

The whole role of advertising in our economy has been one of controversy. Many people say that advertising is an unjustifiable social cost which does nothing more than switch people from one brand of merchandise to another. Other people, who support advertising, claim that it does provide a service to our economy, and it does justify all the expenditures made. Furthermore, they argue that advertising also keeps the economy strong by encouraging expenditures which in turn will increase or keep employment high. The battle of advertising continues to wage hot and heavy, and there certainly is merit in both arguments. For example, it was once argued that advertising tobacco products did nothing more than encourage people to elect between several equally bad alternatives (assuming that any brand of tobacco smoked was harmful). However, it was also argued that the abolition of tobacco advertisements would be harmful to the television industry, possibly reducing the variety of entertainment offered to the public and the number of employed actors. There are still those who like to argue the above points but usually such arguments are far more emotional than rational.

Rather than engage in the argument of whether or not advertising is a worthwhile expenditure of funds, however, the general nature of this chapter will operate under the assumption that: (1) the small business manager's competitors will advertise; (2) if the small business manager intends to make a go of his or her enterprise, he or she, too, must advertise; and (3) advertising is an additional cost to the business. So far as the moral or ethical considerations of advertising are concerned, the general tenor of this chapter will be much like that of the college senior's reply to a prospective employer who was putting her to the task of justifying advertising: "Well, sir, to me advertising is not the practice of enticing people to buy products which they don't need; rather, I feel it is apprising them of needs which they did not know they had."

381

## WHY SMALL BUSINESSES SHOULD ADVERTISE

### The purpose of advertising

Advertising is mass *communication of information*, intended to *persuade* buyers to buy, so as to enable the business to *maximize dollar profits*. Advertising is nothing more than the engagement in the art of communication with the dual purpose of (1) persuading buyers to buy and (2) maximizing the profits of the seller. Advertising thus is a tool which the small business manager might use in attempting to sell more products in an effort to enlarge profits of his or her firm.

While the dual purpose of advertising may be obvious, knowing how to advertise is an entirely different matter. To be persuasive, an ad must be at the right place, at the right time, in the right amount, and done with good taste, proper tone, suitable design, and so on; and it must cost less than the benefits to be derived from it. Thus, knowledge of how, when, and where to advertise is essential in developing an effective advertising campaign.

### Kinds of advertising

*Customer advertising.* One of the primary methods of advertising available to the small businessperson who is considering an effective advertising program is customer advertising. As its name suggests, customer advertising is the orientation of the advertising copy toward the customer. Since all businesses have something to sell—whether it is the owner's time, socks, lawn-sprinkler systems, or bulk gravel—there are always customers. Therefore customer advertising can be used by all small business firms, irrespective of whether they are in the retail, wholesale, manufacturing, or service field.

The form that customer-oriented advertising takes can vary. It is possible to engage in informative advertising or emotional advertising, depending on the nature of the business, product, and customer. For example, if the customer is a business firm buying centrifugal pumps, it will be more interested in delivery capacities and maintenance problems than the color and appearance of the pump; whereas if the customer is a young career woman buying shoes, color and appearance may be of primary importance. Therefore, the approach elected may mean the difference between sizable profits or losses for the small business manager.

*Institutional advertising.* Another form of advertising is called "institutional advertising." Institutional advertising means the promotion of an idea about a firm or institution, rather than a specific product or service provided by the small business. An example of institutional advertising is that which is engaged in by trade associations when they buy space and time in newspapers and on radio and television intending to plant the idea to purchase their members' products. Thus, rather than advertising a specific product or service for a particular business firm, the general need for the product or service of the advertising institution is promoted. The assumption made by the members of the association is that if the demand for their members' products and services is increased, generally all will benefit.

**Product advertising.** In contrast to customer and institutional advertising is product advertising, the third basic type of advertising which may be engaged in by the small business manager. Product advertising emphasizes the product itself, and it can further be broken down into one of two parts: (1) direct action advertising and (2) indirect action advertising.

Direct action product advertising is designed primarily to get people to buy the product now; it is aimed at enticing people to purchase a product immediately, if not sooner. Razor blades at the grocery check-out stand and cigarettes at the cash register in the restaurant are items of this nature. The idea is that the merchandise is there, available, and should be purchased. Of course, direct action advertising may take other forms than simple availability of products. In cereal-box advertising, for example, where the children are urged to buy a "super special ring with the secret compartment *now*" is of this nature. However, the form is of secondary importance as long as the buyer is induced to take action immediately— to buy *now*.

In contrast to the direct action product advertising is the indirect action product advertising. This type of advertising differs from the direct action in the sense that the prospective customer for the product or service is not encouraged to take any particular action immediately but is encouraged to have his or her appetite whetted for the particular product or service through time. An example of the indirect action product advertising might be an ad for expensive china, fine furniture, or other high quality merchandise.

As a basic guide, direct action product advertising is usually considered more effective for the low-cost, high-turnover merchandise, which people buy either impulsively or as a matter of convenience; indirect action product advertising is more effective for the high-cost, low-turnover merchandise. Of course, indirect action product advertising may be used for low-cost, high-turnover advertising (for example, toothpaste or mouth wash manufacturer ads on television which suggest fun, frivolity, and lying on the beach), while direct action product advertising may take the form of urging a customer to put an expensive gift under the Christmas tree. These, however, are not the general rule.

There are, therefore, a variety of advertising methods which can be used by the small business advertiser. The only limitation is that the type of advertising which he or she engages in is dependent upon his or her customers, products, and type of business. Basically the problems are similar to those of the large organization. The fundamental difference between small and big business advertising is that the small businessperson's budget is much smaller, thus limiting his or her ability to afford large advertising campaigns which are designed to appeal to customers, promote the institution, and promote the product all at the same time. The small businessperson must, therefore, learn to get the most out of his or her available advertising budget.

### When and how much to advertise

Knowing when to advertise is an extremely difficult problem for any business, but it is particularly difficult for the small business firm. Basically, it is not a problem of when to advertise but rather how much advertising can be afforded. The use of an advertising budget helps determine whether advertising is a true economy which helps increase net profits of the firm and can therefore be afforded, or whether it is an expense.

Since knowing when to advertise is a direct function of the budget available for advertising, it becomes critical for the small businessperson to know precisely how much money he or she can—or must—allocate toward the advertising budget. In attempting to answer this question one invariably thinks in terms of ideals. Usually this advice is given: the aim in setting the amount of money to be spent on advertising is "to spend enough to obtain the objectives of the advertising campaign but not to waste any money by spending more than is necessary."

It is obvious that what small businesspersons are looking for in determining their advertising budget is the optimum amount of money to be spent. If they spend more than is necessary, they are, of course, losing money, not just because of wasted dollars but because they may have been just as well off had there been no advertising at all. In an effort to help the small businessperson resolve the problem of the right-sized advertising budget, the remainder of this section will concern itself with the variety of techniques which have been employed by small business managers in determining their advertising budgets.

*Percentage-of-sales method.* The percentage of sales method is probably the most widely used method of setting the advertising appropriation, largely because of its relative simplicity and its pseudo-scientific appearance. Basically the percentage-of-sales method determines the advertising budget through the utilization of some percentage figure, which is based on either sales or estimated sales of the firm. For example, the small business manager might decide that he or she should spend ten percent of gross sales for advertising because he or she read in a trade journal that most people in that business spend ten percent of their gross sales for advertising. Thus, in determining what he or she should spend for the business advertising campaigns, all the small business manager needs to do is apply a set percentage figure to gross sales for the past year to determine the amount of funds to spend on his or her various advertising campaigns.

In some cases the percentage-of-sales method works quite well. However, there are difficulties with this method. One problem is determining the percentage figure which should be applied to sales. Another difficulty concerns the base figure—that is, should last year's figure be used, this year's, or a combination of all of them? The problem is basically that both the percentage figure and the base figure are estimations, and the advertising budget itself is no more valid than the estimations on which it is based. Nevertheless, the percentage-of-sales method is simple and easy to use, and many business managers find it expeditious to use in determining their advertising budgets.

*Combating competitors.* A second basic method used in determining the advertising budget is that of spending as much as your competitors spend. This is called the combating competitors method. Although this technique may get results, it is subject to several pitfalls. To begin with, it is rather naïve for one small business manager to feel that his or her basic problem of advertising is identical to a competitor's basic problem. This is simply not true. While it is true that two competitors facing each other across the street may have relatively similar trade areas and clientele, this is certainly not the case for two competitors located a mile apart. Furthermore, there is an additional problem inherent in trying to spend precisely what one's competitor is spending for advertising—it may be nearly impossible to accurately determine how much one's competitor is spending on advertisements. Certainly the competitor will not be inclined to disclose such information, and gleaning such information from the advertising media itself is nearly impossible.

Thus, it is extremely difficult to plan an advertising budget based solely on what a competitor is spending. Not only will there be some area of doubt about the exact amount which the competitors are spending but there is also some question as to whether or not the small business manager ( e.g., a local drugstore operator) can compete effectively with a larger competitor's budget ( e.g., Walgreen's or Woolworth's).

*Fixed dollar method.* Another technique used in determining the advertising budget is the fixed dollar technique. Basically, the way the fixed dollar technique works is that the advertiser determines a fixed amount of dollars which he or she intends to spend for each unit of product which is to be sold. In other words, if he or she intends to sell 5,000 ski jackets next year and figures that it takes $1.25 worth of advertising to sell each jacket, the advertising budget for the next year is $6,250.

Again, as in the other techniques, the fixed dollar method has certain drawbacks. Basically the criticism resides in the fact that it ignores the job which the advertiser must accomplish, and it focuses simply on a mechanical formula method of determining the advertising budget.

One thing which can be said for the fixed dollar method, however, is that it does possess the appearance of being an equitable way in which a manufacturer or wholesaler might allocate advertising funds to their co-operative wholesalers or retailers. That is, the manufacturer might set aside 73 cents per ski jacket for each jacket purchased by a wholesaler; or a wholesaler might agree to share equally in the expenses of a full-page ad for each retailer who purchases more than $2,500 of equipment from the wholesaler each month.

*All-that-can-be-afforded method.* Another technique which many small business managers use in determining their advertising budget is simply that of spending all that they can afford. At first blush, the all-that-can-be-afforded method does appear to be a practical technique. Again, however, there are several problems involved in using this technique. One of the major problems in using the all-that-can-be-afforded technique is that what can be afforded is frequently nothing more than the small business manager is willing to spend. That is, an excessively conservative small businessperson will not spend as much as a swashbuckling, free-spending competitor will.

Ambiguity about what can be afforded, however, is only a minor fault of this technique. The major problem is that the amount which is determined as affordable may be less than what is *required* to do the job of advertising which is needed. For example, if a competitor is spending $4,000 per month for newspaper advertising and another small business operator feels he or she can only afford $400 a month, there is little likelihood that the second small businessperson's ads will be as effective. In that case the second small businessperson might be better off not even spending the $400.

Another major problem which crops up in using the all-that-can-be-afforded method is that of the circuitous nature of the technique. That is, if advertising is conducive to increasing sales, it stands to reason that the more one advertises the more sales one will have. Assuming some net profit on each sale, this in turn means that in the second, third, and fourth go-round one may be able to spend even more on one's advertising budget. Conversely, if all-that-can-be-afforded is insufficient and a net profit is not made on the meager amount of sales fostered by an inadequate advertising program, this in turn will breed on itself, causing less money to be available and fewer sales, etc. Thus less funds will be available for the second, third, and fourth rounds of advertising. Therefore, although the all-that can-be-afforded method is not a highly recommended technique for determining one's advertising budget, still practicality must be considered, and certainly there is a point beyond which funds are not available for additional advertising.

**Profit planning method.** The profit planning technique of determining the advertising budget is based on the small business manager determining what profit he or she intends to make for the forthcoming period. This technique is a good deal more elegant and sophisticated than are some of the other advertising budget techniques mentioned above. Because of this, it is also a good deal more time-consuming. However, it does have the facility for forcing one to plan his or her advertising expenditures and also to have a firm grasp of what net sales figures are likely to be, what one's cost of goods sold and operating expenses are, and finally what anticipated earnings will be for the forthcoming advertising period.

TABLE 22–1

| | | |
|---|---:|---:|
| Anticipated sales | $120,000 | $200,000 |
| Less operating expenses | 95,000 | 143,000 |
| Subtotal | $ 25,000 | $ 57,000 |
| Less desired profit | 20,000 | 35,000 |
| Amount available for advertising | $ 5,000 | $ 22,000 |

Basically the way the profit planning method works is that the small businessperson first determines what his or her gross profit will be at various levels of gross sales by means of break-even analysis. (See Chapter 14.) Once the gross profits are determined for the various levels of sales, the operating expenses are subtracted from the gross profit projections, thereby determining the amount of funds remaining for the advertising budget and the net profit for the period for each projected level of sales. As Table 22–1 shows, for an estimated gross sales figure of $120,000 with a hoped-for net profit figure of $20,000, there is only $5,000 available for advertisement; while at the estimated gross sales figure of $200,000 with a hoped-for profit of $35,000, there is $22,000 available for advertising expense. Obviously in view of the competitive picture of the ski jacket industry, Ski Jacket Incorporated would be well advised to plan for a profit of $35,000 and develop an advertising budget commensurate with that figure.

The above analysis also highlights one of the basic fallacies in the profit planning technique. That is, while profit planning is nice, it may be impossible for Ski Jacket Incorporated to raise sales from $120,000 to $200,-000 a year. Thus their advertising budget would be impractical at the $200,000 figure. Furthermore, these figures are nothing more than estimations, as are all break-even analyses, and are therefore not altogether valid. As mentioned above, they are also exceedingly difficult to determine. Therefore the profit planning technique, although more elegant and sophisticated in nature, is still victimized by the shortcoming of being no better than the estimates which go into it and the practicality of such estimates.

*The objective task method.* The objective task method is a straightforward, well-defined method of approaching the determination of an advertising budget. Basically the objective task method is designed to (1) determine what the objectives for the forthcoming advertising program are, (2) determine how these objectives might be met, and (3) determine what it will cost to meet these objectives. Because the objective task method is objective-oriented, it is an extremely realistic approach to advertising budget setting, and it carries with it the advantage of assuring that the advertising goals will be accomplished. The objective task method is implemented by the small business manager determining what he or she wants his or her organization to accomplish by way of advertising next year, determining how he or she wants it done, and determining what it will cost. This requires that the small business manager have a firmly fixed idea in mind as to what he or she wants his or her advertising campaign to do—whether to increase sales, obtain a larger share of the market, or break into a different geographical area, obtain new customers, or introduce a new product on the market.

The major strength of the objective task method is that it does require the small business manager to state his or her objectives. As in any basic managerial problem, small business managers tend to break down whenever it is necessary to have firmly fixed objectives. Therefore the use of the objective task method, which prevents any advertising except that which is based on firm objectives, is an extreme advantage for the small business manager.

While the objective task method may be very realistic, it also is subject to one basic shortcoming. The problem is that because of ignorance or lack of experience the advertiser may not be able to determine precisely how much advertising and what type of advertising is necessary to achieve the objectives which are established by the program. That is, setting the objectives may be easy, but determining the second and third steps of the sequence may be more difficult. For example, even though a firm may have the objective of increasing customers by ten percent for the forthcoming year, the media that will be most effective in attracting these new customers must still be determined, as well as the amount of advertising that will be required to accomplish the task. Therefore, as in any other method of determining advertising budgets, the objective task method has its strengths and its limitations. However, the objective task method is probably the most realistic technique of setting an advertising budget. For this reason it is receiving wider attention and use, not only by small business managers but also large corporations in the United States.

## Where to advertise

*Selecting advertising media.* Selecting the appropriate medium for advertising is not simple. There are a variety of media available, and each has its own strengths and weaknesses. For example, not only are there radios, newspapers, televisions, and magazines, but there are billboards, trade journals, matchbook covers, taxi cards, flyers, leaflets, and even business cards. To choose the most desirable advertising media from the many sources available to the small business manager is an extremely critical decision for two reasons: (1) usually funds available for advertising are so limited that not all media can be used and (2) some media are more effective for some types of products and some types of corporations and industries than are others. Let us look at some of these.

## Considerations about the media

*1. Product considerations.* In discussing the media which a small businessperson will use in advertising his or her company's product, it must be recognized that the situation itself largely determines the amount and kind of media selected. For example, a retailer in a small town where there is only one newspaper does not have the same problem in advertising as a manufacturer in a large city. The retailer would probably use the newspaper to reach his or her immediate market, while the manufacturer may not even use newspaper advertisements, but instead will advertise in trade journals or use other national types of advertising designed to reach the manufacturer's customers.

Thus, the primary task of the advertiser in selecting media from the standpoint of product consideration is that there be a complete and concise understanding of the market which exists for the company's product. Thus, the small business manager might be well advised to copy his or her competitors when it comes to determining the advertising media available.

The important point, however, is to recognize that different media appeal to different types of buyers, and the type of buyer is largely dependent upon the product which is being sold. Further, even the same medium may appeal to different kinds of buyers, so the problem becomes one of both selecting the right medium and then selecting the specific outlet within that medium which is right for the product. The reason for this is that one advertising outlet may have an entirely different following than another. For example, one newspaper might be conservative, another liberal; or one may appeal largely to the laboring classes, while another will appeal to the managerial classes, and yet another to intellectuals. Thus it is obvious that the small business manager who is trying to increase sales of new Cadillacs will probably not be well advised to advertise in a labor union tabloid, and a man running a special on work gloves should not advertise in the *Wall Street Journal*.

Not only is newspaper, radio, and television advertising more or less suited to a particular type of product advertising but in the case of magazines and trade journals this is even more true. For example, some magazines are sports-oriented, other magazines are literature-oriented, others are general news–oriented, while still others may be specialized for golfers, tennis players, and even chess players. It is obvious that the manufacturer of skin diving equipment would not get the desired results by advertising in a golfing magazine, nor would a retailer of newly popular records be wise to advertise in a magazine entiled *The Senior Citizen*. Therefore, the first lesson is that advertising is a situational problem and the product which is to be advertised largely determines the situation.

**2. Audience considerations.** The second consideration in determining where to advertise concerns the audience to be reached. An audience can be defined as the people who are to be reached by the medium carrying the advertiser's message. Therefore, there is a distinct difference between "circulation" and "audience." Circulation is measured by the *number* of copies printed (and presumably distributed) while the audience is the number of people *actually reached* by the ad. These facts are often confused by the uninitiated, and the small business manager may end up thinking that he or she can reach every person in the entire marketing area by placing an ad on a radio station during his or her favorite listening time—6:30 A.M. It may never occur to him or her that even though everyone *could* hear the ad on the radio station, the fact of the matter is that only a very small percentage of the people are listening to the advertisement. He or she should recognize that the business might be better off with a much smaller potential audience by advertising in a newspaper which will actually reach the potential customers.

Therefore, a study of the audience which is to be reached is critical for the small business advertiser because he or she must reach as many people as possible who are *likely prospects* for the product or service which he or she is advertising. Fortunately most of the various advertising media have some figures available on the size and makeup of audiences which their medium reaches. Thus it would behoove the small business manager to ask about, and discuss, audience composition with any advertiser with whom he or she is considering placing any ads.

**3. Cost versus return considerations.** There is an age-old maxim that you "get what you pay for." This maxim is probably just as apropos of the advertising field as it is of any other field. However, there is one difference which must be made clear to the advertiser. That is, the various media can do different things, and the product and institution which is being advertised must be in need of the advertising service which the particular media can provide before full value will be received from that media. The point is this: a television station covers a specific area (1) if the TV sets in that area are turned on, (2) if there are people paying attention to the TV set, and (3) if the viewers are interested in the product which is being advertised. Thus, while a TV station might claim it has nearly 100 percent coverage of all TV sets existing in its prescribed broadcasting area, it still may in no way be effective for advertising a specific product. An ad placed with a TV station which is not suited for the audience of that station will be an expensive, costly proposition which will return little or nothing to the advertiser. Therefore, one of the first things which must be determined is how many prospective customers an advertiser is reaching and how much it costs per *prospective customer* to place an ad.

Once the above cost-versus-return consideration is made, it can then be decided whether one kind of media would be superior to another kind, and which specific advertiser will be used. Fortunately, answering the latter question is not particularly difficult. In fact, all the advertiser needs to do is look at (1) the advertising media's circulation, (2) the kind of people who compose the audience, and (3) the cost of the ad. For example, assume that after careful consideration, a TV repair shop owner decides (1) that the Sunday supplement of one of the two local metropolitan newspapers would be the best place in which to place an ad and (2) that from the standpoint of audience, both newspapers have approximately the same numbers and kinds of readers. Under these circumstances, the small businessperson has only to divide the line rates (or page rates) of each competing newspaper by the number of prospective customers which they will reach to determine the cost per ad placed per prospective customer. This, then, permits the small businessperson to determine which is the best buy. For example, in Table 22–2, it will be seen that the business should take space with the *Daily Bugle* rather than with the *Daily Herald*, upon review of their published rates and their circulation, *assuming that the two newspapers have the same kind of readership.*

TABLE 22–2

|  | *Daily Bugle* | *Daily Herald* |
|---|---|---|
| Circulation. . . . . . . . . . . . . . . . . . | 50,000 | 60,000 |
| Percent of circulation that are "real audience" or prospective customers. . . . . . . . . . . . . . . . | 40% | 40% |
| Prospective customers reached with ad. . . . . . . . . . . . . . . . | 20,000 | 24,000 |
| Cost of ad . . . . . . . . . . . . . . . . . | $2,000 | $2,500 |
| Cost of ad per prospective customer. . . . . . . . . . . . . . . . | $\frac{\$2,000}{20,000} = 10¢$ per prospective customer | $\frac{\$2,500}{24,000} = 10.4¢$ per prospective customer |

## ASSESSING YOUR ADVERTISING EFFORTS

*Testing and evaluating advertising.* Merely knowing what considerations must be made in selecting the media for advertising is not sufficient for continued advertising by any business operation. Media, products, audiences, and cost all change in time and therefore must be reconsidered from time to time. Furthermore, the ads which are placed in a specific medium need to be changed through time, for no matter how appealing and clever the ad, it ceases to be effective after a certain amount of time. Most people simply prefer the new, improved, or otherwise changed product or ad over the timeless, repetitive ad, or product. Because of this problem, numerous ways for advertisers to test and evaluate the effectiveness of their advertising campaigns have been devised. The following section will explore the more commonly used tests which can be applied.

*Copy testing.* One of the primary tests which must be made in testing any advertising is called copy testing. Copy testing is often thought of as reading over a newspaper ad to make sure that the words are not misspelled and that the sentences are complete. This, however, is not effective copy testing. Advertising copy includes much more than the written word. It also includes the layout, the organization, the emphasis, color, texture, design, etc. The first phase of copy testing (at least for the small business manager) is to insure that the copywriter has a clear idea of the audience to whom he or she is addressing the copy. Secondly, the copywriter must know precisely what he or she intends to say to the audience; and thirdly, he or she must say it in the briefest, clearest, and most concise and forceful manner possible. These are the three preliminary steps which the small business manager can take in testing copy, and he or she must determine whether the ad possesses the preceding three characteristics or whether the advertising agency or newspaper copywriter is aware of these points. If so, he or she has won half the battle. However, to win the war the advertiser must continuously engage in copy testing by evaluating its effectiveness by the amount of sales fostered, the comments which are volunteered by readers, and, of course, by his or her own impression of the ad.

*Consumer jury testing.* Another frequently used method of pre-evaluating advertisements is to select what is called a consumer jury to test the ad. Basically the consumer jury is made up of a representative sample of potential consumers or buyers of the product or the service to be advertised who give their opinion as to which of the several sample ads is the more appealing.

Consumer jury testing of ads, however, is oftentimes criticized as being an invalid method of testing an ad. Most of the opponents to consumer jury testing claim that an ad which appeals to a consumer may not be the same ad which would prompt most customers to buy. Other criticisms which tend to be levied against consumer jury testing is that it is not really effective for institutional advertising and not representative of the buyers to whom the appeal is being made. However, even though there is a good deal of criticism levied against jury testing, many small business managers have found it effective to utilize a sample or jury of people in testing copy before it is released.

*Split-run testing.* Another technique which is often used for testing advertising copy is the split-run test. The basic idea behind the split-run test is to design two sets of copy, one of which is to be inserted one day and the other to be inserted another day—or one which is inserted for half the press run while the other is inserted for the other half of the press run. The purpose of the split-run test is to compare the effectiveness of both the ads in an effort to ascertain which is the most effective. One device often used in newspaper advertising of the split-run variety is to code a coupon in the ad which the reader must redeem at the store for merchandise. This, then, permits the merchant to go through the coupons redeemed and determine the ad from which it was clipped. Variations of the split-run newspaper test include the split-run radio test in which the individual is urged to mention the radio announcer's name. In return for mentioning the ad which he or she heard the individual may receive a discount or win a prize or other token.

Split-run testing can be a very effective method of testing the impact of copy. However, the small businessperson should be cautioned about the possible sources of error which may come about with split-run testing. For example, in testing split-run newspaper copy, the time variable may invalidate the results of the test. One merchant ran a split-run test on soft drinks and discovered that sales were much higher with the first-week ad than they were with the second-week ad. However, he also discovered that there was a correlation between an unseasonably high temperature during the first week and unseasonably cold, damp weather during the second week. Which was cause and which was effect of course is not clear in this circumstance, but obviously the climatic variable probably had an influence on the results of this test.

*Readership testing.* Another form of copy testing is called the readership test. Basically the readership test involves determining how many of the possible readers actually saw the ad and took action as a result of it. The surest way to determine how many people took action as a result of the ad is to check on how many people had read the ad before they purchased the product or service which was advertised. The small businessperson can do this by simply asking a buyer if he or she happened to see the ad which was in the paper. Of course, there are several fallacies in utilizing this technique: the reader may not remember having seen the ad when in fact he or she had; the reader may claim that he or she saw the ad when in fact he or she didn't; or the reader may have decided to buy the product or service *despite* having seen the ad rather than because of it. Therefore, the small business manager is cautioned against putting a great deal of stock in the results of a personally conducted readership test. Further, the small businessperson is cautioned from assuming that a high or low readership response is indicative of a good or bad advertisement. The point is that an ad may be a bad ad, but it may be a notable ad which attracts the reader's attention. Thus, an ad for alcohol which is done in bad taste may get the attention and readership of every member of the WCTU and still not encourage any sales.

*Inquiry.* Another form of copy testing is the analysis of inquiries which are made about a product because of the placement of a particular ad. The use of inquiry testing is open to a good deal of fire from critics who claim that even though someone inquires about a particular ad, this does not in any sense indicate that the ad is effective and will promote sales. In fact, they argue that it may only serve to promote sales resistance upon the part of the inquirer if he or she finds any reason to believe the ad was false, or a "come on." On the other hand, there is strong support for believing that inquiries are indicative of effective ads. In fact, several writers in the field feel that where there is no correlation between the number of inquiries and the number of buyers, it is because of failure upon the part of the small businessperson to follow up on the inquiry rather than a shortcoming on the part of the ad itself.

*Sales test.* A final method of testing and evaluating the effectiveness of advertising is called the sales test. The sales test is probably the ultimate evaluation of an ad because it proves that the ad itself has been effective. It has caused a sale.

A variant of the sales test, which appears to be more effective than simply whether or not total sales for the firm have gone up or down, is a sales test in a controlled market. This test is very difficult for the typical small business to engage in because usually sales are limited to a specific town, region, or kind of customer. However, many small manufacturers and certainly some small wholesalers are able to have sales tests in separate geographic areas. That is, they use their regular advertising copy in 90 percent of their sales territory and use a test ad in that 10 percent segment which they can isolate from their other ads. This allows them to determine whether sales have gone up or down in that test area as compared to the control area. If sales go up in the test area then they know that this is a more effective ad; if sales go down they know that the ad is not effective.

## DEVELOPING A GOOD ADVERTISEMENT

The foregoing has been designed to tell the small business manager how, when, and where to engage in advertising strategy. Still to be answered is the question of how to write or develop good advertising copy. The following section will offer guidelines as to whether or not one should hire a professional advertising agency to help with writing copy or whether one can and should do it themselves.

## How to write advertising copy

In approaching the problem of writing copy for an ad, it is essential that the copywriter have a firm objective in mind. That is, he or she should have the answers to the questions "What am I selling?" "To whom am I selling?" and "What is the best technique for conveying my message?" Developing answers to such questions is not easy. It may seem ridiculous to say that some people don't know what they are advertising or selling, but the fact is that many times in writing advertising copy, small business-people aren't really aware of what they should emphasize in the ad. That is, many times they will emphasize the color or quality aspects of a product when in fact the person who is to be swayed by the advertising would be more effectively swayed by an elaboration of the convenience aspects of the product.

Similarly, copywriters do not always know to whom they are addressing the ad. Many times they just feel that they are advertising at large and they thereby fail to focus on the specific audience that comprises the potential buyers for the product. Such focalization of an ad is essential to effective copy writing. Furthermore, in order to convey the message or concept to the reader of the ad, the copywriter must know how to sway the individual or at least how to win the individual's attention. In short, once the prospective customer is selected, the copywriter must decide on the way to best bring the product or service and the prospective customer together.

## Principles of effective advertising copy

There are several principles for writing effective advertising copy. These principles are basically that the advertising copy should be (1) brief, (2) clear, (3) apt, (4) interesting, (5) personal, (6) sincere, and (7) convincing. It should be patently obvious that such requirements, if met, develop all the salient aspects of effective advertising copy.

*Brevity.* Brevity means clarity and conciseness. Each sentence is studied in detail; each word is considered for relevance, appropriateness, and meaning; all words which seem superfluous are deleted; and, finally, the total advertising message is integrated into a hard-hitting appeal to purchase the product.

*Clarity.* Clarity means that the ad should be easy to understand. Basically, unclear advertising copy is subject to three faults: (1) the words which are used are not clearly understood by the advertising prospect; (2) the words are inappropriate, irrelevant, or poorly selected; or (3) the words which are selected are ambiguous, vague, or otherwise unclear to the subject.

*Aptness.* The third requirement for effective copy writing is that the copy be apt. In other words, the copy must fit the needs and wants of the prospect; it must be appropriate and relevant to the customer's terminology, thought processes, interests and desires. This requires that the copywriter not only have a good deal of insight into the customer's nature but that he or she recognize that there are an infinite variety of human natures. Therefore, the copywriter must recognize that copy which is appealing to him or her—his or her vanity, pride and preferences—may not appeal to others. Effective copy is written with the buyer's interest at heart and from the buyer's point of view, not with the seller's interests in mind and from the seller's viewpoint.

*Interesting.* A fourth principle of effective copy writing is that the ad be interesting. Unfortunately, what interests one person may not interest another. Basically the principle behind writing interesting copy is the appeal to people's emotions.

*Personal.* To be effective, advertising copy also must be personal. This means that the word "you" should be included—or at least implied—in the copy. For example, there is a good deal of difference between the effect of the general statement, "Anyone looking for a new car should visit Kline's Auto," and the statement, "If *you* want a new Ford, visit Kline's Auto for the best deal *you* can get."

*Sincere and convincing.* The final principle of writing effective advertising copy is that the individual must be sincere and convincing in writing the copy. To be sincere and convincing, the individual must be convinced of the worth, merit, quality, and value of the service or product which he or she is trying to sell. It is much easier to say that a product is guaranteed to last 15 years if the product is actually made to last for 15 years. Such sincerity, if obtained, will practically always be convincing.

## USING AN ADVERTISING AGENCY

### Role of the advertising agency

Fundamentally, the role of the advertising agency is to prepare and place effective advertisements for the agency's clientele. However, many advertising agencies have organized themselves to perform many additional functions in addition to the writing and placing of advertisements. Many of them, for example, serve as marketing and advertising consultants or counselors, rather than functional copywriters. In fact, one study found that major advances in the field of advertising and the work of advertising agencies have been made in advertising research, copy testing, audience and readership measurement, merchandising, and sales promotion. Therefore, in most cases the advertising agency serves as a consultant as well as a functional copy-writing service. A good advertising agency should be able to (1) study a client's product or service and determine the advantages or disadvantages to his or her product; (2) analyze the potential market for the client's product or service; (3) give advice on possible sources of distribution and sale of the client's product; (4) advise the client on the types, kinds, costs, and effectiveness of the various media which are available to the client; (5) formulate a definite plan of presentation for the client's product or service to prospective buyers; (6) execute that plan; and (7) cooperate with the client's sales organization in order to insure the greatest amount of cooperation between the advertising campaign and the sales effort which is made by the client.

Therefore, the role of the advertising agency is more than the job of providing an ad. It also includes the role of providing a service to the client in respect to the client's product, market, distribution channels, media, and overall, integrated advertising plan.

## Selection of the advertising agency

Selecting the appropriate advertising agency is difficult. Many advertising agencies are full-service agencies which provide all of the above services, while others are not. Therefore, in selecting the advertising agency the small businessperson must determine exactly what is expected of the advertising agency. Since advertising agencies are experts in the field of selling, especially when it comes to their own services, the small businessperson would do well to answer the following question before approaching an agency: Does the small businessperson want an advertising agency which will simply write copy, or is the advertising agency to provide advice and consultation as well? If the small business person intends to use an advertising agency to help in planning a total advertising campaign, it is imperative that a determination be made of what is expected of the advertising agency and then an agency that can provide the required service must be found. If, on the other hand, one desires only copy writing, this service can be provided by any reputable agency.

In choosing among the various agencies which are available to a business, then, the small businessperson should consider the following questions: Is the agent honest? Has the agent been effective? Does the agency display reasonable expertise in handling technical or otherwise specialized advertising problems? Does the agency have enough personnel and facilities to do an effective job of developing the ad and preparing it for publication by the various media used? Does the agency have sufficient personnel to devote attention to my company's problem at the time and to the extent that is necessary?

## Compensating the advertising agency

In addition to the above questions which must be considered before the small business selects the advertising agency which will be used, one other aspect must be resolved. That is the manner in which the agency is to be compensated for its service.

There are several ways in which advertising agencies have elected to be paid for their services. One of the most common methods is called the commission plan. A commission plan is highly favored by the advertising agency and has some appeal to the advertiser. The commission plan works on a kickback basis, which means that the customer pays the list price to the medium in which the ad is placed by the agency. The medium—whether it is newspaper, magazine, radio, or television—then returns a certain amount to the advertising agency for placing the ad. In other words, the medium rather than the advertiser pays the agency. The advantage to the advertising agency is that it very definitely will be paid. The advertiser, on the other hand, knows what the price of the ad will be and that the advertising agency's fee will be included in that price. The commission plan is so popular that from 75 to 90 percent of most advertising agencies' incomes are receipts from such commissions.

In addition to the commission basis, however, there are other ways in which advertising agencies are paid. Quite obviously, sometimes the advertiser is charged a fee or a cost for services provided by the advertising agency. This oftentimes is simply a service fee for utilizing the agency, plus the cost of the actual media used for a particular ad. At other times, this charge is a cost-plus-percent, in which the agency is compensated for the cost of the ads which are placed plus a given percentage figure of that cost for services performed. Still other advertising agencies charge a flat fee for providing their services.

Basically the method of payment is up to the individual advertiser and the agency which he or she intends to utilize. The possibility of negotiation is always available, and the small businessperson is definitely encouraged to bargain with whatever advertising agency he or she chooses for the best possible deal which can be made for receiving the service. It should be pointed out in speaking about such negotiations, however, that contrary to the statistics, many times the negotiated fee is far more desirable for the small businessperson than is the commission plan. This is so because usually local media will give small businesspeople they deal with directly "local rates," while they will not give such rates to an advertising agency. Thus if the agency places the ad for the small business, the agency cannot get as low a rate from the media as the small business can itself. This, in turn, means that to offset costs, the media would require from the small business (through the media commission) a commission which would cover their fee plus a higher rate than if the small business manager had placed the ad himself or herself. Thus, the small business would end up paying more than is required. Therefore, the small business manager should investigate all opportunities and costs before deciding how or whether to use an agency.

### Doing it yourself

The alternative to using an advertising agency is to do the job yourself. Such a decision, of course, must be based on whether or not the individual can serve as one's own effective advertising agency, whether or not one can afford an advertising agency, and whether or not one feels that, on balance, one can be a more effective advertiser in view of the money that can be saved by doing it oneself, in contrast to the benefits which might be obtained from utilizing an advertising agency. The hazard is that the small businessperson who serves as his or her own advertising agent might well be fooling himself or herself. While it is true that many small businesspeople are forced into being their own advertisers because they lack sufficient funds to hire an agency, other small businesspeople are lured into being their own advertising agency because they fail to see the worth of an advertising agency when they can write what they consider to be good ads.

The really critical question which therefore must be resolved by the small business manager in attempting to be his or her own advertising agency is whether or not he or she can write effective ads. Since this problem is often compounded by ego and bias, it is important for the small businessperson who decides that he or she wants to be his or her own advertising agent and copywriter to be thoroughly familiar with the tests of effective advertising which were developed above. If a person is not familiar with such tests, he or she will not get objective feedback as to whether his or her ads are providing the type of readership, attention, and action which he or she is hoping to receive. In view of this the small business manager is advised not to serve as his or her own advertising agent unless (1) economics dictate it, (2) he or she is a good copywriter, and (3) he or she can get effective feedback on the value of the ads written.

### SELLING AND SALES PROMOTION

One final aspect of advertising must still be discussed. That is what is generally considered sales promotion or the real job of selling.

Very few products are sold without personal salesmanship; and, furthermore, many times personal salesmanship can promote sales which otherwise would not have been made. It is therefore of the essence that the small-businessperson realize that his or her advertising campaign is not a success and may even become a failure if it does not extend to, tie in with, and facilitate the actual purchase of the merchandise.

Most businesspeople who are successful know and recognize the need to advertise. Furthermore, they usually assume that their competitors have a product or service as good as their own at equally competitive prices. Therefore, they recognize that the primary purpose of their advertising is to get people to shop in their stores or sales offices, or to see their salesmen. However, they also recognize that getting the "looker" doesn't sell the product or service. The sale must still be made. Thus, the effective advertiser will extend the advertising campaign to include the actual sale of the product (and any subsequent adjustments that must be made).

Extending an advertising program through the actual sale means a variety of things. For one thing, it means that the salesperson must know what is being advertised, at what price, and for how long. Further, it means that the salesperson must know all the products being sold thoroughly—inside and out, advantages and disadvantages, uses and limitations. Furthermore, good, effective selling means that the salesperson will know the same information about competitors' products and services. Thus, a good advertising program includes well-trained salespeople who know their product, what is said about it, and what can be said.

A thorough advertising program also means that the salesperson knows how to sell the product. Knowing how to sell a product is the very heart and culmination of any successful advertising program. It means that salespersons not only know their own and their competitors' products, they also know and understand the "psychology" of selling: how to tie ads in with sales appeals, when to use the soft-sell approach or the hard-sell approach, how to employ any convincing demonstrations or gimmicks, how to size up customers' needs, and how to suggest companion sales, future sales, or alternative products.

Extending the advertising program through the point of sale is essential. No advertising program is complete without it. An ad cannot make the sale; the salesperson can. Unfortunately, many small businesspeople fail in their advertising campaigns precisely at this critical point. Their salespeople frequently seem not to know what is going on, are limited in the facilities with which they have to do the job, and are not properly motivated to do the job. Therefore, if a final admonishment must be made to the small businessperson in regard to how to conduct a successful advertising program, it might run as follows: know your budget, establish your objectives, prepare your appeals, select your media, but do not forget—a salesperson must make the sale!

## QUESTIONS

1. What is the purpose of advertising?
2. What is meant by customer advertising? Institutional advertising? Product advertising? Distinguish between each kind.
3. How does the small businessperson usually determine when to advertise? How does he or she determine how much to advertise? Are these two questions interrelated? Why?
4. Critically analyze the all-that-can-be-afforded method of advertising budget determination.
5. What considerations need to be made in selecting the appropriate advertising media?
6. How can the small businessperson evaluate the efficacy of his or her advertisements? Explain in detail.
7. The text lists some principles of effective advertising copy. What are these? What do they mean?
8. Compare the advantages and disadvantages of using an advertising agency's services against those of "doing it yourself."
9. How are advertising agencies compensated for their services? Which is the best form for the small business to use?
10. Why is personal selling an important extension of any advertising program? Explain your answer.

## PROBLEMS

1. Develop an advertising strategy for one of the following businesses:
    a. Automatic car wash
    b. Machine shop
    c. Skin diving shop
    d. Jewelry store
    e. Resort hotel
2. Develop a full-page newspaper ad for one of the following businesses, being sure to include all copy, illustrations and other material:
    a. Men's clothing store
    b. Automobile dealership
    c. Fast-food restaurant
    d. Auto rental agency
    e. Shoe shop
3. Write a 400-word essay on the advantages of using an advertising agency.

## BIBLIOGRAPHY

Banks, Russell, ed. *Managing the Smaller Company.* New York: American Management Association, 1969, 347 pp. Sixteen company presidents and/or executives give their advice on managing a small business.

Klatt, Lawrence. *Managing the Dynamic Small Firm.* Belmont, Calif.: Wadsworth Publishing Co., 1971. A good, basic primer on small business management.

"Running Your Own Business." *The Financial Post.* Toronto: MacLean-Hunter Limited, 1971. Excellent article on how to run one's own business, the pro's and con's of it all. Canadian orientation, all of which proves that the basics of good business management are essentially universal.

# 23

# Pricing of products and services

Pricing is one of the principle factors which management uses to ensure an adequate return for productive effort. All products and services must be priced for sale, at prices which reflect a wide assortment of circumstances affecting both buyers and sellers. Every transaction between buyer and seller involves a price—a price, it is hoped, which will amply reward the seller for his contribution.

## THE FRAMEWORK OF PRICES

No system of establishing a single price or an entire line of prices can be set up in a vacuum. A series of reference points, comparisons, and judgments must be taken together to provide some idea what is the right price initially for the particular thing being offered. Even the initial price may be wrong, if in fact no sales are made. It can be argued that the price was right, but nobody understood the correctness of the price. A better approach has to be that a price is set in order to sell something. The inherent fairness or validity of a price is really not a very useful criteria.

*The product or service offered.* Many products or services offered are capable of providing very similar end results to the customer. Other items may be highly unique and capable of providing specialized results. The basic nature of a product or service does provide the opportunity to achieve prices which will vary under different circumstances. Changes can deliberately be incorporated which provide product differentiation—often at very little additional cost. Services can include a wide variation in accommodation. In fact, personal services provided by the small business should be superior if accomplished by knowledgeable and capable people. The combination of administrative backing and personal service by the owner at the point of final sale is the real strength of the franchise system.

403

As differences become more evident the ability to adjust prices is more possible. Some trade-off analysis will show where differentiation can be used and whether it is justified.

*Environment of sale.* The total environment under which a sale takes place has a very definite effect on what price can be charged. The right environment should permit the seller to sell at a higher price than under less favorable conditions. Individuals will often pay prices in specialty shops away from their home community which they would never pay at home. In the past years, restaurants featuring an unusual decorative theme or locale have become very popular and at higher prices for the food and service offered. The environment in which a funeral service is discussed and ultimately priced is apt to be in part a function of the environment in which the discussions take place.

If the right environment does not exist initially the entrepreneurs should think about what is needed. Color schemes, art work, a particular motif, or background music, may all be a low cost environmental feature that can help in pricing.

*Reputation.* The reputation of the company may have a significant impact on the prices to be charged. Reputations have been established by companies that were based on customers' collective opinions that prices were right, about right, or not right. A study conducted by one of the authors revealed that customers in general felt that the prices of retail merchants in their particular community were too high. Customers of the same merchants from two neighboring communities thought that in general the prices were low. A reputation that provides the opportunity to price favorably for the firm should be considered where it can be accomplished.

*Competition.* The efforts of competitors and competitive products will set the price levels for many products and services. Inflationary forces of the mid-1970s have made many buyers much more price conscious than they have been for many years. Certain industries and particular kinds of business have become much more competitive. Some of this has been head-on and very direct, while other sellers have tended to be much more selective.

Most small businesses are competitive to a degree, but try to avoid competition in price and selection alone, where they sell against much larger competitors. The effects of competition can be diluted or sidetracked by changing the total sale package in one or more ways. Services and accommodation are two things that small businesses can provide effectively and they should be used. The total package is what counts in the ultimate sale.

*Value.* A particular product or service has at all times something which determines its value to those who own it and those who want it. The important thing about value is that there may be an overall value which is created by a composite of sellers and buyers and which is recognized by a particular individual at some point in time. Value is reflected in price: the going market price for a widely distributed product or service and the price which a given individual is willing to pay. There must be a willingness on the part of the seller to give it up at that price.

The smaller business is uniquely equipped to utilize value in connection with pricing. The wishes of the customer can often be met by modifying or changing the product to meet what is wanted. If the product or service is tailored for the customer, then value for him has been increased. Often the product or basic service does not have to be changed; other things can be done which add value to the regular transaction.

The conditions under which the sale is made are also a part of value. The idea that the customer is always right is not to be ignored or ridiculed. The purchaser spending his or her money has reason to expect or demand something for it. Here, again, is an area where the smaller business can profit from smallness. Decisions can be made on the spot to accommodate particular situations. The big company attempts to reduce action to a prescribed checklist, or cause and effect method. This format is often inappropriate and frustrating to the customer, but well within the ability of the smaller business to improve on.

*Timing.* Timing is another factor that favors the small business in its pricing structure. Many products and services go through life cycles, as well as seasonal variations in demand and periods of over-supply or shortages. Considerable study is needed to find out what timing factors are important as to price, if the effects of competition are subtle, or it is difficult to assess correctly the effect of timing. On the other hand, the price of a recreational motel unit or service feature may be adjusted to fit a single situation by the small entrepreneur, whose hands are not tied to inflexible company policy.

The nature of timing is very significant in certain well-defined types of business. Convenience food stores and weekend "on-call" plumbers are two examples of the effect of nonconventional hours that provide business, but also permit upward adjustment of prices.

Price timing is also very much related to the action of competitors. Smaller businesses may choose to be leaders or followers in setting prices that are timed to vary over an extended time period. Newspaper advertising often reveals the similarity of price timing that occurs where competitors are aware of what each other is doing.

## PRICING—RELATED TO COSTS

Pricing and the volume of sales are two important factors in developing cash flow for the business. This cash inflow must exceed cash outflow in order to develop profit for the business. Every owner and/or manager of a business must know and understand in detail what influences costs and how these can be adjusted to reflect differences in demand and saleability at differing prices. Costs of producing a product or service, in most cases, do not determine the selling price. They must, however, be understood, otherwise the business operation has no chance of establishing prices that will result in sales.

*Buying costs.* Proper product selection and effective buying are an absolute must for a product-oriented firm. Service firms may not put much reliance on products to any extent, but should instead think in terms of the talents that they are offering. Have they hired and trained the right kind of employees?

The trade-offs in buying generally relate to quantity. Buying is usually referred to when things are being purchased for resale in the same form. If purchasing is involved, materials and components are being purchased for incorporation into other end products. In each case, additional quantities provide volume discounts. The difficulty is in balancing the savings of additional purchases with the anticipated sales levels that follow.

Considerable misinformation and poor forecasting may be a part of the decisions regarding the proper utilization of buying costs along with the quantities to buy. Most small businesses should probably plan to adopt a conservative position on cost-volume trade-offs until substantial experience is gained in what may happen.

*Selling costs.* Costs associated with selling constitute a sizable portion of the ultimate price. These costs are usually identified as the physical facilities for selling, direct sales expense, advertising and promotion, along with credit, delivery, and other personal services for the buyer.

As a product or a service is involved with more and more middlemen, the selling costs rise. The seller at each stage must anticipate whether costs are justified and who may reduce ultimate costs by consolidating or eliminating middleman functions.

Each selling cost should be studied to determine if it has real value, can best be provided by the established businesses, and what potential threats exist against the present cost and yield structure.

*Preparation and conversion costs.* Before something can be sold it must be prepared for sale. Transportation, warehousing, financing, inspection, and preparation for sale are all a part of this process. These costs, taken together are apt to constitute a considerable percent of the added-on costs that are necessary before the sale can be made. No good method is ordinarily available to a small business that can get such costs down to the point where they compare favorably with a larger-scale operation. Constant effort and surveillance is probably the best approach to achieve realistic costs in this area consistent with the level of products or services generated.

*Overhead costs.* Overhead costs are separate from buying, conversion, and selling costs; they usually are not directly associated with the product or service but are a necessary part of getting the job done. They include items such as light, heat, and water. Accountants will distinguish overhead as being separate from direct labor and material in a manufacturing concern, or as being distinct from directly related sales costs in a merchandising concern.

Overhead in a small business will vary substantially from one type of business to another and from one business operator to the next. This is one category of costs where the average small businessperson may have substantial advantages over larger businesses. He or she may be able to hold down the total amount of overhead and spread these costs very efficiently throughout the operation. On the other hand, business volume may not be large enough so that he or she can accurately predict and maintain the correct amount of overhead support consistent with the needs of the business.

**Discounts.** Costs associated with the development of a saleable item at the wholesale level are subject to some adjustment downward through the discount process. Legitimate discounts provided within the established pricing structure are: (1) trade discounts and (2) cash discounts.

Trade discounts are computed by the manufacturer from established list prices and given to middlemen, thus allowing them to make a profit as they move the merchandise on to the customer. Trade discounts increase relative to the volume purchased or the bargaining power of the buyer. Lower prices for volume buyers *if accompanied by lower costs to the seller* are not a violation of the Robinson-Patman Act. However, lower differential prices to various customers without regard to volume or cost-price relationships are unlawful. *Negotiation to establish a price permits considerable freedom to both buyer and seller.*

Cash discounts are provided on the manufacturer's invoice and given to the merchandiser as a reward for payment within a stated period. They are an inducement to the buyer to pay his bills promptly and thus improve the cash flow position of the seller. Ordinarily cash discounts are not confusing except when they are in some way substituted for or made a part of the trade discount. The hypothetical or fictitious discount offered to consumers should not be construed as either a trade or cash discount.

The entrepreneur must understand the various discount structures, know how to obtain the maximum discount on any given purchase, and the effect such discounts should have on pricing structure.

## COSTING-OUT FOR PRICING

When the various costing analyses have been completed, the firm is ready to adopt whatever methods are best to establish the prices on the end products or services.

## Markups

Adding a percent of the total costs related to the thing being sold is markup. For services this may work well, for products it may be difficult or awkward because of competitor's prices or a complex mix of products being sold. A percent of cost or selling price can be used and has the advantage of maintaining some consistency based on costs. It is also defensible in relationship to the costs of doing business.

As volume increases, along with lower costs, markups may be decreased. The great weakness in the markup system is that it is based on predicted levels of costs and sales volume. Varying levels of activity dictate different prices—something which customers may not appreciate and be willing to live with.

## Average costs

Fixed and variable costs can be computed at various levels of sales or output, and prices then set at a level related to the average cost. If sales levels approximate predicted amounts or increase, the method is a good one for maintaining an advantageous price structure. If sales are very unpredictable, then this method is not too good. It also poses problems when the pricing levels need to be changed for one reason or another—particularly when the changes are based on different volume levels.

## Return on investment—time or money

Another method to cost out to a pricing structure is to relate to the investment that is made. For a service business where personal time and effort are the measurement of what is being sold, the pricing can be based on the amount of time involved. All the peripheral costs will be assumed to be a direct function of the charges being made by the individual. This is standard practice for auto repairs, service charges for plumbers, and most professional services. This method is simple, direct, and easy to maintain. Some adjustment may be necessary to camouflage hourly rates, if customer resistance develops. Low-cost extra services may be included to lessen the impact of a higher per-hour or task charge.

Capital investment should always be a criteria for computing prices and rate of return. Dun & Bradstreet or other data sources can be used to find out what rate of return is being developed by businesses in various industry classifications and also by volume of business (sales) being generated.

Smaller business managers and owners often do a very poor job of relating investment to their pricing, and ultimately the return on investment. Some individuals fail to even recognize the going value of time or money.

It is one thing to make a temporary sacrifice to develop a later advantage, as opposed to a basic ignorance of what return is justified on a given investment.

## Break-even analysis

The following break-even chart, Figure 23–1, is shown to illustrate how this technique can be used to analyze various alternatives. It may be used for the analysis of production output or the sale of merchandise by a retail firm. In fact, any form of activity where costs of production and selling prices can be determined can make use of break-even analysis. If costs and prices change at various levels of activity the chart is equally useful, even though some of the decisions as a result become a little more difficult.

FIGURE 23–1
Break-even chart (units or dollar value of units)

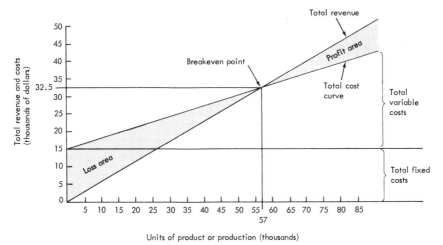

Units of product or production (thousands)

The entrepreneur or manager should develop experience in using break-even analysis and be able to compute rather quickly the changes in break-even point (BEP) when costs and prices change. Anyone who deals with a business, such as financiers or bankers, will require break-even analysis figures along with budget information and return on investment. If a facility in using this technique is apparent, it will be a persuasive factor in gaining support for the business.

The two basic formulas used are:

$$Units\ BEP = \frac{\text{Total fixed costs}}{\text{Fixed cost contribution per unit}}$$

$$Dollars\ BEP = 1 - \frac{\text{Total fixed cost}}{\dfrac{\text{Variable cost/unit}}{\text{Selling price/unit}}}$$

Additional formula information is given at the end of this chapter.

## Marginal costing

The idea behind marginal costing as a means of setting prices is what are the costs involved in producing one more unit of product or service? It is particularly useful in analyzing services such as a transportation, where additional cargo beyond a minimum or average can be handled at virtually no additional expense. In manufacturing, the production of quantities beyond a certain point can be produced at an attractive additional cost.

This method of analysis is useful where the business can divide its productive results, either products or services, in such a way that additional small increments can be produced and perhaps priced so as to develop sales that would otherwise be lost. Working with quantities and costs set up in a table or on a graph, the marginal costs at various operational levels can be determined.

The preceding discussion in this section attempts to give some ideas that are useful in relating the costs of a business to its pricing program, while disregarding or minimizing outside influences. It is very seldom that the outside forces are not a part of any inquiry, but costing-out must be done first to really know what figures are valid prior to moving to the other features to be considered. Review of a good basic marketing or accounting textbook will provide more detailed information about the costing-pricing relationships.

## PRICE SENSITIVITY

The small businessperson must understand that every individual has sensitivities; and in the case of customers, many of them have the same sensitivities. The operator of a business will do well to determine which pricing areas are most sensitive to customers, and what can be done to minimize this feeling and its effect on business.

It is generally conceded that the average person is being offered many more products and services every year than were previously available. As an example, at the time of the advent of the supermarket, the number of items carried in the store might have amounted to no more than 3,500, whereas today large markets are approaching 12,000 items. In other product and service lines similar growth is taking place, although perhaps not to the same magnitude. The question then is, what knowledge do customers have of the products themselves, and to which of these are they particularly price-sensitive? A number of grocery items will be sensitive, but not a sizable number. Some grocery marketers have stated that the sensitive items number no more than 50, although these may be different from one locality to another; all that is necessary to be competitive is for grocery marketers to remain competitive in these 50 items, along with an otherwise efficient operation.

It is important to investigate any particular business and determine what customers know about the products, what type of a pricing pattern they expect, and what products are available from competitors with established prices. Knowing this, the businessperson is faced with the problem of either meeting competitors' prices or attempting to skirt around them in some measure. For nonsensitive products the small businessperson has latitude in the price itself, and can make up for a higher price with the service aspects. Some products are traditionally price-sensitive, whereas others may be sensitive from time to time, but not necessarily continuously. Efforts are made on the part of merchandisers and manufacturers to establish markets or to increase sales potential with the use of price alone; this may result in a price awareness on the part of the customer, forcing the competition to adopt comparable price levels.

Standard and well-advertised products frequently support a higher price; lesser known products may have to be priced downward. This again has nothing to do with quality or value but rather the sensitivity element, established on the basis of judgment that the standard, well-advertised product is the premium product. Numerous examples of a similar type could be given indicating that an area of sensitivity is present; price sensitivity must be recognized for what it is worth, and efforts made to minimize its effect.

## CLASSIFICATION OF PRODUCTS OR GOODS

One step in the pricing analysis process is the examination of products or goods to determine what characteristics tend to place these items in one category or another. Every business owner or manager must view the goods in terms of how they are so classified and why. This process will help the seller to understand more about the inherent nature of goods and why this makes a difference as to how products are priced and how they are sold.

*Suggested-price items.* Some goods carry prices suggested by the manufacturer or distributor. The retailer is expected to use and follow this present pricing structure. There may be no method of legal control or restriction on the ultimate seller if he or she chooses not to comply with the manufacturer's suggested prices. Many products in this category are sold through exclusive sales outlets, and as such, a failure on the part of the merchandiser to respect the suggested selling price may indeed result in the loss of that particular product to his or her operation.

**Leaders or loss leaders.** Leaders are items within the product mix which are used for the purpose of selling at low markup or low price as a means of developing business. Some restriction through state laws are concerned with the selling of products below costs; but generally speaking, enforcement is enacted only on the complaint of a competing merchant, and it is very difficult to determine the individual costs of any particular operation for the purpose of injunction or damages as a result of leader pricing.

**Convenience goods.** Convenience goods are characterized as fast-moving items with wide distribution and available for sale in a great many outlets. They will consistently have fairly low markups, and frequently be carried as a convenience for customers without any particular contribution to profit being expected by the merchant.

**Fashion goods.** Fashion goods possess features which are generally somewhat extreme and possess a short life. These will be shopped for by particular groups of people and will ordinarily carry a high initial markup. Over the salable period of their life, they will gradually depreciate in value, and ultimately if they are not sold, they may have to be disposed of at considerable markdown. Goods which have seasonal characteristics are also generally classified along with fashion goods and sold at prices which contemplate some ultimate markdown.

**Specialties.** Specialties are often presented to the market under special circumstances and probably have particular unique characteristics which allow fairly high initial markups which are reduced as additional competitors recognize their market acceptance. Novelty characteristics are often featured in specialties, although items in this category need not be thought of as special products but rather as special, fast-moving products which enjoy a high degree of popularity for a limited period of time. The "Frisbee" is a good example of a specialty.

**Shopping goods.** Goods possessing certain characteristics which make them unstandardized items that change with the times are rather carefully shopped for by the prospective buyer and called "shopping goods." Varieties of clothing, furniture, automobiles, and certain other items carry a relatively high price, and they create a combination of conditions which cause the buyer to be somewhat more deliberate in his or her investigation and purchase of such items. These are slower selling than other items, develop rather low turnover, and carry fairly high markups to cover additional costs of merchandising.

**Aspinwall's characteristics of goods.** A former professor at the University of Colorado, Professor Leo Aspinwall, has developed some ideas regarding characteristics of goods and their movement through the markets. He classifies goods in terms of the following factors:

1. Replacement rate: the rate at which goods are purchased and consumed.
2. Gross margin: difference between cost and realized sale prices.
3. Adjustment: services applied to meet the exact needs of customers.
4. Time of consumption: the time during which the good gives up the utility desired.
5. Searching time: the time needed to find a suitable item.

He then proceeds to classify goods into three categories which he designates as red, orange, and yellow. As an example, red goods have a high replacement rate and are low in margin, adjustment, time of consumption, and searching. Orange and yellow goods possess other combinations of the five characteristics. The gist of his analysis is that goods possess consumer characteristics in addition to the nature of the goods themselves, which must be analyzed by the seller, for him or her to better understand how to merchandise the mix of goods which are carried in his or her establishment.[1]

## PRICING POLICIES

Policy, which is a guide to action, will apply just as much in guiding the analysis and creation of a pricing program as in any other operating phase of a business. The important thing is to take the time to analyze what factors will affect the area of pricing and establish prices for goods or services which are appropriate to maintain continuity of the business operation.

Activity within any business operation will result in the production of either goods or services, or perhaps both, to be sold by the business to one or more groups of customers. Before policy formation it is advisable to analyze the three divisions of business activity regarding the relationship to price: The first product group is goods *manufactured* and sold which will reach the ultimate buyer through one or more middlemen. These goods are made up from various raw materials and components with the ultimate end product being something different from those items originally bought. The second category of goods and merchandise involves those things which are bought and later resold in the same form, which is a typical activity of the average *final sale merchandising organization* which sells something produced by someone else. The third cate-

---

[1] Leo V. Aspinwall, *Four Marketing Theories* (Boulder, Colo.: Bureau of Business Research, University of Colorado, 1959).

gory involves the *sale of services*, which may be wholly controlled by the seller, or made available by him or her in conjunction with some other organization, such as a franchise service firm.

**Marketing channels.** If the products or services generated by the firm are sold to customers who are located away from point of production, a marketing channel for distribution is needed. Channels can be direct to the consumer, through one or more middlemen, or perhaps some variation involving two or more methods.

Middlemen are not always popular. Ever since the days of Theodore Roosevelt they have been accused of being "nonproductive parasites," who add very little value to the transaction and extract high prices for what they provide. For many smaller businesses, the choice of a marketing channel is often difficult. Small businesses usually represent small and limited output. Middlemen are reluctant to handle small volume business and probably charge a rather high price to do so.

The small businessperson should investigate the channels of distribution to determine what they provide for his or her particular business and whether or not there is any possibility of circumventing certain middlemen to reach a source. Similar opportunities can exist in buying for manufacturing or buying goods for resale. Opportunities to eliminate middleman functions are perhaps more prevalent today than some years ago because of substantial changes in the previously established methods of distribution. Traditional methods of distribution are changing, and "who sells what" is no longer predetermined, along with differences in selling price. Careful analysis and understanding as to the function of marketing channels will be a worthwhile investment.

**Competition.** A pricing policy must consider competitors as well as their prices. The small business entrepreneur may wish to go his or her own way in setting prices and may actually do so, but is more likely to review the competition and try to figure out what policy is best, based on what is found.

Many existing firms will react to a new firm by cutting prices in an attempt to discourage customers from patronizing the new firm. This may continue for some time until it is obviously futile or the new firm manager is compromised. Other tactics, such as increased advertising, may be used.

It is probably well for the newly established business to plan that competitors will develop a direct or indirect price campaign. Some allowance must be made to carry the loss of sales revenue until this period is over.

**Market share.** The market for any given product or service is only so big, and ordinarily if a new business enters the market it must take away business from someone else. There are always a certain number of new products which provide the opportunity for developing a new market. These new products, however, may be incorporated into the sales pattern of an already established market. Pricing is *extremely persuasive* in developing a share of the market, and numerous experimentations and studies have been conducted to determine the effect of *price and advertising* in developing market share. A difficult problem is trying to divide the impact of market penetration between advertising and pricing, and to determine just how much one is independent of the other. If a product is elastic and reducing price increases volume, it is important to know how far to go with price reductions in terms of additional volume and market share. Some theories can be developed about this, but it would probably require trial and error on the part of a businessperson to determine the limits of his or her own potential.

As a means of making a quick entry into the market, some share of the market for a service business is frequently established by using a pricing program below that of competitors. It is apparent that particular market areas are highly individualistic in terms of the pricing structure for services; these pricing levels can be readily determined by a check of the particular market area. The difficult task is for the small businessperson to decide what can be gained if he or she uses differential prices and service pattern to acquire a market share and what the retaliatory effects will be if he or she cuts prices to establish this share.

*Goals of the entrepreneur.* Independent business managers and owners will tend to project a good deal of their own personal ideas into the pricing structure which they establish for their businesses. This personal influence is related to how a person views his or her role as an entrepreneur or business operator, and is a projection of his or her own business ethics. A large business is much less personal and the influence of one person seldom dominates.

There are several ways that the goals of the individual may affect the pricing structure. The person may not wish to "gouge" customers and take advantage of any situation in dealings with customers or clients. On the other hand, the choice may be to charge the infrequent or transient customer a higher price. An individual may view the business as a means of making a reasonable living and as such governs prices so as not to charge a higher price even though the market permits it. The prices set may be considered to be "fair" and bear no relationship to any kind of careful examination of what the market will bear or to the action of competitors. In some cases a price may be set by pure intuition.

*Expansion or change from a previous format.* When a business is scheduled for a substantial change from its previous pattern of operation, it may be time to overhaul the pricing structure. A definite change in the product lines or a change in the "thrust" elements of the business are ample reasons for considering some changes.

The actual price changes may not be as difficult as the planning and strategy which will support the changes in the minds of customers or clients. One technique is to eliminate previous points of reference as to product mix, selection, and shelf space allocations. Another would be a different format as to departmentation and the arrangement of display and shelf space.

The expansion or change may actually be a new "thrust" factor which needs to be highlighted. Pricing is a part of this change in emphasis and should be highlighted to take advantage of a time when such price adjustment can actually be implemented. Prices may or may not be cut. Different price combinations such as averaging may be established and fit well with the other nonprice changes.

*Services.* The pricing of services poses problems that are different from the traditional markup, or pricing to the prices of competitors. It is apparent that many small business owners are not particularly astute in establishing pricing policies for their services.

Certain lines of business adopt uniform or agreed-to prices. These might be unlawful for larger businesses engaged in interstate commerce, but are seldom resisted by legal action at the small enterprise level. The fact that they are agreed to "along Main Street" does not necessarily make them unfair. Standard tasks established and used a great deal rely on "flat rate manuals." These manuals rate a job in time units which are then multiplied by an hourly rate to set the price for a given job. Customers will probably complain if the job time is shortened, resulting in a higher effective rate per hour, but it may be the only reasonable way to justify service rates so that they have a degree of consistency.

Service pricing is difficult and subject to a great deal of customer criticism. The small business owner-manager should think seriously of policies which add "extras" or "sweeteners" to blunt the impact of the price itself. One successful service-business owner describes his policy as: "Smother them (customers) with kindness and charge like hell."

## PRICING STRATEGY

Following the consideration and adoption of basic pricing policies, the next step is to set up the strategy to be used in the actual pricing programs. The process at this point is to set the prices so that the objective policies of the business are met. Considerable change and adjustment will take place before the best workable combinations are found. Some suggestions and ideas about strategy are included in the following part of this section.

*Leaders.* A leader, or formerly a loss leader (before resale price-maintenance laws), is just what the name implies—a low-priced product or service structure to draw customers, who will then purchase other offerings. The leader mechanism is well known and can be examined easily by anyone.

*Random discounts.* Some smaller businesses have had success with marking down products and merchandise on a purely random basis. To be successful, this must include good saleable items, and must be done on a big enough scale to make it pay. Increased customer traffic will search for the unannounced items and in the process be potential buyers of other items.

*Price lining.* In price lining, the strategy is to cluster prices at various points, such as $2.00, $5.00, and $7.50. Based on knowledge about customers, it is probably reasonable in many cases to set prices at these levels. The spread provided is sufficient to provide higher and lower prices and quality without having to maintain a great assortment of different prices.

*Low-cost "extras."* A number of small business enterprises have been very successful in providing a higher image of value with low cost features. This is particularly true in service businesses where a little extra effort and expense can really enhance the price in the mind of the customer. A free newspaper or an evening "slide show" might be a good reason why a motel operator could charge a higher price for his or her units.

*Bargain pricing.* One strategy in pricing is to rely on the trait of human nature that all people love a bargain. The fact that a customer thinks he or she bought at a bargain price is often more important than the price itself. This permits the entrepreneur to plan for a higher price if the image can be conveyed that the price is still a bargain. Discounts from list prices have probably lost their impact, although they are still being used. Pricing up from cost, prices lower than any competitor's, or membership club prices are examples of bargain pricing.

The strategies suggested are a few that have been used with success in the past. Variations and other strategies will occur to alert entrepreneurs as they see what others are doing.

Small business owners are uniquely equipped to develop their own strategies because they operate from flexible positions. They can experiment on a short-run basis, react to conditions as they develop, and develop their own style and methods which are consistent with their own philosophy of how to price.

## PRICING LEGALITY

Because of small size and impact, the small business is not often challenged on the pricing of its products. Service pricing is probably not challenged either, via legal action, although there may be some form of pressure by state regulatory agencies, where such groups may prescribe prices.

As a business becomes larger, and particularly where interstate commerce is involved, the firm's prices may be subject to scrutiny and perhaps challenged as to their legality.

State laws such as "unfair practices acts" or "resale price maintenance" are designed to put a floor under prices, including some reasonable percent as a markup. The laws vary, but their purpose is to prevent pricing below cost as a sales inducement and to prevent "price wars," which are considered unfair and ruinous competition.

The Robinson-Patman Act applies to goods sold in interstate commerce. It provides that a seller may not discriminate in prices between buyers if the goods are the same.

Pricing known as "deceptive pricing" has been attacked by the Federal Trade Commission in the Wheeler-Lea Amendment of 1938 and later guidelines brought out in the 1950s and 1960s. Actions under these guidelines have mainly been to issue warnings and to give private trade organizations a reason to police their own membership.

In the area of state control over pricing, Colorado has a Fair Trade Act, an Unfair Practices Act, a Deceptive Trade Act, and a Restraint of Trade Act. Owners and managers should check for similar laws and their provisions in their own states. (See additional information on laws affecting small business in Chapter 5.)

## SUGGESTIONS FOR PRICING

For the small business, a number of things associated with pricing may be different from what they are for major manufacturers, retailers, or service enterprises. The following suggestions may prove helpful to the small entrepreneur as an aid in setting prices:

1. Never assume that any price established on a product is necessarily correct, or that the product is priced "right."

2. Be willing to experiment with prices and to change them to an extent that is not inconsistent with company policy or likely to affect customer goodwill.

3. Try to avoid head-on price competition with larger companies or others who are better able to achieve a lower pricing structure.

4. Study markets, products, and people continuously and carefully to determine what will work, under what conditions it will succeed, and how such can be incorporated into the goals of the organization.

5. Be realistic as to price changes of products and services over time, and the necessity of setting a pricing structure which allows for reductions and the movement of the goods at the end of seasonal periods. Prepare to meet the pricing of competitors from time to time. Apply the idea of balancing or compensating over the entire range of products and services offered to develop and maintain some average gross margin figure which is consistent with the needs of the business.

6. Constantly utilize service aspects to achieve competitive advantage.

Nothing will support a price as well as having it accompanied with service. Many small business services can be provided with very little cost. In fact, a smile, knowing a customer's name, some conversation, and showing an interest in customers may be all the service that is needed to win and hold them.

7. Make use of the flexibility available to most small businesses. React to changes and make adjustments. Capitalize on developing opportunities and fill voids that have been created, or in some other way prepare for new opportunities and move quickly when they present themselves. Later, if larger competitors move in, or "cutthroat" competition develops, the opportunist is mentally prepared to move out of his or her present operation into something else.

8. Examine all phases of the business constantly in regard to the effect that pricing has on the operation. Examine product sales by individual product, by departments, by seasons of the year, by customers and class, by amount of sales transactions, and any other yardstick that makes sense. In other words, be a leader and an innovator rather than a follower, who must do business on somebody else's terms.

9. Analyze the relationship that credit and installment selling have on the pricing structure. Many times a price is meaningless unless the item or service is available for sale over time or on credit terms.

10. Use your customers as a sounding board to find out what they think about your prices and also your competitors' prices.

## FORMULAS TO AID IN PRICING

A number of quick and easy calculations are needed in every business to determine certain consequences which have an effect on pricing; or conversely, are a result of pricing.

1. *Stock turnover:*

A.  Cost $$\frac{\text{Cost of goods sold}}{\text{Average inventory at cost}} = \text{Stock turnover}$$

B.  Price $$\frac{\text{Net sales}}{\text{Average inventory at selling price}} = \text{Stock turnover}$$

C.  Units $$\frac{\text{Sales in units}}{\text{Average inventory in units}} = \text{Stock turnover}$$

2. *Cost of goods:* $$\frac{\text{Cost of goods}}{\text{Selling price}} = \text{Percent of sales}$$

420

3. *Gross margin:*     Net sales − Cost of goods sold = Gross margin

4. *Markup on cost:*     $\dfrac{\text{Dollar markup}}{\text{Cost}}$ = Percent markup

(Illus.)  $\dfrac{.20}{50./10.00} = 20\%$

5. *Markup on selling price:*     $\dfrac{\text{Dollar markup}}{\text{Selling price}}$ = Percent markup

(Illus.)  $\dfrac{.12\frac{1}{2}}{80./10.00} = 12\frac{1}{2}\%$

6. *Capital turnover:*     $\dfrac{\text{Net sales at retail}}{\text{Capital investment}} = \dfrac{\text{Capital}}{\text{turnover}}$

7. *Break-even points:*

A.  *Units BEP* = $\dfrac{\text{TFC}}{\text{FC contribution per unit}}$

(Illus.) Total fixed cost (TFC)     = \$3,000.00
Variable cost (VC) per unit =     .08
FC contribution (.12 − .08) =     .04
BEP = 75,000 Units

B.  *Dollars BEP* = $\dfrac{\text{TFC}}{1 - \dfrac{\text{VC/unit}}{\text{Selling price/unit}}}$

(Illus.)  $\dfrac{\$3,000.00}{1 - \dfrac{.08}{.12}} = \$9,000.00$

## QUESTIONS

1. Why should each category of costs be analyzed separately before a decision is made on the sales prices of a firm's products or services?
2. What kinds of information about discount structures help the small business to buy more advantageously?
3. Are there ordinarily direct relationships of price and quality over the range of a product line? Why or why not?
4. In theory are all costs variable in the long run?
5. How should a business entrepreneur attempt to find out the price sensitivities of customers?

6. Do inflation and increasingly higher prices tend to change a customer's attitude about the value that a particular purchase represents?

7. What is advantageous about a small entrepreneur setting prices to some extent on the basis of his or her own feel as to what is "right"?

8. How much justification and evidence of costs should be provided to a customer when a price is quoted or stated?

9. How does the smaller business decide what is the best price for a rather different or unique service?

10. What is the advantage of adjusting prices frequently (up and down) instead of maintaining considerable price stability?

## PROBLEMS

1. Study the newspaper advertising of three or four directly competitive retail firms. Compare the prices of the firms over a six-week period on items that are the same or comparable. Attempt to answer the following:

   a. Is there really price competition?

   b. Are the same items repeatedly being featured and priced below the regular prices?

   c. What pricing images are conveyed by the advertising of each establishment?

2. Using the "Yellow Pages" select five service firms and place a call to price a particular well-known type of service job. Carefully note what statements are made in connection with the pricing quoted by each firm.

3. Contact a wholesale firm and inquire about their pricing policies. Try to avoid particular details and names which are apt to be sensitive. Try to establish the following:

   a. Do they use a list price less a discount as a method of pricing?

   b. What conditions warrant differing discount prices?

   c. How do this firm's prices compare with those of other competitors in the area? (This may be only an opinion or conjecture.)

4. Select a small manufacturing firm and make an appointment with the purchasing agent or whoever buys materials and components for the firm. Ask questions that deal with the following circumstances:

   a. What circumstances relating to price uncertainty, shortages, and other problems of the early 1970s have continued to make the buying programs of small businesses difficult and costly?

   b. In what areas have tighter standards of liability tended to raise prices?

   c. How should the buying program of a small business be changed during a period of higher and more frequent price increases than prevail during more normal times?

5. Review the laws and statutes of your state relative to control of businesses through administrative boards and agencies. Contact two or three agencies of your choice and inquire whether the prices within the area of agency regulation are actually controlled.

# BIBLIOGRAPHY

Alpert, Mark I. *Pricing Decisions.* Glenview, Ill.: Scott, Foresman, 1971. A good paperback devoted to pricing. Some information is probably a little more detailed and sophisticated than is needed in a small business, but many different approaches are analyzed which are useful for developing ideas about pricing.

Boone, Louis E., and Kurtz, David L. *Contemporary Marketing.* Hinsdale, Ill.: The Dryden Press, 1974. A recent textbook in the area of basic marketing. Contains up-to-date text material and good graphics explaining how to analyze the various parts of a marketing program. Also has cases.

Consumers Union of the U.S., Inc. *Consumer Reports* (monthly). Mt. Vernon, New York. A consumer advisory periodical which reports in detail about a number of consumer products on a random basis. Pricing information is extensive and useful as a guide to what techniques and policies are being followed by various manufacturers and retail sellers.

Dun & Bradstreet, Inc. *Key Business Ratios.* 99 Church Street, New York, N.Y. 10007; (yearly). The ratios analyses apply to a number of different kinds of businesses. They provide information that can be used to compare a particular firm's ratios with industry averages generated by Dun & Bradstreet. Very useful for comparison.

Klatt, Lawrence A. *Small Business Management: Essentials of Entrepreneurship.* Belmont, Calif.: Wadsworth Publishing Co., 1973. Some very useful chapters on marketing and finance which provide a reference for pricing analysis. Much of this material is not directly presented as related to pricing but is included in a form of analysis which points up how pricing is related to the other functions in a small business.

McGraw-Hill, Inc. *Business Week* (weekly). New York, N.Y. *Business Week* is a weekly news magazine that is devoted entirely to business firms and their activities. No particular articles are referenced here, but feature articles appear frequently which relate to pricing strategies, price levels, costs of doing business, etc. A very worthwhile publication for identifying trends that are emerging and developing.

# 24

# Research—markets, products, and people

No book on small business management would be complete without a chapter devoted to marketing research and sales forecasting. Although marketing research is an essential element of successful small business management, many small business people are skeptical of its values, while others just don't know what it is. Thus, because of the skeptics, and because of ignorance, marketing research is not a commonly used tool of the small business. Much like the element of planning, marketing research is a veritable panacea for the business which does employ it, not because the results are always so informative but because the business's competitors, for the most part, fail to use it.

Marketing research can be defined as the gathering, recording, and analyzing of factual information relating to the transfer and sale of goods and services for the business. Obviously, any definition of marketing research is very broad, inasmuch as it must basically state that any research in respect to markets is marketing research.

Perhaps more important than a definition of marketing research is an understanding of the need for marketing research upon the part of small business managers. It can be argued that the CONSUMER is KING; when sale of merchandise begins to slacken, businesses must get out and sell. However, the admonishment to sell must be backed up with "know-how." Selling is half the marketing battle. But knowing what the customer wants, and when, is an additional problem. It is the task of marketing research to give the necessary insights into a complex picture.

What are these problems? First, there is the problem of finding out what the customer wants. This involves not only ascertaining preferences among existing products and services, but also discovering what new or improved products and services are to be designed. Also, how the customer wants (needs) to have this product delivered is important.

In addition, there is the job of informing the consumer of products that might better serve his or her needs. This requires, among other things, a better-informed sales organization, fully aware of buying intentions and motives in addition to the likes and dislikes of the customer.

Thus, the need to engage in some kind of marketing research emerges because of the need for the small business to (1) know what the customer wants, (2) know how to inform the consumer of the products and services that the business has for sale which might better serve the customer's needs, and (3) know how to optimize the efficiency of the distribution process itself.

## SOURCES AND USES OF INFORMATION FOR SMALL BUSINESSES

### Sources of market information

*Primary information collection.* There are a variety of sources of information about the market which concern the small business. These types of information take the form of unpublished data and published data. Unpublished data is information which the small business itself generates. Usually this requires that the small business person collect information (or someone collects the information for him or her) on a payment-for-services-rendered basis. It is not really important who collects the data, so long as (1) it is reliable and accurate, and (2) it is concerned with the sale or distribution of the products or services of the small business. Examples of such data might include very elementary things such as determining the kind of customers the business serves by analyzing credit information, or determining what geographical area the customers come from by noting the location of the banks on which they draw their checks or the counties in which their automobile license plates are issued. No matter how the small business assembles such data, such sources of information can be invaluable toward informing the manager about his or her clientele, where they live, what they do, and so on. Further, no matter how such data is collected, whether it is by formal random process or by an informal process, one thing is certain: such information is generally accurate and fairly reliable because the studies are made by the business manager (or his or her agent) and the information is gleaned from actual customers. Thus, a great amount of reliable, timely, and accurate information can be amassed by the use of primary information-collection techniques.

*Secondary information collection.* While the primary sources of information are invaluable to a small business there are other sources of good information, many of which are very inexpensive and can be quite reliable and valid. These sources are termed the secondary sources of information, and they include such things as general economic base studies for communities, information from trade associations, U.S. Census reports, and published market analyses.

Although secondary sources of data can be very valuable to a small business, they can also be next to useless, and in some cases, even *worse* than useless. The problem with secondary sources of information is that often they are not readily available, and many times when they are, they are either too comprehensive to be of real benefit to a specific retailer or manufacturer or they are so highly specialized (which often is the case of trade association data) that they are too narrow in their application for a particular small business.

Probably the greatest source of difficulty found in using secondary data comes from using data which is too comprehensive. This tends to lead the small business manager down the primrose path to believing that the information is complete, accurate, and otherwise relevant to his or her particular problem, when it may not be. The manager is then lulled into a sense of security which is often false. Less critical, but sometimes as serious, is the reliance on too well-refined or too narrowly applicable information. In this case, the small business operator is not lulled into a false sense of security, but, by contrast, is driven out of a particular market or business endeavor because he or she fears there is a lack of need for the service or product he or she provides or intends to provide.

Because of the microscopic and macroscopic error element in much of the published information available to the small business, it is not highly recommended that managers rely extensively on such secondary sources of information. Such information, however, can be immensely useful to the small business, and if the business is in a well-defined trade and has trade association data, such material can be invaluable to the manager. The small business operator should be alerted to the fact that many times this information is not relevant or appropriate unless it is intermixed with other data which he or she collects or has an agency collect; still it can be quite useful.

## General-purpose information collection

There is still another source of published information which is available to the small business—information which is usually published in World Almanacs, various statistical abstracts, and current business surveys. However, such data is practically always of a general-purpose character, and rarely, if ever, does it have any specific benefit or meaning for the small business in respect to its particular market or clientele. The only advantage to such information is that it is plentiful, and cheap. Thus, the small business manager who finds these sources of information relevant to the business is wise to use them. But he or she should be apprised of the fact that the reliability and validity of such information is open to question in respect to its relevance to any particular business.

## Uses of market information

There are numerous uses to which the small business manager can put market research data which he or she collects, whether from primary or secondary sources. These are broken down into four decisional areas: price decisions, product decisions, promotional decisions, and place decisions. Inasmuch as price, product, promotional and place decisions are the main points on which most businesses compete, marketing research provides the small business with help in those areas where the manager needs it most. It answers the questions of why customers buy what they buy, and how they are influenced to buy.

In seeking answers to the question of why people buy what they buy the usual practice for the small business manager is to break the marketing research project into one of three kinds of research: motivational research, advertising research, or product research. Because advertising research was dealt with in Chapter 22, only motivational research and product research will be considered in this chapter.

## CUSTOMER MOTIVES: WHY PEOPLE BUY

### Doing research on buyer motivation

One of the first uses for marketing research is to lend insight into the reasons people buy the products that they do—that is, what are their motivations for purchasing the various items which they buy? Many small business managers, for example, feel that people buy products merely because of price. They feel that if a product is priced accurately, it will be purchased. However, such an attitude about people's motivations for purchasing is about as archaic as the concept of the "economic man." People are motivated to purchase products by a variety of impulses, even though they are price-minded. Marketing research of the motivational variety is concerned with the total "mix" of the motives which people have for buying products or services, be they rational or irrational, emotional or calculated, conscious or subconscious.

### Getting a fix on why people buy

Motivational research information lends decisiveness and assurance to otherwise uncertain and confused situations concerning the operation of the business. For example, research into the motivation and buying habits of consumers tells the small business manager that it is wise to place "impulse" items on shelves at eye level rather than floor or ceiling levels, because it is known that people only "see" merchandise at eye level unless they are specifically looking for the product. Thus, a grocery store, if wisely managed, will stock high-margin, profitable items (such as light bulbs, hair spray, etc.) at eye level in order that the shopper, who usually "doesn't think" of such items in a grocery store, can be reminded by means of impulse that this is something he or she needs. At the same time the same grocer will stock staple items at the lower levels of various shelves— knowing that the shopper will deliberately seek out such thing as canned vegetables, eggs, and milk. The idea is to rely on the fact that the staple items attract customers into the store, but that additional sales and revenue are generated by communicating the "impulse" to the customer to purchase other luxury, convenience, or "spur of the moment" items.

Knowledge such as the above "shopper's vision" phenomenon has been developed through years of extensive motivational research. Practically speaking, the information that shoppers have only a limited field of vision, that they buy things in gay colored or bright packages, or that they are inclined to purchase an ostensibly "new" product, has been gleaned through years of research conducted by larger businesses and the nation's colleges and universities. Many small business managers do not develop such information on their own because they neither have the time, the financial resources, or the knowledge. But mere lack of time, money, and know-how is no excuse for the really competitive small business manager. He or she can still speculate about why people buy what they do, and can test these theories by way of a new floor layout, clientele approach, or product ads designed to entice the customer to buy, request, or order a product or service. All that the small business manager really needs to know are the fundamentals of consumer buying behavior as developed by the many motivational research studies. If one stratagem or technique, layout, or design fails, he or she can quickly change to another until the right one is found. In short, a little knowledge of people's motivational drives, coupled with a willingness to arrange and rearrange formats or layouts, can allow the small business manger to capitalize on knowledge that the consumer buys products and services for reasons other than price.

## Understanding customer buying habits

There are a few principles of motivational behavior which have been developed from extensive research. These are, of course, not complete and therefore tend to be very general. But they are sufficient for use by small business managers in developing ideas and approaches as to how to capitalize on the fact that customers purchase things because of a variety of motivations, both conscious and subconsious. These principles include:

*1. A customer's behavior is a function of his or her attitude, plus the facts of the situation.* This principle states that while the given facts of the situation (the price of the product, the extent of the service rendered, etc.) are known and valid, the behavior of the customer is going to vary because of his or her attitude. People's attitudes represent an expression of how they feel about particular factors and, therefore, determine the extent to which they accept or reject the factual circumstances of the product. Attitudes are extremely important in attempting to elicit the desired behavior of the customer, and it is important that the small business manager understand that attitudes are rarely, if ever, all positive or all negative. No product or service will be pleasing and appealing to all customers, and thus the small business operator should try to reach only a particular segment of the market. Further, small business operators should concentrate their conjectures and speculations on the attitudes which the customers display toward their product or service rather than the facts which are given in the situation.

*2. Customers rely on reference points for decision-making.* The second principle of customer motivation simply states that any person will store information learned from living and will use such information as reference points for accepting or rejecting ideas. Thus, people will decide to buy or not to buy a particular product or service on the basis of interpretations which they give to their need for that product or service.

The application of this principle of customer motivation requires that the small business manager recognize that it is far more important to have a knowledge of the assumptions or beliefs held by customers or clients rather than to attempt to tell them how they should perceive the business's product or service. Of course, it must be recognized that assumptions and beliefs often are hard to measure because of customer rationalization. Some people, for example, will hire a gardener because they have convinced themselves consciously that they do not have time to tend their own; however, the real reason may be that they need or want the prestige which having a gardener implies. But whether or not customers rationalize openly about their underlying assumptions and beliefs is immaterial so long as the small business manager *knows* the customers and utilizes this knowledge of their fundamental assumptions and beliefs.

*3. Physical sensations frequently trigger customer behavior.* The third principle of customer motivation states that physical stimuli such as smell, sound, a taste, a touch, or a sight frequently trigger impulsive or spontaneous behavior upon the part of customers or clients. This principle is commonly put to use in various forms: a candy store may make candy within sight of the front window; a grocery store may put the bakery near the front of the store so that the smell of freshly baked goods surrounds customers as they enter; or the record store play music which it feels will appeal to those entering the store. Thus, small business operators, in utilizing this principle of motivation, can promote impulse sales more effectively by solidifying, materializing, or personifying their product or service in order that it will be convenient, handy, and readily accessible to the various physical sensors of customers or clients. Such ready access to the actual product or service can many times trigger immediate purchase or order action by a client while inaccessibility or lag time might leave the customer without any immediate feeling of need for the product or service.

4. *Images, while intangible, give customers very concrete feelings.* The fourth principle of customer motivation states (as developed in Chapter 16) that while it must be recognized that the image which a customer or client holds of a firm, product, or service is wholly intangible, it is nevertheless a very real, solid, concrete sensation—much like frightening dreams which a small child experiences. Therefore, to invoke the principles of customer motivation and enhance the success of a firm, the small business manager must be cognizant of the very real nature of both the corporate and personal image and the impact this image will have on the desire of prospective customers and clients to buy the business's product of service.

5. *People have a variety of motives, but more often than not the individual is not aware of the real motives which compel him or her to action.* Principle number 5 states that customers and clients are always motivated in their actions by some want or need, but that many of their wants or needs are not understood or even known to the individual himself or herself. Therefore, the use of this principle in attempting to direct customer behavior is limited by the fact that there cannot be a complete inventory or cataloging of motives which trigger activity upon the part of anyone or even a group of people. However, even though the real motives for individual activity may not be known to the individual, let alone outsiders, the fact is that a knowledge of general sociopsychological human motives maye be beneficial to the small businessperson in determining crucial aspects of the motivation of people.

The psychologists tell us that underlying practically all basic motives which people have is the desire and need for ego satisfaction. Thus, ego satisfaction becomes a primary source of motivation for people, and oftentimes it is the real (versus rationalized) motive for a particular action or activity. Assuming that people in general (and customers in particular) are striving to satisfy their own egos can, and should, be a fundamental building block in establishing a way to advertise a product, lay out a store, service a customer, or elicit the desired activity on the part of others. The drive for ego satisfaction constantly asserts itself in connection with all people's desire to gain social acceptance or approval, in their desire to feel superior or to be different, and in their attempts to satisfy various ambitions. Because ego satisfaction, or the drive for it, plays such a significant role in the basic motives of people, the small business operator should design marketing gimmicks, devices, or ideas with the ego satisfaction of customers in mind.

## Buying habits and the small business

The foregoing section has been designed to help small business managers gain a knowledge of what motivates people to buy and so establish their own (nonscientific but practical) motivational research program. It pointed out that motivational research is designed to discover why people buy the things they do, but at the same time recognized that the typical manager has neither the time, money, or knowledge required to make a full-blown study of customers' psyches. Thus, with an eye toward the need for true motivational research, but knowing of the practical limitations imposed upon a small business in doing motivational research, a business can test consumer motivational patterns and buying habits in an effort to determine roughly what motivates customers to buy, how to better lay out a store or an operation, assemble merchandise, and present ads. Although this type of motivational research is at best only a trial-and-error method, it can be an immense aid in determining the habits and buying patterns of customers and clientele. The final fact emerges that, unscientific as it may be, some idea of what motivates customer action is better than no knowledge whatsoever.

## PRODUCT RESEARCH: WHAT TO MAKE AND HOW TO SELL IT

### Essentials of product research

Unlike motivation research, product research is something which the small business can engage in and successfully master with a minimum amount of investment. The need for product research is just as important, if not more important, than the need for motivational research on the part of the small business. While motivation research does give answers to why people buy impulsively, product research is needed to help determine what to offer for sale.

Because of the nature of product research and its more readily quantifiable features, product research can be more "scientifically" designed and more readily adapted to the capabilities of most small business managers. For example, most product research requires complying with the following sequence:

1. *Recognizing that a problem needs resolving.* Product research necessitates first the recognition that a problem exists and needs researching. In other words, the small business manufacturer must know whether to continue making existing products, change the existing products slightly, add new products, drop old products, or develop an entirely new line.

2. *Mapping of the strategy to be used in actually researching the problem which exists.* This step should involve discussion with potential customers or clients, reading trade publications, studying competitor's products, and sampling consumers' opinions.

3. *Gathering whatever factual information is avilable.* This is the key to product research because it requires the amassing of *objective* and *pertinent* information which will help resolve the problems which exist. There are numerous techniques which can be used in fact gathering; most of these entail the actual engagement of the strategies decided upon in Step 2 above.

4. *Interpreting the information which is gathered.* Many times small business managers are duped into thinking that the gathering of the factual information has been informative enough to give a solution. Often, however, the really wise solution is not obvious from the factual information gathered. That is, careful interpretation of the information will often disclose much better solutions than snap judgments.

5. *Making a decision.* Decision-making can be a chore, and deciding whether to sink a large investment in a new product, enter a new line, or provide a new service can be a real headache to small business operators. This step—forcing oneself to be decisive and act on a decision—helps eliminate this headache. However, it should be realized that the key to successful decision-making in product research, even that which is carefully carried through the first four steps, is to be *decisive* and *forceful* in the implementation of a decision. There is never absolute certainty that the correct decision has been made, even if the information available is generally accurate and timely. Thus, although decisiveness and forcefulness of implementation has long been recognized as essential ingredients in decision-making by business leaders, many small business managers become procrastinators when faced with a sizable decision which concerns much time and money investment on their part. Therefore, the fifth step—forcing oneself to be decisive—must be just as carefully followed as any of the preceding steps to product research.

## How to do product research

Although product research can be greatly beneficial in the direction and operation of any firm, many small business managers are reluctant to engage in this activity. Many times they feel it is a "frill" which only the giants can afford or they think they're to inexperienced and unschooled in the statistical methodology required for such research. Such an attitude is unfortunate indeed. While it is true that highly involved product research requires some statistical sophistication, it is also true that many of the giants of industry who have product research departments established with hundreds of employees are fond of stating that their product decisions are possibly right only 52 percent of the time. The point is that even with very sophisticated methodology and research design, all that product research provides by way of information to any business is a "guesstimate" of what decision to make. It is then up to the business managers to see to it that this guesstimate is accurate enough to work.

The small business manager is therefore advised to accept the fact that, although he or she is not a $35,000-a-year research manager for a giant soap manufacturer, he or she may be able to muster the wherewithal required to evaluate whether or not he or she should manufacture both genuine and imitation leather jackets, just one, or neither. Further, he or she should have some confidence that if the research is based on a good sample of intelligent people, it will be almost as accurate as that of the $35,000-a-year researcher in determining if "Glide Flakes" will be recognized as the miracle of miracles for the washing of clothes.

### Specific techniques of product research for the small business

What product research is should be clear in the reader's mind. In order to point out some of the questions and pitfalls which can confront the small business manager who is involved with product research, a specific problem which might be tackled is presented.

*Product leadership.* Product leadership is one example of the problems which are analyzed by product research techniques. Many small business managers have no idea whether to engage in a policy of product leadership or whether to wait and see whether a particular product hits the market and is acceptable to the consumer. In other words, it is the age-old problem of deciding whether to be a leader or a follower in the manufacturing of a new product. In designing a research experiment which will shed light on this particular problem, a small business manager should take the steps previously discussed in the following manner:

1. *Recognition of the problem.* A new product or the possibilities of introducing a new product may occur to the small business. Question: Should that product be offered for sale (or produced)?

2. *Planning the investigation.* Once a problem is recognized, a plan must be designed to determine whether or not product leadership is warranted. All relevant information which will be desired or needed must be outlined, and a plan of attack must be formulated for gathering such information. Relevant information desirable in such a situation might include:

1. Prospective customers' preferences and purchasing power.
2. Stability (or lack of it) of the small business's competitive position.
3. The leadership and prestige sought by the business.

4. The possibility of filling an unmet need.
5. Utilization of some excess production capacity or floor space.
6. Possibility of utilizing waste products or personnel who otherwise have nothing to do for part of the day.
7. Possibility of utilizing materials for a higher value use.
8. The possible retaliatory reaction of competitors.
9. The ability to secure supplies needed to make or market the product.
10. The general practice of the trade as to the frequency of new models.
11. Availability of the necessary channels to distribute the new product.
12. The ideas suggested by potential customers or clients.

All the above questions raise problems which should be answered in determining whether or not the small business should be a product leader.

3. *Information gathering.* The third step is to gather the information which will answer (or at least shed light on) the foregoing problems. This involves talking with suppliers to see if supplies are or can be made available, sampling the customers or clients to see if there would be a demand for the product, evaluating operations to see if the productive capacity and personnel are available, and evaluating personal desires as to whether it is preferable to be a leader (and possible failure) or a follower (and possible Johnny-come-lately).

4. *Interpretation of the data.* The fourth step requires that the information gained from customers, suppliers, in-house personnel, and others, be arranged so that it is meaningful to the small business manager in determining whether or not to market a new product. The information can then be evaluated to see if there is a positive or negative indication toward the desirability of introducing a new product or service, and whether the degree of positivism or negativism is high or low. It might be discovered that the prospective buyer of the new product is highly desirous of purchasing such a product but the feasibility of making such a product because of raw material supply is extremely negative. Confusion then reigns in the manager's mind unless he or she is able to determine whether the lack of materials outweighs the degree of desire for the product or vice versa. Thus, it is important that the information be given rank order during Step 3 of the operation.

5. *Making a decision.* At Step 5 the small business manager makes the decision whether or not to be a product leader. If the research has been successful, it will lead to some conclusion. It is possible that uncertainty will still reign, but at least the manager will know more than he or she did at the beginning of the investigation, and this best "guesstimate" should be better informed than a random hunch. At this stage, however, the small business manager must decide whether to go or not go. Refusal to make a decision is, in fact, a negative decision. The decision which is

made should follow logically from the interpretation and reasoning involved from the preceding steps, even though there would still appear to be several intangibles, such as the weight of one group of factual information compared with another. If the intangibles are numerous, this may indicate a negative decision at this stage, but the decision must be made and it must be enacted forcefully.

Therefore, it should be obvious to the reader that in determining whether or not to introduce a new product by means of the formal steps of product research, the small business manager will never have certain knowledge of what to do; but he or she will be in a much better position to make a decision than before. This circumstance is very similar to the situation which large businesses gravitate toward in making their decisions. While it may be true that large businesses will have much more refined data based on larger samples, they will not necessarily have any more definite an idea of the correctness of their decision than will the small business operator. Only time will tell whether the decision was a good one, and no one will ever know whether there could have been a better decision.

The above procedure can be used by the small business manager in making other product decisions, such as measuring the effectiveness of a particular sales campaign, determining how to adjust to a changing market demand or clientele, determining how to package a product, determining whether the firm has been getting the share of the market it should, and so on. An important point to remember is that any research endeavor designed to determine what to do with a product, how to make it, or where to sell it must be based on experimentation and selection.

## SALES FORECASTING: AN ART OR SCIENCE

It has been stated that the small business will engage in market research to determine why people buy what they do. The logical extension and application of such information is to be able to project or predict sales in the future. After all, research information should not be collected for its own sake. Therefore, it can be said that sales forecasting can be one of the most valuable results of market research; and accurate sales forecasts are always the result of careful market research.

Accurate sales forecasts are essential to the success of any small business. As pointed out in Chapter 14, sales forecasts are the foundation of budget determinations. The level of business activity which the small business is expecting must be determined before financing of the operations can occur. This is largely a function of the expected level of sales. An expected doubling in sales volume will require different financing plans, and so forth, than will an anticipated reduction in sales.

## Using market research information in making sales forecasts

Having good information about why people buy what they buy un-fortunately does not insure that good sales forecasts are made. The reason is that market research fundamentally is historical, while sales forecasts are predictive. That is, motivational, product, and advertising research tells why people are buying what they buy now—not what they will buy in the future. Sales *forecasting*, however, by its very definition, means making an estimate of *why* people will buy *what* in the future. Thus, the sales forecast is a guess about the future, and it is either merely a guess or an educated guess. It is an educated guess when it is based on solid market research information.

## Making the sales forecast

Good sales forecasts are immeasurable in value to the small business for it helps in determining what is to be done, when, and by whom. Good sales forecasts, furthermore, are based upon good market information. Therefore, good sales forecasts are made by (1) analyzing what market information is available as a result of the various marketing research projects conducted by the small business, and (2) estimating on the basis of such analysis, what amount of a product or service will actually be sold over some defined period in the light of existing marketing methods.

There is no problem in analyzing the available data generated by the marketing research project. Thus, Step 1 of making the sales forecast is simple (but limited to the thoroughness and accuracy of the marketing research job). However, Step 2—making the actual estimate—is far more difficult.

Normally, one of two methods are used to make the actual estimate of projected sales.[1] One of these is what is called the *unit forecast* procedure, the other is called the *overall forecast* procedure.

## The unit forecast

The unit forecast procedure of sales forecasting is most often used by manufacturers and sellers of items of high unit cost. Therefore, the unit forecast system is not applicable to many areas of small business opera-

---

[1] It should be recognized that some (often times sloppy) sales forecasts are made on the basis of salesmen's estimates or preceding years' sales. Both these methods are not included because (1) salesmen are notorious for their overoptimism and (2) preceding years' sales are far less valuable as a guideline than is research information, particularly valid research information designed to elicit buyers' future intentions. Nevertheless, these methods can and are being used—sometimes with great success—and thus merit mention for sake of completeness.

tion such as retail stores. However, the small business manager who is operating in a high unit cost field should be familiar with the technique.

The unit forecast procedure is nothing more than an estimate, based on marketing research information, about how many units of a given item will be sold. An example of the use of the unit forecast procedure might be an automobile dealer. The dealer will try to predict how many units (automobiles) will be sold in an upcoming period. The dealer will do so by identifying, on the basis of market research information, the types of people who buy cars, evaluating everybody in this group as to their potential for buying a car from that dealership, and making an estimate of how many will actually buy a car in the sales forecast period. Thus it might be said that the unit forecast procedure is nothing more than the adding up of the number of buyers which the small business expects to have, based on market information as to why people buy what they buy when they buy it.

## The overall forecast procedure

The overall forecast procedure is nearly the exact opposite of the unit forecast procedure. That is, whereas the unit forecast can be considered additive, the overall forecast might be considered subtractive or deductive.

The overall forecast procedure starts with an analysis of overall business conditions. That is, an estimate is made for, say, the total market for automobiles in a particular price level, based on expected business conditions. Then an analysis is made of how much or what percent the individual dealer might be able to get of this total market. This analysis is based, again, on the market research information gleaned by the small business as to who are the prospective buyers, where they come from, what they buy, why they buy it, etc.

Obviously the unit forecast procedure is better for some businesses than is the overall forecast procedure. Basically, which is best depends upon the value of the average unit of sale. Estimates of sales of high-unit-cost items are more likely to be accurate using the unit forecast procedure; low-unit-cost item sales are best projected by breaking down the overall sales picture. Whichever method is used, however, the small business manager must be cautioned to recognize that its accuracy and usefulness will correspond to the care used in assembling the market research information.

## RESEARCH: SMALL BUSINESS'S BOON OR BANE?

So far, this chapter has been designed to give the student of small business operations an idea as to the use of research to obtain information on how the small businessperson should act in running his/her business.

However, the small business manager obviously cannot conduct market research continuously. Thus, it is important to know when one is really in need of research information, and when such information is "nice to have" but rather superfluous.

## When research is a necessity

There are numerous times when additional research information must be gleaned by the small business. In fact, one might logically argue that whenever a decision must be made by the small business, market research information would be highly beneficial to that decision. The question then becomes one of relative necessity. It is, of course, difficult to say for sure when something is an absolute necessity and when it would just be convenient to have. However, there are several situations which can arise in which additional information in respect to the market is needed. These instances might include times when the small business is faced with determining whether or not to produce a particular product; whether to develop or expand into a particular market or market area; whether to produce a product which will require an extremely high investment, inventory, or distribution costs; whether or not to expand production capacity; how to allocate advertising and other promotional efforts; how to determine the proper channels of distribution; or how to allocate or control sales personnel.

The foregoing list is not complete and cannot be used as an absolute guide toward determining when a small business should engage in either motivational research, product research, or advertising research. However, those are the areas in which small businesses seem to have the most difficulty and in which they tend to "lose their shirts" when they make a bad or poor decision. For that reason it would appear that in making decisions relevant to the above question, the small business might consider some marketing research effort as a necessity.

## When research is superfluous

Since it has been indicated that market research is necessary when the decision involves significant cost or other serious implications for the small business, it is easy to assume that any other research information sought by the small business is unnecessary and, therefore, perhaps superfluous. However, such a statement gives little or no guide to the manager who is trying to determine whether or not to spend time and money in research activities.

Most superfluous research activity *becomes* superfluous because of the attitude assumed by the small business researcher. That is, many times small business managers get enamored with researching projects and engage in the research merely for the fun of researching rather than for the information obtained. Clearly such activity is superfluous. However, there are other times when the research appears unessential. This can happen if the researcher is totally ignorant of the principles of research design. For example, some pseudo-researchers have been known to engage in completely unscientific product research. A notorious example is one restaurant owner who had *his* family sample *his* wares in an effort to determine whether or not the general public would enjoy *his* food. Obviously, the results of such study are wholly unreliable and invalid because of bias and familiarity.

Time can also have a bearing on the necessity of marketing research activities. If there is not sufficient or adequate time to conduct a research project in totality, the research is completely invalid. Engaging in a "half-baked" plan is fruitless and may lead to erroneous conclusions and decisions. Another instance that constitutes superfluous research is when insufficient funds are available to do the project right. Again, the results of an improperly funded research study can be misleading and, therefore, damaging. Another instance of worthless marketing research may occur if the small business manager fails to consider the scope of the research project; he or she may be unaware of how much area the study should encompass, or how many people, or how many suppliers.

A marketing research study would also appear pointless if the researcher is limited by his or her personal characteristics or the personal characteristics of assistant researchers. For example, caution is the watchword of the successful market researcher, but many times the inexperienced or uninitiated willingly jump into water over their heads. A good researcher will make no predictions until he or she is relatively sure of the information. However, the poorly trained or uninitiated researcher might antagonize the respondents to a questionnaire, or quickly gloss over salient facts in a report because of being in too big a hurry to reach a conclusion.

A final instance when it would appear that marketing research might be an unrewarding task is when the very objectives of the research project are limited. Such a situation rises when the researcher engages in the research task with foregone conclusions or objectives. Thus, while the small business manager may be working to gain knowledge or information as to what to do or how to act, he or she may have decided subconsciously or covertly what the outcome of the research will be. Obviously the results of such research are worthless. In fact, they may be damaging because the decision was made on hunch or intuition and not on the basis of factual information.

## SUMMARY

Marketing research can be a highly useful tool to the small business if the researcher has a fundamental knowledge of the various sources of information available and knows how these sources of information can be used. In most cases, the small business manager is not a sophisticated researcher and does not have the funds and time available to test out various ideas which might enhance business operations. However, even though the small business operation cannot be expected to compete effectively with big business when it comes to sophisticated research design, he or she is still not precluded from being able to effectively utilize general knowledge which exists in respect to motivation research and product research. From the standpoint of motivation research, the small business manager should simply be willing to experiment with the general principles of motivation which years of experience have developed in motivational research studies. In product research all that is needed is a working knowledge of the five steps of information-gathering and decision-making involved in testing a product.

While the small business manager is therefore well advised not to be too cautious in conducting research experiments in order to determine knowledge needed to make business decisions, he or she should also be apprised of the fact that there are times when research is essential and other times when it is basically nonessential and can be damaging. Most of the dangers involved in engaging in research arise because of various limitations on time, money, know-how, and attitude of the researcher rather than because research knowledge itself is unneeded. It must be recognized that some research is *not* better than no research. Rather, any research study must be clearly thought out and actively pursued from start to finish if it is to be of merit. A sloppy, haphazard research project does more harm than good.

It is up to the small business manager to determine when and if he or she should engage in marketing research and whether that research should be of a motivational, product, or promotional nature. Although marketing research is not a subtle, mysterious activity in which only big companies with lots of money can engage, it must also be recognized that it is not a game.

## QUESTIONS

1. Define marketing research and why it is necessary for the small business.
2. What are the various sources to which the small business might look for market information? What are the problems encountered in using these various sources?
3. The text states that marketing research information is useful in making price, product, place, and promotional decisions. How is this so? Use examples.
4. What are "impulse items"? What is "shopper's vision"? Explain what these terms mean and how they are useful.
5. What would you suggest are principles of motivational behavior which the

small business might use in making decisions about how to determine and appeal to people's whims?

6. What is product research? Explain in detail.
7. How might a small business operator decide whether or not to be a product leader? Give an example.
8. How is sales forecasting tied to market research? What are the general forms of sales forecasting methods?
9. How can the small business manager determine how much research to do? How can he or she tell if too much has been done? Explain what would be an ideal amount for an automobile dealer.
10. Write an essay about the statement: "Some research is no better than no research."

## PROBLEM

Develop statistics to support or reject one of your classmate's ideas that Our Town (the town in which your school/college is located) needs one of the following businesses:
1. A Rolls Royce distributorship
2. A fireplace equipment and supply store
3. An airline ticket office
4. A bait shop

Be sure to give detailed data as to the volume of business that could be expected, what competition is in existence or potentially exists, and what that competition might be expected to do. Also assess what and how prospective customers might react to your store opening.

## BIBLIOGRAPHY

Brown, W. E. "Research Project Selection: Part III." *The Creativity Review* vol. 15, no. 3 (August 1973), pp. 2–14. A study of the differing attitudes toward research in smaller companies.

*Businessman's Information Guide.* New York: American Institute of Certified Public Accountants, 1972, 103 pp. A basic information and data guide.

"Competing with the Big Boys." *Industry Week*, July 24, 1972, pp. 46–48. Millionaire's advice on how to make it on your own.

Havelock, R. G. *Planning for Innovation.* Ann Arbor, Mich.: Institute for Social Sciences Research, University of Michigan, 1970. Basic report on innovation and business.

Weaver, Peter. *You, Inc.* New York: Doubleday, 1973. This work looks at you and your business.

# 25

# The management
# of credit sales

One of the more important questions the small business manager must consider is whether customers should be offered credit. The answer depends on a number of factors surrounding the firm's operation. The first factor is whether credit sales are customary in the firm's particular line of business. If so, failure to offer credit could put the business at a competitive disadvantage.

Other important considerations involve the investment necessary to carry credit sales; the type of credit terms to offer; the type of credit analysis to be used in the selection of credit customers; the use of service charges; and the establishment of a systematic and efficient collection system. This chapter considers these various questions and provides a practical approach to managing a credit sales program.

## THE CREDIT SALES DECISION

The decision to establish a credit program involves comparing the earnings on working capital tied up in credit sales with the earnings the funds would produce if they were invested elsewhere. The credit program can only be justified if the benefits exceed the costs. The costs of credit must include the interest charge on any borrowed funds tied up in accounts receivable, as well as the cost of administering credit policy.

When the question of cost versus benefit is considered, many small businesses may be unable to offer credit. For instance, the manager may find it impossible to maintain adequate working capital to support desirable inventory levels and, at the same time, support a credit sales program. In such a case it may be illogical to cut back inventory stocks to finance credit sales.

If the decision is made to establish a credit sales program and the funds are available to finance it, the problem is determining the appro-

441

priate credit terms. This involves determining the credit period and the desirability of offering discount terms to customers for early payment. In deciding what credit terms to offer, it is important to consider the nature of the product or service.

The desirability of a service charge is also an important question. How will a service charge influence sales volume? Will any loss of credit sales because of the service charge be offset by the income resulting from the service charge, plus the earnings on the working capital released from accounts receivable?

Each of the above factors demands serious consideration before the credit decision is made. Although some control over the level of receivables is possible through the rejection and acceptance procedures, and through efficient collection procedures, once the decision has been made to offer credit it is difficult to reverse.

## Controlling the level of credit sales

Controlling the level of credit sales involves determining the quality of credit applicant to accept and the investigative procedures to be used in examining each applicant.

First, consider the quality of the credit applicant to be accepted. As credit customers are accepted, each makes some incremental addition to income, and to expenditures. Thus, the added income must be compared with the added costs. The costs include additional production, administrative, selling, and collection expenses resulting from the credit sales. The increase in costs may be significant, based on the assumption that total demand will increase if credit sales, as well as cash sales, are made.

In theory, credit sales should be added as long as the marginal benefit exceeds the marginal cost. This principle is applied by first determining the amount of additional sales that are produced by accepting a particular group of credit customers, minus the percent of bad debts generated within the group. This result equals the additional revenue produced by the group. Next, additional production, administrative, and selling costs, plus any collection expenses, equals the additional expenditures. The additional revenues minus the additional expenditures equal the net incremental income resulting from the credit sales.

A word of caution is appropriate at this point. Although the marginal principle sounds good in theory; its application is somewhat subjective, and requires sound judgment and experience in the analysis of customers. In addition, there are one or two more subtle questions that must be answered in deciding on the quality of credit applicant to accept. One, is to determine the level of operations necessary to support a particular volume of credit sales, and also any costs that may be associated with increased sales. For instance, in manufacturing there are different sets of incremental or marginal costs at different levels of production. In retailing there are the costs associated with hiring additional sales personnel as credit sales expand, and additional investments in inventory and space.

This means the credit policy of the firm should be flexible, and vary with the level of sales activity. As sales volume decreases in a recessionary period, the manager may go to the marginal credit risk to maintain an acceptable sales volume. On the other hand, as economic conditions improve and sales volume approaches capacity, the manager can be more selective in accepting credit customers.

## TYPES OF CREDIT ARRANGEMENTS AND CREDIT TERMS

The credit investigation procedure used to determine the credit worthiness of applicants depends on the type of credit being extended. There are two classes of credit: *Consumer credit* and *trade credit*. Trade credit is extended by manufacturers and wholesalers to retail establishments, and involves the financing of goods for resale. Consumer credit is granted by retailers to the consumer, who is purchasing for personal or family use. The type of credit that is being offered is important because it dictates the kinds of information available, and the kinds of information desired for an adequate evaluation of the credit applicant.

On the *trade credit* side, goods are usually purchased on an open-book basis; subject to specific terms of sale such as 2/10 net 30. This means that a two percent discount is given by the seller if the buyer pays within ten days. Failure to take the discount within the first ten days, makes the full amount of the invoice due with thirty days. Other possible discount arrangements in common use today appear in Figure 25–1.

Another type of trade credit involves the use of extended datings, common in seasonal selling. By using extended dating, the manufacturer gives the retailer time to obtain funds for payment through resale of the goods. An extended dating program also eliminates the problem of inventory storage at the manufacturing site. An extended dating arrangement simply defers the buyer's payments. For example, payments due on an invoice may be 10 percent after 30 days; 20 percent after 60 days; and the remainder after 120 days. Or, the terms may be 2/10 net 30 with dating from 90 days after the date of sale.

The particular trade credit terms used by the manufacturer depends on the type of product; competitive conditions; and the buyers' and sellers' circumstances. The credit period will normally vary directly with the length of the buyer's inventory turnover period, which depends on the type of product. However, if the seller determines the individual sales terms of each customer, the larger the customer's order and the better the

FIGURE 25–1
Trade credit sales terms

| Sales Term | Explanation |
|---|---|
| 3/10, 1/15, n/60 | Three percent discount for the first 10 days; 1 percent discount for 15 days; bill due net on 60th day. |
| 2/10, n/30, R.O.G. | Two percent discount for 10 days; bill due net on 30th day—but both discount period and 30 days start from the date of receipt of the goods, not from the date of the sale. |
| 2/10, n/30, M.O.M. | Two percent discount for 10 days; bill due net on 30th day—but both periods start from the 15th of the month following the sales date. |
| 2/10, n/30, E.O.M. | Two percent discount for 10 days; bill due net on 30th day—but both periods start from the end of the month in which the sale was made. |
| 2/10, 60 EX | Two percent discount for 10 days; bill due date extended for so many days after the 60-day term allowed. |
| 2/10, PROX. | Terms of 2/10, PROX. in reality are no different from 2/10 E.O.M. E.O.M. is used as the designation of such terms in the textile industry, while PROX. is more generally used in the wholesale grocery line and in the sale of automobile tires. |
| M.O.M. | Billing will be on the 15th of the month, including all purchases made since the middle of the prior month. |
| E.O.M. | Billing at end of month, covering all credit purchases of that month. |
| C.O.D. | Amount of bill will be collected upon delivery of the goods. |

credit standing, the more generous the sales terms. Of course, the seller's sales terms are limited to some extent by financial strength and the liquidity of working capital.

Generally speaking, the manager cannot afford to allow competition to have the advantage in the generosity of sales terms. Furthermore, in many product lines, credit terms are so firmly set by tradition there is little choice other than to conform.

There are four major types of *consumer credit* accounts offered at the retail level: the *ordinary charge account,* the *installment account,* the *budget account,* and the *revolving credit arrangement.* In any particular case, the most desirable account to use will depend upon the type of merchandise, the customer's financial position and income, and the customer's ability to budget expenditures.

An ordinary charge account involves charging for merchandise when purchased, with payment due when the bill is sent to the customer. Typical terms call for payment at the end of the month; but a longer period is allowed if the customer desires an extended payment period. Normally 30-day cash terms are offered; and if the account goes beyond, a service charge is assessed. The ordinary charge account is best suited for frequent family purchases in department stores.

The consumer installment account is most often used in large purchases, such as automobiles, appliances, and furniture, where payment must be spread over a long period of time. A down payment of 10 to 30 percent is normally required, and service charges are added to the cost. The payment period extends from 90 days to 36 months. A service charge of as much as 1½ percent per month on the unpaid balance is typical.

In selling on the installment basis, the credit is usually secured by a chattel mortgage or a conditional sales contract. Both of these arrangements permit the seller to repossess the goods if the customer defaults a payment. Under a chattel mortgage, legal title to the goods passes when the sale is made, but is subject to the seller's lien. When a payment is defaulted the seller can then take court action to repossess the goods. Under the conditional sales contract, legal title does not pass until the buyer makes the last payment; hence immediate repossession is possible when a payment is defaulted.

The consumer budget account is a short-term installment account resulting from charge purchases in amounts typically ranging from $100 to $200. Payment is ordinarily spread over 60 to 120 days, and a service charge is normally added to the price.

Finally, the consumer may be offered a revolving credit account, which is simply another variation of the installment account. A line of credit is granted up to $1,500 or $2,000, and the customer can charge purchases at any time, if the total purchases do not exceed the credit limit given. The buyer must pay a specified percent of the outstanding credit balance monthly, and the interest charge is computed on the unpaid balance at the end of each month. The revolving credit account has the advantage of forcing the consumer to budget; and limits the amount of debt to be carried.

## INVESTIGATION OF THE CREDIT APPLICANT

The credit investigation procedure involves an analysis of costs and benefits. The manager must decide how much time and effort can be spent in analyzing credit worthiness. In adopting a format for analysis, the important relationship is between the time and cost of the analysis, and credit losses. Furthermore, in conducting each investigation the manager must recognize the great importance of time to both parties.

### Sources of credit information

There are a number of sources of credit information that can be used in making the credit decision. Their use will depend upon the time and money available for the investigation.

First, consider the sources of credit information that apply in the extension of consumer credit. In retailing, the first step is to develop a credit application form. An example appears in Figure 25–2.

The credit application will provide all of the basic information necessary for an analysis of the applicant's financial responsibility, and together with information from a local credit bureau or from the customer's banker, will make up the data to be used in the final decision.

The information acquired in the credit application needs no explanation. It is appropriate, however, to discuss the services that a local credit bureau can offer. The credit bureau is an organization supported by its members, who are usually retailers. The basic objectives of the credit bureau is to summarize the credit experience of the various bureau members with particular consumers in the community. In addition, the local bureau may be affiliated with either the National Retail Credit Association or the Associated Credit Bureaus of America, and thus be able to offer credit information on persons who move from one city to another.

One of the important functions of the local credit bureau is to provide credit reports. The report will normally contain a listing of the credit accounts maintained by the applicant, the length of time these accounts have been maintained, the date of the last purchase, the balance due, and the promptness of payment. In addition, the report will indicate the applicant's income and income sources, whether the home is owned or rented, employment data, and a character evaluation.

Another function of the credit bureau is to investigate newcomers to the city, in anticipation of requests for credit data. Notification service is also provided to the member firms which warns them against certain customers that have become poor credit risks in the community. Finally, the local credit bureau can offer valuable assistance in tracing local debtors who have moved from the city without leaving forwarding information, and can assist in the collection of past-due accounts. Most of these local credit bureau services do not require membership for use, but the fees charged for services to nonmembers are considerably higher than those charged to members.

The other source of credit information that usually proves valuable is the banker. This source may be limited, however, because not all bankers will supply credit information about their depositors and borrowers. Many feel such information is confidential and should not be disclosed.

In the extension of trade credit, much more detailed information about the credit applicant is available. First, there are a number of privately operated trade credit agencies which collect credit information on business firms. These data are analyzed and evaluated; then the agency publishes credit ratings that are available to subscribers for a fee. A credit agency may be involved only with a particular line of business, or may be more general in nature, such as Dun & Bradstreet.

# FIGURE 25-2
## ABC store credit application form

NAME_____Phone_____

| | City and | Years at This |
ADDRESS_____State_____Street Address__

Previous
Address_____City and
State_____Years There__

Wife's or
Age__Married__Single__Divorced__Widowed__Dependents__Husband's Name_____

Nearest Relative
Not Living with You_____Relation_____Address_____City and
State_____

EMPLOYED BY:_____ Position_____No. of Years_____
(If in business for self, give firm name)

Address_____ Immediate Superior_____Phone_____

Previous
Employer_____Address_____From_____To_____

Draft Previous Military
Status_____Branch of Service_____From_____To_____

Week        Other        Week
INCOME: Salary $_____Month . . . Income $_____Month . . . Source_____

Wife's or        Week        Years
Husband's Income $.. __Month . . . Employed by_____Phone_____There_____

*OBLIGATIONS: I owe the following banks, mortgage companies, loan and finance com-
panies, and store accounts, medical and other bills and NO others: (If none, so state)

| To Whom Owing | Address | Unpaid Balance | Monthly Payments | Amount to be Paid by this Loan |
|---|---|---|---|---|
| _____ | _____ | $_____ | $_____ | $_____ |
| _____ | _____ | _____ | _____ | _____ |
| _____ | _____ | _____ | _____ | _____ |
| _____ | _____ | _____ | _____ | _____ |

*(If no obligations are owing, give three references above with whom you have had credit dealings, preferably installment credit.)

Real Estate Owned_____Title in Name of_____

Present    Total                                          Monthly
Value $____Mortgage $____Held by_____Payments . $____

Per
Rent from_____Address_____Month . . . $____

Checking
Bank with_____Savings . . . Life Insurance Carried $____Cash Value $____

Automobile Owned: Year____Make____Owing $____To_____

I am not now a co-maker or endorser on any other loans except_____
I have had no suits, judgments, garnishments, or other legal proceedings, except_____

I have not obtained credit, nor intend to obtain credit, elsewhere to make the above purchase, except____

Send Mail To:

Residence____ Business____

First Payment

To Start_____ ☞ SIGN HERE_____

I hereby certify that the above statements are true and correct and are made to obtain a loan from this bank. I agree to notify the bank concerning any material change in my financial condition. I authorize you to obtain any information you may require, and agree that this application shall remain the property of the bank whether the loan is granted or not.

CREDIT BUREAU REPORT FINDINGS_____

TRADE REFERENCES_____

SALES TERMS_____

Dun & Bradstreet is the most well-known credit concern in the United States, with over 100 years of experience in the field of credit reporting. Of primary importance among its many services, are its reference books and written credit reports. The reference book is published six times a year. Through a system of letters, numbers, and symbols, it provides credit information, and Dun & Bradstreet's estimate of the credit standing of the firm.

If additional material is needed, a credit report is obtained. It provides detailed information on the payment record the prospective customer has established with other suppliers; the highest amount of credit that a particular supplier has extended; the amount currently owed to each particular supplier; the promptness with which the customer is making payments; and whether or not the prospective customer has been discounting. The data provided in the written credit report are based on the ledger experience of creditors of the particular company in question.

Data and materials supplied by a local credit bureau may also help in making a trade credit decision. The National Association of Credit Managers operates a credit interchange service. Participating firms provide their local bureaus with listings of their customers. Then when an inquiry is received about the payment habits of some particular company, the bureau acquires reports from each of the firm's suppliers and prepares a summary. The reports are available on both a local and national level.

The banker may be a valuable source of credit information at the trade credit level also. Through the correspondent banking system, commercial banks throughout the nation regularly exchange credit information. For example, suppose a small firm in Denver receives an order from a new customer in Phoenix. Desirous of credit information on the Phoenix customer, the Denver manager approaches his banker and requests that he contact his Phoenix correspondent. It is very likely that credit information on the Phoenix firm can be secured through the correspondent bank network. In fact, firms in smaller communities often can get credit information by using their local bank to go through a chain of four or five banks. The availability of this type of service is another reason why a good banking relationship is so vital to a small business.

It may be that salespeople, with proper training, can be relied upon to provide useful credit information. They may be asked to make periodic reports concerning particular customers as they see them. For instance, by observing the various brands stocked on the retailer's shelves, the salesperson can provide the names of other suppliers. These suppliers can then be contacted to learn of their credit experience with the customer.

In the extension of trade credit, an analysis of financial statement information is important. The latest balance sheets and income statements should be obtained directly from the customer. If the customer is somewhat hesitant in offering the information, the manager should explain that he or she refuses credit to any concern that does not provide its financial statements upon request.

In collecting financial information, the most current statement is not enough; because much of the analysis is based on a comparison of values appearing in the balance sheet and income statement from one period to another. Thus, it is appropriate to obtain the financial statements of the last three or four periods.

A spread sheet will put the financial statement information in a more workable form. An example appears in Figure 25–3. The spread sheet provides space for both recording and analyzing financial information. The spread sheet illustrated is rather detailed; and a more simplified statement may be adequate in some cases. However, regardless of detail, the objective remains the same: to adopt a basic format in the organization and analysis of credit information.

Finally, the manager may find useful credit information from such sources as Better Business Bureaus, Chambers of Commerce, attorneys, trade associations, and the nationally published investment manuals. But regardless of the type and number of sources used, the time and effort expended in the credit analysis function must be consistent with the benefits of the credit analysis program.

## Other credit analysis information

If the manager finds that a large percent of total sales involve a relatively few customers, a more extensive analysis of each customer may be desired. The following paragraphs illustrate the types of information that may be valuable.

1. *Organization and history.* The legal form of organization may be important. Is the customer's business a sole proprietorship, partnership, or corporation? If it's a corporation, the number of shareholders and the distribution of ownership among the shareholders may be important. In a partnership, any formal agreements between the partners and the names of the principal officers and partners are important. In addition to the form of organization, it may be wise for the manager to request a brief history of the firm.

2. *The production function.* The manager should be familiar with the particular products or service offered by the prospective customer. In addition, the names of other suppliers may be important. Finally, the manager may be interested in the prospective customer's physical plant and equipment, whether it is owned or leased, and whether insurance coverage is adequate.

3. *Sales.* The prospective customer's sales experience is important.

**FIGURE 25–3**

Credit information spread sheet

| ASSETS | Date Source | | | | | | | | | |
|---|---|---|---|---|---|---|---|---|---|---|
| Cash | | | | | | | | | | |
| U.S. government securities | | | | | | | | | | |
| | | | | | | | | | | |
| Accounts receivable—trade | | | | | | | | | | |
| Reserve for bad debts | | | | | | | | | | |
| Net receivables | | | | | | | | | | |
|    Total Quick Assets | | | | | | | | | | |
| | | | | | | | | | | |
| Inventory | | | | | | | | | | |
| | | | | | | | | | | |
| Cash value life insurance | | | | | | | | | | |
| Other current assets | | | | | | | | | | |
|    Total Current Assets | | | | | | | | | | |
| | | | | | | | | | | |
| Land | | | | | | | | | | |
| Buildings | | | | | | | | | | |
| Leasehold improvements | | | | | | | | | | |
| Machinery and equipment | | | | | | | | | | |
| Reserve for depreciation | | | | | | | | | | |
|    Net Fixed Assets | | | | | | | | | | |
| | | | | | | | | | | |
| | | | | | | | | | | |
| Prepaid items | | | | | | | | | | |
| Investment and advances affiliates | | | | | | | | | | |
| Intangibles: Goodwill, etc. | | | | | | | | | | |
| | | | | | | | | | | |
| Other noncurrent assets | | | | | | | | | | |
|    Total Assets | | | | | | | | | | |
| **LIABILITIES** | | | | | | | | | | |
| Notes payable banks | | | | | | | | | | |
| Current maturities—long-term debt | | | | | | | | | | |
| Notes payable—other | | | | | | | | | | |
| Notes payable—officers and employees | | | | | | | | | | |
| | | | | | | | | | | |
| Accounts payable trade | | | | | | | | | | |
| | | | | | | | | | | |
| | | | | | | | | | | |
| Accrued expenses | | | | | | | | | | |
| Federal income tax accrual | | | | | | | | | | |
| | | | | | | | | | | |
|    Total Current Liabilities | | | | | | | | | | |
| Long-term debt | | | | | | | | | | |
| | | | | | | | | | | |
| | | | | | | | | | | |
|    Total Liabilities | | | | | | | | | | |
| | | | | | | | | | | |
| | | | | | | | | | | |
| Net worth—partnership or proprietor | | | | | | | | | | |
| Capital stock—preferred | | | | | | | | | | |
| Capital stock—common | | | | | | | | | | |
| Capital or paid-in surplus | | | | | | | | | | |
| Earned surplus | | | | | | | | | | |
| | | | | | | | | | | |
| Treasury stock | | | | | | | | | | |
|    Total Net Worth | | | | | | | | | | |
|    Total Liabilities and Net Worth | | | | | | | | | | |
| | | | | | | | | | | |
| Current assets | | | | | | | | | | |
| Current liabilities | | | | | | | | | | |
|    Net Working Capital | | | | | | | | | | |
| Current ratio | | | | | | | | | | |
| Quick ratio | | | | | | | | | | |
| Net Worth to debt | | | | | | | | | | |
| Sales to receivables | | | | | | | | | | |
| Cost of sales to inventory | | | | | | | | | | |
| Percentage earnings to beginning | | | | | | | | | | |
|    net worth | | | | | | | | | | |
| Net sales | | | | | | | | | | |
| Net profits | | | | | | | | | | |
| Annual provision for depreciation | | | | | | | | | | |
| Officers' salaries | | | | | | | | | | |
| Dividends or withdrawals | | | | | | | | | | |
| Contingent liabilities | | | | | | | | | | |

**FIGURE 25–3** (*continued*)

| | Date | | | | | | | |
|---|---|---|---|---|---|---|---|---|
| | Source | | | | | | | |
| **ANALYSIS WORKING CAPITAL** | | | | | | | | |
| Beginning balance working capital | | | | | | | | |
| Net profit (loss) | | | | | | | | |
| Depreciation, amortization, and depletion | | | | | | | | |
| Increase long–term debt | | | | | | | | |
| Other factors | | | | | | | | |
| | | | | | | | | |
| Total additions | | | | | | | | |
| Dividends: Withdrawals | | | | | | | | |
| Additions to fixed assets | | | | | | | | |
| Reduction long–term debt | | | | | | | | |
| Other factors | | | | | | | | |
| | | | | | | | | |
| Total deductions | | | | | | | | |
| Net increase or (decrease) | | | | | | | | |
| Working Capital End of the Period | | | | | | | | |
| | | | | | | | | |
| **ANALYSIS EARNED SURPLUS** | | | | | | | | |
| Balance beginning of the period | | | | | | | | |
| Net profit (loss) for period | | | | | | | | |
| | | | | | | | | |
| Total additions | | | | | | | | |
| Dividends—preferred | | | | | | | | |
| Dividends—common | | | | | | | | |
| | | | | | | | | |
| Total deductions | | | | | | | | |
| Net increase or (decrease) | | | | | | | | |
| Balance End of the Period | | | | | | | | |
| | | | | | | | | |
| **INCOME STATEMENT (DOLLARS)** | | | | | | | | |
| Gross sales | | | | | | | | |
| Returns and allowances | | | | | | | | |
| Net sales | | | | | | | | |
| Cost of sales | | | | | | | | |
| Gross profit (loss) | | | | | | | | |
| Operating expense—selling expense | | | | | | | | |
| gen. and admin. expense | | | | | | | | |
| officers' salaries | | | | | | | | |
| | | | | | | | | |
| Total operating expenses | | | | | | | | |
| Net profit (loss) from operations | | | | | | | | |
| Other income | | | | | | | | |
| Other expense | | | | | | | | |
| Net profit before federal income tax | | | | | | | | |
| Federal income tax | | | | | | | | |
| Net Profit (Loss) | | | | | | | | |
| Dividends—withdrawals | | | | | | | | |
| **INCOME STATEMENT (PERCENT)** | | | | | | | | |
| Net sales | | | | | | | | |
| Cost of sales | | | | | | | | |
| Gross profit (loss) | | | | | | | | |
| Operating expense—selling expense | | | | | | | | |
| gen. and admin. expense | | | | | | | | |
| officer's salaries | | | | | | | | |
| | | | | | | | | |
| Total operating expenses | | | | | | | | |
| Net profit (loss) from operations | | | | | | | | |
| Other income | | | | | | | | |
| Other expense | | | | | | | | |
| Net profit before federal income tax | | | | | | | | |
| Federal income tax | | | | | | | | |
| Net Profit (Loss) | | | | | | | | |

This involves a familiarity with the applicant's marketing area, the number of customers, and the sales volume with the largest customers. Also important may be the terms of sale offered by the applicant, the backlog of orders, and the lead time necessary to fill an order.

4. *Reputation and prospects.* The prospective customer's position in the industry and the competition he or she faces may be important. Also of interest are industrial trends in new product development; and the growth potential of the prospective customer. Although the applicant's initial purchases may not be large, increases in sales volume may be anticipated as new products are developed and the business grows.

5. *Management.* When one customer represents a relatively large percentage of total sales, the experience of the customer's managerial staff is important. Who are the major officers in the firm, what is their background, and has the question of successor management been resolved? Also of interest is the number of employees, their union affiliation, and the status of the union contract.

6. *Financial.* In addition to an analysis of the information gathered from the financial statements, there are a number of other financial questions to answer before making the credit decision. It may be important to know if the assets are pledged or assigned; the date of the last federal tax clearance; the names of the prospective customer's accountant, banker, and attorney; and whether the prospective customer is affiliated with any other business firms.

The foregoing discussion suggests a rather detailed approach in reaching the credit decision. Although this was intentional, the manager must decide how much time and effort can be spent with each individual applicant in determining the organization and format to be used in gathering credit information.

## THE SUBJECTIVE SIDE OF THE CREDIT DECISION

Once all the information and data desired about the prospective customer have been gathered, the credit decision depends on analytical ability and good judgment. In making the decision, the manager must keep one point in mind: People, not dollars, pay bills. Thus, some attention should be given to examining the credit applicant in terms of what are known as the "four C's of credit": character, capacity, capital, and the conditions of business.

In naming the factors essential to a satisfactory risk, most experienced credit analysts cite character as the most important. There must be a willingness to pay as well as a determination to pay; and the determination to pay varies directly with character.

Character alone, however, is not sufficient for the extension of credit.

Character is a moral endowment, incapable of doing more than directing the force found in capacity and capital. In attempting to appraise character, the manager usually ends up looking at the customer's reputation. The distinction between the two, however, is considerable. Character is within the person, while reputation is in the minds of others. The danger, then, is that those who are responsible for the person's reputation may have erred in their appraisal.

In summary, the best advice is to learn everything possible about the prospective customer's past. Personal habits, manner of living, amusements, environment, and the person's business code of ethics are important.

Capacity, like character, is an intangible factor for which there is no unit of measurement. The appraisal of it, therefore, is comparable. In a sole proprietorship, capacity of the firm may be found solely in one man; but in a partnership or corporation, the managerial ability of many may be considered.

Capacity is both physical and mental. The age of the credit applicant is significant, for it indicates both physical stamina and experience. Energy, aggressiveness, ambition, shrewdness, and judgment should be taken into consideration in evaluating capacity. Also, important are executive ability, general education and training, and general business methods.

In terms of capacity, there are two basic classes of credit applicants: those who have demonstrated their capacity or lack of it; and those who are just beginning in business and have yet to reveal their capacity to run a firm. In summary, capacity and character go hand in hand. The person who possesses character, having a will to pay and capacity, will find a means to pay.

The capital factors is typically given more attention than the character and capacity factors because capital is tangible; a unit of measurement. Capital means the financial strength of the credit applicant. Capital is the amount of money the applicant has at risk in the business. Not only is quantity important, but the nature of the assets in which the capital is invested is also significant.

Capital is the dollars the prospective customer holds out as a guarantee that a credit transaction entered into will be redeemed. Capital represents the extent to which losses resulting from error in business judgment, or adverse business conditions, can be absorbed. The extent of the applicant's capital as well as how it was acquired are important. Was it acquired through the successful operation of the business or by some other means?

In addition to the consideration of character, capacity, and capital, general business conditions must be reviewed. The amount of credit a seasonal business may advantageously use varies with the time of the season.

In considering changes in economic conditions, the manager must look at the general movement of business, as well as the status of the particular business or industry under review. Credit conditions may be generally good in a particular firm, while the status of the industry as a whole may be bad. Or conditions in a certain industry may be good, when general economic conditions are poor.

## MAKING THE CREDIT DECISION

Foremost in the mind of the person involved in the credit decision should be that time is of the essence. This is true for both parties. Once all the necessary information has been collected, the manager owes it to the credit applicant to reach a decision within a relatively short time.

In the case of rejection, it may be that alternative credit terms to those that were applied for can be offered. A clear understanding of the decision by the applicant will avoid stirring up resentment in a credit rejection. Once the decision has been made, the manager must abide by the decision and not be swayed by the prospective customer's pleas for reconsideration.

## COLLECTION PROCEDURE

A systematic means of collection is just as important as a systematic approach to the credit investigation. Once again it is a cost-benefit type of analysis. Ten dollars cannot be spent in the collection of five dollars. The problem is determining just how much pressure should be exerted on customers that are slow paying. Furthermore, the effect of collection procedures on future sales must be considered. Regardless of the collection procedures employed, the manager must avoid becoming known as a "soft touch." The solution is to formulate a clear-cut, reasonable collection plan to be followed in every case without exception. The following discusses such a plan and the various collection tools that have been found to be most effective.

### The customer invoice

The collection procedure should begin with the mailing of the customer invoice at the time the goods are shipped. The invoice informs the customer of the exact amount of total charges and the due date. If a discount is offered on the merchandise for early payment and taken, or if the invoice is paid at maturity, no other collection instrument is necessary. However, the purchaser may not recognize the customer invoice as a collection instrument; hence, the next step in the collection procedure may be necessary.

## The statement

The second step consists of mailing a statement of account to the customer. The statement serves as a reminder to the customer of payments due; and also reconciles the records of the seller and the buyer.

There are three generally accepted methods of handling the statement. First, it may be sent to all customers once a month, regardless of whether there are items due. A second approach is to mail the statements on the first of the month only to those accounts which are already delinquent. A third plan is to mail monthly statements only to those customers who request it.

If the statement is to be used as a payment reminder, it should be mailed on the first day of the month to secure the best results. Furthermore, as an inducement to pay promptly, the terms of payment should be printed prominently on the statement. If an account is delinquent, it is quite a common practice to add a collection appeal by means of a rubber stamp or gummed reminder such as "past due," "please remit," or "kindly send us your check."

## Use of the collection letter

If the customer invoice and the statement of account fail to bring payment, it becomes necessary to use some sort of collection letter. The collection letter is probably the most used tool in the collection procedure; and the most economical and satisfactory method of collecting past-due accounts.

The manager must avoid being offensive in the letter, and at the same time indicate the intention to collect. Regardless of how the collection letter is composed, it has two basic objectives: (1) to let the debtor know the bill must be paid; and (2) to retain the debtor's goodwill. Some use a series of three letters. The first is a reminder; the second more firm; and the last promises drastic action.

## Collections and the telephone

If the collection letter fails, consider direct contact by the telephone. The telephone has certain distinct advantages as a collection instrument. First, it is more definite than the letter, because it brings an answer. The letter can be ignored, but the debtor can hardly refuse to promise a check, or give a reason for not doing so over the telephone.

The primary disadvantage of the telephone is that the manager must still rely on the debtor's promise. The second disadvantage is the difficulty that may be encountered in contacting the debtor, for it may be that he or she simply refuses to talk on the phone.

## Use of the telegram

A number of businesses have been successful in using the telegram as a collection tool. The telegram implies some degree of urgency and has the distinct advantage of getting the debtor's immediate attention. Furthermore, by the time the manager gets to the point of using a telegram, he or she will probably want to use a much stronger appeal. Thus, it is customary to state that the account is overdue and will be referred to an attorney, or to even threaten a civil suit. The telegraph company will have suggested wording available for collection appeals.

## The personal contact

If all collection tools fail, an attempt should be made to establish personal contact with the debtor. If the volume of slow-paying accounts is large enough, the manager may hire an individual solely for the purpose of making these contacts. Although the personal call is often effective, it has the disadvantage of being expensive.

If the manager cannot afford the services of a personal collector, salespeople may be used if properly trained. In fact, in some lines of business it is almost imperative that salespeople act as collector. For instance, the wholesaler selling to retail grocery stores should place full responsibility for collections on the sales force. The salesperson calls on the customer once a week, and the goods bought one week are paid for the next. If payment is not forthcoming, credit is discontinued. This plan has worked well because the individual placing the order is the same individual who writes the check.

Placing the salesperson in the role of collector does have certain disadvantages. First, the salesperson may feel that chances of selling a customer lessen if he or she also plays the part of collector. Furthermore, the salesperson may feel less welcome because the customer has in mind the debt due. This may lead to more conservative buying, and thus lower sales volume.

## Use of the collection agency

Once the manager has exhausted all internal efforts to collect, the account should be referred to a collection agency or an attorney. Both use basically the same procedure.

The advantage of using a collection agency is largely psychological.

Debtors who are habitually slow paying know that creditors themselves are rarely in a position to force collections. Thus, as long as the account remains under the creditor's control, the debtor has nothing to fear. But the situation changes once the account passes to a third party. The debtor knows that the collection agency's only interest in the account is to get payment and earn the commission. Thus, referring an account to a collection agency or an attorney is the creditor's ultimatum. All friendly relations are terminated.

Care should be taken in the selection of a collection agency. The laws relating to collection agency practices do not offer much protection to the creditor, and an agency that is temporarily hard-pressed for funds is tempted to use the creditor's money. Two safeguards that are commonly used in working with the collection agency are ( 1 ) to be sure that the monies collected be carried in a separate bank account from the private funds of the agency, and ( 2 ) to insist that the agency be adequately bonded.

The local attorney is often used by collection agencies in smaller communities, where the agency does not maintain an office. The usual procedure is for the collection agency to make attempts to collect via the mails. When these efforts fail, the account is forwarded to a local attorney who continues the pressure by letter, by telephone, or by personal contact. The local attorney has an influence not possessed by the creditor or the collection agency. Because the lawyer is in a position to start suit at any time, the debtor senses the harm which may be done to his credit reputation.

When the account is forwarded directly to the attorney by the collection agency, the manager will have no direct contact with the local attorney. On the other hand, a lawyer may be used to collect under the direct supervision of the creditor. The advantage of dealing directly with an attorney is that he or she may work harder for collection if he or she is to receive the full fee. When a claim is received through a collection agency, the fee is split. The one disadvantage in using an attorney is the cost involved.

## The charge-off of bad debts

Considerable difference is found among firms in the practice of charging off customer accounts never collected. The problem is to determine those accounts which are to be considered as lost. Who within the business firm is to decide when an account is uncollectible, and when the charge to bad debts should be made? The person most qualified is the credit manager, if the firm has an employee with such a title.

Regardless of the procedure used, accounts receivable should be cleared of all bad accounts before the books are closed for the period.

## SMALL BUSINESS AND THE CREDIT MANAGEMENT FUNCTION

As previously noted, in the small business firm the volume of credit sales may not justify the position of credit manager. However, in those cases where the position of credit manager exists, there must be a clear definition of functions.

If the credit manager is responsible to the treasurer of the firm, sales volume and profits may suffer because of a natural tendency for treasurers to be conservative. On the other hand, making the credit manager responsible to the general sales manager often proves undesirable because the sales manager tends to be optimistic about borderline credit risks. The preferred case is to have the credit manager in an independent position, so he or she may be objective and impartial in decisions about credit risks.

## QUESTIONS

1. In an economic sense, the decision to establish a credit program involves a cost-benefit analysis. Discuss this approach.
2. In controlling the level of credit sales the manager should compare the added income and the added costs associated with selecting a particular credit customer. Discuss the nature of the costs that must be considered.
3. What factors should the manager consider in establishing credit terms?
4. Which of the many sources of credit information do you consider most important?
5. How does the correspondent banking system aid the small business in credit analysis?
6. Discuss the subject side of the credit decision.
7. Outline and discuss what you feel to be the most important steps in an efficient collection procedure.
8. What is the important advantage in using a collection agency?
9. What are the problems associated with charging off bad debts?
10. What factors should be considered in determining the best means of handling the credit management function?

## PROBLEMS

1. Contact two or three successful small businesses in the community that have established credit programs. Review their credit programs with them and discuss the problems most frequently encountered.
2. Make arrangements with a local banker to discuss the credit information services provided to a small business.
3. Contact a local collection agency and become familiar with the procedures it follows in providing credit collection services to small business.

## BIBLIOGRAPHY

Beckman, Theodore N., and Foster, Ronald S.    *Credits and Collections.* 8th ed. New York: McGraw-Hill, 1969.

Cole, Robert H., *Consumer and Commercial Credit Management.* 4th ed. Homewood, Ill.: Richard D. Irwin, 1972.

Credit Research Foundation of the National Association of Credit Men.    *Credit Management Handbook.* Rev. ed. Homewood, Ill.: Richard D. Irwin, 1965.

Miller, Donald E., and Relkin, Donald B.    *Improving Credit Practice.* American Management Association, 1971.

All of these publications are excellent sources of information and guidelines for establishing and operating a credit sales program.

# External sources of help toward better management

The small business manager is frequently confronted with questions and problems that require the help, advice, or guidance of people outside the firm. In most communities, such assistance is readily available.

In addition to the expert advice of the lawyer, the accountant, and the insurance agent, the availability of educational opportunities is important to improve managerial talent and skills. It is also important to recognize the value of a good reference library, and know how to use public and private library facilities as sources of information for better management.

The purpose of this chapter is threefold: the use of consultants in small business is considered; the educational opportunities that may be available to the entrepreneur are examined; and suggestions are made on the use of reference materials or libraries as sources of information.

## SPECIALISTS AND ORGANIZATIONS THAT CAN PROVIDE HELP

### The professional staff

Every small business will periodically need the services of a reliable attorney, a competent certified public accountant, and a knowledgeable insurance agent.

Legal matters will arise from time to time that require the advice of an attorney, and in some firms it may be best to retain one on a continuing basis. Normally, a lawyer will provide continuing services on general legal matters for a retainer fee of $30 to $50 a month. There are two distinct advantages in a retainer arrangement. First, if legal questions come up frequently, a retainer arrangement will prove much less expensive. Second, a lawyer who provides service on a continuing basis becomes more familiar with the firm's legal problems, and may be more sympathetic to its needs.

Chapter 13 stressed the importance of maintaining accurate and complete accounting records in the small business. The investment of time and effort in a good accounting system rewards the manager on a continuing basis by providing accurate and up-to-date accounting information. Inadequate and ill-kept accounting records represent one of the principal causes of small business failure.

These observations point up the need for the services of a competent certified public accountant to establish an efficient record-keeping system, to regularly review the system, and to periodically prepare financial statements. If need dictates, a CPA may be hired on a full-time basis. In most cases, however, the certified public accountant should be hired on a retainer basis. As in the case of the attorney, this is usually more economical than seeking the service only when accounting problems arise.

Chapter 19 stressed the importance of an adequate insurance program. Insurance is a highly technical area of study, and the advice and service of a reliable insurance agent is needed. Insurance agents, both in property and life insurance, are always willing to appraise the need for insurance and recommend the insurance coverage most appropriate.

In the small business, the free advice of an insurance agent should be adequate. However, in some cases the services of an insurance broker are warranted. Acting as the agent of the small business firm, the insurance broker will appraise the risks, make recommendations as to the type of policies that appear necessary, and then go to the market and acquire the coverage at the lowest possible cost. The only real difference between the services of a broker and an insurance agent is that the agent may underwrite policies for only one or a few companies, which may limit the types of coverage available. The broker, on the other hand, is able to place insurance with a number of companies, and thus may be able to offer more complete service in those cases where unique or unusual risks exists.

## The business contact staff

Besides the professional staff, there are people in the community who may be able to provide valuable advice and guidance. Probably the most important person in this category is the local banker. The importance of a favorable banking connection cannot be overemphasized, for the commercial banker offers the most complete financial service at the least cost. In establishing a working relationship with the small business, the banker will avail himself of complete financial information about the business, and be in an excellent position to offer advice on financial matters and management policy. Furthermore, through correspondent relationships with other banks in other communities, the banker is a valuable source of credit information on customers.

The small business manager may be able to gain valuable advice from suppliers. The supplier is obviously operating in the best interests of the customer, and thus will be happy to offer whatever information and advice possible concerning promotional efforts and general marketing procedures.

Other people in the community who may prove helpful include members of the board of directors, real estate agents and brokers, economists, credit bureau managers, newspaper editors, mayors or city managers, councilmen, and county commissioners. All of these individuals are concerned with the economic growth of the community, and thus are willing to provide any aid and assistance they can to small business.

It may be that the manager will want to consider using the services of a management consultant. A management consultant will probably prove most valuable in the larger small business, where basic operational problems exist. The objective is to gather facts, opinions, and suggestions from managers, supervisors, and workers; and to examine the business records and inspect the property, buildings, equipment, and materials used in the operation. From an analysis of the information gathered, any problems are identified, and solutions considered. The consultant normally submits a written report, reviewing the analysis and recommending specific actions. In some cases, help is provided to implement the recommendations.

There are a number of advantages to hiring a management consultant to solve business problems. The management consultant is an unbiased individual, and thus objective in an analysis of the situation. The absence of internal pressures, loyalties, or rivalries permit a proper evaluation of the problems and give a fresh viewpoint to the best solution. Furthermore, the management consultant offers specialized knowledge, combined with wide experience—just the combination many small businesses need to solve their business problems. Poor management practices are quickly detected by the trained consultant, and appropriate corrective measures can be recommended and readily applied.

The third reason for use of a management consultant is that the manager may not have the time or the background to perform a competent analysis of the firm's problems. A good consultant takes the initiative and gets the job done in the most efficient manner and shortest period of time. Meanwhile, the manager can apply all efforts to running the business.

A word of advice is in order in considering the use of a management consultant. It is important there be full cooperation in providing information. The very nature of the consultant's task requires that all information asked for be provided. In addition, the manager must be convinced that the consultant is competent, and be willing to make every effort to cooperate to help execute any changes the consultant may recommend. The management consultant can have little success without full cooperation, even if he or she is an expert.

In selecting a management consultant, the manager should determine the services offered by the firms in the area. The lawyer, accountant, banker, or supplier may be helpful in making recommendations. Furthermore, the local Chamber of Commerce or the Association of Management Consultant Engineers in New York can provide information regarding the reliability and competence of particular consulting organizations. The important questions that must be answered before selecting a consulting firm include the following: How long has the consulting firm been in business? What business firms have they serviced? How have the firms they have serviced reacted to their recommendations? Do they get repeat business from these firms? Who are the principal individuals involved in the firm, and do the principals go out on the job? Have they had any experience in problems in your particular industry or line of business? Finally, are they financially sound?

In the selection process, the manager should be suspicious of consulting firms that use high-pressure selling techniques and advertising. Furthermore, the manager should be skeptical about the firm that sets a fixed fee before examining the actual amount of work to be done, or the firm that offers cut-rate services that may prove to be inadequate. The manager should also probably avoid management consulting firms that ask for payment in advance, that tie in consulting services with the purchase of certain machines or equipment, or will not be specific as to the costs and charges involved.

As for cost, it will depend on the contract arrangement. For example, a consultant may be put on a retainer basis, as are the accountant and the attorney. Such an arrangement would normally involve the consultant coming to the firm three or four days a month, and always being available on short notice to consider problems that may arise. The advantage of the retainer arrangement is that the consultant has a fairly constant control over any changes instituted.

Of course, whatever the manager agrees to pay for consulting services, the total bill will depend on the time spent on the job. The daily fee varies with the person's experience. Generally, a daily fee of $100 per individual is probably minimum.

## What might a trade association do for the small business?

The large business is able to represent its own interests in relationships with labor, government, the public, and other business firms in or out of their industry. But, small businesses are not, and the trade association is a means of joining together for more strength, influence, and protection.

The trade association also offers a variety of services. For example, it may develop accounting and record-keeping systems, organize industry-wide meetings for the interchange of thought and ideas, initiate research in the industry, and keep members informed of government legislation, public events, and technical and trade information that affects the industry. It can also offer statistics and specialized data on sales promotion and the markets for the industry's products. Additionally, a number of trade associations organize and administer training courses and seminars for employees, provide credit reporting services, and maintain a clearinghouse for technical advice for small businesses which cannot afford their own technical staffs.

There are certain costs associated with joining a trade association and the dues vary according to the size of the group and the services provided. Some associations assess a flat, uniform rate, while others base the rate on annual sales volume. Local associations normally collect dues on a monthly basis. Nationwide or statewide associations usually collect annual dues.

## WHAT MIGHT AN ADVERTISING AGENCY DO FOR THE SMALL BUSINESS?

The objective of an advertising agency is to study a firm's product or service by surveying the present and potential market. Based on the survey, the merits of using the various advertising media available are considered and an advertising plan is formulated.

The agency then designs the advertising copy, contracts with the media for space, and forwards the approved copy with complete instructions for presentation. In the use of radio and television, the agency will contract the writing of the commercials, hire the technical staff to produce them, buy the time, and supervise the presentation.

In essence, the services of an advertising agency are free. This results from the fact that the various communication media generally charge the agency 15 percent less than the business would have to pay; and this represents the agency's commission. In other words, the manager must pay the full media rate whether or not the agency is used.[1]

In addition to the services that are provided through compensation to the agency by the media, agency services can be purchased on a fee basis. Packaging designs, sales research, the training of sales personnel, designing merchandise displays, and the preparation of sales and service literature are the typical services available.

The problem in selecting an advertising agency is finding one that will get profitable results from what is typically a limited advertising budget. Some feel the smaller advertising agency gives the small account more

---

[1] Where a local rate is in effect, the media is not allowed to pay the 15 percent commission to the advertising agency; hence the small businessperson in such a case would have to pay a fixed fee to the agency.

attention. On the other hand, the manager may need the specialized services of one of the larger agencies if the product or service is of a highly technical nature.

The Standard Advertising Register lists over 2,500 advertising agencies; thus the manager should have little trouble locating one in the area. An agency should be picked that is financially responsible; that has a staff of sufficient size, ability, and experience; that is free from control of any one media owner; and that is recognized by the various media associations (and hence is eligible for the 15 percent discount). Once the selection has been made, the manager should ask for a demonstration of past work to give some indication of the results that can be expected.

The agency-client agreement should note the services the agency is to perform; the means of billing the business for the services; some understanding that the agency will not handle advertising for a directly competitive product; and that the client's approval is required for all advertising expenditures. Also included should be the statement that the manager is to pay the published rate of the medium, and that the agency is to keep the commission allowed. Finally, the advertising agency will specify it cannot be responsible for the failure of the media to meet their commitments.

As mentioned above, the various media generally allow a 15 percent commission to recognized advertising agencies, which usually covers most of the services rendered. However, if the small business uses so little advertising space or time that the 15 percent commission is too small to cover agency costs, additional fees may be charged. The normal practice is to agree on a minimum fee. Special handling charges may also be added when it is necessary to purchase materials and outside services. All of these conditions should be spelled out in the agency-client agreement.

## EDUCATIONAL OPPORTUNITIES AVAILABLE TO THE SMALL BUSINESS

The successful small business manager typically enjoys hard work, and puts in long hours. Another common trait is the high regard for experience and know-how, plus the continuing need to update that experience and know-how through formal and informal educational training.

Although some with limited formal education have been outstandingly successful in business, the number is small. Only through education can the small business manager learn the elements of a successful venture. No one has yet discovered a method for convincing customers to buy, irrespective of product, price, or service. Without a minium knowledge of business operations, success is nothing more than a matter of chance. The untrained mind is simply not capable of analyzing the problems of operating a small business venture.

To be successful in small business, the manager must be able to identify and evaluate the elements of a problem, then bring them together in a workable course of action. The degree of success the manager has will depend, in large part, on experience, knowledge, and on being up-to-date with new developments in managerial decision-making. Thus, it is important to take advantage of the educational opportunities a community has to offer, and to tap the wealth of information provided by the many libraries, publishers, and government agencies.

Among the many opportunities available, vocational training in business has long been fostered by the U.S. Office of Education and the state supervisors of vocational education. Furthermore, a program of distributive education can be found today in almost every city and town in the United States. These two avenues are very valuable in training young qualified people for eventual ownership and leadership in small business. Such an opportunity should prove valuable in situations where the owner's son or daughter plans to eventually move into a responsible position in the firm.

Within the last decade, university schools of business have recognized the value of education for small business management. Traditionally, collegiate schools of business have offered advanced business training at the graduate level, and training at the undergraduate level, for students interested in middle management positions in medium- and large-sized corporations. Admittedly, this is an essential function of the schools, for big business will continue to need better trained executives. On the other hand, the development and training of the small business owner-manager is also becoming an essential function. Thus, most institutions offer at least a basic course in small business, and in some cases, advanced work is available.

Business educators across the country are also beginning to realize a responsibility in adult training for small business. At the present time, through various night programs across the country, tens of thousands of small business owners are taking one or more short courses under the leadership of trained and experienced business teachers. For example, the University of California at Los Angeles and New York University publish a list of courses which small business owners are encouraged to take. Such programs are a principal ingredient in promoting better, more profitable, small business management.

The Small Business Administration has been an important force in encouraging management training for small business through its administrative management course program. It has co-sponsored over 4,000 courses, in some 900 educational institutions, in which thousands of small business owner-managers have participated.

Business-sponsored organizations have also done much to advance the training of small business owners. Furthermore, chambers of commerce and trade associations often encourage local educational institutions to offer management courses for those members who are small business owners.

Professional associations have had an unusual opportunity to help the small businessperson through research. More and more, the professional journals and publications are recognizing the importance of small business in the American economy and have presented research findings and articles that are very helpful.

The Small Business Administration has pioneered in the field of management assistance, with its previously mentioned administrative management courses; workshops for prospective managers; management publications; management research; and related programs. There are 98 field offices of the Small Business Administration, where a wealth of information and opportunity is available for the asking. Literally hundreds of management aids and management bulletins published by the SBA are distributed free by the field offices. Additionally, there are some excellent SBA publications for sale through the Superintendent of Documents, GPO, Washington, D.C.

In conclusion, a wealth of information and research is being published about small business, and numerous opportunities for self-training and formal education are available in most areas. Thus, the small business manager has little excuse for not enhancing his or her managerial ability. The small business world is extremely competitive. Only those individuals with the foresight, knowledge, experience, and never-ending quest for self-improvement will survive.

## THE SMALL BUSINESS LIBRARY

The advice of many small business experts is available to any manager who knows how to use library materials. Thus, a familiarity with the reference materials in the public library or the library of a nearby educational institution can prove valuable. A good business library and a knowledgeable librarian can represent a source of information comparable to the trade association, banker, supplier, accountant, lawyer, or similar contact. Additionally, the manager should consider building a basic personal library.

The Appendix at the end of this chapter presents a bibliography designed to acquaint the small business manager with the wealth of business information available through library research. It also indicates the kinds of publications that are available, free or by purchase, from the Small Business Administration as well as from several private publishers and organizations. The list is by no means all-inclusive. Trained personnel in the local library will be able to supplement it with additional materials. All U.S. government publications cited are available through the Superintendent of Documents in Washington. Many are free; others are reasonably priced. Those that the manager finds most helpful should be obtained and put on file to afford quick, constant availability.

In addition to the various publications listed in the Appendix, the manager should also consider subscribing to various trade publications pertaining to the firm's line of business; a financial newspaper such as the *Wall Street Journal*, or a daily newspaper with a good business section; and some of the more recognized business magazines, such as *Business Week, Forbes, U.S. News & World Report,* and *Fortune*.

## QUESTIONS

1. Name the three individuals who should make up the professional staff for any small business.
2. What are the advantages of a favorable relationship with a local commercial bank?
3. Describe the functions performed by a management consultant. What are the advantages of hiring such a consultant?
4. Discuss the services that a trade association is prepared to offer.
5. What services are available through an advertising agency? What important problem is associated with selecting an advertising agency?
6. What educational opportunities are normally available in the community which will aid small business?
7. Discuss the functions of the Small Business Administration in terms of educational aid offered to small business.

## PROBLEMS

1. Contact a local management consulting firm and discuss the services being provided to small businesses in the community.
2. Contact a local advertising agency and review the services available to small businesses. Also consider the charges for such services.
3. Examine the educational opportunities in the community that are available to aid small business managers in self-improvement.
4. Examine the library facilities in the community and review the availability of literature that would prove valuable to small business.

# *Appendix*

## Business operating guides and handbooks

Handbooks which treat specific phases of business operation often contain practical information. Only a few examples of the many types available are listed below.[1]

*Prentice-Hall Federal Tax Handbook—1976*. $7.50 a year. Has authentic information with tax control methods for practical and competent guidance to insure effective tax management. Prentice-Hall Inc., Englewood Cliffs, New Jersey 07632.

*Credit Management Handbook*. Credit Research Foundation. 2d ed., 1965. Richard D. Irwin, Inc., 1818 Ridge Rd., Homewood, Ill. 60430. $13.50. Explains how to organize and operate a credit department, to make credit decisions on orders and accounts, to collect overdue accounts, and to use credit reporting and rating agencies.

*Foreign Commerce Handbook*. Chamber of Commerce of the United States, 1615 H St. NW., Washington, D.C. 20006. A guide to sources of information and services for exporters and importers. Gives types of service of U.S. government, intergovernmental and private organizations in foreign trade and related matters. Information sources under 60 major subjects, includes a bibliography of further references.

*Handbook of Practical Public Relations*. A. B. Adams. 1965. Thomas Y. Crowell and Company, 201 Park Ave., South, New York, N.Y. 10003. $6.95. This is a guide for the nonspecialist who wants to get his organization's message to the public. Includes suggestions on preparing news releases, making speeches, and appearing on radio.

*Handbook for Small Business*. 3d ed. 1969. Senate and House Select Committees on Small Business. GPO. $1.75. This survey of small business programs of the federal government describes most of the current federal programs of interest to the small business community.

*Marketing Handbook*. A. W. Frey, editor. 2d ed., 1965. Ronald Press Company, 15 East 26th St., New York, N.Y. 10010. $17.50. A comprehensive reference book for persons concerned with marketing goods and services.

*Office Management Handbook*. Harry L. Wylie, editor. Ronald Press Company, 15 East 26th St., New York, N.Y. 10010. $14. Gives standard principles and practices for running an efficient office, large or small.

*Production Handbook*. Gordon B. Carson, editor. Ronald Press Company, 15 East 26th St., New York, N.Y. 10010. $25. Gives information about plant layout and location, production planning and control, quality control, and manufacturing processes.

*Purchasing Handbook*. George W. Aljian, editor. 3d ed., 1973. McGraw-Hill Book Company, Inc., 330 West 42d St., New York, N.Y. 10036. $34.50.

---

[1] Prices listed in this Appendix are subject to change.

Gives thorough treatment of purchasing department organization, management, and operating procedures.

*Tax Guide for Small Business.* Internal Revenue Service, U.S. Department of the Treasury. Revised annually. GPO or local District Director of Internal Revenue. Designed to assist businesspersons in the preparation of their federal tax returns. Discusses tax problems incident to conducting a trade, business, profession, or acquiring or selling a business.

## Directories

Business firms often need information concerning products, potential buyers, or trade associations. Directories of various types are available. The most obvious are telephone books and their classified sections. Many libraries keep some out-of-town telephone directories for business reference. For further listings of directories, consult the following available at most libraries:

*Directory of Special Libraries and Information Centers.* 2d ed., 1968. $28.50. Gale Research Co., Book Tower, Detroit, Mich. 48226. Has information about more than 13,000 special libraries, information centers, and documentation centers in the U.S. and Canada—arranged alphabetically by the names of supporting organizations. Gives details on information units operated by businesses, government agencies, educational institutions, and trade and professional associations.

*Guide to American Directories.* 9th ed., 1975. B. Klein and Co., 104 Fifth Ave., New York, N.Y. 10011. Gives information on directories classified by industry, by profession, and by function. Useful for identifying specific directories to aid in locating new markets or sources of supply.

Examples of directories which serve the business community are listed below under six group headings: **Associations, Financial, Government, Individuals, Manufacturers,** and **World Trade.**

### Associations

*Directory of National and International Labor Unions in the United States.* (Bulletin 1596). U.S. Department of Labor. GPO. Gives facts about the structure and membership of national and international labor unions.

*Encyclopedia of Associations, vol. I., National Organizations of the United States.* Gale Research Co., Book Tower, Detroit, Mich. 48226. Lists trade, business, professional, labor, scientific, educational, fraternal, and social organizations of the United States, includes historical data.

*National Trade and Professional Associations of the United States.* Annual. 1973 ed., $15. Columbia Books, Publishers, 917 Fifteenth St., Washington, D.C. 20005. Lists the name, telephone number, address, chief executive officer, size of staff and membership, and year formed of more than 4,000 national business and professional associations.

## Financial

*Dun & Bradstreet Reference Book*. Six times a year. Contains the names and ratings of nearly 3 million businesses of all types located throughout the U.S. and Canada. (Dun & Bradstreet also publishes other specialized reference books and directories, for example, *Apparel Trades Book* and *Metalworking Directory*.)

*Moody's Banks and Finance*. Annual with twice-weekly supplements. Moody's Investor Service, 99 Church St., New York, N.Y. 10007. Indexes more than 9,700 American banks and financial institutions, listing their officers, directors, and other top-level personnel.

*Rand-McNally International Bankers' Directory*. Semiannually. Rand-McNally & Company, Box 7600, Chicago, Ill. 60680. Lists over 37,000 banks and branches, giving their officials, and statement figures. It also includes the ABA check routing numbers for all U.S. banks, and a digest of U.S. banking laws.

## Government

The following references include directories of *municipal, state,* and *federal* agencies, their personnel, and functions.

*Municipal Year Book*. Annual. International City Manager's Association, 1313 East 60th St., Chicago, Ill. 60637. $18. A review of municipal events of the year and a directory of city officials in all the states.

*Book of the States*. Biennial. Council of State Governments, 1313 East 60th St., Chicago, Ill. 60637. $19.50. Directory of state officials, state legislatures, state judiciary systems. Also has data on current state programs and legislation. Price includes two supplements.

*State Blue Books*. Many states publish their own "blue books" or directories. Inquire of your local librarian.

*Congressional Directory*. Annual. Joint Committee on Printing. 1970. GPO. $5.05. Biographical data on Members of Congress, membership and staff of Congressional Committees; directory of the Executive and Judiciary, Diplomatic Corps; and other useful information on federal and state agencies.

*Directory of Post Offices*. Annual. U.S. Post Office Department. 1974. GPO. $4.25. List of post offices by state, alphabetical list, and post office addresses for Army and Air Force installations.

*Sources of State Information and State Industrial Directories*. Chamber of Commerce of the United States, 1615 H St. NW., Washington, D.C. 20006. Contains names and addresses of private and public agencies which furnish information about their states. Also listed, under each state, are industrial directories and directories of manufacturers published by state and private organizations. Some regional directories are included.

*United States Government Organization Manual*. Annual. National Archives and Records Service. 1969. GPO. $4.95. The official organization handbook of the federal government, containing descriptive information on the agencies in the legislative, judicial, and executive branches. Abolished or transferred agencies are listed in an appendix.

## Individuals

The following lists only the most general works. *Who's Who* directories are also available for specific occupations and locations.

*Current Biography.* Monthly. H. W. Wilson Company, 950 University Ave., New York, N.Y. 10452. Extensive biographical data on prominent contemporary personalities.

*Poor's Register of Corporations, Directors, and Executives.* Annual. Standard and Poor's Corporation, 345 Hudson St., New York, N.Y. 10014. Listed by corporation and individual.

*Who's Who in America.* Biennial. Marquis—Who's Who, Inc., Marquis Publications Bldg., Chicago, Ill. 60611. A biographical dictionary of notable living men and women.

*Who's Who of American Women.* Biennial. Marquis—Who's Who, Inc., Marquis Publications Bldg., Chicago, Ill. 60611. Biographical information of more than 20,000 distinguished women.

*World's Who's Who in Commerce and Industry.* Marquis—Who's Who, Inc., Marquis Publications Bldg., Chicago, Ill. 60611. Biographical information of men and women prominent in finance, industry, and trade.

## Manufacturers

In addition to the directories listed, there are available many state manufacturer's and industrial directories. These are too numerous to list here. Ask your librarian if such a directory is published for the state in which you are interested.

*Conover-Mast Purchasing Directory.* Seminannual. Conover-Mast Publications, Inc., 95 East Putnam Ave., Greenwich, Conn. 06830. Alphabetical listing of manufacturers, showing product lines, code for number of employees, addresses, and telephone numbers. Classified section lists products with names and addresses of manufacturers. Special chemical and mechanical sections, and trademark and trade name identification.

*MacRae's Blue Book.* Annual. 4 vols. MacRae's Blue Book Co., 903 Burlington, Western Springs, Ill. 60558. Lists sources of industrial equipment, products, and materials; alphabetically arranged by product headings. Separate alphabetical listing of company names and trade names.

*Thomas' Register of American Manufacturers.* Annual. 8 vols. and Index. Thomas Publishing Company, 461 Eighth Ave., New York, N.Y. 10001. Purchasing guide listing names of manufacturers, producers, and similar sources of supply in all lines. Products are classified in six volumes; vol. 7 lists manufacturers, trade names, and commercial organizations; and vol. 8 indexes all product classifications and advertisers.

## World trade

*Trade Directories of the World.* In loose-leaf form, kept current with monthly supplements. Croner Publications, 211–13 Jamaica Ave., Queens Village, N.Y. 11428. Lists 2,000 directories from 151 nations which provide primary sources of information. Cross-indexed to trade and professions, countries, and general export-import publications. Lists over 400 trade categories.

## Economic and marketing information

The Nation's economy and, in turn, its marketing trends are changing constantly. Businesspersons can keep abreast by using the current books, booklets, and periodicals as issued by commercial firms and government agencies. Much of the basic statistical information in the economic and marketing areas is collected by the federal government. Commercial organizations use this data and supplement it with surveys of their own. Listed below are some basic reference publications which present statistical and marketing information; many are issued on a continuing basis.

### Books/booklets

*Bibliography of Publications of Bureaus of Business and Economic Research.* 1957–1975. Associated University Bureaus of Business and Economic Research, West Virginia University, Morgantown, West Virginia. Useful guide to publications primarily concerned with state and local business information.

*Business Literature: An Annotated List for Students and Businessmen.* Baker Library, Graduate School of Business Administration, Harvard University, Soldiers Field, Boston, Mass. 02163. $5. Provides a list of books and magazines in the principal areas of business.

*Business Statistics.* Biennial. U.S. Department of Commerce. Supplementary and historical data for the economic statistics published in the *Survey of Current Business.*

*County and City Data Book: 1967.* Bureau of the Census, U.S. Department of Commerce. 1967. GPO. $5.50. Presents statistical information on business, manufacturers, governments, agriculture, population, housing, vital statistics, bank deposits, and other subjects. Issued every several years.

*Data Sources for Business and Market Analysis.* 2d ed. 1969. Natalie D. Frank. $10. Scarecrow Press, Inc., 257 Park Ave., New York, N.Y. 10010. Provides market research information, its origins and retrieval. Gives basic sources and specific references for the study of business trends.

*Directory of Business and Financial Services.* 6th ed. Special Libraries Association, 31 East 10th St., New York, N.Y. 10003. $6.50. An annotated listing of several hundred business, economic, and financial services.

*Directory of Federal Statistics for Local Areas: A Guide to Sources.* 1966. Bureau of the Census, U.S. Department of Commerce. 1966. GPO. $1. Contains information which should be useful to business firms interested in plant location, to marketers in determining market potentials, and to persons concerned with local or urban conditions.

*Directory of Federal Statistics for States—A Guide to Sources.* Bureau of the

Census, Department of Commerce. 1967. GPO. $2.25. Describes sources of statistics for counties, metropolitan cities, and other geographic units; arranged in 22 categories by subject matter. Indexed.

*Economic Almanac.* Annual. National Industrial Conference Board. Macmillan Co., 866 3d Ave., New York, N.Y. 10022. A business fact book containing statistics of business, labor, and Government. A special Canadian section, a glossary, and an index are included.

*E&P Market Guide.* Annual: 1974 ed. Editor & Publisher Co., 850 Third Ave., New York, N.Y. 10022. $15. Tabulates current estimates of population, households, retail sales for nine major sales classifications, income for states, counties, metropolitan areas, and 1,500 daily newspaper markets. For each area, gives information on transportation and utilities, local newspapers, climate, and employment. Includes state maps.

*McGraw-Hill Dictionary of Modern Economics.* Douglas Greenwald and Associates. 1973. McGraw-Hill Book Co., Inc., 1221 Ave. of Americas, New York, N.Y. 10020. $19.95. Explains the meaning of more than 1300 terms currently used in economics, marketing, and finance. It also describes approximately 200 government and private agencies, and nonprofit associations concerned with the fields of economics and marketing.

*Rand McNally Commercial Atlas and Marketing Guide.* Annual. (Leased on an annual basis.) Rand McNally & Company, Box 7600, Chicago, Ill. 60680. An extensive U.S. atlas presenting marketing data in the form of maps and area statistics.

*SM's Survey of Buying Power.* Annual. *Sales Management,* 630 Third Ave., New York, N.Y. 10017. $25. Gives population, income, and retail sales estimates for state, county, and metropolitan areas (as defined by *Sales Management*).

*Sources of Business Information.* E. T. Coman, editor. 1964. Berkeley, University of California Press, Berkeley, Calif. 94729. $11. Guide to general sources with coverage for specific fields of business and industry.

*The Statesman's Year Book.* Revised annually, edited by S. H. Steinberg and John Paxton. 1969–70. $12.50. St. Martin's Press, Inc., 175 Fifth Ave., New York, N.Y. 10010. This book is a storehouse of information on the United Nations, all countries of the world, and each of the 50 states of the United States.

*Statistical Abstract of the United States: 1974.* Annual. Bureau of the Census, U.S. Department of Commerce. GPO. $9.60. The standard summary of national statistics, includes information on the labor force, population, business enterprises, and national income.

*Statistical Services of the United States Government.* Annual. Bureau of the Budget. 1968. GPO. $1.50. Serves as a basic reference document on U.S. government statistical programs.

*Statistics Sources.* 2d ed., 1971. $27.50. Gale Research Co., Book Tower, Detroit, Mich. 48226. Arranged in dictionary style, it cites periodicals, yearbooks, directories, and other compilations issued by state, federal and foreign agencies, associations, companies, universities, and other organizations.

## Periodicals—U.S.Government

The following are some of the basic federal government periodicals which contain business and general economic reports and are widely used by businesspersons for keeping abreast of developments in their specific areas of interest:

*Construction Review.* Business and Defense Services Administration, U.S. Department of Commerce. Monthly. GPO. $14.50. Brings together virtually all the government's current statistics pertaining to construction, plus some nongovernment statistical information.

*Current Industrial Reports.* Bureau of the Census, U.S. Department of Commerce. Lists of titles and prices available from the Bureau of the Census, Washington, D.C. 20233. These reports give information at the factory level for different industries on inventory, production, shipments, and other business activities.

*Current Business Reports.* Bureau of Census, U.S. Department of Commerce. (Includes a series of four reports: *Weekly Retail Sales Report; Advance Monthly Retail Sales Report; Monthly Retail Trade;* and *Retail Annual Report.*) GPO. $7.20 a year. Estimated sales of retail stores by kinds of business and some data for regions and metropolitan areas.

*Economic Indicators.* Prepared for the Joint Economic Committee by the Council of Economic Advisers. Monthly. GPO. $10.10 a year; 85¢ a copy. Presents tables and charts dealing with prices, employment and wages, production and business activity, purchasing power, credit, and federal finance.

*Federal Reserve Bulletin.* Board of Governors of the Federal Reserve System, Washington, D.C. 20551. Monthly. $8 a year; $2 a copy. Has monthly tables of financial and business statistics. Interest rates, money supply, consumer credit, and industrial production are some of the subjects included. Special articles cover the state of economy, financial institutions, statistical methodology.

*Monthly Labor Review.* U.S. Department of Labor. Monthly. GPO. $22.35 a year; $1.90 a copy. The medium through which the Labor Department publishes its regular monthly reports on such subjects as trends of employment and payrolls, hourly and weekly earnings, working hours, collective agreements, industrial accidents and disputes, as well as special features covering such topics as automation, and profit sharing.

*Monthly Wholesale Trade Reports: Sales and Inventories.* Bureau of the Census, U.S. Department of Commerce. GPO. $7.20 a year; 60¢ a copy. Reports trends in sales and inventories. Also gives some geographic data.

*Survey of Current Business.* Office of Business Economics, U.S. Department of Commerce. Monthly. GPO. $48.30 a year; $3.00 a copy. Subscription includes a weekly statistical supplement. This periodical includes statistics and articles on significant economic developments. It presents statistics on national income, business population, manufacturers sales, inventories, and orders. Carries special articles on personal income, foreign trade, and other aspects of the economy.

## General reference sources

Some of the sources for general information are almanacs, encyclopedias and their yearbooks, and specialized encyclopedias.

### Almanacs

For short factual information, consult the yearly almanacs. These are available for reference at any library or may be purchased from local bookstores. Examples are:

*Information Please Almanac.* Simon and Schuster, 6300 Fifth Ave., New York, N.Y. 10020.

*World Almanac.* Doubleday & Co., Inc., 277 Park Ave., New York, N.Y. 10017.

### Encyclopedias

For information on almost any topic, encyclopedias are readily available. Many contain general information, others are specialized. Often included are illustrations and maps, as well as bibliographies listing standard works on the topic under consideration. They are kept up-to-date by yearbooks.

Among the encyclopedias available are: *Colliers Encyclopedia, Encyclopedia Americana, Encyclopaedia Britannica,* and the *World Book Encyclopedia.*

### Specialized encyclopedias

The more specialized encyclopedias include: *Van Nostrand's Scientific Encyclopedia, McGraw-Hill Encyclopedia of Science and Technology, Encyclopedia of Banking and Finance, Encyclopedia of Chemistry, Encyclopedic Dictionary of Business Finance,* and *Accountant's Encyclopedia.*

### Information services

When the information being sought is too recent for inclusion in almanacs, and encyclopedias, consult the following services which are available at most reference libraries.

*Bulletin of the Public Affairs Information Service.* Weekly. Public Affairs Information Service, Inc., 11 West 40th St., New York, N.Y. 10018. Cumulated five times a year, bound annual volume. This is a selective subject list of the latest books, government publications, reports, and periodical articles, relating to economic conditions, public administration, and international relations. An especially useful feature is the extensive listing of many types of directories.

*Facts on File.* A Weekly Digest of World Events. Facts on File, Inc., 119 West 57th St., New York, N.Y. 10019. This useful and time-saving weekly index digests significant news of the day from a number of metropolitan dailies. The indexes are cumulated quarterly, then annually.

*Funk and Scott Index of Corporations and Industries.* Weekly. Funk and Scott Publishing Company, 10550 Park Lane, University Circle, Cleveland, Ohio 44106. Indexes articles appearing in the leading business, financial, and trade newspapers and magazines. This is an excellent source of current information.

## Where-to-find publications

For the convenience of the user, publication listings are divided into three sections: *Commercial Publications, Federal Government Publications*, and *State Publications*.

### Commercial publications

Most libraries have the following reference sources for identifying *books, periodicals*, and *periodical articles*.

BOOKS: For additional listings of books, consult:

*Books In Print.* Annual. 2 vols.: vol. 1—*Author index;* vol. 2—*Titles and Publishers.* R. R. Bowker Co., 1180 Ave. of the Americas, New York, N.Y. 10036. An author and title index to books currently available from major publishers.

*Cumulative Book Index.* Monthly. H. W. Wilson Co., 950 University Ave., Bronx, N.Y. 10452. A subject, title, author index to books in the English language. Gives price, publisher, number of pages, and date of publication for each book.

*Forthcoming Books.* Bimonthly. R. R. Bowker Co. (in combination with *Subject Guide to Forthcoming Books.*) This service provides a regular updating of *Books In Print.*

*Subject Guide to Books In Print.* 2 vols. alphabetized. R. R. Bowker Co. Useful reference for identifying books currently available on a specific topic.

NEWSPAPERS and PERIODICALS can be identified through use of the following index listings.

*Ayer Directory of Newspaper and Periodicals.* Annual. N. W. Ayer & Son, West Washington Sq., Philadelphia, Pa. 19106. Provides a geographical listing of magazines and newspapers printed in the United Stated and its possessions. Listings are also given for Canada, Bermuda, Panama, and the Philippines. Has an alphabetical index and a classified section which increases its usefulness.

*Business Publication Rates and Data.* Monthly. Standard Rate and Data Service, Inc., 5201 Old Orchard Rd., Skokie, Ill. 60077. Contains a descriptive listing of business magazines and latest advertising rates. Indexed by name of magazine and business fields covered.

*National Directory of Newsletters and Reporting Services.* Gale Research Co. Book Tower, Detroit, Mich. 48226. Provides basic facts concerning the type of periodical publication not covered in the bibliographic tools concerned with the conventional types of periodicals, such as national, international, and selected foreign newsletters, association bulletins, information and financial services.

*Standard Periodical Directory.* 1975. 4th ed. $60. Oxbridge Publishing Co., Inc. 420 Lexington Ave., New York, N.Y. 10017. Gives comprehensive coverage to periodicals in the United States and Canada. Lists over 53,000 entries, including magazines, journals, newsletters, house organs, government publications, advisory services, directories, transactions and proceedings of professional societies, yearbooks, and major city dailies (weekly and small daily newspapers are excluded).

*Ulrich's International Periodicals Directory.* R. R. Bowker Co., 1180 Avenue of the Americas, New York, N.Y. 10036. 16th ed. 1975. $50. Vol. 1 covers scientific, technical, and medical periodicals; vol. 2 covers arts, humanities, business, and social sciences. Classified by subject.

ARTICLES in business and professional magazines provide current information. Specific subject indexes to periodical articles, such as those listed below, are available at libraries for reference.

*Applied Science and Technology Index.* Monthly. H. W. Wilson Co. Subject index covering periodicals in the fields of engineering, applied science, and industry.

*Business Periodicals Index,* Monthly. H. W. Wilson Co. Subject index covering periodicals in the fields of business, finance, labor relations, insurance, advertising, office management, marketing, and related subjects.

*Readers' Guide to Periodical Literature.* Semimonthly, except monthly in July and August. H. W. Wilson Co. A general index to periodicals such as the *New York Times Magazine.*

### Federal government publications

Libraries usually maintain listings of both State and federal government publications. The following are a few examples of such listings that serve as guides to government publications.

Most of the U.S. government publications are the result of research and activities of various Federal agencies. Some are free from the issuing agency, while others cost a nominal fee. Since most of these publications are relatively inexpensive and are usually some of the most recent and authoritative writings in a particular field, this reference material proves most helpful to the public.

By law, the established system of Government Depository Libraries makes federal publications available for public reference. Libraries designated within this system can elect to receive from the Superintendent of Documents, Government Printing Office, those classes of federal publications which are appropriate to their type of library reference service.

Superintendent of Documents (GPO) also issues a number of *Price Lists* (single copy, free) on selected federal (for-sale) publications related to specific subjects. For a complete list of price list subjects, request *How to Keep in Touch with U.S. Government Publications,* free from GPO. Examples of titles which may be of interest to readers of this Bibliography are: *Finance PL 28, Com-*

*merce* PL 62, and *Census* PL 70. These price lists of U.S. government publications on selected subjects give prices and title of publications and may be consulted in depository libraries.

Most libraries have some federal publication listings to identify currently available materials of most of the federal agencies and they keep some of these publications for ready reference.

Some of the guides to federal publications are:

*Monthly Catalog of United States Government Publications.* Superintendent of Documents. GPO. $27.00 a year; $1.85 a copy. The most comprehensive catalog of government publications. It lists by agency both printed and processed publications issued each month, including Congressional hearings, documents, and reports.

*A Survey of Federal Government Publications of Interest to Small Business.* Small Business Administration. 1969. GPO. Nontechnical publications most likely to be of assistance to businesspersons have been selected, annotated, and arranged both by subject and issuing agency.

*SBA 115A—Free Management Assistance Publications,* and *SBA 115B—For-Sale Booklets.* Small Business Administration. Complete listings of currently available management assistance publications issued by SBA. Both lists are free from the nearest SBA field office or SBA, Washington, D.C. 20416.

Publications Lists of other U.S. Government Departments and Agencies. Most Federal agencies issue, periodically or intermittently, lists (titles of the lists vary) of their current publications. If not available at local libraries, these lists are free from the issuing agency—check with the nearest *field office* of the Government agency. (For local office addresses, look for the agency under *U.S. Government* in the telephone directory.)

### State publications

Most reference libraries keep current and historical material of local civic interest, including newspapers, magazines, and books. An example of a guide to state publications is listed below.

*Monthly Checklist of State Publications.* Library of Congress. GPO. $21.90 a year; $1.50 a copy. List by state and agency of the state documents received by the Library of Congress.

## Small Business Administration *free* management-assistance publications

### Management aids

These free leaflets deal with functional problems in small manufacturing plants and concentrate on subjects of interest to administrative executives. Request by number and title.

| *Leaflet* | *Title* |
|---|---|
| 32. | *How Trade Associations Help Small Business* |
| 41. | *How the Public Employment Service Helps Small Business* |

480

207. *Pointers on Scheduling Production*
208. *Problems in Managing a Family-Owned Business*
209. *Preventing Employee Pilferage*
210. *Records Retention: Normal and Disaster*
211. *Termination of DOD Contracts for the Government's Convenience*
212. *The Equipment Replacement Decision*
213. *Selecting Employee Benefit Plans*
214. *The Metric System and Small Business*
215. *How To Prepare a Pre-Award Survey*
216. *Finding a New Product for Your Company*
217. *Reducing Air Pollution in Industry*

## Technical aids

These leaflets are intended for top technical personnel in small concerns or for technical specialists who supervise that part of the company's operations. Request by number and title.

42. *Principles of Plant Layout for Small Plants*
61. *Noise Reduction in the Small Shop*
63. *Cut Corners With Conveyors*
73. *Pointers on In-Plant Trucking*
78. *Controlling Quality in Defense Production*
82. *Inspection on Defense Contracts in Small Firms*
86. *PERT/CPM Management System for the Small Subcontractor*
87. *Value Analysis for Small Business*
90. *Welding and Flame-Cutting Processes and Practices*
91. *A Tested System for Achieving Quality Control*
92. *Using Adhesives in Small Plants*

## Small marketers aids

These leaflets provide suggestions and management guidelines for small retail, wholesale, and service firms. Request by number and title.

25. *Are You Kidding Yourself About Your Profits?*
71. *Checklist for Going Into Business*
95. *Are Your Salespeople Missing Opportunities?*
96. *Checklist for Successful Retail Advertising*
101. *Pointers for Developing Your Top Assistant*
104. *Preventing Accidents in Small Stores*
105. *A Pricing Checklist for Managers*
106. *Finding and Hiring the Right Employees*
107. *Building Strong Relations With Your Bank*
108. *Building Repeat Retail Business*
109. *Stimulating Impulse Buying for Increased Sales*
110. *Controlling Cash in Small Retail and Service Firms*
111. *Interior Display: A Way To Increase Sales*
112. *Sales Potential and Market Shares*
113. *Quality and Taste as Sales Appeals*
114. *Pleasing Your Boss, The Customer*

### Small business bibliographies

These leaflets furnish reference sources for individual types of businesses. Request by number and title.

17.  *Restaurants and Catering*
18.  *Basic Library Reference Sources*
20.  *Advertising—Retail Store*
21.  *Variety Stores*
24.  *Food Stores*
27.  *Suburban Shopping Centers*
29.  *National Mailing-List Houses*
30.  *Voluntary and Cooperative Food Chains*
31.  *Retail Credit and Collections*
33.  *Drugstores*
37.  *Buying for Retail Stores*
41.  *Mobile Homes and Parks*
42.  *Bookstores*
44.  *Job Printing Shop*
45.  *Men's and Boys' Wear Stores*
46.  *Woodworking Shops*
47.  *Soft-Frozen Dessert Stands*
48.  *Furniture Retailing*
50.  *Apparel and Accessories for Women, Misses, & Children*
51.  *Trucking and Cartage*
52.  *Store Arrangement and Display*
53.  *Hobby Shops*
55.  *Wholesaling*
56.  *Training Commercial Salesmen*
58.  *Automation for Small Offices*
60.  *Painting and Wall Decorating*
64.  *Photographic Dealers and Studios*
65.  *Real Estate Business*
66.  *Motels*
67.  *Manufacturers' Sales Representative*
68.  *Discount Retailing*
69.  *Machine Shop—Job Type*
72.  *Personnel Management*
74.  *Retail Florist*
75.  *Inventory Management*
76.  *Pet Shops*

## Small Business Administration *for-sale* booklets

The management-assistance booklets in this list are published by the Small Business Administration, but are *sold* by the Superintendent of Documents, Government Printing Office, Washington, D.C., 20402. *The booklets must be ordered by SBA number on an order blank provided by the Superintendent of Documents.*

### Small business management series

The booklets in this series provide discussions of special management problems in small companies.

484

SBA 1.12:1     *An Employee Suggestion System for Small Companies.* Explains the basic principles for starting and operating a suggestion system. It also warns of various pitfalls and gives examples of suggestions submitted by employees through company suggestion systems.

SBA 1.12:3     *Human Relations in Small Business.* Discusses human relations as the subject involves finding and selecting employees, developing them, and motivating them.

SBA 1.12:4     *Improving Material Handling in Small Business.* A discussion of the basics of the material handling function, the method of laying out workplaces, and other factors to setting up an efficient system.

SBA 1.12:7     *Better Communications in Small Business.* Designed to help smaller manufacturers help themselves in winning cooperation by means of more skillful communications. It also seeks to explain how the controlling of communications within the firm can improve operating efficiency and competetive strength.

SBA 1.12:9     *Cost Accounting for Small Manufacturers.* Stresses the importance of determining and recording costs accurately. Designed for small manufacturers and their accountants. Diagrams, flowcharts, and illustrations are included to make the material easier to use.

SBA 1.12:13     *The Small Manufacturer and His Specialized Staff.* Stresses the necessity of building a competent staff through the use of staff specialist and outside professional advisers so that the small businessperson can be relieved of routine work as the business prospers.

SBA 1.12:15     *Handbook of Small Business Finance.* Written for the small businessperson who wants to improve financial-management skills. Indicates the major areas of financial management and describes a few of the many techniques that can help the small businessperson understand and apply results of his past decisions to those of the future.

SBA 1.12:16     *Health Maintenance Programs for Small Business.* Discusses how smaller firms with limited funds can set up health programs to keep losses due to employee sickness and accidents as low as possible.

SBA 1.12:17     *New Product Introduction for Small Business Owners.* Provides basic information which will help the owners of small businesses to understand better what is involved in placing a new or improved product on the market.

SBA 1.12:19     *Technology and Your New Products.* Designed to inform the small businessperson about the benefits of technology. For example, he or she can use technology to improve a product, to diversify a product line, and to reduce costs.

SBA 1.12:20   *Ratio Analysis for Small Business.* Ratio analysis is the process of determining the relationships between certain financial or operating data of a business to provide a basis for managerial control. The purpose of the booklet is to help the owner/manager in detecting favorable or unfavorable trends in business.

SBA 1.12:21   *Profitable Small Plant Layout.* Help for the small business owner who is in the predicament of rising costs on finished goods, decreasing net profits, and lowered production because of the lack of economical and orderly movement of production materials from one process to another throughut the shop.

SBA 1.12:25   *Guides for Profit Planning.* Guides for computing and using the break-even point, the level of gross profit, and the rate of return on investment. Designed for readers who have no specialized training in accounting and economics.

SBA 1.12:27   *Profitable Community Relations for Small Business.* Practical information on how to build and maintain sound community relations by participation in community affairs.

SBA 1.12:29   *Management Audit for Small Manufacturers.* A series of questions which will indicate whether the owner-manager of a small manufacturing plant is planning, organizing, directing, and coordinating business activities efficiently.

SBA 1.12:30   *Insurance and Risk Management for Small Business.* A discussion of what insurance is, the necessity of obtaining professional advice on buying insurance, and the main types of insurance a small business may need.

SBA 1.12:31   *Management Audit for Small Retailers.* Designed to meet the needs of the owner-manager of a small retail enterprise. The approach is the same as that in SBMS No. 29—a do-it-yourself technique. That is, 149 questions guide the owner-manager in an examination of himself and his business operation.

SBA 1.12:32   *Financial Recordkeeping for Small Stores.* Written primarily for the small store owner or prospective owner whose business doesn't justify hiring a trained, full-time bookkeeper.

SBA 1.12:33   *Small Store Planning for Growth.* A discussion of the nature of growth, the management skills needed, and some techniques for use in promoting growth. Included is a consideration of merchandising, advertising and display, and checklists for increases in transactions and gross margins.

SBA 1.12:34   *Selecting Advertising Media—A Guide for Small Business.* Intended to aid the small businessperson in deciding which medium to select for making a product, service, or store known to potential customers and how to make the most use of advertising money.

## Starting and managing series

This series is designed to help the small entrepreneur in the effort "to look before you leap" into a business. The first volume in the series—*Starting and Managing a Small Business of Your Own*—deals with the subject in general terms. Each of the other volumes deals with one type of business in detail, and their titles are designed to inform of their contents. Available titles are listed below.

| | |
|---|---|
| SBA 1.15:1 | *Starting and Managing a Small Business of Your Own* |
| SBA 1.15:3 | *Starting and Managing a Service Station* |
| SBA 1.15:4 | *Starting and Managing a Small Bookkeeping Service* |
| SBA 1.15:5 | *Starting and Managing a Small Building Business* |
| SBA 1.15:9 | *Starting and Managing a Small Restaurant* |
| SBA 1.15:10 | *Starting and Managing a Small Retail Hardware Store* |
| SBA 1.15:11 | *Starting and Managing a Small Retail Drugstore* |
| SBA 1.15:12 | *Starting and Managing a Small Dry Cleaning Business* |
| SBA 1.15:13 | *Starting and Managing a Small Automatic Vending Business* |
| SBA 1.15:14 | *Starting and Managing a Carwash* |
| SBA 1.15:15 | *Starting and Managing a Swap Shop or Consignment Sale Shop* |
| SBA 1.15:16 | *Starting and Managing a Small Shoe Service Shop* |
| SBA 1.15:17 | *Starting and Managing a Small Retail Camera Shop* |
| SBA 1.15:18 | *Starting and Managing a Retail Flower Shop* |
| SBA 1.15:19 | *Starting and Managing a Pet Shop* |
| SBA 1.15:20 | *Starting and Managing a Small Retail Music Store* |
| SBA 1.15:21 | *Starting and Managing a Small Retail Jewelry Store* |
| SBA 1.15:22 | *Starting and Managing an Employment Agency* |
| SBA 1.15:23 | *Starting and Managing a Small Drive-In Restaurant* |

## Small business research series

SBA 1.20:1　*Cash Planning in Small Manufacturing Companies.* This book reports on research that was done on cash planning for the small manufacturer. It is designed for owners and managers of small firms and the specialists who study and aid small businesses.

SBA 1.20:2　*The First Two Years: Problems of Small Firm Growth and Survival.* This discussion is based on the detailed observation of 81 small retail and service firms over a 2-year period. The operations of each enterprise were systematically followed from the time of launching through the end of the second year.

SBA 1.20:3　*Interbusiness Financing: The Economic Implications for Small Business.* Interbusiness financing can be generally defined as the financial help that one independent business gives another without going through conventional sources such as banks and finance companies. This booklet tries to bring into focus the various methods used for this particular kind of assistance.

SBA 1.20:4    *Personality and Success: An Evaluation of Personal Characteristics of Successful Small Business Managers.* One of the major goals of the study reported in this book was to determine those personality traits of successful business managers which contributed measurably to the success of their enterprises.

### Nonseries publications

SBA 1.18 2:G74/969    *A Survey of Federal Government Publications of Interest to Small Business.* Lists booklets, pamphlets, and leaflets published by the various government agencies which are most likely to be of assistance to the small business community. Both the for-sale and free literature is listed for prospective and established small businesspersons.

SBA 1.19:EX7/971    *Export Marketing for Small Firms.* A manual for owner-managers of smaller firms who seek sales in foreign markets.

SBA 1.13/3:972    *U.S. Government Purchasing and Sales Directory.* A directory for businesses that are interested in selling to the U.S. Government. Lists the purchasing needs of various Agencies.

SBA 1.2:M31/11    *Managing for Profits.* Ten chapters on various aspects of small business management, for example, marketing, production, and credit.

SBA 1.2:B98    *'Buying and Selling a Small Business.* Deals with the problems that confront buyers and sellers of small businesses. Discusses the buy-sell transaction, sources of information for buyer-seller decision, the buy-sell process, using financial statements in the buy-sell transaction, and analyzing the market position of the company.

SBA 1.2:M31/14    *Strengthening Small Business Management.* Twenty-one chapters on small business management. This collection reflects the experience which the author gained in a lifetime of work with the small business community.

## Sources of further information

### Associations

American Management Association, 135 W. 50th Street, New York, N.Y. 10020

Association of Management Consultants, 811 E. Wisconsin Ave., Milwaukee, Wis. 53202

Presidents Association, 135 West 50th Street, New York, N.Y. 10020

488

## Periodicals

*Business Horizons.* Indiana University, Graduate School of Business, Bloomington, Ind. 47401

*California Management Review.* University of California, Graduate School of Business Administration, Berkeley, Calif. 94720

*Harvard Business Review.* Harvard University, Graduate School of Business Administration, Boston, Mass. 02163

*Journal of Small Business Management.* National Council for Small Business Management Development, University of Wisconsin Extension, 600 West Kilbourn Avenue, Milwaukee, Wis. 53203

*Management Review.* American Management Association, Saranac Lake, N.Y. 12983

*Supervisory Management.* American Management Association, Saranac Lake, N.Y. 12983

## Books

*Business Policy in Growing Firms.* Robert B. Buchele, Intext/Chandler Publishing Co., New York, N.Y., 1967.

*Entrepreneurship and Venture Management.* Clifford M. Baumback and Joseph R. Mancuso. Prentice-Hall, Englewood Cliffs, N.J., 1975.

*How to Organize and Operate a Small Business.* P. C. Kelley, K. Lawyer & C. M. Baumback, Prentice-Hall, Englewood Cliffs, N.J., 1968.

*How to Run a Small Business.* J. K. Lasser. McGraw-Hill, New York, N.Y., 1963.

*Manage More by Doing Less.* Raymond O. Loen, McGraw-Hill, New York, N.Y., 1971.

*Managing the Smaller Company.* Russell Bank, editor, American Management Association, New York, N.Y., 1969.

*The Practice of Management.* Peter F. Drucker. Harper & Row, New York, N.Y., 1954.

*Small Business Management.* H. N. Broom & J. G. Longenecker. South-Western Publishing Co., Burlingame, Calif., 1971.

*Small Business Management: Essentials of Entrepreneurship.* Lawrence A. Klatt. Wadsworth Publishing Company, Belmont, Calif., 1973.

*Small Business Management Fundamentals,* by Dan Steinhoff, McGraw-Hill, New York, N.Y., 1974.

*Starting & Succeeding in Your Own Small Business.* Louis L. Allen. Grosset & Dunlap, New York, N.Y., 1968.

*Up Your Own Organization.* Donald M. Dible. Entrepreneur Press, Santa Clara, Calif., 1971.

## Pamphlets

*The Business Failure Record.* Compiled yearly by the Business Economics Department, Dun & Bradstreet, New York, N.Y.

*Cost of Doing Business, Corporations, Key Business Ratios in 185 Lines.* Business Economics Department, Dun & Bradstreet, New York, N.Y., 1973.

*Cost of Doing Business, Partnerships & Proprietorships, Key Business Ratios in 120 Lines.* Business Economics Department, Dun & Bradstreet, New York, N.Y., 1973.

*Terms of Sale for 94 Manufacturing and Wholesale Lines.* Business Information Systems, Services and Sciences, Dun & Bradstreet, New York, N.Y., 1970.

*Venture Capital.* The professional journal of the venture capital and SBIC industry, published by S. M. Rubel & Company, 10 South LaSalle Street, Chicago, Ill., 1974.

*Small Business Reporter.* Published by the Bank of America, San Francisco, Calif. These are a series of pamphlets dealing generally with small business operations, and specifically with particular types of small businesses. The available issues are listed below and can be purchased upon request.

*Business Operations Series*

Advertising
Vol. 9, no. 1, pub. 1969

Opening Your Own Business
A personal appraisal
Vol. 7, no. 7, reissued 1971

How to Buy or Sell a Business
Vol. 8, no. 11, reissued 1973

Understanding Financial Statements
Vol. 7, no. 11, reissued 1972

Financing Small Business
Vol. 8, no. 5, reissued 1973

Franchising
Vol. 9, no. 9, pub. 1970

Avoiding Management Pitfalls
Vol. 11, no. 5, pub. 1973

Business Management
Advice from Consultants
Vol. 11, no. 3, pub. 1973

Management Succession
Vol. 10, no. 12, pub. 1972

Marketing a New Product
Vol. 10, no. 5, pub. 1971

Personnel for the Small Business
Vol. 9, no. 8, pub. 1970

Retail Financial Records
Vol. 10, no. 4, pub. 1971

Steps to Starting Business
Vol. 10, no. 10, pub. 1972

490

Retail Nurseries
Vol. 9, no. 10, pub. 1970

Independent Pet Shops
Vol. 10, no. 2, pub. 1971

Small Job Printing
Vol. 9, no. 5, pub. 1970

Repair Services
Vol. 10, no. 9, pub. 1972

Service Stations
Vol. 10, no .7, pub. 1971

Independent Sporting Goods Stores
Vol. 10, no. 11, pub. 1972

Applying for Minority Business Loans Special issue, 28-page illustrated kit, pub. 1970

*Professional Management Series*

Establishing a Dental Practice
in California, pub. 1969

Establishing a Medical Practice
in California, pub. 1972

Establishing a Veterinary Practice
in California, pub. 1972

# Index

## A

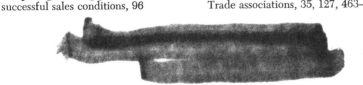

500

*This book has been set in 10 point and 9 point Caledonia, leaded 2 points. Chapter numbers are 48 point Helvetica and chapter titles are 24 point (small) Helvetica. The size of the type page is 27 by 45½ picas.*

## DATE DUE

| | | | |
|---|---|---|---|
| | | | |
| | | | |
| | | | |
| | | | |
| | | | |
| | | | |
| | | | |
| | | | |
| | | | |
| | | | |
| | | | |
| | | | |
| | | | |
| | | | |
| | | | |
| | | | |
| | | | |
| | | | |
| | | | |
| GAYLORD | | | PRINTED IN U.S.A. |